DUMBARTON OAKS
MEDIEVAL LIBRARY

Jan M. Ziolkowski, General Editor

THE VULGATE BIBLE

VOLUME IV

DOML 13

The Vulgate Bible

VOLUME IV

THE MAJOR
PROPHETICAL BOOKS

DOUAY-RHEIMS TRANSLATION

Edited by

ANGELA M. KINNEY

Introduction by

SWIFT EDGAR

DUMBARTON OAKS
MEDIEVAL LIBRARY

HARVARD UNIVERSITY PRESS
CAMBRIDGE, MASSACHUSETTS
LONDON, ENGLAND
2012

Copyright © 2012 by the President and Fellows of Harvard College
ALL RIGHTS RESERVED
Printed in the United States of America

Library of Congress Cataloging-in-Publication Data
Bible, English. Douai. 2012
  The Vulgate Bible : Douay-Rheims translation / edited by Angela M.
  Kinney.
    v.c. — (Dumbarton Oaks medieval library ; DOML 13)
  English and Latin text on facing pages.
  Includes bibliographical references.
  Contents: v. 1. The Pentateuch. v. 2a. The Historical Books, part a. v. 2b.
  The Historical Books, part b. v. 3. The Poetical Books. v. 4. The Major
  Prophetical Books
  ISBN 978-0-674-05534-6 (v. 1: alk. paper)
  ISBN 978-0-674-99667-0 (v. 2a: alk. paper)
  ISBN 978-0-674-06077-7 (v. 2b: alk. paper)
  ISBN 978-0-674-99668-7 (v. 3: alk. paper)
  ISBN 978-0-674-99669-4 (v. 4: alk. paper)
  I. Edgar, Swift, 1985–   II. Dumbarton Oaks.   III. Title.
  BS180 2010
  222′.1047—dc22   2010015238

Contents

Introduction

The Vulgate Bible is a collection of Latin texts compiled and translated in large part by Saint Jerome (ca. 345–420) in the late fourth and early fifth centuries CE. Roughly speaking, Jerome translated the Old Testament—except for the books of Wisdom, Ecclesiasticus, Baruch and 1 and 2 Maccabees—and he revised existing Latin versions of the Psalms and the Gospels. Jerome's Bible was used widely in the Western European Christian (and later, specifically Catholic) tradition from the early Middle Ages through the twentieth century.

The adjective "Vulgate" (from the Latin verb *vulgare,* meaning "to disseminate") lacks the connotation of coarseness often inherent in its relative "vulgar," but both words imply commonness. Indeed, the Vulgate Bible was so widespread that its significance can hardly be overstated. It made critical contributions to literature, visual art, music and education during the Middle Ages and the Renaissance, and it informed much of the Western theological, intellectual, artistic and even political history of that period. Students of almost any aspect of European civilization from the seventh century (when the Latin Bible existed more or less in the form we know today) through the sixteenth century (when translations of scripture into various European vernaculars

became widely available to the public and acceptable to religious authorities) must refer frequently to the Vulgate Bible and have a thorough knowledge of it.

In this edition, the Latin is presented opposite the first English version of the Bible sanctioned by the Roman Catholic Church. This English Bible is typically referred to as the Douay-Rheims Version, after the present-day names of its places of publication. The New Testament was published in 1582 by the English College at Rheims, and the Old Testament (to call it the Hebrew Bible would be inaccurate, since it includes nine books that have never belonged to the Hebrew canon) was published in 1609 and 1610, in two volumes, by the English College at Douay. The entire Douay-Rheims Bible was revised several times, notably by Bishop Dr. Richard Challoner (1691–1781) in 1749 and 1750.

In this introduction, I use the terms "Catholic" and "Protestant" in their current senses. Adherents to the Church of England in the sixteenth century at times referred to themselves as Catholics and to those who followed the religious authorities in Rome as Popish or Papists. The members of the Roman Church called their Anglican rivals various names, such as heretics, Protestants, Lutherans and Calvinists, but they would not have called them Catholics.

Douay and Rheims were major centers of learning for English-speaking Catholics, who faced hostility in Protestant England. The English College, a prominent Catholic institution, was exiled from Douay to Rheims in 1578, near the beginning of the Eighty Years' War between the Netherlands (to which Douay at the time belonged) and Philip II of Spain, who had founded the college.[1] The exile lasted until 1593. The college undertook these translations of the Bi-

ble primarily in response to the English versions produced under the Church of England that did not treat Jerome's text as the ultimate authority. Protestant English translators did use the Vulgate, but they also consulted the German rendering by Martin Luther (1482–1546), the Greek Septuagint and New Testament, testimonia in Hebrew and other sources. In contrast, the Douay-Rheims Version was directly translated from the Latin Bible as it was known to the professors at the English College in 1582.

While the English College was working on its translations at Douay and Rheims, Pope Sixtus V (r. 1585–1590) called for the preparation of an authoritative Latin text. This Latin Bible was published in 1590, just prior to his death, but it contained errors and was soon suppressed for fear that Protestants would use them to attack the Catholic Church.[2] Three corrected printings followed, in 1592, 1593 and 1598, during the papacy of Clement VIII (r. 1592–1605). These four editions, substantially the same, are referred to collectively as the Sixto-Clementine Version. While it strongly resembles the Latin Bible that evidently served as the basis for the Douay-Rheims translation, the two are not identical. The Dumbarton Oaks Medieval Library (DOML) here presents a reconstructed Latin text of the lost Bible used by the professors at Douay and Rheims, and Challoner's revision of the English translation faces the Latin. Challoner's text, discussed in detail below ("The English Text of This Edition"), sometimes reflects the Sixto-Clementine Bible more closely than did the English College translations of 1582, 1609 and 1610, but many of the revision's features are not at all related to the Sixto-Clementine Bible, and some lead the translation even further from the Latin.

Although the Douay Old Testament was not published until 1609–1610, most of the work on the translation seems to have been completed much earlier, before any Sixto-Clementine edition. Despite its publication date, therefore, this section of the English translation still provides a valuable witness to a Latin text that predated the Sixto-Clementine Version. Most scholars accept the conclusion by Charles Dodd that "the work may be entirely ascribed to Mr. [Gregory] Martin [who died a decade before publication of the Sixto-Clementine edition] . . . He translated the whole Bible; tho' it was not publish'd all at one time."[3] There is good reason to believe that Dodd was right: an entry in the "Douay Diaries,"[4] records of the activities at the young English College, attests that Martin began translating the Bible in October 1578 and that he translated two chapters a day, which were revised by two other professors. Since there are 1,353 chapters in the Bible—including the Books of Tobit, Judith, Wisdom, Ecclesiasticus, Baruch, 1 and 2 Maccabees and 3 and 4 Ezra, and counting the Prayer of Manasseh as one chapter—the task would have taken Martin and his team slightly more than 676 days, far less time than the thirty years that elapsed between the project's commencement and the complete publication of the Bible. Indeed, this calculation is confirmed in the address "To the right vvelbeloved English reader" in the first volume of the Old Testament (1609), which states that the Bible was translated "about thirtie yeares since" (fifth page of the section). The translation thus almost certainly preceded the Sixto-Clementine text, which immediately became the standard edition upon its printing in 1592. The lag between translation and publication is explained on the first page of the

same section: "As for the impediments, which hitherto haue hindered this worke, they al proceded (as manie do know) of one general cause, our poore estate in banishment"—that is, the exile of the English College to Rheims.

The Douay-Rheims translation used here mostly follows the version printed in 1899, a slight revision of Challoner's editions, incorporating elements from the 1749, 1750 and 1752 printings. Challoner's principal contribution was to make the original Douay-Rheims easier to read by updating obscure phraseology and obsolete words. This volume modifies the 1899 version to bring the punctuation and the transliteration of proper nouns and adjectives into line with modern practice (see Alternate Spellings in the endmatter for this edition's policies regarding transliterations) and to restore some readings from Challoner's 1750 and 1752 editions that had been changed (mostly due to printers' errors) in the 1899 version. In addition, the whole text has been prepared according to the guidelines of the fifteenth edition of the *Chicago Manual of Style*. This policy has resulted in significant alterations to Challoner's edition, which superabounds in colons and commas, lacks quotation marks and begins each verse on a new line, sometimes making the text difficult to understand. In contrast to most English Bibles, this volume renders all of the text as prose, even the parts that were originally in verse, since neither the Latin nor the English is poetic. The Latin text has been punctuated according to the English translation to allow easy movement between the two languages. In the rare instances when they diverge, the text in each language has been punctuated according to its most natural meaning (see, for example, Gen 31:1–4).

Readers of the Dumbarton Oaks Medieval Library who wish to compare either the English or the Latin version presented here with another Bible should bear in mind that the versification in the Vulgate and the numbering of psalms differ from those in Bibles translated from languages other than Latin. Furthermore, the books in this volume have been selected and ordered according to Challoner's revisions, which follow the Sixto-Clementine Bible. This policy has resulted in the inclusion of some chapters and books commonly considered "apocryphal" or "deuterocanonical" (Tobit, Judith, Wisdom, Ecclesiasticus, Baruch, 1 and 2 Maccabees, Daniel 3:24–90, Daniel 13 and 14) and the omission of others that were relegated to appendices even in early printed versions of the Bible (3 and 4 Ezra and the Prayer of Mannaseh). The names of some books differ from the ones that may be familiar to many readers: for instance, 1 and 2 Kings in this volume are commonly called 1 and 2 Samuel; 3 and 4 Kings are usually 1 and 2 Kings; 1 and 2 Paralipomenon equate to 1 and 2 Chronicles; 1 Ezra is usually simply Ezra, while 2 Ezra is typically Nehemiah; the Canticle of Canticles is also known as the Song of Songs; Ecclesiasticus is Sirach and in some Latin Bibles is known as Iesu Filii Sirach; and, last, the Apocalypse of St. John the Apostle may be known to most readers as the Book of Revelation.

THE LATIN TEXT OF THIS EDITION

The Latin in this edition presents as closely as possible the text from which the Douay-Rheims translators worked. It would have been a version of the Bible known to many Europeans from the eighth through the sixteenth century. Be-

fore Jerome, translations of parts of the Bible into Latin existed; we call these disparate texts the Old Latin Bible. After Jerome finished his work, versions of his Vulgate proliferated. According to one count, a third of the biblical manuscripts we have today dating to about one hundred years after Jerome's death are from the Vulgate, and a century later "manuscripts of the Vulgate start to outnumber those of the Old Latin by about two to one. In the seventh century, the ratio has risen to about six to one."[5] The early ninth century brought the stabilization of a recension that was overseen by Alcuin, the schoolmaster from York who played a major role in the cultural revival promoted by Charlemagne. The so-called Alcuin Bibles, of which some thirty survive, became the standard text outside Italy during the Carolingian period. They were the products of monastic copy centers known as scriptoria. In the thirteenth century, the Alcuin Bibles gave way to the so-called Paris Bibles, which were written by professional scribes. The text of the Paris Bibles, a direct descendent of the Alcuin Bibles, was in turn closely related to the Sixto-Clementine Bibles of the late sixteenth century. In large part, the DOML text corresponds to Robert Weber's edition (2007). Most adjustments to bring the Latin closer to the English coincide with an edition of the Sixto-Clementine Bible (1959) that preserves the majority of the readings from the second Clementine edition (1593) and occasionally replaces that text with readings from the other two Clementine editions, which were very similar to each other. For consistency's sake, the spellings and inflections of adjustments based on the Sixto-Clementine Bible have been brought into line with Weber's text.

When neither the Weber nor the Sixto-Clementine text

provides the reading that the Douay-Rheims translators appear to have seen, the critical apparatuses in Weber and in Quentin's edition (1926–[1995]) have been consulted. Often the readings attested in early printed editions of the Bible, such as the famous "42-line Bible" printed by Johannes Gutenberg in 1454, come closest to the translation. In rare instances it has been necessary to print reconstructions of the text theoretically used by the translators, since neither the Sixto-Clementine, Weber and Quentin editions nor the citations in their apparatus provide a suitable reading. These reconstructions, often closer to the Greek Septuagint than to any Vulgate edition, follow the Old Latin Bible.

In trying to identify the Latin source or sources of the Douay-Rheims translation, some scholars have pointed to the Louvain Bible,[6] an early printed edition that strongly resembles the Sixto-Clementine Version. However, the readings in the Douay-Rheims Version do not support the conclusion that Martin based his translation on either the Louvain Bible of 1547 or the correction of that edition published at Rome in 1574. Furthermore, the preface of the Douay-Rheims Version addressed "To the right vvelbeloved English reader" states (and Greenslade accepts) that the editors of the Old Testament "conformed it to the most perfect Latin Edition"—presumably, given the publication date, the Sixto-Clementine Version.[7] To take just one illustration of the danger of assuming that the translators used a single identifiable source, consider Ex 16:29, which in the Douay translation reads in part, "and let none goe forth": of the many sources considered by Quentin (including the Louvain Bible), only two—both early printed editions and neither of them the Sixto-Clementine or the Louvain edition—begin

the relevant Latin clause with a conjunction. Moreover, while the translators claimed their work was "diligently conferred with the Hebrew, Greeke, and other Editions in diuers languages,"[8] the relative paucity of readings different from well-established Latin sources and the inconsistency in the nature of the divergences suggest that they were working with a now lost Latin text of idiosyncratic nature rather than a still extant one that they chose to ignore from time to time. Since several people collaborated on that translation, the translators may also have followed different editions of the Bible and therefore produced a translation for which there is no single surviving Latin source.

Unlike the Latin as edited by Weber, the Sixto-Clementine edition (to whose family the Douay-Rheims translation belongs) often regularizes the language found in earlier manuscripts. In general, the Sixto-Clementine rarely accepts the *lectio difficilior,* while most editors since the eighteenth century, including Weber, tend to choose the "more difficult reading" from among multiple possibilities. For example, at Gen 32:5, the Weber edition reads, "habeo boves et asinos oves et servos atque ancillas," while the Sixto-Clementine editors preferred to avoid the variations of asyndeton after *asinos* and of *atque,* so their text reads, "Habeo boves et asinos et oves et servos et ancillas." In this instance, the Douay-Rheims translators evidently saw a conjunction between *asinos* and *oves* and also between *servos* and *ancillas.* In this edition, an *et* has been inserted in the former case, but the *atque* has remained in the latter, because we cannot know which of the many options for the English "and" the translators encountered in their Latin.

At times, the translation reflects a base text closer to We-

ber's than to the Sixto-Clementine edition. For example, at Gen 1:14, Weber reads "fiant luminaria in firmamento caeli ut dividant diem ac noctem," while for *ut,* the Sixto-Clementine edition reads *et.* However, the Douay-Rheims translation (as revised by Challoner, but here retaining the grammatical construction of the original) reads, "Let there be lights made in the firmament of heaven to divide the day and the night," clearly translating *ut.* The Sixto-Clementine choice was probably made by analogy to verses like Gen 1:6, which reads in both editions "Fiat firmamentum in medio aquarum, et dividat."

THE ENGLISH TEXT OF THIS EDITION

The "Douay-Rheims Version" is an imperfect name for the translation of the Vulgate Bible used in this volume. Indeed, one anonymous scholar in 1836 went so far as to write that calling a translation similar to the one printed here "the Douay or Rhemish version is an abuse of terms."[9] The English here follows a text that was published in 1899. Although this text has been understood routinely as being the Douay-Rheims Version without any qualification, it in fact offers an English translation that derives not directly from the work of the English College of Douay and Rheims, but rather from a nineteenth-century form of a revision by Challoner. Challoner published at least five revisions of the New Testament and two of the Old (the New Testaments appeared in 1749, 1750, 1752, 1764 and 1772, the Old Testaments in 1750 and 1763–1764); after his death, others produced many more. Since the editions of 1582, 1609 and 1610, many subsequent revisions have purported to be simple reprints.

Indeed, the frontispiece to the 1899 edition has a message of approbation by James Cardinal Gibbons, then archbishop of Baltimore, who writes that the text "is an accurate reprint of the Rheims and Douay edition with Dr. Challoner's notes." But if we are to understand the "Rheims and Douay edition" to mean the translations originally printed in those cities in the late sixteenth and early seventeenth centuries, the text we have is by no means an accurate reprint of that.

Because the versions issued between 1610 and 1899 can be difficult to come by, and because the only work approaching a systematic collation of various "Douay-Rheims" Bibles is a bitterly anti-Catholic work from 1855,[10] many scholars regard the Douay-Rheims translation as a text that has barely changed (if at all) since its first printing. Some are aware of Challoner's extensive revisions in the mid-eighteenth century, which updated the language of the Douay-Rheims Version and toned down the polemical annotations, but few know the extent of his alterations, or that they make it more distant from the Latin Vulgate, or that they took place over several editions or that the editions published after his death often contain the work of other scholars.

Many factors complicate analysis of the modifications that the Douay-Rheims Version has undergone over the past four centuries. The most significant is the doctrinal conservatism of the Catholic Church. Owing to both the primacy of Jerome's Vulgate (another inadequate label, since Jerome hardly produced the Latin text by himself), recognized at the Council of Trent (1545–1563), and the desire of the Church to exert some control over access to scripture, the translation of the Bible into vernacular tongues was dis-

couraged. Yet after Protestant churches made the text of the Bible available to speakers of English and German, it became easier for reformist thinkers to disseminate their teachings. Some English-speaking Catholics then sought to produce their own translation, but since the point of this work was to regulate the message read by the flock, the translation required authorization to insure that it was appropriate. A letter of 1580 from William Allen, the president of the English College at Douay, to a colleague, Professor Jean de Vendeville, expresses the need for papal sanctioning of the translation: "We on our part will undertake, if His Holiness shall think proper, to produce a faithful, pure, and genuine version of the Bible in accordance with the version approved by the Church."[11] The printed edition was approved not by the pope but by three professors at Allen's own college (Douay-Rheims 1609, *Approbatio*).

Conservatism demanded the Church's approbation and made revision difficult. How could a reviser supplant something that had already been declared acceptable to the Church? Revisions required approval of their own, yet they could not directly contradict previously approved editions. For this reason, the only reference to a difference between Challoner's 1750 edition and the printings of 1582, 1609 and 1610 comes on the title page, which describes the work as "Newly revised and corrected, according to the Clementine Edition of the Scriptures." As the phrasing shows, Challoner was careful to note that his version derived from the Latin Bible first authorized by Pope Clement VIII in 1592, ten years after the Rheims New Testament, but he obscured the extent of his revisions. Despite the popularity of Challoner's revision and of the Bibles still in print that descend from it,

the English translations and revisions of scripture were not created under a directive from the Vatican. There is no single, indisputably "official" translation of the Latin Bible into English. All the translations lay claim to official status without criticizing other Catholic versions, and none of them has clear primacy.

This confusing (and confused) climate has misled modern readers into believing precisely what the editors and translators of English Catholic Bibles from the sixteenth through the nineteenth century wanted them to think: a single standard English translation of the Bible existed, and the reader in question was holding a copy of it. One well-respected medievalist cautioned against using the King James Version for medieval studies (because it lacks a close relationship to the Vulgate text), implying that the Douay-Rheims Version is preferable. While correct about the King James Version, he shows himself to be unaware of the Douay-Rheims's own modern tradition, writing, "The English translation of [the Vulgate] is the one known as the 'Douai-Rheims' translation . . . also available in many modern editions," and later quoting the translation of Ct 2:4 in the Douay-Rheims as "he set in order charity in me."[12] This quotation comes from Challoner's revision of the translation from 1750; the 1610 translation reads, "he hath ordered in me charitie."

The particular case of Ct 2:4 does not perfectly illustrate the danger of using Challoner's revision of the Douay-Rheims translation, because his rendering still matches the Vulgate text ("ordinavit in me caritatem"). But in many places (italicized in this edition) Challoner strayed from the Latin, usually to revise some particularly awkward phrasing

in the older Douay-Rheims edition. For example, at Gen 6:13, he changed "the earth is replenished with iniquitie from the face of them" to "the earth is filled with iniquity through them." Four points are important about this revision. The first is that Challoner updated the spelling of "iniquitie." Second, here, as elsewhere, he translated very logically an ordinary Latin word *(repleta)* with an equally common English one ("filled"), rather than with a cognate ("replenished"). Thus, he followed a policy that contrasts with the Latinate qualities that pervade the earlier translation. Third, "through" is not found in any Latin edition; while the meaning of "from the face of them" is obscure in English, it is a literal rendition of all the transmitted Vulgate texts of this verse. The fourth point is the trickiest one to address: the preposition "through" instead of "from the face of" is in fact found in the King James Version, which was in Challoner's day the more or less official Anglican (and of course Protestant) Bible.

Gen 6:13 illustrates how Challoner revised the Douay-Rheims Bible on literary grounds. One peculiarity of Bible studies is that many areas of interest are plagued with partisanship, and it can be difficult to make any argument without seeming to side with one religious (or secular) establishment against another. In trying to articulate the relationship between the King James and Douay-Rheims Versions, many otherwise useful sources emphasize the effects of one on the other according to the publisher's disposition: that is to say, Catholic sources underscore the similarities between the 1582 New Testament and the 1611 King James text, while Protestant reference works point to Challoner's alleged in-

debtedness to the King James Version. A notable exception is the anonymous article quoted above, which in its passionate call for a responsible, authorized translation of the Sixto-Clementine Vulgate rightly commented on a difference between the 1582 New Testament and Challoner's revision: "This correction is taken verbatim from the Protestant version."[13] Without delving into the differences in the theological programs of the editors of the Douay-Rheims and King James Versions or calling one preferable to the other, one could argue convincingly (as many have done) that the King James Bible has far greater—or at the very least, more enduring—literary merit than the original Douay-Rheims Version.

To understand the relative qualities of these English Bibles, compare, for example, the translations of Dt 30:19. The Douay-Rheims reads: "I cal for witnesses this day heauen and earth, that I haue proposed to you life and death, blessing and cursing. Choose therefore life, that both thou mayest liue, and thy seede." The King James Version has "I call heauen and earth to record this day against you, that I haue set before you life and death, blessing and cursing: therefore choose life, that both thou and thy seed may liue." Significantly, the King James Version is more natural and memorable; we should also note that the most awkward phrasing in the Douay-Rheims translation ("proposed to") has, in Challoner, been replaced by "set before," the King James reading.

The literary superiority of the King James Version is worth bearing in mind, because Challoner (whose schoolboy nickname, we are told, was Book)[14] revised the Douay-

Rheims text primarily on the basis of literary sensibilities. His version significantly departs from the Douay-Rheims when that text is most stilted, and not infrequently in such instances, Challoner's revision closely matches the sense or wording (or both) of the King James Bible.

A word of caution should be issued to those who would accept the implication of the subtitle of Challoner's Bible: "Newly revised and corrected, according to the Clementine Edition of the Scriptures." This description suggests that Challoner updated the Douay-Rheims translation in light of the standard text of the Bible that had not been available to the translators at the English College. Through oversight, however, his revision skipped a few phrases that the Douay-Rheims translators had missed as well (mostly when similar Latin words appeared on different parts of the page, causing leaps of the eye).[15] These omissions suggest strongly that Challoner's primary task was to make the English of the Douay-Rheims version more readable; it was not a revision on textual grounds. Otherwise, a careful collation of the Douay-Rheims Version with the Sixto-Clementine Bible would have been essential. More often than not, Challoner appears simply to have read the Douay-Rheims and fixed the poor or awkward style, occasionally turning to the King James, Latin, Greek or possibly Hebrew texts for help. He does not seem to have compared the Douay-Rheims systematically with the Latin (or any other version).

If we are not prepared to credit the magnum opus of the Anglican Church as a major source for Challoner, we can say that many of his revisions came from Hebrew and Greek sources (the same texts that the King James editors read,

possibly accounting for the similarities). Why Challoner often turned to sources other than the Latin Vulgate, which had existed in stable and authorized form since 1592, is unclear, especially in view of his title-page statement that he had updated the Douay-Rheims according to the Sixto-Clementine Bible. The period in which Challoner published his first edition of the New Testament (1749) was one of lively productivity for biblical scholars. The monumental edition of the pre-Vulgate Latin Bible credited to Pierre Sabatier, a Benedictine monk, was in production (Rheims 1739, 1749; Paris 1751). This text was meant to reconstruct the Bible as it was known to the Church fathers writing in Latin before the general acceptance of Jerome's text, and it received the approbation of two vicars general and Sabatier's own abbot. It relies frequently on Greek and Hebrew sources, indicating that the study of those texts was not as distasteful to the Church elite in the eighteenth century as it had been in 1609, when the Douay-Rheims translators prefaced their edition with the following words:

> But here an other question may be proposed: VVhy we translate the Latin text, rather than the Hebrew, or Greke, which Protestantes preferre, as the fountaine tongues, wherin holie Scriptures were first written? To this we answer, that if in dede those first pure Editions were now extant, or if such as be extant, were more pure than the Latin, we would also preferre such fountaines before the riuers, in whatsoeuer they should be found to disagree. But the ancient best lerned Fathers, & Doctors of the Church, do much complaine, and

testifie to vs, that both the Hebrew and Greke Editions are fouly corrupted by Iewes, and Heretikes,
since the Latin was truly translated out of them,
whiles they were more pure.[16]

Indeed, by 1750 the Counter-Reformational motives of
the Douay-Rheims Version of 1582, 1609 and 1610 had become largely irrelevant, and the polemical annotations of
the first translation were either omitted or stripped of their
vehemence. Even the notes in the Old Testament of 1609–
1610 contain less vitriol than those in the 1582 New Testament. Strict adherence to the Vulgate Bible mattered less to
Challoner than to the original translators, although he still
evidently favored literalism in his renderings. Consequently,
he may have preferred to replace poorly worded translations
with a new literal translation of a different source, rather
than to print loose constructions of the Latin text. None-
theless, the translation on the whole adheres faithfully to
the Vulgate, the official Bible of the Catholic Church; after
all, Challoner wrote a pamphlet entitled "The Touchstone
of the New Religion: or, Sixty Assertions of Protestants,
try'd by their own Rule of Scripture alone, and condemned
by clear and express Texts of their own Bible" (London 1735).
Interestingly, this tract reveals Challoner's familiarity with,
or at least access to, the King James Version of the Bible. As
one scholar put it, "He sought to establish the Roman
Church's credentials out of the mouths of her enemies."[17]

It may be fitting that the DOML Bible is an artificial one.
After all, in whatever language or languages the texts collectively called the Bible are read, they are heterogeneous, cob-
bled together over centuries, having been composed (or re-

vealed) and varied by oral tradition throughout the preceding millennia. With only minor revisions, we use Challoner's edition of the Douay-Rheims Bible because his text preserves the character of the English translation that brings us closest to the end of the medieval period while still being fairly elegant and readable. This edition differs from the 1899 printing in restoring readings from the 1750 and 1752 editions which had been spuriously altered in the 1899 version and in updating the biblical names and the punctuation of the earlier edition. Challoner's notes have been excised, though his chapter summaries remain.

With its rich and somewhat thorny history, Challoner's English is important to scholars of many disciplines, and its proximity to the literal translation of the most important book of the medieval period—namely, the Latin Bible— makes it invaluable to English-speakers studying the Middle Ages.

A Note on the Translation

Every discussion of the Douay-Rheims translation— whether praising or condemning it, whether acknowledging or ignoring Challoner's contribution to the text—affirms its proximity to the Latin. The translation in this volume has, however, a few characteristics that are either difficult for contemporary English-speakers to understand or that make the English less literal than it could be.

Challoner's word choice may sometimes puzzle readers. In the service of literalism, the Douay-Rheims translators and Challoner usually rendered *postquam* by the now obsolete phrase "after that," regardless of whether the Latin

word was a conjunction or an adverb. For example, at Gen 24:22, the translation reads, "And after that the camels had drunk, the man took out golden earrings weighing two sicles and as many bracelets of ten sicles weight," whereas a natural, more modern rendering would eliminate the word "that." Possibly by analogy to the case of *postquam,* or possibly because in the seventeenth century there was little distinction between the meanings of "after" and "after that," the translators occasionally rendered other words as "after that" where the phrase makes little sense in modern usage; see, for example, the temporal *cum* at Gen 8:6. On the whole, though, Challoner avoided trying to fit the square peg of English translation into the round hole of the Latin text. He shied away from the Douay-Rheims tendency to translate Latin words with awkward cognates, such as "invocate" for forms of *invoco* (for example, Gen 4:26); he frequently rendered relative pronouns with a conjunction followed by a demonstrative (Gen 3:1 and elsewhere); and he and his antecedents were free with temporal constructions, rendering, to take one example, *de nocte* as "very early" at Ex 34:4. Furthermore, Challoner translated many conjunctions as "now" that literally mean "and," "but," "moreover" or "therefore" (for example, Gen 16:1 and 3 Rg 1:1); the King James translators were also liberal in their use of "now."

Challoner's breaches of the rule of strict (some have said excessive) literalism also occur in areas other than word choice. The most frequent deviations appear in the translation of participles, the passive voice and especially passive participles. The translation of Nm 20:6 illustrates this program: the verse in Latin begins, "Ingressusque Moses et Aaron dimissa multitudine Tabernaculum Foederis coruerunt"; the 1609 translation reads, "And Moyses and Aaron,

the multitude being dismissed, entering into the tabernacle of couenant, fel"; whereas Challoner, preferring not to employ the passive voice or more than one construction with a participle, rendered the verse (with my punctuation), "And Moses and Aaron leaving the multitude went into the Tabernacle of the Covenant and fell." The many ablatives absolute and other participial constructions that have been modified by Challoner to fit more neatly into his preferred English style have not been signaled by italics in this volume because they do not illuminate anything about the Latin text and because the renderings are not so loose as to make their relationship to the Latin difficult to perceive.

Another systematic abandonment of literal translations appears in Challoner's rendering of oath formulas and other invocations of God, especially those that begin in Latin *vivo* or *vivit Dominus* or that employ constructions similar to "haec faciat mihi Deus et haec addat." Usually the first two formulas are rendered by adding "as" in English before the subject of the verb, and if the next clause begins with a conjunction, it is excised in translation. See, for example, 1 Rg 14:39, which begins in Latin, "Vivit Dominus, salvator Israhel, quia si" and was translated in the 1609 edition as "Our Lord the sauiour of Israel liueth, that if," which was modified by Challoner to read, "As the Lord liveth who is the saviour of Israel, if." The constructions that substantially resemble "haec faciat mihi Deus et haec addat" as at 1 Rg 14:44 were translated predictably in 1609 as "These thinges doe God to me, and these thinges adde he." Challoner rendered the prayer as "May God do so and so to me and add still more." Both of these divergences from the Latin are anticipated in the English of the King James Version, and because such renderings are pervasive, they have

been noted only here and are not mentioned in the Notes to the Text.

Challoner's antecedents at Douay and Rheims were also at times a bit lax in their translation. The degrees of adjectives and adverbs are not differentiated: *durius* (Gen 31:29) can be rendered as "roughly," *pessima* (Gen 37:20) as "naughtie." *Haec* (Gen 9:8), especially before verbs of saying, is often translated as "thus." Similar lapses in literalism occur with the verbs *volo* and *debeo,* the future tense, the future perfect tense and the subjunctive mood, which are all often rendered as simple futures in English; yet in most cases when the Douay-Rheims translators stuck to a literal translation and Challoner changed it, his variation and its source have been noted. When the Douay-Rheims translators use a turn of phrase that does not square with the Latin, the divergence has been commented upon only if the translation seems to be a useful key to the Latin they worked from; if they seem simply to have rendered the text loosely, no note appears. The most striking translation choices that the professors from Douay and Rheims made were to translate *utinam* (e.g., Ex 16:3) as "would to God," *absit* (e.g., Gen 44:17) as "God forbid," *salve* (e.g., 2 Rg 18:28) as "God save thee" and *vivat Rex* (e.g., 1 Rg 10:24) as "God save the King," even though there is no reference to the Divine. One other consistent policy of the Douay-Rheims translation was to translate *Dominus* as "our Lord." This practice stemmed from theological rather than philological reasons, and Challoner (like the King James translators) rendered this word as "the Lord." In these cases, there can be no other Latin reading, and since the English is not helpful in illuminating a hitherto unknown Latin text, no note has been made.

Last, the translation and Challoner's revision tried to avoid enjambment as much as possible. For example, Nm 7:18–19 reads in Latin, "Secundo die, obtulit Nathanahel, filius Suar, dux de tribu Isachar:/acetabulum argenteum," whereas at verses 24–25 of the same chapter we find "Tertio die, princeps filiorum Zabulon, Heliab, filius Helon,/obtulit acetabulum argenteum." Syntactically, the verses are identical (the colon is placed in the Latin only on the basis of the translation), but because in the first example *obtulit* appears in a separate verse from its direct object, the translation reads, "The second day, Nethanel, the son of Zuar, prince of the tribe of Issachar, made his offering:/a silver dish," while at verses 24–25 we have "The third day, the prince of the sons of Zebulun, Eliab, the son of Helon,/offered a silver dish."

Apart from these few deviations and the occasional italicized words and phrases, the Challoner revision is an exceptionally literal and readable translation of the Vulgate Bible, and it has proved helpful over the past quarter millennium to those who find the meaning of the Latin obscure.

I am grateful to the many people who have helped me with this project, including readers George Carlisle, Bob Edgar, Sally Edgar, Jim Halporn, Scott Johnson and Christopher Osborne; Alexandra Helprin, for her support and encouragement; Terra Dunham, Ian Stevenson and Sharmila Sen at Harvard University Press; Jesse Rainbow, for answering all my questions about Hebrew with clarity, depth, and precision; Christopher Husch, Philip Kim, and Julian Yolles for their excellent proofreading; Maria Ascher, for her thought-

ful editing of the Introduction; Andy Kelly, whose generosity was particularly helpful in the introductory paragraphs on Richard Challoner; Michael Herren and Danuta Shanzer for their careful reading and helpful suggestions; Angela Kinney for her invaluable editorial assistance; and especially Jan Ziolkowski, who conceived of the series, trusted me to see this project through, and supervised my work.

Swift Edgar

I would like to join in thanking those mentioned above and name additional collaborators without whose assistance this project could not have proceeded. Swift Edgar, of course, provided a treasury of advice and guidance. Two outstanding interns became indispensable to me: Christopher Husch helped with sundry scholarly and organizational aspects, including many useful philological remarks; likewise, Anne Marie Creighton added helpful comments while assisting with everything from punctuation to checking variants. Help with punctuation was also provided by Daniel Kim and Amy Oh; Diana Ferrara assisted with formatting the text. I am grateful to my husband, Robert, for his advice on matters of biblical Greek, his rich library, and his patience. The staff of Dumbarton Oaks and the graduate community and faculty at the University of Illinois continually encouraged me. Special thanks goes to Howard Jacobson for his assistance with Hebrew and to my adviser, Danuta Shanzer, whose brilliance, patience and energy never fail to inspire. Finally, I have the sincerest gratitude for Jan Ziolkowski, not

only for his guidance and consultation on this project, but also for his indefatigable dedication to this series and our field.

Angela M. Kinney

NOTES

1 See Carleton, *The Part of Rheims in the Making of the English Bible,* p. 13.

2 Quentin, *Mémoire sur l'établissement du texte de la Vulgate,* pp. 190–92.

3 Dodd, *The Church History of England,* vol. 2, p. 121, quoted in Pope and Bullough, *English Versions of the Bible,* p. 252.

4 Knox, *The First and Second Diaries of the English College,* p. 145, cited in Carleton, *The Part of Rheims in the Making of the English Bible,* p. 16.

5 de Hamel, *The Book: A History of the Bible,* p. 28.

6 Pope and Bullough, *English Versions of the Bible,* p. 295; Greenslade, *The Cambridge History of the Bible,* p. 163.

7 Greenslade, *The Cambridge History of the Bible,* p. 163.

8 Frontispiece, Douay-Rheims Bible, 1609.

9 A Catholic, "A new Version of the Four Gospels," p. 476, quoted in Cartmell, "English Spiritual Writers," p. 583. Cartmell erroneously cites the passage as appearing on page 276 but attributes it correctly to Nicholas Wiseman, though the review was published anonymously.

10 Cotton, *Rhemes and Doway.*

11 Translated from the Latin by Knox; see Carleton, *The Part of Rheims in the Making of the English Bible,* p. 15.

12 Kaske, *Medieval Christian Literary Imagery,* p. 6.

13 A Catholic, "A new Version of the Four Gospels," p. 476.

14 Duffy, *Challoner and His Church,* p. 6.

15 See Pope and Bullough, *English Versions of the Bible,* pp. 359–71.

16 "To the right vvelbeloved English reader," Douay-Rheims Bible, 1609.

17 Gilley, "Challoner as Controvertionalist," p. 93.

Abbreviations

Ecl	Ecclesiastes
Ct	Canticle of Canticles
Wis	Wisdom
Sir	Ecclesiasticus
Is	Isaiah
Jer	Jeremiah
Lam	Lamentations
Bar	Baruch
Ez	Ezekiel
Dn	Daniel
Hos	Hosea
Joel	Joel
Am	Amos
Ob	Obadiah
Jon	Jonah
Mi	Micah
Na	Nahum
Hab	Habakkuk
Zeph	Zephaniah
Hag	Haggai
Zech	Zechariah
Mal	Malachi
1 Mcc	1 Maccabees
2 Mcc	2 Maccabees
Mt	Matthew
Mk	Mark
Lk	Luke
John	John
Act	Acts of the Apostles

Rom	Romans
1 Cor	1 Corinthians
2 Cor	2 Corinthians
Gal	Galatians
Eph	Ephesians
Phlp	Philippians
Col	Colossians
1 Th	1 Thessalonians
2 Th	2 Thessalonians
1 Tim	1 Timothy
2 Tim	2 Timothy
Tit	Titus
Phlm	Philemon
Hbr	Hebrews
Ja	James
1 Pt	1 Peter
2 Pt	2 Peter
1 John	1 John
2 John	2 John
3 John	3 John
Jud	Jude
Apc	Apocalypse of St. John the Apostle

LATIN NAMES FOR BOOKS IN THE BIBLE

Gen	Genesis
Ex	Exodi
Lv	Levitici
Nm	Numerorum
Dt	Deuteronomii

Ios	Iosue
Idc	Iudicum
Rt	Ruth
1 Rg	1 Regum
2 Rg	2 Regum
3 Rg	3 Regum
4 Rg	4 Regum
1 Par	1 Paralipomenon
2 Par	2 Paralipomenon
1 Esr	1 Ezrae
2 Esr	2 Ezrae
Tb	Tobiae
Idt	Iudith
Est	Hester
Iob	Iob
Ps	Psalmi
Prv	Proverbiorum
Ecl	Ecclesiastes
Ct	Canticum Canticorum
Sap	Sapientiae
Sir	Sirach (Ecclesiasticus *or* Iesu Filii Sirach)
Is	Isaias
Ier	Hieremias
Lam	Lamentationes
Bar	Baruch
Ez	Hiezechiel
Dn	Danihel
Os	Osee
Ioel	Iohel

Am	Amos
Abd	Abdias
Ion	Iona
Mi	Micha
Na	Naum
Hab	Abacuc
So	Sofonias
Agg	Aggeus
Za	Zaccharias
Mal	Malachi
1 Mcc	1 Macchabeorum
2 Mcc	2 Macchabeorum
Mt	Secundum Mattheum
Mc	Secundum Marcum
Lc	Secundum Lucam
Io	Secundum Iohannem
Act	Actus Apostolorum
Rm	Ad Romanos
1 Cor	Ad Corinthios 1
2 Cor	Ad Corinthios 2
Gal	Ad Galatas
Eph	Ad Ephesios
Phil	Ad Philippenses
Col	Ad Colossenes
1 Th	Ad Thessalonicenses 1
2 Th	Ad Thessalonicenses 2
1 Tim	Ad Timotheum
Tit	Ad Titum
Phlm	Ad Philemonem

Hbr	Ad Hebraeos
Iac	Epistula Iacobi
1 Pt	Epistula Petri 1
2 Pt	Epistula Petri 2
1 Io	Epistula Iohannis 1
2 Io	Epistula Iohannis 2
3 Io	Epistula Iohannis 3
Iud	Epistula Iudae
Apc	Apocalypsis Iohannis

ISAIAH

Caput 1

Visio Isaiae, filii Amos, quam vidit super Iudam et Hierusalem in diebus Oziae, Ioatham, Ahaz et Ezechiae, regum Iuda.

2 Audite, caeli, et auribus percipe, terra, quoniam Dominus locutus est. Filios enutrivi et exaltavi, ipsi autem spreverunt me. 3 Cognovit bos possessorem suum, et asinus praesepe domini sui, Israhel autem me non cognovit, et populus meus non intellexit.

4 Vae genti peccatrici, populo gravi iniquitate, semini nequam, filiis sceleratis! Dereliquerunt Dominum; blasphemaverunt Sanctum Israhel; abalienati sunt retrorsum. 5 Super quo percutiam vos ultra, addentes praevaricationem? Omne caput languidum, et omne cor maerens. 6 A planta pedis usque ad verticem non est in eo sanitas; vulnus et livor et plaga tumens, non est circumligata nec curata medicamine neque fota oleo. 7 Terra vestra deserta; civitates vestrae succensae

Chapter 1

The prophet complains of the sins of Judah and Jerusalem
and exhorts them to a sincere conversion.

The vision of Isaiah, the son of Amoz, which he saw concerning Judah and Jerusalem in the days of Uzziah, Jotham,
Ahaz and Hezekiah, kings of Judah.

2 Hear, O ye heavens, and give ear, O earth, for the Lord
hath spoken. I have brought up children and exalted them,
but they have despised me. 3 The ox knoweth his owner, and
the ass his master's crib, but Israel hath not known me, and
my people hath not understood.

4 Woe to the sinful nation, a people laden with iniquity,
a wicked seed, ungracious children! They have forsaken the
Lord; they have blasphemed the Holy One of Israel; they
are gone away backwards. 5 For what shall I strike you any
more, you that increase transgression? The whole head is
sick, and the whole heart is sad. 6 From the sole of the foot
unto the top of the head there is no soundness therein;
wounds and bruises and swelling sores, they are not bound
up nor *dressed* nor fomented with oil. 7 Your land is desolate;

igni. Regionem vestram coram vobis alieni devorant, et desolabitur sicut in vastitate hostili, 8 et derelinquetur filia
Sion ut umbraculum in vinea et sicut tugurium in cucumerario et sicut civitas quae vastatur. 9 Nisi Dominus exercituum
reliquisset nobis semen, quasi Sodoma fuissemus, et quasi
Gomorra similes essemus.

10 Audite verbum Domini, principes Sodomorum; percipite auribus legem Dei nostri, populus Gomorrae. 11 "Quo
mihi multitudinem victimarum vestrarum?" dicit Dominus.
"Plenus sum; holocausta arietum et adipem pinguium et
sanguinem vitulorum et agnorum et hircorum nolui. 12 Cum
veniretis ante conspectum meum, quis quaesivit haec de
manibus vestris ut ambularetis in atriis meis? 13 Ne offeratis
ultra sacrificium frustra; incensum abominatio est mihi.
Neomeniam et sabbatum et festivitates alias non feram; iniqui sunt coetus vestri. 14 Kalendas vestras et sollemnitates
vestras odivit anima mea. Facta sunt mihi molesta; laboravi
sustinens. 15 Et cum extenderitis manus vestras, avertam
oculos meos a vobis, et cum multiplicaveritis orationem,
non audiam, manus enim vestrae sanguine plenae sunt.
16 Lavamini; mundi estote; auferte malum cogitationum vestrarum ab oculis meis; quiescite agere perverse. 17 Discite
benefacere; quaerite iudicium; subvenite oppresso; iudicate
pupillo; defendite viduam. 18 Et venite, et arguite me," dicit
Dominus. "Si fuerint peccata vestra ut coccinum, quasi nix
dealbabuntur, et si fuerint rubra quasi vermiculus, velut lana
alba erunt. 19 Si volueritis et audieritis me, bona terrae come-

your cities are burnt with fire. Your country strangers devour before your face, and it shall be desolate as when wasted by enemies, 8 and the daughter of Zion shall be left as a covert in a vineyard and as a lodge in a garden of cucumbers and as a city that is laid waste. 9 Except the Lord of hosts had left us seed, we had been as Sodom, and we should have been like to Gomorrah.

10 Hear the word of the Lord, ye rulers of Sodom; give ear to the law of our God, ye people of Gomorrah. 11 "To what purpose *do you offer* me the multitude of your victims?" saith the Lord. "I am full; I desire not holocausts of rams and fat of fatlings and blood of calves and lambs and buck-goats. 12 When you came *to appear* before me, who required these things at your hands that you should walk in my courts? 13 Offer sacrifice no more in vain; incense is an abomination to me. The new moons and the sabbaths and other festivals I will not abide; your assemblies are wicked. 14 My soul hateth your *new moons* and your solemnities. They are become troublesome to me; I am weary of bearing them. 15 And when you stretch forth your hands, I will turn away my eyes from you, and when you multiply prayer, I will not hear, for your hands are full of blood. 16 Wash yourselves; be clean; take away the evil of your devices from my eyes; cease to do perversely. 17 Learn to do well; seek judgment; relieve the oppressed; judge for the fatherless; defend the widow. 18 And *then* come, and accuse me," saith the Lord. "If your sins be as scarlet, they shall be made as white as snow, and if they be red as crimson, they shall be white as wool. 19 If you be willing and will hearken to me, you shall eat the good things of

detis. 20 Quod si nolueritis et me provocaveritis ad iracundiam, gladius devorabit vos, quia os Domini locutum est."

21 Quomodo facta est meretrix civitas fidelis plena iudicii? Iustitia habitavit in ea, nunc autem homicidae. 22 Argentum tuum versum est in scoriam; vinum tuum mixtum est aqua. 23 Principes tui infideles, socii furum. Omnes diligunt munera; sequuntur retributiones. Pupillo non iudicant, et causa viduae non ingreditur ad eos.

24 Propter hoc ait Dominus, Deus exercituum, Fortis Israhel, "Heu! Consolabor super hostibus meis, et vindicabor de inimicis meis. 25 Et convertam manum meam ad te, et excoquam ad purum scoriam tuam, et auferam omne stagnum tuum. 26 Et restituam iudices tuos ut fuerunt prius, et consiliarios tuos sicut antiquitus. Post haec vocaberis civitas iusti, urbs fidelis. 27 Sion in iudicio redimetur, et reducent eam in iustitia. 28 Et conteret scelestos et peccatores simul, et qui dereliquerunt Dominum consumentur. 29 Confundentur enim ab idolis quibus sacrificaverunt, et erubescetis super hortis quos elegeratis, 30 cum fueritis velut quercus defluentibus foliis et velut hortus absque aqua. 31 Et erit fortitudo vestra ut favilla stuppae, et opus vestrum quasi scintilla, et succendetur utrumque simul, et non erit qui extinguat."

the land. 20 But if you will not and will provoke me to wrath, the sword shall devour you, because the mouth of the Lord hath spoken it."

21 How is the faithful city that was full of judgment become a harlot? Justice dwelt in it, but now murderers. 22 Thy silver is turned into dross; thy wine is mingled with water. 23 Thy princes are faithless, companions of thieves. They all love bribes; they run after rewards. They judge not for the fatherless, and the widow's cause cometh not in to them.

24 Therefore saith the Lord, the God of hosts, the Mighty One of Israel, "Ah! I will comfort myself over my adversaries, and I will be revenged of my enemies. 25 And I will turn my hand to thee, and I will *clean purge away* thy dross, and I will take away all thy tin. 26 And I will restore thy judges as they were before, and thy counsellors as of old. After this thou shalt be called the city of the just, a faithful city. 27 Zion shall be redeemed in judgment, and they shall bring her back in justice. 28 And he shall destroy the wicked and the sinners together, and they that have forsaken the Lord shall be consumed. 29 For they shall be confounded for the idols to which they have sacrificed, and you shall be ashamed of the gardens which you have chosen, 30 when you shall be as an oak with the leaves falling off and as a garden without water. 31 And your strength shall be as the ashes of tow, and your work as a spark, and both shall burn together, and there shall be none to quench it."

Caput 2

Verbum quod vidit Isaias, filius Amos, super Iudam et Hierusalem.

2 Et erit in novissimis diebus praeparatus mons domus Domini in vertice montium, et elevabitur super colles, et fluent ad eum omnes gentes. 3 Et ibunt populi multi et dicent, "Venite, et ascendamus ad montem Domini et ad domum Dei Iacob, et docebit nos vias suas, et ambulabimus in semitis eius," quia de Sion exibit lex, et verbum Domini de Hierusalem. 4 Et iudicabit Gentes et arguet populos multos, et conflabunt gladios suos in vomeres et lanceas suas in falces. Non levabit gens contra gentem gladium, nec exercebuntur ultra ad proelium.

5 Domus Iacob, venite, et ambulemus in lumine Domini. 6 Proiecisti enim populum tuum, domum Iacob, quia repleti sunt ut olim et augures habuerunt ut Philisthim et pueris alienis adheserunt. 7 Repleta est terra argento et auro, et non est finis thesaurorum eius. 8 Et repleta est terra eius equis, et innumerabiles quadrigae eius. Et repleta est terra eius idolis; opus manuum suarum adoraverunt quod fecerunt digiti eorum. 9 Et incurvavit se homo, et humiliatus est vir; ne ergo

Chapter 2

All nations shall flow to the church of Christ. The Jews shall
be rejected for their sins. Idolatry shall be destroyed.

The word that Isaiah, the son of Amoz, saw concerning
Judah and Jerusalem.

2 And in the last days the mountain of the house of the
Lord shall be prepared on the top of mountains, and it shall
be exalted above the hills, and all nations shall flow unto it.
3 And many people shall go and say, "Come, and let us go up
to the mountain of the Lord and to the house of the God
of Jacob, and he will teach us his ways, and we will walk in
his paths," for the law shall come forth from Zion, and the
word of the Lord from Jerusalem. 4 And he shall judge the
Gentiles and rebuke many people, and they shall turn their
swords into ploughshares and their spears into sickles. Nation shall not lift up sword against nation, neither shall they
be exercised any more to war.

5 O house of Jacob, come ye, and let us walk in the light of
the Lord. 6 For thou hast cast off thy people, the house of
Jacob, because they are filled as in times past and have had
soothsayers as the Philistines and have adhered to strange
children. 7 Their land is filled with silver and gold, and there
is no end of their treasures. 8 And their land is filled with
horses, and their chariots are innumerable. Their land also is
full of idols; they have adored the work of their own hands
which their own fingers have made. 9 And man hath bowed
himself down, and man hath been debased; therefore for-

dimittas eis. 10 Ingredere in petram, et abscondere in fossa humo a facie timoris Domini et a gloria maiestatis eius. 11 Oculi sublimes hominis humiliati sunt, et incurvabitur altitudo virorum, exaltabitur autem Dominus solus in die illa. 12 Quia dies Domini exercituum super omnem superbum et excelsum et super omnem arrogantem, et humiliabitur, 13 et super omnes cedros Libani sublimes et erectas et super omnes quercus Basan, 14 et super omnes montes excelsos et super omnes colles elevatos, 15 et super omnem turrem excelsam et omnem murum munitum, 16 et super omnes naves Tharsis et super omne quod visu pulchrum est. 17 Et incurvabitur sublimitas hominum, et humiliabitur altitudo virorum, et elevabitur Dominus solus in die illa.

18 Et idola penitus conterentur. 19 Et introibunt in speluncas petrarum et in voragines terrae a facie formidinis Domini et a gloria maiestatis eius, cum surrexerit percutere terram. 20 In die illa proiciet homo idola argenti sui et simulacra auri sui quae fecerat sibi ut adoraret, talpas et vespertiliones. 21 Et ingredietur fissuras petrarum et in cavernas saxorum a facie formidinis Domini et a gloria maiestatis eius, cum surrexerit percutere terram. 22 Quiescite ergo ab homine cuius spiritus in naribus eius est, quia excelsus reputatus est ipse.

give them not. 10 Enter thou into the rock, and hide thee in the *pit* from the face of the fear of the Lord and from the glory of his majesty. 11 The lofty eyes of man are humbled, and the haughtiness of men shall be made to stoop, and the Lord alone shall be exalted in that day. 12 Because the day of the Lord of hosts shall be upon every one that is proud and high-minded and upon every one that is arrogant, and he shall be humbled, 13 and upon all the tall and lofty cedars of Lebanon and upon all the oaks of Bashan, 14 and upon all the high mountains and upon all the elevated hills, 15 and upon every high tower and every fenced wall, 16 and upon all the ships of Tarshish and upon all that is fair to behold. 17 And the loftiness of men shall be bowed down, and the haughtiness of men shall be humbled, and the Lord alone shall be exalted in that day.

18 And idols shall be utterly destroyed. 19 And they shall go into the holes of rocks and into the caves of the earth from the face of the fear of the Lord and from the glory of his majesty, when he shall rise up to strike the earth. 20 In that day a man shall cast away his idols of silver and his idols of gold which he had made for himself to adore, moles and bats. 21 And he shall go into the clefts of rocks and into the holes of stones from the face of the fear of the Lord and from the glory of his majesty, when he shall rise up to strike the earth. 22 Cease ye therefore from the man whose breath is in his nostrils, for he is reputed high.

Caput 3

Ecce enim: Dominator, Dominus exercituum, auferet ab Hierusalem et ab Iuda validum et fortem, omne robur panis et omne robur aquae, 2 fortem et virum bellatorem, iudicem et prophetam et ariolum et senem, 3 principem super quinquaginta et honorabilem vultu et consiliarium et sapientem de architectis et prudentem eloquii mystici. 4 Et dabo pueros principes eorum, et effeminati dominabuntur eis. 5 Et inruet populus vir ad virum, et unusquisque ad proximum suum; tumultuabitur puer contra senem, et ignobilis contra nobilem.

6 Adprehendet enim vir fratrem suum, domesticum patris sui, "Vestimentum tibi est; princeps esto noster, ruina autem haec sub manu tua."

7 Respondebit in die illa, dicens, "Non sum medicus, et in domo mea non est panis neque vestimentum. Nolite constituere me principem populi."

8 Ruit enim Hierusalem, et Iudas concidit, quia lingua eorum et adinventiones eorum contra Dominum ut provocarent oculos maiestatis eius. 9 Agnitio vultus eorum respondit eis, et peccatum suum quasi Sodoma praedicaverunt, nec

Chapter 3

*The confusion and other evils that shall come upon the Jews
for their sins. The pride of their women shall be punished.*

For behold: the Sovereign, the Lord of hosts, shall take
away from Jerusalem and from Judah the valiant and the
strong, the whole strength of bread and the whole strength
of water, 2 the strong man and the man of war, the judge and
the prophet and the *cunning man* and the ancient, 3 the captain over fifty and the honourable in countenance and the
counsellor and the *architect* and the skilful in *eloquent* speech.
4 And I will give children to be their princes, and the effemi-
nate shall rule over them. 5 And the people shall rush one
upon another, and every man against his neighbour; the
child shall make a tumult against the ancient, and the base
against the honourable.

6 For a man shall take hold of his brother, one of the house
of his father, *saying,* "Thou hast a garment; be thou our ruler,
and let this ruin be under thy hand."

7 In that day he shall answer, saying, "I am no healer, and
in my house there is no bread nor clothing. Make me not
ruler of the people."

8 For Jerusalem is ruined, and Judah is fallen, because
their tongue and their devices are against the Lord, to provoke the eyes of his majesty. 9 The *shew* of their countenance
hath answered them, and they have proclaimed *abroad* their

absconderunt. Vae animae eorum, quoniam reddita sunt eis mala.

10 Dicite iusto quoniam bene, quoniam fructum adinventionum suarum comedet. 11 Vae impio in malum, retributio enim manuum eius fiet ei. 12 Populum meum, exactores sui spoliaverunt, et mulieres dominatae sunt eis. Popule meus, qui beatum te dicunt, ipsi te decipiunt et viam gressuum tuorum dissipant.

13 Stat ad iudicandum Dominus, et stat ad iudicandos populos. 14 Dominus ad iudicium veniet cum senibus populi sui et principibus eius, vos enim depasti estis vineam, et rapina pauperis in domo vestra. 15 "Quare adteritis populum meum et facies pauperum commolitis?" dicit Dominus, Deus exercituum.

16 Et dixit Dominus, "Pro eo quod elevatae sunt filiae Sion et ambulaverunt extento collo et nutibus oculorum ibant et plaudebant, ambulabant pedibus suis et conposito gradu incedebant, 17 decalvabit Dominus verticem filiarum Sion, et Dominus crinem earum nudabit." 18 In die illa auferet Dominus ornatum calciamentorum et lunulas 19 et torques et monilia et armillas et mitras 20 et discriminalia et periscelidas et murenulas et olfactoriola et inaures 21 et anulos et gemmas in fronte pendentes 22 et mutatoria et palliola et linteamina et acus 23 et specula et sindones et vittas et theristra. 24 Et erit pro suavi odore fetor, et pro zona funiculus, et pro crispanti crine calvitium, et pro fascia pectorali cilicium. 25 Pulcherrimi quoque viri tui gladio cadent, et fortes tui in proelio. 26 Et maerebunt atque lugebunt portae eius, et desolata in terra sedebit.

sin as Sodom, and they have not hid it. Woe to their souls, for evils are rendered to them.

10 Say to the just man that it is well, for he shall eat the fruit of his *doings.* 11 Woe to the wicked unto evil, for the reward of his hands shall be given him. 12 As for my people, their oppressors have stripped them, and women have ruled over them. O my people, they that call thee blessed, the same deceive thee and destroy the way of thy steps.

13 The Lord standeth up to judge, and he standeth to judge the people. 14 The Lord will enter into judgment with the ancients of his people and its princes, for you have devoured the vineyard, and the spoil of the poor is in your house. 15 "Why do you consume my people and grind the faces of the poor?" saith the Lord, the God of hosts.

16 And the Lord said, "Because the daughters of Zion are haughty and have walked with stretched out necks and *wanton* glances of their eyes and *made a noise as* they walked with their feet and moved in a set pace, 17 the Lord will make bald the crown of the head of the daughters of Zion, and the Lord will discover their hair." 18 In that day the Lord will take away the ornaments of shoes and little moons 19 and chains and necklaces and bracelets and bonnets 20 and bodkins and ornaments of the legs and tablets and sweet balls and earrings 21 and rings and jewels hanging on the forehead 22 and changes of apparel and short cloaks and fine linen and *crisping* pins 23 and looking-glasses and lawns and headbands and *fine* veils. 24 And instead of a sweet smell there shall be stench, and instead of a girdle a cord, and instead of curled hair baldness, and instead of a stomacher haircloth. 25 Thy fairest men also shall fall by the sword, and thy valiant ones in battle. 26 And her gates shall lament and mourn, and she shall sit desolate on the ground.

Caput 4

Et adprehendent septem mulieres virum unum in die illa, dicentes, "Panem nostrum comedemus et vestimentis nostris operiemur, tantummodo invocetur nomen tuum super nos; aufer obprobrium nostrum."

2 In die illa erit germen Domini in magnificentia et gloria, et fructus terrae sublimis et exultatio his qui salvati fuerint de Israhel. 3 Et erit omnis qui relictus fuerit in Sion et residuus in Hierusalem sanctus vocabitur, omnis qui scriptus est in vita in Hierusalem, 4 si abluerit Dominus sordes filiarum Sion et sanguinem Hierusalem laverit de medio eius in spiritu iudicii et spiritu ardoris. 5 Et creabit Dominus super omnem locum Montis Sion et ubi invocatus est nubem per diem et fumum et splendorem ignis flammantis in nocte, super omnem enim gloriam protectio. 6 Et tabernaculum erit in umbraculum diei ab aestu et in securitatem et absconsionem a turbine et a pluvia.

Chapter 4

After an extremity of evils that shall fall upon the Jews, a remnant shall be comforted by Christ.

And in that day seven women shall take hold of one man, saying, "We will eat our own bread and wear our own apparel, only let us be called by thy name; take away our reproach."

2 In that day the bud of the Lord shall be in magnificence and glory, and the fruit of the earth shall be high and a great joy to them that shall have escaped of Israel. 3 And it shall come to pass that every one that shall be left in Zion and that shall remain in Jerusalem shall be called holy, every one that is written in life in Jerusalem, 4 if the Lord shall wash away the filth of the daughters of Zion and shall wash away the blood of Jerusalem out of the midst thereof by the spirit of judgment and by the spirit of burning. 5 And the Lord will create upon every place of Mount Zion and where he is called upon a cloud by day and a smoke and the brightness of a flaming fire in the night, for over all the glory shall be a protection. 6 And there shall be a tabernacle for a shade in the daytime from the heat and for a security and covert from the whirlwind and from rain.

Caput 5

Cantabo dilecto meo canticum patruelis mei vineae suae.

Vinea facta est dilecto meo in cornu filio olei. 2 Et sepivit eam et lapides elegit ex illa et plantavit eam electam et aedificavit turrem in medio eius et torcular extruxit in ea, et expectavit ut faceret uvas, et fecit labruscas.

3 Nunc ergo, habitatores Hierusalem et viri Iuda, iudicate inter me et vineam meam. 4 Quid est quod debui ultra facere vineae meae et non feci ei? An quod expectavi ut faceret uvas, et fecit labruscas?

5 Et nunc ostendam vobis quid ego faciam vineae meae. Auferam sepem eius, et erit in direptionem; diruam maceriam eius, et erit in conculcationem. 6 Et ponam eam desertam; non putabitur, et non fodietur, et ascendent super eam vepres et spinae, et nubibus mandabo ne pluant super eam imbrem. 7 Vinea enim Domini exercituum domus Israhel est, et vir Iuda germen delectabile eius. Et expectavi ut faceret iudicium, et ecce: iniquitas, et iustitiam, et ecce:

Chapter 5

The reprobation of the Jews is foreshewn under the parable
of a vineyard. A woe is pronounced against sinners; the army
of God shall send against them.

I will sing to my beloved the canticle of my cousin concerning his vineyard.

My beloved had a vineyard on a *hill in a fruitful place.* 2 And
he fenced it in and picked the stones out of it and planted it
with choicest vines and built a tower in the midst thereof and
set up a winepress therein, and he looked that it should bring
forth grapes, and it brought forth wild grapes.

3 *And* now, O ye inhabitants of Jerusalem and ye men of
Judah, judge between me and my vineyard. 4 What is there
that I ought to do more to my vineyard *that* I have not done
to it? Was it that I looked that it should bring forth grapes,
and it hath brought forth wild grapes?

5 And now I will shew you what I will do to my vineyard.
I will take away the hedge thereof, and it shall be wasted; I
will break down the wall thereof, and it shall be trodden
down. 6 And I will make it desolate; it shall not be pruned,
and it shall not be digged, *but* briers and thorns shall come
up, and I will command the clouds to rain no rain upon
it. 7 For the vineyard of the Lord of hosts is the house of Israel, and the man of Judah his pleasant plant. And I looked
that he should do judgment, and behold: iniquity, and do

clamor. 8 Vae qui coniungitis domum ad domum et agrum agro copulatis usque ad terminum loci; numquid habitabitis soli vos in medio terrae?

9 "In auribus meis sunt haec," dicit Dominus exercituum, "nisi domus multae desertae fuerint grandes et pulchrae absque habitatore." 10 Decem enim iugera vinearum facient lagunculam unam, et triginta modii sementis facient modios tres.

11 Vae qui consurgitis mane ad ebrietatem sectandam et potandum usque ad vesperam, ut vino aestuetis. 12 Cithara et lyra et tympanum et tibia et vinum in conviviis vestris, et opus Domini non respicitis, nec opera manuum eius consideratis. 13 Propterea captivus ductus est populus meus quia non habuit scientiam, et nobiles eius interierunt fame, et multitudo eius siti exaruit. 14 Propterea dilatavit infernus animam suam et aperuit os suum absque ullo termino, et descendent fortes eius et populus eius et sublimes gloriosique eius ad eum. 15 Et incurvabitur homo, et humiliabitur vir, et oculi sublimium deprimentur. 16 Et exaltabitur Dominus exercituum in iudicio, et Deus sanctus sanctificabitur in iustitia. 17 Et pascentur agni iuxta ordinem suum, et deserta in ubertatem versa advenae comedent.

18 Vae qui trahitis iniquitatem in funiculis vanitatis, et quasi vinculum plaustri peccatum, 19 qui dicitis, "Festinet, et cito veniat opus eius ut videamus, et veniat consilium Sancti Israhel, et sciemus illud." 20 Vae qui dicitis malum bonum et bonum malum, ponentes tenebras lucem et lucem tenebras,

justice, and behold: a cry. 8 Woe to you that join house to house and lay field to field even to the end of the place; shall you alone dwell in the midst of the earth?

9 "These things are in my ears," saith the Lord of hosts, "unless many great and fair houses shall become desolate without an inhabitant." 10 For ten acres of vineyards shall yield one little *measure,* and thirty bushels of seed shall yield three bushels.

11 Woe to you that rise up early in the morning to follow drunkenness and to drink till the evening, to be inflamed with wine. 12 The harp and the lyre and the timbrel and the pipe and wine are in your feasts, and the work of the Lord you regard not, nor do you consider the works of his hands. 13 Therefore is my people led away captive because they had not knowledge, and their nobles have perished with famine, and their multitude were dried up with thirst. 14 Therefore hath hell enlarged her soul and opened her mouth without any bounds, and their strong ones and their people and their high and glorious ones shall go down into it. 15 And man shall be brought down, and man shall be humbled, and the eyes of the lofty shall be brought low. 16 And the Lord of hosts shall be exalted in judgment, and the holy God shall be sanctified in justice. 17 And the lambs shall feed according to their order, and strangers shall eat the deserts turned into fruitfulness.

18 Woe to you that draw iniquity with cords of vanity, and sin as the rope of a cart, 19 that say, "Let him make haste, and let his work come quickly that we may see it, and let the counsel of the Holy One of Israel come *that* we may know it." 20 Woe to you that call evil good and good evil, that put darkness *for* light and light *for* darkness, that put bitter for

ponentes amarum in dulce et dulce in amarum. 21 Vae qui sapientes estis in oculis vestris et coram vobismet ipsis prudentes. 22 Vae qui potentes estis ad bibendum vinum et viri fortes ad miscendam ebrietatem, 23 qui iustificatis impium pro muneribus et iustitiam iusti aufertis ab eo. 24 Propter hoc, sicut devorat stipulam lingua ignis et calor flammae exurit, sic radix eorum quasi favilla erit, et germen eorum ut pulvis ascendet, abiecerunt enim legem Domini exercituum et eloquium Sancti Israhel blasphemaverunt. 25 Ideo iratus est furor Domini in populum suum, et extendit manum suam super eum et percussit eum, et conturbati sunt montes, et facta sunt morticina eorum quasi stercus in medio platearum. In omnibus his non est aversus furor eius, sed adhuc manus eius extenta.

26 Et levabit signum in nationibus procul et sibilabit ad eum de finibus terrae, et ecce: festinus velociter veniet. 27 Non est deficiens neque laborans in eo; non dormitabit neque dormiet, neque solvetur cingulum renum eius nec rumpetur corrigia calciamenti eius. 28 Sagittae eius acutae, et omnes arcus eius extenti. Ungulae equorum eius ut silex, et rotae eius quasi impetus tempestatis, 29 rugitus eius ut leonis. Rugiet ut catuli leonum; et frendet et tenebit praedam, et amplexabitur, et non erit qui eruat. 30 Et sonabit super eum in die illa sicut sonitus maris. Aspiciemus in terram, et ecce: tenebrae tribulationis, et lux obtenebrata est in caligine eius.

sweet and sweet for bitter. 21 Woe to you that are wise in your own eyes and prudent in your own conceits. 22 Woe to you that are mighty to drink wine and stout men at drunkenness, 23 that justify the wicked for gifts and take away the justice of the just from him. 24 Therefore, as the tongue of the fire devoureth the stubble and the heat of the flame consumeth it, so shall their root be as ashes, and their bud shall go up as dust, for they have cast away the law of the Lord of hosts and have blasphemed the word of the Holy One of Israel. 25 Therefore is the wrath of the Lord kindled against his people, and he hath stretched out his hand upon them and struck them, and the mountains were troubled, and their carcasses became as dung in the midst of the streets. For all this his anger is not turned away, but his hand is stretched out still.

26 And he will lift up a sign to the nations afar off and will whistle to them from the ends of the earth, and behold: they shall come with speed swiftly. 27 There is none that shall faint nor labour among them; they shall not slumber nor sleep, neither shall the girdle of their loins be loosed nor the latchet of their shoes be broken. 28 Their arrows are sharp, and all their bows are bent. The hoofs of their horses shall be like the flint, and their wheels like the violence of a tempest, 29 their roaring like that of a lion. They shall roar like young lions; yea, they shall *roar* and take hold of the prey, and they shall keep fast hold of it, and there shall be none to deliver it. 30 And they shall make a noise against them that day like the roaring of the sea. We shall look towards the land, and behold: darkness of tribulation, and the light is darkened with the mist thereof.

Caput 6

In anno quo mortuus est Rex Ozias, vidi Dominum seden-
tem super solium excelsum et elevatum, et ea quae sub eo
erant implebant templum. 2 Seraphin stabant super illud;
sex alae uni, et sex alae alteri; duabus velabant faciem eius, et
duabus velabant pedes eius, et duabus volabant. 3 Et clama-
bant alter ad alterum et dicebant, "Sanctus, sanctus, sanctus
Dominus, Deus exercituum; plena est omnis terra gloria
eius." 4 Et commota sunt superliminaria cardinum a voce
clamantis, et domus impleta est fumo.

5 Et dixi, "Vae mihi quia tacui, quia vir pollutus labiis ego
sum, et in medio populi polluta labia habentis ego habito, et
Regem, Dominum exercituum, vidi oculis meis."

6 Et volavit ad me unus de seraphin, et in manu eius carbonem quem forcipe tulerat de altari. 7 Et tetigit os meum
et dixit, "Ecce: tetigit hoc labia tua, et auferetur iniquitas
tua, et peccatum tuum mundabitur."

8 Et audivi vocem Domini dicentis, "Quem mittam? Et
quis ibit nobis?"

Et dixi, "Ecce: ego sum; mitte me."

9 Et dixit, "Vade, et dices populo huic, 'Audite audientes,
et nolite intellegere, et videte visionem, et nolite cognos-

Chapter 6

A glorious vision in which the prophet's lips are cleansed.
He foretelleth the obstinacy of the Jews.

In the year that King Uzziah died, I saw the Lord sitting upon a throne high and elevated, and *his train* filled the temple. 2 Upon it stood the seraphims; the one had six wings, and the other had six wings; with two they covered his face, and with two they covered his feet, and with two they flew. 3 And they cried one to another and said, "Holy, holy, holy the Lord, God of hosts; all the earth is full of his glory." 4 And the lintels of the doors were moved at the voice of him that cried, and the house was filled with smoke.

5 And I said, "Woe is me because I have held my peace, because I am a man of unclean lips, and I dwell in the midst of a people that hath unclean lips, and I have seen with my eyes the King, the Lord of hosts."

6 And one of the seraphims flew to me, and in his hand was a live coal which he had taken with the tongs off the altar. 7 And he touched my mouth and said, "Behold: this hath touched thy lips, and thy *iniquities* shall be taken away, and thy sin shall be cleansed."

8 And I heard the voice of the Lord saying, "Whom shall I send? And who shall go for us?"

And I said, "Lo: here am I; send me."

9 And he said, "Go, and thou shalt say to this people, 'Hearing hear, and understand not, and see the vision, and

cere.' 10 Excaeca cor populi huius, et aures eius adgrava, et oculos eius claude, ne forte videat oculis suis et auribus suis audiat et corde suo intellegat et convertatur, et sanem eum."

11 Et dixi, "Usquequo, Domine?"

Et dixit, "Donec desolentur civitates absque habitatore, et domus sine homine, et terra relinquetur deserta. 12 Et longe faciet Dominus homines, et multiplicabitur quae derelicta fuerat in medio terrae. 13 Et adhuc in ea decimatio, et convertetur et erit in ostensionem sicut terebinthus et sicuti quercus quae expandit ramos suos; semen sanctum erit id quod steterit in ea."

Caput 7

Et factum est in diebus Ahaz, filii Ioatham, filii Oziae, regis Iuda, ascendit Rasin, rex Syriae, et Phacee, filius Romeliae, rex Israhel, in Hierusalem ad proeliandum contra eam, et non potuerunt debellare eam. 2 Et nuntiaverunt domui David, dicentes, "Requievit Syria super Ephraim," et

know it not.' 10 Blind the heart of this people, and make their ears heavy, and shut their eyes, lest they see with their eyes and hear with their ears and understand with their heart and be converted, and I heal them."

11 And I said, "How long, O Lord?"

And he said, "Until the cities be wasted without inhabitant, and the houses without man, and the land shall be left desolate. 12 And the Lord shall remove men far away, and she shall be multiplied that was left in the midst of the earth. 13 And there shall be still a tithing therein, and she shall turn and shall be made a shew as a turpentine tree and as an oak that spreadeth its branches; that which shall stand therein shall be a holy seed."

Chapter 7

The prophet assures King Ahaz that the two kings, his enemies, shall not take Jerusalem. A virgin shall conceive and bear a son.

And it came to pass in the days of Ahaz, the son of Jotham, the son of Uzziah, king of Judah, that Rezin, king of Syria, and Pekah, the son of Remaliah, king of Israel, came up to Jerusalem to fight against it, *but* they could not prevail over it. 2 And they told the house of David, saying, "Syria hath rested upon Ephraim," and his heart was moved, and

commotum est cor eius, et cor populi eius, sicut moventur ligna silvarum a facie venti.

3 Et dixit Dominus ad Isaiam, "Egredere in occursum Ahaz, tu et qui derelictus est, Iasub, filius tuus, ad extremum aquaeductus piscinae superioris in via agri fullonis. 4 Et dices ad eum, 'Vide ut sileas; noli timere, et cor tuum ne formidet a duabus caudis titionum fumigantium istorum in ira furoris Rasin, regis Syriae, et filii Romeliae. 5 Eo quod consilium inierit contra te Syria in malum Ephraim et filius Romeliae, dicentes, 6 "Ascendamus ad Iudam et suscitemus eum et avellamus eum ad nos et ponamus regem in medio eius filium Tabeel," 7 haec dicit Dominus Deus: "Non stabit, et non erit istud. 8 Sed caput Syriae Damascus, et caput Damasci Rasin, et adhuc sexaginta et quinque anni et desinet Ephraim esse populus. 9 Et caput Ephraim Samaria, et caput Samariae filius Romeliae. Si non credideritis, non permanebitis."'"

10 Et adiecit Dominus loqui ad Ahaz, dicens, 11 "Pete tibi signum a Domino, Deo tuo, in profundum inferni sive in excelsum supra."

12 Et dixit Ahaz, "Non petam, et non temptabo Dominum."

13 Et dixit, "Audite ergo, domus David: numquid parum vobis est molestos esse hominibus quia molesti estis et Deo meo? 14 Propter hoc dabit Dominus ipse vobis signum. Ecce: virgo concipiet et pariet filium, et vocabitur nomen eius Emmanuhel. 15 Butyrum et mel comedet ut sciat reprobare

the heart of his people, as the trees of the woods are moved *with* the wind.

3 And the Lord said to Isaiah, "Go forth to meet Ahaz, thou and Jashub, thy son that is left, to the *conduit* of the upper pool in the way of the fuller's field. 4 And thou shalt say to him, 'See thou be quiet; fear not, and let not thy heart be afraid of the two tails of these fire brands smoking with the wrath of the fury of Rezin, king of Syria, and of the son of Remaliah. 5 Because Syria hath taken counsel against thee unto the evil of Ephraim and the son of Remaliah, saying, 6 "Let us go up to Judah and rouse it up and draw it away to us and make the son of Tabeel king in the midst thereof," 7 thus saith the Lord God: "It shall not stand, and this shall not be. 8 But the head of Syria is Damascus, and the head of Damascus is Rezin, and within threescore and five years *Ephraim* shall cease to be a people. 9 And the head of Ephraim is Samaria, and the head of Samaria the son of Remaliah. If you will not believe, you shall not continue."''"

10 And the Lord spoke again to Ahaz, saying, 11 "Ask thee a sign of the Lord, thy God, *either* unto the depth of hell or unto the height above."

12 And Ahaz said, "I will not ask, and I will not tempt the Lord."

13 And he said, "Hear ye therefore, O house of David: is it a small thing for you to be grievous to men that you are grievous to my God also? 14 Therefore the Lord himself shall give you a sign. Behold: a virgin shall conceive and bear a son, and his name shall be called Immanuel. 15 He shall eat butter and honey that he may know to refuse the evil and to

malum et eligere bonum. 16 Quia antequam sciat puer reprobare malum et eligere bonum, derelinquetur terra quam tu
detestaris a facie duum regum suorum. 17 Adducet Dominus
super te et super populum tuum et super domum patris tui
dies qui non venerunt a diebus separationis Ephraim a Iuda
cum rege Assyriorum."

18 Et erit in die illa sibilabit Dominus muscae quae est in
extremo fluminum Aegypti et api quae est in terra Assur.
19 Et venient et requiescent omnes in torrentibus vallium
et in cavernis petrarum et in omnibus frutectis et in universis foraminibus. 20 In die illa radet Dominus in novacula
conducta in his qui trans flumen sunt, in rege Assyriorum,
caput et pilos pedum, et barbam universam.

21 Et erit in die illa nutriet homo vaccam boum et duas
oves. 22 Et prae ubertate lactis comedet butyrum, butyrum
enim et mel manducabit omnis qui relictus fuerit in medio
terrae.

23 Et erit in die illa omnis locus ubi fuerint mille vites
mille argenteis in spinas et in vepres erunt. 24 Cum sagittis
et arcu ingredientur illuc, vepres enim et spinae erunt in
universa terra. 25 Et omnes montes qui in sarculo sarientur,
non veniet illuc terror spinarum et veprium, et erit in pascua
bovis et in conculcationem pecoris.

choose the good. 16 For before the child know to refuse the evil and to choose the good, the land which thou abhorrest shall be forsaken of the face of her two kings. 17 The Lord shall bring upon thee and upon thy people and upon the house of thy father days that have not come since the time of the separation of Ephraim from Judah with the king of the Assyrians."

18 And it shall come to pass in that day that the Lord shall hiss for the fly that is in the uttermost part of the rivers of Egypt and for the bee that is in the land of Assyria. 19 And they shall come and shall all of them rest in the torrents of the valleys and in the holes of the rocks and upon all places set with shrubs and in all hollow places. 20 In that day the Lord shall shave with a razor that is hired by them that are beyond the river, by the king of the Assyrians, the head and the hairs of the feet, and the whole beard.

21 And it shall come to pass in that day that a man shall nourish a young cow and two sheep. 22 And for the abundance of milk he shall eat butter, for butter and honey shall every one eat that shall be left in the midst of the land.

23 And it shall come to pass in that day that every place where there were a thousand vines at a thousand pieces of silver shall become thorns and briers. 24 With arrows and with bows they shall go in thither, for briars and thorns shall be in all the land. 25 And as for all the hills that shall be raked with a rake, the fear of thorns and briers shall not come thither, *but* they shall be for the ox to feed on and the lesser cattle to tread upon.

Caput 8

Et dixit Dominus ad me, "Sume tibi librum grandem, et scribe in eo stilo hominis, 'Velociter spolia detrahe; cito praedare.'"

2 Et adhibui mihi testes fideles: Uriam, sacerdotem, et Zacchariam, filium Barachiae. 3 Et accessi ad prophetissam, et concepit et peperit filium.

Et dixit Dominus ad me, "Voca nomen eius Adcelera spolia detrahere. Festina praedari. 4 Quia antequam sciat puer vocare patrem suum et matrem suam, auferetur fortitudo Damasci et spolia Samariae coram rege Assyriorum."

5 Et adiecit Dominus loqui ad me adhuc, dicens, 6 "Pro eo quod abiecit populus iste aquas Siloae quae vadunt cum silentio et adsumpsit magis Rasin et filium Romeliae, 7 propter hoc ecce: Dominus adducet super eos aquas fluminis fortes et multas, regem Assyriorum et omnem gloriam eius, et ascendet super omnes rivos eius et fluet super universas ripas eius 8 et ibit per Iudam inundans et transiens usque ad collum veniet. Et erit extensio alarum eius implens latitudinem terrae tuae, O Emmanuhel."

9 Congregamini, populi, et vincimini, et audite, universae procul terrae. Confortamini, et vincimini; accingite vos, et

Chapter 8

The name of a child that is to be born. Many evils shall
come upon the Jews for their sins.

And the Lord said to me, "Take thee a great book, and
write in it with a man's pen, 'Take away the spoils with speed;
quickly take the prey.'"

2 And I took unto me faithful witnesses: Uriah, the priest,
and Zechariah, the son of Jeberechiah. 3 And I went to the
prophetess, and she conceived and bore a son.

And the Lord said to me, "Call his name Hasten to take
away the spoils. Make haste to take away the prey. 4 For before the child know to call his father and his mother, the
strength of Damascus and the spoils of Samaria shall be
taken away before the king of the Assyrians."

5 And the Lord spoke to me again, saying, 6 "Forasmuch
as this people hath cast away the waters of Shiloah that go
with silence and hath rather taken Rezin and the son of Remaliah, 7 therefore behold: the Lord will bring upon them
the waters of the river strong and many, the king of the Assyrians and all his glory, and he shall come up over all his
channels and shall overflow all his banks 8 and shall pass
through Judah overflowing and going over shall reach even
to the neck. And the stretching out of his wings shall fill the
breadth of thy land, O Immanuel."

9 Gather yourselves together, O ye people, and be overcome, and give ear, all ye lands afar off. Strengthen yourselves, and be overcome; gird yourselves, and be overcome.

vincimini. 10 Inite consilium, et dissipabitur; loquimini verbum, et non fiet, quia nobiscum Deus.

11 Haec enim ait Dominus ad me, sicut in forti manu erudivit me ne irem in via populi huius, dicens, 12 "Non dicatis, 'Coniuratio,' omnia enim quae loquitur populus iste coniuratio est. Et timorem eius ne timeatis, neque paveatis. 13 Dominum exercituum ipsum sanctificate, ipse pavor vester, et ipse terror vester. 14 Et erit vobis in sanctificationem, in lapidem autem offensionis et in petram scandali duabus domibus Israhel, in laqueum et in ruinam habitantibus Hierusalem. 15 Et offendent ex eis plurimi et cadent et conterentur et inretientur et capientur."

16 Liga testimonium; signa legem in discipulis meis. 17 Et expectabo Dominum, qui abscondit faciem suam a domo Iacob, et praestolabor eum. 18 Ecce: ego et pueri mei quos mihi dedit Dominus in signum et in portentum Israhel a Domino exercituum qui habitat in Monte Sion.

19 Et cum dixerint ad vos, "Quaerite a pythonibus et a divinis qui stridunt in incantationibus suis. Numquid non populus a Deo suo requiret pro vivis a mortuis?"— 20 ad legem magis et ad testimonium. Quod si non dixerint iuxta verbum hoc, non erit eis matutina lux. 21 Et transibit per eam; corruet et esuriet, et cum esurierit, irascetur et maledicet regi suo et Deo suo et suspiciet sursum. 22 Et ad terram intuebitur, et ecce: tribulatio et tenebrae, dissolutio et angustia et caligo persequens, et non poterit avolare de angustia sua.

10 Take counsel together, and it shall be defeated; speak a word, and it shall not be done, because God is with us.

11 For thus saith the Lord to me, as he hath taught me with a strong arm that I should not walk in the way of this people, saying, 12 "Say ye not, 'A conspiracy,' for all that this people speaketh is a conspiracy. Neither fear ye their fear, nor be afraid. 13 Sanctify the Lord of hosts himself, *and let* him be your fear, and *let* him be your dread. 14 And he shall be a sanctification to you, but for a stone of stumbling and for a rock of offence to the two houses of Israel, for a snare and a ruin to the inhabitants of Jerusalem. 15 And very many of them shall stumble and fall and shall be broken in pieces and shall be snared and taken."

16 Bind up the testimony; seal the law among my disciples. 17 And I will wait for the Lord, who hath hid his face from the house of Jacob, and I will look for him. 18 Behold: I and my children whom the Lord hath given me for a sign and for a wonder in Israel from the Lord of hosts who dwelleth in Mount Zion.

19 And when they shall say to you, "Seek of pythons and of diviners who mutter in their enchantments. *Should* not the people seek of their God for the living of the dead?"— 20 to the law rather and to the testimony. And if they speak not according to this word, they shall not have the morning light. 21 And they shall pass by it; they shall fall and be hungry, and when they shall be hungry, they will be angry and curse their king and their God and look upwards. 22 And they shall look to the earth, and behold: trouble and darkness, weakness and distress and a mist following them, and they cannot fly away from their distress.

Caput 9

Primo tempore adleviata est terra Zabulon et terra Nepthalim, et novissimo adgravata est via maris trans Iordanem
Galileae Gentium. 2 Populus qui ambulabat in tenebris vidit
lucem magnam; habitantibus in regione umbrae mortis, lux
orta est eis. 3 Multiplicasti gentem et non magnificasti laetitiam. Laetabuntur coram te sicut qui laetantur in messe,
sicut exultant victores capta praeda quando dividunt spolia.
4 Iugum enim oneris eius et virgam umeri eius et sceptrum
exactoris eius superasti sicut in die Madian. 5 Quia omnis
violenta praedatio cum tumultu et vestimentum mixtum
sanguine erit in conbustionem et cibus ignis.

6 Parvulus enim natus est nobis, et filius datus est nobis,
et factus est principatus super umerum eius, et vocabitur
nomen eius Admirabilis, Consiliarius, Deus Fortis, Pater fu-
turi saeculi, Princeps pacis. 7 Multiplicabitur eius imperium,
et pacis non erit finis. Super solium David et super regnum
eius sedebit ut confirmet illud et corroboret in iudicio et

Chapter 9

What joy shall come after afflictions by the birth and kingdom of Christ which shall flourish for ever. Judgments upon Israel for their sins.

At the first time the land of Zabulun and the land of Naphtali was lightly touched, and at the last the way of the sea beyond the Jordan of the Galilee of the Gentiles was heavily loaded. 2 The people that walked in darkness have seen a great light; to them that dwelt in the region of the shadow of death, light is risen. 3 Thou hast multiplied the nation and hast not increased the joy. They shall rejoice before thee as they that rejoice in the harvest, as conquerors rejoice after taking a prey when they divide the spoils. 4 For the yoke of their burden and the rod of their shoulder and the sceptre of their oppressor thou hast overcome as in the day of Midian. 5 For every violent taking of spoils with tumult and garment mingled with blood shall be burnt and be fuel for the fire.

6 For a child is born to us, and a son is given to us, and the government is upon his shoulder, and his name shall be called Wonderful, Counsellor, God the Mighty, the Father of the world to come, the Prince of peace. 7 His empire shall be multiplied, and there shall be no end of peace. He shall sit upon the throne of David and upon his kingdom to establish it and strengthen it with judgment and with justice

iustitia amodo et usque in sempiternum; zelus Domini exercituum faciet hoc.

8 Verbum misit Dominus in Iacob, et cecidit in Israhel. 9 Et sciet populus omnis Ephraim, et habitantes Samariam in superbia et magnitudine cordis dicentes, 10 "Lateres ceciderunt, sed quadris lapidibus aedificabimus; sycomoros succiderunt, sed cedros inmutabimus." 11 Et elevabit Dominus hostes Rasin super eum et inimicos eius in tumultum vertet, 12 Syriam ab oriente et Philisthim ab occidente, et devorabunt Israhel toto ore. In omnibus his non est aversus furor eius, sed adhuc manus eius extenta.

13 Et populus non est reversus ad percutientem se et Dominum exercituum non inquisierunt. 14 Et disperdet Dominus ab Israhel caput et caudam, incurvantem et refrenantem, die una. 15 Longevus et honorabilis, ipse est caput, et propheta docens mendacium, ipse cauda est. 16 Et erunt qui beatificant populum istum seducentes, et qui beatificantur praecipitati. 17 Propter hoc super adulescentulis eius non laetabitur Dominus, et pupillorum eius et viduarum non miserebitur, quia omnis hypocrita est et nequam, et universum os locutum est stultitiam. In omnibus his non est aversus furor eius, sed adhuc manus eius extenta.

18 Succensa est enim quasi ignis impietas; veprem et spinam vorabit et succendetur in densitate saltus, et convolvetur superbia fumi. 19 In ira Domini exercituum conturbata est terra, et erit populus quasi esca ignis; vir fratri suo non

from henceforth and for ever; the zeal of the Lord of hosts will perform this.

8 The Lord sent a word into Jacob, and it hath lighted upon Israel. 9 And all the people of Ephraim shall know, and the inhabitants of Samaria that say in the pride and *haughtiness* of their heart, 10 "The bricks are fallen down, but we will build with square stones; they have cut down the sycamores, but we will change them for cedars." 11 And the Lord shall set up the enemies of Rezin over him and shall *bring on* his enemies *in a crowd,* 12 *the Syrians* from the east and the Philistines from the west, and they shall devour Israel with *open* mouth. For all this his indignation is not turned away, but his hand is stretched out still.

13 And the people are not returned to him who hath struck them and have not sought after the Lord of hosts. 14 And the Lord shall destroy out of Israel the head and the tail, him that bendeth down and him that holdeth back, in one day. 15 The aged and honourable, he is the head, and the prophet that teacheth lies, he is the tail. 16 And they that call this people blessed *shall* cause them to err, and they that are called blessed shall be thrown down headlong. 17 Therefore the Lord shall have no joy in their young men, neither shall he have mercy on their fatherless and widows, for every one is a hypocrite and wicked, and every mouth hath spoken folly. For all this his indignation is not turned away, but his hand is stretched out still.

18 For wickedness is kindled as a fire; it shall devour the brier and the thorn and shall kindle in the thicket of the forest, and it shall be wrapped up in smoke ascending on high. 19 By the wrath of the Lord of hosts the land is troubled, and the people shall be as fuel for the fire; no man shall spare his

parcet. 20 Et declinabit ad dexteram et esuriet et comedet ad sinistram et non saturabitur. Unusquisque carnem brachii sui vorabit: Manasses, Ephraim, et Ephraim, Manassen, simul ipsi contra Iudam. 21 In omnibus his non est aversus furor eius, sed adhuc manus eius extenta.

Caput 10

Vae qui condunt leges iniquas et scribentes, iniustitiam scripserunt 2 ut opprimerent in iudicio pauperes et vim facerent causae humilium populi mei, ut essent viduae praeda eorum et pupillos diriperent. 3 Quid facietis in die visitationis et calamitatis de longe venientis? Ad cuius fugietis auxilium, et ubi derelinquetis gloriam vestram, 4 ne incurvemini sub vinculo et cum interfectis cadatis? Super omnibus his non est aversus furor eius, sed adhuc manus eius extenta.

5 Vae Assur; virga furoris mei et baculus ipse est; in manu eorum indignatio mea. 6 Ad gentem fallacem mittam eum, et contra populum furoris mei mandabo illi, ut auferat

brother. 20 And he shall turn to the right hand and shall be hungry and shall eat on the left hand and shall not be filled. Every one shall eat the flesh of his own arm: Manasseh, Ephraim, and Ephraim, Manasseh, *and* they together shall be against Judah. 21 After all these things his indignation is not turned away, but his hand is stretched out still.

Chapter 10

Woe to the makers of wicked laws. The Assyrians shall be a rod for punishing Israel, but for their pride they shall be destroyed and a remnant of Israel saved.

W oe to them that make wicked laws and when they write, *write* injustice 2 to oppress the poor in judgment and do violence to the cause of the humble of my people, that widows might be their prey and that they might rob the fatherless. 3 What will you do in the day of visitation and of the calamity which cometh from afar? To whom will ye flee for help, and where will ye leave your glory, 4 that you be not bowed down under the bond and fall with the slain? In all these things his anger is not turned away, but his hand is stretched out still.

5 Woe to the Assyrian; he is the rod and the staff of my anger, *and* my indignation is in their hands. 6 I will send him to a deceitful nation, and I will give him a charge against the

spolia et diripiat praedam et ponat illum in conculcationem quasi lutum platearum. 7 Ipse autem non sic arbitrabitur, et cor eius non ita aestimabit, sed ad conterendum erit cor eius et ad internicionem gentium non paucarum.

8 Dicet enim, 9 "Numquid non principes mei simul reges sunt? Numquid non ut Charchamis sic Chalanno et ut Arfad sic Emath? Numquid non ut Damascus sic Samaria? 10 Quomodo invenit manus mea regna idoli, sic et simulacra eorum de Hierusalem et de Samaria. 11 Numquid non sicut feci Samariae et idolis eius, sic faciam Hierusalem et simulacris eius?"

12 Et erit cum impleverit Dominus cuncta opera sua in Monte Sion et in Hierusalem, visitabo super fructum magnifici cordis regis Assur et super gloriam altitudinis oculorum eius, 13 dixit enim, "In fortitudine manus meae feci, et in sapientia mea intellexi, et abstuli terminos populorum et principes eorum depraedatus sum et detraxi quasi potens in sublime residentes. 14 Et invenit quasi nidum manus mea fortitudinem populorum, et sicut colliguntur ova quae derelicta sunt, sic universam terram ego congregavi, et non fuit qui moveret pinnam et aperiret os et ganniret."

15 Numquid gloriabitur securis contra eum qui secat in ea? Aut exaltabitur serra contra eum a quo trahitur? Quomodo si elevetur virga contra levantem se, et exaltetur baculus qui utique lignum est. 16 Propter hoc mittet Dominator, Dominus exercituum, in pinguibus eius tenuitatem, et subtus gloriam eius succensa ardebit quasi conbustio ignis. 17 Et erit lumen Israhel in igne, et Sanctus eius in flamma,

people of my wrath, to take away the spoils and to lay hold on the prey and to tread them down like the mire of the streets. 7 But he shall not take it so, and his heart shall not think so, but his heart shall be set to destroy and to cut off nations not a few.

8 For he shall say, 9 "Are not my princes *as so many* kings? Is not Calno as Carchemish and Hamath as Arpad? Is not Samaria as Damascus? 10 As my hand hath found the kingdoms of the idol, so also their idols of Jerusalem and of Samaria. 11 Shall I not as I have done to Samaria and her idols, so do to Jerusalem and her idols?"

12 And it shall come to pass that when the Lord shall have performed all his works in Mount Zion and in Jerusalem, I will visit the fruit of the proud heart of the king of Assyria and the glory of the haughtiness of his eyes, 13 for he hath said, "By the strength of my own hand I have done it, and by my own wisdom I have understood, and I have removed the bounds of the people and have taken the spoils of their princes and as a mighty man hath pulled down them that sat on high. 14 And my hand hath found the strength of the people as a nest, and as eggs are gathered that are left, so have I gathered all the earth, and there was none that moved the wing *or* opened the mouth *or* made the least noise."

15 Shall the axe boast itself against him that cutteth with it? Or shall the saw exalt itself against him by whom it is drawn? As if a rod should lift itself up against him that lifteth it up, and a staff exalt itself which is but wood. 16 Therefore the sovereign Lord, the Lord of hosts, shall send leanness among his fat ones, and under his glory shall be kindled a burning, as it were the burning of a fire. 17 And the light of Israel shall be as a fire, and the Holy One thereof as a flame,

et succendetur et devorabitur spina eius et vepres in die una. 18 Et gloria saltus eius et carmeli eius ab anima usque ad carnem consumetur, et erit terrore profugus. 19 Et reliquiae ligni saltus eius pro paucitate numerabuntur, et puer scribet eos.

20 Et erit in die illa non adiciet residuum Israhel et hii qui fugerint de domo Iacob inniti super eo qui percutit eos, sed innitetur super Dominum, Sanctum Israhel, in veritate. 21 Reliquiae convertentur, reliquiae, inquam, Iacob, ad Deum fortem. 22 Si enim fuerit populus tuus, Israhel, quasi harena maris, reliquiae convertentur ex eo; consummatio adbreviata inundabit iustitiam. 23 Consummationem enim et adbreviationem Dominus, Deus exercituum, faciet in medio omnis terrae.

24 Propter hoc haec dicit Dominus, Deus exercituum: "Noli timere, populus meus, habitator Sion, ab Assur; in virga percutiet te, et baculum suum levabit super te in via Aegypti 25 adhuc enim paululum modicumque, et consummabitur indignatio, et furor meus super scelus eorum." 26 Et suscitabit super eum Dominus exercituum flagellum iuxta plagam Madian in petra Oreb et virgam suam super mare, et levabit eam in via Aegypti. 27 Et erit in die illa auferetur onus eius de umero tuo et iugum eius de collo tuo, et conputrescet iugum a facie olei.

28 Veniet in Aiath; transibit in Magro; apud Machmas commendabit vasa sua. 29 Transierunt cursim. Gaba sedes

and his thorns and his briers shall be set on fire and shall be devoured in one day. 18 And the glory of his forest and of his beautiful hill shall be consumed from the soul even to the flesh, and he shall run away through fear. 19 And they that remain of the trees of his forest *shall be so few that* they shall *easily* be numbered, and a child shall write them down.

20 And it shall come to pass in that day that the remnant of Israel and they that shall escape of the house of Jacob shall lean no more upon him that striketh them, but they shall lean upon the Lord, the Holy One of Israel, in truth. 21 The remnant shall be converted, the remnant, I say, of Jacob, to the mighty God. 22 For if thy people, O Israel, shall be as the sand of the sea, a remnant of them shall be converted; the consumption abridged shall overflow *with* justice. 23 For the Lord, God of hosts, shall make a consumption and an abridgment in the midst of all the land.

24 Therefore thus saith the Lord, the God of hosts: "O my people that dwellest in Zion, be not afraid of the Assyrian; he shall strike thee with his rod, and he shall lift up his staff over thee in the way of Egypt 25 for yet a little and a very little while, and my indignation shall cease, and my wrath shall be upon their wickedness." 26 And the Lord of hosts shall raise up a scourge against him according to the slaughter of Midian in the rock of Oreb and his rod over the sea, and he shall lift it up in the way of Egypt. 27 And it shall come to pass in that day that his burden shall be taken away from off thy shoulder and his yoke from off thy neck, and the yoke shall putrify at the presence of the oil.

28 He shall come into Aiath; he shall pass into Migron; at Michmash he shall lay up his carriages. 29 They have passed

nostra; obstipuit Rama; Gabaath Saulis fugit. 30 Hinni voce tua, filia Gallim; adtende, Laisa, pauperculaAnathoth. 31 Migravit Medemena; habitatores Gebim, confortamini. 32 Adhuc dies est ut in Nobe stetur; agitabit manum suam super montem filiae Sion, collem Hierusalem. 33 Ecce: dominator Dominus exercituum confringet lagunculam in terrore, et excelsi statura succidentur, et sublimes humiliabuntur. 34 Et subvertentur condensa saltus ferro, et Libanus cum excelsis cadet.

Caput 11

Et egredietur virga de radice Iesse, et flos de radice eius ascendet. 2 Et requiescet super eum spiritus Domini, spiritus sapientiae et intellectus, spiritus consilii et fortitudinis, spiritus scientiae et pietatis. 3 Et replebit eum spiritus timoris Domini. Non secundum visionem oculorum iudicabit, neque secundum auditum aurium arguet. 4 Sed iudicabit in iustitia pauperes et arguet in aequitate pro mansuetis terrae,

in haste. Geba is our lodging; Ramah was astonished; Gibeah of Saul fled away. 30 *Lift up* thy voice, O daughter of Gallim; attend, O Laishah, poor Anathoth. 31 Madmenah is removed; ye inhabitants of Gebim, take courage. 32 It is yet day enough to remain in Nob; he shall shake his hand against the mountain of the daughter of Zion, the hill of Jerusalem. 33 Behold: the sovereign Lord of hosts shall break the earthen vessel with terror, and the tall of stature shall be cut down, and the lofty shall be humbled. 34 And the thickets of the forest shall be cut down with iron, and Lebanon with its high ones shall fall.

Chapter 11

Of the spiritual kingdom of Christ to which all nations shall repair.

And there shall come forth a rod out of the root of Jesse, and a flower shall rise up out of his root. 2 And the spirit of the Lord shall rest upon him, the spirit of wisdom and of understanding, the spirit of counsel and of fortitude, the spirit of knowledge and of godliness. 3 And he shall be filled with the spirit of the fear of the Lord. He shall not judge according to the sight of the eyes, nor reprove according to the hearing of the ears. 4 But he shall judge the poor with justice and shall reprove with equity for the meek of the earth,

et percutiet terram virga oris sui, et spiritu labiorum suorum interficiet impium. 5 Et erit iustitia cingulum lumborum eius, et fides cinctorium renum eius.

6 Habitabit lupus cum agno, et pardus cum hedo accubabit; vitulus et leo et ovis simul morabuntur, et puer parvulus minabit eos. 7 Vitulus et ursus pascentur; simul requiescent catuli eorum, et leo quasi bos comedet paleas. 8 Et delectabitur infans ab ubere super foramine aspidis, et in caverna reguli qui ablactatus fuerit manum suam mittet. 9 Non nocebunt, et non occident in universo monte sancto meo, quia repleta est terra scientia Domini sicut aquae maris operientes.

10 In die illa radix Iesse, qui stat in signum populorum, ipsum Gentes deprecabuntur, et erit sepulchrum eius gloriosum.

11 Et erit in die illa adiciet Dominus secundo manum suam ad possidendum residuum populi sui quod relinquetur ab Assyriis et ab Aegypto et a Fetros et ab Aethiopia et ab Aelam et a Sennaar et ab Emath et ab insulis maris. 12 Et levabit signum in nationes et congregabit profugos Israhel et dispersos Iuda colliget a quattuor plagis terrae. 13 Et auferetur zelus Ephraim, et hostes Iuda peribunt. Ephraim non aemulabitur Iudam, et Iudas non pugnabit contra Ephraim. 14 Et volabunt in umeros Philisthim per mare; simul praedabuntur filios orientis. Idumea et Moab praeceptum manus

and he shall strike the earth with the rod of his mouth, and with the breath of his lips he shall slay the wicked. 5 And justice shall be the girdle of his loins, and faith the girdle of his reins.

6 The wolf shall dwell with the lamb, and the leopard shall lie down with the kid; the calf and the lion and the sheep shall abide together, and a little child shall lead them. 7 The calf and the bear shall feed; their young ones shall rest together, and the lion shall eat straw like the ox. 8 And the *sucking* child shall play on the hole of the asp, and the weaned child shall thrust his hand into the den of the basilisk. 9 They shall not hurt, nor shall they kill in all my holy mountain, for the earth is filled with the knowledge of the Lord as the covering waters of the sea.

10 In that day the root of Jesse, who standeth for an ensign of the people, him the Gentiles shall beseech, and his sepulchre shall be glorious.

11 And it shall come to pass in that day that the Lord shall set his hand the second time to possess the remnant of his people which shall be left from the Assyrians and from Egypt and from Pathros and from Ethiopia and from Elam and from Shinar and from Hamath and from the islands of the sea. 12 And he shall set up a standard unto the nations and shall assemble the fugitives of Israel and shall gather together the dispersed of Judah from the four quarters of the earth. 13 And the envy of Ephraim shall be taken away, and the enemies of Judah shall perish. Ephraim shall not envy Judah, and Judah shall not fight against Ephraim. 14 But they shall fly upon the shoulders of the Philistines by the sea; they together shall spoil the children of the east. Edom and Moab shall be under the rule of their hand, and the children

eorum, et filii Ammon oboedientes erunt. 15 Et desolabit Dominus linguam maris Aegypti et levabit manum suam super flumen in fortitudine spiritus sui, et percutiet eum in septem rivis ita ut transeant per eum calciati. 16 Et erit via residuo populo meo qui relinquetur ab Assyriis, sicut fuit Israheli in die qua ascendit de terra Aegypti.

Caput 12

Et dices in illa die, "Confitebor tibi, Domine, quoniam iratus es mihi; conversus est furor tuus, et consolatus es me. 2 Ecce: Deus salvator meus. Fiducialiter agam et non timebo, quia fortitudo mea et laus mea Dominus, et factus est mihi in salutem."

3 Haurietis aquas in gaudio de fontibus salvatoris, 4 et dicetis in illa die, "Confitemini Domino, et invocate nomen eius. Notas facite in populis adinventiones eius; mementote quoniam excelsum est nomen eius. 5 Cantate Domino, quoniam magnifice fecit; adnuntiate hoc in universa terra. 6 Exulta, et lauda, habitatio Sion, quia magnus in medio tui, Sanctus Israhel."

of Ammon shall be obedient. 15 And the Lord shall lay waste the tongue of the sea of Egypt and shall lift up his hand over the river in the strength of his spirit, and he shall strike it in the seven streams so that men may pass through it in their shoes. 16 And there shall be a highway for the remnant of my people which shall be left from the Assyrians, as there was for Israel in the day that he came up out of the land of Egypt.

Chapter 12

A canticle of thanksgiving for the benefits of Christ.

And thou shalt say in that day, "I will give thanks to thee, O Lord, for thou wast angry with me; thy wrath is turned away, and thou hast comforted me. 2 Behold: God is my saviour. I will deal confidently and will not fear, because the Lord is my strength and my praise, and he is become my salvation."

3 You shall draw waters with joy out of the saviour's fountains, 4 and you shall say in that day, "Praise ye the Lord, and call upon his name. Make his works known among the people; remember that his name is high. 5 Sing ye to the Lord, for he hath done *great things;* shew this forth in all the earth. 6 Rejoice, and praise, O thou habitation of Zion, for great is he that is in the midst of thee, the Holy One of Israel."

Caput 13

Onus Babylonis quod vidit Isaias, filius Amos.

2 Super montem caligosum levate signum. Exaltate vocem; levate manum, et ingrediantur portas duces. 3 Ego mandavi sanctificatis meis et vocavi fortes meos in ira mea, exultantes in gloria mea. 4 Vox multitudinis in montibus, quasi populorum frequentium; vox sonitus regum, gentium congregatarum. Dominus exercituum praecepit militiae belli, 5 venientibus de terra procul a summitate caeli, Dominus et vasa furoris eius, ut disperdat omnem terram.

6 Ululate, quia prope est dies Domini; quasi vastitas a Domino veniet. 7 Propter hoc omnes manus dissolventur, et omne cor hominis tabescet 8 et conteretur. Torsiones et dolores tenebunt; quasi parturiens dolebunt. Unusquisque ad proximum suum stupebit; facies conbustae vultus eorum. 9 Ecce: dies Domini veniet, crudelis et indignationis plenus et irae furorisque, ad ponendam terram in solitudine et peccatores eius conterendos de ea. 10 Quoniam stellae caeli et splendor earum non expandent lumen suum; obtenebratus est sol in ortu suo, et luna non splendebit in lumine suo.

Chapter 13

The burden of Babylon which Isaiah, the son of Amoz, saw.

2 Upon the dark mountain lift ye up a banner. Exalt the voice; lift up the hand, and let the rulers go into the gates. 3 I have commanded my sanctified ones and have called my strong ones in my wrath, them that rejoice in my glory. 4 The noise of a multitude in the mountains, as it were of many people; the noise of the sound of kings, of nations gathered together. The Lord of hosts hath given charge to the troops of war, 5 to them that come from a country afar off from the end of heaven, the Lord and the instruments of his wrath, to destroy the whole land.

6 Howl ye, for the day of the Lord is near; it shall come as a destruction from the Lord. 7 Therefore shall all hands be faint, and every heart of man shall melt 8 and shall be broken. Gripings and pains shall take hold of them; they shall be in pain as a woman in labour. Every one shall be amazed at his neighbour; their countenances shall be as faces burnt. 9 Behold: the day of the Lord shall come, a cruel day and full of indignation and of wrath and fury, to lay the land desolate and to destroy the sinners thereof out of it. 10 For the stars of heaven and their brightness shall not display their light; the sun shall be darkened in his rising, and the moon shall not shine with her light.

11 Et visitabo super orbis mala et contra impios iniquitatem eorum, et quiescere faciam superbiam infidelium et arrogantiam fortium humiliabo. 12 Pretiosior erit vir auro, et homo mundo obrizo. 13 Super hoc caelum turbabo, et movebitur terra de loco suo, propter indignationem Domini exercituum et propter diem irae furoris eius. 14 Et erit quasi dammula fugiens et quasi ovis, et non erit qui congreget. Unusquisque ad populum suum convertetur, et singuli ad terram suam fugient. 15 Omnis qui inventus fuerit occidetur, et omnis qui supervenerit cadet in gladio. 16 Infantes eorum adlidentur in oculis eorum; diripientur domus eorum, et uxores eorum violabuntur.

17 Ecce: ego suscitabo super eos Medos, qui argentum non quaerant nec aurum velint, 18 sed sagittis parvulos interficiant et lactantibus uteri non misereantur, et super filios non parcat oculus eorum.

19 Et erit Babylon illa, gloriosa in regnis, inclita in superbia Chaldeorum, sicut subvertit Dominus Sodomam et Gomorram. 20 Non habitabitur usque in finem, et non fundabitur usque ad generationem et generationem. Nec ponet ibi tentoria Arabs, nec pastores requiescent ibi. 21 Sed requiescent ibi bestiae, et replebuntur domus eorum draconibus, et habitabunt ibi strutiones, et pilosi saltabunt ibi, 22 et respondebunt ibi ululae in aedibus eius, et sirenae in delubris voluptatis.

11 And I will visit the evils of the world and against the wicked for their iniquity, and I will make the pride of infidels to cease and will bring down the arrogancy of the mighty. 12 A man shall be more precious than gold, yea, a man than the *finest of* gold. 13 For this I will trouble the heaven, and the earth shall be moved out of her place, for the indignation of the Lord of hosts and for the day of his *fierce* wrath. 14 And they shall be as a doe fleeing away and as a sheep, and there shall be none to gather them together. Every man shall turn to his own people, and every one shall flee to his own land. 15 Every one that shall be found shall be slain, and every one that shall come to their aid shall fall by the sword. 16 Their infants shall be dashed in pieces before their eyes; their houses shall be pillaged, and their wives shall be ravished.

17 Behold: I will stir up the Medes against them, who shall not seek silver nor desire gold, 18 but with their arrows they shall kill the children and shall have no pity upon the sucklings of the womb, and their eye shall not spare their sons.

19 And that Babylon, glorious among kingdoms, the famous *pride* of the Chaldeans, shall be even as the Lord destroyed Sodom and Gomorrah. 20 It shall no more be inhabited for ever, and it shall not be founded unto generation and generation. Neither shall the Arabian pitch his tents there, nor shall shepherds rest there. 21 But wild beasts shall rest there, and their houses shall be filled with serpents, and ostriches shall dwell there, and the hairy ones shall dance there, 22 and owls shall answer one another there in the houses thereof, and sirens in the temples of pleasure.

Caput 14

Prope est ut veniat tempus eius, et dies eius non elonga-
buntur. Miserebitur enim Dominus Iacob et eliget adhuc de
Israhel et requiescere eos faciet super humum suam; adiungetur advena ad eos et adherebit domui Iacob. 2Et tenebunt
eos populi et adducent eos in locum suum, et possidebit eos
domus Israhel super terram Domini in servos et ancillas, et
erunt capientes eos qui se ceperant et subicient exactores
suos.

3 Et erit in die illa cum requiem dederit tibi Deus a labore
tuo et a concussione tua et a servitute dura qua ante servisti,
4 sumes parabolam istam contra regem Babylonis et dices,
"Quomodo cessavit exactor? Quievit tributum. 5 Contrivit
Dominus baculum impiorum, virgam dominantium 6 cae-
dentem populos in indignatione plaga insanabili, subicien-
tem in furore gentes, persequentem crudeliter. 7 Conquievit
et siluit omnis terra; gavisa est et exultavit.

8 "Abietes quoque laetatae sunt super te, et cedri Libani:
'Ex quo dormisti, non ascendit qui succidat nos.'

Chapter 14

The restoration of Israel after their captivity. The parable or song insulting over the king of Babylon. A prophecy against the Philistines.

Her time is near at hand, and her days shall not be prolonged. For the Lord will have mercy on Jacob and will yet choose out of Israel and will make them rest upon their own ground, *and* the stranger shall be joined with them and shall adhere to the house of Jacob. 2 And the people shall take them and bring them into their place, and the house of Israel shall possess them in the land of the Lord for servants and handmaids, and they shall make them captives that had taken them and shall subdue their oppressors.

3 And it shall come to pass in that day that when God shall give thee rest from thy labour and from thy vexation and from the hard bondage wherewith thou didst serve before, 4 thou shalt take up this parable against the king of Babylon and shalt say, "How is the oppressor come to nothing? The tribute hath ceased. 5 The Lord hath broken the staff of the wicked, the rod of the rulers 6 that struck the people in wrath with an incurable wound, that brought nations under in fury, that persecuted in a cruel manner. 7 The whole earth is quiet and still; it is glad and hath rejoiced.

8 "The fir trees also have rejoiced over thee, and the cedars of Lebanon, *saying,* 'Since thou hast slept, there hath none come up to cut us down.'

9 "Infernus subter conturbatus est in occursum adventus tui; suscitavit tibi gigantas. Omnes principes terrae surrexerunt de soliis suis, omnes principes nationum. 10 Universi respondebunt et dicent tibi, 'Et tu vulneratus es sicut et nos; nostri similis effectus es.' 11 Detracta est ad inferos superbia tua; concidit cadaver tuum. Subter te sternetur tinea, et operimentum tuum erunt vermes.

12 "Quomodo cecidisti de caelo, Lucifer, qui mane oriebaris? Corruisti in terram, qui vulnerabas gentes? 13 Qui dicebas in corde tuo, 'In caelum conscendam; super astra Dei exaltabo solium meum; sedebo in monte testamenti in lateribus aquilonis. 14 Ascendam super altitudinem nubium; ero similis Altissimo.' 15 Verumtamen ad infernum detraheris in profundum laci.

16 "Qui te viderint ad te inclinabuntur teque prospicient. 'Numquid iste est vir qui conturbavit terram, qui concussit regna, 17 qui posuit orbem desertum et urbes eius destruxit, vinctis eius non aperuit carcerem?' 18 Omnes reges gentium universi dormierunt in gloria, vir in domo sua. 19 Tu autem proiectus es de sepulchro tuo quasi stirps inutilis pollutus et obvolutus cum his qui interfecti sunt gladio et descenderunt ad fundamenta laci quasi cadaver putridum. 20 Non habebis consortium neque cum eis in sepultura, tu enim terram tuam disperdisti; tu populum tuum occidisti. Non vocabitur in aeternum semen pessimorum. 21 Praeparate filios eius occisioni in iniquitate patrum suorum; non consurgent nec hereditabunt terram neque implebunt faciem orbis civitatum."

9 "Hell below was in an uproar to meet thee at thy coming; it stirred up the giants for thee. All the princes of the earth are risen up from their thrones, all the princes of nations. 10 All shall answer and say to thee, 'Thou also art wounded as well as we; thou art become like unto us.' 11 Thy pride is brought down to hell; thy carcass is fallen down. Under thee shall the moth be strewed, and worms shall be thy covering.

12 "How art thou fallen from heaven, O Lucifer, who didst rise in the morning? How art thou fallen to the earth, that didst wound the nations? 13 And thou saidst in thy heart, 'I will ascend into heaven; I will exalt my throne above the stars of God; I will sit in the mountain of the covenant in the sides of the north. 14 I will ascend above the height of the clouds; I will be like the Most High.' 15 But yet thou shalt be brought down to hell into the depth of the pit.

16 "They that shall see thee shall turn toward thee and behold thee. 'Is this the man that troubled the earth, that shook kingdoms, 17 that made the world a wilderness and destroyed the cities thereof, that opened not the prison to his prisoners?' 18 All the kings of the nations have all of them slept in glory, every one in his own house. 19 But thou art cast out of thy grave as an unprofitable branch defiled and wrapped up among them that were slain by the sword and are gone down to the bottom of the pit as a rotten carcass. 20 Thou shalt not keep company with them even in burial, for thou hast destroyed thy land; thou hast slain thy people. The seed of the wicked shall not be named for ever. 21 Prepare his children for slaughter for the iniquity of their fathers; they shall not rise up nor inherit the land nor fill the face of the world with cities."

22 "Et consurgam super eos," dicit Dominus exercituum, "et perdam Babylonis nomen et reliquias et germen et progeniem," ait Dominus. 23 "Et ponam eam in possessionem ericii et in paludes aquarum, et scopabo eam in scopa terens," dicit Dominus exercituum.

24 Iuravit Dominus exercituum, dicens, "Si non ut putavi, ita erit, et quomodo mente tractavi, 25 sic eveniet ut conteram Assyrium in terra mea et in montibus meis conculcem eum, et auferetur ab eis iugum eius, et onus illius ab umero eorum tolletur. 26 Hoc consilium quod cogitavi super omnem terram, et haec est manus extenta super universas gentes. 27 Dominus enim exercituum decrevit, et quis poterit infirmare? Et manus eius extenta, et quis avertet eam?"

28 In anno quo mortuus est Rex Ahaz factum est onus istud.

29 "Ne laeteris, Philisthea omnis tu, quoniam comminuta est virga percussoris tui, de radice enim colubri egredietur regulus, et semen eius absorbens volucrem. 30 Et pascentur primogeniti pauperum, et pauperes fiducialiter requiescent, et interire faciam in fame radicem tuam, et reliquias tuas interficiam. 31 Ulula, porta; clama, civitas; prostrata est Philisthea omnis, ab aquilone enim fumus veniet, et non est qui effugiat agmen eius."

32 Et quid respondebitur nuntiis gentium? Quia Dominus fundavit Sion, et in ipso sperabunt pauperes populi eius.

22 "And I will rise up against them," saith the Lord of hosts, "and I will destroy the name of Babylon and the remains and the bud and the offspring," saith the Lord. 23 "And I will make it a possession for the ericius and pools of waters, and I will sweep it and wear it out with a besom," saith the Lord of hosts.

24 The Lord of hosts hath sworn, saying, "Surely as I have thought, so shall it be, and as I have purposed, 25 so shall it fall out that I will destroy the Assyrian in my land and upon my mountains tread him under foot, and his yoke shall be taken away from them, and his burden shall be taken off their shoulder. 26 This is the counsel that I have purposed upon all the earth, and this is the hand that is stretched out upon all nations. 27 For the Lord of hosts hath decreed, and who can disannul it? And his hand is stretched out, and who shall turn it away?"

28 In the year that King Ahaz died was this burden.

29 "Rejoice not thou, whole Philistia, that the rod of him that struck thee is broken in pieces, for out of the root of the serpent shall come forth a basilisk, and his seed shall swallow the bird. 30 And the firstborn of the poor shall be fed, and the poor shall rest with confidence, and I will make thy root perish with famine, and I will kill thy remnant. 31 Howl, O gate; cry, O city; all Philistia is thrown down, for a smoke shall come from the north, and there is none that shall escape his troop."

32 And what shall be answered to the messengers of the nations? That the Lord hath founded Zion, and the poor of his people shall hope in him.

Caput 15

Onus Moab.

Quia nocte vastata est Ar Moab, conticuit. Quia nocte vastatus est murus Moab, conticuit. 2 Ascendit domus, et Dibon ad excelsa in planctum super Nabo, et super Medaba Moab ululabit. In cunctis capitibus eius calvitium, et omnis barba radetur. 3 In triviis eius accincti sunt sacco; super tecta eius et in plateis eius omnis ululatus descendit in fletum. 4 Clamabit Esebon, et Eleale; usque Iasa audita est vox eorum. Super hoc expediti Moab ululabunt; anima eius ululabit sibi. 5 Cor meum ad Moab clamabit; vectes eius usque ad Segor, vitulam conternantem, per ascensum enim Luith flens ascendet, et in via Oronaim clamorem contritionis levabunt.

6 Aquae enim Nemrim desertae erunt, quia aruit herba. Defecit germen; viror omnis interiit. 7 Secundum magnitudinem operis et visitatio eorum; ad torrentem salicum ducent eos. 8 Quoniam circumiit clamor terminum Moab, usque ad Gallim ululatus eius, et usque ad puteum Helim clamor eius. 9 Quia aquae Dibon repletae sunt sanguine, ponam enim super Dibon additamenta, his qui fugerint de Moab leonem et reliquiis terrae.

Chapter 15

A prophecy of the desolation of the Moabites.

The burden of Moab.

Because in the night Ar of Moab is laid waste, it is silent. Because the wall of Moab is destroyed in the night, it is silent. 2 The house is gone up, and Dibon to the high places to mourn over Nebo, and over Medeba Moab *hath howled*. On all their heads shall be baldness, and every beard shall be shaven. 3 In their streets they are girded with sackcloth; on the tops of their houses and in their streets all *shall* howl and come down weeping. 4 Heshbon shall cry, and Elealeh; their voice is heard even to Jahaz. For this shall the well appointed men of Moab howl; his soul shall howl to itself. 5 My heart shall cry to Moab; the bars thereof shall flee unto Zoar, a heifer of three years old, for by the ascent of Luhith they shall go up weeping, and in the way of Horonaim they shall lift up a cry of destruction.

6 For the waters of Nimrim shall be desolate, for the grass is withered away. The spring is faded; all the greenness is perished. 7 According to the greatness of their work is their visitation also; they shall lead them to the torrent of the willows. 8 For the cry is gone round about the border of Moab, the howling thereof unto Eglaim, and unto the well of Elim the cry thereof. 9 For the waters of Dibon are filled with blood, for I will bring more upon Dibon, the lion upon them that shall flee of Moab and upon the remnant of the land.

Caput 16

Emitte agnum, Domine, dominatorem terrae, de Petra deserti ad montem filiae Sion. 2 Et erit sicut avis fugiens et pulli de nido avolantes, sic erunt filiae Moab in transcensu Arnon.

3 Ini consilium; coge concilium. Pone quasi noctem umbram tuam in meridie; absconde fugientes, et vagos ne prodas. 4 Habitabunt apud te profugi mei, Moab; esto latibulum eorum a facie vastatoris, finitus est enim pulvis. Consummatus est miser; defecit qui conculcabat terram.

5 Et praeparabitur in misericordia solium, et sedebit super illud in veritate in tabernaculo David, iudicans et quaerens iudicium et velociter reddens quod iustum est.

6 Audivimus superbiam Moab. Superbus est valde: superbia eius et arrogantia eius et indignatio eius plus quam fortitudo eius. 7 Idcirco ululabit Moab ad Moab; universus ululabit. His qui laetantur super muros cocti lateris, loquimini plagas suas. 8 Quoniam suburbana Esebon deserta sunt, et vineam Sabama domini gentium exciderunt, flagella eius usque ad Iazer pervenerunt. Erraverunt in deserto; propagines eius relictae sunt; transierunt mare. 9 Super hoc plorabo in fletu Iazer vineam Sabama. Inebriabo te lacrima mea,

Chapter 16

The prophet prayeth for Christ's coming. The affliction of
the Moabites for their pride.

Send forth, O Lord, the lamb, the ruler of the earth, from
Petra of the desert to the mount of the daughter of Zion.
2 And it shall come to pass that as a bird fleeing away and as
young ones flying out of the nest, so shall the daughters of
Moab be in the passage of Arnon.

3 Take counsel; gather a council. Make thy shadow as the
night in the midday; hide them that flee, and betray not
them that wander about. 4 My fugitives shall dwell with thee,
O Moab; be thou a covert to them from the face of the destroyer, for the dust is at an end. The wretch is consumed;
he hath failed that trod the earth under foot.

5 And a throne shall be prepared in mercy, and one shall
sit upon it in truth in the tabernacle of David, judging and
seeking judgment and quickly rendering that which is just.

6 We have heard of the pride of Moab. He is exceeding
proud: his pride and his arrogancy and his indignation is
more than his strength. 7 Therefore shall Moab howl to
Moab; every one shall howl. To them that rejoice upon the
brick walls, tell ye their stripes. 8 For the suburbs of Heshbon are desolate, and the lords of the nations have destroyed
the vineyard of Sibmah; the branches thereof have reached
even to Jazer. They have wandered in the wilderness; the
branches thereof are left; they are gone over the sea. 9 Therefore I will lament with the weeping of Jazer the vineyard of

Esebon et Eleale, quoniam super vindemiam tuam et super messem tuam vox calcantium inruit. 10 Et auferetur laetitia et exultatio de Carmelo, et in vineis non exultabit neque iubilabit. Vinum in torculari non calcabit qui calcare consueverat; vocem calcantium abstuli. 11 Super hoc venter meus ad Moab quasi cithara sonabit, et viscera mea ad murum cocti lateris.

12 Et erit cum apparuerit quod laboravit Moab super excelsis suis, ingredietur ad sancta sua ut obsecret et non valebit.

13 Hoc verbum quod locutus est Dominus ad Moab ex tunc, 14 et nunc locutus est Dominus, dicens, "In tribus annis, quasi anni mercennarii, auferetur gloria Moab super omni populo multo, et relinquetur parvus et modicus, nequaquam multus."

Caput 17

Onus Damasci.

"Ecce: Damascus desinet esse civitas et erit sicut acervus lapidum in ruina. 2 Derelictae civitates Aroer gregibus erunt, et requiescent ibi, et non erit qui exterreat. 3 Et cessabit

Sibmah. I will water thee with my tears, O Heshbon and El-ealeh, for the voice of the treaders hath rushed in upon thy vintage and upon thy harvest. 10 And gladness and joy shall be taken away from Carmel, and there shall be no rejoicing nor shouting in the vineyards. He shall not tread out wine in the press that was wont to tread it out; the voice of the treaders I have taken away. 11 Wherefore my bowels shall sound like a harp for Moab, and my inward parts for the *brick* wall.

12 And it shall come to pass when it is seen that Moab is wearied on his high places, that he shall go in to his sanctuaries to pray and shall not prevail.

13 This is the word that the Lord spoke to Moab from that time, 14 and now the Lord hath spoken, saying, "In three years, as the years of a hireling, the glory of Moab shall be taken away for all the multitude of the people, and it shall be left small and feeble, not many."

Chapter 17

Judgments upon Damascus and Samaria. The overthrow of the Assyrians.

The burden of Damascus.

"Behold: Damascus shall cease to be a city and shall be as a ruinous heap of stones. 2 The cities of Aroer shall be left for flocks, and they shall rest there, and there shall be none to make them afraid. 3 And aid shall cease from Ephraim,

adiutorium ab Ephraim, et regnum a Damasco, et reliquiae Syriae sicut gloria filiorum Israhel erunt," dicit Dominus exercituum.

4 "Et erit in die illa adtenuabitur gloria Iacob, et pinguedo carnis eius marcescet. 5 Et erit sicut congregans in messe quod restiterit, et brachium eius spicas leget, et erit sicut quaerens spicas in valle Rafaim. 6 Et relinquetur in eo sicut racemus et sicut excussio oleae, duarum aut trium olivarum in summitate rami, sive quattuor aut quinque in cacuminibus eius fructus eius," dicit Dominus, Deus Israhel.

7 In die illa inclinabitur homo ad factorem suum, et oculi eius ad Sanctum Israhel respicient. 8 Et non inclinabitur ad altaria quae fecerunt manus eius, et quae operati sunt digiti eius non respiciet, lucos et delubra. 9 In die illa erunt civitates fortitudinis eius derelictae sicut aratra et segetes quae derelictae sunt a facie filiorum Israhel, et eris deserta. 10 Quia oblita es Dei, salvatoris tui, et fortis adiutoris tui non es recordata, propterea plantabis plantationem fidelem et germen alienum seminabis. 11 In die plantationis tuae labrusca, et mane semen tuum florebit; ablata est messis in die hereditatis et dolebit graviter.

12 Vae multitudini populorum multorum, ut multitudo maris sonantis, et tumultus turbarum, sicut sonitus aquarum multarum. 13 Sonabunt populi sicut sonitus aquarum inundantium, et increpabit eum, et fugiet procul, et rapietur

and the kingdom from Damascus, and the remnant of Syria shall be as the glory of the children of Israel," saith the Lord of hosts.

4 "And it shall come to pass in that day that the glory of Jacob shall be made thin, and the fatness of his flesh shall grow lean. 5 And it shall be as when one gathereth in the harvest that which remaineth, and his arm shall gather the ears of corn, and it shall be as he that seeketh ears in the vale of Rephaim. 6 And the fruit thereof that shall be left upon it shall be as one cluster of grapes and as the shaking of the olive tree, two or three *berries* in the top of a bough, or four or five upon the top of the tree," saith the Lord, the God of Israel.

7 In that day man shall bow down himself to his maker, and his eyes shall look to the Holy One of Israel. 8 And he shall not look to the altars which his hands made, and he shall not have respect to the things that his fingers wrought, such as groves and temples. 9 In that day his strong cities shall be forsaken as the ploughs and the corn that were left before the face of the children of Israel, and thou shalt be desolate. 10 Because thou hast forgotten God, thy saviour, and hast not remembered thy strong helper, therefore shalt thou plant good plants and shalt sow strange seed. 11 In the day of thy planting shall be the wild grape, and in the morning thy seed shall flourish; the harvest is taken away in the day of inheritance and shall grieve thee much.

12 Woe to the multitude of many people, like the multitude of the roaring sea, and the tumult of crowds, like the noise of many waters. 13 Nations shall make a noise like the noise of waters overflowing, *but* he shall rebuke him, and he

sicut pulvis montium a facie venti et sicut turbo coram tempestate. 14 In tempore vespere, et ecce: turbatio. In matutino, et non subsistet. Haec est pars eorum qui vastaverunt nos, et sors diripientium nos.

Caput 18

Vae terrae, cymbalo alarum, quae est trans flumina Aethiopiae, 2 qui mittit in mare legatos et in vasis papyri super aquas. Ite, angeli veloces, ad gentem convulsam et dilaceratam, ad populum terribilem post quem non est alius, ad gentem expectantem et conculcatam, cuius diripuerunt flumina terram eius.

3 Omnes habitatores orbis qui moramini in terra, cum elevatum fuerit signum in montibus, videbitis, et clangorem tubae audietis. 4 Quia haec dicit Dominus ad me: "Quiescam et considerabo in loco meo, sicut meridiana lux clara est et sicut nubes roris in die messis."

5 Ante messem enim totus effloruit, et inmatura perfectio germinabit, et praecidentur ramusculi eius falcibus,

shall flee far off, and he shall be carried away as the dust of the mountains before the wind and as a whirlwind before a tempest. 14 In the time of the evening, *behold: there shall be* trouble. The morning *shall come,* and he shall not be. This is the portion of them that have wasted us, and the lot of them that spoiled us.

Chapter 18

A woe to the Ethiopians who fed Israel with vain hopes.
Their future conversion.

Woe to the land, the winged cymbal, which is beyond the rivers of Ethiopia, 2 that sendeth ambassadors by the sea and in vessels of bulrushes upon the waters. Go, ye swift angels, to a nation rent and torn in pieces, to a terrible people after which there is no other, to a nation expecting and trodden under foot, whose land the rivers have spoiled.

3 All ye inhabitants of the world who dwell on the earth, when the sign shall be lifted up on the mountains, you shall see, and you shall hear the sound of the trumpet. 4 For thus saith the Lord to me: "I will take my rest and consider in my place, as the noon light is clear and as a cloud of dew in the day of harvest."

5 For before the harvest it was all flourishing, and it shall bud without perfect ripeness, and the sprigs thereof shall be

et quae derelicta fuerint abscidentur et excutientur. 6 Et relinquentur simul avibus montium et bestiis terrae, et aestate perpetua erunt super eum volucres, et omnes bestiae terrae super illum hiemabunt.

7 In tempore illo deferetur munus Domino exercituum a populo divulso et dilacerato, a populo terribili post quem non fuit alius, a gente expectante, expectante et conculcata, cuius diripuerunt flumina terram eius, ad locum nominis Domini exercituum, Montem Sion.

Caput 19

Onus Aegypti.

"Ecce: Dominus ascendet super nubem levem et ingredietur Aegyptum, et movebuntur simulacra Aegypti a facie eius, et cor Aegypti tabescet in medio eius. 2 Et concurrere faciam Aegyptios adversum Aegyptios, et pugnabit vir contra fratrem suum et vir contra amicum suum, civitas adversus civitatem, regnum adversus regnum. 3 Et disrumpetur spiritus Aegypti in visceribus eius, et consilium eius praecipitabo, et interrogabunt simulacra sua et divinos suos et

cut off with pruning hooks, and what is left shall be cut away and shaken out. 6 And they shall be left together to the birds of the mountains and the beasts of the earth, and the fowls shall be upon them all the summer, and all the beasts of the earth shall winter upon them.

7 At that time shall a present be brought to the Lord of hosts from a people rent and torn in pieces, from a terrible people after which there hath been no other, from a nation expecting, expecting and trodden under foot, whose land the rivers have spoiled, to the place of the name of the Lord of hosts, to Mount Zion.

Chapter 19

The punishment of Egypt. Their call to the church.

The burden of Egypt.

"Behold: the Lord will ascend upon a swift cloud and will enter into Egypt, and the idols of Egypt shall be moved at his presence, and the heart of Egypt shall melt in the midst thereof. 2 And I will set the Egyptians to fight against the Egyptians, and they shall fight brother against brother and friend against friend, city against city, kingdom against kingdom. 3 And the spirit of Egypt shall be broken in the bowels thereof, and I will cast down their counsel, and they shall consult their idols and their diviners and their wizards and

pythones et ariolos. 4 Et tradam Aegyptum in manu dominorum crudelium, et rex fortis dominabitur eorum," ait Dominus, Deus exercituum.

5 Et arescet aqua de mari, et fluvius desolabitur atque siccabitur. 6 Et deficient flumina; adtenuabuntur et siccabun-
tur rivi aggerum. Calamus et iuncus marcescet. 7 Nudabitur
alveus rivi a fonte suo, et omnis sementis inrigua siccabitur;
arescet et non erit.

8 Et maerebunt piscatores, et lugebunt omnes mittentes
in flumen hamum, et expandentes rete super faciem aquae
marcescent. 9 Confundentur qui operabantur linum, pec-
tentes et texentes subtilia. 10 Et erunt inrigua eius flaccentia;
omnes qui faciebant lacunas ad capiendos pisces.

11 Stulti principes Taneos; sapientes consiliarii Pharaonis
dederunt consilium insipiens. Quomodo dicetis Pharaoni,
"Filius sapientium ego, filius regum antiquorum"? 12 Ubi
sunt nunc sapientes tui? Adnuntient tibi, et indicent quid
cogitaverit Dominus exercituum super Aegyptum. 13 Stulti
facti sunt principes Taneos; emarcuerunt principes Mem-
pheos. Deceperunt Aegyptum, angulum populorum eius.
14 Dominus miscuit in medio eius spiritum vertiginis, et errare fecerunt Aegyptum in omni opere suo sicut errat ebrius
et vomens. 15 Et non erit Aegypto opus quod faciat caput et
caudam, incurvantem et refrenantem.

soothsayers. 4 And I will deliver Egypt into the hand of cruel masters, and a strong king shall rule over them," saith the Lord, the God of hosts.

5 And the water of the sea shall be dried up, and the river shall be wasted and dry. 6 And the rivers shall fail; the streams of the banks shall be diminished and be dried up. The reed and the bulrush shall wither away. 7 The channel of the river shall be laid bare from its fountain, and every thing sown *by the water* shall be dried up; it shall wither away and shall be no more.

8 The fishers also shall mourn, and all that cast a hook into the river shall lament, and they that spread nets upon the *waters* shall languish away. 9 They shall be confounded that wrought in flax, combing and weaving fine linen. 10 And its watery places shall be dry; all they *shall mourn* that made pools to take fishes.

11 The princes of Tanis are become fools; the wise counsellors of Pharaoh have given foolish counsel. How will you say to Pharaoh, "I am the son of the wise, the son of ancient kings"? 12 Where are now thy wise men? Let them tell thee, and shew what the Lord of hosts hath purposed upon Egypt. 13 The princes of Tanis are become fools; the princes of Memphis are *gone astray.* They have deceived Egypt, the stay of the people thereof. 14 The Lord hath mingled in the midst thereof the spirit of giddiness, and they have caused Egypt to err in all its works as a drunken man staggereth and vomiteth. 15 And there shall be no work for Egypt to make head or tail, him that bendeth down or that holdeth back.

16 In die illa erit Aegyptus quasi mulieres, et stupebunt et timebunt a facie commotionis manus Domini exercituum quam ipse movebit super eam. 17 Et erit terra Iuda Aegypto in pavorem; omnis qui illius fuerit recordatus pavebit a facie consilii Domini exercituum quod ipse cogitavit super eam.

18 In die illa erunt quinque civitates in terra Aegypti loquentes lingua Chanaan et iurantes per Dominum exercituum; civitas solis vocabitur una.

19 In die illa erit altare Domini in medio terrae Aegypti et titulus iuxta terminum eius Domini. 20 Erit in signum et in testimonium Domino exercituum in terra Aegypti, clamabunt enim ad Dominum a facie tribulantis, et mittet eis salvatorem et propugnatorem qui liberet eos. 21 Et cognoscetur Dominus ab Aegypto, et cognoscent Aegyptii Dominum in die illa et colent eum in hostiis et in muneribus, et vota vovebunt Domino et solvent. 22 Et percutiet Dominus Aegyptum plaga et sanabit eam, et revertentur ad Dominum, et placabitur eis et sanabit eos.

23 In die illa erit via de Aegypto in Assyrios, et intrabit Assyrius Aegyptum, et Aegyptius in Assyrios, et servient Aegyptii Assur.

24 In die illa erit Israhel tertius Aegyptio et Assyrio, benedictio in medio terrae 25 cui benedixit Dominus exercituum, dicens, "Benedictus populus meus Aegypti, et opus manuum mearum Assyrio, hereditas autem mea Israhel."

16 In that day Egypt shall be like unto women, and they shall be amazed and afraid *because* of the moving of the hand of the Lord of hosts which he shall move over it. 17 And the land of Judah shall be a terror to Egypt; every one that shall remember it shall tremble *because* of the counsel of the Lord of hosts which he hath determined concerning it.

18 In that day there shall be five cities in the land of Egypt speaking the language of Canaan and swearing by the Lord of hosts; one shall be called the city of the sun.

19 In that day there shall be an altar of the Lord in the midst of the land of Egypt and a monument of the Lord at the borders thereof. 20 It shall be for a sign and for a testimony to the Lord of hosts in the land of Egypt, for they shall cry to the Lord *because* of the oppressor, and he shall send them a saviour and a defender to deliver them. 21 And the Lord shall be known by Egypt, and the Egyptians shall know the Lord in that day and shall worship him with sacrifices and offerings, and they shall make vows to the Lord and perform them. 22 And the Lord shall strike Egypt with a scourge and shall heal it, and they shall return to the Lord, and he shall be pacified towards them and heal them.

23 In that day there shall be a way from Egypt to the Assyrians, and the Assyrian shall enter into Egypt, and the Egyptian to the Assyrians, and the Egyptians shall serve the Assyrian.

24 In that day shall Israel be the third to the Egyptian and the Assyrian, a blessing in the midst of the land 25 which the Lord of hosts hath blessed, saying, "Blessed be my people of Egypt, and the work of my hands to the Assyrian, but Israel is my inheritance."

Caput 20

In anno quo ingressus est Tharthan in Azotum, cum misisset eum Sargon, rex Assyriorum, et pugnasset contra Azotum et cepisset eam, 2 in tempore illo locutus est Dominus in manu Isaiae, filii Amos, dicens, "Vade, et solve saccum de lumbis tuis, et calciamenta tua tolle de pedibus tuis." Et fecit sic, vadens nudus et disculciatus.

3 Et dixit Dominus, "Sicut ambulavit servus meus, Isaias, nudus et disculciatus—trium annorum signum et portentum erit super Aegyptum et super Aethiopiam— 4 sic minabit rex Assyriorum captivitatem Aegypti et transmigrationem Aethiopiae, iuvenum et senum, nudam et disculciatam, discopertis natibus ad ignominiam Aegypti. 5 Et timebunt et confundentur ab Aethiopia, spe sua, et ab Aegypto, gloria sua. 6 Et dicet habitator insulae huius in die illa, 'Ecce: haec erat spes nostra ad quos confugimus in auxilium ut liberarent nos a facie regis Assyriorum, et quomodo effugere poterimus nos?'"

Chapter 20

The ignominious captivity of the Egyptians and the Ethiopians.

In the year that Tartan entered into Ashdod, when Sargon, the king of the Assyrians, had sent him, and he had fought against Ashdod and had taken it, 2 at that same time the Lord spoke by the hand of Isaiah, the son of Amoz, saying, "Go, and loose the sackcloth from off thy loins, and take off thy shoes from thy feet." And he did so, and went naked and barefoot.

3 And the Lord said, "As my servant, Isaiah, hath walked naked and barefoot—it shall be a sign and a wonder of three years upon Egypt and upon Ethiopia— 4 so shall the king of the Assyrians lead away the prisoners of Egypt and the captivity of Ethiopia, young and old, naked and barefoot, with their buttocks uncovered to the shame of Egypt. 5 And they shall be afraid and ashamed of Ethiopia, their hope, and of Egypt, their glory. 6 And the inhabitants of this isle shall say in that day, 'Lo: this was our hope to whom we fled for help to deliver us from the face of the king of the Assyrians, and how shall we be able to escape?'"

Caput 21

Onus deserti maris.

Sicut turbines ab africo veniunt, de deserto venit, de terra horribili.

2 Visio dura nuntiata est mihi: qui incredulus est infideliter agit, et qui depopulator est vastat.

Ascende, Aelam; obside, Mede; omnem gemitum eius cessare feci.

3 Propterea repleti sunt lumbi mei dolore. Angustia possedit me sicut angustia parturientis. Corrui cum audirem; conturbatus sum cum viderem. 4 Emarcuit cor meum; tenebrae stupefecerunt me. Babylon, dilecta mea, posita est mihi in miraculum. 5 Pone mensam; contemplare in specula comedentes et bibentes. Surgite, principes, arripite clypeum.

6 Haec enim dixit mihi Dominus: "Vade, et pone speculatorem, et quodcumque viderit, adnuntiet." 7 Et vidit currum duorum equitum, ascensorem asini et ascensorem cameli, et contemplatus est diligenter multo intuitu.

8 Et clamavit leo, "Super speculam Domini ego sum stans iugiter per diem, et super custodiam meam ego sum stans

Chapter 21

The destruction of Babylon by the Medes and Persians.
A prophecy against the Edomites and the Arabians.

The burden of the desert of the sea.

As whirlwinds come from the south, it cometh from the desert, from a terrible land.

2 A grievous vision is told me: he that is unfaithful dealeth unfaithfully, and he that is a spoiler spoileth.

Go up, O Elam; besiege, O Mede; I have made all the mourning thereof to cease.

3 Therefore are my loins filled with pain. Anguish hath taken hold of me as the anguish of a woman in labour. I fell down at the hearing of it; I was troubled at the seeing of it. 4 My heart failed; darkness amazed me. Babylon, my beloved, is become a wonder to me. 5 Prepare the table; behold in the watchtower them that eat and drink. Arise, ye princes, take up the shield.

6 For thus hath the Lord said to me: "Go, and set a watchman, and whatsoever he shall see, let him tell." 7 And he saw a chariot with two horsemen, a rider upon an ass and a rider upon a camel, and he beheld them diligently with much heed.

8 And a lion cried out, "I am upon the watchtower of the Lord standing continually by day, and I am upon my ward

totis noctibus. 9 Ecce: iste venit ascensor, vir bigae equitum."

Et respondit et dixit, "Cecidit; cecidit Babylon, et omnia sculptilia deorum eius contrita sunt in terram."

10 Tritura mea et filii areae meae, quae audivi a Domino exercituum, Deo Israhel, adnuntiavi vobis.

11 Onus Duma ad me clamat ex Seir: "Custos, quid de nocte? Custos, quid de nocte?"

12 Dixit custos, "Venit mane et nox. Si quaeritis, quaerite. Convertimini; venite."

13 Onus in Arabia.

In saltu ad vesperam dormietis in semitis Dedanim. 14 Occurrentes sitienti, ferte aquam, qui habitatis terram austri; cum panibus occurrite fugienti. 15 A facie enim gladiorum fugerunt, a facie gladii inminentis, a facie arcus extenti, a facie gravis proelii.

16 Quoniam haec dicit Dominus ad me: "Adhuc in uno anno, quasi in anno mercennarii, et auferetur omnis gloria Cedar. 17 Et reliquiae numeri sagittariorum fortium de filiis Cedar inminuentur, Dominus enim, Deus Israhel, locutus est."

standing whole nights. 9 Behold: this man cometh, the rider upon the chariot with two horsemen."

And he answered and said, "Babylon is fallen; she is fallen, and all the graven gods thereof are broken unto the ground."

10 O my threshing and the children of my floor, that which I have heard of the Lord of hosts, the God of Israel, I have declared unto you.

11 The burden of Dumah calleth to me out of Seir: "Watchman, what of the night? Watchman, what of the night?"

12 The watchman said, "The morning cometh, also the night. If you seek, seek. Return; come."

13 The burden in Arabia.

In the forest at evening you shall sleep in the paths of Dedanim. 14 Meeting the thirsty, bring him water, you that inhabit the land of the south; meet with bread him that fleeth. 15 For they are fled from before the swords, from the sword that hung over them, from the bent bow, from the face of a grievous battle.

16 For thus saith the Lord to me: "Within a year, according to the years of a *hireling*, all the glory of Cedar shall be taken away. 17 And the residue of the number of strong archers of the children of Cedar shall be diminished, for the Lord, the God of Israel, hath spoken it."

Caput 22

Onus vallis visionis.

Quidnam tibi quoque est quia ascendisti et tu omnis in tecta, 2 clamoris plena, urbs frequens, civitas exultans? Interfecti tui non interfecti gladio, nec mortui in bello. 3 Cuncti principes tui fugerunt simul dureque ligati sunt. Omnes qui inventi sunt vincti sunt pariter; procul fugerunt.

4 Propterea dixi, "Recedite a me. Amare flebo; nolite incumbere ut consolemini me super vastitate filiae populi mei." 5 Dies enim interfectionis et conculcationis et fletuum Domino, Deo exercituum, in valle visionis, scrutans murum et magnificus super montem.

6 Et Aelam sumpsit faretram, currum hominis equitis, et parietem nudavit clypeus. 7 Et erunt electae valles tuae plenae quadrigarum, et equites ponent sedes suas in porta. 8 Et revelabitur operimentum Iudae, et videbis in die illa armamentarium domus saltus. 9 Et scissuras civitatis David videbitis, quia multiplicatae sunt. Et congregastis aquas piscinae inferioris 10 et domos Hierusalem numerastis et destruxistis domos ad muniendum murum. 11 Et lacum fecistis inter

Chapter 22

The prophet laments the devastation of Judah. He foretells
the deprivation of Shebna and the substitution of Eliakim, a
figure of Christ.

The burden of the valley of vision.

What aileth thee also that thou too art wholly gone up to
the housetops, 2 full of clamour, a populous city, a joyous
city? Thy slain are not slain by the sword, nor dead in battle.
3 All the princes are fled together and are bound hard. All
that were found are bound together; they are fled far off.

4 Therefore have I said, "Depart from me. I will weep bitterly; labour not to comfort me for the devastation of the
daughter of my people." 5 For it is a day of slaughter and of
treading down and of weeping to the Lord, the God of hosts,
in the valley of vision, searching the wall and magnificent
upon the mountain.

6 And Elam took the quiver, the chariot of the horseman,
and the shield was taken down from the wall. 7 And thy
choice valleys shall be full of chariots, and the horsemen
shall place themselves in the gate. 8 And the covering of Judah shall be discovered, and thou shalt see in that day the
armoury of the house of the forest. 9 And you shall see the
breaches of the city of David, that they are many. And you
have gathered together the waters of the lower pool 10 and
have numbered the houses of Jerusalem and broken down
houses to fortify the wall. 11 And you made a ditch between

duos muros ad aquam piscinae veteris, et non suspexistis ad eum qui fecerat eam, et operatorem eius de longe non vidistis.

12 Et vocabit Dominus, Deus exercituum, in die illa ad fletum et ad planctum, ad calvitium et ad cingulum sacci, 13 et ecce: gaudium et laetitia, occidere vitulos et iugulare arietes, comedere carnes et bibere vinum: "Comedamus et bibamus, cras enim moriemur."

14 Et revelata est in auribus meis vox Domini exercituum: "Si dimittetur iniquitas haec vobis donec moriamini," dicit Dominus, Deus exercituum.

15 Haec dicit Dominus, Deus exercituum: "Vade, ingredere ad eum qui habitat in tabernaculo, ad Sobnam, praepositum templi, et dices ad eum, 16 'Quid tu hic, aut quasi quis hic? Quia excidisti tibi hic sepulchrum; excidisti in excelso memoriam diligenter, in petra tabernaculum tibi. 17 Ecce: Dominus asportari te faciet sicut asportatur gallus gallinacius, et quasi amictum sic sublevabit te. 18 Coronans coronabit te tribulatione; quasi pilam mittet te in terram latam et spatiosam. Ibi morieris, et ibi erit currus gloriae tuae, ignominia domus Domini tui. 19 Et expellam te de statione tua, et de ministerio tuo deponam te.

20 "Et erit in die illa vocabo servum meum Eliachim, filium Helciae, 21 et induam illum tunica tua et cingulo tuo confortabo eum et potestatem tuam dabo in manu eius, et erit quasi pater habitantibus Hierusalem et domui Iuda. 22 Et dabo clavem domus David super umerum eius, et aperiet, et non erit qui claudat, et claudet, et non erit qui ape-

the two walls for the water of the old pool, and you have not looked up to the maker thereof, nor regarded him even at a distance that wrought it long ago.

12 And the Lord, the God of hosts, in that day shall call to weeping and to mourning, to baldness and to girding with sackcloth, 13 and behold: joy and gladness, killing calves and slaying rams, eating flesh and drinking wine: "Let us eat and drink; for tomorrow we shall die."

14 And the voice of the Lord of hosts was revealed in my ears: "Surely this iniquity shall not be forgiven you till you die," saith the Lord, God of hosts.

15 Thus saith the Lord, God of hosts: "Go, get thee in to him that dwelleth in the tabernacle, to Shebna, who is over the temple, and thou shalt say to him, 16 'What dost thou here, or as if thou wert somebody here? For thou hast hewed thee out a sepulchre here; thou hast hewed out a monument carefully in a high place, a dwelling for thyself in a rock. 17 Behold: the Lord will cause thee to be carried away as a cock is carried away, and he will lift thee up as a garment. 18 He will crown thee with *a crown of* tribulation; he will toss thee like a ball into a large and spacious country. There shalt thou die, and there shall the chariot of thy glory be, the shame of the house of thy Lord. 19 And I will drive thee out from thy station, and depose thee from thy ministry.

20 "And it shall come to pass in that day that I will call my servant Eliakim, the son of Hilkiah, 21 and I will clothe him with thy robe and will strengthen him with thy girdle and will give thy power into his hand, and he shall be as a father to the inhabitants of Jerusalem and to the house of Judah. 22 And I will lay the key of the house of David upon his shoulder, and he shall open, and none shall shut, and he shall

riat. 23 Et figam illum paxillum in loco fideli, et erit in solium gloriae domui patris sui. 24 Et suspendent super eum omnem gloriam domus patris eius, vasorum diversa genera, omne vas parvulum, a vasis craterarum usque ad omne vas musicorum.

25 "'In die illa,' dicit Dominus exercituum, 'auferetur paxillus qui fixus fuerat in loco fideli, et frangetur et cadet, et peribit quod pependerat in eo, quia Dominus locutus est.'"

Caput 23

Onus Tyri.

Ululate, naves maris, quia vastata est domus unde venire consueverant; de terra Cetthim revelatum est eis. 2 Tacete, qui habitatis in insula; negotiatores Sidonis transfretantes mare repleverunt te. 3 In aquis multis semen Nili; messis fluminis fruges eius, et facta est negotiatio gentium.

4 Erubesce, Sidon, ait enim mare, fortitudo maris, dicens, "Non parturivi, et non peperi, et non enutrivi iuvenes nec ad

shut, and none shall open. 23 And I will fasten him as a peg in a sure place, and he shall be for a throne of glory to the house of his father. 24 And they shall hang upon him all the glory of his father's house, divers kinds of vessels, every little vessel, from the vessels of cups even to every instrument of music.

25 "'In that day,' saith the Lord of hosts, 'shall the peg be removed that was fastened in the sure place, and it shall be broken and shall fall, and that which hung thereon shall perish, because the Lord hath spoken it.'"

Chapter 23

The destruction of Tyre. It shall be repaired again after seventy years.

The burden of Tyre.

Howl, ye ships of the sea, for the house is destroyed from whence they were wont to come; from the land of Kethim it is revealed to them. 2 Be silent, you that dwell in the island; the merchants of Sidon passing over the sea have filled thee. 3 The seed of the Nile in many waters, the harvest of the river is her revenue, and she is become the mart of the nations.

4 Be thou ashamed, O Sidon, for the sea speaketh, *even* the strength of the sea, saying, "I have not been in labour, nor have I brought forth, nor have I nourished up young

incrementum perduxi virgines." 5 Cum auditum fuerit in Aegypto, dolebunt cum audierint de Tyro.

6 Transite maria; ululate, qui habitatis in insula. 7 Numquid non haec civitas vestra est, quae gloriabatur a diebus
pristinis in antiquitate sua? Ducent eam pedes sui longe ad
peregrinandum.

8 Quis cogitavit hoc super Tyrum, quondam coronatam,
cuius negotiatores principes, institores eius incliti terrae?
9 Dominus exercituum cogitavit hoc ut detraheret superbiam omnis gloriae et ad ignominiam deduceret universos
inclitos terrae. 10 Transi terram tuam quasi flumen, filia maris; non est cingulum ultra tibi.

11 Manum suam extendit super mare; conturbavit regna.
Dominus mandavit adversum Chanaan ut contereret fortes
eius. 12 Et dixit, "Non adicies ultra ut glorieris calumniam,
sustinens virgo filia Sidonis; in Cetthim consurgens trans-
freta; ibi quoque non erit requies tibi.

13 Ecce: terra Chaldeorum. Talis populus non fuit; Assur
fundavit eam. In captivitatem transduxerunt robustos eius;
suffoderunt domos eius; posuerunt eam in ruinam.

14 Ululate, naves maris, quia devastata est fortitudo
vestra.

15 Et erit in die illa in oblivione eris, O Tyre, septuaginta
annis sicut dies regis unius, post septuaginta autem annos
erit Tyro quasi canticum meretricis. 16 Sume citharam; circui
civitatem, meretrix oblivioni tradita. Bene cane; frequenta
canticum ut memoria tui sit. 17 Et erit post septuaginta annos visitabit Dominus Tyrum et reducet eam ad mercedes

men nor brought up virgins." 5 When it shall be heard in Egypt, they will be sorry when they shall hear of Tyre.

6 Pass over the seas; howl, ye inhabitants of the island. 7 Is not this your city, which gloried from of old in her antiquity? Her feet shall carry her afar off to sojourn.

8 Who hath taken this counsel against Tyre, that was formerly crowned, whose merchants were princes, *and* her traders the nobles of the earth? 9 The Lord of hosts hath designed it to pull down the pride of all glory and bring to disgrace all the glorious ones of the earth. 10 Pass thy land as a river, O daughter of the sea; thou hast a girdle no more.

11 He stretched out his hand over the sea; he troubled kingdoms. The Lord hath given a charge against Canaan to destroy the strong ones thereof. 12 And he said, "Thou shalt glory no more, O virgin daughter of Sidon who art oppressed; arise, and sail over to Kethim; there also thou shalt have no rest.

13 Behold: the land of the Chaldeans. There was not such a people; the Assyrian founded it. They have led away the strong ones thereof into captivity; they have destroyed the houses thereof; they have brought it to ruin.

14 Howl, O ye ships of the sea, for your strength is laid waste.

15 And it shall come to pass in that day that thou, O Tyre, shalt be forgotten, seventy years according to the days of one king, but after seventy years there shall be unto Tyre as the song of a harlot. 16 Take a harp; go about the city, thou harlot that hast been forgotten. Sing well; sing many a song that thou mayst be remembered. 17 And it shall come to pass after seventy years that the Lord will visit Tyre and will bring

suas, et rursum fornicabitur cum universis regnis terrae super faciem terrae. 18 Et erunt negotiationes eius et mercedes eius sanctificatae Domino; non condentur neque reponentur, quia his qui habitaverint coram Domino erit negotiatio eius ut manducent in saturitatem et vestiantur usque ad vetustatem.

Caput 24

Ecce: Dominus dissipabit terram et nudabit eam et adfliget faciem eius et disperget habitatores eius. 2 Et erit sicut populus, sic sacerdos et sicut servus, sic dominus eius; sicut ancilla, sic domina eius; sicut emens, sic ille qui vendit; sicut fenerator, sic is qui mutuum accipit; sicut qui repetit, sic qui debet.

3 Dissipatione dissipabitur terra, et direptione praedabitur, Dominus enim locutus est verbum hoc. 4 Luxit et defluxit terra et infirmata est. Defluxit orbis; infirmata est altitudo populi terrae. 5 Et terra infecta est ab habitatoribus

her back again to her traffic, and she shall commit fornication again with all the kingdoms of the world upon the face of the earth. 18 And her merchandise and her hire shall be sanctified to the Lord; they shall not be kept in store nor laid up, for her merchandise shall be for them that shall dwell before the Lord that they may eat unto fulness and be clothed for a continuance.

Chapter 24

The judgments of God upon all the sinners of the world.
A remnant shall joyfully praise him.

Behold: the Lord shall lay waste the earth and shall strip it and shall afflict the face thereof and scatter abroad the inhabitants thereof. 2 And it shall be as with the people, so with the priest and as with the servant, so with his master; as with the handmaid, so with her mistress; as with the buyer, so with the seller; as with the lender, so with the borrower; as with him that calleth for his money, so with him that oweth.

3 With desolation shall the earth be laid waste, and it shall be utterly spoiled, for the Lord hath spoken this word. 4 The earth mourned and faded away and is weakened. The world faded away; the height of the people of the earth is weakened. 5 And the earth is infected by the inhabitants thereof

suis quia transgressi sunt leges, mutaverunt ius, dissipaverunt foedus sempiternum.

6 Propter hoc maledictio vorabit terram, et peccabunt
habitatores eius, ideoque insanient cultores eius, et relinquentur homines pauci. 7 Luxit vindemia; infirmata est vitis;
ingemuerunt omnes qui laetabantur corde. 8 Cessavit gaudium tympanorum; quievit sonitus laetantium; conticuit
dulcedo citharae. 9 Cum cantico non bibent vinum; amara
erit potio bibentibus illam.

10 Adtrita est civitas vanitatis; clausa est omnis domus
nullo introeunte. 11 Clamor erit super vino in plateis. Deserta est omnis laetitia; translatum est gaudium terrae. 12 Relicta est in urbe solitudo, et calamitas opprimet portas.
13 Quia haec erunt in medio terrae, in medio populorum,
quomodo si paucae olivae quae remanserunt excutiantur ex
olea, et racemi cum fuerit finita vindemia.

14 Hii levabunt vocem suam atque laudabunt. Cum glorificatus fuerit Dominus, hinnient de mari. 15 Propter hoc in
doctrinis glorificate Dominum, in insulis maris, nomen Domini, Dei Israhel. 16 A finibus terrae laudes audivimus, gloriam iusti.

Et dixi, "Secretum meum mihi, secretum meum mihi, vae
mihi." Praevaricantes praevaricati sunt, et praevaricatione
transgressorum praevaricati sunt. 17 Formido et fovea et laqueus super te, qui habitator es terrae. 18 Et erit qui fugerit a
voce formidinis cadet in foveam, et qui se explicuerit de fo-

because they have transgressed the laws, they have changed the ordinance, they have broken the everlasting covenant.

6 Therefore shall a curse devour the earth, and the inhabitants thereof shall sin, and therefore they that dwell therein shall be mad, and few men shall be left. 7 The vintage hath mourned; the vine hath languished away; all the merry-hearted have sighed. 8 The mirth of timbrels hath ceased; the noise of them that rejoice is ended; the melody of the harp is silent. 9 They shall not drink wine with a song; the drink shall be bitter to them that drink it.

10 The city of vanity is broken down; every house is shut up; no man cometh in. 11 There shall be a crying for wine in the streets. All mirth is forsaken; the joy of the earth is gone away. 12 Desolation is left in the city, and calamity shall oppress the gates. 13 For it shall be thus in the midst of the earth, in the midst of the people, as if a few olives that remain should be shaken out of the olive tree, *or* grapes when the vintage is ended.

14 These shall lift up their voice and shall give praise. When the Lord shall be glorified, they shall *make a joyful noise* from the sea. 15 Therefore glorify ye the Lord in instruction, the name of the Lord, God of Israel, in the islands of the sea. 16 From the ends of the earth we have heard praises, the glory of the just one.

And I said, "My secret to myself, my secret to myself, woe is me." The prevaricators have prevaricated, and with the prevarication of transgressors they have prevaricated. 17 Fear and the pit and the snare are upon thee, O thou inhabitant of the earth. 18 And it shall come to pass that he that shall flee from the noise of the fear shall fall into the pit, and he that shall rid himself out of the pit shall be taken

vea tenebitur laqueo, quia cataractae de excelsis apertae sunt, et concutientur fundamenta terrae. 19 Confractione confringetur terra; contritione conteretur terra; commotione commovebitur terra. 20 Agitatione agitabitur terra sicut ebrius et auferetur quasi tabernaculum unius noctis, et gravabit eam iniquitas sua, et corruet et non adiciet ut resurgat.

21 Et erit in die illa visitabit Dominus super militiam caeli in excelso et super reges terrae qui sunt super terram. 22 Et congregabuntur in congregationem unius fascis in lacum, et cludentur ibi in carcere, et post multos dies visitabuntur. 23 Et erubescet luna, et confundetur sol, cum regnaverit Dominus exercituum in Monte Sion et in Hierusalem et in conspectu senum suorum fuerit glorificatus.

Caput 25

Domine, Deus meus es tu. Exaltabo te et confitebor nomini tuo, quoniam fecisti mirabilia, cogitationes antiquas fideles. Amen. 2 Quia posuisti civitatem in tumulum, urbem fortem in ruinam, domum alienorum ut non sit civitas et in

in the snare, for the flood-gates from on high are opened, and the foundations of the earth shall be shaken. 19 With breaking shall the earth be broken; with crushing shall the earth be crushed; with trembling shall the earth be moved. 20 With shaking shall the earth be shaken as a drunken man and shall be removed as the tent of one night, and the iniquity thereof shall be heavy upon it, and it shall fall and not rise again.

21 And it shall come to pass that in that day the Lord shall visit upon the host of heaven on high and upon the kings of the earth on the earth. 22 And they shall be gathered together as in the gathering of one bundle into the pit, and they shall be shut up there in prison, and after many days they shall be visited. 23 And the moon shall blush, and the sun shall be ashamed, when the Lord of hosts shall reign in Mount Zion and in Jerusalem and shall be glorified in the sight of his ancients.

Chapter 25

A canticle of thanksgiving for God's judgments and benefits.

O Lord, thou art my God. I will exalt thee and give glory to thy name, for thou hast done wonderful things, thy designs of old faithful. Amen. 2 For thou hast reduced the city to a heap, the strong city to ruin, the house of strangers to

sempiternum non aedificetur. 3 Super hoc laudabit te populus fortis; civitas gentium robustarum timebit te, 4 quia factus es fortitudo pauperi, fortitudo egeno in tribulatione sua, spes a turbine, umbraculum ab aestu. Spiritus enim robustorum quasi turbo inpellens parietem. 5 Sicut aestum in siti tumultum alienorum humiliabis, et quasi calore sub nube torrente, propaginem fortium marcescere facies.

6 Et faciet Dominus exercituum omnibus populis in monte hoc convivium pinguium, convivium vindemiae, pinguium medullatorum, vindemiae defecatae. 7 Et praecipitabit in monte isto faciem vinculi conligati super omnes populos et telam quam orditus est super universas nationes. 8 Praecipitabit mortem in sempiternum, et auferet Dominus Deus lacrimam ab omni facie, et obprobrium populi sui auferet de universa terra, quia Dominus locutus est.

9 Et dicet in die illa, "Ecce: Deus noster iste. Expectavimus eum, et salvabit nos. Iste Dominus; sustinuimus eum; exultabimus et laetabimur in salutari eius."

10 Quia requiescet manus Domini in monte isto, et triturabitur Moab sub eo sicuti teruntur paleae in plaustro. 11 Et extendet manus suas sub eo sicut extendit natans ad natandum, et humiliabit gloriam eius cum adlisione manuum eius. 12 Et munimenta sublimium murorum tuorum concident et humiliabuntur et detrahentur in terram usque ad pulverem.

be no city and to be no more built up for ever. 3 Therefore shall a strong people praise thee; the city of mighty nations shall fear thee, 4 because thou hast been a strength to the poor, a strength to the needy in his distress, a *refuge* from the whirlwind, a shadow from the heat. For the blast of the mighty is like a whirlwind beating against a wall. 5 Thou shalt bring down the tumult of strangers as heat in thirst, and as with heat under a burning cloud, thou shalt make the branch of the mighty to wither away.

6 And the Lord of hosts shall make unto all people in this mountain a feast of fat things, a feast of wine, of fat things full of marrow, of wine purified from the lees. 7 And he shall destroy in this mountain the face of the bond with which all people were tied and the web that he began over all nations. 8 He shall cast death down headlong for ever, and the Lord God shall wipe away tears from every face, and the reproach of his people he shall take away from off the whole earth, for the Lord hath spoken it.

9 And *they* shall say in that day, "Lo: this is our God. We have waited for him, and he will save us. This is the Lord; we have patiently waited for him; we shall rejoice and be joyful in his salvation."

10 For the hand of the Lord shall rest in this mountain, and Moab shall be trodden down under him as straw is broken in pieces with the wain. 11 And he shall stretch forth his hands under him as he that swimmeth stretcheth forth his hands to swim, and he shall bring down his glory with the dashing of his hands. 12 And the bulwarks of thy high walls shall fall and be brought low and shall be pulled down to the ground even to the dust.

Caput 26

In die illa cantabitur canticum istud in terra Iuda:

Urbs fortitudinis nostrae, Sion, salvator ponetur in ea, murus et antemurale. 2 Aperite portas, et ingrediatur gens iusta custodiens veritatem. 3 Vetus error abiit; servabis pacem, pacem, quia in te speravimus. 4 Sperastis in Domino in saeculis aeternis, in Domino Deo, forti in perpetuum.

5 Quia incurvabit habitantes in excelso; civitatem sublimem humiliabit. Humiliabit eam usque ad terram; detrahet eam usque ad pulverem. 6 Conculcabit eam pes, pedes pauperis, gressus egenorum.

7 Semita iusti recta est; rectus callis iusti ad ambulandum. 8 Et in semita iudiciorum tuorum, Domine, sustinuimus te; nomen tuum et memoriale tuum in desiderio animae. 9 Anima mea desideravit te in nocte, sed et spiritu meo in praecordiis meis de mane vigilabo ad te. Cum feceris iudicia tua in terra, iustitiam discent habitatores orbis. 10 Misereamur impio, et non discet iustitiam; in terra sanctorum iniqua gessit, et non videbit gloriam Domini.

11 Domine, exaltetur manus tua, et non videant; videant et confundantur zelantes populi, et ignis hostes tuos devo-

Chapter 26

A canticle of thanks for the deliverance of God's people.

In that day shall this canticle be sung in the land of Judah:
Zion, the city of our strength, a saviour, a wall and a bulwark, shall be set therein. 2 Open ye the gates, and let the just nation that keepeth the truth enter in. 3 The old error is passed away; thou wilt keep peace, peace, because we have hoped in thee. 4 You have hoped in the Lord for evermore, in the Lord God, mighty for ever.

5 For he shall bring down them that dwell on high; the high city he shall lay low. He shall bring it down even to the ground; he shall pull it down even to the dust. 6 The foot shall tread it down, the feet of the poor, the steps of the needy.

7 The way of the just is right; the path of the just is right to walk in. 8 And in the way of thy judgments, O Lord, we have patiently waited for thee; thy name and thy remembrance are the desire of the soul. 9 My soul hath desired thee in the night, yea and with my spirit within me in the morning early I will watch to thee. When thou shalt do thy judgments on the earth, the inhabitants of the world shall learn justice. 10 Let us have pity on the wicked, *but* he will not learn justice; in the land of the saints he hath done wicked things, and he shall not see the glory of the Lord.

11 Lord, let thy hand be exalted, and let them not see; let the envious people see and be confounded, and let fire de-

ret. 12 Domine, dabis pacem nobis, omnia enim opera nostra operatus es nobis. 13 Domine, Deus noster, possederunt nos domini absque te; tantum in te recordemur nominis tui. 14 Morientes non vivant; gigantes non resurgant; propterea visitasti et contrivisti eos et perdidisti omnem memoriam eorum.

15 Indulsisti genti, Domine, indulsisti genti; numquid glorificatus es? Elongasti omnes terminos terrae.

16 Domine, in angustia requisierunt te; in tribulatione murmuris doctrina tua eis. 17 Sicut quae concipit cum appropinquaverit ad partum dolens clamat in doloribus suis, sic facti sumus a facie tua, Domine. 18 Concepimus et quasi parturivimus et peperimus spiritum. Salutes non fecimus in terra; ideo non ceciderunt habitatores terrae.

19 Vivent mortui tui; interfecti mei resurgent. Expergiscimini, et laudate, qui habitatis in pulvere, quia ros lucis ros tuus, et terram gigantum detrahes in ruinam.

20 Vade, populus meus, intra in cubicula tua; claude ostia tua super te; abscondere modicum ad momentum, donec pertranseat indignatio. 21 Ecce enim: Dominus egredietur de loco suo ut visitet iniquitatem habitatoris terrae contra eum, et revelabit terra sanguinem suum et non operiet ultra interfectos suos.

vour thy enemies. 12 Lord, thou wilt give us peace, for thou hast wrought all our works for us. 13 O Lord, our God, other lords besides thee have had dominion over us; only in thee let us remember thy name. 14 Let not the dead live; let not the giants rise again; therefore hast thou visited and destroyed them and hast destroyed all their memory.

15 Thou hast been favourable to the nation, O Lord, thou hast been favourable to the nation; art thou glorified? Thou hast removed all the ends of the earth far off.

16 Lord, they have sought after thee in distress; in the tribulation of murmuring thy instruction was with them. 17 As a woman with child when she draweth near the time of her delivery is in pain and crieth out in her pangs, so are we become in thy presence, O Lord. 18 We have conceived and been as it were in labour and have brought forth wind. We have not wrought salvation on the earth; therefore the inhabitants of the earth have not fallen.

19 Thy dead men shall live; my slain shall rise again. Awake, and give praise, ye that dwell in the dust, for thy dew is the dew of the light, and the land of the giants thou shalt pull down into ruin.

20 Go, my people, enter into thy chambers; shut thy doors upon thee; hide thyself a little for a moment, until the indignation pass away. 21 For behold: the Lord will come out of his place to visit the iniquity of the inhabitant of the earth against him, and the earth shall disclose her blood and shall cover her slain no more.

Caput 27

In die illa visitabit Dominus in gladio suo duro et grandi et forti super Leviathan, serpentem vectem, et super Leviathan, serpentem tortuosum, et occidet cetum qui in mari est.

2 In die illa vinea meri cantabit ei. 3 Ego Dominus qui servo eam; repente propinabo ei. Ne forte visitetur contra eam, nocte et die servo eam. 4 Indignatio non est mihi. Quis dabit me spinam et veprem in proelio? Gradiar super eam, succendam eam pariter? 5 An potius tenebit fortitudinem meam? Faciet pacem mihi, pacem faciet mihi?

6 Qui ingrediuntur impetu ad Iacob, florebit et germinabit Israhel, et implebunt faciem orbis semine.

7 Numquid iuxta plagam percutientis se percussit eum? Aut sicut occidit interfectos eius sic occisus est? 8 In mensura contra mensuram, cum abiecta fuerit, iudicabis eam. Meditatus est in spiritu suo duro per diem aestus.

9 Idcirco super hoc dimittetur iniquitas domui Iacob, et iste omnis fructus, ut auferatur peccatum eius; cum posuerit omnes lapides altaris sicut lapides cineris adlisos, non stabunt luci et delubra. 10 Civitas enim munita desolata erit,

Chapter 27

The punishment of the oppressors of God's people. The Lord's favour to his church.

In that day the Lord with his hard and great and strong sword shall visit Leviathan, the bar serpent, and Leviathan, the crooked serpent, and shall slay the whale that is in the sea.

2 In that day there shall be singing *to* the vineyard of pure wine. 3 I am the Lord that keep it; I will suddenly give it drink. Lest any hurt come to it, I keep it night and day. 4 There is no indignation in me. Who shall make me a thorn and a brier in battle? Shall I march against it, shall I set it on fire together? 5 Or rather shall it take hold of my strength? Shall it make peace with me, shall it make peace with me?

6 *When* they *shall* rush in unto Jacob, Israel shall blossom and bud, and they shall fill the face of the world with seed.

7 Hath he struck him according to the stroke of him that struck him? Or is he slain as he killed them that were slain by him? 8 In measure against measure, when it shall be cast off, thou shalt judge it. He hath meditated with his severe spirit in the day of heat.

9 Therefore upon this shall the iniquity of the house of Jacob be forgiven, and this is all the fruit, that the sin thereof should be taken away; when he shall have made all the stones of the altar as burnt stones broken in pieces, the groves and temples shall not stand. 10 For the strong city shall be deso-

speciosa relinquetur et dimittetur quasi desertum. Ibi pascetur vitulus, et ibi accubabit et consumet summitates eius.
11 In siccitate messes illius conterentur; mulieres venientes
et docentes eam, non est enim populus sapiens. Propterea
non miserebitur eius qui fecit eum, et qui formavit eum non
parcet ei.

12 Et erit in die illa percutiet Dominus ab alveo fluminis
usque ad torrentem Aegypti, et vos congregabimini unus et
unus, filii Israhel.

13 Et erit in die illa clangetur in tuba magna, et venient
qui perditi fuerant de terra Assyriorum et qui eiecti erant in
terra Aegypti, et adorabunt Dominum in monte sancto in
Hierusalem.

Caput 28

Vae coronae superbiae, ebriis Ephraim et flori decidenti,
gloriae exultationis eius, qui erant in vertice vallis pinguissi-
mae, errantes a vino.

2 Ecce: validus et fortis Dominus, sicut impetus grandinis, turbo confringens, sicut impetus aquarum multarum

late, the beautiful city shall be forsaken and shall be left as a wilderness. There the calf shall feed, and there shall he lie down and shall consume its *branches.* 11 Its harvests shall be destroyed with drought; women shall come and teach it, for it is not a wise people. Therefore he that made it shall not have mercy on it, and he that formed it shall not spare it.

12 And it shall come to pass that in that day the Lord will strike from the channel of the river even to the torrent of Egypt, and you shall be gathered together one by one, O ye children of Israel.

13 And it shall come to pass that in that day a noise shall be made with a great trumpet, and they that were lost shall come from the land of the Assyrians and they that were outcasts in the land of Egypt, and they shall adore the Lord in the holy mount in Jerusalem.

Chapter 28

The punishment of the Israelites for their pride, intemperance and contempt of religion. Christ, the cornerstone.

Woe to the crown of pride, to the drunkards of Ephraim and to the fading flower, the glory of his joy, who were on the head of the *fat* valley, staggering with wine.

2 Behold: the Lord is mighty and strong, as a storm of hail, a destroying whirlwind, as the violence of many waters over-

inundantium et emissarum super terram spatiosam. 3 Pedibus conculcabitur corona superbiae ebriorum Ephraim. 4 Et
erit flos decidens, gloriae exultationis eius, qui est super verticem vallis pinguium, quasi temporaneum ante maturita-
tem autumni, quod cum aspexerit videns, statim ut manu
tenuerit devorabit illud.

5 In die illa erit Dominus exercituum corona gloriae et
sertum exultationis residuo populi sui 6 et spiritus iudicii
sedenti super iudicium et fortitudo revertentibus de bello
ad portam. 7 Verum hii quoque prae vino nescierunt et prae
ebrietate erraverunt. Sacerdos et propheta nescierunt prae
ebrietate; absorti sunt a vino; erraverunt in ebrietate. Nescierunt videntem; ignoraverunt iudicium. 8 Omnes enim
mensae repletae sunt vomitu sordiumque ita ut non esset ultra locus.

9 "Quem docebit scientiam, et quem intellegere faciet
auditum? Ablactatos a lacte, avulsos ab uberibus. 10 Quia
manda, remanda; manda, remanda; expecta, reexpecta; expecta, reexpecta; modicum ibi, modicum ibi."

11 In loquella enim labii et lingua altera loquetur ad populum istum 12 cui dixit, "Haec est requies mea. Reficite las-
sum, et hoc est meum refrigerium," et noluerunt audire.
13 Et erit eis verbum Domini: "Manda, remanda; manda, remanda; expecta, reexpecta; expecta, reexpecta; modicum
ibi, modicum ibi," ut vadant et cadant retrorsum et conte-
rantur et inlaqueentur et capiantur.

flowing and sent forth upon a spacious land. 3 The crown of pride of the drunkards of Ephraim shall be trodden under feet. 4 And the fading flower, *the* glory of his joy, who is on the head of the *fat* valley, shall be as a hasty fruit before the ripeness of autumn, which when he that seeth it shall behold, as soon as he taketh it in his hand he will eat it up.

5 In that day the Lord of hosts shall be a crown of glory and a garland of joy to the residue of his people 6 and a spirit of judgment to him that sitteth in judgment and strength to them that return out of the battle to the gate. 7 But these also have been ignorant through wine and through drunkenness have erred. The priest and the prophet have been ignorant through drunkenness; they are swallowed up with wine; they have gone astray in drunkenness. They have not known him that seeth; they have been ignorant of judgment. 8 For all tables were full of vomit and filth so that there was no more place.

9 "Whom shall he teach knowledge, and whom shall he make to understand the hearing? Them that are weaned from the milk, that are drawn away from the breasts. 10 For command, command again; command, command again; expect, expect again; expect, expect again; a little there, a little there."

11 For with the speech of lips and with another tongue he will speak to this people 12 to whom he said, "This is my rest. Refresh the weary, and this is my refreshing," and they would not hear. 13 And the word of the Lord shall be to them: "Command, command again; command, command again: expect, expect again; expect, expect again; a little there, a little there," that they may go and fall backward and be broken and snared and taken.

14 Propter hoc audite verbum Domini, viri inlusores qui dominamini super populum meum qui est in Hierusalem. 15 Dixistis enim, "Percussimus foedus cum morte, et cum inferno fecimus pactum. Flagellum inundans cum transierit, non veniet super nos, quia posuimus mendacium spem nostram, et mendacio protecti sumus."

16 Idcirco haec dicit Dominus Deus: "Ecce: ego mittam in fundamentis Sion lapidem, lapidem probatum, angularem, pretiosum, in fundamento fundatum. (Qui crediderit, non festinet.) 17 Et ponam iudicium in pondere et iustitiam in mensura, et subvertet grando spem mendacii, et protectionem aquae inundabunt. 18 Et delebitur foedus vestrum cum morte, et pactum vestrum cum inferno non stabit. Flagellum inundans cum transierit, eritis ei in conculcationem. 19 Quandocumque pertransierit, tollet vos, quoniam mane diluculo pertransibit in die et in nocte, et tantummodo sola vexatio intellectum dabit auditui."

20 Coangustatum est enim stratum ita ut alter decidat, et pallium breve utrumque operire non potest. 21 Sicut enim in monte divisionum stabit Dominus; sicut in valle quae est in Gabaon irascetur ut faciat opus suum, alienum opus eius, ut operetur opus suum; peregrinum est opus eius ab eo. 22 Et nunc nolite inludere, ne forte constringantur vincula vestra. Consummationem enim et adbreviationem audivi a Domino, Deo exercituum, super universam terram.

23 Auribus percipite, et audite vocem meam; adtendite, et audite eloquium meum. 24 Numquid tota die arabit arans ut serat? Proscindet et sariet humum suam? 25 Nonne, cum

14 Wherefore hear the word of the Lord, ye scornful men who rule over my people that is in Jerusalem. 15 For you have said, "We have entered into a league with death, and we have made a covenant with hell. When the overflowing scourge shall pass through, it shall not come upon us, for we have placed our hope in lies, and by falsehood we are protected."

16 Therefore thus saith the Lord God: "Behold: I will lay a stone in the foundations of Zion, a tried stone, a corner stone, a precious stone, founded in the foundation. (He that believeth, let him not hasten.) 17 And I will set judgment in weight and justice in measure, and hail shall overturn the hope of falsehood, and waters shall overflow its protection. 18 And your league with death shall be abolished, and your covenant with hell shall not stand. When the overflowing scourge shall pass, you shall be trodden down by it. 19 Whensoever it shall pass through, it shall take you away, because in the morning early it shall pass through in the day and in the night, and vexation alone shall make you understand what you hear."

20 For the bed is straitened so that one must fall out, and a short covering cannot cover both. 21 For the Lord shall stand up as in the mountain of divisions; he shall be angry as in the valley which is in Gibeon that he may do his work, his strange work, that he may perform his work; his work is strange to him. 22 And now do not mock, *lest* your bonds be tied strait. For I have heard of the Lord, the God of hosts, a consumption and a cutting short upon all the earth.

23 Give ear, and hear my voice; hearken, and hear my speech. 24 Shall the ploughman plough all the day to sow? Shall he open and harrow his ground? 25 Will he not, when

adaequaverit faciem eius, seret gith et cyminum sparget et ponet triticum per ordinem et hordeum et milium et viciam in finibus suis? 26 Et erudiet illum in iudicio; Deus suus docebit illum. 27 Non enim in serris triturabitur gith, nec rota plaustri super cyminum circumiet, sed in virga excutietur gith, et cyminum in baculo. 28 Panis autem comminuetur, verum non in perpetuum triturans triturabit illum, neque vexabit eum rota plaustri nec in ungulis suis comminuet eum. 29 Et hoc a Domino, Deo exercituum, exivit ut mirabile faceret consilium et magnificaret iustitiam.

Caput 29

Vae Arihel, Arihel, civitas quam expugnavit David. Additus est annus ad annum; sollemnitates evolutae sunt. 2 Et circumvallabo Arihel, et erit tristis et maerens, et erit mihi quasi Arihel. 3 Et circumdabo quasi spheram in circuitu tuo et iaciam contra te aggerem et munimenta ponam in obsidionem tuam. 4 Humiliaberis. De terra loqueris, et de humo

he hath made plain the surface thereof, sow gith and scatter cumin and put wheat in order and barley and millet and vetches in their bounds? 26 For he will instruct him in judgment; his God will teach him. 27 For gith shall not be threshed with saws, neither shall the cart wheel turn about upon cumin, but gith shall be beaten out with a rod, and cumin with a staff. 28 But bread corn shall be broken small, but the thresher shall not thresh it for ever, neither shall the cart wheel hurt it nor break it with its teeth. 29 This also is come forth from the Lord, God of hosts, to make his counsel wonderful and magnify justice.

Chapter 29

God's heavy judgments upon Jerusalem for their obstinacy,
with a prophecy of the conversion of the Gentiles.

Woe to Ariel, to Ariel, the city which David took. Year is added to year; the solemnities are at an end. 2 And I will make a trench about Ariel, and it shall be in sorrow and mourning, and it shall be to me as Ariel. 3 And I will make *a* circle round about thee and will cast up a rampart against thee and raise up bulwarks to besiege thee. 4 Thou shalt be brought down. Thou shalt speak out of the earth, and thy

audietur eloquium tuum, et erit quasi pythonis de terra vox tua, et de humo eloquium tuum mussitabit.

5 Et erit sicut pulvis tenuis multitudo ventilantium te, et sicut favilla pertransitens multitudo eorum qui contra te praevaluerunt. 6 Eritque repente confestim. A Domino exercituum visitabitur in tonitru et commotione terrae et voce magna turbinis et tempestatis et flamma ignis devorantis. 7 Et erit sicut somnium visionis nocturnae multitudo omnium gentium quae dimicaverunt contra Arihel, et omnes qui militaverunt et obsederunt et praevaluerunt adversus eam. 8 Et sicuti somniat esuriens et comedit, cum autem fuerit expergefactus vacua est anima eius, et sicut somniat sitiens et bibit, et postquam fuerit expergefactus lassus adhuc sitit, et anima eius vacua est, sic erit multitudo omnium Gentium quae dimicaverunt contra Montem Sion.

9 Obstupescite, et admiramini; fluctuate, et vacillate. Inebriamini, et non a vino; movemini, et non ab ebrietate. 10 Quoniam miscuit vobis Dominus spiritum soporis. Claudet oculos vestros; prophetas et principes vestros qui vident visiones operiet.

11 Et erit vobis visio omnium sicut verba libri signati, quem cum dederint scienti litteras, dicent, "Lege istum," et respondebit, "Non possum, signatus est enim." 12 Et dabitur liber nescienti litteras, diceturque ei, "Lege," et respondebit, "Nescio litteras."

13 Et dixit Dominus, "Eo quod adpropinquat populus iste ore suo et labiis suis glorificat me, cor autem eius longe est a

speech shall be heard out of the ground, and thy voice shall be from the earth like that of the python, and out of the ground thy speech shall mutter.

5 And the multitude of them that fan thee shall be like small dust, and as ashes passing away the multitude of them that have prevailed against thee. 6 And it shall be at an instant suddenly. A visitation shall come from the Lord of hosts in thunder and with earthquake and with a great noise of whirlwind and tempest and with the flame of devouring fire. 7 And the multitude of all nations that have fought against Ariel shall be as the dream of a vision by night, and all that have fought and besieged and prevailed against it. 8 And as he that is hungry dreameth and eateth, but when he is awake his soul is empty, and as he that is thirsty dreameth and drinketh, and after he is awake is yet faint with thirst, and his soul is empty, so shall be the multitude of all the Gentiles that have fought against Mount Zion.

9 Be astonished, and wonder; waver, and stagger. Be drunk, and not with wine; stagger, and not with drunkenness. 10 For the Lord hath mingled for you the spirit of a deep sleep. He will shut up your eyes; he will cover your prophets and princes that see visions.

11 And the vision of all shall be unto you as the words of a book that is sealed, which when they shall deliver to one that is learned, they shall say, "Read this," and he shall answer, "I cannot, for it is sealed." 12 And the book shall be given to one that knoweth no letters, and it shall be said to him, "Read," and he shall answer, "I know no letters."

13 And the Lord said, "Forasmuch as this people draw near me with their mouth and with their lips glorify me, but

me, et timuerunt me mandato hominum et doctrinis, 14 ideo ecce: ego addam ut admirationem faciam populo huic miraculo grandi et stupendo, peribit enim sapientia a sapientibus eius, et intellectus prudentium eius abscondetur."

15 Vae qui profundi estis corde ut a Domino abscondatis consilium, quorum sunt in tenebris opera, et dicunt, "Quis videt nos, et quis novit nos?" 16 Perversa est haec vestra cogitatio, quasi lutum contra figulum cogitet, et dicat opus factori suo, "Non fecisti me," aut figmentum dicat fictori suo, "Non intellegis."

17 Nonne adhuc in modico et in brevi convertetur Libanus in Chermel, et Chermel in saltum reputabitur? 18 Et audient in die illa surdi verba libri, et de tenebris et caligine oculi caecorum videbunt. 19 Et addent mites in Domino laetitiam, et pauperes homines in Sancto Israhel exultabunt. 20 Quoniam defecit qui praevalebat; consummatus est inlusor, et succisi sunt omnes qui vigilabant super iniquitatem, 21 qui peccare faciebant homines in verbo et arguentem in porta subplantabant et declinaverunt frustra a iusto.

22 Propter hoc haec dicit Dominus ad domum Iacob, qui redemit Abraham: "Non modo confundetur Iacob, nec modo vultus eius erubescet, 23 sed cum viderit filios suos, opera manuum mearum, in medio sui sanctificantes nomen meum, et sanctificabunt Sanctum Iacob et Deum Israhel praedicabunt, 24 et scient errantes spiritu intellectum, et mussitatores discent legem."

their heart is far from me, and they have feared me with the commandment and doctrines of men, 14 therefore behold: I will proceed to cause an admiration in this people by a great and wonderful miracle, for wisdom shall perish from their wise men, and the understanding of their prudent men shall be hid."

15 Woe to you that are deep of heart to hide your counsel from the Lord, and their works are in the dark, and they say, "Who seeth us, and who knoweth us?" 16 This thought of yours is perverse, as if the clay should think against the potter, and the work should say to the maker thereof, "Thou madest me not," or the thing framed should say to him that fashioned it, "Thou understandest not."

17 Is it not yet a very little while and Lebanon shall be turned into *charmel,* and *charmel* shall be esteemed as a forest? 18 And in that day the deaf shall hear the words of the book, and out of darkness and obscurity the eyes of the blind shall see. 19 And the meek shall increase their joy in the Lord, and the poor men shall rejoice in the Holy One of Israel. 20 For he that did prevail hath failed; the scorner is consumed, and they are all cut off that watched for iniquity, 21 that made men sin by word and supplanted him that reproved them in the gate and declined in vain from the just.

22 Therefore thus saith the Lord to the house of Jacob, he that redeemed Abraham: "Jacob shall not now be confounded, neither shall his countenance now be ashamed, 23 but when he shall see his children, the work of my hands, in the midst of him sanctifying my name, and they shall sanctify the Holy One of Jacob and shall glorify the God of Israel, 24 and they that erred in spirit shall know understanding, and they that murmured shall learn the law."

Caput 30

"Vae, filii desertores," dicit Dominus, "ut faceretis consilium et non ex me et ordiremini telam et non per spiritum meum, ut adderetis peccatum super peccatum, 2 qui ambulatis ut descendatis in Aegyptum et os meum non interrogastis, sperantes auxilium in fortitudine Pharaonis et habentes fiduciam in umbra Aegypti. 3 Et erit vobis fortitudo Pharaonis in confusionem, et fiducia umbrae Aegypti in ignominiam. 4 Erant enim in Tani principes tui, et nuntii tui usque ad Hanes pervenerunt. 5 Omnes confusi sunt super populo qui eis prodesse non potuit. Non fuerunt in auxilium et in aliquam utilitatem, sed in confusionem et in obprobrium."

6 Onus iumentorum austri.

In terra tribulationis et angustiae—leaena et leo ex eis, vipera et regulus volans—portantes super umeros iumentorum divitias suas et super gibbum camelorum thesauros suos ad populum qui eis prodesse non poterit. 7 Aegyptus enim frustra et vane auxiliabitur. Ideo clamavi super hoc, "Superbia tantum est; quiesce."

8 Nunc ergo ingressus scribe ei super buxum, et in libro diligenter exara illud, et erit in die novissimo in testimonium usque in aeternum. 9 Populus enim ad iracundiam provocans est et filii mendaces, filii nolentes audire legem

Chapter 30

The people are blamed for their confidence in Egypt. God's mercies towards his church. The punishment of sinners.

"Woe to you, apostate children," saith the Lord, "that you would take counsel and not of me and would begin a web and not by my spirit, that you might add sin upon sin, 2 who walk to go down into Egypt and have not asked at my mouth, hoping for help in the strength of Pharaoh and trusting in the shadow of Egypt. 3 And the strength of Pharaoh shall be to your confusion, and the confidence of the shadow of Egypt to your shame. 4 For thy princes were in Tanis, and thy messengers came even to Hanes. 5 They were all confounded at a people that could not profit them. They were no help nor to any profit, but to confusion and to reproach."

6 The burden of the beasts of the south.

In a land of trouble and distress—from whence come the lioness and the lion, the viper and the flying basilisk—they carry their riches upon the shoulders of beasts and their treasures upon the bunches of camels to a people that shall not be able to profit them. 7 For Egypt shall help in vain and to no purpose. Therefore have I cried concerning this, "It is pride only; sit still."

8 Now therefore go in and write for them upon box, and note it diligently in a book, and it shall be in the latter days for a testimony for ever. 9 For it is a people that provoketh to wrath and lying children, children that will not hear the

Dei, 10 qui dicunt videntibus, "Nolite videre," et aspicientibus, "Nolite aspicere nobis ea quae recta sunt. Loquimini nobis placentia; videte nobis errores. 11 Auferte a me viam; declinate a me semitam; cesset a facie nostra Sanctus Israhel."

12 Propterea haec dicit Sanctus Israhel: "Pro eo quod reprobastis verbum hoc et sperastis in calumniam et tumultum et innixi estis super eo, 13 propterea erit vobis iniquitas haec sicut interruptio cadens et requisita in muro excelso, quoniam subito, dum non speratur, veniet contritio eius. 14 Et comminuetur sicut conteritur lagoena figuli contritione pervalida, et non invenietur de fragmentis eius testa in qua portetur igniculus de incendio, aut hauriatur parum aquae de fovea.

15 Quia haec dicit Dominus Deus, Sanctus Israhel: "Si revertamini et quiescatis, salvi eritis; in silentio et in spe erit fortitudo vestra. Et noluistis, 16 et dixistis, 'Nequaquam, sed ad equos fugiemus'; ideo fugietis. 'Et super veloces ascendemus'; ideo velociores erunt qui persequentur vos. 17 Mille homines a facie terroris unius, et a facie terroris quinque fugietis, donec relinquamini quasi malus navis in vertice montis et quasi signum super collem."

18 Propterea expectat Dominus ut misereatur vestri, et ideo exaltabitur parcens vobis, quia Deus iudicii Dominus; beati omnes qui expectant eum. 19 Populus enim Sion habitabit in Hierusalem. Plorans, nequaquam plorabis; miserans

law of God, 10 who say to the seers, "See not," and to them that behold, "Behold not for us those things that are right. Speak unto us pleasant things; see errors for us. 11 Take away from me the way; turn away the path from me; let the Holy One of Israel cease from before us."

12 Therefore thus saith the Holy One of Israel: "Because you have rejected this word and have trusted in oppression and tumult and have leaned upon it, 13 therefore shall this iniquity be to you as a breach that falleth and is found wanting in a high wall, for the destruction thereof shall come on a sudden, when it is not looked for. 14 And it shall be broken small as the potter's vessel is broken all to pieces with mighty breaking, and there shall not a shard be found of the pieces thereof wherein a little fire may be carried from the hearth, or a little water be drawn out of the pit.

15 For thus saith the Lord God, the Holy One of Israel: "If you return and be quiet, you shall be saved; in silence and in hope shall your strength be. And you would not, 16 *but* have said, 'No, but we will flee to horses'; therefore shall you flee. 'And we will mount upon swift ones'; therefore shall they be swifter that shall pursue after you. 17 A thousand men shall flee for fear of one, and for fear of five shall you flee, till you be left as the mast of a ship on the top of a mountain and as an ensign upon a hill."

18 Therefore the Lord waiteth that he may have mercy on you, and therefore shall he be exalted sparing you, because the Lord is the God of judgment; blessed are all they that wait for him. 19 For the people of Zion shall dwell in Jerusalem. Weeping, thou shalt not weep; he will surely have pity

miserebitur tui. Ad vocem clamoris tui, statim ut audierit respondebit tibi. 20 Et dabit vobis Dominus panem artum et aquam brevem et non faciet avolare a te ultra doctorem tuum, et erunt oculi tui videntes praeceptorem tuum. 21 Et aures tuae audient verbum post tergum monentis, "Haec est via; ambulate in ea, et non declinetis neque ad dexteram neque ad sinistram." 22 Et contaminabis lamminas sculptilium argenti tui et vestimentum conflatilis auri tui et disperges ea sicut inmunditiam menstruatae. "Egredere," dices ei.

23 Et dabitur pluvia semini tuo ubicumque seminaveris in terra, et panis frugum terrae erit uberrimus et pinguis. Pascetur in possessione tua in die illo agnus spatiose, 24 et tauri tui et pulli asinorum qui operantur terram commixtum migma comedent sicut in area ventilatum est. 25 Et erunt super omnem montem excelsum et super omnem collem elevatum rivi currentium aquarum in die interfectionis multorum cum ceciderint turres. 26 Et erit lux lunae sicut lux solis, et lux solis erit septempliciter, sicut lux septem dierum, in die qua alligaverit Dominus vulnus populi sui et percussuram plagae eius sanaverit.

27 Ecce: nomen Domini venit de longinquo; ardens furor eius et gravis ad portandum. Labia eius repleta sunt indignatione, et lingua eius quasi ignis devorans. 28 Spiritus eius velut torrens inundans usque ad medium colli ad perdendas gentes in nihilum et frenum erroris quod erat in maxillis populorum.

on thee. At the voice of thy cry, as soon as he shall hear he will answer thee. 20 And the Lord will give you spare bread and short water and will not cause thy teacher to flee away from thee any more, and thy eyes shall see thy teacher. 21 And thy ears shall hear the word of one admonishing thee behind thy back, "This is the way; walk ye in it, and go not aside neither to the right hand nor to the left." 22 And thou shalt defile the plates of thy graven things of silver and the garment of thy molten things of gold and shalt cast them away as the uncleanness of a menstruous woman. Thou shalt say to it, "Get thee hence."

23 And rain shall be given to thy seed wheresoever thou shalt sow in the land, and the bread of the corn of the land shall be most plentiful and fat. The lamb in that day shall feed at large in thy possession, 24 and thy oxen and the ass colts that till the ground shall eat mingled provender as it was winnowed in the floor. 25 And there shall be upon every high mountain and upon every elevated hill rivers of running waters in the day of the slaughter of many when the towers shall fall. 26 And the light of the moon shall be as the light of the sun, and the light of the sun shall be sevenfold, as the light of seven days, in the day when the Lord shall bind up the wound of his people and shall heal the stroke of their wound.

27 Behold: the name of the Lord cometh from afar; his wrath burneth and is heavy to bear. His lips are filled with indignation, and his tongue as a devouring fire. 28 His breath as a torrent overflowing even to the midst of the neck to destroy the nations unto nothing and the bridle of error that was in the jaws of the people.

29 Canticum erit vobis sicut nox sanctificatae sollemnitatis et laetitia cordis, sicut qui pergit cum tibia ut intret in montem Domini ad Fortem Israhel. 30 Et auditam faciet Dominus gloriam vocis suae et terrorem brachii sui ostendet in comminatione furoris et flamma ignis devorantis. Adlidet in turbine et in lapide grandinis. 31 A voce enim Domini pavebit Assur virga percussus. 32 Et erit transitus virgae fundatus quam requiescere faciet Dominus super eum in tympanis et citharis, et in bellis praecipuis expugnabit eos. 33 Praeparata est enim ab heri Thofeth, a rege praeparata profunda et dilatata. Nutrimenta eius ignis et ligna multa; flatus Domini sicut torrens sulphuris succendens eam.

Caput 31

V ae qui descendunt in Aegyptum ad auxilium, in equis sperantes et habentes fiduciam super quadrigis quia multae sunt et super equitibus, quia praevalidi nimis, et non sunt

29 You shall have a song as in the night of the sanctified solemnity and joy of heart, as when one goeth with a pipe to come into the mountain of the Lord to the Mighty One of Israel. 30 And the Lord shall make the glory of his voice to be heard and shall shew the terror of his arm in the threatening of wrath and the flame of devouring fire. He shall crush to pieces with whirlwind and hailstones. 31 For at the voice of the Lord the Assyrian shall fear being struck with the rod. 32 And the passage of the rod shall be strongly grounded which the Lord shall make to rest upon him with timbrels and harps, and in great battles he shall overthrow them. 33 For Topheth is prepared from yesterday, prepared by the king deep and wide. The nourishment thereof is fire and much wood; the breath of the Lord as a torrent of brimstone kindling it.

Chapter 31

The folly of trusting to Egypt and forgetting God. He will fight for his people against the Assyrians.

Woe to them that go down to Egypt for help, trusting in horses and putting their confidence in chariots because they are many and in horsemen, because they are very strong, and

confisi super Sanctum Israhel et Dominum non requisierunt. 2 Ipse autem sapiens adduxit malum et verba sua non
abstulit, et consurget contra domum pessimorum et contra
auxilium operantium iniquitatem. 3 Aegyptus homo et non
Deus, et equi eorum caro et non spiritus. Et Dominus incli-
nabit manum suam, et corruet auxiliator, et cadet cui prae-
statur auxilium, simulque omnes consumentur.

4 Quia haec dicit Dominus ad me: "Quomodo si rugiat
leo, et catulus leonis super praedam suam, et cum occurrerit
ei multitudo pastorum, a voce eorum non formidabit et a
multitudine eorum non pavebit, sic descendet Dominus exercituum ut proelietur super Montem Sion et super collem
eius. 5 Sicut aves volantes, sic proteget Dominus exercituum
Hierusalem, protegens et liberans, transiens et salvans."

6 Convertimini sicut in profundum recesseratis, filii Israhel. 7 In die enim illa abiciet vir idola argenti sui et idola auri
sui quae fecerunt vobis manus vestrae in peccatum. 8 Et cadet Assur in gladio non viri, et gladius non hominis vorabit
eum, et fugiet non a facie gladii, et iuvenes eius vectigales
erunt. 9 Et fortitudo eius a terrore transibit, et pavebunt fugientes principes eius. Dixit Dominus, cuius ignis est in Sion
et caminus eius in Hierusalem.

have not trusted in the Holy One of Israel and have not sought after the Lord. 2 But he that is the wise one hath brought evil and hath not removed his words, and he will rise up against the house of the wicked and against the aid of them that work iniquity. 3 Egypt is man and not God, and their horses flesh and not spirit. And the Lord shall put down his hand, and the helper shall fall, and he that is helped shall fall, and they shall all be confounded together.

4 For thus saith the Lord to me: "Like as the lion roareth, and the lion's whelp upon his prey, and when a multitude of shepherds shall come against him, he will not fear at their voice nor be afraid of their multitude, so shall the Lord of hosts come down to fight upon Mount Zion and upon the hill thereof. 5 As birds dying, so will the Lord of hosts protect Jerusalem, protecting and delivering, passing over and saving."

6 Return as you had deeply revolted, O children of Israel. 7 For in that day a man shall cast away his idols of silver and his idols of gold which your hands have made for you to sin. 8 And the Assyrian shall fall by the sword not of a man, and the sword not of a man shall devour him, and he shall flee not at the face of the sword, and his young men shall be tributaries. 9 And his strength shall pass away with dread, and his princes fleeing shall be afraid. The Lord hath said it, whose fire is in Zion and his furnace in Jerusalem.

Caput 32

Ecce: in iustitia regnabit rex, et principes in iudicio praeerunt. 2 Et erit vir sicut qui absconditur a vento et celat se a tempestate, sicut rivi aquarum in siti et umbra petrae prominentis in terra deserta. 3 Non caligabunt oculi videntium, et aures audientium diligenter auscultabunt. 4 Et cor stultorum intelleget scientiam, et lingua balborum velociter loquetur et plane. 5 Non vocabitur ultra is qui insipiens est princeps, neque fraudulentus appellabitur maior, 6 stultus enim fatua loquetur et cor eius faciet iniquitatem ut perficiat simulationem et loquatur ad Dominum fraudulenter et vacuefaciat animam esurientis et potum sitienti auferat.

7 Fraudulenti vasa pessima sunt, ipse enim cogitationes concinnavit ad perdendos mites in sermone mendacii cum loqueretur pauper iudicium. 8 Princeps vero ea quae digna sunt principe cogitabit, et ipse super duces stabit.

9 Mulieres opulentae, surgite, et audite vocem meam. Filiae confidentes, percipite auribus eloquium meum. 10 Post dies enim et annum, vos conturbabimini confidentes, consummata est enim vindemia; collectio ultra non veniet. 11 Obstupescite, opulentae; conturbamini, confidentes: exuite vos, et confundimini; accingite lumbos vestros. 12 Super

Chapter 32

The blessings of the reign of Christ. The desolation of the
Jews and prosperity of the church of Christ.

Behold: a king shall reign in justice, and princes shall rule
in judgment. 2 And a man shall be as when one is hid from
the wind and hideth himself from a storm, as rivers of waters in drought and the shadow of a rock that standeth out
in a desert land. 3 The eyes of them that see shall not be dim,
and the ears of them that hear shall hearken diligently. 4 And
the heart of fools shall understand knowledge, and the
tongue of stammerers shall speak readily and plain. 5 The
fool shall no more be called prince, neither shall the deceitful be called *great,* 6 for the fool will speak foolish things and
his heart will work iniquity to practise hypocrisy and speak
to the Lord deceitfully and to make empty the soul of the
hungry and take away drink from the thirsty.

7 The vessels of the deceitful are most wicked, for he hath
framed devices to destroy the meek with *lying* words when
the poor man speaketh judgment. 8 But the prince will devise such things as are worthy of a prince, and he shall stand
above the rulers.

9 Rise up, ye rich women, and hear my voice. Ye confident
daughters, give ear to my speech. 10 For after days and a year,
you that are confident shall be troubled, for the vintage is
at an end; the gathering shall come no more. 11 Be astonished, ye rich women; be troubled, ye confident ones; strip
you, and be confounded; gird your loins. 12 Mourn for your

ubera plangite, super regione desiderabili, super vinea fertili. 13 Super humum populi mei spinae et vepres ascendent. Quanto magis super omnes domos gaudii civitatis exultantis? 14 Domus enim dimissa est; multitudo urbis relicta est; tenebrae et palpatio factae sunt super speluncas usque in aeternum. Gaudium onagrorum, pascua gregum, 15 donec effundatur super nos spiritus de excelso, et erit desertum in charmel, et charmel in saltum reputabitur.

16 Et habitabit in solitudine iudicium, et iustitia in charmel sedebit. 17 Et erit opus iustitiae pax, et cultus iustitiae silentium et securitas usque in sempiternum. 18 Et sedebit populus meus in pulchritudine pacis et in tabernaculis fiduciae et in requie opulenta. 19 Grando autem in descensione saltus, et humilitate humiliabitur civitas. 20 Beati qui seminatis super omnes aquas, inmittentes pedem bovis et asini.

Caput 33

Vae qui praedaris; nonne et ipse praedaberis? Et qui spernis, nonne et ipse sperneris? Cum consummaveris depraedationem, depraedaberis; cum fatigatus desiveris contemnere, contemneris.

breasts, for the delightful country, for the fruitful vineyard. 13 Upon the land of my people shall thorns and briers come up. How much more upon all the houses of joy of the city that rejoiced? 14 For the house is forsaken; the multitude of the city is left; darkness and obscurity are come upon its dens for ever. A joy of wild asses, the pastures of flocks, 15 until the spirit be poured upon us from on high, and the desert shall be as a charmel, and charmel shall be counted for a forest.

16 And judgment shall dwell in the wilderness, and justice shall sit in charmel. 17 And the work of justice shall be peace, and the service of justice quietness and security for ever. 18 And my people shall sit in the beauty of peace and in the tabernacles of confidence and in wealthy rest. 19 But hail shall be in the descent of the forest, and the city shall be made very low. 20 Blessed are ye that sow upon all waters, sending thither the foot of the ox and the ass.

Chapter 33

God's revenge against the enemies of his church. The happiness of the heavenly Jerusalem.

Woe to thee that spoilest; shalt not thou thyself also be spoiled? And thou that despisest, shalt not thyself also be despised? When thou shalt have made an end of spoiling, thou shalt be spoiled; when being wearied thou shalt cease to despise, thou shalt be despised.

2 Domine, miserere nostri, te enim expectavimus; esto brachium nostrum in mane et salus nostra in tempore tribulationis. 3 A voce angeli fugerunt populi, et ab exaltatione tua dispersae sunt gentes. 4 Et congregabuntur spolia vestra sicut colligitur brucus, velut cum fossae plenae fuerint de eo. 5 Magnificatus est Dominus, quoniam habitavit in excelso; implevit Sion iudicio et iustitia. 6 Et erit fides in temporibus tuis, divitiae salutis, sapientia et scientia; timor Domini ipse est thesaurus eius.

7 Ecce: videntes clamabunt foris; angeli pacis amare flebunt. 8 Dissipatae sunt viae; cessavit transiens per semitam. Irritum factum est pactum. Proiecit civitates; non reputavit homines. 9 Luxit et elanguit terra; confusus est Libanus et obsorduit, et factus est Saron sicut desertum, et concussa est Basan et Carmelus.

10 "Nunc consurgam," dicit Dominus. "Nunc exaltabor; nunc sublevabor. 11 Concipietis ardorem; parietis stipulam; spiritus vester ut ignis vorabit vos. 12 Et erunt populi quasi de incendio cinis; spinae congregatae igni conburentur. 13 Audite, qui longe estis, quae fecerim, et cognoscite, vicini, fortitudinem meam."

14 Conterriti sunt in Sion peccatores; possedit tremor hypocritas. Quis poterit habitare de vobis cum igne devorante? Quis habitabit ex vobis cum ardoribus sempiternis? 15 Qui ambulat in iustitiis et loquitur veritatem, qui proicit avaritiam ex calumnia et excutit manus suas ab omni munere, qui obturat aures suas ne audiat sanguinem et claudit oculos

2 O Lord, have mercy on us, for we have waited for thee; be thou our arm in the morning and our salvation in the time of trouble. 3 At the voice of the angel the people fled, and at the lifting up thyself the nations are scattered. 4 And your spoils shall be gathered together as the locusts are gathered, as when the ditches are full of them. 5 The Lord is magnified, for he hath dwelt on high; he hath filled Zion with judgment and justice. 6 And there shall be faith in thy times, riches of salvation, wisdom and knowledge; the fear of the Lord is his treasure.

7 Behold: they that see shall cry without; the angels of peace shall weep bitterly. 8 The ways are made desolate; no one passeth by the road. The covenant is made void. He hath rejected the cities; he hath not regarded the men. 9 The land hath mourned and languished; Lebanon is confounded and become foul, and Sharon is become as a desert, and Bashan and Carmel are shaken.

10 "Now will I rise up," saith the Lord. "Now will I be exalted; now will I lift up myself. 11 You shall conceive heat; you shall bring forth stubble; your breath as fire shall devour you. 12 And the people shall be as ashes after a fire; as a bundle of thorns they shall be burnt with fire. 13 Hear, you that are far off, what I have done, and you that are near, know my strength."

14 The sinners in Zion are afraid; trembling hath seized upon the hypocrites. Which of you can dwell with devouring fire? Which of you shall dwell with everlasting burnings? 15 He that walketh in justices and speaketh truth, that casteth away avarice by oppression and shaketh his hands from all bribes, that stoppeth his ears lest he hear blood and

suos ne videat malum, 16 iste in excelsis habitabit. Munimenta saxorum sublimitas eius; panis ei datus est; aquae eius fideles sunt. 17 Regem in decore suo videbunt oculi eius; cernent terram de longe.

18 Cor tuum meditabitur timorem; ubi est litteratus? Ubi legis verba ponderans? Ubi doctor parvulorum? 19 Populum inpudentem non videbis, populum alti sermonis, ita ut non possis intellegere disertitudinem linguae eius in quo nulla est sapientia. 20 Respice Sion, civitatem sollemnitatis nostrae. Oculi tui videbunt Hierusalem, habitationem opulentam, tabernaculum quod nequaquam transferri poterit, nec auferentur clavi eius in sempiternum, et omnes funiculi eius non rumpentur, 21 quia solummodo ibi magnificus est Dominus noster. Locus fluviorum, rivi latissimi et patentes; non transibit per eum navis remigum, neque trieris magna transgredietur eum. 22 Dominus enim iudex noster; Dominus legifer noster; Dominus rex noster. Ipse salvabit nos.

23 Laxati sunt funiculi tui, et non praevalebunt; sic erit malus tuus ut dilatare signum non queas. Tunc dividentur spolia praedarum multarum; claudi diripient rapinam. 24 Nec dicet vicinus, "Elangui." Populus qui habitat in ea, auferetur ab eo iniquitas.

shutteth his eyes that he may see no evil, 16 he shall dwell on high. The fortifications of rocks shall be his highness; bread is given him; his waters are sure. 17 His eyes shall see the king in his beauty; they shall see the land far off.

18 Thy heart shall meditate fear; where is the learned? Where is he that pondereth the words of the law? Where is the teacher of little ones? 19 The shameless people thou shalt not see, the people of profound speech, so that thou canst not understand the eloquence of his tongue in whom there is no wisdom. 20 Look upon Zion, the city of our solemnity. Thy eyes shall see Jerusalem, a rich habitation, a tabernacle that cannot be removed, neither shall the nails thereof be taken away for ever, neither shall any of the cords thereof be broken, 21 because only there our Lord is magnificent. A place of rivers, very broad and spacious streams; no ship with oars shall pass by it, neither shall the great galley pass through it. 22 For the Lord is our judge; the Lord is our lawgiver; the Lord is our king. He will save us.

23 Thy tacklings are loosed, and they shall be of no strength; thy mast shall be in such condition that thou shalt not be able to spread the flag. Then shall the spoils of much prey be divided; the lame shall take the spoil. 24 Neither shall he that is near say, "I am feeble." The people that dwell therein shall have their iniquity taken away from them.

Caput 34

Accedite, Gentes, et audite, et populi, adtendite; audiat terra et plenitudo eius, orbis et omne germen eius. 2 Quia indignatio Domini super omnes gentes, et furor super universam militiam eorum; interfecit eos et dedit eos in occisionem. 3 Interfecti eorum proicientur, et de cadaveribus eorum ascendet fetor; tabescent montes sanguine eorum. 4 Et tabescet omnis militia caelorum, et conplicabuntur sicut liber caeli, et omnis militia eorum defluet sicut defluit folium de vinea et de ficu. 5 "Quoniam inebriatus est in caelo gladius meus, ecce: super Idumeam descendet et super populum interfectionis meae ad iudicium."

6 Gladius Domini repletus est sanguine; incrassatus est adipe de sanguine agnorum et hircorum, de sanguine medullatorum arietum, victima enim Domini in Bosra et interfectio magna in terra Edom. 7 Et descendent unicornes cum eis, et tauri cum potentibus. Inebriabitur terra eorum sanguine, et humus eorum adipe pinguium. 8 Quia dies ultionis Domini, annus retributionum iudicii Sion.

Chapter 34

The general judgment of the wicked.

Come near, ye Gentiles, and hear, and hearken, ye people; let the earth hear and all that is therein, the world and every thing that cometh forth of it. 2 For the indignation of the Lord is upon all nations, and his fury upon all their armies; he hath killed them and delivered them to slaughter. 3 Their slain shall be cast forth, and out of their carcasses shall rise a stink; the mountains shall be melted with their blood. 4 And all the host of the heavens shall pine away, and the heavens shall be folded together as a book, and all their host shall fall down as the leaf falleth from the vine and from the fig tree. 5 "For my sword is inebriated in heaven, behold: it shall come down upon Idumea and upon the people of my slaughter unto judgment."

6 The sword of the Lord is filled with blood; it is made thick with the blood of lambs and buck goats, with the blood of rams full of marrow, for there is a victim of the Lord in Bozrah and a great slaughter in the land of Edom. 7 And the unicorns shall go down with them, and the bulls with the mighty. Their land shall be soaked with blood, and their ground with the fat of fat ones. 8 For it is the day of the vengeance of the Lord, the year of recompenses of the judgment of Zion.

9 Et convertentur torrentes eius in picem et humus eius in sulphur, et erit terra eius in picem ardentem. 10 Nocte et die non extinguetur; in sempiternum ascendet fumus eius. A generatione in generationem desolabitur; in saeculum saeculorum non erit transiens per eam. 11 Et possidebunt illam onocrotalus et ericius, et ibis et corvus habitabunt in ea, et extendetur super eam mensura ut redigatur ad nihilum et perpendiculum in desolationem. 12 Nobiles eius non erunt ibi; regem potius invocabunt, et omnes principes eius erunt in nihilum. 13 Et orientur in domibus eius spinae et urticae, et paliurus in munitionibus eius, et erit cubile draconum et pascua strutionum. 14 Et occurrent daemonia onocentauris, et pilosus clamabit alter ad alterum; ibi cubavit lamia et invenit sibi requiem. 15 Ibi habuit foveam ericius et enutrivit catulos et circumfodit et fovit in umbra eius; illuc congregati sunt milvi alter ad alterum.

16 Requirite diligenter in libro Domini, et legite: "Unum ex eis non defuit, alter alterum non quaesivit, quia quod ex ore meo procedit ille mandavit, et spiritus eius, ipse congregavit ea. 17 Et ipse misit eis sortem, et manus eius divisit eam illis in mensuram. Usque in aeternum possidebunt eam; in generatione et generatione habitabunt in ea."

9 And the streams thereof shall be turned into pitch and the ground thereof into brimstone, and the land thereof shall become burning pitch. 10 Night and day it shall not be quenched; the smoke thereof shall go up for ever. From generation to generation it shall lie waste; none shall pass through it for ever and ever. 11 *The* bittern and ericius shall possess it, and the ibis and the raven shall dwell in it, and a line shall be stretched out upon it to bring it to nothing and a plummet unto desolation. 12 The nobles thereof shall not be there; they shall call rather upon the king, and all the princes thereof shall be nothing. 13 And thorns and nettles shall grow up in its houses, and the thistle in the fortresses thereof, and it shall be the habitation of dragons and the pasture of ostriches. 14 And demons and monsters shall meet, and the hairy ones shall cry out one to another; there hath the lamia lain down and found rest for herself. 15 There hath the ericius had its hole and brought up its young ones and hath dug round about and cherished them in the shadow thereof; thither are the kites gathered together one to another.

16 Search ye diligently in the book of the Lord, and read: "Not one of them was wanting, one hath not sought for the other, for that which proceedeth out of my mouth he hath commanded, and his spirit, it hath gathered them. 17 And he hath cast the lot for them, and his hand hath divided it to them by line. They shall possess it for ever; *from* generation *to* generation they shall dwell therein."

Caput 35

Laetabitur deserta et invia, et exultabit solitudo et florebit quasi lilium. 2 Germinans germinabit et exultabit laetabunda et laudans. Gloria Libani data est ei, decor Carmeli et Saron; ipsi videbunt gloriam Domini et decorem Dei nostri.

3 Confortate manus dissolutas, et genua debilia roborate. 4 Dicite pusillanimis, "Confortamini, et nolite timere. Ecce: Deus vester ultionem adducet retributionis. Deus ipse veniet et salvabit vos."

5 Tunc aperientur oculi caecorum, et aures surdorum patebunt. 6 Tunc saliet sicut cervus claudus, et aperta erit lingua mutorum, quia scissae sunt in deserto aquae et torrentes in solitudine. 7 Et quae erat arida erit in stagnum, et sitiens in fontes aquarum. In cubilibus in quibus prius dracones habitabant orietur viror calami et iunci.

8 Et erit ibi semita et via, et via sancta vocabitur. Non transibit per eam pollutus, et haec erit vobis directa via, ita ut stulti non errent per eam. 9 Non erit ibi leo, et mala bestia non ascendet per eam nec invenietur ibi, et ambulabunt qui

Chapter 35

The joyful flourishing of Christ's kingdom. In his church
shall be a holy and secure way.

The land that was desolate and impassable shall be glad,
and the wilderness shall rejoice and shall flourish like the lily.
2 It shall bud forth and blossom and shall rejoice with joy
and praise. The glory of Lebanon is given to it, the beauty of
Carmel and Sharon; they shall see the glory of the Lord and
the beauty of our God.

3 Strengthen ye the feeble hands, and confirm the weak
knees. 4 Say to the fainthearted, "Take courage, and fear not.
Behold: your God will bring the revenge of recompense.
God himself will come and will save you."

5 Then shall the eyes of the blind be opened, and the ears
of the deaf shall be unstopped. 6 Then shall the lame man
leap as a hart, and the tongue of the dumb shall be free, for
waters are broken out in the desert and streams in the wilderness. 7 And that which was dry land shall become a pool,
and the thirsty land springs of water. In the dens where dragons dwelt before shall rise up the verdure of the reed and the
bulrush.

8 And a path and a way shall be there, and it shall be called
the holy way. The unclean shall not pass over it, and this shall
be unto you a straight way, so that fools shall not err therein.
9 No lion shall be there, nor shall any mischievous beast go
up by it nor be found there, *but* they shall walk *there* that

liberati fuerint. 10 Et redempti a Domino convertentur, et venient in Sion cum laude, et laetitia sempiterna super caput eorum. Gaudium et laetitiam obtinebunt, et fugiet dolor et gemitus.

Caput 36

Et factum est in quartodecimo anno Regis Ezechiae ascendit Sennacherib, rex Assyriorum, super omnes civitates Iuda munitas et cepit eas. 2 Et misit rex Assyriorum Rabsacen de Lachis in Hierusalem, ad regem Ezechiam, in manu gravi, et stetit in aquaeductu piscinae superioris in via agri fullonis. 3 Et egressus est ad eum Eliachim, filius Helciae, qui erat super domum, et Sobna, scriba, et Ioae, filius Asaph, a commentariis.

4 Et dixit ad eos Rabsaces, "Dicite Ezechiae, 'Haec dicit rex magnus, rex Assyriorum: "Quae est ista fiducia qua confidis? 5 Aut quo consilio vel fortitudine rebellare disponis? Super quem habes fiduciam quia recessisti a me? 6 Ecce: confidis super baculum harundineum confractum istum, super Aegyptum, cui si innisus fuerit homo, intrabit in manum

shall be delivered. 10 And the redeemed of the Lord shall return and shall come into Zion with praise, and everlasting joy shall be upon their heads. They shall obtain joy and gladness, and sorrow and mourning shall flee away.

Chapter 36

Sennacherib invades Judah. His blasphemies.

And it came to pass in the fourteenth year of King Hezekiah that Sennacherib, king of the Assyrians, came up against all the fenced cities of Judah and took them. 2 And the king of the Assyrians sent Rabshakeh from Lachish to Jerusalem, to King Hezekiah, with a great army, and he stood by the conduit of the upper pool in the way of the fuller's field. 3 And there went out to him Eliakim, the son of Hilkiah, who was over the house, and Shebna, the scribe, and Joah, the son of Asaph, the recorder.

4 And Rabshakeh said to them, "Tell Hezekiah, 'Thus saith the great king, the king of the Assyrians: "What is this confidence wherein thou trustest? 5 Or with what counsel or strength dost thou prepare for war? On whom dost thou trust that thou art revolted from me? 6 Lo: thou trustest upon this broken staff of a reed, upon Egypt, upon which if

eius et perforabit eam. Sic Pharao, rex Aegypti, omnibus qui confidunt in eo. 7 Quod si responderis mihi, 'In Domino, Deo nostro, confidimus,' nonne ipse est cuius abstulit Ezechias excelsa et altaria et dixit Iudae et Hierusalem, 'Coram altari isto adorabitis'?"

8 "'Et nunc trade te domino meo, regi Assyriorum, et dabo tibi duo milia equorum, nec poteris ex te praebere ascensores eorum. 9 Et quomodo sustinebis faciem iudicis unius loci ex servis domini mei minoribus? Quod si confidis in Aegypto, in quadrigis et in equitibus: 10 et nunc numquid sine Domino ascendi ad terram istam ut disperderem eam? Dominus dixit ad me, "Ascende super terram istam, et disperde eam."'"

11 Et dixit Eliachim et Sobna et Ioae ad Rabsacen, "Loquere ad servos tuos Syra lingua, intellegimus enim. Ne loquaris ad nos Iudaice in auribus populi qui est super murum."

12 Et dixit ad eos Rabsaces, "Numquid ad dominum tuum et ad te misit me dominus meus ut loquerer omnia verba ista et non potius ad viros qui sedent in muro, ut comedant stercora sua et bibant urinam pedum suorum vobiscum?"

13 Et stetit Rabsaces et clamavit voce magna Iudaice et dixit, "Audite verba regis magni, regis Assyriorum. 14 Haec dicit rex: 'Non seducat vos Ezechias, quia non poterit eruere vos. 15 Et non vobis tribuat fiduciam Ezechias super Domino, dicens, "Eruens liberabit nos Dominus; non dabitur

a man lean, it will go into his hand and pierce it. So is Pharaoh, king of Egypt, to all that trust in him. 7 But if thou wilt answer me, 'We trust in the Lord, our God,' is it not he whose high places and altars Hezekiah hath taken away and hath said to Judah and Jerusalem, 'You shall worship before this altar'?"

8 "'And now deliver thyself up to my lord, the king of the Assyrians, and I will give thee two thousand horses, and thou wilt not be able on thy part to find riders for them. 9 And how wilt thou stand against the face of the judge of one place of the *least* of my master's servants? But if thou trust in Egypt, in chariots and in horsemen: 10 and am I now come up without the Lord against this land to destroy it? The Lord said to me, "Go up against this land, and destroy it."'"

11 And Eliakim and Shebna and Joah said to Rabshakeh, "Speak to thy servants in the Syrian tongue, for we understand it. Speak not to us in the Jews' language in the hearing of the people that are upon the wall."

12 And Rabshakeh said to them, "Hath my master sent me to thy master and to thee to speak all these words and not rather to the men that sit on the wall, that they may eat their own dung and drink *their urine* with you?"

13 Then Rabshakeh stood and cried out with a loud voice in the Jews' language and said, "Hear the words of the great king, the king of the Assyrians. 14 Thus saith the king: 'Let not Hezekiah deceive you, for he shall not be able to deliver you. 15 And let not Hezekiah make you trust in the Lord, saying, "The Lord will surely deliver us, *and* this city shall

civitas ista in manu regis Assyriorum."' 16 Nolite audire Ezechiam, haec enim dicit rex Assyriorum: 'Facite mecum
benedictionem, et egredimini ad me, et comedite unusquisque vineam suam, et unusquisque ficum suam, et bibite
unusquisque aquam cisternae suae, 17 donec veniam et tollam vos ad terram quae est ut terra vestra, terram frumenti
et vini, terram panum et vinearum.

18 "'Nec conturbet vos Ezechias, dicens, "Dominus liberabit nos." Numquid liberaverunt dii gentium unusquisque
terram suam de manu regis Assyriorum? 19 Ubi est deus
Emath et Arfad? Ubi est deus Seffarvaim? Numquid liberaverunt Samariam de manu mea? 20 Quis est ex omnibus diis
terrarum istarum qui eruerit terram suam de manu mea, ut
eruat Dominus Hierusalem de manu mea?'"

21 Et siluerunt, et non responderunt ei verbum, mandave-
rat enim rex, dicens, "Ne respondeatis ei." 22 Et ingressus est
Eliachim, filius Helciae, qui erat super domum, et Sobna,
scriba, et Ioae, filius Asaph, a commentariis, ad Ezechiam
scissis vestibus et nuntiaverunt ei verba Rabsacis.

not be given into the hands of the king of the Assyrians.'"
16 Do not hearken to Hezekiah, for thus saith the king of
the Assyrians: 'Do with me that which is for your advantage,
and come out to me, and eat ye every one of his vine, and
every one of his fig tree, and drink ye every one the water of
his cistern, 17 till I come and take you away to a land like to
your own, a land of corn and of wine, a land of bread and
vineyards.

18 "'Neither let Hezekiah trouble you, saying, "The Lord
will deliver us." Have any of the gods of the nations delivered their land out of the hand of the king of the Assyrians?
19 Where is the god of Hamath and of Arpad? Where is the
god of Sepharvaim? Have they delivered Samaria out of my
hand? 20 Who is there among all the gods of these lands that
hath delivered his country out of my hand, that the Lord
may deliver Jerusalem out of my hand?'"

21 And they held their peace and answered him not a
word, for the king had commanded, saying, "Answer him
not." 22 And Eliakim, the son of Hilkiah, that was over the
house, and Shebna, the scribe, and Joah, the son of Asaph,
the recorder, went in to Hezekiah with their garments rent
and told him the words of Rabshakeh.

Caput 37

Et factum est cum audisset Rex Ezechias scidit vestimenta sua et obvolutus est sacco et intravit in domum Domini. 2 Et misit Eliachim, qui erat super domum, et Sobnam, scribam, et seniores de sacerdotibus opertos saccis ad Isaiam, filium Amos, prophetam.

3 Et dixerunt ad eum, "Haec dicit Ezechias: 'Dies tribulationis et correptionis et blasphemiae dies haec, quia venerunt filii usque ad partum et virtus non est pariendi. 4 Si quo modo audiat Dominus, Deus tuus, verba Rabsacis, quem misit rex Assyriorum, dominus suus, ad blasphemandum Deum viventem et obprobrandum sermonibus quos audivit Dominus, Deus tuus; leva ergo orationem pro reliquiis quae reppertae sunt.'"

5 Et venerunt servi regis Ezechiae ad Isaiam, 6 et dixit ad eos Isaias, "Haec dicetis domino vestro: 'Haec dicit Dominus: "Ne timeas a facie verborum quae audisti, quibus blasphemaverunt pueri regis Assyriorum me. 7 Ecce: ego dabo ei spiritum, et audiet nuntium et revertetur ad terram suam, et corruere eum faciam gladio in terra sua."'"

8 Reversus est autem Rabsaces et invenit regem Assyrio-

Chapter 37

Hezekiah, his mourning and prayer. God's promise of protection. The Assyrian army is destroyed. Sennacherib is slain.

And it came to pass when King Hezekiah had heard it that he rent his garments and covered himself with sackcloth and went into the house of the Lord. 2 And he sent Eliakim, who was over the house, and Shebna, the scribe, and the ancients of the priests covered with sackcloth to Isaiah, the son of Amoz, the prophet.

3 And they said to him, "Thus saith Hezekiah: 'This day is a day of tribulation and of rebuke and of blasphemy, for the children are come to the birth and there is not strength to bring forth. 4 It may be the Lord, thy God, will hear the words of Rabshakeh, whom the king of the Assyrians, his master, hath sent to blaspheme the living God and to reproach with words which the Lord, thy God, hath heard; wherefore lift up thy prayer for the remnant that is left.'"

5 And the servants of Hezekiah came to Isaiah, 6 and Isaiah said to them, "Thus shall you say to your master: 'Thus saith the Lord: "Be not afraid of the words that thou hast heard, with which the servants of the king of the Assyrians have blasphemed me. 7 Behold: I will send a spirit upon him, and he shall hear a message and shall return to his own country, and I will cause him to fall by the sword in his own country.'""

8 And Rabshakeh returned and found the king of the As-

rum proeliantem adversus Lobnam, audierat enim quia profectus esset de Lachis. 9 Et audivit de Tharaca, rege Aethiopiae, dicentes, "Egressus est ut pugnet contra te."

Quod cum audisset misit nuntios ad Ezechiam, dicens, 10 "Haec dicetis Ezechiae, regi Iudae, loquentes, 'Non te decipiat Deus tuus, in quo tu confidis, dicens, "Non dabitur Hierusalem in manu regis Assyriorum." 11 Ecce: tu audisti omnia quae fecerunt reges Assyriorum omnibus terris quas subverterunt, et tu poteris liberari? 12 Numquid eruerunt eos dii gentium quos subverterunt patres mei, Gozan et Aran et Reseph et filios Eden qui erant in Thalassar? 13 Ubi est rex Emath et rex Arfad et rex urbis Seffarvaim, Ana et Ava?'"

14 Et tulit Ezechias libros de manu nuntiorum et legit eos et ascendit in domum Domini, et expandit eos Ezechias coram Domino. 15 Et oravit Ezechias ad Dominum, dicens, 16 "Domine exercituum, Deus Israhel, qui sedes super cherubin, tu es Deus solus omnium regnorum terrae; tu fecisti caelum et terram. 17 Inclina, Domine, aurem tuam, et audi; aperi, Domine, oculos tuos, et vide, et audi omnia verba Sennacherib quae misit ad blasphemandum Deum viventem. 18 Vere enim, Domine, desertas fecerunt reges Assyriorum terras et regiones earum. 19 Et dederunt deos earum igni, non enim erant dii sed opera manuum hominum, lignum et lapis, et comminuerunt eos. 20 Et nunc, Domine, Deus noster, salva nos de manu eius, et cognoscant omnia regna terrae quia tu es Dominus solus."

syrians besieging Libnah, for he had heard that he was departed from Lachish. 9 And he heard say about Tirhakah, the king of Ethiopia: "He is come forth to fight against thee."

And when he heard it he sent messengers to Hezekiah, saying, 10 "Thus shall you speak to Hezekiah, the king of Judah, saying, 'Let not thy God deceive thee, in whom thou trustest, saying, "Jerusalem shall not be given into the hands of the king of the Assyrians." 11 Behold: thou hast heard all that the kings of the Assyrians have done to all countries which they have destroyed, and canst thou be delivered? 12 Have the gods of the nations delivered them whom my fathers have destroyed, Gozan and Haran and Rezeph and the children of Eden that were in Telassar? 13 Where is the king of Emath and the king of Arpad and the king of the city of Sepharvaim, of Hena and of Ivvah?'"

14 And Hezekiah took the letter from the hand of the messengers and read it and went up to the house of the Lord, and Hezekiah spread it before the Lord. 15 And Hezekiah prayed to the Lord, saying, 16 "O Lord of hosts, God of Israel, who sittest upon the cherubims, thou alone art the God of all the kingdoms of the earth; thou hast made heaven and earth. 17 Incline, O Lord, thy ear, and hear; open, O Lord, thy eyes, and see, and hear all the words of Sennacherib which he hath sent to blaspheme the living God. 18 For of a truth, O Lord, the kings of the Assyrians have laid waste lands and their countries. 19 And they have cast their gods into the fire, for they were not gods but the works of men's hands, of wood and stone, and they broke them in pieces. 20 And now, O Lord, our God, save us out of his hand, and let all the kingdoms of the earth know that thou only art the Lord."

21 Et misit Isaias, filius Amos, ad Ezechiam, dicens, "Haec dicit Dominus, Deus Israhel: 'Pro quibus rogasti me de Sennacherib, rege Assyriorum, 22 hoc est verbum quod locutus est Dominus super eum:

""'Despexit te et subsannavit te virgo, filia Sion. Post te caput movit filia Hierusalem. 23 Cui exprobrasti, et quem blasphemasti, et super quem exaltasti vocem et levasti altitudinem oculorum tuorum? Ad Sanctum Israhel. 24 In manu servorum tuorum exprobrasti Domino et dixisti, 'In multitudine quadrigarum mearum ego ascendi altitudinem montium, iuga Libani, et succidam excelsa cedrorum eius et electas abietes illius, et introibo altitudinem summitatis eius, saltum Carmeli eius. 25 Ego fodi et bibi aquam et exsiccavi vestigio pedis mei omnes rivos aggerum.'

26 ""'Numquid non audisti quae olim fecerim ei? Ex diebus antiquis ego plasmavi illud, et nunc adduxi, et factum est in eradicationem collium conpugnantium et civitatum munitarum. 27 Habitatores earum breviata manu; contremuerunt et confusi sunt. Facti sunt sicut faenum agri et gramen pascuae et herba tectorum, quae exaruit antequam maturesceret.

28 ""'Habitationem tuam et egressum tuum et introitum tuum cognovi et insaniam tuam contra me. 29 Cum fureres adversum me, superbia tua ascendit in aures meas. Ponam ergo circulum in naribus tuis et frenum in labiis tuis, et reducam te in viam per quam venisti.

21 And Isaiah, the son of Amoz, sent to Hezekiah, saying, "Thus saith the Lord, the God of Israel: 'For the prayer thou hast made to me concerning Sennacherib, the king of the Assyrians, 22 this is the word which the Lord hath spoken of him:

""The virgin, the daughter of Zion, hath despised thee and laughed thee to scorn. The daughter of Jerusalem hath wagged the head after thee. 23 Whom hast thou reproached, and whom hast thou blasphemed, and against whom hast thou exalted thy voice and lifted up thy eyes on high? Against the Holy One of Israel. 24 By the hand of thy servants thou hast reproached the Lord and hast said, 'With the multitude of my chariots I have gone up to the height of the mountains, to the top of Lebanon, and I will cut down its tall cedars and its choice fir trees and will enter to the top of its height, to the forest of its Carmel. 25 I have digged and drunk water and have dried up with the sole of my foot all the rivers *shut up in* banks.'

26 ""Hast thou not heard what I have done to him of old? From the days of old I have formed it, and now I have brought it to effect, and it hath come to pass that hills fighting together and fenced cities should be destroyed. 27 The inhabitants of them *were weak of* hand; they trembled and were confounded. They became like the grass of the field and the herb of the pasture and like the grass of the housetops, which withered before it was ripe.

28 ""I know thy dwelling and thy going out and thy coming in and thy rage against me. 29 When thou wast mad against me, thy pride came up to my ears. Therefore I will put a ring in thy nose and a bit between thy lips, and I will turn thee back by the way by which thou camest.

30 """"Tibi autem hoc erit signum: Comede hoc anno quae sponte nascuntur, et in anno secundo pomis vescere, in anno autem tertio seminate, et metite, et plantate vineas, et comedite fructum earum. 31 Et mittet id quod salvatum fuerit de domo Iuda et quod reliquum est radicem deorsum et faciet fructum sursum, 32 quia de Hierusalem exibunt reliquiae, et salvatio de Monte Sion. Zelus Domini exercituum faciet istud.

33 """"Propterea haec dicit Dominus de rege Assyriorum: 'Non introibit civitatem hanc et non iaciet ibi sagittam et non occupabit eam clypeus et non mittet in circuitu eius aggerem. 34 In via qua venit per eam revertetur, et civitatem hanc non ingredietur,' dicit Dominus. 35 'Et protegam civitatem istam ut salvem eam propter me et propter David, servum meum.'"""

36 Egressus est autem angelus Domini et percussit in castris Assyriorum centum octoginta quinque milia. Et surrexerunt mane, et ecce: omnes cadavera mortuorum. 37 Et egressus est et abiit et reversus est Sennacherib, rex Assyriorum, et habitavit in Nineve.

38 Et factum est cum adoraret in templo Nesroch, deum suum, Adramelech et Sarasar, filii eius, percusserunt eum gladio, fugeruntque in terram Ararat, et regnavit Asarhaddon, filius eius, pro eo.

30 """But to thee this shall be a sign: Eat this year the things that spring of themselves, and in the second year eat fruits, but in the third year sow, and reap, and plant vineyards, and eat the fruit of them. 31 And that which shall be saved of the house of Judah and which is left shall take root downward and shall bear fruit upward, 32 for out of Jerusalem shall go forth a remnant, and salvation from Mount Zion. The zeal of the Lord of hosts shall do this.

33 """Wherefore thus saith the Lord concerning the king of the Assyrians: 'He shall not come into this city nor shoot an arrow *into it* nor *come before it with shield* nor cast a trench about it. 34 By the way that he came he shall return, and into this city he shall not come,' saith the Lord. 35 'And I will protect this city *and will* save it for my own sake and for the sake of David, my servant.'"""

36 And the angel of the Lord went out and slew in the camp of the Assyrians a hundred and eighty-five thousand. And they arose in the morning, and behold: they were all dead corpses. 37 And Sennacherib, the king of the Assyrians, went out and departed and returned and dwelt in Nineveh.

38 And it came to pass as he was worshipping in the temple of Nisroch, his god, that Adrammelech and Sharezer, his sons, slew him with the sword, and they fled into the land of Ararat, and Esar-haddon, his son, reigned in his stead.

Caput 38

In diebus illis aegrotavit Ezechias usque ad mortem, et introivit ad eum Isaias, filius Amos, propheta, et dixit ei, "Haec dicit Dominus: 'Dispone domui tuae, quia morieris tu et non vives.'"

2 Et convertit Ezechias faciem suam ad parietem et oravit ad Dominum, 3 et dixit "Obsecro, Domine, memento quaeso quomodo ambulaverim coram te in veritate et in corde perfecto et quod bonum est in oculis tuis fecerim." Et flevit Ezechias fletu magno.

4 Et factum est verbum Domini ad Isaiam, dicens, 5 "Vade, et dic Ezechiae, 'Haec dicit Dominus, Deus David, patris tui: "Audivi orationem tuam, et vidi lacrimas tuas. Ecce: ego adiciam super dies tuos quindecim annos, 6 et de manu regis Assyriorum eruam te et civitatem istam, et protegam eam. 7 Hoc autem tibi erit signum a Domino quia faciet Dominus verbum hoc quod locutus est. 8 Ecce: ego reverti faciam umbram linearum, per quas descenderat in horologio Ahaz in sole, retrorsum decem lineis."'"

Et reversus est sol decem lineis per gradus quos descenderat.

Chapter 38

Hezekiah, being advertised that he shall die, obtains by
prayer a prolongation of his life, in confirmation of which
the sun goes back. The canticle of Hezekiah.

In those days Hezekiah was sick even to death, and Isaiah,
the son of Amoz, the prophet, came unto him and said to
him, "Thus saith the Lord: 'Take order with thy house, for
thou shalt die and not live.'"

2 And Hezekiah turned his face toward the wall and
prayed to the Lord 3 and said, "I beseech thee, O Lord, remember *how* I have walked before thee in truth and with a
perfect heart and have done that which is good in thy sight."
And Hezekiah wept with great weeping.

4 And the word of the Lord came to Isaiah, saying, 5 "Go,
and say to Hezekiah, 'Thus saith the Lord, the God of David, thy father: "I have heard thy prayer, and I have seen thy
tears. Behold: I will add to thy days fifteen years, 6 and I will
deliver thee and this city out of the hand of the king of the
Assyrians, and I will protect it. 7 And this shall be a sign to
thee from the Lord that the Lord will do this word which he
hath spoken. 8 Behold: I will bring again the shadow of the
lines, by which it is now gone down in the sundial of Ahaz
with the sun, ten lines backward."'"

And the sun returned ten lines by the degrees by which it
was gone down.

9 Scriptura Ezechiae, regis Iuda, cum aegrotasset et convaluisset de infirmitate sua:

10 "Ego dixi, 'In dimidio dierum meorum vadam ad portas inferi; quaesivi residuum annorum meorum.' 11 Dixi, 'Non videbo Dominum Deum in terra viventium. Non aspiciam hominem ultra et habitatorem quietis. 12 Generatio mea ablata est, et convoluta est a me quasi tabernaculum pastorum. Praecisa est velut a texente vita mea; dum adhuc ordirer, succidit me. De mane usque ad vesperam finies me. 13 Sperabam usque ad mane; quasi leo sic contrivit omnia ossa mea. De mane usque ad vesperam finies me. 14 Sicut pullus hirundinis sic clamabo; meditabor ut columba. Adtenuati sunt oculi mei suspicientes in excelsum. Domine, vim patior; responde pro me.'

15 "Quid dicam, aut quid respondebit mihi, cum ipse fecerit? Recogitabo tibi omnes annos meos in amaritudine animae meae. 16 Domine, si sic vivitur, et in talibus vita spiritus mei, corripies me et vivificabis me. 17 Ecce: in pace amaritudo mea amarissima, tu autem eruisti animam meam ut non periret. Proiecisti post tergum tuum omnia peccata mea. 18 Quia non infernus confitebitur tibi, neque mors laudabit te; non expectabunt qui descendunt in lacum veritatem tuam. 19 Vivens, vivens, ipse confitebitur tibi sicut et ego hodie; pater filiis notam faciet veritatem tuam. 20 Domine, salvum me fac, et psalmos nostros cantabimus cunctis diebus vitae nostrae in domo Domini."

21 Et iussit Isaias ut tollerent massam de ficis et cataplasmarent super vulnus, et sanaretur. 22 Et dixit Ezechias, "Quod erit signum quia ascendam in domum Domini?"

9 The writing of Hezekiah, king of Judah, when he had been sick and was recovered of his sickness:

10 "I said, 'In the midst of my days I shall go to the gates of hell; I sought for the residue of my years.' 11 I said, 'I shall not see the Lord God in the land of the living. I shall behold man no more nor the inhabitant of rest. 12 My generation is at an end, and it is rolled away from me as a shepherd's tent. My life is cut off as by a weaver; whilst I was yet but beginning, he cut me off. From morning even to night thou wilt make an end of me. 13 I hoped till morning; as a lion so hath he broken all my bones. From morning even to night thou wilt make an end of me. 14 I will cry like a young swallow; I will meditate like a dove. My eyes are weakened looking upward. Lord, I suffer violence; answer thou for me.'

15 "What shall I say, or what shall he answer for me, whereas he himself hath done it? I will recount to thee all my years in the bitterness of my soul. 16 O Lord, if man's life be such, and the life of my spirit be in such things as these, thou shalt correct me and make me to live. 17 Behold: in peace is my bitterness most bitter, but thou hast delivered my soul that it should not perish. Thou hast cast all my sins behind thy back. 18 For hell shall not confess to thee, neither shall death praise thee, *nor* shall they that go down into the pit look for thy truth. 19 The living, the living, he shall give praise to thee as I *do* this day; the father shall make thy truth known to the children. 20 O Lord, save me, and we will sing our psalms all the days of our life in the house of the Lord."

21 Now Isaiah *had* ordered that they should take a lump of figs and lay it as it plaster upon the wound, and that he should be healed. 22 And Hezekiah *had* said, "What shall be the sign that I shall go up to the house of the Lord?"

Caput 39

In tempore illo misit Merodach Baladan, filius Baladan, rex Babylonis, libros et munera ad Ezechiam, audierat enim quod aegrotasset et convaluisset. 2 Laetatus est autem super eis Ezechias, et ostendit eis cellam aromatum et argenti et auri et odoramentorum et unguenti optimi et omnes apothecas supellectilis suae et universa quae inventa sunt in thesauris eius. Non fuit verbum quod non ostenderet eis Ezechias in domo sua et in omni potestate sua.

3 Introiit autem Isaias, propheta, ad Regem Ezechiam et dixit ei, "Quid dixerunt viri isti, et unde venerunt ad te?"

Et dixit Ezechias, "De terra longinqua venerunt ad me, de Babylone."

4 Et dixit, "Quid viderunt in domo tua?"

Et dixit Ezechias, "Omnia quae in domo mea sunt viderunt; non fuit res quam non ostenderim eis in thesauris meis."

5 Et dixit Isaias ad Ezechiam, "Audi verbum Domini exercituum: 6 'Ecce: dies venient et auferentur omnia quae in domo tua sunt et quae thesaurizaverunt patres tui usque ad diem hanc in Babylonem. Non relinquetur quicquam,' dicit

Chapter 39

Hezekiah shews all his treasures to the ambassadors of Babylon, upon which Isaiah foretells the Babylonish captivity.

At that time Merodach-baladan, the son of Baladan, king of Babylon, sent letters and presents to Hezekiah, for he had heard that he had been sick and was recovered. 2 And Hezekiah rejoiced *at their coming,* and he shewed them the storehouse of his aromatical spices and of the silver and of the gold and of the sweet odours and of the *precious* ointment and all the storehouses of his furniture and all things that were found in his treasures. There was nothing in his house nor in all his dominion that Hezekiah shewed them not.

3 Then Isaiah, the prophet, came to King Hezekiah and said to him, "What said these men, and from whence came they to thee?"

And Hezekiah said, "From a far country they came to me, from Babylon."

4 And he said, "What saw they in thy house?"

And Hezekiah said, "All things that are in my house have they seen; there was not any thing which I have not shewn them in my treasures."

5 And Isaiah said to Hezekiah, "Hear the word of the Lord of hosts: 6 'Behold: the days shall come *that* all that is in thy house and that thy fathers have laid up in store until this day shall be carried away into Babylon. There shall not

Dominus. 7 'Et de filiis tuis qui exibunt de te, quos genueris tollent, et erunt eunuchi in palatio regis Babylonis.'"

8 Et dixit Ezechias ad Isaiam, "Bonum verbum Domini quod locutus est," et dixit, "Fiat tantum pax et veritas in diebus meis."

Caput 40

"Consolamini; consolamini, popule meus," dicit Deus vester. 2 Loquimini ad cor Hierusalem, et advocate eam, quoniam conpleta est malitia eius. Dimissa est iniquitas illius; suscepit de manu Domini duplicia pro omnibus peccatis suis.

3 Vox clamantis in deserto: "Parate viam Domini; rectas facite in solitudine semitas Dei nostri. 4 Omnis vallis exaltabitur, et omnis mons et collis humiliabitur, et erunt prava in directa, et aspera in vias planas. 5 Et revelabitur gloria Domini, et videbit omnis caro pariter quod os Domini locutum est.

6 Vox dicentis, "Clama."

Et dixi, "Quid clamabo?"

any thing be left,' saith the Lord. 7 'And of thy children that shall issue from thee, whom thou shalt beget they shall take away, and they shall be eunuchs in the palace of the king of Babylon.'"

8 And Hezekiah said to Isaiah, "The word of the Lord which he hath spoken is good," and he said, "Only let peace and truth be in my days."

Chapter 40

The prophet comforts the people with the promise of the coming of Christ to forgive their sins. God's almighty power and majesty.

"Be comforted; be comforted, my people," saith your God. 2 Speak ye to the heart of Jerusalem, and call to her, for her evil is come to an end. Her iniquity is forgiven; she hath received of the hand of the Lord double for all her sins.

3 The voice of one crying in the desert: "Prepare ye the way of the Lord; make straight in the wilderness the paths of our God. 4 Every valley shall be exalted, and every mountain and hill shall be made low, and the crooked shall become straight, and the rough ways plain. 5 And the glory of the Lord shall be revealed, and all flesh together shall see that the mouth of the Lord hath spoken.

6 The voice of one saying, "Cry."

And I said, "What shall I cry?"

"Omnis caro faenum, et omnis gloria eius quasi flos agri. 7 Exsiccatum est faenum, et cecidit flos, quia spiritus Domini sufflavit in eo. Vere faenum est populus; 8 exsiccatum est faenum, et cecidit flos, verbum autem Domini nostri manet in aeternum."

9 Super montem excelsum ascende, tu qui evangelizas Sion; exalta in fortitudine vocem tuam, qui evangelizas Hierusalem. Exalta; noli timere. Dic civitatibus Iudae, "Ecce Deus vester." 10 Ecce: Dominus Deus in fortitudine veniet, et brachium eius dominabitur. Ecce: merces eius cum eo, et opus illius coram illo. 11 Sicut pastor gregem suum pascet. In brachio suo congregabit agnos et in sinu suo levabit, et fetas ipse portabit.

12 Quis mensus est pugillo aquas et caelos palmo ponderavit? Quis adpendit tribus digitis molem terrae et libravit in pondere montes et colles in statera? 13 Quis adiuvit spiritum Domini? Aut quis consiliarius eius fuit et ostendit illi? 14 Cum quo iniit consilium, et instruxit eum et docuit eum semitam iustitiae et erudivit eum scientiam et viam prudentiae ostendit illi? 15 Ecce: gentes quasi stilla situlae et quasi momentum staterae reputatae sunt. Ecce: insulae quasi pulvis exiguus. 16 Et Libanus non sufficiet ad succendendum, et animalia eius non sufficient ad holocaustum. 17 Omnes gentes quasi non sint sic sunt coram eo et quasi nihilum et inane reputatae sunt ei.

18 Cui ergo similem fecistis Deum? Aut quam imaginem ponetis ei? 19 Numquid sculptile conflavit faber? Aut

"All flesh is grass, and all the glory thereof as the flower of the field. 7 The grass is withered, and the flower is fallen, because the spirit of the Lord hath blown upon it. Indeed the people is grass; 8 the grass is withered, and the flower is fallen, but the word of our Lord endureth for ever."

9 Get thee up upon a high mountain, thou that bringest good tidings to Zion; lift up thy voice with strength, thou that bringest good tidings to Jerusalem. Lift it up; fear not. Say to the cities of Judah, "Behold your God." 10 Behold: the Lord God shall come with strength, and his arm shall rule. Behold: his reward is with him, and his work is before him. 11 He shall feed his flock like a shepherd. He shall gather together the lambs with his arm and shall take them up in his bosom, and he himself shall carry them that are with young.

12 Who hath measured the waters in the hollow of his hand and weighed the heavens with his palm? Who hath poised with three fingers the bulk of the earth and weighed the mountains in scales and the hills in a balance? 13 Who hath forwarded the spirit of the Lord? Or who hath been his counsellor and hath taught him? 14 With whom hath he consulted, and who hath instructed him and taught him the path of justice and taught him knowledge and shewed him the way of understanding? 15 Behold: the nations are as a drop of a bucket and are counted as the smallest grain of a balance. Behold: the islands are as a little dust. 16 And Lebanon shall not be enough to burn, nor the beasts thereof sufficient for a burnt offering. 17 All nations are before him as if they had no being at all and are counted to him as nothing and vanity.

18 To whom then have you likened God? Or what image will you make for him? 19 Hath the workman cast a graven

aurifex auro figuravit illud, et lamminis argenteis argenta-
rius? 20 Forte lignum et inputribile elegit; artifex sapiens
quaerit quomodo statuat simulacrum quod non moveatur.

21 Numquid non scitis? Numquid non audistis? Numquid
non adnuntiatum est ab initio vobis? Numquid non intel-
lexistis fundamenta terrae? 22 Qui sedet super gyrum terrae,
et habitatores eius sunt quasi lucustae, qui extendit velut nihilum caelos et expandit eos sicut tabernaculum ad inhabi-
tandum. 23 Qui dat secretorum scrutatores quasi non sint,
iudices terrae velut inane fecit. 24 Et quidem neque plantatus neque satus neque radicatus in terra truncus eorum; repente flavit in eos, et aruerunt, et turbo quasi stipulam auferet eos.

25 "Et cui adsimilastis me et adaequastis?" dicit Sanctus.
26 Levate in excelsum oculos vestros, et videte quis creavit
haec, qui educit in numero militiam eorum et omnes ex nomine vocat. Prae multitudine fortitudinis et roboris virtutis-
que eius neque unum reliquum fuit.

27 Quare dicis, Iacob, et loqueris, Israhel, "Abscondita est
via mea a Domino, et a Deo meo iudicium meum transivit"?
28 Numquid nescis, aut non audisti? Deus sempiternus Dominus qui creavit terminos terrae. Non deficiet neque labo-
rabit, nec est investigatio sapientiae eius. 29 Qui dat lasso
virtutem et his qui non sunt fortitudinem et robur multiplicat. 30 Deficient pueri et laborabunt, et iuvenes in infirmi-

statue? Or hath the goldsmith formed it with gold, or the silversmith with plates of silver? 20 He hath chosen strong wood and that will not rot; the skilful workman seeketh how he may set up an idol that may not be moved.

21 Do you not know? *Hath it* not *been* heard? Hath it not been told you from the beginning? Have you not understood the foundations of the earth? 22 It is he that sitteth upon the *globe* of the earth, and the inhabitants thereof are as locusts, he that stretcheth out the heavens as nothing and spreadeth them out as a tent to dwell in. 23 He that *bringeth* the searchers of secrets *to nothing*, that hath made the judges of the earth as vanity. 24 And surely their stock was neither planted nor sown nor rooted in the earth; suddenly he hath blown upon them, and they are withered, and a whirlwind shall take them away as stubble.

25 "And to whom have ye likened me or made me equal?" saith the Holy One. 26 Lift up your eyes on high, and see who hath created these things, who bringeth out their host by number and calleth them all by their names. By the *greatness* of his might and strength and power not one of them was missing.

27 Why sayest thou, O Jacob, and speakest, O Israel, "My way is hid from the Lord, and my judgment is passed over from my God"? 28 Knowest thou not, or hast thou not heard? The Lord is the everlasting God who hath created the ends of the earth. He shall not faint nor labour, neither is there any searching out of his wisdom. 29 It is he that giveth strength to the weary and increaseth force and might to them that are not. 30 Youths shall faint and labour, and young

tate cadent. 31 Qui autem sperant in Domino mutabunt fortitudinem; adsument pinnas sicut aquilae. Current et non
laborabunt; ambulabunt et non deficient.

Caput 41

"Taceant ad me insulae, et gentes mutent fortitudinem.
Accedant et tunc loquantur; simul ad iudicium propinque-
mus.

2 "Quis suscitavit ab oriente iustum, vocavit eum ut se-
queretur se? Dabit in conspectu eius gentes, et reges obtinebit. Dabit quasi pulverem gladio eius, sicut stipulam vento
raptam arcui eius. 3 Persequetur eos; transibit in pace; semita
in pedibus eius non apparebit. 4 Quis haec operatus est et
fecit, vocans generationes ab exordio? Ego, Dominus; primus et novissimus ego sum.

5 "Viderunt insulae et timuerunt; extrema terrae obstipuerunt; adpropinquaverunt et accesserunt. 6 Unusquisque
proximo suo auxiliabitur et fratri suo dicet, 'Confortare.'
7 Confortavit faber aerarius percutiens malleo eum qui cu-
debat tunc temporis, dicens, "Glutino bonum est," et
confortavit eum in clavis ut non moveretur.

men shall fall by infirmity. 31 But they that hope in the Lord shall renew their strength; they shall take wings as eagles. They shall run and not be weary; they shall walk and not faint.

Chapter 41

The reign of the just one. The vanity of idols.

"Let the islands keep silence before me, and the nations *take new* strength. Let them come near and then speak; let us come near to judgment together.

2 "Who hath raised up the just one from the east, hath called him to follow him? He shall give the nations in his sight, and he shall rule over kings. He shall give them as the dust to his sword, as stubble driven by the wind to his bow. 3 He shall pursue them; he shall pass in peace; no path shall appear after his feet. 4 Who hath wrought and done these things, calling the generations from the beginning? I, the Lord; I am the first and the last.

5 "The islands saw it and feared; the ends of the earth were astonished; they drew near and came. 6 Every one shall help his neighbour and shall say to his brother, 'Be of good courage.' 7 The coppersmith striking with the hammer encouraged him that forged at that time, saying, "It is ready for soldering," and he strengthened it with nails that it should not be moved.

8 "Et tu, Israhel, serve meus, Iacob, quem elegi, semen Abraham, amici mei, 9 in quo adprehendi te ab extremis terrae et a longinquis eius vocavi te et dixi tibi, 'Servus meus es tu; elegi te et non abieci te.' 10 Ne timeas, quia tecum sum ego; ne declines, quia ego Deus tuus. Confortavi te et auxiliatus sum tibi, et suscepit te dextera iusti mei.

11 "Ecce: confundentur et erubescent omnes qui pugnant adversum te. Erunt quasi non sint, et peribunt viri qui contradicunt tibi. 12 Quaeres eos et non invenies viros rebelles tuos. Erunt quasi non sint et veluti consumptio, homines bellantes adversum te. 13 Quia ego Dominus, Deus tuus, adprehendens manum tuam dicensque tibi, 'Ne timeas; ego adiuvi te.'

14 "Noli timere, vermis Iacob, qui mortui estis ex Israhel; ego auxiliatus sum tibi," dicit Dominus et redemptor tuus, Sanctus Israhel. 15 "Ego posui te quasi plaustrum triturans novum habens rostra serrantia. Triturabis montes et comminues et colles quasi pulverem pones. 16 Ventilabis eos, et ventus tollet, et turbo disperget eos, et tu exultabis in Domino. In Sancto Israhel laetaberis.

17 "Egeni et pauperes quaerunt aquas, et non sunt; lingua eorum siti aruit. Ego, Dominus, exaudiam eos; Deus Israhel, non derelinquam eos. 18 Aperiam in supernis collibus flumina et in medio camporum fontes. Ponam desertum in stagna aquarum et terram inviam in rivos aquarum. 19 Dabo in solitudinem cedrum et spinam et myrtum et lignum

8 "But thou, Israel, art my servant, Jacob, whom I have chosen, the seed of Abraham, my friend, 9 in whom I have taken thee from the ends of the earth and from the remote parts thereof have called thee and said to thee, 'Thou art my servant; I have chosen thee and have not cast thee away.' 10 Fear not, for I am with thee; turn not aside, for I am thy God. I have strengthened thee and have helped thee, and the right hand of my just one hath upheld thee.

11 "Behold: all that fight against thee shall be confounded and ashamed. They shall be as nothing, and the men shall perish that strive against thee. 12 Thou shalt seek them and shalt not find the men that resist thee. They shall be as nothing and as a thing consumed, the men that war against thee. 13 For I am the Lord, thy God, who take thee by the hand and say to thee, 'Fear not; I have helped thee.'

14 "Fear not, thou worm of Jacob, you that are dead of Israel; I have helped thee," saith the Lord and thy redeemer, the Holy One of Israel. 15 "I have made thee as a new threshing wain with teeth like a saw. Thou shall thresh the mountains and break them in pieces and shalt make the hills as chaff. 16 Thou shalt fan them, and the wind shall carry them away, and the whirlwind shall scatter them, and thou shalt rejoice in the Lord. In the Holy One of Israel thou shalt be joyful.

17 "The needy and the poor seek for waters, and there are none; their tongue hath been dry with thirst. I, the Lord, will hear them; I, the God of Israel, will not forsake them. 18 I will open rivers in the high hills and fountains in the midst of the plains. I will turn the desert into pools of waters and the impassable land into streams of waters. 19 I will *plant in* the wilderness the cedar and the thorn and the

olivae. Ponam in deserto abietem, ulmum et buxum simul, 20 ut videant et sciant et recogitent et intellegant pariter quia manus Domini fecit hoc, et Sanctus Israhel creavit illud.

21 "Prope facite iudicium vestrum," dicit Dominus. "Adferte si quid forte habetis," dixit Rex Iacob. 22 "Accedant et nuntient nobis quaecumque ventura sunt. Priora, quae fuerunt, nuntiate, et ponemus cor nostrum et sciemus novissima eorum, et quae ventura sunt indicate nobis. 23 Adnuntiate quae ventura sunt in futurum, et sciemus quia dii estis vos. Bene quoque aut male, si potestis, facite, et loquamur et videamus simul. 24 Ecce: vos estis ex nihilo, et opus vestrum ex eo quod non est. Abominatio est qui elegit vos.

25 "Suscitavi ab aquilone, et veniet ab ortu solis. Vocabit nomen meum, et adducet magistratus quasi lutum et velut plastes conculcans humum.

26 "Quis adnuntiavit ab exordio ut sciamus, et a principio ut dicamus, 'Iustus es'? Non est neque adnuntians neque praedicens neque audiens sermones vestros. 27 Primus ad Sion dicet, 'Ecce: adsunt,' et Hierusalem evangelistam dabo. 28 Et vidi, et non erat neque ex istis quisquam qui iniret consilium et interrogatus responderet verbum. 29 Ecce: omnes iniusti, et vana opera eorum; ventus et inane simulacra eorum."

myrtle and the olive tree. I will set in the desert the fir tree, the elm and the box tree together, 20 that they may see and know and consider and understand together that the hand of the Lord hath done this, and the Holy One of Israel hath created it.

21 "Bring your cause near," saith the Lord. "Bring hither *if* you have any thing to *allege*," said the King of Jacob. 22 "Let them come and tell us all things that are to come. Tell us the former things, what they were, and we will set our heart upon them and shall know the latter end of them, and tell us the things that are to come. 23 Shew the things that are to come hereafter, and we shall know that ye are gods. Do ye also good or evil, if you can, and let us speak and see together. 24 Behold: you are of nothing, and your work of that which hath no being. He that hath chosen you is an abomination.

25 "I have raised up one from the north, and he shall come from the rising of the sun. He shall call upon my name, and he shall make princes to be as dirt and as the potter treading clay.

26 "Who hath declared from the beginning that we may know, and from time of old that we may say, 'Thou art just'? There is none that sheweth nor that foretelleth nor that heareth your words. 27 The first shall say to Zion, 'Behold: they are here,' and to Jerusalem I will give an evangelist. 28 And I saw, and there was no one even among them to consult *or* who, when I asked, could answer a word. 29 Behold: they are all in the wrong, and their works are vain; their idols are wind and vanity."

Caput 42

"Ecce servus meus. Suscipiam eum, electus meus; conplacuit sibi in illo anima mea. Dedi spiritum meum super eum; iudicium Gentibus proferet. 2 Non clamabit neque accipiet personam, nec audietur foris vox eius. 3 Calamum quassatum non conteret, et linum fumigans non extinguet; in veritate educet iudicium. 4 Non erit tristis neque turbulentus donec ponat in terra iudicium, et legem eius insulae expectabunt."

5 Haec dicit Dominus Deus creans caelos et extendens eos, firmans terram et quae germinant ex ea, dans flatum populo qui est super eam et spiritum calcantibus eam: 6 "Ego, Dominus, vocavi te in iustitia et adprehendi manum tuam et servavi te. Et dedi te in foedus populi, in lucem Gentium, 7 ut aperires oculos caecorum et educeres de conclusione vinctum et de domo carceris sedentes in tenebris. 8 Ego, Dominus: hoc est nomen meum; gloriam meam alteri non dabo et laudem meam sculptilibus. 9 Quae prima fuerunt, ecce: venerunt, nova quoque ego adnuntio. Antequam oriantur, audita vobis faciam."

10 Cantate Domino canticum novum—laus eius ab extremis terrae—qui descenditis in mare et plenitudo eius,

Chapter 42

The office of Christ. The preaching of the gospel to the
Gentiles. The blindness and reprobation of the Jews.

"Behold my servant. I will uphold him, my elect; my soul
delighteth in him. I have given my spirit upon him; he shall
bring forth judgment to the Gentiles. 2 He shall not cry nor
have respect to person, neither shall his voice be heard
abroad. 3 The bruised reed he shall not break, and smoking
flax he shall not quench; he shall bring forth judgment unto
truth. 4 He shall not be sad nor troublesome till he set judgment in the earth, and the islands shall wait for his law."

5 Thus saith the Lord God that created the heavens and
stretched them out, that established the earth and the
things that spring out of it, that giveth breath to the people
upon it and spirit to them that tread thereon: 6 "I, the Lord,
have called thee in justice and taken thee by the hand and
preserved thee. And I have given thee for a covenant of the
people, for a light of the Gentiles, 7 that thou mightest open
the eyes of the blind and bring forth the prisoner out of
prison and them that sit in darkness out of the prison house.
8 I, the Lord: this is my name; I will not give my glory to another nor my praise to graven things. 9 The things that were
first, behold: they are come, and new things do I declare.
Before they spring forth, I will make you hear them."

10 Sing ye to the Lord a new song—his praise is from the
ends of the earth—you that go down to the sea and all that

insulae et habitatores earum. 11 Sublevetur desertum et civitates eius; in domibus habitabit Cedar. Laudate, habitatores Petrae! De vertice montium clamabunt; 12 ponent Domino gloriam et laudem eius in insulis nuntiabunt. 13 Dominus sicut fortis egredietur; sicut vir proeliator suscitabit zelum. Vociferabitur et clamabit; super inimicos suos confortabitur.

14 "Tacui semper; silui; patiens fui. Sicut parturiens loquar; dissipabo et absorbebo simul. 15 Desertos faciam montes et colles et omne gramen eorum exsiccabo, et ponam flumina in insulas et stagna arefaciam. 16 Et ducam caecos in viam quam nesciunt, et in semitis quas ignoraverunt ambulare eos faciam. Ponam tenebras coram eis in lucem, et prava in recta; haec verba feci eis et non dereliqui eos. 17 Conversi sunt retrorsum; confundantur confusione qui confidunt in sculptili, qui dicunt conflatili, 'Vos dii nostri.'

18 "Surdi, audite, et caeci, intuemini, ad videndum. 19 Quis caecus nisi servus meus? Et surdus nisi ad quem nuntios meos misi? Quis caecus nisi qui venundatus est? Et quis caecus nisi servus Domini? 20 Qui vides multa, nonne custodies? Qui apertas habes aures, nonne audies?"

21 Et Dominus voluit ut sanctificaret eum et magnificaret legem et extolleret. 22 Ipse autem populus direptus et vastatus; laqueus iuvenum omnes, et in domibus carcerum absconditi sunt. Facti sunt in rapinam, nec est qui eruat, in

are therein, ye islands and ye inhabitants of them. 11 Let the desert and the cities thereof be exalted; Kedar shall dwell in houses. Ye inhabitants of Petra, give praise! They shall cry from the top of the mountains; 12 they shall give glory to the Lord and shall declare his praise in the islands. 13 The Lord shall go forth as a mighty man; as a man of war shall he stir up zeal. He shall shout and cry; he shall prevail against his enemies.

14 "I have always held my peace; I have kept silence; I have been patient. I will speak now as a woman in labour; I will destroy and swallow up at once. 15 I will lay waste the mountains and hills and will make all their grass to wither, and I will turn rivers into islands and will dry up the standing pools. 16 And I will lead the blind into the way which they know not, and in the paths which they were ignorant of I will make them walk. I will make darkness light before them, and crooked things straight; these things have I done to them and have not forsaken them. 17 They are turned back; let them be greatly confounded that trust in a graven thing, that say to a molten thing, 'You are our gods.'

18 "Hear, ye deaf, and ye blind, behold, that you may see. 19 Who is blind but my servant? *Or* deaf but he to whom I have sent my messengers? Who is blind but he that is sold? *Or* who is blind but the servant of the Lord? 20 Thou that seest many things, wilt thou not observe them? Thou that hast ears open, wilt thou not hear?"

21 And the Lord was willing to sanctify him and to magnify the law and exalt it. 22 But this is a people that is robbed and wasted; they are all the snare of young men, and they are hid in the houses of prisons. They are made a prey, and there is none to deliver them, a spoil, and there is none that

direptionem, nec est qui dicat, "Redde." 23 Quis est in vobis qui audiat hoc, adtendat et auscultet futura? 24 Quis dedit in direptionem Iacob et Israhel vastantibus? Nonne Dominus ipse, cui peccavimus? Et noluerunt in viis eius ambulare, et non audierunt legem eius. 25 Et effudit super eum indignationem furoris sui et forte bellum et conbusit eum in circuitu, et non cognovit, et succendit eum, et non intellexit.

Caput 43

Et nunc haec dicit Dominus creans te, Iacob, et formans te, Israhel: "Noli timere, quia redemi te et vocavi te nomine tuo; meus es tu. 2 Cum transieris per aquas, tecum ero, et flumina non operient te; cum ambulaveris in igne, non conbureris, et flamma non ardebit in te, 3 quia ego Dominus, Deus tuus, Sanctus Israhel, salvator tuus. Dedi propitiationem tuam Aegyptum, Aethiopiam et Saba pro te. 4 Ex quo honorabilis factus es in oculis meis et gloriosus, ego dilexi te, et dabo homines pro te, et populos pro anima tua. 5 Noli

saith, "Restore." 23 Who is there among you that will give ear to this, that will attend and hearken for times to come? 24 Who hath given Jacob for a spoil and Israel to robbers? Hath not the Lord himself, against whom we have sinned? And they would not walk in his ways, and they have not hearkened to his law. 25 And he hath poured out upon him the indignation of his fury and a strong battle and hath burnt him round about, and he knew not, and set him on fire, and he understood not.

Chapter 43

God comforts his church, promising to protect her for ever.
He expostulates with the Jews for their ingratitude.

And now thus saith the Lord that created thee, O Jacob, and formed thee, O Israel: "Fear not, for I have redeemed thee and called thee by thy name; thou art mine. 2 When thou shalt pass through the waters, I will be with thee, and the rivers shall not cover thee; when thou shalt walk in the fire, thou shalt not be burnt, and the flame shall not burn in thee, 3 for I am the Lord, thy God, the Holy One of Israel, thy saviour. I have given Egypt for thy atonement, Ethiopia and Seba for thee. 4 Since thou becamest honourable in my eyes, *thou art* glorious; I have loved thee, and I will give men for thee, and people for thy life. 5 Fear not, for I am with

timere, quoniam tecum ego sum. Ab oriente adducam semen tuum, et ab occidente congregabo te. 6 Dicam aquiloni,
'Da,' et austro, 'Noli prohibere; adfer filios meos de longinquo et filias meas ab extremis terrae.'

7 "Et omnem qui invocat nomen meum, in gloriam meam
creavi eum; formavi eum et feci eum.

8 "Educ foras populum caecum et oculos habentem, sur-
dum et aures ei sunt. 9 Omnes gentes congregatae sunt simul, et collectae sunt tribus; quis in vobis adnuntiet istud et
quae prima sunt audire nos faciet? Dent testes eorum et ius-
tificentur et audiant et dicant, 'Vere.'

10 "Vos testes mei," dicit Dominus, "et servus meus quem
elegi, ut sciatis et credatis mihi et intellegatis quia ego ipse
sum. Ante me non est formatus deus, et post me non erit.
11 Ego sum, ego sum Dominus, et non est absque me salvator. 12 Ego adnuntiavi et salvavi. Auditum feci, et non fuit in
vobis alienus. Vos testes mei," dicit Dominus, "et ego Deus.
13 Et ab initio ego ipse, et non est qui de manu mea eruat.
Operabor, et quis avertet illud?"

14 Haec dicit Dominus, redemptor vester, Sanctus Israhel: "Propter vos misi in Babylonem et detraxi vectes universos et Chaldeos in navibus suis gloriantes. 15 Ego Dominus, Sanctus vester, creans Israhel, Rex vester."

16 Haec dicit Dominus, qui dedit in mari viam et in aquis
torrentibus semitam, 17 qui eduxit quadrigam et equum,
agmen et robustum; simul obdormierunt, nec resurgent;

thee. I will bring thy seed from the east, and gather thee from the west. 6 I will say to the north, 'Give up,' and to the south, 'Keep not back; bring my sons from afar and my daughters from the ends of the earth.'

7 "And every one that calleth upon my name, I have created him for my glory; I have formed him and made him.

8 "Bring forth the people that are blind and have eyes, that are deaf and have ears. 9 All the nations are assembled together, and the tribes are gathered; who among you can declare this and shall make us hear the former things? Let them bring forth their witnesses; *let* them be justified and hear and say, 'It is truth.'

10 "You are my witnesses," saith the Lord, "and my servant whom I have chosen, that you may know and believe me and understand that I myself am. Before me there was no god formed, and after me there shall be none. 11 I am, I am the Lord, and there is no saviour besides me. 12 I have declared and have saved. I have made it heard, and there was no strange one among you. You are my witnesses," saith the Lord, "and I am God. 13 And from the beginning I am the same, and there is none that can deliver out of my hand. I will work, and who shall turn it away?"

14 Thus saith the Lord, your redeemer, the Holy One of Israel: "For your sake I sent to Babylon and have brought down all their bars and the Chaldeans glorying in their ships. 15 I am the Lord, your Holy One, the creator of Israel, your King."

16 Thus saith the Lord, who made a way in the sea and a path in the mighty waters, 17 who brought forth the chariot and the horse, the army and the strong; they lay down to sleep together, and they shall not rise again; they are broken

contriti sunt quasi linum et extincti sunt: 18 "Ne memineritis priorum, et antiqua ne intueamini. 19 Ecce: ego facio nova, et nunc orientur. Utique cognoscetis ea; ponam in deserto viam, et in invio flumina. 20 Glorificabit me bestia agri, dracones et strutiones, quia dedi in deserto aquas, flumina in invio, ut darem potum populo meo, electo meo.

21 "Populum istum formavi mihi; laudem meam narrabit. 22 Non me invocasti, Iacob, nec laborasti in me, Israhel. 23 Non obtulisti mihi arietem holocausti tui, et victimis tuis non glorificasti me. Non te servire feci in oblatione, nec laborem tibi praebui in ture. 24 Non emisti mihi argento calamum, et adipe victimarum tuarum non inebriasti me. Verumtamen servire me fecisti in peccatis tuis; praebuisti mihi laborem in iniquitatibus tuis.

25 "Ego sum, ego sum ipse qui deleo iniquitates tuas propter me, et peccatorum tuorum non recordabor. 26 Reduc me in memoriam, et iudicemur simul; narra si quid habes ut iustificeris. 27 Pater tuus primus peccavit, et interpretes tui praevaricati sunt in me. 28 Et contaminavi principes sanctos; dedi ad internicionem Iacob et Israhel in blasphemiam."

as flax and are extinct: 18 "Remember not former things, and look not on things of old. 19 Behold: I do new things, and now they shall spring forth. Verily you shall know them; I will make a way in the wilderness, and rivers in the desert. 20 The beast of the field shall glorify me, the dragons and the ostriches, because I have given waters in the wilderness, rivers in the desert, to give drink to my people, to my chosen.

21 "This people have I formed for myself; they shall shew forth my praise. 22 *But* thou hast not called upon me, O Jacob, neither hast thou laboured about me, O Israel. 23 Thou hast not offered me the ram of thy holocaust, nor hast thou glorified me with thy victims. I have not caused thee to serve with oblations, nor wearied thee with incense. 24 Thou hast bought me no sweet cane with money, neither hast thou filled me with the fat of thy victims. But thou hast made me to serve with thy sins; thou hast wearied me with thy iniquities.

25 "I am, I am he that blot out thy iniquities for my own sake, and I will not remember thy sins. 26 Put me in remembrance, and let us plead together; tell if thou hast any thing to justify thyself. 27 Thy first father sinned, and thy teachers have transgressed against me. 28 And I have profaned the holy princes; I have given Jacob to slaughter and Israel to reproach."

Caput 44

"Et nunc audi, Iacob, serve meus, et Israhel, quem elegi."
2 Haec dicit Dominus faciens et formans te, ab utero auxiliator tuus: "Noli timere, serve meus Iacob, et rectissime, quem elegi. 3 Effundam enim aquas super sitientem et fluenta super aridam; effundam spiritum meum super semen tuum et benedictionem meam super stirpem tuam. 4 Et germinabunt inter herbas quasi salices iuxta praeterfluentes aquas. 5 Iste dicet, 'Domini ego sum,' et ille vocabit in nomine Iacob, et hic scribet manu sua, 'Domino,' et in nomine Israhel adsimilabitur."

6 Haec dicit Dominus, Rex Israhel, et redemptor eius, Dominus exercituum: "Ego primus, et ego novissimus, et absque me non est Deus. 7 Quis similis mei? Vocet et adnuntiet, et ordinem exponat mihi, ex quo constitui populum antiquum. Ventura et quae futura sunt, adnuntient eis. 8 Nolite timere, neque conturbemini ex tunc audire te feci et adnuntiavi, 'Vos estis testes mei.' Numquid est Deus absque me et formator quem ego non noverim?"

9 Plastae idoli omnes nihil sunt, et amantissima eorum non proderunt eis. Ipsi sunt testes eorum quia non vident

Chapter 44

God's favour to his church. The folly of idolatry. The people shall be delivered from captivity.

"And now hear, O Jacob, my servant, and Israel, whom I have chosen." 2 Thus saith the Lord that made and formed thee, thy helper from the womb: "Fear not, O my servant Jacob, and thou, most righteous, whom I have chosen. 3 For I will pour out waters upon the thirsty ground and streams upon the dry land; I will pour out my spirit upon thy seed and my blessing upon thy stock. 4 And they shall spring up among the herbs as willows beside the running waters. 5 One shall say, 'I am the Lord's,' and another shall call himself by the name of Jacob, and another shall subscribe with his hand, 'To the Lord,' and surname himself by the name of Israel."

6 Thus saith the Lord, the King of Israel, and his redeemer, the Lord of hosts: "I am the first, and I am the last, and beside me there is no God. 7 Who is like to me? Let him call and declare, and let him set before me the order, since I appointed the ancient people. *And* the things to come and that shall be hereafter, let them shew unto them. 8 Fear ye not, neither be ye troubled from that time I have made thee to hear and have declared, 'You are my witnesses.' Is there a God besides me, *a* maker whom I have not known?"

9 The makers of idols are all of them nothing, and their best beloved things shall not profit them. They are their

neque intellegunt, ut confundantur. 10 Quis formavit deum et sculptile conflavit ad nihil utile? 11 Ecce: omnes participes eius confundentur, fabri enim sunt ex hominibus. Convenient omnes; stabunt et pavebunt et confundentur simul.

12 Faber ferrarius lima operatus est; in prunis et in malleis formavit illud et operatus est in brachio fortitudinis suae. Esuriet et deficiet; non bibet aquam et lassescet.

13 Artifex lignarius extendit normam; formavit illud in runcina; fecit illud in angularibus et in circino tornavit illud, et fecit imaginem viri quasi speciosum hominem habitantem in domo. 14 Succidit cedros, tulit ilicem et quercum quae steterat inter ligna saltus; plantavit pinum quam pluvia nutrivit. 15 Et facta est hominibus in focum; sumpsit ex eis et calefactus est, et succendit et coxit panes, de reliquo autem operatus est deum et adoravit; fecit sculptile et curvatus est ante illud. 16 Medium conbusit igni, et de medio carnes coxit et comedit; coxit pulmentum et saturatus est et calefactus est et dixit, "Va, calefactus sum; vidi focum." 17 Reliquum autem eius deum fecit et sculptile sibi; curvatur ante illud et adorat illud et obsecrat, dicens, "Libera me, quia Deus meus es tu."

18 Nescierunt neque intellexerunt, obliti enim sunt ne videant oculi eorum et ne intellegant corde suo. 19 Non

witnesses that they do not see nor understand, that they may be ashamed. 10 Who hath formed a god and made a graven thing that is profitable for nothing? 11 Behold: all the partakers thereof shall be confounded, for the makers are men. They shall all assemble together; they shall stand and fear and shall be confounded together.

12 The smith hath wrought with his file; with coals and with hammers he hath formed it and hath wrought with the *strength* of his *arm*. He shall hunger and faint; he shall drink no water and shall be weary.

13 The carpenter hath stretched out his rule; he hath formed it with a plane; he hath made it with corners and hath fashioned it round with the compass, and he hath made the image of a man as it were a beautiful man dwelling in a house. 14 He hath cut down cedars, taken the holm and the oak that stood among the trees of the forest; he hath planted the pine tree which the rain hath nourished. 15 And it hath served men for fuel; he took thereof and warmed himself, and he kindled it and baked bread, but of the rest he made a god and adored it; he made a graven thing and bowed down before it. 16 *Part of it* he burnt with fire, and with *part of it* he dressed *his meat;* he boiled pottage and was filled and was warmed and said, "Aha, I am warm; I have seen the fire." 17 But the residue thereof he made a god and a graven thing for himself; he boweth down before it and adoreth it and prayeth unto it, saying, "Deliver me, for thou art my God."

18 They have not known nor understood, for their eyes are covered that they may not see and that they may not understand with their heart. 19 They do not consider in their

recogitant in mente sua neque cognoscunt neque sentiunt ut dicant, "Medietatem eius conbusi igne, et coxi super carbones eius panes. Coxi carnes et comedi, et de reliquo eius idolum faciam? Ante truncum ligni procidam?"

20 Pars eius cinis est; cor insipiens adoravit illud, et non liberabit animam suam neque dicet, "Forte mendacium est in dextera mea."

21 "Memento horum, Iacob, et Israhel, quoniam servus meus es tu. Formavi te. Servus meus es tu, Israhel; ne obliviscaris mei. 22 Delevi ut nubem iniquitates tuas et quasi nebulam peccata tua; revertere ad me, quoniam redemi te."

23 Laudate, caeli, quoniam misericordiam fecit Dominus! Iubilate, extrema terrae; resonate, montes, laudationem, saltus et omne lignum eius, quoniam redemit Dominus Iacob, et Israhel gloriabitur.

24 Haec dicit Dominus, redemptor tuus et formator tuus ex utero: "Ego sum Dominus faciens omnia, extendens caelos solus, stabiliens terram, et nullus mecum. 25 Irrita faciens signa divinorum et ariolos in furorem vertens. Convertens sapientes retrorsum et scientiam eorum stultam faciens. 26 Suscitans verbum servi sui et consilium nuntiorum suorum conplens, qui dico Hierusalem, 'Habitaberis,' et civitatibus Iuda, 'Aedificabimini,' et deserta eius suscitabo. 27 Qui dico profundo, 'Desolare, et flumina tua arefaciam.' 28 Qui dico Cyro, 'Pastor meus es, et omnem voluntatem meam conplebis.' Qui dico Hierusalem, 'Aedificaberis,' et templo, 'Fundaberis.'"

mind nor know nor have the thought to say, "I have burnt part of it in the fire, and I have baked bread upon the coals thereof. I have broiled flesh and have eaten, and of the residue thereof shall I make an idol? Shall I fall down before the stock of a tree?

20 Part thereof is ashes; his foolish heart adoreth it, and he will not save his soul nor say, "Perhaps there is a lie in my right hand."

21 "Remember these things, O Jacob, and Israel, for thou art my servant. I have formed thee. Thou art my servant, O Israel; forget me not. 22 I have blotted out thy iniquities as a cloud and thy sins as a mist; return to me, for I have redeemed thee."

23 Give praise, O ye heavens, for the Lord hath shewn mercy! Shout with joy, ye ends of the earth; ye mountains, resound with praise, thou, O forest and every tree therein, for the Lord hath redeemed Jacob, and Israel shall be glorified.

24 Thus saith the Lord, thy redeemer and thy maker from the womb: "I am the Lord that make all things, that alone stretch out the heavens, that establish the earth, and there is none with me. 25 That make void the tokens of diviners and make the soothsayers mad. That turn the wise backward and that make their knowledge foolish. 26 That raise up the word of my servant and perform the counsel of my messengers, who say to Jerusalem, 'Thou shalt be inhabited,' and to the cities of Judah, 'You shall be built,' and I will raise up the wastes thereof. 27 Who say to the deep, 'Be thou desolate, and I will dry up thy rivers.' 28 Who say to Cyrus, 'Thou art my shepherd, and thou shalt perform all my pleasure.' Who say to Jerusalem, 'Thou shalt be built,' and to the temple, 'Thy foundations shall be laid.'"

Caput 45

Haec dicit Dominus christo meo, Cyro, cuius adprehendi dexteram ut subiciam ante faciem eius gentes et dorsa regum vertam et aperiam coram eo ianuas, et portae non cludentur: 2 "Ego ante te ibo et gloriosos terrae humiliabo. Portas aereas conteram et vectes ferreos confringam, 3 et dabo tibi thesauros absconditos et arcana secretorum, ut scias quia ego Dominus qui voco nomen tuum, Deus Israhel. 4 Propter servum meum, Iacob, et Israhel, electum meum, et vocavi te nomine tuo; adsimilavi te, et non cognovisti me.

5 "Ego Dominus, et non est amplius; extra me non est Deus. Accinxi te, et non cognovisti me, 6 ut sciant hii qui ab ortu solis et qui ab occidente quoniam absque me non est. Ego Dominus, et non est alter. 7 Formans lucem et creans tenebras, faciens pacem et creans malum, ego, Dominus faciens omnia haec."

8 "Rorate, caeli, desuper, et nubes pluant iustum; aperiatur terra et germinet salvatorem, et iustitia oriatur simul. Ego, Dominus, creavi eum."

Chapter 45

A prophecy of Cyrus as a figure of Christ, the great deliverer of God's people.

Thus saith the Lord to my anointed, Cyrus, whose right hand I have taken hold of to subdue nations before his face and to turn the backs of kings and to open the doors before him, and the gates shall not be shut: 2 "I will go before thee and will humble the great ones of the earth. I will break in pieces the gates of brass and will burst the bars of iron, 3 and I will give thee hidden treasures and the concealed riches of secret places, that thou mayest know that I am the Lord who call thee by thy name, the God of Israel. 4 For the sake of my servant, Jacob, and Israel, my elect, I have even called thee by thy name; I have made a likeness of thee, and thou hast not known me.

5 "I am the Lord, and there is none else; there is no God besides me. I girded thee, and thou hast not known me, 6 that they may know who are from the rising of the sun and they who are from the west that there is none besides me. I am the Lord, and there is none else. 7 I form the light and create darkness; I make peace and create evil, I, the Lord that do all these things."

8 "Drop down dew, ye heavens, from above, and let the clouds rain the just; let the earth be opened and bud forth a saviour, and let justice spring up together. I, the Lord, have created him."

9 Vae qui contradicit fictori suo, testa de samiis terrae. Numquid dicet lutum figulo suo, "Quid facis?" et "Opus tuum absque manibus est"? 10 Vae qui dicit patri, "Quid generas?" et mulieri, "Quid parturis?"

11 Haec dicit Dominus, Sanctus Israhel, plastes eius: "Ventura interrogate me super filios meos, et super opus manuum mearum mandate mihi. 12 Ego feci terram, et hominem super eam creavi ego. Manus meae tetenderunt caelos, et omni militiae eorum mandavi. 13 Ego suscitavi eum ad iustitiam, et omnes vias eius dirigam; ipse aedificabit civitatem meam et captivitatem meam dimittet, non in pretio neque in muneribus," dicit Dominus, Deus exercituum.

14 Haec dicit Dominus: "Labor Aegypti et negotiatio Aethiopiae et Sabaim, viri sublimes, ad te transibunt et tui erunt. Post te ambulabunt; vincti manicis pergent, et te adorabunt teque deprecabuntur: 'Tantum in te est Deus, et non est absque te Deus.'"

15 Vere tu es Deus absconditus, Deus Israhel, salvator. 16 Confusi sunt et erubuerunt omnes; simul abierunt in confusionem fabricatores errorum. 17 Israhel salvatus est in Domino salute aeterna; non confundemini, et non erubescetis usque in saeculum saeculi.

18 Quia haec dicit Dominus creans caelos, ipse Deus formans terram et faciens eam, ipse plastes eius (non in vanum creavit eam; ut habitaretur formavit eam): "Ego Dominus, et non est alius. 19 Non in abscondito locutus sum, in loco terrae tenebroso. Non dixi semini Iacob, 'Frustra quaerite me.' Ego Dominus, loquens iustitiam, adnuntians recta.

9 Woe to him that gainsayeth his maker, a shard of the earthen pots. Shall the clay say to him that fashioneth it, "What art thou making?" and "Thy work is without hands"? 10 Woe to him that saith to his father, "Why begettest thou?" and to the woman, "Why dost thou bring forth?"

11 Thus saith the Lord, the Holy One of Israel, his maker: "Ask me of things to come concerning my children, and concerning the work of my hands give ye charge to me. 12 I made the earth, and I created man upon it. My hand stretched forth the heavens, and I have commanded all their host. 13 I have raised him up to justice, and I will direct all his ways; he shall build my city and let go my captives, not for ransom nor for presents," saith the Lord, the God of hosts.

14 Thus saith the Lord: "The labour of Egypt and the merchandise of Ethiopia and of Sabaim, men of stature, shall come over to thee and shall be thine. They shall walk after thee; they shall go bound with manacles, and they shall worship thee and shall make supplication to thee: 'Only in thee is God, and there is no God besides thee.'"

15 Verily thou art a hidden God, the God of Israel, the saviour. 16 They are all confounded and ashamed; the forgers of errors are gone together into confusion. 17 Israel is saved in the Lord with an eternal salvation; you shall not be confounded, and you shall not be ashamed for ever and ever.

18 For thus saith the Lord that created the heavens, God himself that formed the earth and made it, the very maker thereof (he did not create it in vain; he formed it to be inhabited): "I am the Lord, and there is no other. 19 I have not spoken in secret, in a dark place of the earth. I have not said to the seed of Jacob, 'Seek me in vain.' I am the Lord, that speak justice, that declare right things.

20 "Congregamini, et venite, et accedite simul, qui salvati estis ex Gentibus; nescierunt qui levant lignum sculpturae suae et rogant deum non salvantem. 21 Adnuntiate, et venite, et consiliamini simul; quis auditum fecit hoc ab initio? Ex tunc praedixit illud? Numquid non ego, Dominus, et non est ultra Deus absque me? Deus iustus et salvans; non est praeter me. 22 Convertimini ad me, et salvi eritis, omnes fines terrae, quia ego Deus, et non est alius. 23 In memet ipso iuravi; egredietur de ore meo iustitiae verbum et non revertetur, quia mihi curvabitur omne genu, et iurabit omnis lingua.

24 "Ergo 'In Domino,' dicet, 'meae sunt iustitiae et imperium; ad eum venient, et confundentur omnes qui repugnant ei. 25 In Domino iustificabitur et laudabitur omne semen Israhel.'"

Caput 46

"Confractus est Bel; contritus est Nabo; facta sunt simulacra eorum bestiis et iumentis, onera vestra gravi pondere usque ad lassitudinem. 2 Contabuerunt et contrita sunt

20 "Assemble yourselves, and come, and draw near together, ye that are saved of the Gentiles; they have no knowledge that set up the wood of their graven work and pray to a god that cannot save. 21 Tell ye, and come, and consult together; who hath declared this from the beginning? Who hath foretold this from that time? Have not I, the Lord, and there is no God else besides me? A just God and a saviour; there is none besides me. 22 Be converted to me, and you shall be saved, all ye ends of the earth, for I am God, and there is no other. 23 I have sworn by myself; the word of justice shall go out of my mouth and shall not return, 24 for every knee shall be bowed to me, and every tongue shall swear.

25 "Therefore shall he say, 'In the Lord are my justices and empire; they shall come to him, and all that resist him shall be confounded. 26 In the Lord shall all the seed of Israel be justified and praised.'"

Chapter 46

The idols of Babylon shall be destroyed. Salvation is promised through Christ.

"Bel is broken; Nebo is destroyed; their idols are put upon beasts and cattle, your burdens of heavy weight even unto weariness. 2 They are consumed and are broken to-

simul. Non potuerunt salvare portantem, et anima eorum in captivitatem ibit.

3 "Audite me, domus Iacob, et omne residuum domus Israhel qui portamini a meo utero gestamini a mea vulva. 4 Usque ad senectam ego ipse, et usque ad canos ego portabo. Ego feci, et ego feram; ego portabo et salvabo.

5 "Cui adsimilastis me et adaequastis et conparastis me et fecistis similem? 6 Qui confertis aurum de sacculo et argentum statera ponderatis conducentes aurificem ut faciat deum, et procidunt et adorant. 7 Portant illum in umeris gestantes et ponentes in loco suo, et stabit ac de loco suo non movebitur. Sed et cum clamaverint ad eum non audiet; de tribulatione non salvabit eos.

8 "Mementote istud, et confundamini; redite, praevaricatores, ad cor. 9 Recordamini prioris saeculi, quoniam ego sum Deus, et non est ultra Deus, nec est similis mei, 10 adnuntians ab exordio novissimum, et ab initio quae necdum facta sunt, dicens, "Consilium meum stabit, et omnis voluntas mea fiet," 11 vocans ab oriente avem et de terra longinqua virum voluntatis meae, et locutus sum et adducam illud; creavi, et faciam illud.

12 "Audite me, duro corde qui longe estis a iustitia. 13 Prope feci iustitiam meam; non elongabitur, et salus mea non morabitur. Dabo in Sion salutem et Israheli gloriam meam."

gether. They could not save him that carried them, and they themselves shall go into captivity.

3 "Hearken unto me, O house of Jacob, *all* the remnant of the house of Israel who are carried by my bowels are borne up by my womb. 4 Even to your old age I am the same, and to your grey hairs I will carry you. I have made you, and I will bear; I will carry and will save.

5 "To whom have you likened me and made me equal and compared me and made me like? 6 You that contribute gold out of the bag and weigh out silver in the scales and hire a goldsmith to make a god, and they fall down and worship. 7 They bear him on their shoulders and carry him and set him in his place, and he shall stand and shall not stir out of his place. Yea, when they shall cry also unto him he shall not hear; he shall not save them from tribulation.

8 "Remember this, and be ashamed; return, ye transgressors, to the heart. 9 Remember the former age, for I am God, and there is no God beside, neither is there the like to me, 10 who shew from the beginning the things that shall be at last, and from ancient times the things that as yet are not done, saying, "My counsel shall stand, and all my will shall be done," 11 who call a bird from the east and from a far country the man of my own will, and I have spoken and will bring it to pass; I have created, and I will do it.

12 "Hear me, O ye hardhearted who are far from justice. 13 I have brought my justice near; it shall not be afar off, and my salvation shall not tarry. I will give salvation in Zion and my glory in Israel."

Caput 47

"Descende; sede in pulvere, virgo filia Babylon; sede in terra. Non est solium filiae Chaldeorum, quia ultra non vocaberis mollis et tenera. 2 Tolle molam, et mole farinam; denuda turpitudinem tuam; discoperi umerum; revela crura; transi flumina. 3 Revelabitur ignominia tua, et videbitur obprobrium tuum. Ultionem capiam, et non resistet mihi homo. 4 Redemptor noster, Dominus exercituum nomen illius, Sanctus Israhel.

5 "Sede tacens, et intra in tenebras, filia Chaldeorum, quia non vocaberis ultra domina regnorum. 6 Iratus sum super populum meum; contaminavi hereditatem meam et dedi eos in manu tua. Non posuisti eis misericordias; super senem adgravasti iugum tuum valde. 7 Et dixisti, 'In sempiternum ero domina'; non posuisti haec super cor tuum, neque recordata es novissimi tui.

8 "Et nunc audi haec, delicata et habitans confidenter, quae dicis in corde tuo, 'Ego sum, et non est praeter me amplius. Non sedebo vidua, et ignorabo sterilitatem.' 9 Venient tibi duo haec subito in die una sterilitas et viduitas.

Chapter 47

God's judgment upon Babylon.

"Come down; sit in the dust, O virgin daughter of Babylon; sit on the ground. There is no throne for the daughter of the Chaldeans, for thou shalt no more be called delicate and tender. 2 Take a millstone, and grind meal; uncover thy shame; strip thy shoulder; make bare thy legs; pass over the rivers. 3 Thy nakedness shall be discovered, and thy shame shall be seen. I will take vengeance, and no man shall resist me. 4 Our redeemer, the Lord of hosts is his name, the Holy One of Israel.

5 "Sit thou silent, and get thee into darkness, O daughter of the Chaldeans, for thou shalt no more be called the lady of kingdoms. 6 I was angry with my people; I have polluted my inheritance and have given them into thy hand. Thou hast shewed no mercy to them; upon the ancient thou hast laid thy yoke exceeding heavy. 7 And thou hast said, 'I shall be a lady for ever'; thou hast not laid these things to thy heart, neither hast thou remembered thy latter end.

8 "And now hear these things, thou that art delicate and dwellest confidently, that sayest in thy heart, 'I am, and there is none else besides me. I shall not sit as a widow, and I shall not know barrenness.' 9 These two things shall come upon thee suddenly in one day: barrenness and widowhood.

Universa venerunt super te propter multitudinem maleficiorum tuorum et propter duritiam incantatorum tuorum vehementem. 10 Et fiduciam habuisti in malitia tua et dixisti, 'Non est qui videat me.' Sapientia tua et scientia tua, haec decepit te. Et dixisti in corde tuo, 'Ego sum, et praeter me non est altera.' 11 Veniet super te malum, et nescies ortum eius, et inruet super te calamitas quam non poteris expiare. Veniet super te repente miseria quam nescies.

12 "Sta cum incantatoribus tuis et cum multitudine maleficiorum tuorum in quibus laborasti ab adulescentia tua, si forte quid prosit tibi aut si possis fieri fortior. 13 Defecisti in multitudine consiliorum tuorum; stent et salvent te augures caeli, qui contemplabantur sidera et supputabant menses, ut ex eis adnuntiarent ventura tibi. 14 Ecce: facti sunt quasi stipula. Ignis conbusit eos; non liberabunt animam suam de manu flammae; non sunt prunae quibus calefiant, nec focus ut sedeant ad eum. 15 Sic facta sunt tibi in quibuscumque laboraveras; negotiatores tui ab adulescentia tua, unusquisque in via sua erraverunt; non est qui salvet te."

All things are come upon thee because of the multitude of thy sorceries and for the great hardness of thy enchanters. 10 And thou hast trusted in thy wickedness and hast said, 'There is none that seeth me.' Thy wisdom and thy knowledge, this hath deceived thee. And thou hast said in thy heart, 'I am, and besides me there is no other.' 11 Evil shall come upon thee, and thou shalt not know the rising thereof, and calamity shall fall violently upon thee which thou canst not keep off. Misery shall come upon thee suddenly which thou shalt not know.

12 "Stand now with thy enchanters and with the multitude of thy sorceries in which thou hast laboured from thy youth, if so be it may profit thee any thing or if thou mayst become stronger. 13 Thou hast failed in the multitude of thy counsels; let now the astrologers stand and save thee, they that gazed at the stars and counted the months, that from them they might tell the things that shall come to thee. 14 Behold: they are as stubble. Fire hath burnt them; they shall not deliver themselves from the power of the flames; there are no coals wherewith they may be warmed, nor fire that they may sit thereat. 15 Such are all the things become to thee in which thou hast laboured; thy merchants from thy youth, every one hath erred in his own way; there is none that can save thee."

Caput 48

"Audite haec, domus Iacob, qui vocamini nomine Israhel et de aquis Iuda existis, qui iuratis in nomine Domini et Dei Israhel recordamini non in veritate neque in iustitia. 2 De civitate enim sancta vocati sunt et super Deum Israhel constabiliti sunt; Dominus exercituum nomen eius.

3 "Priora ex tunc adnuntiavi, et ex ore meo exierunt, et audita feci ea. Repente operatus sum, et venerunt, 4 scivi enim quia durus es tu, et nervus ferreus cervix tua, et frons tua aerea. 5 Praedixi tibi ex tunc; antequam venirent indicavi tibi, ne forte diceres, 'Idola mea fecerunt haec, et sculptilia mea et conflatilia mandaverunt ista.'

6 "Quae audisti vide omnia, vos autem num adnuntiastis? Audita feci tibi nova ex tunc, et conservata sunt quae nescis. 7 Nunc creata sunt et non ex tunc et ante diem et non audisti ea, ne forte dicas, 'Ecce: cognovi ea.' 8 Neque audisti neque cognovisti, neque ex tunc aperta est auris tua. Scio enim quia praevaricans praevaricabis, et transgressorem ex utero vocavi te.

Chapter 48

He reproaches the Jews for their obstinacy. He will deliver
them out of their captivity for his own name's sake.

"Hear ye these things, O house of Jacob, you that are
called by the name of Israel and are come forth out of the
waters of Judah, you who swear by the name of the Lord and
make mention of the God of Israel *but* not in truth nor in
justice. 2 For they are called of the holy city and are established upon the God of Israel; the Lord of hosts is his name.

3 "The former things of old I have declared, and they
went forth out of my mouth, and I have made them to be
heard. I did them suddenly, and they came to pass, 4 for I
knew that thou art stubborn, and thy neck is an iron sinew,
and thy forehead of brass. 5 I foretold thee of old; before
they came to pass I told thee, *lest* thou shouldst say, 'My idols
have done these things, and my graven and molten things
have commanded them.'

6 "See *now* all the things which thou hast heard, but have
you declared them? I have shewn thee new things from that
time, and things are kept which thou knowest not. 7 They
are created now and not of old and before the day *when* thou
heardest them not, *lest* thou shouldst say, 'Behold: I knew
them.' 8 Thou hast neither heard nor known, neither was
thy ear opened of old. For I know that transgressing thou
wilt transgress, and I have called thee a transgressor from
the womb.

9 "Propter nomen meum longe faciam furorem meum, et laude mea infrenabo te ne intereas. 10 Ecce: excoxi te, sed non quasi argentum. Elegi te in camino paupertatis. 11 Propter me, propter me faciam, ut non blasphemer, et gloriam meam alteri non dabo.

12 "Audi me, Iacob, et Israhel, quem ego voco. Ego ipse, ego primus, et ego novissimus. 13 Manus quoque mea fundavit terram, et dextera mea mensa est caelos; ego vocabo eos, et stabunt simul.

14 "Congregamini, omnes vos, et audite. Quis de eis adnuntiavit haec? Dominus dilexit eum; faciet voluntatem suam in Babylone, et brachium suum in Chaldeis. 15 Ego, ego locutus sum et vocavi eum; adduxi eum, et directa est via eius. 16 Accedite ad me, et audite hoc: non a principio in abscondito locutus sum; ex tempore antequam fieret ibi eram, et nunc Dominus Deus misit me et spiritus eius."

17 Haec dicit Dominus, redemptor tuus, Sanctus Israhel: "Ego Dominus, Deus tuus, docens te utilia, gubernans te in via qua ambulas. 18 Utinam adtendisses mandata mea, facta fuisset sicut flumen pax tua, et iustitia tua sicut gurgites maris, 19 et fuisset quasi harena semen tuum, et stirps uteri tui ut lapilli eius; non interisset et non fuisset adtritum nomen eius a facie mea."

20 Egredimini de Babylone; fugite a Chaldeis. In voce exultationis adnuntiate; auditum facite hoc, et efferte illud usque ad extrema terrae. Dicite: "Redemit Dominus servum suum Iacob."

9 "For my name's sake I will remove my wrath far off, and for my praise I will bridle thee lest thou shouldst perish. 10 Behold: I have refined thee, but not as silver. I have chosen thee in the furnace of poverty. 11 For my own sake, for my own sake will I do it, that I may not be blasphemed, and I will not give my glory to another.

12 "Hearken to me, O Jacob, and thou, Israel, whom I call. I am he, I am the first, and I am the last. 13 My hand also hath founded the earth, and my right hand hath measured the heavens; I shall call them, and they shall stand together.

14 "Assemble yourselves together, all you, and hear. Who among them hath declared these things? The Lord hath loved him; he will do his pleasure in Babylon, and his arm shall be on the Chaldeans. 15 I, even I have spoken and called him; I have brought him, and his way is made prosperous. 16 Come ye near unto me, and hear this: I have not spoken in secret from the beginning; from the time before it was done I was there, and now the Lord God hath sent me and his spirit."

17 Thus saith the Lord, thy redeemer, the Holy One of Israel: "I am the Lord, thy God, that teach thee profitable things, that govern thee in the way that thou walkest. 18 O that thou hadst hearkened to my commandments, thy peace had been as a river, and thy justice as the waves of the sea, 19 and thy seed had been as the sand, and the offspring of thy bowels like the gravel thereof; his name should not have perished nor have been destroyed from before my face."

20 Come forth out of Babylon; flee ye from the Chaldeans. Declare it with the voice of joy; make this to be heard, and speak it out even to the ends of the earth. Say: "The Lord hath redeemed his servant Jacob."

21 Non sitierunt in deserto cum educeret eos; aquam de petra produxit eis, et scidit petram, et fluxerunt aquae. 22 "Non est pax," dicit Dominus, "impiis."

Caput 49

Audite, insulae, et adtendite, populi de longe. Dominus ab utero vocavit me; de ventre matris meae recordatus est nominis mei. 2 Et posuit os meum quasi gladium acutum. In umbra manus suae protexit me et posuit me sicut sagittam electam. In faretra sua abscondit me.

3 Et dixit mihi, "Servus meus es tu, Israhel, quia in te gloriabor."

4 Et ego dixi, "In vacuum laboravi; sine causa et vane fortitudinem meam consumpsi. Ergo iudicium meum cum Domino, et opus meum cum Deo meo."

5 Et nunc dicit Dominus, formans me ex utero servum sibi, ut reducam Iacob ad eum, et Israhel non congregabitur, et glorificatus sum in oculis Domini, et Deus meus factus est fortitudo mea,—6 et dixit, "Parum est ut sis mihi servus

21 They thirsted not in the desert when he led them out; he brought forth water out of the rock for them, and he clove the rock, and the waters gushed out. 22 "There is no peace to the wicked," saith the Lord.

Chapter 49

Christ shall bring the Gentiles to salvation. God's love to his church is perpetual.

G ive ear, ye islands, and hearken, ye people from afar. The Lord hath called me from the womb; from the bowels of my mother he hath been mindful of my name. 2 And he hath made my mouth like a sharp sword. In the shadow of his hand he hath protected me and hath made me as a chosen arrow. In his quiver he hath hidden me.

3 And he said to me, "Thou art my servant, Israel, for in thee will I glory."

4 And I said, "I have laboured in vain; I have spent my strength without cause and in vain. Therefore my judgment is with the Lord, and my work with my God."

5 And now saith the Lord, that formed me from the womb to be his servant, that I may bring back Jacob unto him, and Israel will not be gathered together, and I am glorified in the eyes of the Lord, and my God is made my strength,—6 and he said, "It is a small thing that thou shouldst be my servant

ad suscitandas tribus Iacob et feces Israhel convertendas. Ecce: dedi te in lucem Gentium, ut sis salus mea usque ad extremum terrae."

7 Haec dicit Dominus, redemptor Israhel, Sanctus eius, ad contemptibilem animam, ad abominatam gentem, ad servum dominorum: "Reges videbunt, et consurgent principes et adorabunt propter Dominum, quia fidelis est, et Sanctum Israhel qui elegit te."

8 Haec dicit Dominus: "In tempore placito exaudivi te, et in die salutis auxiliatus sum tui, et servavi te et dedi te in foedus populi, ut suscitares terram et possideres hereditates dissipatas, 9 ut diceres his qui vincti sunt, 'Exite,' et his qui in tenebris, 'Revelamini.' Super vias pascentur, et in omnibus planis pascua eorum. 10 Non esurient neque sitient, et non percutiet eos aestus et sol, quia qui miseretur eorum reget eos, et ad fontes aquarum potabit eos. 11 Et ponam omnes montes meos in viam, et semitae meae exaltabuntur. 12 Ecce: isti de longe venient, et ecce: illi ab aquilone et mari, et isti de terra australi."

13 Laudate, caeli, et exulta, terra; iubilate, montes, laudem, quia consolatus est Dominus populum suum et pauperum suorum miserebitur.

14 Et dixit Sion, "Dereliquit me Dominus, et Dominus oblitus est mei."

to raise up the tribes of Jacob and to convert the dregs of Israel. Behold: I have given thee to be the light of the Gentiles, that thou mayst be my salvation even to the farthest part of the earth."

7 Thus saith the Lord, the redeemer of Israel, his Holy One, to the soul that is despised, to the nation that is abhorred, to the servant of rulers: "Kings shall see, and princes shall rise up and adore for the Lord's sake, because he is faithful, and for the Holy One of Israel who hath chosen thee."

8 Thus saith the Lord: "In an acceptable time I have heard thee, and in the day of salvation I have helped thee, and I have preserved thee and given thee to be a covenant of the people, that thou mightest raise up the earth and possess the inheritances that were destroyed, 9 that thou mightest say to them that are bound, 'Come forth,' and to them that are in darkness, 'Shew yourselves.' They shall feed in the ways, and their pastures shall be in every plain. 10 They shall not hunger nor thirst, neither shall the heat nor the sun strike them, for he that is merciful to them shall be their shepherd, and at the fountains of waters he shall give them drink. 11 And I will make all my mountains a way, and my paths shall be exalted. 12 Behold: these shall come from afar, and behold: these from the north and from the sea, and these from the south country."

13 Give praise, O ye heavens, and rejoice, O earth; ye mountains, give praise with jubilation, because the Lord hath comforted his people and will have mercy on his poor ones.

14 And Zion said, "The Lord hath forsaken me, and the Lord hath forgotten me."

15 "Numquid oblivisci potest mulier infantem suum ut non misereatur filio uteri sui? Et si illa oblita fuerit, ego tamen non obliviscar tui. 16 Ecce: in manibus meis descripsi te. Muri tui coram oculis meis semper. 17 Venerunt structores tui; destruentes te et dissipantes a te exibunt. 18 Leva in circuitu oculos tuos, et vide: omnes isti congregati sunt; venerunt tibi. Vivo ego," dicit Dominus, "quia omnibus his velut ornamento vestieris, et circumdabis tibi eos quasi sponsa."

19 Quia deserta tua et solitudines tuae et terra ruinae tuae nunc angusta erunt prae habitatoribus, et longe fugabuntur qui absorbebant te. 20 Adhuc dicent in auribus tuis filii sterilitatis tuae, "Angustus mihi est locus; fac spatium mihi ut habitem."

21 Et dices in corde tuo, "Quis genuit mihi istos? Ego sterilis et non pariens, transmigrata et captiva, et istos quis enutrivit? Ego destituta et sola, et isti, ubi erant?"

22 Haec dicit Dominus Deus: "Ecce: levabo ad Gentes manum meam et ad populos exaltabo signum meum. Et adferent filios tuos in ulnis et filias tuas super umeros portabunt. 23 Et erunt reges nutricii tui, et reginae nutrices tuae; vultu in terram demisso adorabunt te, et pulverem pedum tuorum lingent. Et scies quia ego Dominus, super quo non confundentur qui expectant eum."

24 Numquid tolletur a forte praeda? Aut quod captum fuerit a robusto salvum esse poterit? 25 Quia haec dicit Dominus: "Equidem et captivitas a forte tolletur, et quod abla-

15 "Can a woman forget her infant so as not to have pity on the son of her womb? And if she should forget, yet will not I forget thee. 16 Behold: I have graven thee in my hands. Thy walls are always before my eyes. 17 Thy builders are come; they that destroy thee and make thee waste shall go out of thee. 18 Lift up thy eyes round about, and see: all these are gathered together; they are come to thee. As I live," saith the Lord, "thou shalt be clothed with all these as with an ornament, and as a bride thou shalt put them about thee."

19 For thy deserts and thy desolate places and the land of thy destruction shall now be too narrow by reason of the inhabitants, and they that swallowed thee up shall be chased far away. 20 The children of thy barrenness shall still say in thy ears, "The place is too strait for me; make me room to dwell in."

21 And thou shalt say in thy heart, "Who hath *begotten* these? I was barren and brought not forth, led away and captive, and who hath brought up these? I was destitute and alone, and these, where were they?"

22 Thus saith the Lord God: "Behold: I will lift up my hand to the Gentiles and will set up my standard to the people. And they shall bring thy sons in their arms and carry thy daughters upon their shoulders. 23 And kings shall be thy nursing fathers, and queens thy nurses; they shall worship thee with their face toward the earth, and they shall lick up the dust of thy feet. And thou shalt know that I am the Lord, for they shall not be confounded that wait for him."

24 Shall the prey be taken from the strong? Or can that which was taken by the mighty be delivered? 25 For thus saith the Lord: "Yea verily even the captivity shall be taken away from the strong, and that which was taken by the

tum fuerit a robusto salvabitur. Eos vero qui iudicaverunt te ego iudicabo, et filios tuos ego salvabo. 26 Et cibabo hostes tuos carnibus suis, et quasi musto sanguine suo inebriabuntur, et sciet omnis caro quia ego Dominus salvans te et redemptor tuus, Fortis Iacob."

Caput 50

Haec dicit Dominus: "Quis est hic liber repudii matris vestrae quo dimisi eam? Aut quis est creditor meus cui vendidi vos? Ecce: in iniquitatibus vestris venditi estis, et in sceleribus vestris dimisi matrem vestram. 2 Quia veni, et non erat vir; vocavi, et non erat qui audiret. Numquid adbreviata et parvula facta est manus mea, ut non possim redimere? Aut non est in me virtus ad liberandum? Ecce: in increpatione mea desertum faciam mare; ponam flumina in siccum; conputrescent pisces sine aqua et morientur in siti. 3 Induam caelos tenebris et saccum ponam operimentum eorum."

mighty shall be delivered. But I will judge those that have judged thee, and thy children I will save. 26 And I will feed thy enemies with their own flesh, and they shall be made drunk with their own blood as with new wine, and all flesh shall know that I am the Lord that save thee and thy redeemer, the Mighty One of Jacob."

Chapter 50

The synagogue shall be divorced for her iniquities. Christ for her sake will endure ignominious afflictions.

Thus saith the Lord: "What is this bill of the divorce of your mother with which I have put her away? Or who is my creditor to whom I sold you? Behold: you are sold for your iniquities, and for your wicked deeds have I put your mother away. 2 Because I came, and there was not a man; I called, and there was none that would hear. Is my hand shortened and become little, that I cannot redeem? Or is there no strength in me to deliver? Behold: at my rebuke I will make the sea a desert, I will turn the rivers into dry land; the fishes shall rot for want of water and shall die for thirst. 3 I will clothe the heavens with darkness and will make sackcloth their covering."

4 Dominus dedit mihi linguam eruditam, ut sciam susten-
tare eum qui lassus est verbo. Erigit mane; mane erigit mihi
aurem ut audiam quasi magistrum. 5 Dominus Deus aperuit
mihi aurem, ego autem non contradico; retrorsum non abii.
6 Corpus meum dedi percutientibus, et genas meas vellenti-
bus. Faciem meam non averti ab increpantibus et conspuentibus.

7 Dominus Deus auxiliator meus. Ideo non sum confusus;
ideo posui faciem meam ut petram durissimam, et scio quoniam non confundar. 8 Iuxta est qui iustificat me; quis con-
tradicet mihi? Stemus simul. Quis est adversarius meus? Ac-
cedat ad me. 9 Ecce: Dominus Deus auxiliator meus. Quis
est qui condemnet me? Ecce: omnes quasi vestimentum
conterentur; tinea comedet eos.

10 Quis ex vobis timens Dominum, audiens vocem servi
sui, qui ambulavit in tenebris et non est lumen ei? Speret in
nomine Domini et innitatur super Deum suum.

11 Ecce: omnes vos accendentes ignem, accincti flammis,
ambulate in lumine ignis vestri et in flammis quas succen-
distis. De manu mea factum est hoc vobis; in doloribus dormietis.

4 The Lord hath given me a learned tongue, that I should know how to uphold by word him that is weary. He wakeneth in the morning; in the morning he wakeneth my ear that I may hear him as a master. 5 The Lord God hath opened my ear, and I do not resist; I have not gone back. 6 I have given my body to the strikers, and my cheeks to them that plucked them. I have not turned away my face from them that rebuked me and spit *upon me*.

7 The Lord God is my helper. Therefore am I not confounded; therefore have I set my face as a most hard rock, and I know that I shall not be confounded. 8 He is near that justifieth me; who will contend with me? Let us stand together. Who is my adversary? Let him come near to me. 9 Behold: the Lord God is my helper. Who is he that shall condemn me? Lo: they shall all be destroyed as a garment; the moth shall eat them up.

10 Who is there among you that feareth the Lord, that heareth the voice of his servant, that hath walked in darkness and hath no light? Let him hope in the name of the Lord and lean upon his God.

11 Behold: all you that kindle a fire, encompassed with flames, walk in the light of your fire and in the flames which you have kindled. This is done to you by my hand; you shall sleep in sorrows.

Caput 51

"Audite me, qui sequimini quod iustum est et quaeritis Dominum. Adtendite ad petram unde excisi estis et ad cavernam laci de qua praecisi estis. 2 Adtendite ad Abraham, patrem vestrum, et ad Sarram quae peperit vos, quia unum vocavi eum et benedixi ei et multiplicavi eum. 3 Consolabitur ergo Dominus Sion et consolabitur omnes ruinas eius, et ponet desertum eius quasi delicias et solitudinem eius quasi hortum Domini. Gaudium et laetitia invenietur in ea, gratiarum actio et vox laudis.

4 "Adtendite ad me, popule meus, et tribus mea, me audite, quia lex a me exiet, et iudicium meum in lucem populorum requiescet. 5 Prope est iustus meus. Egressus est salvator meus, et brachia mea populos iudicabunt. Me insulae expectabunt et brachium meum sustinebunt. 6 Levate in caelum oculos vestros, et videte sub terra deorsum, quia caeli sicut fumus liquescent, et terra sicut vestimentum adteretur, et habitatores eius sicut haec interibunt, salus autem mea in sempiternum erit, et iustitia mea non deficiet.

7 "Audite me, qui scitis iustum, populus meus cuius lex mea in corde eorum; nolite timere obprobrium hominum, et blasphemias eorum ne metuatis. 8 Sicut enim vestimentum sic comedet eos vermis, et sicut lanam sic devorabit eos

Chapter 51

An exhortation to trust in Christ. He shall protect the children of his church.

"Give ear to me, you that follow that which is just and you that seek the Lord. Look unto the rock whence you are hewn and to the hole of the pit from which you are dug out. 2 Look unto Abraham, your father, and to Sarah that bore you, for I called him alone and blessed him and multiplied him. 3 The Lord therefore will comfort Zion and will comfort all the ruins thereof, and he will make her desert as a place of pleasure and her wilderness as the garden of the Lord. Joy and gladness shall be found therein, thanksgiving and the voice of praise.

4 "Hearken unto me, O my people, and give ear to me, O my tribes, for a law shall go forth from me, and my judgment shall rest to be a light of the nations. 5 My just one is near at hand. My saviour is gone forth, and my arms shall judge the people. The islands shall look for me and shall patiently wait for my arm. 6 Lift up your eyes to heaven, and look down to the earth beneath, for the heavens shall vanish like smoke, and the earth shall be worn away like a garment, and the inhabitants thereof shall perish in like manner, but my salvation shall be for ever, and my justice shall not fail.

7 "Hearken to me, you that know what is just, my people who have my law in your heart; fear ye not the reproach of men, and be not afraid of their blasphemies. 8 For the worm shall eat them up as a garment, and the moth shall consume

tinea, salus autem mea in sempiternum erit, et iustitia mea in generationes generationum."

9 Consurge; consurge; induere fortitudinem, brachium Domini; consurge sicut in diebus antiquis, in generationibus saeculorum. Numquid non tu percussisti superbum; vulnerasti draconem? 10 Numquid non tu siccasti mare, aquam abyssi vehementis, qui posuisti profundum maris viam ut transirent liberati? 11 Et nunc qui redempti sunt a Domino revertentur et venient in Sion laudantes, et laetitia sempiterna super capita eorum. Gaudium et laetitiam tenebunt; fugiet dolor et gemitus.

12 "Ego, ego ipse consolabor vos; quis tu ut timeres ab homine mortali et a filio hominis qui quasi faenum ita arescet? 13 Et oblitus es Domini, factoris tui, qui tetendit caelos et fundavit terram, et formidasti iugiter tota die a facie furoris eius qui te tribulabat et paraverat ad perdendum; ubi nunc est furor tribulantis? 14 Cito veniet gradiens ad aperiendum, et non interficiet usque ad internicionem, nec deficiet panis eius. 15 Ego autem sum Dominus, Deus tuus, qui conturbo mare, et intumescunt fluctus eius; Dominus exercituum nomen meum. 16 Posui verba mea in ore tuo et in umbra manus meae protexi te, ut plantes caelos et fundes terram et dicas ad Sion, 'Populus meus es tu.'"

17 Elevare; elevare; consurge, Hierusalem, quae bibisti de manu Domini calicem irae eius. Usque ad fundum calicis soporis bibisti, et epotasti usque ad feces. 18 Non est qui sustentet eam ex omnibus filiis quos genuit, et non est qui

them as wool, but my salvation shall be for ever, and my justice *from generation to generation.*"

9 Arise; arise; put on strength, O thou arm of the Lord; arise as in the days of old, in the ancient generations. Hast not thou struck the proud one *and* wounded the dragon? 10 Hast not thou dried up the sea, the water of the mighty deep, who madest the depth of the sea a way that the delivered might pass over? 11 And now they that are redeemed by the Lord shall return and shall come into Zion *singing* praises, and joy everlasting shall be upon their heads. They shall obtain joy and gladness; sorrow and mourning shall flee away.

12 "I, I myself will comfort you; who art thou that thou shouldst be afraid of a mortal man and of the son of man who shall wither away like grass? 13 And thou hast forgotten the Lord, thy maker, who stretched out the heavens and founded the earth, and thou hast been afraid continually all the day at the presence of his fury who afflicted thee and had prepared himself to destroy thee; where is now the fury of the oppressor? 14 He shall quickly come that is going to open *unto you,* and he shall not kill unto utter destruction, neither shall his bread fail. 15 But I am the Lord, thy God, who trouble the sea, and the waves thereof swell; the Lord of hosts is my name. 16 I have put my words in thy mouth and have protected thee in the shadow of my hand, that thou mightest plant the heavens and found the earth and mightest say to Zion, 'Thou art my people.'"

17 Arise; arise; stand up, O Jerusalem, which hast drunk at the hand of the Lord the cup of his wrath. Thou hast drunk even to the bottom of the cup of dead sleep, and thou hast drunk even to the dregs. 18 There is none that can uphold her among all the children that she hath brought forth, and

adprehendat manum eius ex omnibus filiis quos enutrivit. 19 Duo sunt quae occurrerunt tibi; quis contristabitur super te? Vastitas et contritio et fames et gladius—quis consolabitur te? 20 Filii tui proiecti sunt; dormierunt in capite omnium viarum sicut oryx inlaqueatus, pleni indignatione Domini, increpatione Dei tui.

21 Idcirco audi hoc, paupercula et ebria non a vino. 22 Haec dicit Dominator tuus, Dominus, et Deus tuus, qui pugnavit pro populo suo: "Ecce: tuli de manu tua calicem soporis, fundum calicis indignationis meae; non adicies ut bibas illum ultra. 23 Et ponam illum in manu eorum qui te humiliaverunt et dixerunt animae tuae, 'Incurvare ut transeamus,' et posuisti ut terram corpus tuum et quasi viam transeuntibus."

Caput 52

Consurge; consurge; induere fortitudine tua, Sion. Induere vestimentis gloriae tuae, Hierusalem, civitas Sancti, quia non adiciet ultra ut pertranseat per te incircumcisus et

there is none that taketh her by the hand among all the children that she hath brought up. 19 There are two things that have happened to thee; who shall be sorry for thee? Desolation and destruction and the famine and the sword—who shall comfort thee? 20 Thy children are cast forth; they have slept at the head of all the ways as the wild ox that is snared, full of the indignation of the Lord, of the rebuke of thy God.

21 Therefore hear this, thou poor little one and thou that art drunk but not with wine. 22 Thus saith thy Sovereign, the Lord, and thy God, who *will fight* for his people: "Behold: I have taken out of thy hand the cup of dead sleep, the *dregs* of the cup of my indignation; thou shalt not drink it again any more. 23 And I will put it in the hand of them that have oppressed thee and have said to thy soul, 'Bow down that we may go over,' and thou hast laid thy body as the ground and as a way to them that went over."

Chapter 52

Under the figure of the deliverance from the Babylonish captivity, the church is invited to rejoice for her redemption from sin. Christ's kingdom shall be exalted.

Arise; arise; put on thy strength, O Zion. Put on the garments of thy glory, O Jerusalem, the city of the Holy One, for henceforth the uncircumcised and unclean shall

inmundus. 2 Excutere de pulvere; consurge; sede, Hierusalem. Solve vincula colli tui, captiva filia Sion.

3 Quia haec dicit Dominus: "Gratis venundati estis, et
sine argento redimemini." 4 Quia haec dicit Dominus Deus:
"In Aegyptum descendit populus meus in principio ut colonus esset ibi, et Assur absque ulla causa calumniatus est eum.
5 Et nunc quid mihi est hic," dicit Dominus, "quoniam abla-
tus est populus meus gratis? Dominatores eius inique agunt,"
dicit Dominus, "et iugiter tota die nomen meum blasphe-
matur. 6 Propter hoc sciet populus meus nomen meum in die
illa, quia ego ipse qui loquebar, ecce: adsum."

7 Quam pulchri super montes pedes adnuntiantis et praedicantis pacem, adnuntiantis bonum, praedicantis salutem,
dicentis Sion, "Regnabit Deus tuus!" 8 Vox speculatorum
tuorum—levaverunt vocem; simul laudabunt, quia oculo ad
oculum videbunt cum converterit Dominus Sion. 9 Gaudete,
et laudate simul, deserta Hierusalem, quia consolatus est
Dominus populum suum; redemit Hierusalem. 10 Paravit
Dominus brachium sanctum suum in oculis omnium Gentium, et videbunt omnes fines terrae salutare Dei nostri.

11 Recedite; recedite; exite inde. Pollutum nolite tangere;
exite de medio eius. Mundamini, qui fertis vasa Domini.
12 Quoniam non in tumultu exibitis, nec in fuga properabi-
tis, praecedet enim vos Dominus, et congregabit vos Deus
Israhel.

no more pass through thee. 2 Shake thyself from the dust; arise; sit up, O Jerusalem. Loose the bonds from off thy neck, O captive daughter of Zion.

3 For thus saith the Lord: "You were sold for nought, and you shall be redeemed without money." 4 For thus saith the Lord God: "My people went down into Egypt at the beginning to sojourn there, and the Assyrian hath oppressed them without any cause at all. 5 And now what have I here," saith the Lord, "for my people is taken away for nought? They that rule over them treat them unjustly," saith the Lord, "and my name is continually blasphemed all the day long. 6 Therefore my people shall know my name in that day, for I myself that spoke, behold: I am here."

7 How beautiful upon the mountains are the feet of him that bringeth good tidings and that preacheth peace, of him that sheweth forth good, that preacheth salvation, that saith to Zion, "Thy God shall reign!" 8 The voice of thy watchmen—they have lifted up their voice; they shall praise together, for they shall see eye to eye when the Lord shall convert Zion. 9 Rejoice, and give praise together, O ye deserts of Jerusalem, for the Lord hath comforted his people; he hath redeemed Jerusalem. 10 The Lord hath prepared his holy arm in the sight of all the Gentiles, and all the ends of the earth shall see the salvation of our God.

11 Depart; depart; go ye out from thence. Touch no unclean thing; go out of the midst of her. Be ye clean, you that carry the vessels of the Lord. 12 For you shall not go out in a tumult, neither shall you make haste by flight, for the Lord will go before you, and the God of Israel will gather you together.

13 Ecce: intelleget servus meus. Exaltabitur et elevabitur et sublimis erit valde. 14 Sicut obstipuerunt super te multi, sic inglorius erit inter viros aspectus eius, et forma eius inter filios hominum. 15 Iste asperget gentes multas. Super ipsum continebunt reges os suum, quia quibus non est narratum de eo viderunt, et qui non audierunt contemplati sunt.

Caput 53

Quis credidit auditui nostro? Et brachium Domini cui revelatum est? 2 Et ascendet sicut virgultum coram eo et sicut radix de terra sitienti. Non est species ei neque decor, et vidimus eum, et non erat aspectus, et desideravimus eum, 3 despectum et novissimum virorum, virum dolorum et scientem infirmitatem. Et quasi absconditus vultus eius et despectus, unde nec reputavimus eum. 4 Vere languores nostros ipse tulit et dolores nostros ipse portavit, et nos putavimus eum quasi leprosum et percussum a Deo et humiliatum. 5 Ipse autem vulneratus est propter iniquitates nostras; adtritus est propter scelera nostra. Disciplina pacis nostrae

13 Behold: my servant shall understand. He shall be exalted and extolled and shall be exceeding high. 14 As many have been astonished at thee, so shall his visage be inglorious among men, and his form among the sons of men. 15 He shall sprinkle many nations. Kings shall shut their mouth at him, for they to whom it was not told of him have seen, and they that had not heard have beheld.

Chapter 53

A prophecy of the passion of Christ.

Who hath believed our report? And to whom is the arm of the Lord revealed? 2 And he shall grow up as a tender plant before him and as a root out of a thirsty ground. There is no beauty in him nor comeliness, and we have seen him, and there was no sightliness *that* we *should be* desirous of him, 3 despised and the most abject of men, a man of sorrows and acquainted with infirmity. And his look was as it were hidden and despised, whereupon we esteemed him not. 4 Surely he hath borne our infirmities and carried our sorrows, and we have thought him as it were a leper and as one struck by God and afflicted. 5 But he was wounded for our iniquities; he was bruised for our sins. The chastisement of our peace

super eum, et livore eius sanati sumus. 6 Omnes nos quasi oves erravimus; unusquisque in viam suam declinavit, et Dominus posuit in eo iniquitatem omnium nostrum.

7 Oblatus est quia ipse voluit, et non aperuit os suum. Sicut ovis ad occisionem ducetur et quasi agnus coram tondente obmutescet, et non aperiet os suum. 8 De angustia et de iudicio sublatus est. Generationem eius quis enarrabit? Quia abscisus est de terra viventium; propter scelus populi mei percussi eum. 9 Et dabit impios pro sepultura, et divitem pro morte sua, eo quod iniquitatem non fecerit, neque dolus fuerit in ore eius.

10 Et Dominus voluit conterere eum in infirmitate; si posuerit pro peccato animam suam, videbit semen longevum, et voluntas Domini in manu eius dirigetur. 11 Pro eo quod laboravit anima eius, videbit et saturabitur. In scientia sua iustificabit ipse, iustus servus meus, multos, et iniquitates eorum ipse portabit. 12 Ideo dispertiam ei plurimos, et fortium dividet spolia pro eo quod tradidit in mortem animam suam et cum sceleratis reputatus est, et ipse peccata multorum tulit et pro transgressoribus rogavit.

was upon him, and by his bruises we are healed. 6 All we like sheep have gone astray; every one hath turned aside into his own way, and the Lord hath laid on him the iniquity of us all.

7 He was offered because it was his own will, and he opened not his mouth. He shall be led as a sheep to the slaughter and shall be dumb as a lamb before his shearer, and he shall not open his mouth. 8 He was taken away from distress and from judgment. Who shall declare his generation? Because he is cut off out of the land of the living; for the wickedness of my people have I struck him. 9 And he shall give the ungodly for his burial, and the rich for his death, because he hath done no iniquity, neither was there deceit in his mouth.

10 And the Lord was pleased to bruise him in infirmity; if he shall lay down his life for sin, he shall see a long-lived seed, and the will of the Lord shall be prosperous in his hand. 11 Because his soul hath laboured, he shall see and be filled. By his knowledge shall this, my just servant, justify many, and he shall bear their iniquities. 12 Therefore will I distribute to him very many, and he shall divide the spoils of the strong because he hath delivered his soul unto death and was reputed with the wicked, and he hath borne the sins of many and hath prayed for the transgressors.

Caput 54

"Lauda, sterilis quae non paris. Decanta laudem, et hinni, quae non pariebas, quoniam multi filii desertae magis quam eius quae habet virum," dicit Dominus. 2 "Dilata locum tentorii tui, et pelles tabernaculorum tuorum extende. Ne parcas; longos fac funiculos tuos, et clavos tuos consolida. 3 Ad dexteram enim et ad levam penetrabis, et semen tuum Gentes hereditabit et civitates desertas inhabitabit.

4 "Noli timere, quia non confunderis neque erubesces, non enim te pudebit, quia confusionis adulescentiae tuae oblivisc
eris et obprobrii viduitatis tuae non recordaberis amplius. 5 Quia dominabitur tui qui fecit te; Dominus exercituum nomen eius, et redemptor tuus, Sanctus Israhel, Deus omnis terrae vocabitur. 6 Quia ut mulierem derelictam et maerentem spiritu vocavit te Dominus et uxorem ab adulescentia abiectam," dixit Deus tuus. 7 "Ad punctum in modico dereliqui te, et in miserationibus magnis congregabo te. 8 In momento indignationis abscondi faciem meam parumper a te, et in misericordia sempiterna misertus sum tui," dixit redemptor tuus, Dominus.

Chapter 54

The Gentiles, who were barren before, shall multiply in the church of Christ, from which God's mercy shall never depart.

"Give praise, O thou barren that bearest not. Sing forth praise, and *make a joyful noise,* thou that didst not travail with child, for many are the children of the desolate more than of her that hath a husband," saith the Lord. 2 "Enlarge the place of thy tent, and stretch out the skins of thy tabernacles. Spare not; lengthen thy cords, and strengthen thy stakes. 3 For thou shalt pass on to the right hand and to the left, and thy seed shall inherit the Gentiles and shall inhabit the desolate cities.

4 "Fear not, for thou shalt not be confounded nor blush, for thou shalt not be put to shame, because thou shalt forget the shame of thy youth and shalt remember no more the reproach of thy widowhood. 5 For he that made thee shall rule over thee; the Lord of hosts is his name, and thy redeemer, the Holy One of Israel, shall be called the God of all the earth. 6 For the Lord hath called thee as a woman forsaken and mourning in spirit and as a wife cast off from her youth," said thy God. 7 "For a small moment have I forsaken thee, *but* with great mercies will I gather thee. 8 In a moment of indignation have I hid my face a little while from thee, *but* with everlasting kindness have I had mercy on thee," said the Lord, thy redeemer.

9 "Sicut in diebus Noe istud mihi est, cui iuravi ne inducerem aquas Noe ultra super terram, sic iuravi ut non irascar tibi et non increpem te. 10 Montes enim commovebuntur, et colles contremescent, misericordia autem mea non recedet a te, et foedus pacis meae non movebitur," dixit miserator tuus, Dominus.

11 "Paupercula, tempestate convulsa, absque ulla consolatione, ecce: ego sternam per ordinem lapides tuos et fundabo te in sapphyris, 12 et ponam iaspidem propugnacula tua et portas tuas in lapides sculptos et omnes terminos tuos in lapides desiderabiles. 13 Universos filios tuos doctos a Domino, et multitudinem pacis filiis tuis. 14 Et in iustitia fundaberis. Recede procul a calumnia, quia non timebis, et a pavore, quia non adpropinquabit tibi.

15 "Ecce: accola veniet qui non erat mecum; advena quondam tuus adiungetur tibi. 16 Ecce: ego creavi fabrum sufflantem in igne prunas et proferentem vas in opus suum, et ego creavi interfectorem ad disperdendum. 17 Omne vas quod fictum est contra te non dirigetur, et omnem linguam resistentem tibi in iudicio iudicabis. Haec est hereditas servorum Domini et iustitia eorum apud me," dicit Dominus.

9 "This thing is to me as in the days of Noah, to whom I swore that I would no more bring in the waters of Noah upon the earth, so have I sworn not to be angry with thee and not to rebuke thee. 10 For the mountains shall be moved, and the hills shall tremble, but my mercy shall not depart from thee, and the covenant of my peace shall not be moved," said the Lord, that hath mercy on thee.

11 "O poor little one, tossed with tempest, without all comfort, behold: I will lay thy stones in order and will lay thy foundations with sapphires, 12 and I will make thy bulwarks of jasper and thy gates of graven stones and all thy borders of desirable stones. 13 All thy children shall be taught of the Lord, and great shall be the peace of thy children. 14 And thou shalt be founded in justice. Depart far from oppression, for thou shalt not fear, and from terror, for it shall not come near thee.

15 "Behold: an inhabitant shall come who was not with me; he that was a stranger to thee before shall be joined to thee. 16 Behold: I have created the smith that bloweth the coals in the fire and bringeth forth an instrument for his work, and I have created the killer to destroy. 17 No weapon that is formed against thee shall prosper, and every tongue that resisteth thee in judgment thou shalt condemn. This is the inheritance of the servants of the Lord and their justice with me," saith the Lord.

Caput 55

 ⁶⁶Omnes sitientes, venite ad aquas, et qui non habetis argentum, properate; emite, et comedite. Venite; emite absque argento et absque ulla commutatione vinum et lac. 2 Quare adpenditis argentum non in panibus, et laborem vestrum non in saturitate? Audite audientes me, et comedite bonum, et delectabitur in crassitudine anima vestra. 3 Inclinate aurem vestram, et venite ad me; audite, et vivet anima vestra, et feriam vobiscum pactum sempiternum, misericordias David fideles. 4 Ecce: testem populis dedi eum, ducem ac praeceptorem Gentibus. 5 Ecce: gentem quam nesciebas vocabis, et gentes quae non cognoverunt te ad te current propter Dominum, Deum tuum, et Sanctum Israhel, quia glorificavit te.

6 "Quaerite Dominum dum inveniri potest; invocate eum dum prope est. 7 Derelinquat impius viam suam et vir iniquus cogitationes suas, et revertatur ad Dominum, et miserebitur eius, et ad Deum nostrum, quoniam multus est ad ignoscendum.

8 "Non enim cogitationes meae cogitationes vestrae neque viae vestrae viae meae," dicit Dominus. 9 "Quia sicut exaltantur caeli a terra, sic exaltatae sunt viae meae a viis vestris et cogitationes meae a cogitationibus vestris. 10 Et quomodo

Chapter 55

God promises abundance of spiritual graces to the faithful
that shall believe in Christ out of all nations and sincerely
serve him.

"All you that thirst, come to the waters, and you that
have no money, make haste; buy, and eat. Come ye; buy wine
and milk without money and without any price. 2 Why do
you spend money for that which is not bread, and your labour for that which doth not satisfy you? Hearken diligently
to me, and eat that which is good, and your soul shall be delighted in fatness. 3 Incline your ear, and come to me; hear,
and your soul shall live, and I will make an everlasting covenant with you, the faithful mercies of David. 4 Behold: I
have given him for a witness to the people, for a leader and a
master to the Gentiles. 5 Behold: thou shalt call a nation
which thou knewest not, and the nations that knew not thee
shall run to thee because of the Lord, thy God, and for the
Holy One of Israel, for he hath glorified thee.

6 "Seek ye the Lord while he may be found; call upon him
while he is near. 7 Let the wicked forsake his way and the unjust man his thoughts, and let him return to the Lord, and
he will have mercy on him, and to our God, for he is bounti-
ful to forgive.

8 "For my thoughts are not your thoughts nor your ways
my ways," saith the Lord. 9 "For as the heavens are exalted
above the earth, so are my ways exalted above your ways and
my thoughts above your thoughts. 10 And as the rain and the

descendit imber et nix de caelo et illuc ultra non revertitur, sed inebriat terram et infundit eam et germinare eam facit et dat semen serenti et panem comedenti, 11 sic erit verbum meum quod egredietur de ore meo. Non revertetur ad me vacuum, sed faciet quaecumque volui et prosperabitur in his ad quae misi illud. 12 Quia in laetitia egrediemini et in pace deducemini; montes et colles cantabunt coram vobis laudem, et omnia ligna regionis plaudent manu. 13 Pro saliunca ascendet abies, et pro urtica crescet myrtus, et erit Dominus nominatus in signum aeternum quod non auferetur."

Caput 56

Haec dicit Dominus: "Custodite iudicium, et facite iustitiam, quia iuxta est salus mea ut veniat et iustitia mea ut reveletur. 2 Beatus vir qui facit hoc et filius hominis qui adprehendet istud, custodiens sabbatum, ne polluat illud, custodiens manus suas ne faciat omne malum."

snow come down from heaven and return no more thither, but soak the earth and water it and make it to spring and give seed to the sower and bread to the eater, 11 so shall my word be which shall go forth from my mouth. It shall not return to me void, but it shall do whatsoever I please and shall prosper in the things for which I sent it. 12 For you shall go out with joy and be led forth with peace; the mountains and the hills shall sing praise before you, and all the trees of the country shall clap their hands. 13 Instead of the shrub shall come up the fir tree, and instead of the nettle shall come up the myrtle tree, and the Lord shall be named for an everlasting sign that shall not be taken away."

Chapter 56

God invites all to keep his commandments. The Gentiles that keep them shall be the people of God. The Jewish pastors are reproved.

Thus saith the Lord: "Keep ye judgment, and do justice, for my salvation is near to come and my justice to be revealed. 2 Blessed is the man that doth this and the son of man that shall lay hold on this, that keepeth the sabbath, from profaning it, that keepeth his hands from doing any evil."

3 Et non dicat filius advenae qui adheret Domino, dicens, "Separatione dividet me Dominus a populo suo." Et non dicat eunuchus, "Ecce: ego lignum aridum."

4 Quia haec dicit Dominus eunuchis: "Qui custodierint sabbata mea et elegerint quae volui et tenuerint foedus meum, 5 dabo eis in domo mea et in muris meis locum et nomen melius a filiis et filiabus. Nomen sempiternum dabo eis quod non peribit. 6 Et filios advenae qui adherent Domino ut colant eum et diligant nomen eius, ut sint ei in servos, omnem custodientem sabbatum, ne polluat illud, et tenentem foedus meum, 7 adducam eos in montem sanctum meum et laetificabo eos in domo orationis meae. Holocausta eorum et victimae eorum placebunt mihi super altari meo, quia domus mea domus orationis vocabitur cunctis populis."

8 Ait Dominus Deus qui congregat dispersos Israhel, "Adhuc congregabo ad eum congregatos eius."

9 Omnes bestiae agri, venite ad devorandum, universae bestiae saltus. 10 Speculatores eius caeci omnes; nescierunt universi, canes muti non valentes latrare, videntes vana, dormientes et amantes somnia. 11 Et canes inpudentissimi: nescierunt saturitatem. Ipsi pastores ignoraverunt intellegentiam; omnes in viam suam declinaverunt, unusquisque ad avaritiam suam, a summo usque ad novissimum: 12 "Venite; sumamus vinum, et impleamur ebrietate, et erit sicut hodie sic et cras et multo amplius."

3 And let not the son of the stranger that adhereth to the Lord speak, saying: "The Lord will divide *and separate* me from his people." And let not the eunuch say, "Behold: I am a dry tree."

4 For thus saith the Lord to the eunuchs: "They that shall keep my sabbaths and shall choose the things that please me and shall hold fast my covenant, 5 I will give to them in my house and within my walls a place and a name better than sons and daughters. I will give them an everlasting name which shall never perish. 6 And the children of the stranger that adhere to the Lord to worship him and to love his name, to be his servants, every one that keepeth the sabbath, from profaning it, and that holdeth fast my covenant, 7 I will bring them into my holy mount and will make them joyful in my house of prayer. Their holocausts and their victims shall please me upon my altar, for my house shall be called the house of prayer for all nations."

8 The Lord God who gathereth the scattered of Israel saith, "I will still gather unto him his congregation."

9 All ye beasts of the field, come to devour, all ye beasts of the forest. 10 His watchmen are all blind; they are all ignorant, dumb dogs not able to bark, seeing vain things, sleeping and loving dreams. 11 And most impudent dogs: they never had enough. The shepherds themselves knew no understanding; all have turned aside into their own way, every one after his own gain, from the first even to the last: 12 "Come, let us take wine, and be filled with drunkenness, and it shall be as today so also tomorrow and much more."

Caput 57

Iustus perit, et nemo est qui recogitet in corde suo, et viri misericordiae colliguntur quia non est qui intellegat, a facie enim malitiae collectus est iustus. 2 Veniat pax; requiescat in cubili suo qui ambulavit in directione sua.

3 "Vos autem accedite huc, filii auguratricis, semen adulteri et fornicariae. 4 Super quem lusistis? Super quem dilatastis os et eiecistis linguam? Numquid non vos filii scelesti, semen mendax, 5 qui consolamini in diis subter omne lignum frondosum, immolantes parvulos in torrentibus subter eminentes petras? 6 In partibus torrentis pars tua; haec est sors tua, et ipsis effudisti libamen; obtulisti sacrificium. Numquid super his non indignabor? 7 Super montem excelsum et sublimem posuisti cubile tuum et illuc ascendisti ut immolares hostias. 8 Et post ostium et retro postem posuisti memoriale tuum, quia iuxta me discoperuisti et suscepisti adulterum. Dilatasti cubile tuum et pepigisti cum eis foedus; dilexisti stratum eorum manu aperta. 9 Et ornasti te regi unguento et multiplicasti pigmenta tua. Misisti legatos tuos

Chapter 57

The infidelity of the Jews. Their idolatry. Promises to humble penitents.

The just perisheth, and no man layeth it to heart, and men of mercy are taken away because there is none that understandeth, for the just man is taken away from before the face of evil. 2 Let peace come; let him rest in his bed that hath walked in his uprightness.

3 "But draw near hither, you sons of the sorceress, the seed of the adulterer and of the harlot. 4 Upon whom have you jested? Upon whom have you opened your mouth wide and put out your tongue? Are not you wicked children, a false seed, 5 who seek your comfort in idols under every green tree, sacrificing children in the torrents under the high rocks? 6 In the parts of the torrent is thy portion; this is thy lot, and thou hast poured out libations to them; thou hast offered sacrifice. Shall I not be angry at these things? 7 Upon a high and lofty mountain thou hast laid thy bed and hast gone up thither to offer victims. 8 And behind the door and behind the post thou hast set up thy remembrance, for thou hast discovered thyself near me and hast received an adulterer. Thou hast enlarged thy bed and made a covenant with them; thou hast loved their bed with open hand. 9 And thou hast adorned thyself for the king with ointment and hast multiplied thy *perfumes*. Thou hast sent thy messengers

procul et humiliata es usque ad inferos. 10 In multitudine viae tuae laborasti; non dixisti, 'Quiescam.' Vitam manus tuae invenisti; propterea non rogasti.

11 "Pro quo sollicita timuisti, quia mentita es et mei non es recordata neque cogitasti in corde tuo? Quia ego tacens et quasi non videns, et mei oblita es. 12 Ego adnuntiabo iustitiam tuam, et opera tua non proderunt tibi. 13 Cum clamaveris, liberent te congregati tui, et omnes eos auferet ventus; tollet aura. Qui autem fiduciam habet mei hereditabit terram et possidebit montem sanctum meum.

14 "Et dicam, 'Viam facite; praebete iter. Declinate de semita; auferte offendicula de via populi mei.'"

15 Quia haec dicit Excelsus et Sublimis habitans aeternitatem, et sanctum nomen eius, in excelso et in sancto habitans et cum contrito et humili spiritu, ut vivificet spiritum humilium et vivificet cor contritorum: 16 "Non enim in sempiternum litigabo, neque usque ad finem irascar, quia spiritus a facie mea egredietur, et flatus ego faciam. 17 Propter iniquitatem avaritiae eius iratus sum, et percussi eum; abscondi a te faciem meam et indignatus sum, et abiit vagus in via cordis sui. 18 Vias eius vidi, et sanavi eum et reduxi eum et reddidi consolationes ipsi et lugentibus eius. 19 Creavi fructum labiorum. Pacem, pacem ei qui longe est et qui prope," dixit Dominus, "et sanavi eum."

far off and wast debased even to hell. 10 Thou hast been wearied in the multitude of thy *ways, yet* thou saidst not, 'I will rest.' Thou hast found life of thy hand; therefore thou hast not asked.

11 "For whom hast thou been solicitous and afraid, that thou hast lied and hast not been mindful of me nor thought on me in thy heart? For I am silent and as one that seeth not, and thou hast forgotten me. 12 I will declare thy justice, and thy works shall not profit thee. 13 When thou shalt cry, let thy companies deliver thee, *but* the wind shall carry them all off; a breeze shall take them away. But he that putteth his trust in me shall inherit the land and shall possess my holy mount.

14 "And I will say, 'Make a way; give free passage. Turn out of the path; take away the stumbling blocks out of the way of my people.'"

15 For thus saith the High and the Eminent that inhabiteth eternity, and his name is holy, who dwelleth in the high and holy place and with a contrite and humble spirit, to revive the spirit of the humble and to revive the heart of the contrite: 16 "For I will not contend for ever, neither will I be angry unto the end, because the spirit shall go forth from my face, and breathings I will make. 17 For the iniquity of his covetousness I was angry, and I struck him; I hid my face from thee and was angry, and he went away wandering in the way of his own heart. 18 I saw his ways, and I healed him and brought him back and restored comforts to him and to them that mourn for him. 19 I created the fruit of the lips. Peace, peace to him that is far off and to him that is near," said the Lord, "and I healed him."

20 "Impii autem quasi mare fervens quod quiescere non potest, et redundant fluctus eius in conculcationem et lutum. 21 Non est pax impiis," dicit Dominus Deus.

Caput 58

Clama; ne cesses; quasi tuba exalta vocem tuam, et adnuntia populo meo scelera eorum, et domui Iacob peccata eorum. 2 Me etenim de die in diem quaerunt et scire vias meas volunt quasi gens quae iustitiam fecerit et iudicium Dei sui non reliquerit. Rogant me iudicia iustitiae; adpropinquare Deo volunt.

3 "Quare ieiunavimus et non aspexisti? Humiliavimus animas nostras, et nescisti?" Ecce: in die ieiunii vestri invenitur voluntas vestra, et omnes debitores vestros repetitis. 4 Ecce: ad lites et contentiones ieiunatis et percutitis pugno impie. Nolite ieiunare sicut usque ad hanc diem ut audiatur in excelso clamor vester. 5 Numquid tale est ieiunium quod elegi, per diem adfligere hominem animam suam? Numquid contorquere quasi circulum caput suum et saccum et cinerem sternere? Numquid istud vocabis ieiunium et diem acceptabilem Domino?

6 Nonne hoc est magis ieiunium quod elegi? Dissolve conligationes impietatis; solve fasciculos deprimentes.

CHAPTER 58

20 "But the wicked are like the raging sea which cannot rest, and the waves thereof *cast up dirt* and mire. 21 There is no peace to the wicked," saith the Lord God.

Chapter 58

God rejects the hypocritical fasts of the Jews, recommends works of mercy and sincere godliness.

Cry; cease not; lift up thy voice like a trumpet, and shew my people their wicked doings and the house of Jacob their sins. 2 For they seek me from day to day and desire to know my ways as a nation that hath done justice and hath not forsaken the judgment of their God. They ask of me the judgments of justice; they are willing to approach to God.

3 "Why have we fasted, and thou hast not regarded? Have we humbled our souls, and thou hast not taken notice?" Behold: in the day of your fast your own will is found, and you exact of all your debtors. 4 Behold: you fast for debates and strife and strike with the fist wickedly. Do not fast as you have done until this day to make your cry to be heard on high. 5 Is this such a fast as I have chosen, for a man to afflict his soul for a day? Is this it, to wind his head about like a circle and to spread sackcloth and ashes? Wilt thou call this a fast and a day acceptable to the Lord?

6 Is not this rather the fast that I have chosen? Loose the bands of wickedness; undo the bundles that oppress. Let

Dimitte eos qui confracti sunt liberos, et omne onus disrumpe. 7 Frange esurienti panem tuum, et egenos vagosque induc in domum tuam. Cum videris nudum, operi eum, et carnem tuam ne despexeris. 8 Tunc erumpet quasi mane lumen tuum, et sanitas tua citius orietur, et anteibit faciem tuam iustitia tua, et gloria Domini colliget te. 9 Tunc invocabis, et Dominus exaudiet; clamabis, et dicet, "Ecce: adsum."

Si abstuleris de medio tui catenam et desieris digitum extendere et loqui quod non prodest, 10 cum effuderis esurienti animam tuam et animam adflictam repleveris, orietur in tenebris lux tua et tenebrae tuae erunt sicut meridies.

11 Et requiem tibi dabit Dominus semper et implebit splendoribus animam tuam et ossa tua liberabit, et eris quasi hortus inriguus et sicut fons aquarum cuius non deficient aquae. 12 Et aedificabuntur in te deserta saeculorum. Fundamenta generationis et generationis suscitabis, et vocaberis aedificator sepium, avertens semitas in quietem.

13 Si averteris a sabbato pedem tuum, ne facias voluntatem tuam in die sancto meo, et vocaveris sabbatum delicatum et sanctum Domini gloriosum et glorificaveris eum, dum non facis vias tuas et non invenitur voluntas tua ut loquaris sermonem, 14 tunc delectaberis super Domino, et sustollam te super altitudines terrae et cibabo te hereditate Iacob, patris tui. Os enim Domini locutum est.

them that are broken go free, and break asunder every burden. 7 *Deal* thy bread to the hungry, and bring the needy and the harbourless into thy house. When thou shalt see one naked, cover him, and despise not thy own flesh. 8 Then shall thy light break forth as the morning, and thy health shall speedily arise, and thy justice shall go before thy face, and the glory of the Lord shall gather thee up. 9 Then shalt thou call, and the Lord shall hear; thou shalt cry, and he shall say, "Here I am."

If thou wilt take away the chain out of the midst of thee and cease to stretch out the finger and to speak that which profiteth not, 10 when thou shalt pour out thy soul to the hungry and shalt satisfy the afflicted soul, then shall thy light rise up in darkness and thy darkness shall be as the noon day.

11 And the Lord will give thee rest continually and will fill thy soul with brightness and deliver thy bones, and thou shalt be like a watered garden and like a fountain of water whose waters shall not fail. 12 And the places that have been desolate for ages shall be built in thee. Thou shalt raise up the foundations of generation and generation, and thou shalt be called the *repairer* of the fences, turning the paths into rest.

13 If thou turn away thy foot from the sabbath, from doing thy own will in my holy day and call the sabbath delightful and the holy of the Lord glorious and glorify him, while thou dost not thy own ways and thy own will is not found to speak a word, 14 then shalt thou be delighted in the Lord, and I will lift thee up above the high places of the earth and will feed thee with the inheritance of Jacob, thy father. For the mouth of the Lord hath spoken it.

Caput 59

Ecce: non est adbreviata manus Domini ut salvare nequeat, neque adgravata est auris eius ut non exaudiat. 2 Sed iniquitates vestrae diviserunt inter vos et Deum vestrum, et peccata vestra absconderunt faciem eius a vobis ne exaudiret, 3 manus enim vestrae pollutae sunt sanguine, et digiti vestri iniquitate; labia vestra locuta sunt mendacium, et lingua vestra iniquitatem fatur. 4 Non est qui invocet iustitiam, neque est qui iudicet vere, sed confidunt in nihili et loquuntur vanitates. Conceperunt laborem et pepererunt iniquitatem.

5 Ova aspidum ruperunt et telas araneae texuerunt; qui comederit de ovis eorum morietur, et quod confotum est erumpet in regulum. 6 Telae eorum non erunt in vestimentum, neque operientur operibus suis; opera eorum opera inutilia, et opus iniquitatis in manibus eorum. 7 Pedes eorum ad malum currunt et festinant ut effundant sanguinem innocentem; cogitationes eorum cogitationes inutiles; vastitas et contritio in viis eorum. 8 Viam pacis nescierunt, et non est iudicium in gressibus eorum. Semitae eorum incurvatae sunt eis; omnis qui calcat in eis ignorat pacem.

Chapter 59

The dreadful evil of sin is displayed as the great obstacle to
all good from God, yet he will send a redeemer and make an
everlasting covenant with his church.

Behold: the hand of the Lord is not shortened that it cannot save, neither is his ear heavy that it cannot hear. 2 But
your iniquities have divided between you and your God, and
your sins have hid his face from you that he should not hear,
3 for your hands are defiled with blood, and your fingers with
iniquity; your lips have spoken lies, and your tongue uttereth
iniquity. 4 There is none that calleth upon justice, neither is
there any one that judgeth truly, but they trust in a mere
nothing and speak vanities. They have conceived labour and
brought forth iniquity.

5 They have broken the eggs of asps and have woven the
webs of spiders; he that shall eat of their eggs shall die, and
that which is *brought out* shall be hatched into a basilisk.
6 Their webs shall not be for clothing, neither shall they
cover themselves with their works; their works are unprofitable works, and the work of iniquity is in their hands. 7 Their
feet run to evil and make haste to shed innocent blood; their
thoughts are unprofitable thoughts; wasting and destruction are in their ways. 8 They have not known the way of
peace, and there is no judgment in their steps. Their paths
are become crooked to them; every one that treadeth in
them knoweth no peace.

9 Propter hoc elongatum est iudicium a nobis, et non adprehendet nos iustitia. Expectavimus lucem, et ecce: tenebrae; splendorem, et in tenebris ambulavimus. 10 Palpavimus sicut caeci parietem, et quasi absque oculis adtrectavimus. Inpegimus meridie quasi in tenebris; in caligosis quasi mortui.

11 Rugiemus quasi ursi omnes et quasi columbae meditantes gememus. Expectavimus iudicium, et non est; salutem, et elongata est a nobis. 12 Multiplicatae sunt enim iniquitates nostrae coram te, et peccata nostra responderunt nobis, quia scelera nostra nobiscum, et iniquitates nostras cognovimus, 13 peccare et mentiri contra Dominum. Et aversi sumus ne iremus post tergum Dei nostri, ut loqueremur calumniam et transgressionem. Concepimus et locuti sumus de corde verba mendacii.

14 Et conversum est retrorsum iudicium, et iustitia longe stetit, quia corruit in platea veritas et aequitas non potuit ingredi. 15 Et facta est veritas in oblivionem, et qui recessit a malo praedae patuit, et vidit Dominus, et malum apparuit in oculis eius quia non est iudicium. 16 Et vidit quia non est vir, et aporiatus est quia non est qui occurrat, et salvavit sibi brachium suum, et iustitia eius ipsa confirmavit eum. 17 Indutus est iustitia ut lorica et galea salutis in capite eius; indutus est vestimentis ultionis et opertus est quasi pallio zeli. 18 Sicut ad vindictam, quasi ad retributionem indignationis hostibus suis et vicissitudinem inimicis suis, insulis vicem reddet. 19 Et timebunt qui ab occidente nomen Domini, et qui ab

9 Therefore is judgment far from us, and justice shall not overtake us. We looked for light, and behold: darkness; brightness, and we have walked in the dark. 10 We have groped for the wall, *and* like the blind *we* have groped as if we had no eyes. We have stumbled at noonday as in darkness; we are in dark places as dead men.

11 We shall roar all of us like bears and shall lament as mournful doves. We have looked for judgment, and there is none; for salvation, and it is far from us. 12 For our iniquities are multiplied before thee, and our sins have testified against us, for our wicked doings are with us, and we have known our iniquities, 13 in sinning and lying against the Lord. And we have turned away so that we went not after our God, *but* spoke calumny and transgression. We have conceived and uttered from the heart words of falsehood.

14 And judgment is turned away backward, and justice hath stood far off, because truth hath fallen down in the street and equity could not come in. 15 And truth hath been forgotten, and he that departed from evil lay open to be a prey, and the Lord saw, and it appeared evil in his eyes because there is no judgment. 16 And he saw that there is not a man, and he stood astonished because there is none to oppose himself, and his own arm brought salvation to him, and his own justice supported him. 17 He put on justice as a breastplate and a helmet of salvation upon his head; he put on the garments of vengeance and was clad with zeal as with a cloak. 18 As unto revenge, as it were to repay wrath to his adversaries and a reward to his enemies, he will repay the like to the islands. 19 And they from the west shall fear the name of the Lord, and they from the rising of the sun, his

ortu solis, gloriam eius, cum venerit quasi fluvius violentus quem spiritus Domini cogit.

20 "Et venerit Sion redemptor et eis qui redeunt ab iniquitate in Iacob," dicit Dominus.

21 "Hoc foedus meum cum eis," dicit Dominus: "Spiritus meus qui est in te et verba mea quae posui in ore tuo non recedent de ore tuo et de ore seminis tui et de ore seminis seminis tui," dicit Dominus, "amodo et usque in sempiternum."

Caput 60

Surge; inluminare, Hierusalem, quia venit lumen tuum, et gloria Domini super te orta est. 2 Quia ecce: tenebrae operient terram, et caligo populos, super te autem orietur Dominus, et gloria eius in te videbitur. 3 Et ambulabunt Gentes in lumine tuo et reges in splendore ortus tui.

4 Leva in circuitu oculos tuos, et vide: omnes isti congregati sunt; venerunt tibi. Filii tui de longe venient, et filiae tuae de latere surgent. 5 Tunc videbis et afflues, et mirabitur et dilatabitur cor tuum, quando conversa fuerit ad te multi-

glory, when he shall come as a violent stream which the spirit of the Lord driveth on.

20 "And there shall come a redeemer to Zion and to them that return from iniquity in Jacob," saith the Lord.

21 "This is my covenant with them," saith the Lord: "My spirit that is in thee and my words that I have put in thy mouth shall not depart out of thy mouth nor out of the mouth of thy seed nor out of the mouth of thy seed's seed," saith the Lord, "from henceforth and for ever."

Chapter 60

The light of true faith shall shine forth in the church of Christ and shall be spread through all nations and continue for all ages.

Arise; be enlightened, O Jerusalem, for thy light is come, and the glory of the Lord is risen upon thee. 2 For behold: darkness shall cover the earth, and a mist the people, but the Lord shall arise upon thee, and his glory shall be seen upon thee. 3 And the Gentiles shall walk in thy light and kings in the brightness of thy rising.

4 Lift up thy eyes round about, and see: all these are gathered together; they are come to thee. Thy sons shall come from afar, and thy daughters shall rise up at thy side. 5 Then shalt thou see and abound, and thy heart shall wonder and be enlarged, when the multitude of the sea shall be con-

tudo maris; fortitudo Gentium venerit tibi. 6 Inundatio camelorum operiet te, dromedariae Madian et Efa; omnes de Saba venient aurum et tus deferentes et laudem Domino adnuntiantes. 7 Omne pecus Cedar congregabitur tibi. Arietes Nabaioth ministrabunt tibi; offerentur super placabili altari meo, et domum maiestatis meae glorificabo.

8 Qui sunt isti qui ut nubes volant et quasi columbae ad fenestras suas? 9 Me enim insulae expectant et naves maris in principio, ut adducam filios tuos de longe, argentum eorum et aurum eorum cum eis, nomini Domini, Dei tui, et Sancto Israhel, quia glorificavit te. 10 Et aedificabunt filii peregrinorum muros tuos, et reges eorum ministrabunt tibi, in indignatione enim mea percussi te, et in reconciliatione mea misertus sum tui.

11 Et aperientur portae tuae iugiter; die et nocte non claudentur, ut adferatur ad te fortitudo Gentium et reges earum adducantur. 12 Gens enim et regnum quod non servierit tibi peribit, et Gentes solitudine vastabuntur. 13 Gloria Libani ad te veniet, abies et buxus et pinus simul, ad ornandum locum sanctificationis meae, et locum pedum meorum glorificabo. 14 Et venient ad te curvi filii eorum qui humiliaverunt te, et adorabunt vestigia pedum tuorum omnes qui detrahebant tibi et vocabunt te civitatem Domini, Sion Sancti Israhel.

verted to thee; the strength of the Gentiles shall come to thee. 6 The multitude of camels shall cover thee, the dromedaries of Midian and Ephah; all they from Sheba shall come bringing gold and frankincense and shewing forth praise to the Lord. 7 All the flocks of Kedar shall be gathered together unto thee. The rams of Nebaioth shall minister to thee; they shall be offered upon my acceptable altar, and I will glorify the house of my majesty.

8 Who are these that fly as clouds and as doves to their windows? 9 For the islands wait for me and the ships of the sea in the beginning, that I may bring thy sons from afar, their silver and their gold with them, to the name of the Lord, thy God, and to the Holy One of Israel, because he hath glorified thee. 10 And the children of strangers shall build up thy walls, and their kings shall minister to thee, for in my wrath have I struck thee, and in my reconciliation have I had mercy upon thee.

11 And thy gates shall be open continually; they shall not be shut day nor night, that the strength of the Gentiles may be brought to thee and their kings may be brought. 12 For the nation and the kingdom that will not serve thee shall perish, and the Gentiles shall be wasted with desolation. 13 The glory of Lebanon shall come to thee, the fir tree and the box tree and the pine tree together, to beautify the place of my sanctuary, and I will glorify the place of my feet. 14 And the children of them that afflict thee shall come bowing down to thee, and all that slandered thee shall worship the steps of thy feet and shall call thee the city of the Lord, the Zion of the Holy One of Israel.

15 Pro eo quod fuisti derelicta et odio habita et non erat qui per te transiret, ponam te in superbiam saeculorum, gaudium in generationem et generationem, 16 et suges lac Gentium, et mamilla regum lactaberis, et scies quia ego Dominus, salvans te, et redemptor tuus, Fortis Iacob.

17 Pro aere adferam aurum, et pro ferro adferam argentum, et pro lignis, aes, et pro lapidibus, ferrum, et ponam visitationem tuam pacem, et praepositos tuos iustitiam. 18 Non audietur ultra iniquitas in terra tua, vastitas et contritio in terminis tuis, et occupabit salus muros tuos, et portas tuas laudatio. 19 Non erit tibi amplius sol ad lucendum per diem, nec splendor lunae inluminabit te, sed erit tibi Dominus in lucem sempiternam, et Deus tuus in gloriam tuam. 20 Non occidet ultra sol tuus, et luna tua non minuetur, quia erit tibi Dominus in lucem sempiternam, et conplebuntur dies luctus tui. 21 Populus autem tuus omnes iusti; in perpetuum hereditabunt terram, germen plantationis meae, opus manus meae ad glorificandum. 22 Minimus erit in mille, et parvulus in gentem fortissimam. Ego, Dominus, in tempore eius subito faciam istud.

15 Because thou wast forsaken and hated and there was none that passed through thee, I will make thee to be an everlasting glory, a joy unto generation and generation, 16 and thou shalt suck the milk of the Gentiles, and thou shalt be nursed with the breasts of kings, and thou shalt know that I am the Lord, thy saviour, and thy redeemer, the Mighty One of Jacob.

17 For brass I will bring gold, and for iron I will bring silver, and for wood, brass, and for stones, iron, and I will make thy visitation peace, and thy overseers justice. 18 Iniquity shall no more be heard in thy land, wasting nor destruction in thy borders, and salvation shall possess thy walls, and praise thy gates.19 Thou shalt no more have the sun for thy light by day, neither shall the brightness of the moon enlighten thee, but the Lord shall be unto thee for an everlasting light, and thy God for thy glory. 20 Thy sun shall go down no more, and thy moon shall not decrease, for the Lord shall be unto thee for an everlasting light, and the days of thy mourning shall be ended. 21 And thy people shall be all just; they shall inherit the land for ever, the branch of my planting, the work of my hand to glorify me. 22 The least shall become a thousand, and a little one a most strong nation. I, the Lord, will suddenly do this thing in its time.

Caput 61

Spiritus Domini super me eo quod unxerit Dominus me. Ad adnuntiandum mansuetis misit me, ut mederer contritis corde et praedicarem captivis indulgentiam et clausis apertionem, 2 ut praedicarem annum placabilem Domino et diem ultionis Deo nostro, ut consolarer omnes lugentes, 3 ut ponerem lugentibus Sion et darem eis coronam pro cinere, oleum gaudii pro luctu, pallium laudis pro spiritu maeroris. Et vocabuntur in ea fortes iustitiae, plantatio Domini ad glorificandum. 4 Et aedificabunt deserta a saeculo et ruinas antiquas erigent et instaurabunt civitates desertas dissipatas in generationem et generationem. 5 Et stabunt alieni et pascent pecora vestra, et filii peregrinorum agricolae et vinitores vestri erunt.

6 Vos autem sacerdotes Domini vocabimini. "Ministri Dei nostri," dicetur vobis. Fortitudinem Gentium comedetis, et in gloria earum superbietis. 7 Pro confusione vestra duplici et rubore laudabunt partem suam; propter hoc in terra sua duplicia possidebunt. Laetitia sempiterna erit eis.

8 Quia ego Dominus diligens iudicium et odio habens

Chapter 61

The office of Christ. The mission of the apostles. The happiness of their converts.

The spirit of the Lord is upon me because the Lord hath anointed me. He hath sent me to preach to the meek, to heal the contrite of heart and to preach a release to the captives and deliverance to them that are shut up, 2 to proclaim the acceptable year of the Lord and the day of vengeance of our God, to comfort all that mourn, 3 to appoint to the mourners of Zion and to give them a crown for ashes, the oil of joy for mourning, a garment of praise for the spirit of grief. And they shall be called in it the mighty ones of justice, the planting of the Lord to glorify him. 4 And they shall build the places that have been waste from of old and shall raise up ancient ruins and shall repair the desolate cities that were destroyed for generation and generation. 5 And strangers shall stand and shall feed your flocks, and the sons of strangers shall be your husbandmen and the dressers of your vines.

6 But you shall be called the priests of the Lord. To you it shall be said, "Ye ministers of our God." You shall eat the *riches* of the Gentiles, and you shall pride yourselves in their glory. 7 For your double confusion and shame they shall praise their part; therefore shall they receive double in their land. Everlasting joy shall be unto them.

8 For I am the Lord that love judgment and hate robbery

rapinam in holocausto, et dabo opus eorum in veritate, et foedus perpetuum feriam eis. 9 Et scient in Gentibus semen eorum, et germen eorum in medio populorum. Omnes qui viderint eos cognoscent eos, quia isti sunt semen cui benedixit Dominus.

10 Gaudens gaudebo in Domino, et exultabit anima mea in Deo meo, quia induit me vestimentis salutis et indumento iustitiae circumdedit me, quasi sponsum decoratum corona et quasi sponsam ornatam monilibus suis. 11 Sicut enim terra profert germen suum et sicut hortus semen suum germinat, sic Dominus Deus germinabit iustitiam et laudem coram universis gentibus.

Caput 62

Propter Sion non tacebo, et propter Hierusalem non quiescam donec egrediatur ut splendor iustus eius et salvator eius ut lampas accendatur. 2 Et videbunt Gentes iustum tuum, et cuncti reges inclitum tuum, et vocabitur tibi nomen novum quod os Domini nominabit. 3 Et eris corona

in a holocaust, and I will make their work in truth, and I will make a perpetual covenant with them. 9 And they shall know their seed among the Gentiles, and their offspring in the midst of people. All that shall see them shall know them, that these are the seed which the Lord hath blessed.

10 I will greatly rejoice in the Lord, and my soul shall be joyful in my God, for he hath clothed me with the garments of salvation and with the robe of justice he hath covered me, as a bridegroom decked with a crown and as a bride adorned with her jewels. 11 For as the earth bringeth forth her bud and as the garden causeth her seed to shoot forth, so shall the Lord God make justice to spring forth and praise before all the nations.

Chapter 62

The prophet will not cease from preaching Christ, to whom all nations shall be converted and whose church shall continue for ever.

For Zion's sake I will not hold my peace, and for the sake of Jerusalem I will not rest till her just one come forth as brightness and her saviour be lighted as a lamp. 2 And the Gentiles shall see thy just one, and all kings thy glorious one, and thou shalt be called by a new name which the mouth of the Lord shall name. 3 And thou shalt be a crown of glory in

gloriae in manu Domini, et diadema regni in manu Dei tui.
4 Non vocaberis ultra "Derelicta," et terra tua non vocabitur
amplius "Desolata," sed vocaberis "Voluntas mea in ea," et
terra tua, "Inhabitata," quia conplacuit Domino in te, et
terra tua inhabitabitur. 5 Habitabit enim iuvenis cum vir-
gine, et habitabunt in te filii tui. Et gaudebit sponsus super
sponsam, et gaudebit super te Deus tuus. 6 Super muros
tuos, Hierusalem, constitui custodes tota die, et tota nocte
perpetuo non tacebunt.

Qui reminiscimini Domini, ne taceatis, 7 et ne detis silentium ei donec stabiliat et donec ponat Hierusalem laudem
in terra. 8 Iuravit Dominus in dextera sua et in brachio fortitudinis suae, "Si dedero triticum tuum ultra cibum inimicis
tuis, et si biberint filii alieni vinum tuum, in quo laborasti.
9 Quia qui congregabunt illud comedent et laudabunt Dominum, et qui conportant illud bibent in atriis sanctis
meis."

10 Transite; transite per portas; praeparate viam populo.
Planum facite iter, et eligite lapides, et elevate signum ad populos. 11 Ecce: Dominus auditum fecit in extremis terrae:
"Dicite filiae Sion, 'Ecce: salvator tuus venit; ecce: merces
eius cum eo, et opus eius coram illo.'" 12 Et vocabunt eos populus sanctus, redempti a Domino. Tu autem vocaberis
quaesita civitas et non derelicta.

the hand of the Lord, and a royal diadem in the hand of thy God. 4 Thou shalt no more be called "Forsaken," and thy land shall no more be called "Desolate," but thou shalt be called "My pleasure in her," and thy land, "Inhabited," because the Lord hath been well pleased with thee, and thy land shall be inhabited. 5 For the young man shall dwell with the virgin, and thy children shall dwell in thee. And the bridegroom shall rejoice over the bride, and thy God shall rejoice over thee. 6 Upon thy walls, O Jerusalem, I have appointed watchmen all the day, and all the night they shall never hold their peace.

You that are mindful of the Lord, hold not your peace, 7 and give him no silence till he establish and till he make Jerusalem a praise in the earth. 8 The Lord hath sworn by his right hand and by the arm of his strength, "Surely I will no more give thy corn to be meat for thy enemies, and the sons of the strangers shall not drink thy wine, for which thou hast laboured. 9 For they that *gather* it shall eat it and shall praise the Lord, and they that bring it together shall drink it in my holy courts."

10 Go through; go through the gates; prepare the way for the people. Make the road plain; *pick* out the stones, and lift up the standard to the people. 11 Behold: the Lord hath made it to be heard in the ends of the earth: "Tell the daughter of Zion, 'Behold: thy Saviour cometh; behold: his reward is with him, and his work before him.'" 12 And they shall call them the holy people, the redeemed of the Lord. But thou shalt be called a city sought after and not forsaken.

Caput 63

"Quis est iste qui venit de Edom tinctis vestibus de Bosra, iste formonsus in stola sua, gradiens in multitudine fortitudinis suae?"

"Ego, qui loquor iustitiam et propugnator sum ad salvandum."

2 "Quare ergo rubrum est indumentum tuum, et vestimenta tua sicut calcantium in torculari?"

3 "Torcular calcavi solus, et de Gentibus non est vir mecum; calcavi eos in furore meo et conculcavi eos in ira mea, et aspersus est sanguis eorum super vestimenta mea, et omnia indumenta mea inquinavi. 4 Dies enim ultionis in corde meo; annus redemptionis meae venit. 5 Circumspexi, et non erat auxiliator; quaesivi, et non fuit qui adiuvaret, et salvavit mihi brachium meum, et indignatio mea ipsa auxiliata est mihi. 6 Et conculcavi populos in furore meo et inebriavi eos in indignatione mea et detraxi in terram virtutem eorum."

7 Miserationum Domini recordabor, laudem Domini, super omnibus quae reddidit nobis Dominus et super multitudinem bonorum domui Israhel, quae largitus est eis secundum indulgentiam suam et secundum multitudinem

Chapter 63

Christ's victory over his enemies. His mercies to his people.
Their complaint.

"Who is this that cometh from Edom with dyed garments from Bozrah, this beautiful one in his robe, walking in the greatness of his strength?"

"I, that speak justice and am a defender to save."

2 "Why then is thy apparel red, and thy garments like theirs that tread in the winepress?"

3 "I have trodden the winepress alone, and of the Gentiles there is not a man with me; I have trampled on them in my indignation and have trodden them down in my wrath, and their blood is sprinkled upon my garments, and I have stained all my apparel. 4 For the day of vengeance is in my heart; the year of my redemption is come. 5 I looked about, and there was none to help; I sought, and there was none to give aid, and my own arm hath saved for me, and my indignation itself hath helped me. 6 And I have trodden down the people in my wrath and have made them drunk in my indignation and have brought down their strength to the earth."

7 I will remember the tender mercies of the Lord, the praise of the Lord, for all the things that the Lord hath bestowed upon us and for the multitude of his good things to the house of Israel, which he hath given them according to his kindness and according to the multitude of his

misericordiarum suarum. 8 Et dixit, "Verumtamen populus meus est, filii non negantes," et factus est eis salvator. 9 In omni tribulatione eorum non est tribulatus, et angelus faciei eius salvavit eos. In dilectione sua et in indulgentia sua ipse redemit eos, et portavit eos et levavit eos cunctis diebus saeculi. 10 Ipsi autem ad iracundiam provocaverunt et adflixerunt spiritum Sancti eius, et conversus est eis in inimicum, et ipse debellavit eos.

11 Et recordatus est dierum saeculi Mosi et populi sui; ubi est qui eduxit eos de mari cum pastoribus gregis sui? Ubi est qui posuit in medio eius spiritum Sancti sui, 12 qui eduxit ad dexteram Mosen brachio maiestatis suae, qui scidit aquas ante eos ut faceret sibi nomen sempiternum, 13 qui eduxit eos per abyssos, quasi equum in deserto non inpingentem.

14 Quasi animal in campo descendens spiritus Domini ductor eius fuit; sic adduxisti populum tuum ut faceres tibi nomen gloriae. 15 Adtende de caelo, et vide de habitaculo sancto tuo et gloriae tuae: ubi est zelus tuus et fortitudo tua, multitudo viscerum tuorum et miserationum tuarum?

"Super me continuerunt se."

16 Tu enim pater noster, et Abraham nescivit nos, et Israhel ignoravit nos. Tu, Domine, pater noster, redemptor noster; a saeculo nomen tuum. 17 Quare errare nos fecisti, Domine, de viis tuis? Indurasti cor nostrum ne timeremus te? Convertere propter servos tuos, tribus hereditatis tuae. 18 Quasi nihilum possederunt populum sanctum tuum;

mercies. 8 And he said, "*Surely* they are my people, children that *will* not deny," *so* he became their saviour. 9 In all their affliction he was not troubled, and the angel of his presence saved them. In his love and in his mercy he redeemed them, and he carried them and lifted them up all the days of old. 10 But they provoked to wrath and afflicted the spirit of his Holy One, and he was turned to be their enemy, and he fought against them.

11 And he remembered the days of old of Moses and of his people; where is he that brought them up out of the sea with the shepherds of his flock? Where is he that put in the midst of them the spirit of his Holy One, 12 he that brought out Moses by the right hand by the arm of his majesty, that divided the waters before them to make himself an everlasting name, 13 he that led them out through the deep, as a horse in the wilderness that stumbleth not.

14 As a beast that goeth down in the field the spirit of the Lord was their leader; so didst thou lead thy people to make thyself a glorious name. 15 Look down from heaven, and behold from thy holy habitation and *the place* of thy glory: where is thy zeal and thy strength, the multitude of thy bowels and of thy mercies?

"They have held back themselves from me."

16 For thou art our father, and Abraham hath not known us, and Israel hath been ignorant of us. Thou, O Lord, art our father, our redeemer; from everlasting is thy name. 17 Why hast thou made us to err, O Lord, from thy ways? Why hast thou hardened our heart that we should not fear thee? Return for the sake of thy servants, the tribes of thy inheritance. 18 They have possessed thy holy people as noth-

hostes nostri conculcaverunt sanctificationem tuam. 19 Facti sumus quasi in principio, cum non dominareris nostri, neque invocaretur nomen tuum super nos.

Caput 64

Utinam disrumperes caelos et descenderes: a facie tua montes defluerent; 2 sicut exustio ignis tabescerent; aquae arderent igni ut notum fieret nomen tuum inimicis tuis, a facie tua gentes turbarentur. 3 Cum feceris mirabilia, non sustinebimus. Descendisti, et a facie tua montes defluxerunt.

4 A saeculo non audierunt neque auribus perceperunt; oculus non vidit, Deus, absque te, quae praeparasti expectantibus te. 5 Occurristi laetanti et facienti iustitiam. In viis tuis recordabuntur tui; ecce: tu iratus es, et peccavimus. In ipsis fuimus semper, et salvabimur. 6 Et facti sumus ut inmundus omnes nos et quasi pannus menstruatae universae iustitiae nostrae, et cecidimus quasi folium universi, et

ing; our enemies have trodden down thy sanctuary. 19 We are become as in the beginning, when thou didst not rule over us, and when we were not called by thy name.

Chapter 64

The prophet prays for the release of his people and for the remission of their sins.

That thou wouldst rend the heavens and wouldst come down: the mountains would melt away at thy presence; 2 they would melt as at the burning of fire; the waters would burn with fire that thy name might be made known to thy enemies, that the nations might tremble at thy presence. 3 When thou shalt do wonderful things, we shall not bear them. Thou didst come down, and at thy presence the mountains melted away.

4 From the beginning of the world they have not heard nor perceived with the ears; the eye hath not seen, O God, besides thee, what things thou hast prepared for them that wait for thee. 5 Thou hast met him that rejoiceth and doth justice. In thy ways they shall remember thee; behold: thou art angry, and we have sinned. In them we have been always, and we shall be saved. 6 And we are all become as one unclean and all our justices as the rag of a menstruous woman, and we have all fallen as a leaf, and our iniquities

iniquitates nostrae quasi ventus abstulerunt nos. 7 Non est qui invocet nomen tuum, qui consurgat et teneat te. Abscondisti faciem tuam a nobis et adlisisti nos in manu iniquitatis nostrae.

8 Et nunc, Domine, pater noster es tu, nos vero lutum, et fictor noster es tu, et opera manuum tuarum omnes nos. 9 Ne irascaris, Domine, satis, et ne ultra memineris iniquitatis nostrae. Ecce: respice; populus tuus omnes nos. 10 Civitas sancti tui facta est deserta. Sion deserta facta est; Hierusalem desolata est. 11 Domus sanctificationis nostrae et gloriae nostrae ubi laudaverunt te patres nostri facta est in exustionem ignis, et omnia desiderabilia nostra versa sunt in ruinas. 12 Numquid super his continebis te, Domine? Tacebis et adfliges nos vehementer?

Caput 65

"Quaesierunt me qui ante non interrogabant; invenerunt qui non quaesierunt me. Dixi, 'Ecce ego, ecce ego,' ad gentem quae non invocabat nomen meum. 2 Expandi manus meas tota die ad populum incredulum qui graditur in via

like the wind have taken us away. 7 There is none that calleth upon thy name, that riseth up and taketh hold of thee. Thou hast hid thy face from us and hast crushed us in the hand of our iniquity.

8 And now, O Lord, thou art our father, and we are clay, and thou art our maker, and we all are the works of thy hands. 9 Be not very angry, O Lord, and remember no longer our iniquity. Behold: see; we are all thy people. 10 The city of thy sanctuary is become a desert. Zion is made a desert; Jerusalem is desolate. 11 The house of our holiness and of our glory where our fathers praised thee is burnt with fire, and all our lovely things are turned into ruins. 12 Wilt thou refrain thyself, O Lord, upon these things? Wilt thou hold thy peace and afflict us vehemently?

Chapter 65

The Gentiles shall seek and find Christ, but the Jews will persecute him and be rejected; only a remnant shall be reserved. The church shall multiply and abound with graces.

"They have sought me that before asked not *for me;* they have found me that sought me not. I said, 'Behold me, behold me,' to a nation that did not call upon my name. 2 I have spread forth my hands all the day to an unbelieving people who walk in a way that is not good after their

non bona post cogitationes suas, 3 populus qui ad iracundiam provocat me ante faciem meam semper, qui immolant in hortis et sacrificant super lateres, 4 qui habitant in sepulchris et in delubris idolorum dormiunt, qui comedunt carnem suillam, et ius profanum in vasis eorum, 5 qui dicunt, 'Recede a me; non adpropinques mihi quia inmundus es.' Isti fumus erunt in furore meo, ignis ardens tota die.

6 "Ecce: scriptum est coram me; Non tacebo, sed reddam et retribuam in sinum eorum 7 iniquitates vestras et iniquitates patrum vestrorum simul," dicit Dominus, "qui sacrificaverunt super montes et super colles exprobraverunt mihi, et remetiar opus eorum primum in sinu eorum."

8 Haec dicit Dominus: "Quomodo si inveniatur granum in botro, et dicatur, 'Ne dissipes illud quoniam benedictio est,' sic faciam propter servos meos, ut non disperdam totum. 9 Et educam de Iacob semen et de Iuda possidentem montes meos, et hereditabunt eam electi mei, et servi mei habitabunt ibi. 10 Et erunt campestria in caulas gregum, et Vallis Achor in cubile armentorum, populo meo qui requisierunt me.

11 "Et vos qui dereliquistis Dominum, qui obliti estis montem sanctum meum, qui ponitis Fortunae mensam et libatis super eam, 12 numerabo vos in gladio, et omnes in caede corruetis, pro eo quod vocavi, et non respondistis; locutus sum, et non audistis, et faciebatis ·malum in oculis meis, et quae nolui elegistis." 13 Propter hoc haec dicit Dominus Deus: "Ecce: servi mei comedent, et vos esurietis. Ecce: servi mei bibent, et vos sitietis. 14 Ecce: servi mei

own thoughts, 3 a people that continually provoke me to anger before my face, that immolate in gardens and sacrifice upon bricks, 4 that dwell in sepulchres and sleep in the temple of idols, that eat swine's flesh, and profane broth is in their vessels, 5 that say, 'Depart from me; come not near me because thou art unclean.' These shall be smoke in my anger, a fire burning all the day.

6 "Behold: it is written before me; I will not be silent, but I will render and repay into their bosom 7 your iniquities and the iniquities of your fathers together," saith the Lord, "who have sacrificed upon the mountains and have reproached me upon the hills, and I will measure back their first work in their bosom."

8 Thus saith the Lord: "As if a grain be found in a cluster, and it be said, 'Destroy it not because it is a blessing,' so will I do for the sake of my servants, that I may not destroy the whole. 9 And I will bring forth a seed out of Jacob and out of Judah a possessor of my mountains, and my elect shall inherit it, and my servants shall dwell there. 10 And the plains shall be turned to folds of flocks, and the Valley of Achor into a place for the herds to lie down in, for my people that have sought me.

11 "And you that have forsaken the Lord, that have forgotten my holy mount, that set a table for Fortune and offer libations upon it, 12 I will number you in the sword, and you shall all fall by slaughter, because I called, and you did not answer; I spoke, and you did not hear, and you did evil in my eyes, and you have chosen the things that displease me."
13 Therefore thus saith the Lord God: "Behold: my servants shall eat, and you shall be hungry. Behold: my servants shall drink, and you shall be thirsty. 14 Behold: my servants shall

laetabuntur, et vos confundemini. Ecce: servi mei laudabunt prae exultatione cordis, et vos clamabitis prae dolore cordis et prae contritione spiritus ululabitis. 15 Et dimittetis nomen vestrum in iuramentum electis meis, et interficiet te Dominus Deus et servos suos vocabit nomine alio, 16 in quo qui benedictus est super terram benedicetur in Deo (amen), et qui iurat in terra iurabit in Deo (amen), quia oblivioni traditae sunt angustiae priores et quia absconditae sunt ab oculis meis.

17 "Ecce enim: ego creo caelos novos et terram novam, et non erunt in memoria priora, et non ascendent super cor. 18 Sed gaudebitis et exultabitis usque in sempiternum in his quae ego creo, quia ecce: ego creo Hierusalem exultationem et populum eius gaudium. 19 Et exultabo in Hierusalem et gaudebo in populo meo, et non audietur in eo ultra vox fletus et vox clamoris. 20 Non erit ibi amplius infans dierum et senex qui non impleat dies suos, quoniam puer centum annorum morietur, et peccator centum annorum maledictus erit.

21 "Et aedificabunt domos et habitabunt, et plantabunt vineas et comedent fructus earum. 22 Non aedificabunt, et alius habitabit; non plantabunt, et alius comedet, secundum enim dies ligni erunt dies populi mei, et opera manuum eorum inveterabunt. 23 Electi mei non laborabunt frustra neque generabunt in conturbatione, quia semen benedictorum Domini est et nepotes eorum cum eis. 24 Eritque antequam clament ego, exaudiam; adhuc illis loquentibus ego audiam.

rejoice, and you shall be confounded. Behold: my servants shall praise for joyfulness of heart, and you shall cry for sorrow of heart and shall howl for grief of spirit. 15 And you shall leave your name for an execration to my elect, and the Lord God shall slay thee and call his servants by another name, 16 in which he that is blessed upon the earth shall be blessed in God (amen), and he that sweareth in the earth shall swear by God (amen), because the former distresses are forgotten and because they are hid from my eyes.

17 "For behold: I create new heavens and a new earth, and the former things shall not be in remembrance, and they shall not come upon the heart. 18 But you shall be glad and rejoice for ever in these things which I create, for behold: I create Jerusalem a rejoicing and the people thereof joy. 19 And I will rejoice in Jerusalem and joy in my people, and the voice of weeping shall no more be heard in her, nor the voice of crying. 20 There shall no more be an infant of days there nor an old man that shall not fill up his days, for the child shall die a hundred years old, and the sinner being a hundred years old shall be accursed.

21 "And they shall build houses and inhabit them, and they shall plant vineyards and eat the fruits of them. 22 They shall not build, and another inhabit; they shall not plant, and another eat, for as the days of a tree so shall be the days of my people, and the works of their hands shall be of long continuance. 23 My elect shall not labour in vain nor bring forth in trouble, for they are the seed of the blessed of the Lord and their posterity with them. 24 And it shall come to pass that before they call, I will hear; as they are yet speaking I

25 Lupus et agnus pascentur simul; leo et bos comedent paleas, et serpenti pulvis panis eius. Non nocebunt neque occident in omni monte sancto meo," dicit Dominus.

Caput 66

Haec dicit Dominus: "Caelum sedis mea, et terra scabillum pedum meorum. Quae est ista domus quam aedificabitis mihi? Et quis est iste locus quietis meae? 2 Omnia haec manus mea fecit, et facta sunt universa ista," dicit Dominus. "Ad quem autem respiciam nisi ad pauperculum et contritum spiritu et trementem sermones meos?

3 "Qui immolat bovem quasi qui interficiat virum, qui mactat pecus quasi qui excerebret canem, qui offert oblationem quasi qui sanguinem suillum offerat, qui recordatur turis quasi qui benedicat idolo. Haec omnia elegerunt in viis suis, et in abominationibus suis anima eorum delectata est. 4 Unde et ego eligam inlusiones eorum et quae timebant adducam eis, quia vocavi, et non erat qui responderet; locutus sum, et non audierunt, feceruntque malum in oculis meis et quae nolui elegerunt."

will hear. 25 The wolf and the lamb shall feed together; the lion and the ox shall eat straw; and dust shall be the serpent's food. They shall not hurt nor kill in all my holy mountain," saith the Lord.

Chapter 66

More of the reprobation of the Jews and of the call of the Gentiles.

Thus saith the Lord: "Heaven is my throne, and the earth my footstool. What is this house that you will build to me? And what is this place of my rest? 2 My hand made all these things, and all these things were made," saith the Lord. "But to whom shall I have respect but to him that is poor and little and of a contrite spirit and that trembleth at my words?

3 "He that sacrificeth an ox is as if he slew a man, he that killeth a sheep in sacrifice as if he should brain a dog, he that offereth an oblation as if he should offer swine's blood, he that remembereth incense as if he should bless an idol. All these things have they chosen in their ways, and their soul is delighted in their abominations. 4 Wherefore I also will choose their mockeries and will bring upon them the things they feared, because I called, and there was none that would answer; I have spoken, and they heard not, and they have done evil in my eyes and have chosen the things that displease me."

5 Audite verbum Domini, qui tremitis ad verbum eius: "Dixerunt fratres vestri odientes vos et abicientes propter nomen meum, 'Glorificetur Dominus, et videbimus in laetitia vestra,' ipsi autem confundentur."

6 Vox populi de civitate, vox de templo, vox Domini reddentis retributionem inimicis suis.

7 Antequam parturiret peperit; antequam veniret partus eius peperit masculum. 8 Quis audivit umquam tale? Et quis vidit huic simile? Numquid parturiet terra in die una? Aut parietur gens simul, quia parturivit et peperit Sion filios suos?

9 "Numquid ego, qui alios parere facio, ipse non pariam?" dicit Dominus. "Si ego, qui generationem ceteris tribuo, sterilis ero?" ait Dominus, Deus tuus. 10 Laetamini cum Hierusalem, et exultate in ea, omnes qui diligitis eam. Gaudete cum ea gaudio universi, qui lugetis super eam, 11 ut sugatis et repleamini ab ubere consolationis eius, ut mulgeatis et deliciis affluatis ab omnimoda gloria eius.

12 Quia haec dicit Dominus: "Ecce: ego declinabo super eam quasi fluvium pacis, et quasi torrentem inundantem gloriam Gentium, quam sugetis. Ad ubera portabimini, et super genua blandientur vobis. 13 Quomodo si cui mater blandiatur, ita ego consolabor vos, et in Hierusalem consolabimini. 14 Videbitis, et gaudebit cor vestrum, et ossa vestra quasi herba germinabunt, et cognoscetur manus Domini servis eius, et indignabitur inimicis suis. 15 Quia ecce: Dominus in igne veniet, et quasi turbo quadrigae eius reddere in

5 Hear the word of the Lord, you that tremble at his word: "Your brethren that hate you and cast you out for my name's sake have said, 'Let the Lord be glorified, and we shall see in your joy,' but they shall be confounded."

6 A voice of the people from the city, a voice from the temple, the voice of the Lord that rendereth recompense to his enemies.

7 Before she was in labour she brought forth; before her time came to be delivered she brought forth a man child. 8 Who hath ever heard such a thing? And who hath seen the like to this? Shall the earth bring forth in one day? Or shall a nation be brought forth at once, because Zion hath been in labour and hath brought forth her children?

9 "Shall not I, that make others to bring forth children, myself bring forth?" saith the Lord. "Shall I, that give generation to others, be barren?" saith the Lord, thy God. 10 Rejoice with Jerusalem, and be glad with her, all you that love her. Rejoice for joy with her, all you that mourn for her, 11 that you may suck and be filled with the breasts of her consolations, that you may milk out and flow with delights from the abundance of her glory.

12 For thus saith the Lord: "Behold: I will bring upon her as it were a river of peace, and as an overflowing torrent the glory of the Gentiles, which you shall suck. You shall be carried at the breasts, and upon the knees they shall caress you. 13 As one whom the mother caresseth, so will I comfort you, and you shall be comforted in Jerusalem. 14 You shall see, and your heart shall rejoice, and your bones shall flourish like an herb, and the hand of the Lord shall be known to his servants, and he shall be angry with his enemies. 15 For behold: the Lord will come with fire, and his chariots are like a

indignatione furorem suum, et increpationem suam in flamma ignis. 16 Quia in igne Dominus diiudicabit et in gladio suo ad omnem carnem, et multiplicabuntur interfecti a Domino. 17 Qui sanctificabantur et mundos se putabant in hortis post ianuam intrinsecus, qui comedebant carnem suillam et abominationem et murem, simul consumentur," dicit Dominus.

18 "Ego autem opera eorum et cogitationes eorum novi; venio ut congregem cum omnibus gentibus et linguis, et venient et videbunt gloriam meam. 19 Et ponam in eis signum, et mittam ex eis qui salvati fuerint ad Gentes, in mare, in Africam et Lydiam, tenentes sagittam, in Italiam et Graeciam, ad insulas longe, ad eos qui non audierunt de me et non viderunt gloriam meam. Et adnuntiabunt gloriam meam Gentibus, 20 et adducent omnes fratres vestros de cunctis gentibus donum Domino in equis et in quadrigis et in lecticis et in mulis et in carrucis ad montem sanctum meum, Hierusalem," dicit Dominus, "quomodo si inferant filii Israhel munus in vase mundo in domum Domini. 21 Et adsumam ex eis in sacerdotes et Levitas," dicit Dominus.

22 "Quia sicut caeli novi et terra nova, quae ego facio stare coram me," dicit Dominus, "sic stabit semen vestrum et nomen vestrum. 23 Et erit mensis ex mense et sabbatum ex sabbato; veniet omnis caro ut adoret coram facie mea," dicit Dominus.

24 "Et egredientur et videbunt cadavera virorum qui praevaricati sunt in me; vermis eorum non morietur, et ignis eorum non extinguetur, et erunt usque ad satietatem visionis omni carni."

whirlwind to render his wrath in indignation, and his rebuke with flames of fire. 16 For the Lord shall judge by fire and by his sword unto all flesh, and the slain of the Lord shall be many. 17 They that were sanctified and thought themselves clean in the gardens behind the gate within, they that did eat swine's flesh and the abomination and the mouse, they shall be consumed together," saith the Lord.

18 "But I know their works and their thoughts; I come that I may gather them together with all nations and tongues, and they shall come and shall see my glory. 19 And I will set a sign among them, and I will send of them that shall be saved to the Gentiles, into the sea, into Africa and Lydia, them that *draw the bow,* into Italy and Greece, to the islands afar off, to them that have not heard of me and have not seen my glory. And they shall declare my glory to the Gentiles, 20 and they shall bring all your brethren out of all nations for a gift to the Lord upon horses and in chariots and in litters and on mules and in coaches to my holy mountain, Jerusalem," saith the Lord, "as if the children of Israel should bring an offering in a clean vessel into the house of the Lord. 21 And I will take of them to be priests and Levites," saith the Lord.

22 "For as the new heavens and the new earth, which I make to stand before me," saith the Lord, "so shall your seed stand and your name. 23 And there shall be month after month and sabbath after sabbath, *and* all flesh shall come to adore before my face," saith the Lord.

24 "And they shall go out and see the carcasses of the men that have transgressed against me; their worm shall not die, and their fire shall not be quenched, and they shall be a loathsome sight to all flesh."

JEREMIAH

Caput 1

Verba Hieremiae, filii Helciae, de sacerdotibus qui fuerunt in Anathoth, in terra Beniamin. 2 Quod factum est verbum Domini ad eum in diebus Iosiae, filii Amon, regis Iuda, in tertiodecimo anno regni eius, 3 et factum est in diebus Ioachim, filii Iosiae, regis Iuda, usque ad consummationem undecimi anni Sedeciae, filii Iosiae, regis Iuda, usque ad transmigrationem Hierusalem in mense quinto.

4 Et factum est verbum Domini ad me, dicens, 5 "Priusquam te formarem in utero, novi te, et antequam exires de vulva, sanctificavi te et prophetam in gentibus dedi te."

6 Et dixi, "A, a, a, Domine Deus, ecce: nescio loqui, quia puer ego sum."

7 Et dixit Dominus ad me, "Noli dicere, 'Puer sum,' quoniam ad omnia quae mittam te ibis, et universa quaecumque mandavero tibi loqueris. 8 Ne timeas a facie eorum, quia tecum ego sum ut eruam te," dicit Dominus. 9 Et misit Dominus manum suam et tetigit os meum, et dixit Dominus ad me, "Ecce: dedi verba mea in ore tuo. 10 Ecce: consti-

Chapter 1

The time and the calling of Jeremiah. His prophetical visions. God encourages him.

The words of Jeremiah, the son of Hilkiah, of the priests that were in Anathoth, in the land of Benjamin. 2 The word of the Lord which came to him in the days of Josiah, the son of Amon, king of Judah, in the thirteenth year of his reign, 3 and which came *to him* in the days of Jehoiakim, the son of Josiah, king of Judah, unto the end of the eleventh year of Zedekiah, the son of Josiah, king of Judah, even unto the *carrying away* of Jerusalem *captive* in the fifth month.

4 And the word of the Lord came to me, saying, 5 "Before I formed thee in the *bowels of thy mother,* I knew thee, and before thou camest forth out of the womb, I sanctified thee and made thee a prophet unto the nations."

6 And I said, "Ah, ah, ah, Lord God, behold: I cannot speak, for I am a child."

7 And the Lord said to me, "Say not, 'I am a child,' for thou shalt go to all that I shall send thee, and *whatsoever* I shall command thee, thou shalt speak. 8 Be not afraid at their presence, for I am with thee to deliver thee," saith the Lord. 9 And the Lord put forth his hand and touched my mouth, and the Lord said to me, "Behold: I have given my words in thy mouth. 10 Lo: I have set thee this day over the

tui te hodie super gentes et super regna ut evellas et destruas et disperdas et dissipes et aedifices et plantes."

11 Et factum est verbum Domini ad me, dicens, "Quid tu vides Hieremia ?"

Et dixi, "Virgam vigilantem ego video."

12 Et dixit Dominus ad me, "Bene vidisti, quia vigilabo ego super verbo meo ut faciam illud." 13 Et factum est verbum Domini secundo ad me, dicens, "Quid tu vides?"

Et dixi, "Ollam succensam ego video et faciem eius a facie aquilonis."

14 Et dixit Dominus ad me, "Ab aquilone pandetur malum super omnes habitatores terrae. 15 Quia ecce: ego convocabo omnes cognationes regnorum aquilonis," ait Dominus, "et venient et ponent unusquisque solium suum in introitu portarum Hierusalem et super omnes muros eius in circuitu et super universas urbes Iuda. 16 Et loquar iudicia mea cum eis, super omni malitia eorum, qui dereliquerunt me et libaverunt diis alienis et adoraverunt opus manuum suarum. 17 Tu, ergo, accinge lumbos tuos, et surge, et loquere ad eos omnia quae ego praecipio tibi. Ne formides a facie eorum, nec enim timere te faciam vultum eorum. 18 Ego quippe dedi te hodie in civitatem munitam et in columnam ferream et in murum aereum super omnem terram regibus Iuda, principibus eius, et sacerdotibus et populo terrae. 19 Et bellabunt adversum te et non praevalebunt quia tecum ego sum," ait Dominus, "ut liberem te."

nations and over the kingdoms to root up and to pull down and to waste and to destroy and to build and to plant."

11 And the word of the Lord came to me, saying, "What seest thou, Jeremiah?"

And I said, "I see a rod watching."

12 And the Lord said to me, "Thou hast seen well, for I will watch over my word to perform it." 13 And the word of the Lord came to me a second time, saying, "What seest thou?"

And I said, "I see a boiling caldron and the face thereof from the face of the north."

14 And the Lord said to me, "From the north shall an evil break forth upon all the inhabitants of the land. 15 For behold: I will call together all the families of the kingdoms of the north," saith the Lord, "and they shall come and shall set every one his throne in the entrance of the gates of Jerusalem and upon all the walls thereof round about and upon all the cities of Judah. 16 And I will pronounce my judgments against them, touching all their wickedness, who have forsaken me and have sacrificed to strange gods and have adored the work of their own hands. 17 Thou, therefore, gird up thy loins, and arise, and speak to them all that I command thee. Be not afraid at their presence, for I will make thee not to fear their countenance. 18 For *behold:* I have made thee this day a fortified city and a pillar of iron and a wall of brass over all the land to the kings of Judah, to the princes thereof, and to the priests and to the people of the land. 19 And they shall fight against thee and shall not prevail, for I am with thee," saith the Lord, "to deliver thee."

Caput 2

Et factum est verbum Domini ad me, dicens, 2 "Vade, et clama in auribus Hierusalem, dicens, 'Haec dicit Dominus: "Recordatus sum tui, miserans adulescentiam tuam et caritatem disponsationis tuae, quando secuta me es in deserto in terra quae non seminatur. 3 Sanctus Israhel Domino, primitiae frugum eius. Omnes qui devorant eum delinquent; mala venient super eos," dicit Dominus.'"

4 Audite verbum Domini, domus Iacob, et omnes cognationes domus Israhel. 5 Haec dicit Dominus: "Quid invenerunt patres vestri in me iniquitatis quia elongaverunt a me et ambulaverunt post vanitatem et vani facti sunt? 6 Et non dixerunt, 'Ubi est Dominus qui ascendere nos fecit de terra Aegypti, qui transduxit nos per desertum, per terram inhabitabilem et inviam, per terram sitis et imaginem mortis, per terram in qua non ambulavit vir, neque habitavit homo?' 7 Et induxi vos in terram Carmeli ut comederetis fructum eius et optima illius, et ingressi contaminastis terram meam et hereditatem meam posuistis in abominationem.

8 "Sacerdotes non dixerunt, 'Ubi est Dominus?' Et tenentes legem nescierunt me, et pastores praevaricati sunt in me, et prophetae prophetaverunt in Baal et idola secuti sunt. 9 Propterea adhuc iudicio contendam vobiscum," ait

Chapter 2

God expostulates with the Jews for their ingratitude and infidelity.

And the word of the Lord came to me, saying, 2 "Go, and cry in the ears of Jerusalem, saying, 'Thus saith the Lord: "I have remembered thee, pitying thy youth and the love of thy *espousals,* when thou followest me in the desert in a land that is not sown. 3 Israel is holy to the Lord, the first fruits of his increase. All they that devour him offend; evils shall come upon them," saith the Lord.'"

4 Hear ye the word of the Lord, O house of Jacob, and all ye families of the house of Israel. 5 Thus saith the Lord: "What iniquity have your fathers found in me that they are gone far from me and have walked after vanity and are become vain? 6 And they have not said, 'Where is the Lord that made us come up out of the land of Egypt, that led us through the desert, through a land uninhabited and unpassable, through a land of drought and the image of death, through a land wherein no man walked, nor any man dwelt?' 7 And I brought you into the land of Carmel to eat the fruit thereof and the best things thereof, and when ye entered in you defiled my land and made my inheritance an abomination.

8 "The priests did not say, 'Where is the Lord?' And they that held the law knew me not, and the pastors transgressed against me, and the prophets prophesied in Baal, and followed idols. 9 Therefore will I yet contend in judgment with

Dominus, "et cum filiis vestris disceptabo. 10 Transite ad insulas Cetthim, et videte, et in Cedar mittite, et considerate vehementer, et videte si factum est huiuscemodi. 11 Si mutavit gens deos suos, et certe ipsi non sunt dii, populus vero meus mutavit gloriam suam in idolum. 12 Obstupescite, caeli, super hoc, et portae eius, desolamini vehementer," dicit Dominus.

13 "Duo enim mala fecit populus meus. Me dereliquerunt, fontem aquae vivae, et foderunt sibi cisternas, cisternas dissipatas quae continere non valent aquas. 14 Numquid servus est Israhel aut vernaculus? Quare ergo est factus in praedam? 15 Super eum rugierunt leones, et dederunt vocem suam; posuerunt terram eius in solitudinem; civitates eius exustae sunt, et non est qui habitet in eis.

16 "Filii quoque Memfeos et Tafnes, constupraverunt te usque ad verticem. 17 Numquid non istud factum est tibi quia dereliquisti Dominum, Deum tuum, eo tempore quo ducebat te per viam? 18 Et nunc quid tibi vis in via Aegypti, ut bibas aquam turbidam? Et quid tibi cum via Assyriorum, ut bibas aquam fluminis? 19 Arguet te malitia tua, et aversio tua increpabit te. Scito, et vide quia malum et amarum est reliquisse te Dominum, Deum tuum, et non esse timorem mei apud te," dicit Dominus, Deus exercituum. 20 "A saeculo confregisti iugum meum; rupisti vincula mea, et dixisti, 'Non serviam.' In omni enim colle sublimi et sub omni ligno frondoso tu prosternebaris meretrix.

21 "Ego autem plantavi te vineam electam, omne semen verum; quomodo ergo conversa es mihi in pravum, vinea aliena? 22 Si laveris te nitro et multiplicaveris tibi herbam

you," saith the Lord, "and I will plead with your children. 10 Pass over to the isles of Kethim, and see, and send into Kedar, and consider diligently, and see if there hath been done any thing like this. 11 If a nation hath changed their gods, and indeed they are not gods, but my people have changed their glory into an idol. 12 Be astonished, O ye heavens, at this, and ye gates thereof, be very desolate," saith the Lord.

13 "For my people have done two evils. They have forsaken me, the fountain of living water, and have digged to themselves cisterns, broken cisterns that can hold no *water.* 14 Is Israel a bondman or a homeborn slave? Why then is he become prey? 15 The lions have roared upon him and have made a noise; they have made his land a wilderness; his cities are burnt down, and there is none to dwell in them.

16 "The children also of Memphis and of Tahpanhes have deflowered thee even to the crown of the head. 17 Hath not this been done to thee because thou hast forsaken the Lord, thy God, at that time when he led thee by the way? 18 And now what hast thou to do in the way of Egypt, to drink the troubled water? And what hast thou to do with the way of the Assyrians, to drink the water of the river? 19 Thy own wickedness shall reprove thee, and thy apostasy shall rebuke thee. Know thou, and see that it is an evil and a bitter thing for thee to have left the Lord, thy God, and that my fear is not with thee," saith the Lord, the God of hosts. 20 "Of old time thou hast broken my yoke; thou hast burst my bands, and thou sadist, 'I will not serve.' For on every high hill and under every green tree thou didst prostitute thyself.

21 "Yet I planted thee a chosen vineyard, all true seed; how then art thou turned unto me into that which is *good for nothing,* O strange vineyard? 22 Though thou wash thy-

borith, maculata es in iniquitate tua coram me," dicit Dominus Deus. 23 "Quomodo dicis, 'Non sum polluta; post Baalim non ambulavi'? Vide vias tuas in convalle; scito quid feceris, cursor levis explicans vias suas. 24 Onager adsuetus in solitudine in desiderio animae suae, adtraxit ventum amoris sui. Nullus avertet eam; omnes qui quaerunt eam non deficient; in menstruis eius invenient eam. 25 Prohibe pedem tuum a nuditate et guttur tuum a siti. Et dixisti, 'Desperavi; nequaquam faciam, adamavi quippe alienos, et post eos ambulabo.'

26 "Quomodo confunditur fur quando deprehenditur, sic confusi sunt domus Israhel, ipsi et reges eorum, principes et sacerdotes, et prophetae eorum. 27 Dicentes ligno, 'Pater meus es tu,' et lapidi, 'Tu me genuisti,' verterunt ad me tergum et non faciem, et in tempore adflictionis suae dicent, 'Surge, et libera nos.' 28 Ubi sunt dii tui, quos fecisti tibi? Surgant et liberent te in tempore adflictionis tuae, secundum numerum quippe civitatum tuarum erant dii tui, Iuda. 29 Quid vultis mecum iudicio contendere? Omnes dereliquistis me," dicit Dominus. 30 "Frustra percussi filios vestros; disciplinam non receperunt. Devoravit gladius vester prophetas vestros: quasi leo vastator generatio vestra."

31 Videte verbum Domini: "Numquid solitudo factus sum Israheli, aut terra serotina? Quare ergo dixit populus meus, 'Recessimus; non veniemus ultra ad te'? 32 Numquid obliviscetur virgo ornamenti sui aut sponsa fasciae

self with nitre and multiply to thyself the herb borith, thou art stained in thy iniquity before me," saith the Lord God. 23 "How canst thou say, 'I am not polluted, *and* I have not walked after Baalim'? See thy ways in the valley; know what thou hast done *as* a swift runner pursuing his course. 24 A wild ass accustomed to the wilderness in the desire of his heart, snuffed up the wind of his love. None shall turn her away; all that seek her shall not fail; in her monthly *filth* they shall find her. 25 Keep thy foot from being bare and thy throat from thirst. *But* thou saidst, 'I have lost all hope; I will not do it, for I have loved strangers, and I will walk after them.'

26 "As the thief is confounded when he is taken, so is the house of Israel confounded, they and their kings, their princes and their priests, and their prophets. 27 Saying to a stock, 'Thou art my father,' and to a stone, 'Thou hast begotten me,' they have turned their back to me and not their face, and in the time of their affliction they will say, 'Arise, and deliver us.' 28 Where are the gods, whom thou hast made thee? Let them arise and deliver thee in the time of thy affliction, for according to the number of thy cities were thy gods, O Judah. 29 Why will you contend with me in judgment? You have all forsaken me," saith the Lord. 30 "In vain have I struck your children; they have not received correction. Your sword hath devoured your prophets; your generation is like a ravaging lion."

31 See ye the word of the Lord: "Am I become a wilderness to Israel, or a lateward springing land? Why then have my people said, 'We are revolted; we will come to thee no more'? 32 Will a virgin forget her ornament, or a bride her

pectoralis suae? Populus vero meus oblitus est mei diebus innumeris. 33 Quid niteris bonam ostendere viam tuam ad quaerendam dilectionem, quae insuper et malitias tuas docuisti vias tuas, 34 et in alis tuis inventus est sanguis animarum pauperum et innocentium? Non in fossis inveni eos sed in omnibus quae supra memoravi. 35 Et dixisti, 'Absque peccato et innocens ego sum, et propterea avertatur furor tuus a me.' Ecce: ego iudicio contendam tecum, eo quod dixeris, 'Non peccavi.' 36 Quam vilis es facta nimis, iterans vias tuas! Et ab Aegypto confunderis, sicut confusa es ab Assur. 37 Nam et ab ista egredieris, et manus tuae erunt super caput tuum, quoniam obtrivit Dominus confidentiam tuam, et nihil habebis prosperum in ea."

Caput 3

"Vulgo dicitur, 'Si dimiserit vir uxorem suam, et recedens ab eo duxerit virum alterum, numquid revertetur ad eam ultra? Numquid non polluta et contaminata erit mulier illa?' Tu autem fornicata es cum amatoribus multis, tamen revertere ad me," dicit Dominus, "et ego suscipiam te.

stomacher? But my people hath forgotten me days without number. 33 Why dost thou endeavour to shew thy way good to seek my love, thou who has *also* taught thy malices to be thy ways, 34 and in thy *skirts* is found the blood of the souls of the poor and innocent? Not in ditches have I found them but in all places which I mentioned before. 35 And thou hast said, 'I am without sin and am innocent, and therefore let thy anger be turned away from me.' Behold: I will contend with thee in judgment, because thou hast said, 'I have not sinned.' 36 How exceeding base art thou become, going the same ways over again! And thou shalt be *ashamed* of Egypt, as thou wast *ashamed* of Assyria. 37 For from thence also thou shalt go, and thy hand shall be upon thy head, for the Lord hath destroyed thy trust, and thou shalt have nothing prosperous therein."

Chapter 3

God invites the rebel Jews to return to him, with a promise
to receive them. He foretells the conversion of the Gentiles.

"It is commonly said, 'If a man put away his wife, and she go from him and marry another man, shall he return to her any more? Shall not that woman be polluted and defiled?' But thou hast prostituted thyself to many lovers, nevertheless return to me," saith the Lord, "and I will receive thee.

2 Leva oculos tuos in directum, et vide ubi non prostrata sis. In viis sedebas, expectans eos quasi latro in solitudine, et polluisti terram in fornicationibus tuis et in malitiis tuis. 3 Quam ob rem prohibitae sunt stillae pluviarum, et serotinus imber non fuit; frons meretricis facta est; tibi noluisti erubescere. 4 Ergo saltim amodo voca me, 'Pater meus, dux virginitatis meae, tu es. 5 Numquid irasceris in perpetuum, aut perseverabis in finem?' Ecce: locuta es et fecisti mala et potuisti."

6 Et dixit Dominus ad me in diebus Iosiae Regis, "Numquid vidisti quae fecerit aversatrix Israhel? Abiit sibimet super omnem montem excelsum et sub omni ligno frondoso et fornicata est ibi. 7 Et dixi, cum fecisset haec omnia, 'Ad me revertere,' et non est reversa. Et vidit praevaricatrix soror eius Iuda 8 quia pro eo quod moechata esset aversatrix Israhel, dimisissem eamet dedissem ei libellum repudii, et non timuit praevaricatrix Iuda, soror eius, sed abiit et fornicata est etiam ipsa. 9 Et facilitate fornicationis suae contaminavit terram et moechata est cum lapide et ligno. 10 Et in omnibus his non est reversa ad me praevaricatrix soror eius Iuda in toto corde suo sed in mendacio," ait Dominus.

11 Et dixit Dominus ad me, "Iustificavit animam suam aversatrix Israhel conparatione praevaricatricis Iuda. 12 Vade, et clama sermones istos contra aquilonem, et dices, '"Revertere, aversatrix Israhel," ait Dominus, "et non avertam faciem meam a vobis, quia sanctus ego sum," dicit Dominus, "et non irascar in perpetuum. 13 Verumtamen scito iniquitatem tuam, quia in Dominum, Deum tuum, praevaricata es, et dispersisti vias tuas alienis sub omni ligno fron-

2 Lift up thy eyes *on high,* and see where thou hast not prostituted thyself. Thou didst sit in the ways, waiting for them as a robber in the wilderness, and thou hast polluted the land with thy fornications and with thy wickedness. 3 Therefore the showers were withholden, and there was no lateward rain; thou hadst a harlot's forehead, thou wouldst not blush. 4 Therefore at least at this time call to me, 'Thou art my father, the guide of my virginity. 5 Wilt thou be angry for ever, or wilt thou continue until the end?' Behold: thou hast spoken and hast done evil things and hast been able."

6 And the Lord said to me in the days of King Josiah, "Hast thou seen what rebellious Israel hast done? She hath gone of herself upon every high mountain and under every green tree and hath played the harlot there. 7 And when she had done all these things, I said, 'Return to me,' and she did not return. And her treacherous sister Judah saw 8 that because the rebellious Israel had played the harlot, I had put her away, and had given her a bill of divorce, *yet* her treacherous sister Judah was not afraid, but went and played the harlot also herself. 9 And by the facility of her fornication she defiled the land and played the harlot with *stones* and *with stocks.* 10 And *after* all this, her treacherous sister Judah hath not returned to me with her whole heart, but with falsehood," saith the Lord.

11 And the Lord said to me, "The rebellious Israel hath justified her soul in comparison of the treacherous Judah. 12 Go, and proclaim these words toward the north, and thou shalt say, '"Return, O rebellious Israel," saith the Lord, "and I will not turn away my face from you, for I am holy," saith the Lord, "and I will not be angry for ever. 13 But yet *acknowledge* thy iniquity, that thou hast transgressed against the Lord, thy God, and thou hast scattered thy ways to strang-

doso et vocem meam non audisti," ait Dominus. 14 "Convertimini, filii revertentes," dicit Dominus, "quia ego vir vester, et adsumam vos, unum de civitate et duos de cognatione, et introducam vos in Sion. 15 Et dabo vobis pastores iuxta cor meum, et pascent vos scientia et doctrina.

16 "Cumque multiplicati fueritis et creveritis in terra in diebus illis," ait Dominus, "non dicent ultra. Arca testamenti Domini, neque ascendet super cor, neque recordabuntur illius, nec visitabitur, nec fiet ultra. 17 In tempore illo vocabunt Hierusalem solium Domini, et congregabuntur ad eam omnes gentes in nomine Domini in Hierusalem, et non ambulabunt post pravitatem cordis sui pessimi. 18 In diebus illis ibit domus Iuda ad domum Israhel, et venient simul de terra aquilonis ad terram quam dedi patribus vestris. 19 Ego autem dixi, 'Quomodo ponam te in filiis et tribuam tibi terram desiderabilem, hereditatem praeclaram exercituum Gentium?' Et dixi, 'Patrem vocabis me et post me ingredi non cessabis.' 20 Sed quomodo si contemnat mulier amatorem suum, sic contempsit me domus Israhel," dicit Dominus.

21 "Vox in viis audita est: ploratus et ululatus filiorum Israhel, quoniam iniquam fecerunt viam suam; obliti sunt Domini, Dei sui. 22 Convertimini, filii revertentes, et sanabo aversiones vestras."

"Ecce: nos venimus ad te, tu enim es Dominus, Deus noster. 23 Vere mendaces erant colles et multitudo montium;

ers under every green tree and hast not heard my voice," saith the Lord. 14 "Return, O ye revolting children," saith the Lord, "for I am your husband, and I will take you, one of a city and two of a kindred, and will bring you into Zion. 15 And I will give you pastors according to my own heart, and they shall feed you with knowledge and doctrine.

16 "And when you shall be multiplied and increase in the land in those days," saith the Lord, "they shall say no more. The ark of the covenant of the Lord, neither shall it come upon the heart, neither shall they remember it, neither shall it be visited, neither shall that be done any more. 17 At that time Jerusalem shall be called the throne of the Lord, and all the nations shall be gathered together to it in the name of the Lord to Jerusalem, and they shall not walk after the perversity of their most wicked heart. 18 In those days the house of Judah shall go to the house of Israel, and they shall come together out of the land of the north to the land which I gave to your fathers. 19 But I said, 'How shall I put thee among the children and give thee a *lovely* land, the goodly inheritance of the armies of the Gentiles?' And I said, 'Thou shalt call me father and shalt not cease to walk after me.' 20 But as a woman that despiseth her lover, so hath the house of Israel despised me," saith the Lord.

21 "A voice was heard in the highways: weeping and howling of the children of Israel, because they have made their way wicked; they have forgotten the Lord, their God. 22 Return, you rebellious children, and I will heal your rebellions."

"Behold: we come to thee, for thou art the Lord, our God. 23 In very deed the hills were liars and the multitude of the

vere in Domino, Deo nostro, salus Israhel. ²⁴ Confusio comedit laborem patrum nostrorum ab adulescentia nostra,
greges eorum et armenta eorum, filios eorum et filias eorum.
²⁵ Dormiemus in confusione nostra, et operiet nos ignominia nostra, quoniam Domino, Deo nostro, peccavimus, nos
et patres nostri ab adulescentia nostra usque ad hanc diem,
et non audivimus vocem Domini, Dei nostri."

Caput 4

"Si converteris, Israhel," ait Dominus, "ad me convertere.
Si abstuleris offendicula tua a facie mea, non commoveberis.
² Et iurabis, vivit Dominus, in veritate et in iudicio et in iustitia, et benedicent eum Gentes ipsumque laudabunt."

³ Haec enim dicit Dominus viro Iuda et Hierusalem: "No-
vate vobis novale, et nolite serere super spinas. ⁴ Circumci-
dimini Domino, et auferte praeputia cordium vestrorum,
viri Iuda et habitatores Hierusalem, ne forte egrediatur ut
ignis indignatio mea et succendatur, et non sit qui extinguat
propter malitiam cogitationum vestrarum.

mountains; truly in the Lord, our God, is the salvation of Israel. 24 Confusion hath devoured the labor of our fathers from our youth, their flocks and their herds, their sons and their daughters. 25 We shall sleep in our confusion, and our shame shall cover us, because we have sinned against the Lord, our God, we and our fathers from our youth even to this day, and we have not hearkened to the voice of the Lord, our God."

Chapter 4

An admonition to sincere repentance and circumcision of the heart, with threats of grievous punishment to those that persist in sin.

"If thou wilt return, O Israel," saith the Lord, "return to me. If thou wilt take away thy stumbling blocks out of my sight, thou shalt not be moved. 2 And thou shalt swear, as the Lord liveth, in truth and in judgment and in justice, and the Gentiles shall bless him and shall praise him."

3 For thus saith the Lord to the *men* of Judah and Jerusalem: "Break up anew your fallow ground, and sow not upon thorns. 4 Be circumcised to the Lord, and take away the foreskins of your hearts, ye men of Judah and ye inhabitants of Jerusalem, *lest* my indignation come forth like fire and burn, and there be none that can quench it because of the wickedness of your thoughts.

5 "Adnuntiate in Iuda, et in Hierusalem auditum facite; loquimini, et canite tuba in terra; clamate fortiter, et dicite, 'Congregamini, et ingrediamur civitates munitas.' 6 Levate signum in Sion. Confortamini; nolite stare, quia malum ego adduco ab aquilone et contritionem magnam. 7 Ascendit leo de cubili suo, et praedo gentium se levavit; egressus est de loco suo ut ponat terram tuam in desolationem; civitates tuae vastabuntur, remanentes absque habitatore. 8 Super hoc accingite vos ciliciis, plangite, et ululate, quia non est aversa ira furoris Domini a nobis.

9 "Et erit in die illa," dicit Dominus. "Peribit cor regis et cor principum, et obstupescent sacerdotes, et prophetae consternabuntur."

10 Et dixi, "Heu, heu, heu, Domine Deus, ergone decepisti populum istum et Hierusalem, dicens, 'Pax erit vobis, et ecce: pervenit gladius usque ad animam'?"

11 In tempore illo dicetur populo huic et Hierusalem: "Ventus urens in viis quae sunt in deserto viae filiae populi mei, non ad ventilandum et ad purgandum. 12 Spiritus plenus ex his veniet mihi, et nunc ego loquar iudicia mea cum eis. 13 Ecce: quasi nubes ascendet, et quasi tempestas currus eius; velociores aquilis equi illius, vae nobis, quoniam vastati sumus. 14 Lava a malitia cor tuum, Hierusalem, ut salva fias; usquequo morabuntur in te cogitationes noxiae?

15 "Vox enim adnuntiantis a Dan, et notum facientis idolum de Monte Ephraim: 16 'Dicite gentibus, "Ecce: auditum est in Hierusalem custodes venire de terra longinqua

5 "Declare ye in Judah, and make it heard in Jerusalem; speak, and sound with the trumpet in the land; cry *aloud,* and say, 'Assemble yourselves, and let us go into strong cities.' 6 Set up the standard in Zion. Strengthen yourselves; stay not, for I bring evil from the north and great destruction. 7 The lion is come up out of his den, and the robber of nations hath roused himself; he is come forth out of his place to make thy land desolate; thy cities shall be laid waste, remaining without an inhabitant. 8 For this gird yourselves with haircloth, lament, and howl, for the fierce anger of the Lord is not turned away from us.

9 "And it shall come to pass in that day," saith the Lord, *"that* the heart of the king shall perish and the heart of the princes, and the priests shall be astonished, and the prophets shall be amazed."

10 And I said, "Alas, alas, alas, O Lord God, hast thou then deceived this people and Jerusalem, saying, 'You shall have peace, and behold: the sword reacheth even to the soul'?"

11 At that time it shall be said to this people and to Jerusalem: "A burning wind is in the ways that are in the desert of the way of the daughter of my people not to fan, nor to cleanse. 12 A full wind from these places shall come to me, and now I will speak my judgments with them. 13 Behold: he shall come up as a cloud, and his chariots as a tempest; his horses are swifter than eagles; woe unto us, for we are laid waste. 14 Wash thy heart from wickedness, O Jerusalem, that thou mayst be saved; how long shall hurtful thoughts abide in thee?

15 "For a voice of one declaring from Dan, and giving notice of the idol from Mount Ephraim: 16 'Say ye to the nations, "Behold: it is heard in Jerusalem that guards are

et dare super civitates Iuda vocem suam. 17 'Quasi custodes agrorum facti sunt super eam in gyro quia me ad iracundiam provocavit,' ait Dominus. 18 Viae tuae et cogitationes tuae fecerunt haec tibi; ista malitia tua quia amara, quia tetigit cor tuum.""'"

19 Ventrem meum, ventrem meum doleo; sensus cordis mei turbati sunt in me; non tacebo, quoniam vocem bucinae audivit anima mea, clamorem proelii. 20 Contritio super contritionem vocata est, et vastata est omnis terra; repente vastata sunt tabernacula mea, subito pelles meae. 21 Usquequo videbo fugientem, audiam vocem bucinae? 22 Quia stultus populus meus me non cognovit; filii insipientes sunt et vecordes; sapientes sunt ut faciant mala, bene autem facere nescierunt.

23 Aspexi terram, et ecce: vacua erat et nihili, et caelos, et non erat lux in eis. 24 Vidi montes, et ecce: movebantur, et omnes colles conturbati sunt. 25 Intuitus sum, et non erat homo, et omne volatile caeli recessit. 26 Aspexi, et ecce: Carmelus desertus, et omnes urbes eius destructae sunt a facie Domini et a facie irae furoris eius.

27 Haec enim dicit Dominus, "Deserta erit omnis terra, sed tamen consummationem non faciam. 28 Lugebit terra, et maerebunt caeli desuper, eo quod locutus sum; cogitavi, et non paenituit me, nec aversus sum ab eo."

29 A voce equitis et mittentis sagittam, fugit omnis civitas; ingressi sunt ardua et ascenderunt rupes; universae

coming from a far country and give out their voice against the cities of Judah. 17 'They are set round about her as keepers of fields because she hath provoked me to wrath,' saith the Lord. 18 Thy ways and thy devices have brought these things upon thee; this is thy wickedness because it is bitter, because it hath touched thy heart."'"

19 My bowels, my bowels are in pain; the senses of my heart are troubled within me; I will not hold my peace, for my soul hath heard the sound of the trumpet, the cry of battle. 20 Destruction upon destruction is called for, and all the earth is laid waste; my tents are destroyed on a sudden *and* my pavilions in a moment. 21 How long shall I see men fleeing away, how long shall I hear the sound of the trumpet? 22 For my foolish people have not known me, they are foolish and senseless children; they are wise to do evil, but to do good they have no knowledge.

23 I beheld the earth, and lo: it was void and *nothing,* and the heavens, and there was no light in them. 24 I looked upon the mountains, and behold: they trembled, and all the hills were troubled. 25 I beheld, and *lo:* there was no man, and all the birds of the air were gone. 26 I looked, and behold: Carmel was a wilderness, and all its cities were destroyed at the presence of the Lord and at the presence of the wrath of his indignation.

27 For thus saith the Lord, "All the land shall be desolate, but yet I will not utterly destroy. 28 The earth shall mourn, and the heavens shall lament from above, because I have spoken; I have purposed, and I have not repented, neither am I turned away from it."

29 At the voice of the horsemen and the archers, all the city is fled away; they have entered into thickets and have

urbes derelictae sunt, et non habitat in eis homo. 30 Tu autem vastata quid facies? Cum vestieris te coccino, cum ornata fueris monili aureo, et pinxeris stibio oculos tuos, frustra conponeris; contempserunt te amatores tui; animam tuam quaerent. 31 Vocem enim quasi parturientis audivi, angustias ut puerperae, vox filiae Sion inter morientes expandentesque manus suas: "Vae mihi, quia defecit anima mea propter interfectos."

Caput 5

Circuite vias Hierusalem, et aspicite, et considerate, et quaerite in plateis eius, an inveniatis virum facientem iudicium et quaerentem fidem, et propitius ero ei. 2 Quod si etiam, "Vivit Dominus," dixerint, et hoc falso iurabunt. 3 Domine, oculi tui respiciunt fidem; percussisti eos, et non doluerunt; adtrivisti eos, et rennuerunt accipere disciplinam; induraverunt facies suas supra petram, et noluerunt reverti. 4 Ego autem dixi, "Forsitan pauperes sunt et stulti,

climbed up the rocks; all the cities are forsaken, and there dwelleth not a man in them. 30 But when thou art spoiled what wilt thou do? Though thou deckest thee with ornaments of gold, and paintest thy eyes with stibic stone, thou shalt dress thyself out in vain; thy lovers have despised thee; they will seek thy life. 31 For I have heard the voice as of a woman in travail, anguishes as of a woman in labour of a child, the voice of the daughter of Zion *dying away, spreading* her hands: "Woe is me, for my soul hath fainted because of them that are slain."

Chapter 5

The judgments of God shall fall upon the Jews for their manifold sins.

G o *about through* the streets of Jerusalem, and see, and consider, and seek in the broad places thereof, if you can find a man that executeth judgment, and seeketh faith, and I will be merciful unto it. 2 And though they say, "The Lord liveth," this also they will swear falsely. 3 O Lord, thy eyes are upon truth; thou hast struck them, and they have not grieved; thou hast bruised them, and they have refused to receive correction; they have made their faces harder than the rock, and they have refused to return. 4 But I said, "Perhaps these are poor and foolish, that know not the way of

ignorantes viam Domini, iudicium Dei sui. 5 Ibo igitur ad optimates, et loquar eis, ipsi enim cognoverunt viam Domini, iudicium Dei sui." Et ecce: magis hii simul confregerunt iugum; ruperunt vincula. 6 Idcirco percussit eos leo de silva; lupus ad vesperam vastavit eos, pardus vigilans super civitates eorum; omnis qui egressus fuerit ex eis capietur, quia multiplicatae sunt praevaricationes eorum; confortatae sunt aversiones eorum.

7 "Super quo propitius tibi esse potero? Filii tui dereliquerunt me et iurant in his qui non sunt dii; saturavi eos, et moechati sunt, et in domo meretricis luxuriabantur. 8 Equi amatores et admissarii facti sunt; unusquisque ad uxorem proximi sui hinniebat. 9 Numquid super his non visitabo," dicit Dominus, "et in gente tali non ulciscetur anima mea? 10 Ascendite muros eius, et dissipate, consummationem autem nolite facere; auferte propagines eius, quia non sunt Domini. 11 Praevaricatione enim praevaricata est in me domus Israhel et domus Iuda," ait Dominus.

12 Negaverunt Dominum et dixerunt, "Non est ipse, neque veniet super nos malum; gladium et famem non videbimus. 13 Prophetae fuerunt in ventum locuti, et responsum non fuit in eis; haec ergo evenient illis."

14 Haec dicit Dominus, Deus exercituum: "Quia locuti estis verbum istud, ecce: ego do verba mea in ore tuo in ignem, et populum istum in ligna, et vorabit eos. 15 Ecce: ego adducam super vos gentem de longinquo, domus Israhel," ait Dominus, "gentem robustam, gentem antiquam, gentem cuius ignorabis linguam, nec intelleges quid loqua-

the Lord, the judgment of their God. 5 I will go therefore to the great men, and I will speak to them, for they have known the way of the Lord, the judgment of their God." And behold: these have together broken the yoke more, *and* have burst the bonds. 6 Wherefore a lion out of the wood hath slain them; a wolf in the evening hath spoiled them; a leopard watcheth for their cities; every one that shall go out thence shall be taken, because their transgressions are multiplied; their rebellions are strengthened.

7 *"How* can I be merciful to thee? Thy children have forsaken me and swear by them that are not gods; I fed them to the full, and they committed adultery, and rioted in the harlot's house. 8 They are become as amorous horses and stallions; every one neighed after his neighbour's wife. 9 Shall I not visit for these things," saith the Lord, "and shall not my soul take revenge on such a nation? 10 Scale the walls thereof, and throw them down, but do not *utterly destroy;* take away the branches thereof, because they are not the Lord's. 11 For the house of Israel and the house of Judah have *greatly* transgressed against me," saith the Lord.

12 They have denied the Lord and said, "It is not he, and the evil shall not come upon us; we shall not see the sword and famine. 13 The prophets have spoken in the wind, and there was no *word of God* in them; these things therefore shall befall them."

14 Thus saith the Lord, the God of hosts: "Because you have spoken this word, behold: I will make my words in thy mouth as fire, and this people as wood, and it shall devour them. 15 Behold: I will bring upon you a nation from afar, O house of Israel," saith the Lord, "a strong nation, an ancient nation, a nation whose language thou shalt not know, nor

tur. 16 Faretra eius quasi sepulchrum patens: universi fortes.
17 Et comedet segetes tuas et panem tuum; devorabit filios
tuos et filias tuas; comedet gregem tuum et armenta tua;
comedet vineam tuam et ficum tuam, et conteret urbes munitas tuas, in quibus tu habes fiduciam, gladio. 18 Verumtamen in diebus illis," ait Dominus, "non faciam vos in
consummationem. 19 Quod si dixeritis, 'Quare fecit Dominus, Deus noster, nobis haec omnia?' dices ad eos, 'Sicut dereliquistis me et servistis deo alieno in terra vestra, sic servietis alienis in terra non vestra.'

20 "Adnuntiate hoc domui Iacob et auditum facite in Iuda,
dicentes, 21 'Audi, popule stulte, qui non habes cor, qui habentes oculos non videtis, et aures et non auditis. 22 "Me
ergo non timebitis," ait Dominus, "et a facie mea non dole-
bitis, qui posui harenam terminum mari, praeceptum sempiternum quod non praeteribit, et commovebuntur et non
poterunt, et intumescent fluctus eius et non transibunt illud? 23 Populo autem huic factum est cor incredulum et
exasperans; recesserunt et abierunt. 24 Et non dixerunt in
corde suo, 'Metuamus Dominum, Deum nostrum, qui dat
nobis pluviam temporaneam et serotinam in tempore suo,
plenitudinem annuae messis custodientem nobis.' 25 Iniquitates vestrae declinaverunt haec, et peccata vestra prohibue-
runt bonum a vobis.

26 ""Quia inventi sunt in populo meo impii insidiantes
quasi aucupes, laqueos ponentes et pedicas ad capiendos viros. 27 Sicut decipula plena avibus, sic domus eorum plenae
dolo; ideo magnificati sunt et ditati. 28 Incrassati sunt et

understand what they say. 16 Their quiver is as an open sepulchre: they are all valiant. 17 And they shall eat up thy corn
and thy bread; they shall devour thy sons and thy daughters;
they shall eat up thy flocks and thy herds; they shall eat thy
vineyards and thy figs, and with the sword they shall destroy
thy strong cities, wherein thou trustest. 18 Nevertheless in
those days," saith the Lord, "I will not bring you to *utter
destruction*. 19 And if you shall say, 'Why hath the Lord, our
God, done all these things to us?' thou shalt say to them, 'As
you have forsaken me and served a strange god in your own
land, so shall you serve strangers in a land that is not your
own.'

20 "Declare ye this to the house of Jacob, and publish it in
Judah, saying, 21 'Hear, O foolish people, *and without understanding,* who have eyes and see not, and ears and hear not.
22 "Will not you then fear me," saith the Lord, "and will you
not *repent* at my presence? I have set the sand a bound for
the sea, an everlasting ordinance which it shall not pass over,
and the waves thereof shall toss themselves and shall not
prevail, *they* shall swell, and shall not pass over it. 23 But the
heart of this people is become hard of belief and provoking,
they are revolted and gone away. 24 And they have not said in
their heart, 'Let us fear the Lord, our God, who giveth us the
early and the latter rain in due season, who preserveth for
us the fullness of the yearly harvest.' 25 Your iniquities have
turned these things away, and your sins have withholden
good *things* from you.

26 ""For among my people are found wicked men that lie
in wait as fowlers, setting snares and traps to catch men.
27 As a net is full of birds, so their houses are full of deceit;
therefore are they become great and enriched. 28 They are

inpinguati et praeterierunt sermones meos pessime. Causam viduae non iudicaverunt; causam pupilli non direxerunt, et iudicium pauperum non iudicaverunt. 29 Numquid super his non visitabo," dicit Dominus, "aut super gentem huiuscemodi non ulciscetur anima mea? 30 Stupor et mirabilia facta sunt in terra. 31 Prophetae prophetabant mendacium, et sacerdotes adplaudebant manibus suis, et populus meus dilexit talia. Quid igitur fiet in novissimo eius?""""

Caput 6

Confortamini, filii Beniamin, in medio Hierusalem, et in Thecua clangite bucina, et super Bethaccharem levate vexillum, quia malum visum est ab aquilone et contritio magna. 2 Speciosae et delicatae adsimilavi filiam Sion. 3 Ad eam venient pastores et greges eorum; fixerunt in ea tentoria in circuitu pascet; unusquisque eos qui sub manu sua sunt. 4 Sanctificate super eam bellum; consurgite, et ascendamus in meridie. Vae nobis, quia declinavit dies, quia longiores

grown gross and fat and have most wickedly transgressed my words. They have not judged the cause of the widow; they have not managed the cause of the fatherless; and they have not judged the judgment of the poor. 29 Shall I not visit for these things," saith the Lord, "or shall not my soul take revenge on such a nation? 30 Astonishing and wonderful things have been done in the land. 31 The prophets prophesied falsehood, and the priests clapped their hands, and my people loved such things. What then shall be done in the end thereof?""

Chapter 6

The evils that threaten Jerusalem. She is invited to return and walk in the good way and not to rely on sacrifices without obedience.

Strengthen yourselves, ye sons of Benjamin, in the midst of Jerusalem, and sound the trumpet in Tekoa, and set up the standard over Beth-haccherem, for evil is seen out of the north and a great destruction. 2 I have likened the daughter of Zion to a beautiful and delicate woman. 3 The shepherds shall come to her with their flocks; they have pitched their tents against her round about; every one shall feed them that are under his hand. 4 Prepare ye war against her; arise, and let us go up at midday. Woe unto us, for the day is

factae sunt umbrae vesperi. 5 Surgite, et ascendamus in nocte, et dissipemus domos eius.

6 Quia haec dicit Dominus exercituum: "Caedite lignum eius, effundite circa Hierusalem aggerem. Haec est civitas visitationis; omnis calumnia in medio eius. 7 Sicut frigidam facit cisterna aquam suam, sic frigidam fecit malitiam suam; iniquitas et vastitas audietur in ea; coram me semper infirmitas et plaga. 8 Erudire, Hierusalem, ne forte recedat anima mea a te, ne forte ponam te desertam, terram inhabitabilem."

9 Haec dicit Dominus exercituum: "Usque ad racemum colligent quasi in vinea reliquias Israhel; converte manum tuam quasi vindemiator ad cartallum."

10 Cui loquar, et quem contestabor, ut audiat? Ecce: incircumcisae aures eorum, et audire non possunt. Ecce: verbum Domini factum est eis in obprobrium, et non suscipient illud. 11 Idcirco furore Domini plenus sum; laboravi sustinens. Effunde super parvulum foris et super concilium iuvenum simul, vir enim cum muliere capietur, senex cum pleno dierum.

12 "Et transibunt domus eorum ad alteros, agri et uxores pariter, quia extendam manum meam super habitantes terram," dicit Dominus. 13 "A minore quippe usque ad maiorem, omnes avaritiae student, et a propheta usque ad sacerdotem, cuncti faciunt dolum. 14 Et curabant contritionem filiae populi mei cum ignominia, dicentes, 'Pax, pax,' et non erat pax. 15 Confusi sunt quia abominationem fecerunt, quin potius

declined, for the shadows of the evening are grown longer.
5 Arise, and let us go up in the night, and destroy her houses."

6 For thus saith the Lord of hosts, "Hew down her trees; cast up a trench about Jerusalem. This is the city to be visited; all oppression is in the midst of her. 7 As a cistern maketh its water cold, so hath she made her wickedness cold; violence and spoil shall be heard in her; infirmity and stripes are continually before me. 8 Be thou instructed, O Jerusalem, *lest* my soul depart from thee, *lest* I make thee desolate, a land uninhabited."

9 Thus saith the Lord of hosts, "They shall gather the remains of Israel as in a vine, even to one cluster; turn back thy hand as a grape-gatherer into the basket."

10 To whom shall I speak, and to whom shall I testify, that he may hear? Behold: their ears are uncircumcised, and they cannot hear. Behold: the word of the Lord is become unto them a reproach, and they will not receive it. 11 Therefore am I full of the fury of the Lord; I am weary with holding in; pour it out upon the child abroad, and upon the council of the young men together, for man and woman shall be taken, the ancient and he that is full of days.

12 "And their houses shall be turned over to others, with their lands and their wives together, for I will stretch for my hand upon the inhabitants of the land," saith the Lord. 13 "For from the *least* of them even to the *greatest,* all *are given* to covetousness, and from the prophet even to the priest, all *are guilty of* deceit. 14 And they healed the *breach* of the daughter of my people disgracefully, saying, 'Peace, peace,' and there was no peace. 15 They were confounded because they committed abomination, yea, rather they were not

confusione non sunt confusi, et erubescere nescierunt, quam ob rem cadent inter ruentes; in tempore visitationis suae corruent," dicit Dominus.

16 Haec dicit Dominus: "State super vias, et videte, et interrogate de semitis antiquis quae sit via bona, et ambulate in ea, et invenietis refrigerium animabus vestris. Et dixerunt, 'Non ambulabimus.' 17 Et constitui super vos speculatores: 'Audite vocem tubae.' Et dixerunt 'Non audiemus.' 18 Ideo audite, gentes, et cognosce, congregatio, quanta ego faciam eis. 19 Audi, terra; ecce: ego adducam mala super populum istum, fructum cogitationum eius, quia verba mea non audierunt, et legem meam proiecerunt. 20 Ut quid mihi tus de Saba adfertis et calamum suave olentem de terra longinqua? Holocaustomata vestra non sunt accepta, et victimae vestrae non placuerunt mihi."

21 Propterea haec dicit Dominus: "Ecce: ego dabo in populum istum ruinas, et ruent in eis patres et filii simul; vicinus et proximus et peribunt."

22 Haec dicit Dominus: "Ecce: populus venit de terra aquilonis, et gens magna consurget a finibus terrae. 23 Sagittam et scutum arripiet; crudelis est et non miserebitur. Vox eius quasi mare sonabit, et super equos ascendent, praeparati quasi vir ad proelium adversum te, filia Sion!"

24 Audivimus famam eius; dissolutae sunt manus nostrae. Tribulatio adprehendit nos dolores ut parturientem. 25 Nolite exire ad agros, et in via ne ambuletis, quoniam gladius inimici pavor in circuitu. 26 Filia populi mei, accingere

confounded with confusion, and they knew not how to blush, wherefore they shall fall among them that fall; in the time of their visitation they shall fall down," saith the Lord.

16 Thus saith the Lord: "Stand ye on the ways, and see, and ask *for* the old paths which is the good way, and walk ye in it, and you shall find refreshment for your souls. And they said, 'We will not walk.' 17 And I appointed watchmen over you, *saying,* 'Hearken ye to the sound of the trumpet.' And they said, 'We will not hearken.' 18 Therefore hear, ye nations, and know, O congregation, what great things I will do to them. 19 Hear, O earth; behold: I will bring evils upon this people, the fruits of their own thoughts, because they have not heard my words, and they have cast away my law. 20 To what purpose do you bring me frankincense from Sheba and the sweet smelling cane from a far country? Your holocausts are not acceptable, nor are your sacrifices pleasing to me."

21 Therefore thus saith the Lord, "Behold: I will bring destruction upon this people, by which fathers and sons together shall fall, neighbour and *kinsman* shall perish."

22 Thus saith the Lord, "Behold: a people cometh from the land of the north, and a great nation shall rise up from the ends of the earth. 23 They shall lay hold on arrow and shield; they are cruel and will have no mercy. Their voice shall roar like the sea, and they shall mount upon horses, prepared as *men* for war against thee, O daughter of Zion!"

24 We have heard the fame thereof; our hands grow feeble. Anguish hath taken hold of us as a woman in labor. 25 Go not out into the fields, nor walk in the high way, for the sword of the enemy *and* fear is on every side. 26 Gird thee with sackcloth, O daughter of my people, and sprinkle thee

cilicio, et conspergere cinere; luctum unigeniti fac tibi, planctum amarum, quia repente veniet vastator super nos.

27 "Probatorem dedi te in populo meo robustum, et scies et probabis viam eorum. 28 Omnes isti principes declinantes, ambulantes fraudulenter; aes et ferrum: universi corrupti sunt. 29 Defecit sufflatorium; in igne consumptum est plumbum; frustra conflavit conflator, malitiae enim eorum non sunt consumptae. 30 Argentum reprobum vocate eos, quia Dominus proiecit illos."

Caput 7

Verbum quod factum est ad Hieremiam a Domino, dicens, 2 "Sta in porta domus Domini, et praedica ibi verbum istud, et dic 'Audite verbum Domini, omnis Iuda qui ingredimini per portas has ut adoretis Dominum. 3 Haec dicit Dominus exercituum, Deus Israhel: "Bonas facite vias vestras et studia vestra, et habitabo vobiscum in loco isto. 4 Nolite confidere in verbis mendacii, dicentes, 'Templum Domini, templum Domini, templum Domini est.' 5 Quoniam si bene direxeritis vias vestras et studia vestra, si feceritis iudicium

with ashes; make thee mourning as for an only son, a bitter lamentation, because the destroyer shall suddenly come upon us.

27 "I have set thee for a strong trier among my people, and thou shalt know and prove their way. 28 All of these princes go out of the way; they walk deceitfully; *they are* brass and iron; they are all corrupted. 29 The bellows have failed; the lead is consumed in the fire; the founder hath melted in vain, for their wicked deeds are not consumed. 30 Call them reprobate silver, for the Lord hath rejected them."

Chapter 7

The temple of God shall not protect a sinful people without a sincere conversion. The Lord will not receive the prayers of the prophet for them because they are obstinate in their sins.

The word that came to Jeremiah from the Lord, saying, 2 "Stand in the gate of the house of the Lord, and proclaim there this word, and say, 'Hear ye the word of the Lord, all ye men of Judah, that enter in at these gates to adore the Lord. 3 Thus saith the Lord of hosts, the God of Israel, "Make your ways and your doings good, and I will dwell with you in this place. 4 Trust not in lying words, saying, 'The temple of the Lord, the temple of the Lord, it is the temple of the Lord.' 5 For if you will order well your ways and your doings, if you

inter virum et proximum eius, 6 advenae et pupillo et viduae non feceritis calumniam, nec sanguinem innocentem effuderitis in loco hoc, et post deos alienos non ambulaveritis in malum vobismet ipsis, 7 habitabo vobiscum in loco isto in terra quam dedi patribus vestris a saeculo et usque in saeculum.

8 ""Ecce: vos confiditis vobis in sermonibus mendacii qui non proderunt vobis, 9 furari, occidere, adulterari, iurare mendaciter, libare Baalim, et ire post deos alienos quos ignoratis. 10 Et venistis, et stetistis coram me in domo hac, in qua invocatum est nomen meum, et dixistis, 'Liberati sumus eo quod fecerimus omnes abominationes istas.'

11 ""Numquid ergo spelunca latronum facta est domus ista, in qua invocatum est nomen meum, in oculis vestris? Ego, ego sum. Ego vidi," dicit Dominus. 12 "Ite ad locum meum in Silo, ubi habitavit nomen meum a principio, et videte quae fecerim ei propter malitiam populi mei Israhel. 13 Et nunc quia fecistis omnia opera haec," dicit Dominus, "et locutus sum ad vos mane consurgens et loquens, et non audistis, et vocavi vos, et non respondistis, 14 faciam domui huic, in qua invocatum est nomen meum et in qua vos habetis fiduciam, et loco quem dedi vobis et patribus vestris, sicut feci Silo. 15 Et proiciam vos a facie mea sicut proieci omnes fratres vestros, universum semen Ephraim. 16 Tu, ergo, noli orare pro populo hoc, nec adsumas pro eis laudem et orationem, et non obsistas mihi, quia non exaudiam te. 17 Nonne vides quid isti faciant in civitatibus Iuda et in plateis Hierusalem? 18 Filii colligunt ligna, et patres succendunt

will execute judgment between a man and his neighbour, 6 if you oppress not the stranger, *the* fatherless, and the widow, and shed not innocent blood in this place, and walk not after strange gods to your own hurt, 7 I will dwell with you in this place, in the land, which I gave to your fathers from the beginning and for evermore.

8 ""Behold: you put your trust in lying words which shall not profit you. 9 To steal, to murder, to commit adultery, to swear falsely, to offer to Baalim, and to go after strange gods which you know not. 10 And you have come, and stood before me in this house, in which my name is called upon, and have said, 'We are delivered because we have done all these abominations.'

11 ""Is this house then, in which my name hath been called upon, in your eyes become a den of robbers? I, I am he. I have seen it," saith the Lord. 12 "Go ye to my place in Shiloh, where my name dwelt from the beginning, and see what I did to it for the wickedness of my people Israel. 13 And now because you have done all these works," saith the Lord, "and I have spoken to you rising up early and speaking, and you have not heard, and I have called you, and you have not answered, 14 I will do to this house, in which my name is called upon and in which you trust, and to the place which I have given you and your fathers, as I did to Shiloh. 15 And I will cast you away from before my face as I have cast away all your brethren, the whole seed of Ephraim. 16 Therefore, do not thou pray for this people, nor take to thee praise and supplication for them, and do not withstand me, for I will not hear thee. 17 Seest thou not what they do in the cities of Judah, and in the streets of Jerusalem? 18 The children gather wood, and the fathers kindle the fire, and

ignem, et mulieres conspergunt adipem ut faciant placentas reginae caeli et libent diis alienis et me ad iracundiam provocent. 19 Numquid me ad iracundiam provocant?" dicit Dominus. "Nonne semet ipsos, in confusionem vultus sui?"

20 "'Ideo haec dicit Dominus Deus: "Ecce: furor meus et indignatio mea conflatur super locum istum, super viros et super iumenta et super lignum regionis et super fruges terrae, et succendetur et non extinguetur."

21 "'Haec dicit Dominus exercituum, Deus Israhel, "Holocaustomata vestra addite victimis vestris, et comedite carnes. 22 Quia non sum locutus cum patribus vestris, et non praecepi eis, in die qua eduxi eos de terra Aegypti, de verbo holocaustomatum et victimarum. 23 Sed hoc verbum praecepi eis, dicens, 'Audite vocem meam, et ero vobis Deus, et vos eritis mihi populus, et ambulate in omni via quam mandavi vobis, ut bene sit vobis.' 24 Et non audierunt nec inclinaverunt aurem suam, sed abierunt in voluntatibus et in pravitate cordis sui mali, factique sunt retrorsum et non in ante, 25 a die qua egressi sunt patres eorum de terra Aegypti usque ad diem hanc. Et misi ad vos omnes servos meos, prophetas, per diem consurgens diluculo et mittens. 26 Et non audierunt me nec inclinaverunt aurem suam, sed induraverunt cervicem suam et peius operati sunt quam patres eorum.""

the women knead the dough to make cakes to the queen of heaven, and to offer libations to strange gods, and to provoke me to anger. 19 Do they provoke me to anger?" saith the Lord. "Is it not themselves, to the confusion of their own countenance?"

20 "'Therefore thus saith the Lord God, "Behold: my wrath and my indignation was enkindled against this place, upon men and upon beasts and upon the trees of the field and upon the fruits of the land, and it shall burn and shall not be quenched."

21 "'Thus saith the Lord of hosts, the God of Israel, "Add your burnt offerings to your sacrifices, and eat ye the flesh. 22 For I spoke not to your fathers, and I commanded them not, in the day that I brought them out of the land of Egypt, concerning the matter of burnt offerings and sacrifices. 23 But this thing I commanded them, saying, 'Hearken to my voice, and I will be your God, and you shall be my people, and walk ye in all the way that I have commanded you, that it may be well with you.' 24 *But* they hearkened not, nor inclined their ear, but walked in their own will and in the perversity of their wicked heart, and went backward and not forward 25 from the day that their fathers came out of the land of Egypt, even to this day. And I have sent to you all my servants, the prophets, *from day to day* rising up early and sending. 26 And they have not hearkened to me nor inclined their ear, but have hardened their neck and have done worse than their fathers."'"

27 "Et loqueris ad eos omnia verba haec, et non audient te, et vocabis eos, et non respondebunt tibi. 28 Et dices ad eos, 'Haec est gens quae non audivit vocem Domini, Dei sui, nec recepit disciplinam. Periit fides et ablata est de ore eorum. 29 Tonde capillum tuum, et proice, et sume in directum planctum. Quia proiecit Dominus et reliquit generationem furoris sui 30 quia "Fecerunt filii Iuda malum in oculis meis," dicit Dominus. "Posuerunt offendicula sua in domo in qua invocatum est nomen meum ut polluerent eam, 31 et aedificaverunt excelsa Thofeth, qui est in valle filii Ennom, ut incenderent filios suos et filias suas igni, quae non praecepi nec cogitavi in corde meo. 32 Ideo ecce: dies venient," dicit Dominus, "et non dicetur amplius Thofeth et vallis filii Ennom, sed vallis interfectionis, et sepelient in Thofeth eo quod non sit locus. 33 Et erit morticinum populi huius in cibum volucribus caeli et bestiis terrae, et non erit qui abigat. 34 Et quiescere faciam de urbibus Iuda et de plateis Hierusalem vocem gaudii et vocem laetitiae, vocem sponsi et vocem sponsae, in desolatione enim erit terra.""'"

27 "And thou shalt speak to them all these words, *but* they will not hearken to thee, and thou shalt call them, *but* they will not answer thee. 28 And thou shalt say to them, 'This is a nation which hath not hearkened to the voice of the Lord, their God, nor received instruction. Faith is lost and is carried away out of their mouth. 29 Cut off thy hair, and cast it away, and take up a lamentation on high. For the Lord hath rejected and forsaken the generation of his wrath 30 because "The children of Judah have done evil in my eyes," saith the Lord. "They have set their abominations in the house in which my name is called upon to pollute it, 31 and they have built the high places of Topheth, which is in the valley of the son of Hinnom, to burn their sons and their daughters in the fire, which I commanded not nor thought on in my heart. 32 Therefore behold: the days shall come," saith the Lord, "and it shall no more be called Topheth *nor* the valley of the son of Hinnom, but the valley of slaughter, and they shall bury in Topheth, because there is no place. 33 And the carcasses of this people shall be meat for the fowls of the air, and for the beasts of the earth, and there shall be none to drive them away. 34 And I will cause to cease out of the cities of Judah and out of the streets of Jerusalem the voice of joy, and the voice of gladness, the voice of the bridegroom and the voice of the bride, for the land shall be desolate.""""

Caput 8

"In tempore illo," ait Dominus, "eicient ossa regum Iuda et ossa principum eius et ossa sacerdotum et ossa prophetarum et ossa eorum qui habitaverunt Hierusalem de sepulchris suis. 2 Et expandent ea ad solem et lunam et omnem militiam caeli, quae dilexerunt, et quibus servierunt, et post quae ambulaverunt, et quae quaesierunt et adoraverunt; non colligentur, et non sepelientur; in sterquilinium super faciem terrae erunt. 3 Et eligent magis mortem quam vitam omnes qui residui fuerint de cognatione hac pessima in universis locis quae derelicta sunt, ad quae eieci eos," dicit Dominus exercituum.

4 "Et dices ad eos, 'Haec dicit Dominus: "Numquid qui cadit non resurget, et qui aversus est, non revertetur? 5 Quare ergo aversus est populus iste in Hierusalem aversione contentiosa? Adprehenderunt mendacium, et noluerunt reverti. 6 "Adtendi et auscultavi: nemo quod bonum est loquitur; nullus est qui agat paenitentiam super peccato suo, dicens, 'Quid feci?' Omnes conversi sunt ad cursum suum quasi equus impetu vadens ad proelium. 7 Milvus in caelo cognovit tempus suum; turtur et hirundo et ciconia custodierunt tempus adventus sui, populus autem meus non cognovit iudicium Domini. 8 Quomodo dicitis, 'Sapientes nos sumus, et

Chapter 8

Other evils that shall fall upon the Jews for their impenitence.

"At that time," saith the Lord, "they shall cast out the bones of the kings of Judah and the bones of the princes thereof and the bones of the priests and the bones of the inhabitants of Jerusalem out of their graves. 2 And they shall spread them abroad to the sun and the moon and all the host of heaven, whom they have loved, and whom they have served, and after whom they have walked, and whom they have sought and adored; they shall not be gathered, and they shall not be buried; they shall be as dung upon the face of the earth. 3 And *death shall be chosen rather than life by all* that shall remain of this wicked kindred in all places which are left, to which I have cast them out," saith the Lord of hosts.

4 "And thou shalt say to them, 'Thus saith the Lord: "Shall not he that falleth rise again, and he that is turned away, shall he not turn again? 5 Why then is this people in Jerusalem turned away with a stubborn revolting? They have laid hold on lying, and have refused to return. 6 I attended and hearkened: no man speaketh what is good; there is none that doth penance for his sin, saying, 'What have I done?' They are all turned to their own course as a horse rushing to the battle. 7 The kite in the air hath known her time; the turtle and the swallow, and the stork have observed the time of their coming, but my people have not known the judgment of the Lord. 8 How do you say, 'We are wise, and the law of

lex Domini nobiscum est'? Vere mendacium operatus est stilus mendax scribarum. 9 Confusi sunt sapientes; perterriti et capti sunt, verbum enim Domini proiecerunt, et sapientia nulla est in eis. 10 Propterea dabo mulieres eorum exteris, agros eorum heredibus, quia a minimo usque ad maximum, omnes avaritiam sequuntur; a propheta usque ad sacerdotem, cuncti faciunt mendacium.

11 ""Et sanabant contritionem filiae populi mei ad ignominiam, dicentes, 'Pax, pax,' cum non esset pax. 12 Confusi sunt quia abominationem fecerunt; quinimmo, confusione non sunt confusi, et erubescere nescierunt, idcirco cadent inter corruentes; in tempore visitationis suae corruent," dicit Dominus.

13 ""Congregans congregabo eos," ait Dominus. "Non est uva in vitibus, et non sunt ficus in ficulnea; folium defluxit, et dedi eis quae praetergressa sunt."

14 "Quare sedemus? Convenite, et ingrediamur civitatem munitam, et sileamus ibi, quia Dominus, Deus noster, silere nos fecit, et potum dedit nobis aquam fellis, peccavimus enim Domino. 15 Expectavimus pacem, et non erat bonum tempus medellae, et ecce: formido. 16 A Dan auditus est fremitus equorum eius; a voce hinnituum pugnatorum eius commota est omnis terra, et venerunt et devoraverunt terram et plenitudinem eius, urbem et habitatores eius.

17 ""Quia ecce: ego mittam vobis serpents, regulos, quibus non est incantatio, et mordebunt vos," ait Dominus.'"

the Lord is with us'? Indeed the lying pen of the scribes hath wrought falsehood. 9 The wise men are confounded; they are dismayed and taken, for they have cast away the word of the Lord, and there is no wisdom in them. 10 Therefore I will give their women to strangers, their fields to *others for an inheritance,* because from the least even to the greatest, all follow covetousness; from the prophet even to the priest, all deal deceitfully.

11 ""And they healed the *breach* of the daughter of my people disgracefully, saying, 'Peace, peace,' when there was no peace. 12 They are confounded because they have committed abomination; yea rather, they are not confounded with confusion, and they have not known how to blush, therefore shall they fall among them that fall; in the time of their visitation they shall fall," saith the Lord.

13 ""Gathering I will gather them together," saith the Lord. "There is no grape on the vines, and there are no figs on the fig tree; the leaf is fallen, and I have given them the things that are passed away."""

14 "'Why do we sit still? Assemble yourselves, and let us enter into the fenced city, and let us be silent there, for the Lord, our God, hath put us to silence, and hath given us water of gall to drink, for we have sinned against the Lord. 15 We looked for peace, and no good *came,* for a time of healing, and behold: fear. 16 The snorting of his horse was heard from Dan; all the land was moved at the sound of the neighing of his warriors, and they came and devoured the land and all that was in it, the city and its inhabitants.

17 ""For behold: I will send *among* you serpents, basilisks, against which there is no charm, and they shall bite you," saith the Lord.'"

18 Dolor meus super dolorem; in me cor meum maerens. 19 Ecce vox clamoris filiae populi mei de terra longinqua: "Numquid Dominus non est in Sion, aut rex eius non est in ea?"

Quare ergo me ad iracundiam concitaverunt in sculptilibus suis et in vanitatibus alienis? 20 Transiit messis; finita est aestas, et nos salvati non sumus. 21 Super contritione filiae populi mei contritus sum et contristatus; stupor obtinuit me. 22 Numquid resina non est in Galaad, aut medicus non est ibi? Quare igitur non est obducta cicatrix filiae populi mei?

Caput 9

Quis dabit capiti meo aquam et oculis meis fontem lacrimarum? Et plorabo die et nocte interfectos filiae populi mei. 2 Quis dabit me in solitudine diversorium viatorum? Et derelinquam populum meum et recedam ab eis, quia omnes adulteri sunt, coetus praevaricatorum.

3 "Et extenderunt linguam suam quasi arcum mendacii et non veritatis; confortati sunt in terra, quia de malo ad malum egressi sunt, et me non cognoverunt," dicit Dominus.

18 My sorrow is above sorrow; my heart mourneth within me. 19 Behold the voice of the daughter of my people from a far country: "Is not the Lord in Zion, or is not her king in her?"

Why then have they provoked me to wrath with their idols and strange vanities? 20 The harvest is passed; the summer is ended, and we are not saved. 21 For the affliction of the daughter of my people I am afflicted and made sorrowful; astonishment hath taken hold on me. 22 Is there no balm in Gilead, or is no physician there? Why then is not the wound of the daughter of my people closed?

Chapter 9

The prophet laments the miseries of his people and their sins which are the cause of them. He exhorts them to repentance.

Who will give water to my head, and a fountain of tears to my eyes? And I will weep day and night for the slain of the daughter of my people. 2 Who will give me in the wilderness a lodging place of wayfaring men? And I will leave my people and depart from them, because they are all adulterers, an assembly of transgressors.

3 "And they have bent their tongue as a bow for lies and not for truth; they have strengthened themselves upon the earth, for they have proceeded from evil to evil, and me they have not known," saith the Lord.

4 "Unusquisque se a proximo suo custodiat, et in omni fratre suo non habeat fiduciam, quia omnis frater subplantans subplantabit, et omnis amicus fraudulenter incedet. 5 Et vir fratrem suum deridebit, et veritatem non loquentur, docuerunt enim linguam suam loqui mendacium; ut inique agerent laboraverunt. 6 Habitatio tua in medio doli; in dolo rennuerunt scire me," dicit Dominus.

7 Propterea haec dicit Dominus exercituum: "Ecce: ego conflabo et probabo eos. Quid enim aliud faciam a facie filiae populi mei? 8 Sagitta vulnerans lingua eorum; dolum locuta est. In ore suo pacem cum amico suo loquitur, et occulte ponit ei insidias. 9 Numquid super his non visitabo?" dicit Dominus, "aut in gentem huiuscemodi non ulciscetur anima mea? 10 Super montes adsumam fletum ac lamentum, et super speciosa deserti, planctum, quoniam incensa sunt, eo quod non sit vir pertransitens, et non audierunt vocem possidentis. A volucre caeli usque ad pecora transmigraverunt et recesserunt. 11 Et dabo Hierusalem in acervos harenae et cubilia draconum, et civitates Iuda dabo in desolationem, eo quod non sit habitator."

12 Quis est vir sapiens qui intellegat hoc, et ad quem verbum oris Domini fiat ut adnuntiet istud: quare perierit terra et exusta sit quasi desertum eo quod non sit qui pertranseat?

13 Et dixit Dominus, "Quia dereliquerunt legem meam quam dedi eis et non audierunt vocem meam et non ambula-

4 "Let every man take heed of his neighbour, and let him not trust in any brother of his, for every brother will *utterly* supplant, and every friend will walk deceitfully. 5 And a man shall mock his brother, and they will not speak the truth, for they have taught their tongue to speak lies; they have laboured to commit iniquity. 6 Thy habitation is in the midst of deceit; through deceit they have refused to know me," saith the Lord.

7 Therefore thus saith the Lord of hosts: "Behold: I will melt and try them. For what else shall I do *before* the daughter of my people? 8 Their tongue is a piercing arrow; it hath spoken deceit. With his mouth one speaketh peace with his friend, and secretly he lieth in wait for him. 9 Shall I not visit them for these things," saith the Lord, "or shall not my soul be revenged on such a nation? 10 For the mountains I will take up weeping and lamentation, and for the beautiful places of the desert, mourning, because they are burnt up, for that there is not a man that passeth through them, and they have not heard the voice of the owner. From the fowl of the air to the beasts they are gone away and departed. 11 And I will make Jerusalem to be heaps of sand and dens of dragons, and I will make the cities of Judah desolate, for want of an inhabitant."

12 Who is the wise man that may understand this, and to whom the word of the mouth of the Lord may come that he may declare this: why the land hath perished and is burnt up like a wilderness *which* none passeth through?

13 And the Lord said, "Because they have forsaken my law which I gave them, and have not heard my voice, and have

verunt in ea. 14 Et abierunt post pravitatem cordis sui et post Baalim, quod didicerunt a patribus suis."

15 Idcirco haec dicit Dominus exercituum, Deus Israhel: "Ecce: ego cibabo populum istum absinthio, et potum dabo eis aquam fellis. 16 Et dispergam eos in gentibus quas non noverunt ipsi et patres eorum, et mittam post eos gladium donec consumantur."

17 Haec dicit Dominus exercituum, Deus Israhel: "Contemplamini, et vocate lamentatrices, et veniant, et ad eas quae sapientes sunt mittite, et properent. 18 Festinent et adsumant super nos lamentum; deducant oculi nostri lacrimas, et palpebrae nostrae defluant aquis. 19 Quia vox lamentationis audita est de Sion: 'Quomodo vastati sumus et confusi vehementer? Quia dereliquimus terram, quoniam deiecta sunt tabernacula nostra.'"

20 Audite ergo, mulieres, verbum Domini, et adsumant aures vestrae sermonem oris eius, et docete filias vestras lamentum, et unaquaeque proximam suam planctum. 21 Quia ascendit mors per fenestras nostras; ingressa est domos nostras disperdere parvulos de foris, iuvenes de plateis. 22 Loquere, "Haec dicit Dominus: 'Et cadet morticinum hominis quasi stercus super faciem regionis, et quasi faenum post tergum metentis, et non est qui colligat.'"

23 Haec dicit Dominus, "Non glorietur sapiens in sapientia sua, et non glorietur fortis in fortitudine sua, et non glorietur dives in divitiis suis, 24 sed in hoc glorietur qui gloriatur: scire et nosse me, quia ego sum Dominus qui facio

not walked in it. 14 *But* they have gone after the perverseness of their own heart, and after Baalim, which their fathers taught them.

15 Therefore thus saith the Lord of hosts, the God of Israel: "Behold: I will feed this people with wormwood, and give them water of gall to drink. 16 And I will scatter them among the nations which they and their fathers have not known, and I will send the sword after them till they be consumed."

17 Thus saith the Lord of hosts, the God of Israel: "Consider ye, and call for the mourning women, and let them come, and send to them that are wise women, and let them make haste. 18 Let them hasten and take up a lamentation for us; let our eyes shed tears, and our eyelids run down with waters. 19 For a voice of wailing is heard out of Zion: 'How are we wasted and greatly confounded? Because we have left the land, because our dwellings are cast down.'"

20 Hear therefore, ye women, the word of the Lord, and let your ears receive the word of his mouth, and teach your daughters wailing, and every one her neighbour mourning. 21 For death is come up through our windows; it is entered into our houses to destroy the children from without, the young men from the streets. 22 Speak, "Thus saith the Lord: 'Even the carcass of man shall fall as dung upon the face of the country, and as grass behind the back of the mower, and there is none to gather it.'"

23 Thus saith the Lord: "Let not the wise man glory in his wisdom, and let not the strong man glory in his strength, and let not the rich man glory in his riches, 24 but let him that glorieth glory in this: that he understandeth and knoweth me, for I am the Lord that exercise mercy and

misericordiam et iudicium et iustitiam in terra, haec enim placent mihi," ait Dominus.

25 "Ecce: dies veniunt," dicit Dominus, "et visitabo super omnem qui circumcisum habet praeputium. 26 Super Aegyptum et super Iudam et super Edom et super filios Ammon et super Moab et super omnes qui adtonsi sunt in comam, habitantes in deserto, quia omnes gentes habent praeputium, omnis autem domus Israhel incircumcisi sunt corde."

Caput 10

Audite verbum quod locutus est Dominus super vos, domus Israhel. 2 Haec dicit Dominus: "Iuxta vias Gentium nolite discere, et a signis caeli nolite metuere quae timent gentes, 3 quia leges populorum vanae sunt, quia lignum de saltu praecidit opus manus artificis in ascia. 4 Argento et auro decoravit illud, clavis et malleis conpegit ut non dissolvatur. 5 In similitudinem palmae fabricata sunt et non loquentur;

judgment and justice in the earth, for these things please me," saith the Lord.

25 "Behold: the days come," saith the Lord, "and I will visit upon every one that hath the foreskin circumcised. 26 Upon Egypt and upon Judah and upon Edom and upon the children of Ammon and upon Moab and upon all that have their hair polled round, that dwell in the desert, for all the nations *are uncircumcised in the flesh,* but all the house of Israel are uncircumcised in the heart."

Chapter 10

Neither stars nor idols are to be feared, but the great creator of all things. The chastisement of Jerusalem for her sins.

Hear ye the word which the Lord hath spoken concerning you, O house of Israel. 2 Thus saith the Lord: "Learn not according to the ways of the Gentiles, and be not afraid of the signs of heaven which the heathens fear, 3 for the laws of the people are vain, for the works of the hand of the workman hath cut a tree out of the forest with an axe. 4 He hath decked it with silver and gold, he hath put it together with nails and hammers that it may not fall asunder. 5 They are framed after the likeness of a palm tree and shall not speak; they *must be* carried *to be* removed because they cannot go.

portata tollentur quia incedere non valent. Nolite ergo timere ea, quia nec male possunt facere nec bene.

6 Non est similis tui, Domine; magnus es tu, et magnum nomen tuum in fortitudine. 7 Quis non timebit te, O rex gentium? Tuum est enim decus inter cunctos sapientes gentium, et in universis regnis eorum nullus est similis tui. 8 Pariter insipientes et fatui probabuntur; doctrina vanitatis eorum lignum est. 9 Argentum involutum de Tharsis adfertur et aurum de Ofaz, opus artificis et manus aerarii; hyacinthus et purpura indumentum eorum; opus artificum universa haec. 10 Dominus autem Deus verus est, ipse Deus vivens et rex sempiternus: ab indignatione eius commovebitur terra, et non sustinebunt gentes comminationem eius.

11 Sic ergo dicetis eis: "Dii qui caelos et terram non fecerunt, pereant de terra et de his quae sub caelo sunt."

12 Qui facit terram in fortitudine sua, praeparat orbem in sapientia sua et prudentia sua extendit caelos. 13 Ad vocem suam dat multitudinem aquarum in caelo et elevat nebulas ab extremitatibus terrae; fulgura in pluviam facit et educit ventum de thesauris suis. 14 Stultus factus est omnis homo ab scientia; confusus est omnis artifex in sculptili, quoniam falsum est quod conflavit, et non est spiritus in eis. 15 Vana sunt et opus risu dignum; in tempore visitationis suae peribunt.

Therefore fear them not, for they can neither do evil nor good.

6 There is none like to thee, O Lord; thou art great, and great is thy name in might. 7 Who shall not fear thee, O king of nations? For thine is the glory among all the wise men of the nations, and in all their kingdoms there is none like unto thee. 8 They shall be all proved together to be senseless and foolish; the doctrine of their vanity is wood. 9 Silver *spread into plates* is brought from Tarshish, and gold from Uphaz, the work of the artificer and of the hand of the coppersmith; violet and purple is their clothing; all these things are the work of artificers. 10 But the Lord is the true God, he is the living God, and the everlasting king: at his wrath the earth shall tremble, and the nations shall not *be able to* abide his threatening.

11 Thus then shall you say to them, The gods that have not made heaven and earth, let them perish from the earth and from among these things that are under heaven.

12 He that maketh the earth by his power, *that* prepareth the world by his wisdom and stretcheth out the heavens by his knowledge. 13 At his voice he giveth a multitude of waters in the heaven and lifteth up the clouds from the ends of the earth; he maketh lightnings for rain, and bringeth forth the wind out of his treasures. 14 Every man is become a fool for knowledge; every artist is confounded in his graven idol, for what he hath cast is false, and there is no spirit in them. 15 They are vain things and a ridiculous work; in the time of their visitation they shall perish.

16 Non est his similis pars Iacob, qui enim formavit omnia ipse est, et Israhel virga hereditatis eius: Dominus exercituum nomen illi. 17 Congrega de terra confusionem tuam, quae habitas in obsidione. 18 Quia haec dicit Dominus: "Ecce: ego longe proiciam habitatores terrae in hac vice, et tribulabo eos ita ut inveniantur."

19 Vae mihi super contritione mea, pessima plaga mea. Ego autem dixi, "Plane haec infirmitas mea est, et portabo illam."

20 Tabernaculum meum vastatum est; omnes funiculi mei disrupti sunt; filii mei exierunt a me, et non subsistunt; non est qui extendat ultra tentorium meum et erigat pelles meas. 21 Quia stulte egerunt pastores et Dominum non quaesierunt, propterea non intellexerunt, et omnis grex eorum dispersus est. 22 Vox auditionis, ecce: venit et commotio magna de terra aquilonis ut ponat civitates Iuda solitudinem et habitaculum draconum.

23 Scio, Domine, quia non est hominis via eius, nec viri est ut ambulet et dirigat gressus suos. 24 Corripe me, Domine, verumtamen in iudicio et non in furore tuo, ne forte ad nihilum redigas me.

25 Effunde indignationem tuam super gentes quae non cognoverunt te et super provincias quae nomen tuum non invocaverunt, quia comederunt Iacob et devoraverunt eum et consumpserunt illum et decus eius dissipaverunt.

16 "The portion of Jacob is not like these, for it is he who formed all things, and Israel is the rod of his inheritance: the Lord of hosts is his name. 17 Gather up thy shame out of the land, thou that dwellest in a siege. 18 For thus saith the Lord: "Behold: I will cast away far off the inhabitants of the land at this time, and I will afflict them so that they may be found.

19 Woe is me for my destruction; my wound is very grievous. But I said, "Truly this is my own *evil,* and I will bear it."

20 My tabernacle is laid waste; all my cords are broken; my children are gone out from me, and they are not; there is none to stretch forth my tent any more and to set up my curtains. 21 Because the pastors have done foolishly and have not sought the Lord, therefore have they not understood, and all their flock is scattered. 22 Behold: the sound of a noise cometh, a great commotion out of the land of the north to make the cities of Judah a desert and a dwelling for dragons.

23 I know, O Lord, that the way of a man is not his, neither is it in a man to walk and to direct his steps. 24 Correct me, O Lord, but yet with judgment, and not in thy fury, *lest* thou bring me to nothing.

25 Pour out thy indignation upon the nations that have not known thee and upon the provinces that have not called upon thy name, because they have eaten up Jacob and devoured him and consumed him and have destroyed his glory.

Caput 11

Verbum quod factum est ad Hieremiam a Domino, dicens, 2 "Audite verba pacti huius, et loquimini ad viros Iuda et ad habitatores Hierusalem, 3 et dices ad eos, 'Haec dicit Dominus, Deus Israhel: "Maledictus vir qui non audierit verba pacti huius, 4 quod praecepi patribus vestris in die qua eduxi eos de terra Aegypti de fornace ferrea, dicens 'Audite vocem meam, et facite omnia quae praecipio vobis, et eritis mihi in populum, et ego ero vobis in Deum,' 5 ut suscitem iuramentum quod iuravi patribus vestris: daturum me eis terram fluentem lacte et melle, sicut est dies haec.""'"

Et respondi et dixi, "Amen, Domine."

6 Et dixit Dominus ad me, "Vociferare omnia verba haec in civitatibus Iuda et foris Hierusalem, dicens, 'Audite verba pacti huius, et facite illa. 7 Quia contestans contestatus sum patres vestros in die qua eduxi eos de terra Aegypti usque ad diem hanc; mane surgens contestatus sum et dixi, "Audite vocem meam." 8 Et non audierunt nec inclinaverunt aurem suam, sed abierunt unusquisque in pravitate cordis sui mali, et induxi super eos omnia verba pacti huius, quod praecepi ut facerent, et non fecerunt.'"

Chapter 11

The prophet proclaims the covenant of God and denounces
evils to the obstinate transgressors of it. The conspiracy of the
Jews against him, a figure of their conspiracy against Christ.

The word that came from the Lord to Jeremiah, saying,
2 "Hear ye the words of this covenant, and speak to the men
of Judah and to the inhabitants of Jerusalem, 3 and thou shalt
say to them, 'Thus saith the Lord, the God of Israel: "Cursed
is the man that shall not hearken to the words of this covenant, 4 which I commanded your fathers in the day that I
brought them out of the land of Egypt from the iron furnace, saying, 'Hear ye my voice, and do all things that I command you, and you shall be my people, and I will be your
God,' 5 that I may accomplish the oath which I swore to
your fathers: to give them a land flowing with milk and
honey, as it is this day.'"'"

And I answered and said, "Amen, O Lord."

6 And the Lord said to me, "Proclaim aloud all these words
in the cities of Judah, and in the streets of Jerusalem, saying, 'Hear ye the words of the covenant, and do them. 7 For
protesting I conjured your fathers in the day that I brought
them out of the land of Egypt even to this day; rising early
I conjured them, and said, "Hearken ye to my voice." 8 And
they obeyed not, nor inclined their ear, but walked every
one in the perverseness of his own wicked heart, and I
brought upon them all the words of this covenant, which I
commanded them to do, but they did them not.'"

9 Et dixit Dominus ad me, "Inventa est coniuratio in viris Iuda et in habitatoribus Hierusalem. 10 Reversi sunt ad iniquitates patrum suorum priores, qui noluerunt audire verba mea, et hii ergo abierunt post deos alienos, ut servirent eis; irritum fecerunt domus Israhel et domus Iuda pactum meum quod pepigi cum patribus eorum.

11 Quam ob rem haec dicit Dominus: "Ecce: ego inducam super eos mala de quibus exire non poterunt, et clamabunt ad me, et non exaudiam eos. 12 Et ibunt civitates Iuda et habitatores Hierusalem et clamabunt ad deos quibus libant, et non salvabunt eos in tempore adflictionis eorum. 13 Secundum numerum enim civitatum tuarum erant dii tui, Iuda, et secundum numerum viarum Hierusalem posuisti aras confusionis, aras ad libandum Baalim. 14 Tu, ergo, noli orare pro populo hoc, et ne adsumas pro eis laudem et orationem, quia non exaudiam in tempore clamoris eorum ad me, in tempore adflictionis eorum."

15 Quid est quod dilectus meus in domo mea fecit scelera multa? Numquid carnes sanctae auferent a te malitias tuas in quibus gloriata es?

16 Olivam uberem, pulchram, fructiferam, speciosam vocavit Dominus nomen tuum; ad vocem loquellae grandis exarsit ignis in ea, et conbusta sunt frutecta eius. 17 Et Dominus exercituum qui plantavit te locutus est super te malum, pro malis domus Israhel et domus Iuda quae fecerunt sibi ad inritandum me, libantes Baalim.

18 Tu autem, Domine, demonstrasti mihi, et cognovi; tunc

9 And the Lord said to me, "A conspiracy is found among the men of Judah and among the inhabitants of Jerusalem. 10 They are returned to the former iniquities of their fathers, who refused to hear my words, so these likewise have gone after strange gods, to serve them, the house of Israel, and the house of Judah have made void my covenant, which I made with their fathers."

11 Wherefore thus saith the Lord: "Behold: I will bring in evils upon them which they shall not be able to escape, and they shall cry to me, and I will not hearken to them. 12 And the cities of Judah and the inhabitants of Jerusalem shall go and cry to the gods to whom they offer sacrifice, and they shall not save them in the time of their affliction. 13 For according to the number of thy cities were thy gods, O Judah, and according to the number of the streets of Jerusalem thou hast set up altars of confusion, altars to offer sacrifice to Baalim. 14 Therefore, do not thou pray for this people, and do not take up praise and prayer for them, for I will not hear them in the time of their cry to me, in the time of their affliction."

15 What is the meaning that my beloved hath wrought much wickedness in my house? Shall the holy flesh take away from thee thy crimes in which thou hast boasted?

16 The Lord called thy name a plentiful olive tree, fair, fruitful *and* beautiful; at the noise of a word, a great fire was kindled in it, and the branches thereof are burnt. 17 And the Lord of hosts that planted thee hath pronounced evil against thee, for the evils of the house of Israel and the house of Judah which they have done to themselves to provoke me, offering sacrifice to Baalim.

18 But thou, O Lord, hast shewn me, and I have known;

ostendisti mihi studia eorum. 19 Et ego quasi agnus mansuetus qui portatur ad victimam, et non cognovi quia super me cogitaverunt consilia, dicentes, "Mittamus lignum in panem eius et eradamus eum de terra viventium, et nomen eius non memoretur amplius." 20 Tu autem, Domine Sabaoth, qui iudicas iuste et probas renes et corda, videam ultionem tuam ex eis, tibi enim revelavi causam meam.

21 Propterea haec dicit Dominus ad viros Anathoth, qui quaerunt animam tuam et dicunt, "Non prophetabis in nomine Domini, et non morieris in manibus nostris." 22 Propterea haec dicit Dominus exercituum: "Ecce: ego visitabo super eos; iuvenes morientur in gladio; filii eorum et filiae eorum morientur in fame. 23 Et reliquiae non erunt ex eis, inducam enim malum super viros Anathoth, annum visitationis eorum."

Caput 12

Iustus quidem tu es, Domine, si disputem tecum, verumtamen iusta loquar ad te. Quare via impiorum prosperatur, bene est omnibus qui praevaricantur et inique agunt? 2 Plantasti eos, et radicem miserunt; proficiunt et faciunt

then thou shewedst me their doings. 19 And I was as a meek lamb that is carried to be a victim, and I knew not that they had devised counsels against me, saying, "Let us put wood on his bread and cut him off from the land of the living, and let his name be remembered no more." 20 But thou, O Lord of Sabaoth, who judgest justly and triest the reins and hearts, let me see thy revenge on them, for to thee I have revealed my cause.

21 Therefore thus saith the Lord to the men of Anathoth, who seek thy life, and say, "Thou shalt not prophesy in the name of the Lord, and thou shalt not die in our hands." 22 Therefore thus saith the Lord of hosts: "Behold: I will visit upon them; their young men shall die by the sword; their sons and their daughters shall die by famine. 23 And there shall be no remains of them, for I will bring in evil upon the men of Anathoth, the year of their visitation."

Chapter 12

The prosperity of the wicked shall be but for a short time. The desolation of the Jews for their sins. Their return from their captivity.

Thou indeed, O Lord, art just, if I plead with thee, but yet I will speak what is just to thee. Why doth the way of the wicked prosper, why is it well with all them that transgress and do wickedly? 2 Thou hast planted them, and they have

fructum. Prope es tu ori eorum et longe a renibus eorum. 3 Et tu, Domine, nosti me; vidisti me et probasti cor meum tecum: congrega eos quasi gregem ad victimam, et sanctifica eos in die occisionis. 4 Usquequo lugebit terra et herba omnis regionis siccabitur propter malitiam habitantium in ea? Consumptum est animal et volucre, quoniam dixerunt, "Non videbit novissima nostra."

5 Si cum peditibus currens laborasti, quomodo contendere poteris cum equis, cum autem in terra pacis secura fueris, quid facies in superbia Iordanis? 6 Nam et fratres tui et domus patris tui, etiam ipsi pugnaverunt adversum te et clamaverunt post te plena voce. Ne credas eis cum locuti fuerint tibi bona.

7 Reliqui domum meam; dimisi hereditatem meam; dedi dilectam animam meam in manu inimicorum eius. 8 Facta est mihi hereditas mea quasi leo in silva; dedit contra me vocem, ideo odivi eam. 9 Numquid avis discolor hereditas mea mihi? Numquid avis tincta per totum? Venite; congregamini, omnes bestiae terrae; properate ad devorandum.

10 Pastores multi demoliti sunt vineam meam; conculcaverunt partem meam; dederunt portionem meam desiderabilem in desertum solitudinis. 11 Posuerunt eam in dissipationem, luxitque super me. Desolatione desolata est omnis terra, quia nullus est qui recogitet corde. 12 Super omnes vias deserti venerunt vastatores, quia gladius Domini devorabit ab extremo terrae usque ad extremum eius; non

taken root, they prosper and bring forth fruit. Thou art near in their mouth, and far from their reins. 3 And thou, O Lord, hast known me, thou hast seen me and proved my heart with thee: gather them together as sheep for a sacrifice, and *prepare* them for the day of slaughter. 4 How long shall the land mourn and the herb of every field wither for the wickedness of them that dwell therein? The beasts and the birds are consumed, because they have said, "He shall not see our last end."

5 If thou hast wearied with running with footmen, how canst thou contend with horses? And if thou hast been secure in a land of peace, what wilt thou do in the *swelling* of the Jordan? 6 For even thy brethren and the house of thy father, even they have fought against thee, and have cried after thee with full voice. Believe them not when they speak good things to thee.

7 I have forsaken my house; I have left my inheritance; I have given my dear soul into the hand of her enemies. 8 My inheritance is become to me as a lion in the wood; it hath cried out against me, therefore have I hated it. 9 Is my inheritance to me as a speckled bird? Is it as a bird dyed throughout? Come ye; assemble yourselves, all the beasts of the earth; make haste to devour.

10 Many pastors have destroyed my vineyard; they have trodden my portion under foot; they have changed my delightful portion into a desolate wilderness. 11 They have laid it waste, and it hath mourned for me. With desolation is all the land made desolate, because there is none that considereth in the heart. 12 The spoilers are come upon all the ways of the wilderness, for the sword of the Lord shall devour from one end of the land to the other end thereof;

est pax universae carni. 13 Seminaverunt triticum et spinas messuerunt; hereditatem acceperunt, et non eis proderit. Confundemini a fructibus vestris propter iram furoris Domini.

14 Haec dicit Dominus adversum omnes vicinos meos pessimos qui tangunt hereditatem quam distribui populo meo Israhel: "Ecce: ego evellam eos de terra eorum, et domum Iuda evellam de medio eorum. 15 Et cum evellero eos, convertar et miserebor eorum, et reducam eos, virum ad hereditatem suam, et virum in terram suam. 16 Et erit, si eruditi didicerint vias populi mei, ut iurent in nomine meo, 'Vivit Dominus,' sicut docuerunt populum meum iurare in Baal; aedificabuntur in medio populi mei. 17 Quod si non audierint, evellam gentem illam evulsione et perditione ait Dominus.

Caput 13

Haec dicit Dominus ad me: "Vade, et posside tibi lumbare lineum, et pones illud super lumbos tuos et in aquam non inferes illud." 2 Et possedi lumbare iuxta verbum

there is no peace for all flesh. 13 They have sown wheat and reaped thorns; they have received an inheritance, and it shall not profit them. You shall be ashamed of your fruits because of the *fierce* wrath of the Lord.

14 Thus saith the Lord against all my wicked neighbours that touch the inheritance that I have shared out to my people Israel: "Behold: I will pluck them out of their land, and I will pluck the house of Judah out of the midst of them. 15 And when I shall have plucked them out, I will return and have mercy on them, and I will bring them back, every man to his inheritance, and every man to his land. 16 And it shall come to pass, if they will be taught and will learn the ways of my people, to swear by my name, 'The Lord liveth,' as they have taught my people to swear by Baal, that they shall be built up in the midst of my people. 17 But if they will not hear, I will utterly pluck out and *destroy* that nation," saith the Lord.

Chapter 13

Under the figure of a linen girdle is foretold the destruction of the Jews. Their obstinacy in sin brings all miseries upon them.

Thus saith the Lord to me: "Go, and get thee a linen girdle, and thou shalt put it about thy loins and shalt not put it into water." 2 And I got a girdle according to the word of the

Domini, et posui circa lumbos meos. 3 Et factus est sermo Domini ad me secundo, dicens, 4 "Tolle lumbare quod possedisti, quod est circa lumbos tuos, et surgens vade ad Eufraten, et absconde illud ibi in foramine petrae." 5 Et abii et abscondi illud in Eufrate, sicut praeceperat mihi Dominus.

6 Et factum est post dies plurimos dixit Dominus ad me, "Surge; vade ad Eufraten, et tolle inde lumbare quod praecepi tibi ut absconderes illud ibi." 7 Et abii ad Eufraten, et fodi, et tuli lumbare de loco ubi absconderam illud, et ecce: conputruerat lumbare, ita ut nullo usui aptum esset.

8 Et factum est verbum Domini ad me, dicens, 9 "Haec dicit Dominus: 'Sic putrescere faciam superbiam Iuda et superbiam Hierusalem multam. 10 Populum istum pessimum qui nolunt audire verba mea et ambulant in pravitate cordis sui abieruntque post deos alienos ut servirent eis et adorarent eos: et erunt sicut lumbare istud quod nullo usui aptum est. 11 Sicut enim adheret lumbare ad lumbos viri, sic adglutinavi mihi omnem domum Israhel et omnem domum Iuda,' dicit Dominus, 'ut essent mihi in populum, et in nomen, et in laudem, et in gloriam, et non audierunt.

12 "'Dices ergo ad eos sermonem istum: "Haec dicit Dominus, Deus Israhel: 'Omnis laguncula implebitur vino.' Et dicent ad te, 'Numquid ignoramus quia omnis laguncula implebitur vino?' 13 Et dices ad eos, 'Haec dicit Dominus: "Ecce: ego implebo omnes habitatores terrae huius et reges qui sedent de stirpe David super thronum eius et sacerdotes

Lord, and put it about my loins. 3 And the word of the Lord came to me the second time, saying, 4 "Take the girdle which thou hast got, which is about thy loins, and arise, and go to the Euphrates, and hide it there in a hole of the rock." 5 And I went and hid it *by* the Euphrates, as the Lord had commanded me.

6 And it came to pass after many days that the Lord said to me, "Arise; go to the Euphrates, and take from thence the girdle which I commanded thee to hide there." 7 And I went to the Euphrates, and digged, and took the girdle out of the place where I had hid it, and behold: the girdle was rotten, so that it was fit for no use.

8 And the word of the Lord came to me, saying, 9 "Thus saith the Lord: 'After this manner will I make the pride of Judah and the great pride of Jerusalem to rot. 10 This wicked people that will not hear my words and that walk in the perverseness of their heart and have gone after strange gods to serve them and to adore them: and they shall be as this girdle which is fit for no use. 11 For as the girdle sticketh close to the loins of a man, so have I brought close to me all of the house of Israel and all the house of Judah,' saith the Lord, 'that they might be my people, and for a name, and for a praise, and for a glory, *but* they *would* not *hear.*

12 "'Thou shalt speak therefore to them this word: "Thus saith the Lord, God of Israel: 'Every bottle shall be filled with wine.' And they shall say to thee, 'Do we not know that every bottle shall be filled with wine?' 13 And thou shalt say to them, 'Thus saith the Lord, "Behold: I will fill all the inhabitants of this land and the kings of the race of David that sit upon his throne and the priests and the prophets and

et prophetas et omnes habitatores Hierusalem ebrietate. 14 Et dispergam eos virum a fratre suo, et patres et filios pariter," ait Dominus. "Non parcam, et non concedam, neque miserebor ut non disperdam eos."''"''

15 Audite, et auribus percipite. Nolite elevari, quia Dominus locutus est. 16 Date Domino, Deo vestro, gloriam antequam contenebrescat, et antequam offendant pedes vestri ad montes caligosos; expectabitis lucem, et ponet eam in umbram mortis et in caliginem. 17 Quod si hoc non audieritis, in abscondito plorabit anima mea a facie superbiae; plorans plorabit, et deducet oculus meus lacrimam, quia captus est grex Domini.

18 Dic regi et dominatrici, "Humiliamini; sedete, quoniam descendit de capite vestro corona gloriae vestrae." 19 Civitates austri clausae sunt, et non est qui aperiat; translata est omnis Iudaea transmigratione perfecta.

20 Levate oculos vestros, et videte, qui venitis ab aquilone: ubi est grex qui datus est tibi, pecus inclitum tuum? 21 Quid dices cum visitaverit te? Tu enim docuisti eos adversum te et erudisti in caput tuum. Numquid non dolores adprehendent te quasi mulierem parturientem? 22 Quod si dixeris in corde tuo, "Quare venerunt mihi haec?" Propter multitudinem iniquitatis tuae, revelata sunt verecundiora tua; pollutae sunt plantae tuae. 23 Si mutare potest Aethiops pellem suam aut pardus varietates suas, et vos poteritis bene facere cum didiceritis malum. 24 Et disseminabo eos quasi stipulam quae vento raptatur in deserto.

25 "Haec sors tua parsque mensurae tuae a me," dicit

all the inhabitants of Jerusalem with drunkenness. 14 And I will scatter them every man from his brother, and fathers and sons in like manner," saith the Lord. "I will not spare, and I will not pardon, nor will I have mercy, *but* to destroy them.""""

15 Hear ye, and give ear. Be not proud, for the Lord hath spoken. 16 Give ye glory to the Lord, your God, before it be dark, and before your feet stumble upon the dark mountains; you shall look for light, and he will turn it into the shadow of death and into darkness. 17 But if you will not hear this, my soul shall weep in secret *for* your pride; weeping it shall weep, and my eyes shall run down with tears, because the flock of the Lord is carried away captive.

18 Say to the king and to the queen, "Humble yourselves; sit down, for the crown of your glory is come down from your head." 19 The cities of the south are shut up, and there is none to open them; all Judah is carried away captive with an *entire* captivity.

20 Lift up your eyes, and see, you that come from the north: where is the flock that is given thee, thy beautiful cattle? 21 What wilt thou say when he shall visit thee? For thou hast taught them against thee and instructed them against thy own head. Shall not sorrows lay hold on thee as a woman in labour? 22 And if thou shalt say in thy heart, "Why are these things come upon me?" For the greatness of thy iniquity, thy *nakedness* is discovered; the soles of thy feet are defiled. 23 If the Ethiopian can change his skin or the leopard his spots, you may also do well when you have learned evil. 24 And I will scatter them as stubble which is carried away by the wind in the desert.

25 "This is thy lot and the portion of thy measure from

Dominus, "quia oblita es mei et confisa es in mendacio. 26 Unde et ego nudavi femora tua contra faciem tuam, et apparuit ignominia tua. 27 Adulteria tua et hinnitus tuus, scelus fornicationis tuae, super colles in agro vidi abominationes tuas. Vae tibi, Hierusalem: non mundaberis post me? Usquequo adhuc?"

Caput 14

Quod factum est verbum Domini ad Hieremiam de sermonibus siccitatis.

2 Luxit Iudaea, et portae eius corruerunt, et obscuratae sunt in terra, et clamor Hierusalem ascendit. 3 Maiores miserunt minores suos ad aquam: venerunt ad hauriendum; non invenerunt aquam; reportaverunt vasa sua vacua; confusi sunt et adflicti, et operuerunt capita sua. 4 Propter terrae vastitatem, quia non venit pluvia in terram, confusi sunt agricolae; operuerunt capita sua. 5 Nam et cerva in agro peperit et reliquit, quia non erat herba.

6 Et onagri steterunt in rupibus; traxerunt ventum quasi

me," saith the Lord, "because thou hast forgotten me and hast trusted in falsehood. 26 Wherefore I have also bared thy thighs against thy face, and thy shame hath appeared. 27 I have seen thy adulteries and thy neighing, the wickedness of thy fornication, *and* thy abominations upon the hills in the field. Woe to thee, Jerusalem: wilt thou not be made clean after me? How long yet?"

Chapter 14

A grievous famine, and the prophet's prayer on that occasion. Evils denounced to false prophets. The prophet mourns for his people.

The word of the Lord that came to Jeremiah concerning the words of the drought.

2 Judea hath mourned, and the gates thereof are fallen, and are become obscure on the ground, and the cry of Jerusalem is gone up. 3 The great ones sent their inferiors to the water: they came to draw; they found no water; they carried back their vessels empty; they were confounded and afflicted, and covered their heads. 4 For the destruction of the land, because there came no rain upon the earth, the husbandmen were confounded, they covered their heads. 5 Yea, the hind also brought forth in the field and left it, because there was no grass.

6 And the wild asses stood upon the rocks; they snuffed

dracones; defecerunt oculi eorum, quia non erat herba. 7 Si iniquitates nostrae responderint nobis, Domine, fac propter nomen tuum, quoniam multae sunt aversiones nostrae; tibi peccavimus.

8 Expectatio Israhel salvator eius in tempore tribulationis, quare quasi colonus futurus es in terra, et quasi viator declinans ad manendum? 9 Quare futurus es velut vir vagus, ut fortis qui non potest salvare?

Tu autem in nobis es, Domine, et nomen tuum super nos invocatum est; ne derelinquas nos. 10 Haec dicit Dominus populo huic, qui dilexit movere pedes suos et non quievit et Domino non placuit. Nunc recordabitur iniquitatum eorum et visitabit peccata eorum.

11 Et dixit Dominus ad me, "Noli orare pro populo isto in bonum. 12 Cum ieiunaverint non exaudiam preces eorum, et si obtulerint holocaustomata et victimas, non suscipiam ea, quoniam gladio et fame et peste ego consumam eos."

13 Et dixi, "A, a, a, Domine Deus, prophetae dicunt eis, 'Non videbitis gladium, et famis non erit in vobis, sed pacem veram dabit vobis in loco isto.'"

14 Et dixit Dominus ad me, "Falso prophetae vaticinantur in nomine meo: non misi eos, et non praecepi eis, neque locutus sum ad eos. Visionem mendacem et divinationem et fraudulentiam et seductionem cordis sui prophetant vobis. 15 Ideo haec dicit Dominus de prophetis qui prophetant in nomine meo, quos ego non misi, dicentes, 'Gladius et famis non erit in terra hac': in gladio et fame consumentur prophetae illi. 16 Et populi quibus prophetant erunt proiecti in viis

up the wind like dragons; their eyes failed, because there was no grass. 7 If our iniquities have *testified against* us, O Lord, do thou it for thy name's sake, for our rebellions are many; we have sinned against thee.

8 O expectation of Israel, the saviour thereof in time of trouble, why wilt thou be a stranger in the land, and as a wayfaring man turning in to lodge? 9 Why wilt thou be as a wandering man, as a mighty man that cannot save?

But thou, O Lord, art among us, and thy name is called upon us; forsake us not. 10 Thus saith the Lord to his people, that have loved to move their feet and have not rested, and have not pleased the Lord,. He will now remember their iniquities and visit their sins.

11 And the Lord said to me, "Pray not for this people for their good. 12 When they fast I will not hear their prayers, and if they offer holocausts and victims, I will not receive them, for I will consume them by the sword, and by famine, and by the pestilence."

13 And I said, "Ah, ah, ah, O Lord God, the prophets say to them, 'You shall not see the sword, and there shall be no famine among you, but he will give you true peace in this place.'"

14 And the Lord said to me, "The prophets prophesy falsely in my name: I sent them not, neither have I commanded them, nor have I spoken to them. They prophesy unto you a lying vision and divination and deceit and the seduction of their own heart. 15 Therefore thus saith the Lord concerning the prophets that prophecy in my name, whom I did not send, that say, 'Sword and famine shall not be in this land': by sword and famine shall those prophets be consumed. 16 And the people to whom they prophesy shall be

Hierusalem prae fame et gladio, et non erit qui sepeliat eos, ipsi et uxores eorum, filii et filiae eorum, et effundam super eos malum suum.

17 "Et dices ad eos verbum istud: 'Deducant oculi mei lacrimas per noctem et diem, et non taceant, quoniam contritione magna contrita est virgo filia populi mei, plaga pessima vehementer.'"

18 Si egressus fuero ad agros, ecce, occisi gladio, et si introiero in civitatem, ecce, adtenuati fame. Propheta quoque et sacerdos abierunt in terram quam ignorabant. 19 Numquid proiciens abiecisti Iudam, aut Sion abominata est anima tua? Quare ergo percussisti nos ita ut nulla sit sanitas? Expectavimus pacem, et non est bonum, et tempus curationis, et ecce: turbatio. 20 Cognovimus, Domine, impietates nostras, iniquitates patrum nostrorum, quia peccavimus tibi.

21 Ne nos des in obprobrium, propter nomen tuum, neque facias nobis contumeliam solii gloriae tuae. Recordare: ne irritum facias foedus tuum nobiscum. 22 Numquid sunt in sculptilibus Gentium qui pluant? Aut caeli possunt dare imbres? Nonne tu es Dominus, Deus noster, quem expectavimus? Tu enim fecisti omnia haec.

cast out in the streets of Jerusalem because of the famine and the sword, and there shall be none to bury them, they and their wives, their sons and their daughters, and I will pour out their wickedness upon them.

17 "And thou shalt speak this word to them: 'Let my eyes shed down tears night and day, and let them not cease, because the virgin daughter of my people is afflicted with a great affliction, with an exceeding grievous evil.'"

18 If I go forth into the fields, behold, the slain with the sword, and if I enter into the city, behold, them that are consumed with famine. The prophet also and the priest are gone into a land which they knew not. 19 Hast thou utterly cast away Judah, or hath thy soul abhorred Zion? Why then hast thou struck us so that there is no healing *for us?* We have looked for peace, and there is no good, and for the time of healing, and behold: trouble. 20 We acknowledge, O Lord, our wickedness, the iniquities of our fathers, because we have sinned against thee.

21 Give us not to be a reproach, for thy name's sake, and do not disgrace in us the throne of thy glory. Remember: break not thy covenant with us. 22 Are there any among the graven things of the Gentiles that can send rain? Or can the heavens give showers? Art not thou the Lord our God, whom we have looked for? For thou hast made all these things.

Caput 15

Et dixit Dominus ad me, "Si steterit Moses et Samuhel coram me, non est anima mea ad populum istum; eice illos a facie mea, et egrediantur. 2 Quod si dixerint ad te 'Quo egrediemur?' dices ad eos, 'Haec dicit Dominus: "Qui ad mortem, ad mortem, et qui ad gladium, ad gladium, et qui ad famem, ad famem, et qui ad captivitatem, ad captivitatem.'"

3 "Et visitabo super eos quattuor species," dicit Dominus, "gladium ad occisionem et canes ad lacerandum et volatilia caeli et bestias terrae ad devorandum et dissipandum. 4 Et dabo eos in fervorem universis regnis terrae propter Manassem, filium Ezechiae, regis Iuda, super omnibus quae fecit in Hierusalem. 5 Quis enim miserebitur tui Hierusalem? Aut quis contristabitur pro te? Aut quis ibit ad rogandum pro pace tua?

6 "Tu reliquisti me," dicit Dominus. "Retrorsum abisti, et extendam manum meam super te, et interficiam te; laboravi rogans. 7 Et dispergam eos ventilabro in portis terrae. Interfeci et perdidi populum meum, et tamen a viis suis non sunt reverse. 8 Multiplicatae sunt mihi viduae eius super harenam maris. Induxi eis super matrem adulescentis vasta-

Chapter 15

God is determined to punish the Jews for their sins. The
prophet's complaint and God's promise to him.

And the Lord said to me, "If Moses and Samuel shall
stand before me, my soul is not towards this people; cast
them out from my sight, and let them go forth. 2 And if they
shall say unto thee, 'Whither shall we go forth?' thou shalt
say to them, 'Thus saith the Lord, "Such as are for death, to
death, and such as are for the sword, to the sword, and such
as are for famine, to famine, and such as are for captivity, to
captivity."'"

3 "And I will visit them with four kinds," saith the Lord,
"the sword to kill and the dogs to tear and the fowls of the
air and the beasts of the earth to devour and destroy. 4 And I
will give them up to the rage of all the kingdoms of the earth
because of Manasseh, the son of Hezekiah, the king of Judah, for all that he did in Jerusalem. 5 For who shall have pity
on thee, O Jerusalem? Or who shall bemoan thee? Or who
shall go to pray for thy peace?

6 "Thou hast forsaken me," saith the Lord. "Thou art
gone backward, and I will stretch out my hand against thee,
and I will destroy thee; I am weary of entreating thee. 7 And
I will scatter them with a fan in the gates of the land. I have
killed and destroyed my people, and yet they are not returned from their ways. 8 Their widows are multiplied unto
me above the sand of the sea. I have brought upon them

torem meridie; misi super civitates repente terrorem. 9 Infirmata est quae peperit septem; defecit anima eius. Occidit ei sol cum adhuc esset dies. Confusa est et erubuit, et residuos eius in gladium dabo in conspectu inimicorum eorum," ait Dominus.

10 Vae mihi, mater mea, quare genuisti me virum rixae, virum discordiae in universa terra? Non feneravi, nec feneravit mihi quisquam; omnes maledicunt mihi.

11 Dicit Dominus, "Si non reliquiae tuae in bonum, si non occurri tibi in tempore adflictionis et in tempore tribulationis adversum inimicum. 12 Numquid foederabitur ferrum ferro ab aquilone, et aes? 13 Divitias tuas et thesauros tuos in direptionem dabo gratis, in omnibus peccatis tuis, et in omnibus terminis tuis. 14 Et adducam inimicos tuos de terra quam nescis, quia ignis succensus est in furore meo super vos ardebit."

15 Tu scis, Domine, recordare mei, et visita me, et tuere me ab his qui persequuntur me. Noli in patientia tua suscipere me. Scito quoniam sustinui pro te obprobrium. 16 Inventi sunt sermones tui, et comedi eos, et factum est mihi verbum tuum in gaudium et in laetitiam cordis mei, quoniam invocatum est nomen tuum super me, Domine, Deus exercituum. 17 Non sedi in concilio ludentium, et gloriatus sum a facie manus tuae. Solus sedebam quoniam comminatione replesti me. 18 Quare factus est dolor meus perpetuus, et plaga mea desperabilis rennuit curari? Facta est mihi quasi mendacium aquarum infidelium.

19 Propter hoc haec dicit Dominus: "Si converteris, con-

against the mother of the young man a spoiler at noonday; I have cast a terror on a sudden upon the cities. 9 She that hath borne seven is become weak; her soul hath fainted away. Her sun is gone down while it was yet day. She is confounded and ashamed, and the residue of them I will give up to the sword in the sight of their enemies," saith the Lord.

10 Woe is me, my mother, why hast thou borne me a man of strife, a man of contention to all the earth? I have not lent on usury, neither hath any man lent to me on usury, yet all curse me.

11 The Lord saith to me, "Assuredly it shall be well with thy remnant, assuredly I shall help thee in the time of affliction and in the time of tribulation against the enemy. 12 Shall iron be allied with the iron from the north, and the brass? 13 Thy riches and thy treasures I will give unto spoil for nothing, because of all thy sins, even in all thy borders. 14 And I will bring thy enemies out of a land which thou knowest not, for a fire is kindled in my rage, it shall burn upon you."

15 O Lord, thou knowest, remember me, and visit me, and defend me from them that persecute me. Do not defend me in thy patience. Know that for thy sake I have suffered reproach. 16 Thy words were found, and I did eat them, and thy word was to me a joy and gladness of my heart, for thy name is called upon me, O Lord God of hosts. 17 I sat not in the assembly of jesters, nor did I make a boast of the presence of thy hand. I sat alone because thou hast filled me with threats. 18 Why is my sorrow become perpetual, and my wound desperate *so as to* refuse to be healed? It is become to me as the falsehood of deceitful waters that cannot be trusted.

19 Therefore thus saith the Lord: "If thou wilt be con-

vertam te, et ante faciem meam stabis. Et si separaveris pretiosum a vili, quasi os meum eris; convertentur ipsi ad te, et tu non converteris ad eos. 20 Et dabo te populo huic in murum aereum fortem, et bellabunt adversum te et non praevalebunt, quia ego tecum sum ut salvem te et eruam te," dicit Dominus. 21 "Et liberabo te de manu pessimorum, et redimam te de manu fortium."

Caput 16

Et factum est verbum Domini ad me, dicens, 2 "Non accipies uxorem, et non erunt tibi filii et filiae in loco isto. 3 Quia haec dicit Dominus super filios et filias qui generantur in loco isto et super matres eorum quae genuerunt eos et super patres eorum de quorum stirpe sunt nati in terra hac: 4 'Mortibus aegrotationum morientur; non plangentur, et non sepelientur. In sterquilinium super faciem terrae erunt, et gladio et fame consumentur, et erit cadaver eorum in escam volatilibus caeli et bestiis terrae.'

verted, I will convert thee, and thou shalt stand before my face. And if thou wilt separate the precious from the vile, thou shalt be as my mouth; they shall be turned to thee, and thou shalt not be turned to them. 20 And I will make thee to this people as a strong wall of brass, and they shall fight against thee and shall not prevail, for I am with thee to save thee and to deliver thee," saith the Lord. 21 "And I will deliver thee out of the hand of the wicked, and I will redeem thee out of the hand of the mighty."

Chapter 16

The prophet is forbid to marry. The Jews shall be utterly ruined for their idolatry but shall at length be released from their captivity, and the Gentiles shall be converted.

And the word of the Lord came to me, saying, 2 "Thou shalt not take thee a wife, neither shalt thou have thee sons and daughters in this place. 3 For thus saith the Lord concerning the sons and daughters that are born in this place and concerning their mothers that bore them and concerning their fathers of whom they were born in this land: 4 'They shall die by the death of grievous illnesses; they shall not be lamented, and they shall not be buried. They shall be as dung upon the face of the earth, and they shall be consumed with the sword and with famine, and their carcasses shall be meat for the fowls of the air and for the beasts of the earth.'

5 "Haec enim dicit Dominus, 'Ne ingrediaris domum convivii, neque vadas ad plangendum neque consoleris eos, quia abstuli pacem meam a populo isto,' dicit Dominus, 'misericordiam et miserationes.'

6 "Et morientur grandes et parvi in terra ista. Non sepelientur neque plangentur, et non se incident neque calvitium fiet pro eis. 7 Et non frangent inter eos lugenti panem ad consolandum super mortuo, et non dabunt eis potum calicis ad consolandum super patre suo et matre. 8 Et domum convivii non ingrediaris ut sedeas cum eis et comedas et bibas. 9 Quia haec dicit Dominus exercituum, Deus Israhel: 'Ecce: ego auferam de loco isto in oculis vestris et in diebus vestris vocem gaudii et vocem laetitiae, vocem sponsi et vocem sponsae.'

10 "Et cum adnuntiaveris populo huic omnia verba haec et dixerint tibi, 'Quare locutus est Dominus super nos omne malum grande istud? Quae iniquitas nostra? Et quod peccatum nostrum quod peccavimus Domino, Deo nostro?' 11 dices ad eos, '"Quia dereliquerunt patres vestri me," ait Dominus, "et abierunt post deos alienos et servierunt eis et adoraverunt eos, et me dereliquerunt et legem meam non custodierunt. 12 Sed et vos peius operati estis quam patres vestri, ecce enim: ambulat unusquisque post pravitatem cordis sui mali ut me non audiat. 13 Et eiciam vos de terra hac in terram quam ignoratis vos, et patres vestri, et servietis ibi diis alienis die ac nocte, qui non dabunt vobis requiem.'"

5 "For thus saith the Lord: 'Enter not into the house of feasting, neither go thou to mourn nor to comfort them, because I have taken away my peace from this people,' saith the Lord, 'my mercy and commiserations.'

6 "Both the great and the little shall die in this land. They shall not be buried nor lamented, and men shall not cut themselves nor make themselves bald for them. 7 And they shall not break bread among them to him that mourneth to comfort him for the dead, neither shall they give them to drink of the cup to comfort them for their father and mother. 8 And do not thou go into the house of feasting to sit with them and to eat and drink. 9 For thus saith the Lord of hosts, the God of Israel: 'Behold: I will take away out of this place in your sight and in your days the voice of mirth and the voice of gladness, the voice of the bridegroom, and the voice of the bride.'

10 "And when thou shalt tell this people all these words, and they shall say to thee, 'Wherefore hath the Lord pronounced against us all this great evil? What is our iniquity? And what is our sin that we have sinned against the Lord, our God?' 11 thou shalt say to them, '"Because your fathers forsook me," saith the Lord, "and went after strange gods and served them and adored them, and they forsook me and kept not my law. 12 And you also have done worse than your fathers, for behold: every one of you walketh after the perverseness of his evil heart so as not to hearken to me. 13 *So* I will cast you forth out of this land into a land which you know not, nor your fathers, and there you shall serve strange gods day and night, which shall not give you any rest."'

14 "Propterea ecce: dies veniunt," dicit Dominus, "et non dicetur ultra, 'Vivit Dominus, qui eduxit filios Israhel de terra Aegypti,' 15 sed 'Vivit Dominus, qui eduxit filios Israhel de terra aquilonis et de universis terris ad quas eieci eos,' et reducam eos in terram suam quam dedi patribus eorum."

16 "Ecce: ego mittam piscatores multos," dicit Dominus, "et piscabuntur eos, et post haec mittam eis multos venatores, et venabuntur eos de omni monte et de omni colle et de cavernis petrarum, 17 quia oculi mei super omnes vias eorum: non sunt absconditae a facie mea, et non fuit occulta iniquitas eorum ab oculis meis. 18 Et reddam primum duplices iniquitates et peccata eorum, quia contaminaverunt terram meam in morticinis idolorum suorum, et abominationibus suis impleverunt hereditatem meam."

19 Domine, fortitudo mea et robur meum et refugium meum in die tribulationis, ad te Gentes venient ab extremis terrae et dicent, "Vere mendacium possederunt patres nostri, vanitatem quae eis non profuit. 20 Numquid faciet sibi homo deos, et ipsi non sunt dii?"

21 "Idcirco ecce: ego ostendam eis per vicem hanc: ostendam eis manum meam et virtutem meam, et scient quia nomen mihi Dominus."

14 "Therefore behold: the days come," saith the Lord, "when it shall be said no more, 'The Lord liveth, that brought forth the children of Israel out of the land of Egypt,' 15 but 'The Lord liveth, that brought the children of Israel out of the land of the north, and out of all the lands to which I cast them out,' and I will bring them again into their land which I gave to their fathers."

16 "Behold: I will send many fishers," saith the Lord, "and they shall fish them, and after this I will send them many hunters, and they shall hunt them from every mountain and from every hill and out of the holes of the rocks, 17 for my eyes are upon all their ways: they are not hid from my face, and their iniquity hath not been hid from my eyes. 18 And I will repay first their double iniquities and their sins, because they have defiled my land with the carcasses of their idols, and they have filled my inheritance with their abominations."

19 O Lord, my might and my strength and my refuge in the day of tribulation, to thee the Gentiles shall come from the ends of the earth, and shall say, "Surely our fathers have possessed *lies,* a vanity which hath not profited them. 20 Shall a man make gods unto himself, and they are no gods?"

21 "Therefore, behold: I will this once cause them to know: I will shew them my hand and my power, and they shall know that my name is the Lord."

Caput 17

"Peccatum Iuda scriptum est stilo ferreo, in ungue adamantino; exaratum super latitudinem cordis eorum et in cornibus ararum eorum. 2 Cum recordati fuerint filii eorum ararum suarum et lucorum suorum lignorumque frondentium in montibus excelsis, 3 sacrificantes in agro, fortitudinem tuam et omnes thesauros tuos in direptionem dabo, excelsa tua propter peccata in universis finibus tuis. 4 Et relinqueris sola ab hereditate tua quam dedi tibi, et servire te faciam inimicis tuis in terra quam ignoras, quoniam ignem succendisti in furore meo; usque in aeternum ardebit."

5 Haec dicit Dominus: "Maledictus homo qui confidit in homine et ponit carnem brachium suum et a Domino recedit cor eius. 6 Erit enim quasi myricae in deserto, et non videbit cum venerit bonum, sed habitabit in siccitate in deserto, in terra salsuginis et inhabitabili."

7 Benedictus vir qui confidit in Domino, et erit Dominus fiducia eius. 8 Et erit quasi lignum quod transplantatur super aquas quod ad humorem mittit radices suas, et non timebit cum venerit aestus, et erit folium eius viride, et in tempore

Chapter 17

For their obstinacy in sin the Jews shall be led captive. He is cursed that trusteth in flesh. God alone searcheth the heart, giving to every one as he deserves. The prophet prayeth to be delivered from his enemies and preacheth up the observance of the sabbath.

"The sin of Judah is written with a pen of iron, with the point of a diamond, it is graven upon the table of their heart and upon the horns of their altars. 2 When their children shall remember their altars and their groves and their green trees upon the high mountains, 3 sacrificing in the field, I will give thy strength and all thy treasures to the spoil, *and* thy high places for sin in all thy borders. 4 And thou shalt be left stripped of thy inheritance which I gave thee, and I will make thee serve thy enemies in a land which thou knowest not, because thou hast kindled a fire in my wrath; it shall burn for ever."

5 Thus saith the Lord: "Cursed be the man that trusteth in man and maketh flesh his arm and whose heart departeth from the Lord. 6 For he shall be like tamarick in the desert, and he shall not see when good shall come, but he shall dwell in dryness in the desert, in a salt land and not inhabited."

7 Blessed be the man that trusteth in the Lord, and the Lord shall be his confidence. 8 And he shall be as a tree that is planted by the waters that spreadeth out its roots towards moisture, and it shall not fear when the heat cometh, and the leaf thereof shall be green, and in the time of drought it

siccitatis non erit sollicitum, nec aliquando desinet facere fructum. 9 Pravum est cor hominis et inscrutabile: quis cognoscet illud?

10 "Ego Dominus scrutans cor et probans renes qui do unicuique iuxta viam suam et iuxta fructum adinventionum suarum."

11 Perdix fovit quae non peperit; fecit divitias et non in iudicio: in dimidio dierum suorum derelinquet eas, et in novissimo suo erit insipiens.

12 Solium gloriae altitudinis a principio locus sanctificationis nostrae. 13 Expectatio Israhel, Domine, omnes qui te derelinquunt confundentur; recedentes a te in terra scribentur quoniam dereliquerunt venam aquarum viventium, Dominum. 14 Sana me, Domine, et sanabor; salvum me fac, et salvus ero, quoniam laus mea tu es. 15 Ecce: ipsi dicunt ad me, "Ubi est verbum Domini? Veniat!"

16 Et ego non sum turbatus, te pastorem sequens, et diem hominis non desideravi; tu scis. Quod egressum est de labiis meis rectum in conspectu tuo fuit. 17 Non sis mihi tu formidini; spes mea tu in die adflictionis. 18 Confundantur qui persequuntur me, et non confundar ego; paveant illi, et non paveam ego; induc super eos diem adflictionis, et duplici contritione contere eos.

19 Haec dicit Dominus ad me: "Vade, et sta in porta filiorum populi, per quam ingrediuntur reges Iuda et egrediuntur, et in cunctis portis Hierusalem. 20 Et dices ad eos, 'Audite verbum Domini, reges Iuda et omnis Iuda cunctique habitatores Hierusalem qui ingredimini per portas istas.

shall not be solicitous, neither shall it cease at any time to bring forth fruit. 9 The heart is perverse *above all things* and unsearchable: who can know it?

10 "I am the Lord who search the heart and prove the reins, who give to every one according to his way, and according to the fruit of his devices."

11 *As* the partridge hath *hatched eggs* which she did not lay, *so is* he that hath gathered riches and not by right: in the midst of his days he shall leave them, and in his latter end he shall be a fool.

12 A high and glorious throne from the beginning is the place of our sanctification. 13 O Lord, the hope of Israel, all that forsake thee shall be confounded; they that depart from thee shall be written in the earth because they have forsaken the Lord, the vein of living waters. 14 Heal me, O Lord, and I shall be healed, save me, and I shall be saved, for thou art my praise. 15 Behold: they say to me, "Where is the word of the Lord? Let it come!"

16 And I am not troubled, following thee for my pastor, and I have not desired the day of man; thou knowest. That which went out of my lips hath been right in thy sight. 17 Be not thou a terror unto me; thou art my hope in the day of affliction. 18 Let them be confounded that persecute me, and let not me be confounded; let them be afraid, and let not me be afraid; bring upon them the day of affliction, and with a double destruction destroy them.

19 Thus saith the Lord to me, "Go, and stand in the gate of the children of the people, by which the kings of Judah come in and go out, and in all the gates of Jerusalem. 20 And thou shalt say to them, 'Hear the word of the Lord, ye kings of Judah and all Judah and all the inhabitants of Jerusalem

21 Haec dicit Dominus: "Custodite animas vestras, et nolite portare pondera in die sabbati, nec inferatis per portas Hierusalem. 22 Et nolite eicere onera de domibus vestris in die sabbati, et omne opus non facietis; sanctificate diem sabbati, sicut praecepi patribus vestris. 23 Et non audierunt nec inclinaverunt aurem suam, sed induraverunt cervicem suam ne audirent me et ne acciperent disciplinam. 24 Et erit, si audieritis me," dicit Dominus, "ut non inferatis onera per portas civitatis huius in die sabbati, et si sanctificaveritis diem sabbati, ne faciatis in ea omne opus, 25 ingredientur per portas civitatis huius reges et principes, sedentes super solium David et ascendentes in curribus et equis, ipsi et principes eorum, viri Iuda et habitatores Hierusalem, et habitabitur civitas haec in sempiternum.

26 ""Et venient de civitatibus Iuda et de circuitu Hierusalem et de terra Beniamin et de campestribus et de montuosis et ab austro, portantes holocaustum et victimam et sacrificium et tus, et inferent oblationem in domum Domini. 27 Si autem non audieritis me ut sanctificetis diem sabbati et ne portetis onus et ne inferatis per portas Hierusalem in die sabbati, succendam ignem in portis eius, et devorabit domos Hierusalem, et non extinguetur.""""

that enter in by these gates. 21 Thus saith the Lord: "Take heed to your souls, and carry no burdens on the sabbath day, and bring them not in by the gates of Jerusalem. 22 And do not bring burdens out of your houses on the sabbath day, neither do ye any work; sanctify the sabbath day, as I commanded your fathers. 23 But they did not hear nor incline their ear, but hardened their neck that they might not hear me and might not receive instruction. 24 And it shall come to pass, if you will hearken to me," saith the Lord, "to bring in no burdens by the gates of this city on the sabbath day, and if you will sanctify the sabbath day, to do no work therein, 25 *then* shall there enter in by the gates of this city kings and princes, sitting upon the throne of David and *riding in* chariots and on horses, they and their princes, the men of Judah and the inhabitants of Jerusalem, and this city shall be inhabited forever.

26 ""And they shall come from the cities of Judah and from the places round about Jerusalem and from the land of Benjamin and from the plains and from the mountains and from the south, bringing holocausts and victims and sacrifices and frankincense, and they shall bring in an offering into the house of the Lord. 27 But if you will not hearken to me to sanctify the sabbath day and not to carry burdens and not to bring them in by the gates of Jerusalem on the sabbath day, I will kindle a fire in the gates thereof, and it shall devour the houses of Jerusalem, and it shall not be quenched.""

Caput 18

Verbum quod factum est ad Hieremiam a Domino, dicens, 2 "Surge, et descende in domum figuli, et ibi audies verba mea." 3 Et descendi in domum figuli, et ecce: ipse faciebat opus super rotam. 4 Et dissipatum est vas quod ipse faciebat e luto manibus suis, conversusque fecit illud vas alterum sicut placuerat in oculis eius ut faceret.

5 Et factum est verbum Domini ad me, dicens, 6 "'Numquid sicut figulus iste non potero facere vobis, domus Israhel?' ait Dominus. Ecce: sicut lutum in manu figuli, sic vos in manu mea, domus Israhel. 7 Repente loquar adversum gentem et adversum regnum ut eradicem et destruam et disperdam illud. 8 Si paenitentiam egerit gens illa a malo suo quod locutus sum adversum eam, agam et ego paenitentiam super malo quod cogitavi ut facerem ei. 9 Et subito loquar de gente et de regno ut aedificem et plantem illud. 10 Si fecerit malum in oculis meis, ut non audiat vocem meam, paenitentiam agam super bono quod locutus sum ut facerem ei.

11 "Nunc ergo dic viro Iudae et habitatoribus Hierusalem, dicens, 'Haec dicit Dominus: "Ecce: ego fingo contra vos malum et cogito contra vos cogitationem. Revertatur unus-

Chapter 18

As the clay in the hand of the potter, so is Israel in God's hand. He pardoneth penitents and punisheth the obstinate. They conspire against Jeremiah, for which he denounceth to them the miseries that hang over them.

The word that came to Jeremiah from the Lord, saying, 2 "Arise, and go down into the potter's house, and there thou shalt hear my words." 3 And I went down into the potter's house, and behold: he was doing a work on the wheel. 4 And the vessel was broken which he was making of clay with his hands, and turning he *made* another vessel as it seemed good in his eyes to make it.

5 Then the word of the Lord came to me, saying, 6 "'Cannot I do with you as this potter, O house of Israel?' saith the Lord. Behold: as clay is in the hand of the potter, so are you in my hand, O house of Israel. 7 I will suddenly speak against a nation and against a kingdom to root out and to pull down and to destroy it. 8 If that nation against which I have spoken shall repent of their evil, I also will repent of the evil that I have thought to do to them. 9 And I will suddenly speak of a nation and of a kingdom, to build up and plant it. 10 If it shall do evil in my sight, that it obey not my voice, I will repent of the good that I have spoken to do unto it.

11 "Now therefore tell the men of Judah and the inhabitants of Jerusalem, saying, 'Thus saith the Lord: "Behold: I frame evil against you and devise a device against you. Let

quisque a via sua mala, et dirigite vias vestras et studia vestra.""""

12 Qui dixerunt, "Desperavimus, post cogitationes enim nostras ibimus, et unusquisque pravitatem cordis sui mali faciemus."

13 Ideo haec dicit Dominus: "Interrogate gentes, 'Quis audivit talia horribilia quae fecit nimis virgo Israhel? 14 Numquid deficiet de petra agri nix Libani? Aut evelli possunt aquae erumpentes frigidae et defluentes?" 15 Quia oblitus est mei populus meus, frustra libantes et inpingentes in viis suis in semitis saeculi, ut ambularent per eas in itinere non trito, 16 ut fieret terra eorum in desolationem et in sibilum sempiternum; omnis qui praeterierit per eam obstupescet et movebit caput suum. 17 Sicut ventus urens dispergam eos coram inimico; dorsum et non faciem ostendam eis in die perditionis eorum.'"

18 Et dixerunt, "Venite, et cogitemus contra Hieremiam cogitationes, non enim peribit lex a sacerdote, neque consilium a sapiente, nec sermo a propheta; venite, et percutiamus eum lingua, et non adtendamus ad universos sermones eius."

19 Adtende, Domine, ad me, et audi vocem adversariorum meorum. 20 Numquid redditur pro bono malum quia foderunt foveam animae meae? Recordare quod steterim in conspectu tuo ut loquerer pro eis bonum et averterem indignationem tuam ab eis. 21 Propterea da filios eorum in famem, et deduc eos in manus gladii; fiant uxores eorum absque liberis et viduae, et viri earum interficiantur morte; iuvenes eorum confodiantur gladio in proelio. 22 Audiatur clamor de

every man of you return from his evil way, and *make* ye your ways and your doings *good*."'"

12 And they said, "We have no hopes, for we will go after our own thoughts, and we will do every one according to the perverseness of his evil heart."

13 Therefore thus saith the Lord: "Ask among the nations, 'Who hath heard such horrible things as the virgin of Israel hath done to excess? 14 Shall the snow of Lebanon fail from the rock of the field? Or can the cold waters that gush out and run down be taken away?" 15 Because my people have forgotten me, sacrificing in vain and stumbling in their ways in ancient paths, to walk by them in a way not trodden, 16 that their land might be given up to desolation and to a perpetual hissing; every one that shall pass by it shall be astonished and wag his head. 17 As a burning wind will I scatter them before the enemy; I will shew them the back and not the face in the day of their destruction.'"

18 And they said, "Come, and let us invent devices against Jeremiah, for the law shall not perish from the priest, nor counsel from the wise, nor the word from the prophet; come, and let us strike him with the tongue, and let us give no heed to all his words."

19 Give heed to me, O Lord, and hear the voice of my adversaries. 20 Shall evil be rendered for good because they have digged a pit for my soul? Remember that I have stood in thy sight to speak good for them and turn away thy indignation from them. 21 Therefore deliver up their children to famine, and bring them into the hands of the sword; let their wives be bereaved of children and widows, and let their husbands be slain by death; let their young men be stabbed with the sword in battle. 22 Let a cry be heard out of their houses,

domibus eorum, adduces enim super eos latronem repente, quia foderunt foveam ut caperent me et laqueos absconderunt pedibus meis. 23 Tu autem, Domine, scis omne consilium eorum adversum me in mortem. Ne propitieris iniquitati eorum, et peccatum eorum a facie tua non deleatur; fiant corruentes in conspectu tuo; in tempore furoris tui abutere eis.

Caput 19

Haec dicit Dominus: "Vade, et accipe lagunculam figuli testeam a senioribus populi et a senioribus sacerdotum, 2 et egredere ad vallem filii Ennom, quae est iuxta introitum portae fictilis, et praedicabis ibi verba quae ego loquar ad te. 3 Et dices, 'Audite verbum Domini, reges Iuda et habitatores Hierusalem. Haec dicit Dominus exercituum, Deus Israhel: "Ecce: ego inducam adflictionem super locum istum ita ut omnis qui audierit illam, tinniant aures eius, 4 eo quod dereliquerint me et alienum fecerint locum istum et libaverint in eo diis alienis quos nescierunt ipsi et patres eorum et reges Iuda, et repleverunt locum istum sanguine innocentium.

for thou shalt bring the robber upon them suddenly, because they have digged a pit to take me and have hid snares for my feet. 23 But thou, O Lord, knowest all their counsel against me unto death. Forgive not their iniquity, and let not their sin be blotted out from thy sight; let them be overthrown before thy eyes; in the time of thy wrath do thou destroy them.

Chapter 19

Under the type of breaking a potter's vessel the prophet foresheweth the desolation of the Jews for their sins.

Thus saith the Lord: "Go, and take a potter's earthen bottle, *and take* of the ancients of the people and of the ancients of the priests, 2 and go forth into the valley of the son of Hinnom, which is by the entry of the earthen gate, and there thou shalt proclaim the words that I shall tell thee. 3 And thou shalt say, 'Hear the word of the Lord, O ye kings of Judah and ye inhabitants of Jerusalem. Thus saith the Lord of hosts, the God of Israel: "Behold: I will bring an affliction upon this place so that whoever shall hear it, his ears shall tingle, 4 because they have forsaken me and have *profaned* this place and have sacrificed therein to strange gods whom neither they nor their fathers knew nor the kings of Judah, and they have filled this place with the blood of innocents.

5 Et aedificaverunt excelsa Baalim ad conburendos filios suos igni in holocaustum Baalim, quae non praecepi nec locutus sum, nec ascenderunt in cor meum.

6 """Propterea ecce: dies veniunt," dicit Dominus, "et non vocabitur locus iste amplius Thofeth et Vallis Filii Ennom, sed Vallis Occisionis. 7 Et dissipabo consilium Iudae et Hierusalem in loco isto, et subvertam eos gladio in conspectu inimicorum suorum et in manu quaerentium animas eorum, et dabo cadavera eorum escam volatilibus caeli et bestiis terrae. 8 Et ponam civitatem hanc in stuporem et in sibilum; omnis qui praeterierit per eam obstupescet et sibilabit super universa plaga eius. 9 Et cibabo eos carnibus filiorum suorum et carnibus filiarum suarum, et unusquisque carnes amici sui comedet in obsidione et in angustia in qua concludent eos inimici eorum et qui quaerunt animas eorum.'"

10 "Et conteres lagunculam in oculis virorum qui ibunt tecum. 11 Et dices ad eos, 'Haec dicit Dominus exercituum: "Sic conteram populum istum et civitatem istam sicut conteritur vas figuli quod non potest ultra instaurari, et in Thofeth sepelientur eo quod non sit alius locus ad sepeliendum. 12 Sic faciam loco huic," ait Dominus, "et habitatoribus eius, et ponam civitatem istam sicut Thofeth. 13 Et erunt domus Hierusalem et domus regum Iuda sicut locus Thofeth inmundae, omnes domus in quarum domatibus sacrificaverunt omni militiae caeli et libaverunt libamina diis alienis."'"

5 And they have built the high places of Baalim to burn their children with fire for a holocaust to Baalim, which I did not command nor speak of, neither did it once come into my mind."

6 """Therefore behold: the days come," saith the Lord, "*that* this place shall no more be called Topheth nor the Valley of the Son of Hinnom, but the Valley of Slaughter. 7 And I will defeat the counsel of Judah and of Jerusalem in this place, and I will destroy them with the sword in the sight of their enemies and by the hands of them that seek their lives, and I will give their carcasses to be meat for the fowls of the air and for the beasts of the earth. 8 And I will make this city an astonishment and a hissing; every one that shall pass by it shall be astonished and shall hiss because of all the *plagues* thereof. 9 And I will feed them with the flesh of their sons and with the flesh of their daughters, and they shall eat every one the flesh of his friend in the siege and in the distress wherewith their enemies and they that seek their lives shall straiten them.'"

10 "And thou shalt break the bottle in the sight of the men that shall go with thee. 11 And thou shalt say to them, 'Thus saith the Lord of hosts: "*Even* so will I break this people and this city as the potter's vessel is broken which cannot be made whole again, and they shall be buried in Topheth because there is no other place to bury in. 12 Thus will I do to this place," saith the Lord, "and to the inhabitants thereof, and I will make this city as Topheth. 13 And the houses of Jerusalem and the houses of the kings of Judah shall be unclean as the place of Topheth, all the houses upon whose roofs they have sacrificed to all the host of heaven and have poured out drink offerings to strange gods."""

14 Venit autem Hieremias de Thofeth, quo miserat eum Dominus ad prophetandum, et stetit in atrio domus Domini et dixit ad omnem populum, 15 "Haec dicit Dominus exercituum, Deus Israhel: 'Ecce: ego inducam super civitatem hanc et super omnes urbes eius universa mala quae locutus sum adversum eam, quoniam induraverunt cervicem suam ut non audirent sermones meos.'"

Caput 20

Et audivit Phassur, filius Emmer, sacerdos, qui constitutus erat princeps in domo Domini, Hieremiam prophetantem sermones istos. 2 Et percussit Phassur Hieremiam, prophetam, et misit eum in nervum quod erat in porta Beniamin superiori in domo Domini. 3 Cumque inluxisset in crastinum, eduxit Phassur Hieremiam de nervo, et dixit ad eum Hieremias, "Non Phassur vocavit Dominus nomen tuum, sed Pavorem Undique. 4 Quia haec dicit Dominus: 'Ecce: ego dabo te in pavorem, te et omnes amicos tuos, et corruent gladio inimicorum suorum, et oculi tui videbunt. Et omnem Iudam dabo in manum regis Babylonis, et traducet eos in Babylonem et percutiet eos gladio. 5 Et dabo univer-

14 Then Jeremiah came from Topheth, whither the Lord had sent him to prophesy, and he stood in the court of the house of the Lord and said to all the people, 15 "Thus saith the Lord of hosts, the God of Israel: 'Behold: I will bring in upon this city and upon all the cities thereof all the evils that I have spoken against it, because they have hardened their necks that they might not hear my words.'"

Chapter 20

The prophet is persecuted. He denounces captivity to his persecutors and bemoans himself.

Now Pashhur, the son of Immer, the priest, who was appointed chief in the house of the Lord, heard Jeremiah prophesying these words. 2 And Pashhur struck Jeremiah, the prophet, and put him in the stocks that were in the upper gate of Benjamin in the house of the Lord. 3 And when it was light the next day, Pashhur brought Jeremiah out of the stocks, and Jeremiah said to him, "The Lord hath not called thy name Pashhur, but Fear on Every Side. 4 For thus saith the Lord: 'Behold: I will deliver thee up to fear, thee and all thy friends, and they shall fall by the sword of their enemies, and thy eyes shall see it. And I will give all Judah into the hand of the king of Babylon, and he shall carry them away to Babylon and shall strike them with the sword. 5 And I will

sam substantiam civitatis huius et omnem laborem eius omneque pretium et cunctos thesauros regum Iuda dabo in manu inimicorum eorum, et diripient eos et tollent et ducent in Babylonem. 6 Tu autem, Phassur, et omnes habitatores domus tuae ibitis in captivitatem, et in Babylonem venies, et ibi morieris ibique sepelieris, tu et omnes amici tui quibus prophetasti mendacium.'"

7 Seduxisti me, Domine, et seductus sum; fortior me fuisti, et invaluisti. Factus sum in derisum tota die; omnes subsannant me, 8 quia iam olim loquor, vociferans iniquitatem, et vastitatem clamito, et factus est mihi sermo Domini in obprobrium et in derisum tota die.

9 Et dixi, "Non recordabor eius neque loquar ultra in nomine illius," et factus est in corde meo quasi ignis exaestuans claususque in ossibus meis, et defeci, ferre non sustinens. 10 Audivi enim contumelias multorum et terrorem in circuitu: "Persequimini," et "Persequamur eum," ab omnibus viris qui erant pacifici mei et custodientes latus meum, "si quo modo decipiatur, et praevaleamus adversus eum et consequamur ultionem ex eo."

11 Dominus autem mecum est quasi bellator fortis, idcirco qui persequuntur me cadent et infirmi erunt; confundentur vehementer quia non intellexerunt obprobrium sempiternum quod numquam delebitur. 12 Et tu, Domine exercituum, probator iusti, qui vides renes et cor, videam quaeso ultionem tuam ex eis, tibi enim revelavi causam meam.

13 Cantate Domino; laudate Dominum, quia liberavit animam pauperis de manu malorum.

give all the substance of this city and all its labour and every *precious thing thereof* and all the treasures of the kings of Judah will I give into the hands of their enemies, and they shall pillage them and take them away and carry them to Babylon. 6 But thou, Pashhur, and all that dwell in thy house shall go into captivity, and thou shalt go to Babylon, and there thou shalt die and there thou shalt be buried, thou and all thy friends to whom thou hast prophesied a lie.'"

7 Thou hast deceived me, O Lord, and I am deceived; thou hast been stronger than I, and thou hast prevailed. I am become a laughing-stock all the day; all scoff at me, 8 for I am speaking now this long time, crying out *against* iniquity, and I often proclaim devastation, and the word of the Lord is made a reproach to me and a derision all the day.

9 *Then* I said, "I will not make mention of him nor speak any more in his name," and there came in my heart as a burning fire *shut* up in my bones, and I was wearied, not being able to bear it. 10 For I heard the reproaches of many and terror on every side: "Persecute him," and "Let us persecute him," from all the men that were my *familiars* and *continued at* my side, "if by any means he may be deceived, and we may prevail against him and be revenged on him."

11 But the Lord is with me as a strong warrior, therefore they that persecute me shall fall and shall be weak; they shall be greatly confounded because they have not understood the everlasting reproach which never shall be effaced. 12 And thou, O Lord of hosts, who provest the just, who seest the reins and the heart, let me see, I beseech thee, thy vengeance on them, for to thee I have laid open my cause.

13 Sing ye to the Lord; praise the Lord, because he hath delivered the soul of the poor out of the hand of the wicked.

14 Maledicta dies in qua natus sum; dies in qua peperit me mater mea non sit benedicta. 15 Maledictus vir qui adnuntiavit patri meo, dicens, "Natus est tibi puer masculus," et quasi gaudio laetificavit eum. 16 Sit homo ille ut sunt civitates quas subvertit Dominus et non paenituit; eum audiat clamorem mane et ululatum in tempore meridiano 17 qui non me interfecit a vulva, ut fieret mihi mater mea sepulchrum et vulva eius conceptus aeternus. 18 Quare de vulva egressus sum ut viderem laborem et dolorem, et consumerentur in confusione dies mei?

Caput 21

Verbum quod factum est ad Hieremiam a Domino, quando misit ad eum Rex Sedecias Phassur, filium Melchiae, et Sophoniam, filium Maasiae, sacerdotem, dicens, 2 "Interroga pro nobis Dominum, quia Nabuchodonosor, rex Babylonis, proeliatur adversum nos, si forte faciat Dominus nobiscum secundum omnia mirabilia sua, et recedat a nobis."

3 Et dixit Hieremias ad eos, "Sic dicetis Sedeciae: 4 'Haec dicit Dominus, Deus Israhel: "Ecce: ego convertam vasa

14 Cursed be the day wherein I was born; let not the day in which my mother bore me be blessed. 15 Cursed be the man that brought the tidings to my father, saying, "A manchild is born to thee," and made him *greatly* rejoice. 16 Let that man be as the cities that the Lord hath overthrown and hath not repented; let him hear a cry in the morning and howling at noontide 17 who slew me not from the womb, that my mother might have been my grave and her womb an everlasting conception. 18 Why came I out of the womb to see labour and sorrow, and that my days should be spent in confusion?

Chapter 21

The prophet's answer to the messengers of Zedekiah when Jerusalem was besieged.

The word that came to Jeremiah from the Lord, when King Zedekiah sent unto him Pashhur, the son of Malchiah, and Zephaniah, the son of Maaseiah, the priest, saying, 2 "Inquire of the Lord for us, for Nebuchadnezzar, king of Babylon, maketh war against us, if so be the Lord will deal with us according to all his wonderful works, *that* he may depart from us."

3 And Jeremiah said to them, "Thus shall you say to Zedekiah: 4 'Thus saith the Lord, the God of Israel: "Behold:

belli quae in manibus vestris sunt et quibus vos pugnatis adversum regem Babylonis et Chaldeos qui obsident vos in circuitu murorum, et congregabo ea in medio civitatis huius. 5 Et debellabo ego vos in manu extenta et in brachio forti et in furore et in indignatione et in ira grandi. 6 Et percutiam habitatores civitatis huius: homines et bestiae pestilentia magna morientur. 7 Et post haec," ait Dominus, "dabo Sedeciam, regem Iuda, et servos eius et populum eius et qui derelicti sunt in civitate hac a peste et gladio et fame in manu Nabuchodonosor, regis Babylonis, et in manu inimicorum eorum et in manu quaerentium animam eorum, et percutiet eos in ore gladii, et non movebitur neque parcet nec miserebitur.""""

8 Et ad populum hunc dices, "Haec dicit Dominus: 'Ecce: ego do coram vobis viam vitae et viam mortis. 9 Qui habitaverit in urbe hac morietur gladio et fame et peste, qui autem egressus fuerit et transfugerit ad Chaldeos qui obsident vos vivet, et erit ei anima sua quasi spolium. 10 Posui enim faciem meam super civitatem hanc in malum et non in bonum,' ait Dominus. 'In manu regis Babylonis dabitur, et exuret eam igni.'"

11 Et domui regis Iuda: "Audite verbum Domini. 12 Domus David, haec dicit Dominus: 'Iudicate mane iudicium, et eruite vi oppressum de manu calumniantis, ne forte egrediatur ut ignis indignatio mea et succendatur et non sit qui extinguat propter malitiam studiorum vestrorum. 13 Ecce: ego

I will turn back the weapons of war that are in your hands, *with* which you fight against the king of Babylon and the Chaldeans that besiege you round about the walls, and I will gather them together in the midst of this city. 5 And I myself will fight against you with an outstretched hand and with a strong arm and in fury and in indignation and in great wrath. 6 And I will strike the inhabitants of this city: men and beasts shall die of a great pestilence. 7 And after this," saith the Lord, "I will give Zedekiah, the king of Judah, and his servants and his people and such as are left in this city from the pestilence and the sword and the famine into the hand of Nebuchadnezzar, the king of Babylon, and into the hand of their enemies and into the hand of them that seek their life, and he shall strike them with the edge of the sword, and he shall not be moved *to pity* nor spare them nor shew mercy on them.""

8 And to this people thou shalt say, "Thus saith the Lord: 'Behold: I set before you the way of life and the way of death. 9 He that shall abide in this city shall die by the sword and by the famine and by the pestilence, but he that shall go out and flee over to the Chaldeans that besiege you shall live, and his life shall be to him as a spoil. 10 For I have set my face against this city for evil and not for good,' saith the Lord. 'It shall be given into the hand of the king of Babylon, and he shall burn it with fire.'"

11 And to the house of the king of Judah: "Hear ye the word of the Lord. 12 O house of David, thus saith the Lord: 'Judge ye judgment in the morning, and deliver him that is oppressed by violence out of the hand of the oppressor, *lest* my indignation go forth like a fire and be kindled and there be none to quench it because of the evil of your ways. 13 Be-

ad te habitatricem vallis solidae atque campestris,' ait Dominus, 'qui dicitis, "Quis percutiet nos? Et quis ingredietur domos nostras?" 14 Et visitabo super vos iuxta fructum studiorum vestrorum,' dicit Dominus, 'et succendam ignem in saltu eius, et devorabit omnia in circuitu eius.'"

Caput 22

Haec dicit Dominus: "Descende in domum regis Iuda, et loqueris ibi verbum hoc. 2 Et dices, 'Audi verbum Domini, rex Iuda qui sedes super solium David, tu et servi tui et populus tuus qui ingredimini per portas istas. 3 Haec dicit Dominus: "Facite iudicium et iustitiam, et liberate vi oppressum de manu calumniatoris, et advenam et pupillum et viduam nolite contristare, neque opprimatis inique, et sanguinem innocentem ne effundatis in loco isto. 4 Si enim facientes feceritis verbum istud, ingredientur per portas domus huius reges sedentes de genere David super thronum eius et ascendentes currus et equos, ipsi et servi et populus eorum. 5 Quod si non audieritis verba haec, in memet ipso iuravi," dicit Dominus, "quia in solitudinem erit domus haec."

hold: I come to thee that dwellest in a valley *upon a rock above a plain,'* saith the Lord, 'and you say, "Who shall strike us? And who shall enter into our houses?" 14 *But* I will visit upon you according to the fruit of your doings,' saith the Lord, 'and I will kindle a fire in the forest thereof, and it shall devour all things round about it.'"

Chapter 22

An exhortation both to king and people to return to God. The sentence of God upon Jehoahaz, Jehoiakim and Jeconiah.

Thus saith the Lord: "Go down to the house of the king of Judah, and there thou shalt speak this word. 2 And thou shalt say, 'Hear the word of the Lord, O king of Judah that sittest upon the throne of David, thou and thy servants and thy people who enter in by these gates. 3 Thus saith the Lord: "Execute judgment and justice, and deliver him that is *oppressed* out of the hand of the oppressor, and afflict not the stranger, *the* fatherless nor the widow, nor oppress them unjustly, and shed not innocent blood in this place. 4 For if you will do this thing indeed, *then* shall there enter in by the gates of this house kings of the race of David sitting upon his throne and *riding in* chariots and on horses, they and their servants and their people. 5 But if you will not hearken to these words, I swear by myself," saith the Lord, "that this house shall become a desolation."

6 "'Quia haec dicit Dominus super domum regis Iuda: "Galaad tu mihi, caput Libani, si non posuero te solitudinem, urbes inhabitabiles. 7 Et sanctificabo super te interficientem virum et arma eius, et succident electas cedros tuas et praecipitabunt in ignem. 8 Et pertransibunt gentes multae per civitatem hanc, et dicet unusquisque proximo suo, 'Quare fecit Dominus sic civitati huic grandi?' 9 Et respondebunt, 'Eo quod dereliquerint pactum Domini, Dei sui, et adoraverint deos alienos et servierint eis.'"

10 "'Nolite flere mortuum, neque lugeatis super eum fletu; plangite eum qui egreditur, quia non revertetur ultra nec videbit terram nativitatis suae. 11 Quia haec dicit Dominus ad Sellum, filium Iosiae, regem Iuda, qui regnavit pro Iosia, patre suo, qui egressus est de loco isto: "Non revertetur huc amplius, 12 sed in loco ad quem transtuli eum, ibi morietur, et terram istam non videbit amplius."

13 "'Vae qui aedificat domum suam in iniustitia et cenacula sua non in iudicio; amicum suum opprimet frustra et mercedem eius non reddet ei, 14 qui dicit, "Aedificabo mihi domum latam et cenacula spatiosa," qui aperit sibi fenestras et facit laquearia cedrina pingitque sinopide.

15 "''Numquid regnabis quoniam confers te cedro? Pater tuus numquid non comedit et bibit et fecit iudicium et iustitiam, tunc cum bene erat ei? 16 Iudicavit causam pauperis et egeni in bonum suum; numquid non ideo quia cognovit me?" dicit Dominus. 17 Tui vero oculi et cor ad avaritiam et ad

6 "'For thus saith the Lord to the house of the king of Judah: "Thou art to me Gilead, the head of Lebanon, *yet* surely I will make thee a wilderness *and* cities not habitable. 7 And I will *prepare against* thee the *destroyer* and his weapons, and they shall cut down thy chosen cedars and shall cast them headlong into the fire. 8 And many nations shall pass by this city, and they shall say every man to his neighbour, 'Why hath the Lord done so to this great city?' 9 And they shall answer, 'Because they have forsaken the covenant of the Lord, their God, and have adored strange gods and served them.'"

10 "'Weep not for him that is dead, nor bemoan him with *your tears;* lament him that goeth away, for he shall return no more nor see his native country. 11 For thus saith the Lord to Shallum, the son of Josiah, the king of Judah, who reigned instead of *his* father, who went forth out of this place, "He shall return hither no more, 12 but in the place to which I have removed him, there shall he die, and he shall not see this land any more."

13 "'Woe to him that buildeth up his house by injustice and his chambers not in judgment, *that* will oppress his friend without cause and will not pay him his wages, 14 who saith, "I will build me a wide house and large chambers," who openeth to himself windows and maketh roofs of cedar and painteth them with vermilion.

15 "'Shalt thou reign because thou comparest thyself to the cedar? Did not thy father eat and drink and do judgment and justice, *and* it was then well with him? 16 He judged the cause of the poor and needy for his own good; was it not therefore because he knew me?" saith the Lord. 17 But thy eyes and thy heart are set upon covetousness and upon

sanguinem innocentem fundendum et ad calumniam et ad cursum mali operis.

18 "'Propterea haec dicit Dominus ad Ioachim, filium Iosiae, regem Iuda: "Non plangent eum, 'Vae, frater!' et 'Vae, soror!' Non concrepabunt ei, 'Vae, domine!' et 'Vae, inclite!' 19 Sepultura asini sepelietur: putrefactus et proiectus extra portas Hierusalem."

20 "Ascende Libanum, et clama, et in Basan da vocem tuam, et clama ad transeuntes, quia contriti sunt omnes amatores tui. 21 Locutus sum ad te in abundantia tua, et dixisti, "Non audiam." Haec est via tua ab adulescentia tua, quia non audisti vocem meam. 22 Omnes pastores tuos pascet ventus, et amatores tui in captivitatem ibunt, et tunc confunderis et erubesces ab omni malitia tua. 23 Quae sedes in Libano et nidificas in cedris, quomodo congemuisti cum venissent tibi dolores quasi dolores parturientis?

24 ""Vivo ego," dicit Dominus, "quia si fuerit Iechonias, filius Ioachim, regis Iuda anulus in manu dextera mea, inde avellam eum. 25 Et dabo te in manu quaerentium animam tuam et in manu quorum tu formidas faciem et in manu Nabuchodonosor, regis Babylonis, et in manu Chaldeorum. 26 Et mittam te et matrem tuam quae genuit te in terram alienam in qua nati non estis, ibique moriemini, 27 et in terram ad quam ipsi levant animam suam ut revertantur illuc non revertentur."

28 "'Numquid vas fictile atque contritum vir iste Iechonias? Numquid vas absque omni voluptate? Quare abiecti sunt, ipse et semen eius, et proiecti in terram quam ignora-

shedding innocent blood and upon oppression and running after evil works.

18 "'Therefore thus saith the Lord concerning Jehoiakim, the son of Josiah, king of Judah: "They shall not mourn for him, 'Alas, my brother!' and 'Alas, sister!' They shall not lament for him, 'Alas, my lord!' or 'Alas, the noble one!' 19 He shall be buried with the burial of an ass: rotten and cast forth without the gates of Jerusalem."

20 "'Go up to Lebanon, and cry, and lift up thy voice in Bashan, and cry to them that pass by, for all thy lovers are destroyed. 21 I spoke to thee in thy prosperity, and thou saidst, "I will not hear." This hath been thy way from thy youth, because thou hast not heard my voice. 22 The wind shall feed all thy pastors, and thy lovers shall go into captivity, and then shalt thou be confounded and ashamed of all thy wickedness. 23 Thou that sittest in Libanus and makest thy nest in the cedars, how hast thou mourned when sorrows came upon thee as the pains of a woman in labour?

24 ""As I live," saith the Lord, "if Jeconiah, the son of Jehoiakim, the king of Judah were a ring on my right hand, I would pluck him thence. 25 And I will give thee into the hand of them that seek thy life and into the hand of them whose face thou fearest and into the hand of Nebuchadnezzar, king of Babylon, and into the hand of the Chaldeans. 26 And I will send thee and thy mother that bore thee into a strange country in which you were not born, and there you shall die, 27 and they shall not return into the land whereunto they lift up their mind to return thither."

28 "'Is this man Jeconiah an earthen and a broken vessel? Is he a vessel wherein there is no pleasure? Why are they cast out, he and his seed, and are cast into a land which they

verunt? 29 Terra, terra, terra, audi sermonem Domini! 30 Haec dicit Dominus: "Scribe virum istum sterilem, virum qui in diebus suis non prosperabitur, nec enim erit de semine eius vir qui sedeat super solium David et potestatem habeat ultra in Iuda."'"

Caput 23

"Vae pastoribus qui disperdunt et dilacerant gregem pascuae meae!" dicit Dominus. 2 "Ideo haec dicit Dominus, Deus Israhel, ad pastores qui pascunt populum meum: 'Vos dispersistis gregem meum et eiecistis eos et non visitastis eos. Ecce: ego visitabo super vos malitiam studiorum vestrorum,' ait Dominus. 3 'Et ego congregabo reliquias gregis mei de omnibus terris ad quas eiecero eos illuc, et convertam eos ad rura sua, et crescent et multiplicabuntur. 4 Et suscitabo super eos pastores, et pascent eos; non formidabunt ultra, et non pavebunt, et nullus quaeretur ex numero,' dicit Dominus.

know not? 29 O earth, earth, earth, hear the word of the Lord! 30 Thus saith the Lord: "Write this man barren, a man that shall not prosper in his days, for there shall not be a man of his seed that shall sit upon the throne of David and have power any more in Judah."'"

Chapter 23

God reproves evil governors and promises to send good pastors and Christ himself, the prince of the pastors. He inveighs against false prophets preaching without being sent.

"Woe to the pastors that destroy and tear the sheep of my pasture!" saith the Lord. 2 "Therefore thus saith the Lord, the God of Israel, to the pastors that feed my people: 'You have scattered my flock and driven them away and have not visited them. Behold: I will visit upon you *for* the evil of your doings,' saith the Lord. 3 'And I will gather together the remnant of my flock out of all the lands into which I have cast them out, and I will make them return to their own fields, and they shall increase and be multiplied. 4 And I will set up pastors over them, and they shall feed them; they shall fear no more, and they shall not be dismayed, and none shall be wanting of their number,' saith the Lord.

5 "Ecce: dies veniunt," ait Dominus, "et suscitabo David germen iustum, et regnabit rex et sapiens erit et faciet iudicium et iustitiam in terra. 6 In diebus illis salvabitur Iuda, et Israhel habitabit confidenter, et hoc est nomen quod vocabunt eum: Dominus, Iustus Noster. 7 Propter hoc ecce: dies veniunt," dicit Dominus, "et non dicent ultra, 'Vivit Dominus qui eduxit filios Israhel de terra Aegypti,' 8 sed 'Vivit Dominus qui eduxit et adduxit semen domus Israhel de terra aquilonis et de cunctis terris,' ad quas eieceram eos illuc, et habitabunt in terra sua."

9 Ad prophetas: Contritum est cor meum in medio mei; contremuerunt omnia ossa mea. Factus sum quasi vir ebrius et quasi homo madidus a vino a facie Domini et a facie verborum sanctorum eius. 10 Quia adulteris repleta est terra, quia a facie maledictionis luxit terra, arefacta sunt arva deserti, et factus est cursus eorum malus, et fortitudo eorum dissimilis.

11 "Propheta namque et sacerdos polluti sunt, et in domo mea inveni malum eorum," ait Dominus. 12 "Idcirco via eorum erit quasi lubricum in tenebris, inpellentur enim et corruent in ea, adferam enim super eos mala, annum visitationis eorum," ait Dominus. 13 "Et in prophetis Samariae vidi fatuitatem: prophetabant in Baal et decipiebant populum meum Israhel. 14 Et in prophetis Hierusalem vidi similitudinem adulterantium et iter mendacii, et confortaverunt manus pessimorum, ut non converteretur unusquisque a malitia sua; facti sunt mihi omnes ut Sodoma, et habitatores eius quasi Gomorra."

5 "Behold: the days come," saith the Lord, "and I will raise up to David a just branch, and a king shall reign and shall be wise and shall execute judgment and justice in the earth. 6 In those days shall Judah be saved, and Israel shall dwell confidently, and this is the name that they shall call him: The Lord, Our Just One. 7 Therefore behold: the days come," saith the Lord, "and they shall say no more, 'The Lord liveth who brought up the children of Israel out of the land of Egypt,' 8 but 'The Lord liveth who hath brought out and brought hither the seed of the house of Israel from the land of the north and out of all the lands,' to which I had cast them forth, and they shall dwell in their own land."

9 To the prophets: My heart is broken within me; all my bones tremble. I am become as a drunken man and as a man full of wine at the presence of the Lord and at the presence of his holy words. 10 Because the land is full of adulterers, because the land hath mourned *by reason* of cursing, the fields of the desert are dried up, and their course is become evil, and their strength unlike.

11 "For the prophet and the priest are defiled, and in my house I have found their wickedness," saith the Lord. 12 "Therefore their way shall be as a slippery way in the dark, for they shall be driven on and fall therein, for I will bring evils upon them, the year of their visitation," saith the Lord. 13 "And I have seen folly in the prophets of Samaria: they prophesied in Baal and deceived my people Israel. 14 And I have seen the likeness of adulterers and the way of lying in the prophets of Jerusalem, and they strengthened the hands of the *wicked,* that no man should return from his evil doings; they are all become unto me as Sodom, and the inhabitants thereof as Gomorrah."

15 Propterea haec dicit Dominus exercituum ad prophetas: "Ecce: ego cibabo eos absinthio et potabo eos felle, a
prophetis enim Hierusalem est egressa pollutio super omnem terram."

16 Haec dicit Dominus exercituum: "Nolite audire verba
prophetarum qui prophetant vobis et decipiunt vos; visionem cordis sui loquuntur, non de ore Domini. 17 Dicunt his
qui blasphemant me, 'Locutus est Dominus, "Pax erit vobis,"' et omni qui ambulat in pravitate cordis sui dixerunt,
'Non veniet super vos malum.'"

18 Quis enim adfuit in consilio Domini et vidit et audivit
sermonem eius? Quis consideravit verbum illius et audivit?
19 Ecce: turbo dominicae indignationis egredietur, et tempestas erumpens super caput impiorum veniet. 20 Non
revertetur furor Domini usque dum faciat et usque dum
conpleat cogitationem cordis sui; in novissimis diebus intellegetis consilium eius.

21 "Non mittebam prophetas, et ipsi currebant; non loquebar ad eos, et ipsi prophetabant. 22 Si stetissent in consilio meo et nota fecissent verba mea populo meo, avertissem
utique eos a via sua mala et a pessimis cogitationibus suis.
23 Putasne Deus e vicino ego sum," dicit Dominus, "et non
Deus de longe? 24 Occultabitur vir in absconditis, et ego non
videbo eum?" dicit Dominus. "Numquid non caelum et terram ego impleo?" ait Dominus. 25 "Audivi quae dixerunt prophetae prophetantes in nomine meo mendacium atque dicentes, 'Somniavi; somniavi.' 26 Usquequo istud in corde est
prophetarum vaticinantium mendacium et prophetantium
seductiones cordis sui, 27 qui volunt facere ut obliviscatur

15 Therefore thus saith the Lord of hosts to the prophets: "Behold: I will feed them with wormwood and will give them gall to drink, for from the prophets of Jerusalem corruption has gone forth into all the land.

16 Thus saith the Lord of hosts: "Hearken not to the words of the prophets that prophesy to you and deceive you; they speak a vision of their own heart *and* not out of the mouth of the Lord. 17 They say to them that blaspheme me, 'The Lord hath said, "You shall have peace," and to every one that walketh in the perverseness of his own heart they have said, "No evil shall come upon you."

18 For who hath stood in the counsel of the Lord and hath seen and heard his word? Who hath considered his word and heard it? 19 Behold: the whirlwind of the Lord's indignation shall come forth, and a tempest shall break out and come upon the head of the wicked. 20 The wrath of the Lord shall not return till he execute it and till he accomplish the thought of his heart; in the latter days you shall understand his counsel.

21 "I did not send prophets, *yet* they ran; I have not spoken to them, *yet* they prophesied. 22 If they had stood in my counsel and had made my words known to my people, I *should* have turned them from their evil way and from their wicked doings. 23 Am I, think ye, a God at hand," saith the Lord, "and not a God afar off? 24 Shall a man be hid in secret places, and I not see him?" saith the Lord. "Do not I fill heaven and earth?" saith the Lord. 25 "I have heard what the prophets said that prophesy lies in my name and say, 'I have dreamed; I have dreamed.' 26 How long *shall* this *be* in the heart of the prophets that prophesy lies and that prophesy the delusions of their own heart, 27 who seek to make my

populus meus nominis mei propter somnia eorum, quae narrat unusquisque ad proximum suum, sicut obliti sunt patres eorum nominis mei propter Baal? 28 Propheta qui habet somnium, narret somnium, et qui habet sermonem meum, loquatur sermonem meum vere; quid paleis ad triticum?" dicit Dominus. 29 "Numquid non verba mea sunt quasi ignis," ait Dominus, "et quasi malleus conterens petram? 30 Propterea ecce: ego ad prophetas," ait Dominus, "qui furantur verba mea, unusquisque a proximo suo. 31 Ecce: ego ad prophetas," ait Dominus, "qui adsumunt linguas suas et aiunt, 'Dicit Dominus.' 32 Ecce: ego ad prophetas somniantes mendacium," ait Dominus, "qui narraverunt ea et seduxerunt populum meum in mendacio suo et in miraculis suis, cum ego non misissem eos nec mandassem eis, qui nihil profuerunt populo huic," dicit Dominus.

33 "Si igitur interrogaverit te populus iste vel propheta aut sacerdos, dicens, 'Quod est onus Domini?' dices ad eos, '"Vos estis onus, proiciam quippe vos," dicit Dominus.' 34 Et propheta et sacerdos et populus qui dicit, 'Onus Domini,' visitabo super virum illum et super domum eius. 35 Haec dicetis, unusquisque ad proximum et ad fratrem suum: 'Quid respondit Dominus?' et 'Quid locutus est Dominus?'

36 "Et onus Domini ultra non memorabitur, quia onus erit unicuique sermo suus, et pervertistis verba Dei viventis, Domini exercituum, Dei nostri. 37 Haec dices ad prophetam: 'Quid respondit tibi Dominus?' et 'Quid locutus est Dominus?' 38 Si autem 'Onus Domini,' dixeritis, propter hoc haec dicit Dominus: 'Quia dixistis sermonem istum, "Onus Domini," et misi ad vos, dicens, "Nolite dicere 'Onus Domini,'"' 39 propterea ecce: ego tollam vos portans et derelin-

people forget my name through their dreams, which they tell every man to his neighbour, as their fathers forgot my name for Baal? 28 The prophet that hath a dream, let him tell a dream, and he that hath my word, let him speak my word with truth; what hath the chaff to do with the wheat?" saith the Lord. 29 "Are not my words as a fire," saith the Lord, "and as a hammer that breaketh the rock in pieces? 30 Therefore behold: I am against the prophets," saith the Lord, "who steal my words, every one from his neighbour. 31 Behold: I am against the prophets," saith the Lord, "who use their tongues and say, 'The Lord saith it.' 32 Behold: I am against the prophets that have lying dreams," saith the Lord, "and *tell* them and *cause* my people to err by their lying and by their wonders, when I sent them not nor commanded them, who have not profited this people at all," saith the Lord.

33 "If therefore this people or the prophet or the priest shall ask thee, saying, 'What is the burden of the Lord?' thou shalt say to them, '"You are the burden, for I will cast you away," saith the Lord.' 34 And as for the prophet and the priest and the people that *shall* say, 'The burden of the Lord,' I will visit upon that man and upon his house. 35 Thus shall you say, every one to his neighbour and to his brother: 'What hath the Lord answered?' and 'What hath the Lord spoken?'

36 "And the burden of the Lord shall be mentioned no more, for every man's word shall be his burden, *for* you have perverted the words of the living God, of the Lord of hosts, our God. 37 Thus shalt thou say to the prophet: 'What hath the Lord answered thee?' and 'What hath the Lord spoken?' 38 But if you shall say, 'The burden of the Lord,' therefore thus saith the Lord: 'Because you have said this word, "The burden of the Lord," and I have sent to you saying, "Say not 'The burden of the Lord,'" 39 therefore behold: I will take

quam vos et civitatem quam dedi vobis et patribus vestris a facie mea. ⁴⁰ Et dabo vos in obprobrium sempiternum et in ignominiam aeternam quae numquam oblivione delebitur.'"

Caput 24

Ostendit mihi Dominus, et ecce: duo calathi pleni ficis positi ante templum Domini, postquam transtulit Nabuchodonosor, rex Babylonis, Iechoniam, filium Ioachim, regem Iuda, et principes eius et fabrum et inclusorem de Hierusalem, et adduxit eos in Babylonem. 2 Calathus unus ficus bonas habebat nimis, ut solent ficus esse primi temporis, et calathus unus ficus habebat malas nimis quae comedi non poterant eo quod essent malae.

3 Et dixit Dominus ad me, "Quid tu vides Hieremia?"

Et dixi, "Ficus, ficus bonas, bonas valde, et malas, malas valde, quae comedi non possunt eo quod sint malae."

4 Et factum est verbum Domini ad me, dicens, 5 "Haec dicit Dominus, Deus Israhel: 'Sicut ficus hae bonae, sic cognoscam transmigrationem Iuda, quam emisi de loco isto in terram Chaldeorum in bonum. 6 Et ponam oculos meos

you away, carrying you, and will forsake you and the city which I gave to you and to your fathers out of my presence. 40 And I will bring an everlasting reproach upon you and a perpetual shame which shall never be *forgotten.*'"

Chapter 24

Under the type of good and bad figs he foretells the restoration of the Jews that had been carried away captive with Jeconiah and the desolation of those that were left behind.

The Lord shewed me, and behold: two baskets full of figs set before the temple of the Lord, after that Nebuchadnezzar, king of Babylon, had carried away Jeconiah, the son of Jehoiakim, the king of Judah, and his chief men and the *craftsmen* and *engravers* of Jerusalem, and had brought them to Babylon. 2 One basket had very good figs, like the figs of the first *season,* and the other basket had very bad figs which could not be eaten because they were bad.

3 And the Lord said to me, "What seest thou, Jeremiah?"

And I said, "Figs, the good figs, very good, and the bad figs, very bad, which cannot be eaten because they are bad."

4 And the word of the Lord came to me, saying, 5 "Thus saith the Lord, the God of Israel: 'Like these good figs, so will I regard the *captives* of Judah, whom I have sent forth out of this place into the land of the Chaldeans for *their* good. 6 And I will set my eyes upon them to be pacified, and

super eos ad placandum, et reducam eos in terram hanc, et aedificabo eos et non destruam, et plantabo eos et non evellam. 7 Et dabo eis cor ut sciant me, quia ego sum Dominus, et erunt mihi in populum, et ego ero eis in Deum, quia revertentur ad me in toto corde suo.'

8 "Et sicut ficus pessimae quae comedi non possunt eo quod sint malae, haec dicit Dominus: 'Sic dabo Sedeciam, regem Iuda, et principes eius et reliquos de Hierusalem qui remanserunt in urbe hac et qui habitant in terra Aegypti. 9 Et dabo eos in vexationem adflictionemque omnibus regnis terrae, in obprobrium et in parabolam et in proverbium et in maledictionem in universis locis ad quos eieci eos. 10 Et mittam in eis gladium et famem et pestem donec consumantur de terra quam dedi eis et patribus eorum.'"

Caput 25

Verbum quod factum est ad Hieremiam de omni populo Iudae in anno quarto Ioachim, filii Iosiae, regis Iuda, (ipse est annus primus Nabuchodonosor, regis Babylonis) 2 quod locutus est Hieremias propheta ad omnem popu-

I will bring them again into this land, and I will build them up and not pull them down, and I will plant them and not pluck them up. 7 And I will give them a heart to know me, that I am the Lord, and they shall be my people, and I will be their God, because they shall return to me with their whole heart.'

8 "And as the very bad figs that cannot be eaten because they are bad, thus saith the Lord: 'So will I give Zedekiah, the king of Judah, and his princes and the residue of Jerusalem that have remained in this city and that dwell in the land of Egypt. 9 And I will deliver them up to vexation and affliction to all the kingdoms of the earth, to be a reproach and a byword and a proverb and to be a curse in all places to which I have cast them out. 10 And I will send among them the sword and the famine and the pestilence till they be consumed out of the land which I gave to them and their fathers.'"

Chapter 25

The prophet foretells the seventy years captivity and after that, the destruction of Babylon and other nations.

The word that came to Jeremiah concerning all the people of Judah in the fourth year of Jehoiakim, the son of Josiah, king of Judah, (the same is the first year of Nebuchadnezzar, king of Babylon) 2 which Jeremiah the prophet spoke

lum Iuda et ad universos habitatores Hierusalem, dicens, 3 "A tertiodecimo anno Iosiae, filii Amon, regis Iuda, usque ad diem hanc (iste est tertius et vicesimus annus), factum est verbum Domini ad me, et locutus sum ad vos, de nocte consurgens et loquens, et non audistis. 4 Et misit Dominus ad vos omnes servos suos, prophetas, consurgens diluculo mittensque, et non audistis neque inclinastis aures vestras ut audiretis 5 cum diceret, 'Revertimini, unusquisque a via sua mala et a pessimis cogitationibus vestris, et habitabitis in terra quam dedit Dominus vobis et patribus vestris a saeculo et usque in saeculum. 6 Et nolite ire post deos alienos ut serviatis eis adoretisque eos, neque me ad iracundiam provocetis in operibus manuum vestrarum, et non adfligam vos.'

7 "'Et non audistis me,' dicit Dominus, 'ut me ad iracundiam provocaretis in operibus manuum vestrarum in malum vestrum.'

8 "Propterea haec dicit Dominus exercituum: 'Pro eo quod non audistis verba mea, 9 ecce: ego mittam et adsumam universas cognationes aquilonis,' ait Dominus, 'et Nabuchodonosor, regem Babylonis, servum meum, et adducam eos super terram istam et super habitatores eius et super omnes nationes quae in circuitu illius sunt, et interficiam eos et ponam eos in stuporem et in sibilum et in solitudines sempiternas. 10 Perdamque ex eis vocem gaudii et vocem laetitiae, vocem sponsi et vocem sponsae, vocem molae et lumen lucernae. 11 Et erit universa terra haec in solitudinem et in stuporem, et servient omnes gentes istae regi Babylonis septuaginta annis. 12 Cumque impleti fuerint anni septuaginta, visitabo super regem Babylonis et super gentem illam,' dicit

to all the people of Judah and to all the inhabitants of Jerusalem, saying, 3 "From the thirteenth year of Josiah, the son of Amon, king of Judah, until this day (this is the three and twentieth year), the word of the Lord hath come to me, and I have spoken to you, rising before day and speaking, and you have not hearkened. 4 And the Lord hath sent to you all his servants, the prophets, rising early and sending, and you have not hearkened nor inclined your ears to hear 5 when he said, 'Return ye, every one from his evil way and from your wicked devices, and you shall dwell in the land which the Lord hath given to you and your fathers for ever and ever. 6 And go not after strange gods to serve them and adore them, nor provoke me to wrath by the works of your hands, and I will not afflict you.'

7 "'And you have not heard me,' saith the Lord, 'that you might provoke me to anger with the works of your hands to your own hurt.'

8 "Therefore thus saith the Lord of hosts: 'Because you have not heard my words, 9 behold: I will send and take all the kindreds of the north,' saith the Lord, 'and Nebuchadnezzar, the king of Babylon, my servant, and I will bring them against this land and against the inhabitants thereof and against all the nations that are round about it, and I will destroy them and make them an astonishment and a hissing and perpetual desolations. 10 And I will take away from them the voice of mirth and the voice of gladness, the voice of the bridegroom and the voice of the bride, the sound of the mill and the light of the lamp. 11 And all this land shall be a desolation and an astonishment, and all these nations shall serve the king of Babylon seventy years. 12 And when the seventy years shall be expired, I will punish the king of Babylon and

Dominus, 'iniquitatem eorum et super terram Chaldeorum, et ponam illam in solitudines sempiternas. 13 Et adducam super terram illam omnia verba mea quae locutus sum contra eam, omne quod scriptum est in libro isto, quaecumque prophetavit Hieremias adversum omnes gentes, 14 quia servierunt eis, cum essent gentes multae et reges magni, et reddam eis secundum opera eorum et secundum facta manuum suarum.'"

15 Quia sic dicit Dominus exercituum, Deus Israhel: "Sume calicem vini furoris huius de manu mea, et propinabis de illo cunctis gentibus ad quas ego mittam te. 16 Et bibent et turbabuntur et insanient a facie gladii quem ego mittam inter eos."

17 Et accepi calicem de manu Domini, et propinavi cunctis gentibus ad quas misit me Dominus, 18 Hierusalem et civitatibus Iudae et regibus eius et principibus eius, ut darem eos in solitudinem et in stuporem et in sibilum et in maledictionem, sicut est dies ista: 19 Pharaoni, regi Aegypti, et servis eius et principibus eius et omni populo eius 20 et universis generaliter, cunctis regibus terrae Ausitidis et cunctis regibus terrae Philisthim et Ascaloni et Gazae et Accaroni et reliquiis Azoti 21 et Idumeae et Moab et filiis Ammon 22 et cunctis regibus Tyri et cunctis regibus Sidonis et regibus terrae insularum qui sunt trans mare 23 et Dedan et Theman et Buz et universis qui adtonsi sunt in comam 24 et cunctis regibus Arabiae et cunctis regibus occidentis qui habitant in deserto 25 et cunctis regibus Zambri et cunctis regibus Aelam et cunctis regibus Medorum 26 et cunctis regibus aquilonis de prope et de longe, unicuique contra fratrem suum, et

that nation,' saith the Lord, '*for* their iniquity and the land of the Chaldeans, and I will make it perpetual desolations. 13 And I will bring upon that land all my words that I have spoken against it, all that is written in this book, all that Jeremiah hath prophesied against all nations, 14 for they have served them, whereas they were many nations and great kings, and I will repay them according to their deeds and according to the works of their hands.'"

15 For thus saith the Lord of hosts, the God of Israel: "Take the cup of wine of this fury at my hand, and thou shalt make all the nations to drink thereof unto which I shall send thee. 16 And they shall drink and be troubled and be mad *because* of the sword which I shall send among them."

17 And I took the cup at the hand of the Lord, and I presented it to all the nations to drink of it to which the Lord sent me, 18 *to wit,* Jerusalem and the cities of Judah and the kings thereof and the princes thereof, to make them a desolation and an astonishment and a hissing and a curse, as it is at this day: 19 Pharaoh, the king of Egypt, and his servants and his princes and all his people 20 and all in general, all the kings of the land of Ausitis and all the kings of the land of the Philistines and Ashkelon and Gaza and Ekron and the remnant of Ashdod 21 and Edom and Moab and the children of Ammon 22 and all the kings of Tyre and all the kings of Sidon and the kings of the land of the islands that are beyond the sea 23 and Dedan and Tema and Buz and all that have their hair cut round 24 and all the kings of Arabia and all the kings of the west that dwell in the desert 25 and all the kings of Zimri and all the kings of Elam and all the kings of the Medes 26 and all the kings of the north far and near, every one against his brother, and all the kingdoms of the earth

omnibus regnis terrae quae super faciem eius sunt et rex Sesach bibet post eos.

27 "Et dices ad eos, 'Haec dicit Dominus exercituum,
Deus Israhel: "Bibite, et inebriamini, et vomite, et cadite,
neque surgatis a facie gladii quem ego mittam inter vos."'
28 Cumque noluerint accipere calicem de manu tua ut bibant, dices ad eos, 'Haec dicit Dominus exercituum: "Bibentes bibetis, 29 quia ecce: in civitate in qua invocatum est nomen meum ego incipiam adfligere, et vos quasi innocentes
et inmunes eritis? Non eritis inmunes, gladium enim ego
voco super omnes habitatores terrae," dicit Dominus exercituum.'

30 "Et tu prophetabis ad eos omnia verba haec, et dices ad
illos, 'Dominus de excelso rugiet et de habitaculo sancto suo
dabit vocem suam; rugiens rugiet super decorem suum; celeuma quasi calcantium concinetur adversus omnes habitatores terrae. 31 Pervenit sonitus usque ad extrema terrae,
quia iudicium Domino cum gentibus; iudicatur ipse cum
omni carne. "Impios tradidi gladio," dicit Dominus.'"

32 Haec dicit Dominus exercituum: "Ecce: adflictio egredietur de gente in gentem, et turbo magnus egredietur a
summitatibus terrae. 33 Et erunt interfecti Domini in die illa
a summo terrae usque ad summum eius. Non plangentur, et
non colligentur neque sepelientur; in sterquilinium super faciem terrae iacebunt. 34 Ululate, pastores, et clamate, et
aspergite vos cinere, optimates gregis, quia conpleti sunt
dies vestri ut interficiamini et dissipationes vestrae, et cade-

which are upon the face thereof and the king of Sheshach shall drink after them.

27 "And thou shalt say to them, 'Thus saith the Lord of hosts, the God of Israel: "Drink ye, and be drunken, and vomit, and fall, and rise no more *because* of the sword which I shall send among you."' 28 And if they refuse to take the cup at thy hand to drink, thou shalt say to them, 'Thus saith the Lord of hosts: "Drinking you shall drink, 29 for behold: I *begin to bring evil* on the city wherein my name is called upon, and shall you be as innocent and escape free? You shall not escape free, for I will call for the sword upon all the inhabitants of the earth," saith the Lord of hosts.'

30 "And thou shalt prophesy unto them all these words, and thou shalt say to them, 'The Lord shall roar from on high and shall utter his voice from his holy habitation; roaring he shall roar upon *the place of* his beauty; the shout as it were of them that tread grapes shall be given out against all the inhabitants of the earth. 31 The noise is come even to the ends of the earth, for the Lord entereth into judgment with the nations; he entereth into judgment with all flesh. "The wicked I have delivered up to the sword," saith the Lord.'"

32 Thus saith the Lord of hosts: "Behold: evil shall go forth from nation to nation, and a great whirlwind shall go forth from the ends of the earth. 33 And the slain of the Lord shall be at that day from one end of the earth even to the other end thereof. They shall not be lamented, and they shall not be gathered up nor buried; they shall lie as dung upon the face of the earth. 34 Howl, ye shepherds, and cry, and sprinkle yourselves with ashes, ye leaders of the flock, for the days *of your slaughter* and your dispersion are accom-

tis quasi vasa pretiosa. 35 Et peribit fuga a pastoribus, et salvatio ab optimatibus gregis."

36 Vox clamoris pastorum et ululatus optimatium gregis, quia vastavit Dominus pascua eorum. 37 Et conticuerunt arva pacis a facie irae furoris Domini. 38 Dereliquit quasi leo umbraculum suum, quia facta est terra eorum in desolationem a facie irae columbae et a facie irae furoris Domini.

Caput 26

In principio regni Ioachim, filii Iosiae, regis Iuda, factum est verbum istud a Domino, dicens, 2 "Haec dicit Dominus: 'Sta in atrio domus Domini, et loqueris ad omnes civitates Iuda de quibus veniunt ut adorent in domo Domini, universos sermones quos ego mandavi tibi ut loquaris ad eos. Noli subtrahere verbum, 3 si forte audiant et convertantur unusquisque a via sua mala, et paeniteat me mali quod cogito facere eis propter malitia studiorum eorum. 4 Et dices ad eos, "Haec dicit Dominus: 'Si non audieritis me ut ambuletis in

plished, and you shall fall like precious vessels. 35 And *the shepherds shall have no way to flee, nor the leaders* of the flock *to save themselves."*

36 A voice of the cry of the shepherds and a howling of the principal of the flock, because the Lord hath wasted their pastures. 37 And the fields of peace have been silent *because* of the fierce anger of the Lord. 38 He has forsaken his covert as the lion, for the land is laid waste *because* of the wrath of the dove and *because* of the *fierce* anger of the Lord.

Chapter 26

The prophet is apprehended and accused by the priests, but discharged by the princes.

In the beginning of the reign of Jehoiakim, the son of Josiah, king of Judah, came this word from the Lord, saying, 2 "Thus saith the Lord: 'Stand in the court of the house of the Lord, and speak to all the cities of Judah out of which they come to adore in the house of the Lord, all the words which I have commanded thee to speak unto them. Leave not out one word, 3 if so be they will hearken and be converted every one from his evil way, *that* I may repent me of the evil that I think to do unto them for the wickedness of their doings. 4 And thou shalt say to them, "Thus saith the Lord: 'If you will not hearken to me to walk in my law which

lege mea quam dedi vobis, 5 ut audiatis sermones servorum meorum, prophetarum, quos ego misi ad vos de nocte consurgens et dirigens (et non audistis), 6 dabo domum istam sicut Silo, et urbem hanc dabo in maledictionem cunctis gentibus terrae.'"'"

7 Et audierunt sacerdotes et prophetae et omnis populus Hieremiam loquentem verba haec in domo Domini. 8 Cumque conplesset Hieremias loquens omnia quae praeceperat ei Dominus ut loqueretur ad universum populum, adprehenderunt eum sacerdotes et prophetae et omnis populus, dicens, "Morte moriatur! 9 Quare prophetavit in nomine Domini, dicens, 'Sicut Silo erit domus haec, et urbs ista desolabitur eo quod non sit habitator?'" Et congregatus est omnis populus adversum Hieremiam in domo Domini.

10 Et audierunt principes Iuda verba haec, et ascenderunt de domo regis in domum Domini et sederunt in introitu portae domus Domini novae. 11 Et locuti sunt sacerdotes et prophetae ad principes et ad omnem populum, dicentes, "Iudicium mortis est viro huic, quia prophetavit adversum civitatem istam, sicut audistis auribus vestris."

12 Et ait Hieremias ad omnes principes et ad universum populum, dicens, "Dominus misit me ut prophetarem ad domum istam et ad civitatem hanc omnia verba quae audistis. 13 Nunc ergo bonas facite vias vestras et studia vestra et audite vocem Domini, Dei vestri, et paenitebit Dominum mali quod locutus est adversum vos. 14 Ego autem, ecce: in manibus vestris sum; facite mihi quod bonum et rectum est in oculis vestris. 15 Verumtamen scitote, et cognoscite quod si occideritis me, sanguinem innocentem tradetis contra

I have given to you, 5 to give ear to the words of my servants, the prophets, whom I sent to you rising up early and sending (and you have not hearkened), 6 I will make this house like Shiloh, and I will make this city a curse to all the nations of the earth.'"'"

7 And the priests and the prophets and all the people heard Jeremiah speaking these words in the house of the Lord. 8 And when Jeremiah made an end of speaking all that the Lord had commanded him to speak to all the people, the priests and the prophets and all the people laid hold on him, saying, "Let him be put to death! 9 Why hath he prophesied in the name of the Lord, saying, 'This house shall be like Shiloh, and this city shall be made desolate, *without* an inhabitant?'" And all the people were gathered together against Jeremiah in the house of the Lord.

10 And the princes of Judah heard these words, and they went up from the king's house into the house of the Lord and sat in the entry of the new gate of the house of the Lord. 11 And the priests and the prophets spoke to the princes and to all the people, saying, "The judgment of death is for this man, because he hath prophesied against this city, as you have heard with your ears."

12 *Then* Jeremiah spoke to all the princes, and to all the people, saying, "The Lord sent me to prophesy concerning this house and concerning this city all the words that you have heard. 13 Now therefore amend your ways and your doings and hearken to the voice of the Lord, your God, and the Lord will repent him of the evil that he hath spoken against you. 14 But as for me, behold: I am in your hands; do with me what is good and right in your eyes. 15 But know ye, and understand that if you put me to death, you will *shed* innocent

vosmet ipsos et contra civitatem istam et habitatores eius, in veritate enim misit me Dominus ad vos ut loquerer in auribus vestris omnia verba haec."

16 Et dixerunt principes et omnis populus ad sacerdotes et ad prophetas, "Non est viro huic iudicium mortis, quia in nomine Domini, Dei nostri, locutus est ad nos."

17 Surrexerunt ergo viri de senioribus terrae, et dixerunt ad omnem coetum populi, loquentes, 18 "Micheas de Morasthim fuit propheta in diebus Ezechiae, regis Iudae, et ait ad omnem populum Iudae, dicens, 'Haec dicit Dominus exercituum: "Sion quasi ager arabitur, et Hierusalem in acervum lapidum erit, et mons domus in excelsa silvarum."' 19 Numquid morte condemnavit eum Ezechias, rex Iuda, et omnis Iuda? Numquid non timuerunt Dominum et deprecati sunt faciem Domini, et paenituit Dominum mali quod locutus erat adversum eos? Itaque nos facimus malum grande contra animas nostras."

20 Fuit quoque vir prophetans in nomine Domini, Urias, filius Semei de Cariathiarim, et prophetavit adversum civitatem istam et adversum terram hanc, iuxta universa verba Hieremiae. 21 Et audivit Rex Ioachim et omnes potentes et principes eius verba haec, et quaesivit rex interficere eum. Et audivit Urias et timuit fugitque et ingressus est Aegyptum. 22 Et misit Rex Ioachim viros in Aegyptum: Elnathan, filium Achobor, et viros cum eo in Aegyptum. 23 Et eduxerunt Uriam de Aegypto et adduxerunt eum ad Regem Ioachim, et percussit eum gladio, et proiecit cadaver eius in

blood against your own selves and against this city and the inhabitants thereof, for in truth the Lord sent me to you to speak all these words in your hearing."

16 *Then* the princes and all the people said to the priests and to the prophets, "There is no judgment of death for this man, for he hath spoken to us in the name of the Lord, our God."

17 *And some* of the ancients of the land rose up, and they spoke to all the assembly of the people, saying, 18 "Micah of Moresheth was a prophet in the days of Hezekiah, king of Judah, and he spoke to all the people of Judah, saying, 'Thus saith the Lord of hosts: "Zion shall be ploughed like a field, and Jerusalem shall be a heap of stones, and the mountain of the house the high places of woods. 19 Did Hezekiah, king of Judah, and all Judah condemn him to death? Did they not fear the Lord and beseech the face of the Lord, and the Lord repented of the evil that he had spoken against them? Therefore we are doing a great evil against our souls."

20 There was also a man that prophesied in the name of the Lord, Uriah, the son of Shemaiah of Kiriath-jearim, and he prophesied against this city and against this land, according to all the words of Jeremiah. 21 And King Jehoiakim and all his men in power and his princes heard these words, and the king sought to put him to death. And Uriah heard it and was afraid and fled and went into Egypt. 22 And King Jehoiakim sent men into Egypt: Elnathan, the son of Achbor, and men with him into Egypt. 23 And they brought Uriah out of Egypt and brought him to King Jehoiakim, and he slew him with the sword, and he cast his dead body into the graves of

sepulchris vulgi ignobilis. 24 Igitur manus Ahicam, filii Saphan, fuit cum Hieremia, ut non traderetur in manus populi, et interficerent eum.

Caput 27

In principio regni Ioachim, filii Iosiae, regis Iuda, factum est verbum istud ad Hieremiam a Domino, dicens, 2 "Haec dicit Dominus ad me: 'Fac tibi vincula et catenas, et pones eas in collo tuo, 3 et mittes eas ad regem Edom et ad regem Moab et ad regem filiorum Ammon et ad regem Tyri et ad regem Sidonis in manu nuntiorum qui venerunt Hierusalem ad Sedeciam, regem Iuda. 4 Et praecipies eis ut ad dominos suos loquantur: "Haec dicit Dominus exercituum, Deus Israhel: 'Haec dicetis ad dominos vestros: 5 "Ego feci terram et homines et iumenta quae sunt super faciem terrae in fortitudine mea magna et in brachio meo extento, et dedi eam ei qui placuit in oculis meis. 6 Et nunc itaque ego dedi

the *common* people. 24 So the hand of Ahikam, the son of Shaphan, was with Jeremiah, that he should not be delivered into the hands of the people *to* put him to death.

Chapter 27

The prophet sends chains to divers kings, signifying that they must bend their necks under the yoke of the king of Babylon. The vessels of the temple shall not be brought back till all the rest are carried away.

In the beginning of the reign of Jehoiakim, the son of Josiah, king of Judah, this word came to Jeremiah from the Lord, saying, 2 "Thus saith the Lord to me, 'Make thee bands and chains, and thou shalt put them on thy neck, 3 and thou shalt send them to the king of Edom and to the king of Moab and to the king of the children of Ammon and to the king of Tyre and to the king of Sidon by the hand of the messengers that are come to Jerusalem to Zedekiah, the king of Judah. 4 And thou shalt command them to speak to their masters: "Thus saith the Lord of hosts, the God of Israel: 'Thus shall you say to your masters: "I made the earth and the men and the beasts that are upon the face of the earth by my great power and by my stretched out arm, and I have given it to whom it seemed good in my eyes. 6 And now I

omnes terras istas in manu Nabuchodonosor, regis Babylonis, servi mei; insuper et bestias agri dedi ei ut serviant illi. 7 Et servient ei omnes gentes et filio eius et filio filii eius, donec veniat tempus terrae eius et ipsius, et servient ei gentes multae et reges magni. 8 Gens autem et regnum quod non servierit Nabuchodonosor, regi Babylonis, et quicumque non curvaverit collum suum sub iugo regis Babylonis, in gladio et in fame et in peste visitabo super gentem illam," ait Dominus, "donec consumam eos in manu eius. 9 Vos ergo nolite audire prophetas vestros et divinos et somniatores et augures et maleficos qui dicunt vobis, 'Non servietis regi Babylonis,' 10 quia mendacium prophetant vobis ut longe faciant vos de terra vestra et eiciant vos et pereatis. 11 Porro gens quae subiecerit cervicem suam sub iugo regis Babylonis et servierit ei, dimittam eam in terra sua," dicit Dominus, "et colet eam et habitabit in ea.""""

12 Et ad Sedeciam, regem Iuda, locutus sum secundum omnia verba haec, dicens, "Subicite colla vestra sub iugo regis Babylonis et servite ei et populo eius, et vivetis. 13 Quare moriemini, tu et populus tuus, gladio et fame et peste, sicut locutus est Dominus ad gentem quae servire noluerit regi Babylonis? 14 Nolite audire verba prophetarum dicentium vobis, 'Non servietis regi Babylonis,' quia mendacium ipsi loquuntur vobis. 15 Quia 'Non misi eos,' ait Dominus, 'et ipsi prophetant in nomine meo mendaciter ut eiciant vos et pereatis, tam vos quam prophetae qui vaticinantur vobis.'"

have given all these lands into the hand of Nebuchadnezzar, king of Babylon, my servant; moreover also the beasts of the field I have given him to serve him. 7 And all nations shall serve him and his son and his son's son, till the time come for his land and himself, and many nations and great kings shall serve him. 8 But the nation and kingdom that will not serve Nebuchadnezzar, king of Babylon, and whosoever will not bend his neck under the yoke of the king of Babylon, I will visit upon that nation with the sword and with famine and with pestilence," saith the Lord, "till I consume them by his hand. 9 Therefore hearken not to your prophets and diviners and dreamers and soothsayers and sorcerers that say to you, 'You shall not serve the king of Babylon,' 10 for they prophesy lies to you to remove you far from your country and cast you out and to make you perish. 11 But the nation that shall bend down their neck under the yoke of the king of Babylon and shall serve him, I will let them remain in their own land," saith the Lord, "and they shall till it and dwell in it."'"'"

12 And I spoke to Zedekiah, the king of Judah, according to all these words, saying, "Bend down your necks under the yoke of the king of Babylon and serve him and his people, and you shall live. 13 Why will you die, thou and thy people, by the sword and by famine and by the pestilence, as the Lord hath spoken against the nation that will not serve the king of Babylon? 14 Hearken not to the words of the prophets that say to you, 'You shall not serve the king of Babylon,' for they tell you a lie. 15 For 'I have not sent them,' saith the Lord, 'and they prophesy in my name falsely to drive you out and that you may perish, both you and the prophets that prophesy to you.'"

16 Et ad sacerdotes et ad populum istum locutus sum, dicens, "Haec dicit Dominus: 'Nolite audire verba prophetarum vestrorum qui prophetant vobis, dicentes, "Ecce: vasa Domini revertentur de Babylone nunc cito," mendacium enim prophetant vobis. 17 Nolite ergo audire eos, sed servite regi Babylonis ut vivatis. Quare datur haec civitas in solitudinem? 18 Et si prophetae sunt, et est verbum Domini in eis, occurrant Domino exercituum, ut non veniant vasa quae derelicta fuerant in domo Domini et in domo regis Iuda et in Hierusalem in Babylonem.'

19 "Quia haec dicit Dominus exercituum ad columnas et ad mare et ad bases et ad reliqua vasorum quae remanserunt in civitate hac, 20 quae non tulit Nabuchodonosor, rex Babylonis, cum transferret Iechoniam, filium Ioachim, regem Iuda, de Hierusalem in Babylonem, et omnes optimates Iuda et Hierusalem, 21 quia haec dicit Dominus exercituum, Deus Israhel, ad vasa quae derelicta sunt in domo Domini et in domo regis Iuda et Hierusalem: 22 'In Babylonem transferentur, et ibi erunt usque ad diem visitationis suae,' dicit Dominus, 'et adferri faciam ea et restitui in loco isto.'"

16 I spoke also to the priests and to this people, saying, "Thus saith the Lord: 'Hearken not to the words of your prophets that prophesy to you, saying, "Behold: the vessels of the Lord shall now in a short time be brought again from Babylon," for they prophesy a lie unto you. 17 Therefore hearken not to them, but serve the king of Babylon that you may live. Why *should* this city *be* given up to desolation? 18 But if they be prophets, and the word of the Lord be in them, let them interpose themselves before the Lord of hosts, that the vessels which were left in the house of the Lord and in the house of the king of Judah and in Jerusalem may not go to Babylon.'

19 "For thus saith the Lord of hosts to the pillars and to the sea and to the bases and to the rest of the vessels that remain in this city, 20 which Nebuchadnezzar, the king of Babylon, did not take when he carried away Jeconiah, the son of Jehoiakim, the king of Judah, from Jerusalem to Babylon, and all the great men of Judah and Jerusalem, 21 for thus saith the Lord of hosts, the God of Israel, to the vessels that are left in the house of the Lord and in the house of the king of Judah and Jerusalem: 22 'They shall be carried to Babylon, and there they shall be until the day of their visitation,' saith the Lord, 'and I will cause them to be brought and to be restored in this place.'"

Caput 28

Et factum est in anno illo, in principio regni Sedeciae, regis Iuda, in anno quarto in mense quinto, dixit ad me Ananias, filius Azur, propheta de Gabaon, in domo Domini coram sacerdotibus et omni populo, dicens, 2 "Haec dicit Dominus exercituum, Deus Israhel: 'Contrivi iugum regis Babylonis; 3 adhuc duo anni dierum et ego referri faciam ad locum istum omnia vasa domus Domini, quae tulit Nabuchodonosor, rex Babylonis, de loco isto et transtulit ea in Babylonem. 4 Et Iechoniam, filium Ioachim, regem Iuda, et omnem transmigrationem Iudae qui ingressi sunt in Babylonem, ego convertam ad locum istum,' ait Dominus, 'conteram enim iugum regis Babylonis.'"

5 Et dixit Hieremias, propheta, ad Ananiam, prophetam, in oculis sacerdotum et in oculis omnis populi qui stabat in domo Domini, 6 et ait Hieremias, propheta, "Amen: sic faciat Dominus; suscitet Dominus verba tua quae prophetasti, ut referantur vasa in domum Domini et omnis transmigratio de Babylone ad locum istum. 7 Verumtamen audi verbum hoc quod ego loquor in auribus tuis et in auribus universi

Chapter 28

The false prophecy of Hananiah. He dies that same year, as Jeremiah foretold.

And it came to pass in that year, in the beginning of the reign of Zedekiah, king of Judah, in the fourth year in the fifth month, that Hananiah, the son of Azzur, a prophet of Gibeon, spoke to me in the house of the Lord before the priests and all the people, saying, 2 "Thus saith the Lord of hosts, the God of Israel: 'I have broken the yoke of the king of Babylon; 3 as yet two years of days, and I will cause all the vessels of the house of the Lord to be brought back into this place, which Nebuchadnezzar, king of Babylon, took away from this place and carried them to Babylon. 4 And I will bring back to this place Jeconiah, the son of Jehoiakim, king of Judah, and all the *captives* of Judah that are gone to Babylon,' saith the Lord, 'for I will break the yoke of the king of Babylon.'"

5 And Jeremiah, the prophet, said to Hananiah, the prophet, in *the presence* of the priests and in *the presence* of all the people that stood in the house of the Lord, 6 and Jeremiah, the prophet, said, "Amen: the Lord do so; the Lord perform thy words which thou hast prophesied, that the vessels may be brought again into the house of the Lord and all the *captives* may return out of Babylon to this place. 7 Nevertheless hear this word that I speak in thy ears and in

populi. 8 Prophetae qui fuerunt ante me et ante te ab initio et prophetaverunt super terras multas et super regna magna, de proelio et de adflictione et de fame— 9 propheta qui vaticinatus est pacem, cum venerit verbum eius, scietur propheta quem misit Dominus in veritate."

10 Et tulit Ananias, propheta, catenam de collo Hieremiae, prophetae, et confregit eam. 11 Et ait Ananias in conspectu omnis populi, dicens, "Haec dicit Dominus: 'Sic confringam iugum Nabuchodonosor, regis Babylonis, post duos annos dierum de collo omnium gentium.'"

12 Et abiit Hieremias, propheta, in viam suam. Et factum est verbum Domini ad Hieremiam, postquam confregit Ananias, propheta, catenam de collo Hieremiae, prophetae, dicens, 13 "Vade, et dices Ananiae, 'Haec dicit Dominus: "Catenas ligneas contrivisti, et facies pro eis catenas ferreas." 14 Quia haec dicit Dominus exercituum, Deus Israhel: "Iugum ferreum posui super collum cunctarum gentium istarum, ut serviant Nabuchodonosor, regi Babylonis, et servient ei; insuper et bestias terrae dedi ei."'"

15 Et dixit Hieremias, propheta, ad Ananiam, prophetam, "Audi, Anania; non misit te Dominus, et tu confidere fecisti populum istum in mendacio. 16 Idcirco haec dicit Dominus: 'Ecce: emittam te a facie terrae; hoc anno morieris, adversum Dominum enim locutus es.'" 17 Et mortuus est Ananias, propheta, in anno illo mense septimo.

the ears of all the people. 8 The prophets that have been before me and before thee from the beginning and have prophesied concerning many countries and concerning great kingdoms, of war and of affliction and of famine— 9 the prophet that prophesied peace, when his word shall come to pass, the prophet shall be known whom the Lord hath sent in truth."

10 And Hananiah, the prophet, took the chain from the neck of Jeremiah, the prophet, and broke it. 11 And Hananiah spoke in the presence of all the people, saying, "Thus saith the Lord, *'Even* so will I break the yoke of Nebuchadnezzar, the king of Babylon, after two *full* years from off the neck of all the nations.'"

12 And Jeremiah, the prophet, went his way. And the word of the Lord came to Jeremiah, after that Hananiah, the prophet, *had broken* the chain from off the neck of Jeremiah, the prophet, saying, 13 "Go, and *tell* Hananiah, 'Thus saith the Lord: "Thou hast broken chains of wood, and thou shalt make for them chains of iron." 14 For thus saith the Lord of hosts, the God of Israel: "I have put a yoke of iron upon the neck of all these nations, to serve Nebuchadnezzar, king of Babylon, and they shall serve him; moreover also I have given him the beasts of the earth."'"

15 And Jeremiah, the prophet, said to Hananiah, the prophet, "Hear *now,* Hananiah; the Lord hath not sent thee, and thou hast made this people to trust in a lie. 16 Therefore thus saith the Lord: 'Behold: I will send thee away from off the face of the earth; this year shalt thou die, for thou hast spoken against the Lord.'" 17 And Hananiah, the prophet, died in that year in the seventh month.

Caput 29

Et haec sunt verba libri quem misit Hieremias, propheta, de Hierusalem ad reliquias seniorum transmigrationis et ad sacerdotes et ad prophetas et ad omnem populum quem transduxerat Nabuchodonosor de Hierusalem in Babylonem, 2 postquam egressus est Iechonias, rex, et domina et eunuchi et principes Iuda et Hierusalem et faber et inclusor de Hierusalem 3 in manu Ellasa, filii Saphan, et Gamariae, filii Helciae, quos misit Sedecias, rex Iuda, ad Nabuchodonosor, regem Babylonis, in Babylonem, dicens, 4 "Haec dicit Dominus exercituum, Deus Israhel, omni transmigrationi, quam transtuli de Hierusalem in Babylonem: 5 'Aedificate domos, et habitate, et plantate pomaria, et comedite fructum eorum. 6 Accipite uxores, et generate filios et filias, et date filiis vestris uxores, et filias vestras date viris, et pariant filios et filias, et multiplicamini ibi, et nolite esse pauci

Chapter 29

Jeremiah writeth to the captives in Babylon, exhorting them
to be easy there and not to hearken to false prophets. That
they shall be delivered after seventy years, but those that remain in Jerusalem shall perish by the sword, famine and pestilence, and that Ahab, Zedekiah and Shemaiah, false
prophets, shall die miserably.

Now these are the words of the letter which Jeremiah, the prophet, sent from Jerusalem to the residue of the ancients *that were carried into* captivity and to the priests and to the prophets and to all the people whom Nebuchadnezzar had carried away from Jerusalem to Babylon, 2 after that Jeconiah, the king, and the queen and the eunuchs and the princes of Judah and of Jerusalem and the *craftsmen* and the *engravers* were departed out of Jerusalem 3 by the hand of Elasah, the son of Shaphan, and Gemariah, the son of Hilkiah, whom Zedekiah, king of Judah, sent to Babylon to Nebuchadnezzar, king of Babylon, saying, 4 "Thus saith the Lord of hosts, the God of Israel, to all *that are carried away captives,* whom I have *caused to be* carried away from Jerusalem to Babylon: 5 'Build ye houses, and dwell in them, and plant orchards, and eat the fruit of them. 6 Take ye wives, and beget sons and daughters, and *take* wives for your sons, and give your daughters to husbands, and let them bear sons and daughters, and be ye multiplied there, and be not few in

numero. 7 Et quaerite pacem civitatis ad quam transmigrare vos feci, et orate pro ea ad Dominum, quia in pace illius erit pax vobis.'

8 "Haec enim dicit Dominus exercituum, Deus Israhel: 'Non vos inducant prophetae vestri qui sunt in medio vestrum et divini vestri, et ne adtendatis ad somnia vestra quae vos somniatis, 9 quia falso ipsi prophetant vobis in nomine meo, et non misi eos,' dicit Dominus.

10 "Quia haec dicit Dominus: 'Cum coeperint impleri in Babylone septuaginta anni, visitabo vos, et suscitabo super vos verbum meum bonum ut reducam vos ad locum istum. 11 Ego enim scio cogitationes quas cogito super vos,' ait Dominus, 'cogitationes pacis et non adflictionis, ut dem vobis finem et patientiam. 12 Et invocabitis me, et ibitis, et orabitis me, et exaudiam vos. 13 Quaeretis me et invenietis cum quaesieritis me in toto corde vestro, 14 et inveniar a vobis,' ait Dominus, 'et reducam captivitatem vestram, et congregabo vos de universis gentibus et de cunctis locis ad quae expuli vos,' dicit Dominus, 'et reverti vos faciam de loco ad quem transmigrare vos feci 15 quia dixistis, "Suscitavit nobis Dominus prophetas in Babylone."'

16 "Quia haec dicit Dominus ad regem qui sedet super solium David et ad omnem populum habitatorem urbis huius, ad fratres vestros qui non sunt egressi vobiscum in transmigrationem, 17 haec dicit Dominus exercituum: 'Ecce: mittam in eos gladium et famem et pestem, et ponam eos quasi ficus malas quae comedi non possunt eo quod pessimae sint. 18 Et persequar eos in gladio et in fame et in pestilentia, et

number. 7 And seek the peace of the city to which I have caused you to be carried away captives, and pray to the Lord for it, for in the peace thereof shall be your peace.'

8 "For thus saith the Lord of hosts, the God of Israel: 'Let not your prophets that are in the midst of you and your diviners deceive you, and give no heed to your dreams which you dream, 9 for they prophesy falsely to you in my name, and I have not sent them,' saith the Lord.

10 "For thus saith the Lord, 'When the seventy years shall begin to be accomplished in Babylon, I will visit you, and I will perform my good word *in your favour* to bring you again to this place. 11 For I know the thoughts that I think towards you,' saith the Lord, 'thoughts of peace and not of affliction, to give you an end and patience. 12 And you shall call upon me, and you shall go, and you shall pray to me, and I will hear you. 13 You shall seek me and shall find me when you shall seek me with all your heart, 14 and I will be found by you,' saith the Lord, 'and I will bring back your captivity, and I will gather you out of all nations and from all the places to which I have driven you out,' saith the Lord, 'and I will *bring* you back from the place to which I caused you to be carried away captive 15 because you have said, "The Lord hath raised us up prophets in Babylon."'

16 "For thus saith the Lord to the king that sitteth upon the throne of David and to all the people that dwell in this city, to your brethren that are not gone forth with you into captivity, 17 thus saith the Lord of hosts: 'Behold: I will send upon them the sword, and the famine and the pestilence, and I will make them like bad figs that cannot be eaten because they are very bad. 18 And I will persecute them with the sword and with famine and with the pestilence, and I

dabo eos in vexationem universis regnis terrae in maledictionem et in stuporem et in sibilum et in obprobrium cunctis gentibus ad quas ego eieci eos, 19 eo quod non audierint
verba mea,' dicit Dominus, 'quae misi ad eos per servos
meos, prophetas, de nocte consurgens et mittens, et non
audistis,' dicit Dominus. 20 'Vos ergo audite verbum Domini,
omnis transmigratio quam emisi de Hierusalem in Babylonem.'

21 "Haec dicit Dominus exercituum, Deus Israhel, ad
Ahab, filium Coliae, et ad Sedeciam, filium Maasiae, qui
prophetant vobis in nomine meo mendaciter: 'Ecce: ego tradam eos in manus Nabuchodonosor, regis Babylonis, et percutiet eos in oculis vestris. 22 Et adsumetur ex eis maledictio
omni transmigrationi Iuda quae est in Babylone, dicentium,
"Ponat te Dominus sicut Sedeciam et sicut Ahab, quos frixit
rex Babylonis in igne," 23 pro eo quod fecerint stultitiam in
Israhel et moechati sunt in uxores amicorum suorum et locuti sunt verbum in nomine meo mendaciter, quod non
mandavi eis. Ego sum iudex et testis,' dicit Dominus.

24 "Et ad Semeiam, Neelamiten, dices, 25 'Haec dicit Dominus exercituum, Deus Israhel: "Pro eo quod misisti in nomine tuo libros ad omnem populum qui est in Hierusalem et
ad Sophoniam, filium Maasiae, sacerdotem, et ad universos
sacerdotes, dicens, 26 'Dominus dedit te sacerdotem pro
Ioiadae, sacerdote, ut sis dux in domo Domini super omnem
virum arrepticium et prophetantem, ut mittas eum in nervum et in carcerem.' 27 Et nunc quare non increpasti Hieremiam, Anathothiten, qui prophetat vobis? 28 Quia super hoc

will give them up unto affliction to all the kingdoms of the earth to be a curse and an astonishment and a hissing and a reproach to all the nations to which I have driven them out, 19 because they have not hearkened to my words,' saith the Lord, 'which I sent to them by my servants, the prophets, rising by night and sending, and you have not heard,' saith the Lord. 20 'Hear ye therefore the word of the Lord, all ye of the captivity whom I have sent out from Jerusalem to Babylon.'

21 "Thus saith the Lord of hosts, the God of Israel, to Ahab, the son of Kolaiah, and to Zedekiah, the son of Maaseiah, who prophesy unto you in my name falsely: 'Behold: I will deliver them up into the hands of Nebuchadnezzar, the king of Babylon, and he shall kill them before your eyes. 22 And of them shall be taken up a curse by all the captivity of Judah that are in Babylon, saying, "The Lord make thee like Zedekiah and like Ahab, whom the king of Babylon fried in the fire," 23 because they have acted folly in Israel and have committed adultery with the wives of their friends and have spoken lying *words* in my name, which I commanded them not. I am the judge and the witness,' saith the Lord.

24 "And to Shemaiah, the Nehelamite, thou shalt say, 25 'Thus saith the Lord of hosts, the God of Israel: "Because thou hast sent letters in thy name to all the people that are in Jerusalem and to Zephaniah, the son of Maaseiah, the priest, and to all the priests, saying, 26 'The Lord hath made thee priest instead of Jehoiada, the priest, that thou shouldst be ruler in the house of the Lord over every man that raveth and prophesieth, to put him in the stocks and into prison.' 27 And now why hast thou not rebuked Jeremiah, the Anathothite, who prophesieth to you? 28 *For* he hath also sent to

misit ad nos in Babylonem, dicens, 'Longum est: aedificate domos, et habitate, et plantate hortos, et comedite fructus eorum.'""

29 Legit ergo Sophonias, sacerdos, librum istum in auribus Hieremiae, prophetae. 30 Et factum est verbum Domini ad Hieremiam, dicens, 31 "Mitte ad omnem transmigrationem, dicens, 'Haec dicit Dominus ad Semeiam, Neelamiten: "Pro eo quod prophetavit vobis Semeias, et ego non misi eum, et fecit vos confidere in mendacio, 32 idcirco haec dicit Dominus: 'Ecce: ego visitabo super Semeiam, Neelamiten, et super semen eius; non erit ei vir sedens in medio populi huius, et non videbit bonum quod ego faciam populo meo,' ait Dominus, 'quia praevaricationem locutus est adversum Dominum.'""

Caput 30

Hoc verbum quod factum est ad Hieremiam a Domino, dicens, 2 "Haec dicit Dominus, Deus Israhel, dicens, 'Scribe tibi omnia verba quae locutus sum ad te in libro. 3 Ecce enim: dies veniunt,' dicit Dominus, 'et convertam conversionem populi mei, Israhel et Iuda,' ait Dominus, 'et convertam eos ad terram quam dedi patribus eorum, et possidebunt eam.'"

us in Babylon, saying, 'It is a long time: build ye houses, and dwell in them, and plant gardens, and eat the fruits of them.'"'"

29 So Zephaniah, the priest, read this letter in the hearing of Jeremiah, the prophet. 30 And the word of the Lord came to Jeremiah, saying, 31 "Send to all them of the captivity, saying, 'Thus saith the Lord to Shemaiah, the Nehelamite: "Because Shemaiah hath prophesied to you, and I sent him not, and hath caused you to trust in a lie, 32 therefore thus saith the Lord: 'Behold: I will visit upon Shemaiah, the Nehelamite, and upon his seed; he shall not have a man *to* sit in the midst of this people, and he shall not see the good that I will do to my people,' saith the Lord, 'because he hath spoken treason against the Lord.'"'"

Chapter 30

God will deliver his people from their captivity. Christ shall be their king, and his church shall be glorious for ever.

This is the word that came to Jeremiah from the Lord, saying, 2 "Thus saith the Lord, the God of Israel, saying, 'Write thee all the words that I have spoken to thee in a book. 3 For behold: the days come,' saith the Lord, 'and I will bring again the *captivity* of my people, Israel and Judah,' saith the Lord, 'and I will cause them to return to the land which I gave to their fathers, and they shall possess it.'"

4 Et haec verba quae locutus est Dominus ad Israhel et ad Iudam, 5 quoniam haec dicit Dominus: "Vocem terroris audivimus; formido et non est pax. 6 Interrogate, et videte si generat masculus? Quare ergo vidi omnis viri manum super lumbum suum quasi parturientis, et conversae sunt universae facies in auruginem? 7 Vae, quia magna dies illa, nec est similis eius tempusque tribulationis est Iacob, et ex ipso salvabitur. 8 Et erit in die illa," ait Dominus exercituum, "conteram iugum eius de collo tuo et vincula eius disrumpam, et non dominabuntur ei amplius alieni. 9 Sed servient Domino, Deo suo, et David, regi suo, quem suscitabo eis. 10 Tu ergo ne timeas, serve meus Iacob," ait Dominus, "neque paveas, Israhel, quia ecce: ego salvabo te de terra longinqua et semen tuum de terra captivitatis eorum, et revertetur Iacob et quiescet et cunctis affluet bonis, et non erit quem formidet.

11 "Quoniam tecum ego sum," ait Dominus "ut salvem te, faciam enim consummationem in cunctis gentibus in quibus dispersi te, te autem non faciam in consummationem. Sed castigabo te in iudicio, ut non tibi videaris innoxius."

12 Quia haec dicit Dominus: "Insanabilis fractura tua; pessima plaga tua. 13 Non est qui iudicet iudicium tuum ad alligandum; curationum utilitas non est tibi. 14 Omnes amatores tui obliti sunt tui teque non quaerent, plaga enim inimici percussi te, castigatione crudeli; propter multitudinem iniquitatis tuae, dura facta sunt peccata tua. 15 Quid clamas super contritione tua? Insanabilis est dolor tuus. Propter

4 And these are the words that the Lord hath spoken to Israel and to Judah, 5 for thus saith the Lord: "We have heard a voice of terror; there is fear and no peace. 6 Ask ye, and see if a man bear children? Why then have I seen every man with his *hands* on his *loins* like a woman in labour, and all faces are turned yellow? 7 Alas, for that day is great, neither is there the like to it, and it is the time of tribulation to Jacob, *but* he shall be saved out of it. 8 And it shall come to pass in that day," saith the Lord of hosts, "that I will break his yoke from off thy neck and will burst his bands, and strangers shall no more rule over him. 9 But they shall serve the Lord, their God, and David, their king, whom I will raise up to them. 10 Therefore fear thou not, my servant Jacob," saith the Lord, "neither be dismayed, O Israel, for behold: I will save thee from a country afar off and thy seed from the land of their captivity, and Jacob shall return and be at rest and abound with all good things, and there shall be none whom he may fear.

11 "For I am with thee," saith the Lord, "to save thee, for I will *utterly consume* all the nations among which I have scattered thee, but I will not *utterly consume* thee. But I will chastise thee in judgment, that thou mayst not seem to thyself innocent."

12 For thus saith the Lord: "Thy *bruise* is incurable; thy wound is very grievous. 13 There is none to judge thy judgment to bind it up; thou hast no healing medicines. 14 All thy lovers have forgotten thee and will not seek after thee, for I have wounded thee with the wound of an enemy, with a cruel chastisement; by reason of the multitude of thy iniquities, thy sins are hardened. 15 Why criest thou for thy affliction?

multitudinem iniquitatis tuae et propter dura peccata tua feci haec tibi. 16 Propterea omnes qui comedunt te devorabuntur, et universi hostes tui in captivitatem ducentur, et qui te vastant vastabuntur cunctosque praedatores tuos dabo in praedam. 17 Obducam enim cicatricem tibi et a vulneribus tuis sanabo te," dicit Dominus, "quia eiectam vocaverunt te, Sion: 'Haec est quae non habebat requirentem.'"

18 Haec dicit Dominus: "Ecce: ego convertam conversionem tabernaculorum Iacob et tectis eius miserebor, et aedificabitur civitas in excelso suo, et templum iuxta ordinem suum fundabitur. 19 Et egredietur de eis laus voxque ludentium, et multiplicabo eos, et non inminuentur, et glorificabo eos, et non adtenuabuntur. 20 Et erunt filii eius sicut a principio, et coetus eius coram me permanebit, et visitabo adversum omnes qui tribulant eum. 21 Et erit dux eius ex eo, et princeps de medio eius producetur, et adplicabo eum, et accedet ad me. Quis enim iste est qui adplicet cor suum ut adpropinquet mihi?" ait Dominus. 22 "Et eritis mihi in populum, et ego ero vobis in Deum."

23 Ecce turbo Domini, furor egrediens, procella ruens: in capite impiorum conquiescet. 24 Non avertet iram indignationis Dominus donec faciat et conpleat cogitationem cordis sui. In novissimo dierum intellegetis ea.

Thy sorrow is incurable. For the multitude of thy iniquity and for thy hardened sins I have done these things to thee. 16 Therefore all they that devour thee shall be devoured, and all thy enemies shall be carried into captivity, and they that waste thee shall be wasted, and all that prey upon thee will I give for a prey. 17 For I will close up thy scar and will heal thee of thy wounds," saith the Lord, "because they have called thee, O Zion, an outcast: 'This is she that hath none to seek after her.'"

18 Thus saith the Lord: "Behold: I will bring back the *captivity* of the pavilions of Jacob and will have pity on his houses, and the city shall be built in her high place, and the temple shall be founded according to the order thereof. 19 And out of them shall come forth praise and the voice of them that play, and I will multiply them, and they shall not be made few, and I will glorify them, and they shall not be lessened. 20 And their children shall be as from the beginning, and their assembly shall be permanent before me, and I will visit against all that afflict them. 21 And their leader shall be of themselves, and their prince shall come forth from the midst of them, and I will bring him near, and he shall come to me. For who is this that setteth his heart to approach to me?" saith the Lord. 22 "And you shall be my people, and I will be your God."

23 Behold the whirlwind of the Lord, his fury going forth, a violent storm: it shall rest upon the head of the wicked. 24 The Lord will not turn away the wrath of his indignation till he have executed and performed the thought of his heart. In the latter days you shall understand these things.

Caput 31

"In tempore illo," dicit Dominus, "ero Deus universis cognationibus Israhel, et ipsi erunt mihi in populum."

2 Haec dicit Dominus: "Invenit gratiam in deserto populus qui remanserat a gladio; vadet ad requiem suam Israhel."

3 Longe Dominus apparuit mihi.

"Et in caritate perpetua dilexi te, ideo adtraxi te miserans. 4 Rursumque aedificabo te, et aedificaberis, virgo Israhel; adhuc ornaberis tympanis tuis et egredieris in choro ludentium. 5 Adhuc plantabis vineas in montibus Samariae; plantabunt plantantes, et donec tempus veniat non vindemiabunt."

6 Quia erit dies in qua clamabunt custodes in Monte Ephraim, "Surgite, et ascendamus in Sion ad Dominum, Deum nostrum."

7 Quia haec dicit Dominus: "Exultate in laetitia Iacob, et hinnite contra caput Gentium; personate, et canite, et dicite, 'Salva, Domine, populum tuum, reliquias Israhel.' 8 Ecce: ego adducam eos de terra aquilonis et congregabo eos ab extremis terrae, inter quos erunt caecus et claudus, praegnans et pariens, simul coetus magnus revertentium

Chapter 31

The restoration of Israel. Rachel shall cease from mourning.
The new covenant. The church shall never fail.

"At that time," saith the Lord, "I will be the God of all the families of Israel, and they shall be my people."

2 Thus saith the Lord: "The people that were left and escaped from the sword found grace in the desert; Israel shall go to his rest."

3 The Lord hath appeared from afar to me.

"Yea I have loved thee with an everlasting love, therefore have I drawn thee, taking pity on thee. 4 And I will build thee again, and thou shalt be built, O virgin of Israel; thou shalt again be adorned with thy timbrels and shalt go forth in the *dances* of them that make merry. 5 Thou shalt yet plant vineyards in the mountains of Samaria; the planters shall plant, and they shall not gather the vintage before the time.

6 For there shall be a day in which the watchmen on Mount Ephraim shall cry, "Arise, and let us go up to Zion to the Lord, our God."

7 For thus saith the Lord: "Rejoice ye in the joy of Jacob, and neigh before the head of the Gentiles; shout ye, and sing, and say, 'Save, O Lord, thy people, the remnant of Israel.' 8 Behold: I will bring them from the north country and will gather them from the ends of the earth, and among them shall be the blind and the lame, the woman with child and she that is bringing forth, together a great company of

huc. 9 In fletu venient, et in misericordia reducam eos, et adducam eos per torrentes aquarum in via recta, et non inpingent in ea, quia factus sum Israheli pater, et Ephraim primogenitus meus est."

10 Audite verbum Domini, gentes, et adnuntiate in insulis quae procul sunt, et dicite, "Qui dispersit Israhel congregabit eum, et custodiet eum sicut pastor gregem suum." 11 Redemit enim Dominus Iacob et liberavit eum de manu potentioris.

12 "Et venient et laudabunt in Monte Sion, et confluent ad bona Domini, super frumento et vino et oleo et fetu pecorum et armentorum eritque anima eorum quasi hortus inriguus, et ultra non esurient. 13 Tunc laetabitur virgo in choro, iuvenes et senes simul, et convertam luctum eorum in gaudium et consolabor eos et laetificabo a dolore suo. 14 Et inebriabo animam sacerdotum pinguedine, et populus meus bonis meis adimplebitur," ait Dominus.

15 Haec dicit Dominus: "Vox in excelso audita est lamentationis, fletus et luctus, Rachel plorantis filios suos et nolentis consolari super eis, quia non sunt."

16 Haec dicit Dominus: "Quiescat vox tua a ploratu, et oculi tui a lacrimis, quia est merces operi tuo," ait Dominus, "et revertentur de terra inimici. 17 Et est spes novissimis tuis," ait Dominus, "et revertentur filii ad terminos suos."

18 "Audiens audivi Ephraim transmigrantem: 'Castigasti

them returning hither. 9 They shall come with weeping, and I will bring them back in mercy, and I will bring them through the torrents of waters in a right way, and they shall not stumble in it, for I am a father to Israel, and Ephraim is my firstborn."

10 Hear the word of the Lord, O ye nations, and declare it in the islands that are afar off, and say, "He that scattered Israel will gather him, and he will keep him as the shepherd doth his flock." 11 For the Lord hath redeemed Jacob and delivered him out of the hand of one that was mightier than he.

12 "And they shall come and shall give praise in Mount Zion, and they shall flow together to the good things of the Lord, for the corn and wine and oil and the increase of cattle and herds, and their soul shall be as a watered garden, and they shall be hungry no more. 13 Then shall the virgin rejoice in the dance, the young men and old men together, and I will turn their mourning into joy and will comfort them and make them joyful after their sorrow. 14 And I will fill the soul of the priests with fatness, and my people shall be filled with my good things," saith the Lord.

15 Thus saith the Lord: "A voice was heard on high of lamentation, of mourning and weeping, of Rachel weeping for her children and refusing to be comforted for them, because they are not."

16 Thus saith the Lord: "Let thy voice cease from weeping, and thy eyes from tears, for there is a reward for thy work," saith the Lord, "and they shall return out of the land of the enemy. 17 And there is hope for thy last end," saith the Lord, "and the children shall return to their own borders."

18 "Hearing I heard Ephraim when he went into captivity:

me, et eruditus sum quasi iuvenculus indomitus. Converte me, et convertar, quia tu Dominus, Deus meus. 19 Postquam enim convertisti me, egi paenitentiam, et postquam ostendisti mihi, percussi femur meum. Confusus sum et erubui quoniam sustinui obprobrium adulescentiae meae.'

20 "Si filius honorabilis mihi Ephraim, si puer delicatus, quia ex quo locutus sum de eo, adhuc recordabor eius. Idcirco conturbata sunt viscera mea super eum: miserans miserebor eius," ait Dominus.

21 Statue tibi speculam; pone tibi amaritudines; dirige cor tuum in viam rectam in qua ambulasti; revertere, virgo Israhel, revertere ad civitates tuas istas. 22 Usquequo deliciis dissolveris, filia vaga? Quia creavit Dominus novum super terram: femina circumdabit virum.

23 Haec dicit Dominus exercituum, Deus Israhel: "Adhuc dicent verbum istud in terra Iuda et in urbibus eius cum convertero captivitatem eorum: 'Benedicat tibi Dominus, pulchritudo iustitiae, mons sanctus.' 24 Et habitabunt in eo Iudas et omnes civitates eius simul, agricolae et minantes greges, 25 quia inebriavi animam lassam, et omnem animam esurientem saturavi."

26 Ideo quasi de somno suscitatus sum, et vidi, et somnus meus dulcis mihi.

27 "Ecce: dies veniunt," dicit Dominus, "et seminabo domum Israhel et domum Iuda semine hominum et semine iumentorum. 28 Et sicut vigilavi super eos ut evellerem et demolirer et dissiparem et disperderem et adfligerem, sic vigilabo super eos ut aedificem et plantem," ait Dominus. 29 In

'Thou hast chastised me, and I was instructed as a young bullock *unaccustomed to the yoke.* Convert me, and I shall be converted, for thou art the Lord, my God. 19 For after thou didst convert me, I did penance, and after thou didst shew unto me, I struck my thigh. I am confounded and ashamed because I have borne the reproach of my youth.'

20 "Surely Ephraim is an honourable son to me, surely he is a tender child, for since I spoke of him, I will still remember him. Therefore are my bowels troubled for him: pitying I will pity him," saith the Lord.

21 Set thee up a watchtower; make to thee bitterness; direct thy heart into the right way wherein thou hast walked; return, O virgin of Israel, return to these thy cities. 22 How long wilt thou be dissolute in deliciousness, O wandering daughter? For the Lord hath created a new thing upon the earth: a woman shall compass a man.

23 Thus saith the Lord of hosts, the God of Israel: "As yet shall they say this word in the land of Judah and in the cities thereof when I shall bring back their captivity: 'The Lord bless thee, the beauty of justice, the holy mountain.' 24 And Judah and all his cities shall dwell therein together, the husbandmen and they that drive the flocks, 25 for I have inebriated the weary soul, and I have filled every hungry soul."

26 Upon this I was as it were awaked out of a sleep, and I saw, and my sleep was sweet to me.

27 "Behold: the days come," saith the Lord, "and I will sow the house of Israel and the house of Judah with the seed of men and with the seed of beasts. 28 And as I have watched over them to pluck up and to throw down and to scatter and destroy and afflict, so will I watch over them to build up and to plant them, saith the Lord. 29 In those days they

diebus illis non dicent ultra, 'Patres comederunt uvam acerbam, et dentes filiorum obstipuerunt.' 30 Sed unusquisque in iniquitate sua morietur, omnis homo qui comederit uvam acerbam, obstupescent dentes eius.

31 "Ecce: dies venient," dicit Dominus, "et feriam domui Israhel et domui Iuda foedus novum, 32 non secundum pactum quod pepigi cum patribus eorum in die qua adprehendi manum eorum ut educerem eos de terra Aegypti, pactum quod irritum fecerunt, et ego dominatus sum eorum," dicit Dominus. 33 "Sed hoc erit pactum quod feriam cum domo Israhel post dies illos," dicit Dominus. "Dabo legem meam in visceribus eorum, et in corde eorum scribam eam, et ero eis in Deum, et ipsi erunt mihi in populum. 34 Et non docebit ultra, vir proximum suum et vir fratrem suum, dicens, 'Cognoscite Dominum,' omnes enim cognoscent me a minimo eorum usque ad maximum," ait Dominus, "quia propitiabor iniquitati eorum, et peccati eorum non memorabor amplius."

35 Haec dicit Dominus, qui dat solem in lumine diei ,ordinem lunae et stellarum in lumine noctis, qui turbat mare, et sonant fluctus eius; Dominus exercituum nomen illi. 36 "Si defecerint leges istae coram me," dicit Dominus, "tunc et semen Israhel deficiet, ut non sit gens coram me cunctis diebus."

37 Haec dicit Dominus: "Si mensurari potuerint caeli sursum, et investigari fundamenta terrae deorsum, et ego abiciam universum semen Israhel propter omnia quae fecerunt," dicit Dominus. 38 "Ecce: dies veniunt," dicit Dominus, "et aedificabitur civitas Domino a turre Ananehel usque ad

shall say no more, 'The fathers have eaten a sour grape, and the teeth of the children are set on edge.' 30 But every one shall die for his own iniquity, every man that shall eat the sour grape, his teeth shall be set on edge.

31 "Behold: the days shall come," saith the Lord, "and I will make a new covenant with the house of Israel and with the house of Judah, 32 not according to the covenant which I made with their fathers in the day that I took them by the hand to bring them out of the land of Egypt, the covenant which they made void, and I had dominion over them," saith the Lord. 33 "But this shall be the covenant that I will make with the house of Israel after those days," saith the Lord. "I will give my law in their bowels, and I will write it in their heart, and I will be their God, and they shall be my people. 34 And they shall teach no more, every man his neighbour and every man his brother, saying, 'Know the Lord,' for all shall know me from the least of them even to the greatest," saith the Lord, "for I will forgive their iniquity, and I will remember their sin no more."

35 Thus saith the Lord, who giveth the sun for the light of the day, the order of the moon and of the stars for the light of the night, who stirreth up the sea, and the waves thereof roar; the Lord of hosts is his name. 36 "If these ordinances shall fail before me," saith the Lord, "then also the seed of Israel shall fail, so as not to be a nation before me for ever."

37 Thus saith the Lord: "If the heavens above can be measured, and the foundations of the earth searched out beneath, I also will cast away all the seed of Israel for all that they have done," saith the Lord. 38 "Behold: the days come, saith the Lord, "*that* the city shall be built to the Lord from

portam anguli. 39 Et exibit ultra norma mensurae in conspectu eius super collem Gareb, et circuibit Goatha, 40 et
omnem vallem cadaverum et cineris et universam regionem
mortis usque ad torrentem Cedron et usque ad angulum
portae equorum orientalis, Sanctum Domini; non evelletur,
et non destruetur ultra in perpetuum.

Caput 32

Verbum quod factum est ad Hieremiam a Domino in
anno decimo Sedeciae, regis Iuda; ipse est annus octavusdecimus Nabuchodonosor. 2 Tunc exercitus regis Babylonis
obsidebat Hierusalem, et Hieremias, propheta, erat clausus
in atrio carceris qui erat in domo regis Iuda. 3 Clauserat enim
eum Sedecias, rex Iuda, dicens, "Quare vaticinaris, dicens,
'Haec dicit Dominus: "Ecce: ego dabo civitatem istam in
manu regis Babylonis, et capiet eam. 4 Et Sedecias, rex Iuda,
non effugiet de manu Chaldeorum, sed tradetur in manus
regis Babylonis, et loquetur os eius cum ore illius, et oculi

the tower of Hananel even to the gate of the corner. 39 And the measuring line shall go out farther in his sight upon the hill Gareb, and it shall compass Goah, 40 and the whole valley of dead bodies and of ashes and all the country of death even to the torrent Kidron and to the corner of the horse gate towards the east, the Holy of the Lord; it shall not be plucked up, and it shall not be destroyed any more for ever.

Chapter 32

Jeremiah by God's commandment purchases a field of his kinsman and prophesies the return of the people out of captivity and the everlasting covenant God will make with his church.

The word that came to Jeremiah from the Lord in the tenth year of Zedekiah, king of Judah; the same is the eighteenth year of Nebuchadnezzar. 2 At that time the army of the king of Babylon besieged Jerusalem, and Jeremiah, the prophet, was shut up in the court of the prison which was in the house of the king of Judah. 3 For Zedekiah, king of Judah, had shut him up, saying, "Why dost thou prophesy, saying, 'Thus saith the Lord: "Behold: I will give this city into the hand of the king of Babylon, and he shall take it. 4 And Zedekiah, king of Judah, shall not escape out of the hand of the Chaldeans, but he shall be delivered into the hands of the king of Babylon, and *he* shall speak *to him mouth to mouth,*

eius oculos illius videbunt. 5 Et in Babylonem ducet Sedeciam, et ibi erit donec visitem eum," ait Dominus. Si autem
dimicaveritis adversum Chaldeos, nihil prosperum habebitis'?"

6 Et dixit Hieremias, "Factum est verbum Domini ad me,
dicens, 7 'Ecce: Anamehel, filius Sellum, patruelis tuus, veniet ad te, dicens, "Eme tibi agrum meum qui est in Anathoth, tibi enim conpetit ex propinquitate ut emas."' 8 Et
venit ad me Anamehel, filius patrui mei, secundum verbum
Domini, ad vestibulum carceris, et ait ad me, 'Posside agrum
meum qui est in Anathoth in terra Beniamin, quia tibi
conpetit hereditas, et tu propinquus es ut possideas.' Intellexi autem quod verbum Domini esset. 9 Et emi agrum ab
Anamehel, filio patrui mei, qui est in Anathoth, et adpendi
ei argentum: septem stateres et decem argenteos. 10 Et
scripsi in libro et signavi et adhibui testes, et adpendi argentum in statera. 11 Et accepi librum possessionis signatum et
stipulationes et rata et signa forinsecus. 12 Et dedi librum
possessionis Baruch, filio Neri, filii Maasiae, in oculis Anamehel, patruelis mei, et in oculis testium qui scripti erant in
libro emptionis et in oculis omnium Iudaeorum qui sedebant in atrio carceris. 13 Et praecepi Baruch coram eis, dicens, 14 'Haec dicit Dominus exercituum, Deus Israhel:
"Sume libros istos, librum emptionis hunc signatum et librum hunc qui apertus est, et pone illos in vase fictili, ut per-
manere possint diebus multis." 15 Haec enim dicit Dominus
exercituum, Deus Israhel: "Adhuc possidebuntur domus et
agri et vineae in terra ista."'

and his eyes shall see his eyes. 5 And he shall lead Zedekiah to Babylon, and he shall be there till I visit him," saith the Lord. But if you will fight against the Chaldeans, you shall have no success'?"

6 And Jeremiah said, "The word of the Lord came to me, saying, 7 'Behold: Hanamel, the son of Shallum, thy cousin, shall come to thee, saying, "Buy thee my field which is in Anathoth, for it is thy right to buy it, being next akin."' 8 And Hanamel, my uncle's son, came to me according to the word of the Lord, to the entry of the prison, and said to me, *Buy* my field which is in Anathoth in the land of Benjamin, for the right of inheritance is thine, and thou art next of kin to possess it.' And I understood that *this* was the word of the Lord. 9 And I bought the field of Hanamel, my uncle's son, that is in Anathoth, and I weighed him the money: seven staters and ten pieces of silver. 10 And I wrote it in a book and sealed it and took witnesses, and I weighed him the money in the balances. 11 And I took the deed of the purchase that was sealed and the stipulations and the ratifications with the seals that were on the outside. 12 And I gave the deed of the purchase to Baruch, the son of Neriah, the son of Mahseiah, in the sight of Hanamel, my uncle's son, *in* the presence of the witnesses that subscribed the book of the purchase, and before all the Jews that sat in the court of the prison. 13 And I charged Baruch before them, saying, 14 'Thus saith the Lord of hosts, the God of Israel: "Take these writings, this deed of the purchase that is sealed up and this deed that is open, and put them in an earthen vessel, that they may continue many days." 15 For thus saith the Lord of hosts, the God of Israel: "Houses and fields and vineyards shall be possessed again in this land."'

16 "Et oravi ad Dominum postquam tradidi librum possessionis Baruch, filio Neri, dicens, 17 'Heu, heu, heu, Domine Deus, ecce: tu fecisti caelum et terram in fortitudine
tua magna et in brachio tuo extento. Non erit tibi difficile
omne verbum, 18 qui facis misericordiam in milibus et reddis
iniquitatem patrum in sinum filiorum eorum post eos, for-
tissime, magne et potens: Dominus exercituum nomen tibi.
19 Magnus consilio et inconprehensibilis cogitatu, cuius
oculi aperti sunt super omnes vias filiorum Adam, ut reddas
unicuique secundum vias suas et secundum fructum adinventionum eius, 20 qui posuisti signa et portenta in terra Aegypti usque ad diem hanc et in Israhel et in hominibus et fecisti tibi nomen sicut est dies haec, 21 et eduxisti populum
tuum Israhel de terra Aegypti in signis et in portentis et in
manu robusta et in brachio extento et in terrore magno 22 et
dedisti eis terram hanc quam iurasti patribus eorum, ut da-
res eis terram fluentem lacte et melle.

23 "'Et ingressi sunt et possederunt eam, et non oboedierunt voci tuae, et in lege tua non ambulaverunt, omnia quae
mandasti eis ut facerent non fecerunt, et evenerunt eis omnia mala haec. 24 Ecce: munitiones extructae sunt adversum
civitatem ut capiatur, et urbs data est in manus Chaldeorum,
qui proeliantur adversum eam a facie gladii et famis et pesti-
lentiae, et quaecumque locutus es acciderunt, ut ipse tu cer-
nis. 25 Et tu dicis mihi, Domine Deus, "Eme agrum argento,
et adhibe testes," cum urbs data sit in manus Chaldeorum?'"

26 Et factum est verbum Domini ad Hieremiam, dicens,

16 "And after I *had* delivered the deed of purchase to Baruch, the son of Neriah, I prayed to the Lord, saying, 17 'Alas, alas, alas, O Lord God, behold: thou hast made heaven and earth by thy great power and thy stretched out arm. No word shall be hard to thee; 18 thou shewest mercy unto thousands and returnest the iniquity of the fathers into the bosom of their children after them, O most mighty, great and powerful: the Lord of hosts is thy name. 19 Great in counsel and incomprehensible in thought, whose eyes are open upon all the ways of the children of Adam, to render unto every one according to his ways and according to the fruit of his devices, 20 who hast set signs and wonders in the land of Egypt even until this day and in Israel and amongst men and hast made thee a name as at this day, 21 and hast brought forth thy people Israel out of the land of Egypt with signs and with wonders and with a strong hand and a stretched out arm and with great terror 22 and hast given them this land which thou didst swear to their fathers, to give them a land flowing with milk and honey.

23 "And they came in and possessed it, *but* they obeyed not thy voice, and they walked not in thy law, *and* they did not any of those things that thou didst command them to do, and all these evils are come upon them. 24 Behold: works are built up against the city to take it, and the city is given into the hands of the Chaldeans, who fight against it *by* the sword and the famine and the pestilence, and what thou hast spoken is all come to pass, as thou thyself seest. 25 And sayest thou to me, O Lord God, "Buy a field for money, and take witnesses," whereas the city is given into the hands of the Chaldeans?'"

26 And the word of the Lord came to Jeremiah, saying,

27 "Ecce: ego Dominus, Deus universae carnis: numquid mihi difficile erit omne verbum? 28 Propterea haec dicit Dominus: 'Ecce: ego tradam civitatem istam in manus Chaldeorum et in manus regis Babylonis, et capient eam. 29 Et venient Chaldei proeliantes adversum urbem hanc et succendent eam igni et conburent eam et domos in quarum domatibus sacrificabant Baal et libabant diis alienis libamina ad inritandum me. 30 Erant enim filii Israhel et filii Iuda iugiter facientes malum in oculis meis ab adulescentia sua, filii Israhel qui usque nunc exacerbant me in opere manuum suarum,' dicit Dominus. 31 'Quia in furore et in indignatione mea facta est mihi civitas haec a die qua aedificaverunt eam usque ad diem istam qua auferetur de conspectu meo 32 propter malitiam filiorum Israhel et filiorum Iuda, quam fecerunt, ad iracundiam me provocantes, ipsi et reges eorum, principes eorum et sacerdotes eorum et prophetae eorum, viri Iuda et habitatores Hierusalem. 33 Et verterunt ad me terga et non facies, cum docerem eos diluculo et erudirem, et nollent audire ut acciperent disciplinam. 34 Et posuerunt idola sua in domo in qua invocatum est nomen meum ut polluerent eam. 35 Et aedificaverunt excelsa Baal quae sunt in Valle Filii Ennom ut initiarent filios suos et filias suas Moloch, quod non mandavi eis, nec ascendit in cor meum ut facerent abominationem hanc et in peccatum deducerent Iudam.'

36 "Et nunc, propter ista, haec dicit Dominus, Deus Israhel, ad civitatem hanc, de qua vos dicitis quod tradatur in

27 "Behold: I am the Lord, the God of all flesh: shall any thing be hard for me? 28 Therefore thus saith the Lord: 'Behold: I will deliver this city into the hands of the Chaldeans and into the hands of the king of Babylon, and they shall take it. 29 And the Chaldeans that fight against this city shall come and set it on fire and burn it with the houses upon whose roofs they offered sacrifice to Baal and poured out drink offerings to strange gods to provoke me to wrath. 30 For the children of Israel and the children of Judah have continually done evil in my eyes from their youth, the children of Israel who even till now provoke me with the work of their hands,' saith the Lord. 31 'For this city hath been to me a provocation and indignation from the day that they built it until this day in which it shall be taken out of my sight 32 because of all the evil of the children of Israel and of the children of Judah, which they have done, provoking me to wrath, they and their kings, their princes and their priests and their prophets, the men of Judah and the inhabitants of Jerusalem. 33 And they have turned their backs to me and not their faces, when I taught them early in the morning and instructed them, and they would not hearken to receive instruction. 34 And they have set their idols in the house in which my name is called upon to defile it. 35 And they have built the high places of Baal which are in the Valley of the Son of Hinnom to consecrate their sons and their daughters to Molech, which I commanded them not, neither entered it into my heart that they should do this abomination and cause Judah to sin.'

36 "And now, therefore, thus saith the Lord, the God of Israel, to this city, whereof you say that it *shall be* delivered

manus regis Babylonis in gladio et in fame et in peste: 37 'Ecce: ego congregabo eos de universis terris ad quas eieci eos in furore meo et in ira mea et in indignatione grandi, et reducam eos ad locum istum et habitare eos faciam confidenter. 38 Et erunt mihi in populum, et ego ero eis in Deum. 39 Et dabo eis cor unum et viam unam, ut timeant me universis diebus et bene sit eis et filiis eorum post eos. 40 Et feriam eis pactum sempiternum et non desinam eis benefacere, et timorem meum dabo in corde eorum, ut non recedant a me. 41 Et laetabor super eis cum bene eis fecero, et plantabo eos in terra ista in veritate in toto corde meo et in tota anima mea.' 42 Quia haec dicit Dominus: 'Sicut adduxi super populum istum omne malum hoc grande, sic adducam super eos omne bonum quod ego loquor ad eos.'

43 "'Et possidebuntur agri in terra ista, de qua vos dicitis quod deserta sit, eo quod non remanserit homo et iumentum, et data sit in manus Chaldeorum. 44 Agri pecunia ementur, et scribentur in libro et inprimetur signum, et testis adhibebitur in terra Beniamin et in circuitu Hierusalem in civitatibus Iuda et in civitatibus montanis et in civitatibus campestribus et in civitatibus quae ad austrum sunt, quia convertam captivitatem eorum,' ait Dominus."

into the hands of the king of Babylon by the sword and by famine and by pestilence: 37 'Behold: I will gather them together out of all the lands to which I have cast them out in my anger and in my wrath and in my great indignation, and I will bring them again into this place and will cause them to dwell securely. 38 And they shall be my people, and I will be their God. 39 And I will give them one heart and one way, that they may fear me all days and that it may be well with them and with their children after them. 40 And I will make an everlasting covenant with them and will not cease to do them good, and I will give my fear in their heart, that they may not revolt from me. 41 And I will rejoice over them when I shall do them good, and I will plant them in this land in truth with my whole heart and with all my soul.' 42 For thus saith the Lord: 'As I have brought upon this people all this great evil, so will I bring upon them all the good that I now speak to them.'

43 "'And fields shall be purchased in this land, whereof you say that it is desolate, because there remaineth neither man nor beast, and it is given into the hands of the Chaldeans. 44 Fields shall be bought for money, and *deeds* shall be written and sealed, and witnesses shall be taken in the land of Benjamin and round about Jerusalem in the cities of Judah and in the cities on the mountains and in the cities of the plains and in the cities that are towards the south, for I will bring back their captivity,' saith the Lord."

Caput 33

Et factum est verbum Domini ad Hieremiam secundo, cum adhuc clausus esset in atrio carceris, dicens, 2 "Haec dicit Dominus qui facturus est et formaturus illud et paraturus; Dominus nomen eius: 3 'Clama ad me, et exaudiam te, et adnuntiabo tibi grandia et firma quae nescis.' 4 Quia haec dicit Dominus, Deus Israhel, ad domos urbis huius et ad domos regis Iuda, quae destructae sunt, et ad munitiones et ad gladium 5 venientium ut dimicent cum Chaldeis et impleant eas cadaveribus hominum quos percussi in furore meo et in indignatione mea, abscondens faciem meam a civitate hac propter omnem malitiam eorum: 6 'Ecce: ego obducam eis cicatricem et sanitatem, et curabo eos, et revelabo illis deprecationem pacis et veritatis. 7 Et convertam conversionem Iuda et conversionem Hierusalem, et aedificabo eos sicut a principio. 8 Et emundabo illos ab omni iniquitate sua in qua peccaverunt mihi, et propitius ero cunctis iniquitatibus eorum in quibus deliquerunt mihi et spreverunt me. 9 Et erit mihi in nomen et in gaudium et in laudem et in exultationem cunctis gentibus terrae quae audierint omnia bona

Chapter 33

God promises reduction from captivity and other blessings,
especially the coming of Christ, whose reign in his church
shall be glorious and perpetual.

And the word of the Lord came to Jeremiah the second
time, while he was yet shut up in the court of the prison, saying, 2 "Thus saith the Lord that will do this thing and will
form it and prepare it; the Lord is his name: 3 'Cry to me,
and I will hear thee, and I will shew thee great things and
sure things which thou knowest not.' 4 For thus saith the
Lord, the God of Israel, to the houses of this city and to the
houses of the king of Judah, which are destroyed, and to the
bulwarks and to the sword 5 of them that come to fight with
the Chaldeans and to fill them with the dead bodies of the
men whom I have slain in my wrath and in my indignation,
hiding my face from this city because of all their wickedness:
6 'Behold: I will close their wounds and give them health,
and I will cure them, and I will reveal to them the prayer of
peace and truth. 7 And I will bring back the *captivity* of Judah and the *captivity* of Jerusalem, and I will build them as
from the beginning. 8 And I will cleanse them from all their
iniquity whereby they have sinned against me, and I will forgive all their iniquities whereby they have sinned against me
and despised me. 9 And it shall be to me a name and a joy and
a praise and a gladness before all the nations of the earth
that shall hear of all the good things which I will do to them,

quae ego facturus sum eis, et pavebunt et turbabuntur in universis bonis et in omni pace quam ego faciam eis.'

10 "Haec dicit Dominus, 'Adhuc audietur in loco isto (quem vos dicitis esse desertum eo quod non sit homo nec iumentum in civitatibus Iuda et foris Hierusalem, quae desolatae sunt absque homine et absque habitatore et absque pecore) 11 vox gaudii et vox laetitiae, vox sponsi et vox sponsae, vox dicentium, "Confitemini Domino exercituum, quoniam bonus Dominus, quoniam in aeternum misericordia eius," et portantium vota in domum Domini, reducam enim conversionem terrae sicut a principio,' dicit Dominus. 12 Haec dicit Dominus exercituum: 'Adhuc erit in loco isto deserto absque homine et absque iumento et in cunctis civitatibus eius habitaculum pastorum accubantium gregum. 13 In civitatibus montuosis et in civitatibus campestribus et in civitatibus quae ad austrum sunt et in terra Beniamin et in circuitu Hierusalem et in civitatibus Iuda adhuc transibunt greges ad manum numerantis,' ait Dominus.

14 "'Ecce: dies veniunt,' dicit Dominus, 'et suscitabo verbum bonum quod locutus sum ad domum Israhel et ad domum Iuda. 15 In diebus illis et in tempore illo germinare faciam David germen iustitiae, et faciet iudicium et iustitiam in terra. 16 In diebus illis salvabitur Iuda, et Hierusalem habitabit confidenter, et hoc est nomen quod vocabunt eum:

and they shall fear and be troubled for all the good things and for all the peace that I will make for them.'

10 "Thus saith the Lord: 'There shall be heard again in this place (which you say is desolate because there is neither man nor beast in the cities of Judah and without Jerusalem, which are desolate without man and without inhabitant and without beast) 11 the voice of joy and the voice of gladness, the voice of the bridegroom and the voice of the bride, the voice of them that *shall* say, "Give ye glory to the Lord of hosts, for the Lord is good, for his mercy endureth for ever," and of them that *shall* bring their vows into the house of the Lord, for I will bring back the *captivity* of the land as at the first,' saith the Lord. 12 Thus saith the Lord of hosts: 'There shall be again in this place that is desolate without man and without beast and in all the cities thereof an habitation of shepherds causing their flocks to lie down. 13 *And* in the cities on the mountains and in the cities of the plains and in the cities that are towards the south and in the land of Benjamin and round about Jerusalem and in the cities of Judah shall the flocks pass again under the hand of him that numbereth them,' saith the Lord.

14 "'Behold: the days come,' saith the Lord, *'that* I will perform the good word that I have spoken to the house of Israel and to the house of Judah. 15 In those days and at that time I will make the bud of justice to spring forth unto David, and he shall do judgment and justice in the earth.16 In those days shall Judah be saved, and Jerusalem shall dwell securely, and this is the name that they shall call him: The

Dominus, Iustus Noster.' 17 Quia haec dicit Dominus: 'Non interibit de David vir qui sedeat super thronum domus Israhel. 18 Et de sacerdotibus et Levitis non interibit vir a facie mea qui offerat holocaustomata et incendat sacrificium et caedat victimas cunctis diebus.'"

19 Et factum est verbum Domini ad Hieremiam, dicens, 20 "Haec dicit Dominus: 'Si irritum fieri potest pactum meum cum die, et pactum meum cum nocte, ut non sit dies et nox in tempore suo, 21 et pactum meum irritum esse poterit cum David, servo meo, ut non sit ex eo filius qui regnet in throno eius, et Levitae et sacerdotes, ministri mei. 22 Sicuti numerari non possunt stellae caeli, et metiri harena maris, sic multiplicabo semen David, servi mei, et Levitas, ministros meos.'"

23 Et factum est verbum Domini ad Hieremiam, dicens, 24 "Numquid non vidisti quid populus hic locutus sit, dicens, 'Duae cognationes quas elegerat Dominus abiectae sunt,' et populum meum despexerunt eo quod non sit ultra gens coram eis? 25 Haec dicit Dominus: 'Si pactum meum inter diem et noctem et leges caelo et terrae non posui, 26 equidem et semen Iacob et David, servi mei, proiciam, ut non adsumam de semine eius principes seminis Abraham, Isaac et Iacob, reducam enim conversionem eorum et miserebor eis.'"

Lord, Our Just One.' 17 For thus saith the Lord: 'There shall not be cut off from David a man to sit upon the throne of the house of Israel. 18 Neither shall there be cut off from the priests and Levites a man before my face to offer holocausts and to burn sacrifices and to kill victims continually.'"

19 And the word of the Lord came to Jeremiah, saying, 20 "Thus saith the Lord: 'If my covenant with the day can be made void, and my covenant with the night, that there should not be day and night in their season, 21 also my covenant with David, my servant, may be made void, that he should not have a son to reign upon his throne, and with the Levites and priests, my ministers. 22 As the stars of heaven cannot be numbered, nor the sand of the sea be measured, so will I multiply the seed of David, my servant, and the Levites, my ministers.'"

23 And the word of the Lord came to Jeremiah, saying, 24 "Hast thou not seen what this people hath spoken, saying, 'The two families which the Lord had chosen are cast off,' and they have despised my people *so that* it is no more a nation before them? 25 Thus saith the Lord: 'If I have not set my covenant between day and night and laws to heaven and earth, 26 surely I will also cast off the seed of Jacob and of David, my servant, so as not to take any of his seed to be rulers of the seed of Abraham, Isaac and Jacob, for I will bring back their *captivity* and will have mercy on them.'"

Caput 34

Verbum quod factum est ad Hieremiam a Domino (quando Nabuchodonosor, rex Babylonis et omnis exercitus eius universaque regna terrae quae erant sub potestate manus eius et omnes populi bellabant contra Hierusalem et contra omnes urbes eius), dicens, 2 "Haec dicit Dominus, Deus Israhel: 'Vade, et loquere ad Sedeciam, regem Iuda, et dices ad eum, "Haec dicit Dominus: 'Ecce: ego tradam civitatem hanc in manus regis Babylonis, et succendet eam igni. 3 Et tu non effugies de manu eius, sed conprehensione capieris, et in manu eius traderis, et oculi tui oculos regis Babylonis videbunt, et os eius cum ore tuo loquetur, et Babylonem introibis.' 4 Attamen audi verbum Domini, Sedecia, rex Iuda! Haec dicit Dominus ad te: 'Non morieris in gladio, 5 sed in pace morieris, et secundum conbustiones patrum tuorum, regum priorum qui fuerunt ante te, sic conburent te, et "Vae, Domine!" plangent te, quia verbum ego locutus sum,' dicit Dominus."'"

Chapter 34

The prophet foretells that Zedekiah shall fall into the hands of Nebuchadnezzar. God's sentence upon the princes and people that had broken his covenant.

The word that came to Jeremiah from the Lord (when Nebuchadnezzar, king of Babylon, and all his army and all the kingdoms of the earth that were under the power of his hand and all the people fought against Jerusalem and against all the cities thereof), saying, 2 "Thus saith the Lord, the God of Israel, 'Go, and speak to Zedekiah, king of Judah, and say to him, "Thus saith the Lord: 'Behold: I will deliver this city into the hands of the king of Babylon, and he shall burn it with fire. 3 And thou shalt not escape out of his hand, but thou shalt surely be taken, and thou shalt be delivered into his hand, and thy eyes shall see the eyes of the king of Babylon, and his mouth shall speak with thy mouth, and thou shalt go to Babylon.' 4 Yet hear the word of the Lord, O Zedekiah, king of Judah! Thus saith the Lord to thee: 'Thou shalt not die by the sword, 5 but thou shalt die in peace, and according to the burnings of thy fathers, the former kings that were before thee, so shall they burn thee, and they shall mourn for thee, *saying,* "Alas, Lord!" for I have spoken the word,' saith the Lord.""

6 Et locutus est Hieremias, propheta, ad Sedeciam, regem Iuda, universa verba haec in Hierusalem. 7 Et exercitus regis Babylonis pugnabat contra Hierusalem et contra omnes civitates Iuda quae reliquae erant, contra Lachis et contra Azeca, haec enim supererant de civitatibus Iuda, urbes munitae.

8 Verbum quod factum est ad Hieremiam a Domino, postquam percussit Rex Sedecias foedus cum omni populo in Hierusalem, praedicans 9 ut dimitteret unusquisque servum suum et unusquisque ancillam suam, Hebraeum et Hebraeam, liberos, et nequaquam dominarentur eis, id est, in Iudaeo et fratre suo. 10 Audierunt ergo omnes principes et universus populus qui inierant pactum ut dimitteret unusquisque servum suum et unusquisque ancillam suam liberos et ultra non dominarentur eis, audierunt igitur, et dimiserunt. 11 Et conversi sunt deinceps et retraxerunt servos et ancillas suas quos dimiserant liberos et subiugaverunt in famulos et famulas.

12 Et factum est verbum Domini ad Hieremiam a Dominom, dicens, 13 "Haec dicit Dominus, Deus Israhel: 'Ego percussi foedus cum patribus vestris in die qua eduxi eos de terra Aegypti, de domo servitutis, dicens, 14 "Cum conpleti fuerint septem anni, dimittat unusquisque fratrem suum Hebraeum qui venditus est ei, et serviet tibi sex annis, et dimittes eum a te liberum." Et non audierunt patres vestri me, nec inclinaverunt aurem suam. 15 Et conversi estis vos hodie et fecistis quod rectum est in oculis meis, ut praedicaretis

6 And Jeremiah, the prophet, spoke all these words to Zedekiah, the king of Judah, in Jerusalem. 7 And the army of the king of Babylon fought against Jerusalem and against all the cities of Judah that were left, against Lachish and against Azekah, for these remained of the cities of Judah, fenced cities.

8 The word that came to Jeremiah from the Lord, after that King Zedekiah had made a covenant with all the people in Jerusalem, making a proclamation 9 that every man should let his manservant and every man his maidservant, being a Hebrew man or a Hebrew woman, go free, and that they should not lord it over them, to wit, over the *Jews, their brethren.* 10 And all the princes and all the people who entered into the covenant heard that every man should let his manservant and every man his maidservant go free, and should no more have dominion over them, and they obeyed, and let them go free. 11 But afterwards they turned and brought back again their servants and their handmaids whom they had let go free and brought them into subjection as menservants and maidservants.

12 And the word of the Lord came to Jeremiah from the Lord, saying, 13 "Thus saith the Lord, the God of Israel: 'I made a covenant with your fathers in the day that I brought them out of the land of Egypt, out of the house of bondage, saying, 14 "At the end of seven years, let ye go every man his brother, being a Hebrew, who hath been sold to thee, so he shall serve thee six years, and thou shalt let him go free from thee." And your fathers did not hearken to me, nor did they incline their ear. 15 And you turned today and did that which was right in my eyes, in proclaiming liberty every one to his

libertatem unusquisque ad amicum suum, et inistis pactum in conspectu meo, in domo in qua invocatum est nomen meum super eam. 16 Et reversi estis et commaculastis nomen meum, et reduxistis unusquisque servum suum et unusquisque ancillam suam quos dimiseratis ut essent liberi et suae potestatis, et subiugastis eos ut sint vobis servi et ancillae. 17 Propterea haec dicit Dominus: "Vos non audistis me ut praedicaretis libertatem unusquisque fratri suo et unusquisque amico suo. Ecce: ego praedico vobis libertatem," ait Dominus, "ad gladium, ad pestem et ad famem, et dabo vos in commotionem cunctis regnis terrae. 18 Et dabo viros qui praevaricantur foedus meum et non observaverunt verba foederis quibus adsensi sunt in conspectu meo—vitulum quem conciderunt in duas partes et transierunt inter divisiones eius, 19 principes Iuda et principes Hierusalem, eunuchi et sacerdotes et omnis populus terrae qui transierunt inter divisiones vituli— 20 et dabo eos in manus inimicorum suorum et in manus quaerentium animam eorum, et erit morticinum eorum in escam volatilibus caeli et bestiis terrae. 21 Et Sedeciam, regem Iuda, et principes eius dabo in manus inimicorum suorum et in manus quaerentium animas eorum et in manus exercituum regis Babylonis, qui recesserunt a vobis. 22 Ecce: ego praecipio," dicit Dominus, "et reducam eos in civitatem hanc, et proeliabuntur adversum eam et capient eam et incendent igni, et civitates Iuda dabo in solitudinem eo quod non sit habitator.""

brother, and you made a covenant in my sight, in the house upon which my name is invoked. 16 And you are fallen back and have defiled my name, and you have brought back again every man his manservant and every man his maidservant whom you had let go free and set at liberty, and you have brought them into subjection to be your servants and handmaids. 17 Therefore thus saith the Lord: "You have not hearkened to me in proclaiming liberty every man to his brother and every man to his friend. Behold: I proclaim a liberty for you," saith the Lord, "to the sword, to the pestilence and to the famine, and I will cause you to be removed to all the kingdoms of the earth. 18 And I will give the men that have transgressed my covenant and have not performed the words of the covenant which they agreed to in my presence—when they cut the calf in two and passed between the parts thereof, 19 the princes of Judah and the princes of Jerusalem, the eunuchs and the priests and all the people of the land that passed between the parts of the calf— 20 and I will give them into the hands of their enemies and into the hands of them that seek their life, and their dead bodies shall be for meat to the fowls of the air and to the beasts of the earth. 21 And Zedekiah, the king of Judah, and his princes I will give into the hands of their enemies and into the hands of them that seek their lives and into the hands of the armies of the king of Babylon, which are gone from you. 22 Behold: I will command," saith the Lord, "and I will bring them again to this city, and they shall fight against it and take it and burn it with fire, and I will make the cities of Judah a desolation without an inhabitant.""

Caput 35

Verbum quod factum est ad Hieremiam a Domino in diebus Ioachim, filii Iosiae, regis Iuda, dicens, 2 "Vade ad domum Rechabitarum, et loquere eis, et introduces eos in domum Domini, in unam exedram thesaurorum, et dabis eis bibere vinum."

3 Et adsumpsi Iezoniam, filium Hieremiae, filii Absaniae, et fratres eius et omnes filios eius et universam domum Rechabitarum. 4 Et introduxi eos in domum Domini, ad gazofilacium filiorum Anan, filii Hiegedeliae, hominis Dei, quod erat iuxta gazofilacium principum, super thesaurum Maasiae, filii Sellum, qui erat custos vestibuli. 5 Et posui coram filiis domus Rechabitarum scyphos plenos vino et calices, et dixi ad eos, "Bibite vinum."

6 Qui responderunt, "Non bibemus vinum quia Ionadab, filius Rechab, pater noster, praecepit nobis, dicens, 'Non bibetis vinum, vos et filii vestri, usque in sempiternum. 7 Et domum non aedificabitis et sementem non seretis et vineas non plantabitis nec habebitis, sed in tabernaculis habitabitis cunctis diebus vestris, ut vivatis diebus multis super faciem terrae in qua vos peregrinamini.' 8 Oboedivimus ergo voci Ionadab, filii Rechab, patris nostri, in omnibus quae praece-

Chapter 35

The obedience of the Rechabites condemns the disobedience of the Jews. The reward of the Rechabites.

The word that came to Jeremiah from the Lord in the days of Jehoiakim, the son of Josiah, king of Judah, saying, 2 "Go to the house of the Rechabites, and speak to them, and bring them into the house of the Lord, into one of the chambers of the treasures, and thou shalt give them wine to drink."

3 And I took Jaazaniah, the son of Jeremiah, the son of Habazziniah, and his brethren and all his sons and the whole house of the Rechabites. 4 And I brought them into the house of the Lord, to the treasure house of the sons of Hanan, the son of Igdaliah, the man of God, which was by the treasure house of the princes, above the treasure of Maaseiah the son of Shallum, who was keeper of the entry. 5 And I set before the sons of the house of the Rechabites pots full of wine and cups, and I said to them, "Drink ye wine."

6 And they answered, "We will not drink wine because Jonadab, the son of Rechab, our father, commanded us, saying, 'You shall drink no wine, neither you nor your children, for ever. 7 Neither shall ye build houses nor sow seed nor plant vineyards nor have any, but you shall dwell in tents all your days, that you may live many days upon the face of the earth in which you are strangers.' 8 Therefore we have obeyed the voice of Jonadab, the son of Rechab, our father,

pit nobis, ita ut non biberemus vinum cunctis diebus nostris, nos et mulieres nostrae, filii et filiae nostrae, 9 et non aedificaremus domos ad habitandum et vineam et agrum et sementem non habuimus. 10 Sed habitavimus in tabernaculis et oboedientes fuimus iuxta omnia quae praecepit nobis Ionadab, pater noster. 11 Cum autem ascendisset Nabuchodonosor, rex Babylonis, ad terram nostram, diximus, 'Venite, et ingrediamur Hierusalem a facie exercitus Chaldeorum et a facie exercitus Syriae,' et mansimus in Hierusalem."

12 Et factum est verbum Domini ad Hieremiam, dicens, 13 "Haec dicit Dominus exercituum, Deus Israhel: 'Vade, et dic viris Iuda et habitatoribus Hierusalem, "'Numquid non recipietis disciplinam ut oboediatis verbis meis?' dicit Dominus. 14 'Praevaluerunt sermones Ionadab, filii Rechab, quos praecepit filiis suis ut non biberent vinum, et non biberunt usque ad diem hanc quia oboedierunt praecepto patris sui. Ego autem locutus sum ad vos, de mane consurgens et loquens, et non oboedistis mihi. 15 Misique ad vos omnes servos meos, prophetas, consurgens diluculo mittensque et dicens, "Convertimini unusquisque a via sua pessima, et bona facite studia vestra, et nolite sequi deos alienos neque colatis eos, et habitabitis in terra quam dedi vobis et patribus vestris," et non inclinastis aurem vestram neque audistis me. 16 Firmaverunt igitur filii Ionadab, filii Rechab, praeceptum patris sui, quod praeceperat eis, populus autem iste non oboedivit mihi.' 17 Idcirco haec dicit Dominus exercituum, Deus Israhel: 'Ecce: ego adducam super Iudam et super

in all things that he commanded us, so as to drink no wine all our days, neither we nor our wives *nor* our sons nor our daughters, 9 nor to build houses to dwell in nor to have vineyard or field or seed. 10 But we have dwelt in tents and have been obedient according to all that Jonadab, our father, commanded us. 11 But when Nebuchadnezzar, king of Babylon, came up to our land, we said, 'Come; *let* us go into Jerusalem from the face of the army of the Chaldeans and from the face of the army of Syria,' and we have remained in Jerusalem."

12 And the word of the Lord came to Jeremiah, saying, 13 "Thus saith the Lord of hosts, the God of Israel: 'Go, and say to the men of Judah and to the inhabitants of Jerusalem, "'Will you not receive instruction to obey my words?' saith the Lord. 14 'The words of Jonadab, the son of Rechab, by which he commanded his sons not to drink wine, have prevailed, and they have drunk none to this day because they have obeyed the commandment of their father. But I have spoken to you, rising early and speaking, and you have not obeyed me. 15 And I have sent to you all my servants, the prophets, rising early and sending and saying, "Return ye every man from his wicked way, and make your ways good, and follow not strange gods nor worship them, and you shall dwell in the land which I gave you and your fathers," and you have not inclined your ear nor hearkened to me. 16 So the sons of Jonadab, the son of Rechab, have constantly kept the commandment of their father, which he commanded them, but this people hath not obeyed me.' 17 Therefore thus saith the Lord of hosts, the God of Israel: 'Behold: I will bring upon Judah and upon all the inhabitants

omnes habitatores Hierusalem universam adflictionem quam locutus sum adversum illos eo quod locutus sum ad illos, et non audierunt; vocavi illos, et non responderunt mihi.'"'"

18 Domui autem Rechabitarum dixit Hieremias, "Haec dicit Dominus exercituum, Deus Israhel: 'Pro eo quod oboedistis praecepto Ionadab, patris vestri, et custodistis omnia mandata eius et fecistis universa quae praecepit vobis, 19 propterea haec dicit Dominus exercituum, Deus Israhel: "Non deficiet vir de stirpe Ionadab, filii Rechab, stans in conspectu meo cunctis diebus."'"

Caput 36

Et factum est in anno quarto Ioachim, filii Iosiae, regis Iuda, factum est verbum hoc ad Hieremiam a Domino, dicens, 2 "Tolle volumen libri, et scribes in eo omnia verba quae locutus sum tibi adversum Israhel et Iudam et adversum omnes gentes a die qua locutus sum ad te, ex diebus Iosiae usque ad diem hanc, 3 si forte, audiente domo Iuda universa mala quae ego cogito facere eis, revertatur unusquisque

of Jerusalem all the evil that I have pronounced against them because I have spoken to them, and they have not heard; I have called to them, and they have not answered me.'"''"

18 And Jeremiah said to the house of the Rechabites, "Thus saith the Lord of hosts, the God of Israel: 'Because you have obeyed the commandment of Jonadab, your father, and have kept all his precepts and have done all that he commanded you, 19 therefore thus saith the Lord of hosts, the God of Israel: "There shall not be wanting a man of the race of Jonadab, the son of Rechab, standing before me for ever."'"

Chapter 36

Jeremiah sends Baruch to read his prophecies in the temple. The book is brought to King Jehoiakim, who burns it. The prophet denounces his judgment and causes Baruch to write a new copy.

And it came to pass in the fourth year of Jehoiakim, the son of Josiah, king of Judah, that this word came to Jeremiah by the Lord, saying, 2 "Take thee a roll of a book, and thou shalt write in it all the words that I have spoken to thee against Israel and Judah and against all the nations from the day that I spoke to thee, from the days of Josiah even to this day, 3 if so be, when the house of Judah shall hear all the evils that I purpose to do unto them, that they may return every

a via sua pessima, et propitius ero iniquitati et peccato eorum."

4 Vocavit ergo Hieremias Baruch, filium Neriae, et scripsit Baruch ex ore Hieremiae omnes sermones Domini quos locutus est ad eum in volumine libri. 5 Et praecepit Hieremias Baruch, dicens, "Ego clausus sum, nec valeo ingredi domum Domini. 6 Ingredere ergo tu, et lege de volumine, in quo scripsisti ex ore meo, verba Domini, audiente populo in domo Domini in die ieiunii, insuper et audiente universo Iuda qui veniunt de civitatibus suis leges eis, 7 si forte cadat oratio eorum in conspectu Domini, et revertatur unusquisque a via sua pessima, quoniam magnus furor et indignatio est quam locutus est Dominus adversum populum hunc."

8 Et fecit Baruch, filius Neriae, iuxta omnia quae praeceperat ei Hieremias, propheta, legens ex volumine sermones Domini in domo Domini. 9 Factum est autem in anno quinto Ioachim, filii Iosiae, regis Iuda, in mense nono, praedicaverunt ieiunium in conspectu Domini omni populo in Hierusalem et universae multitudini quae confluxerat de civitatibus Iuda in Hierusalem. 10 Legitque Baruch ex volumine sermones Hieremiae in domo Domini, in gazofilacio Gamariae, filii Saphan, scribae, in vestibulo superiori, in introitu portae novae domus Domini, audiente omni populo.

11 Cumque audisset Micheas, filius Gamariae, filii Saphan, omnes sermones Domini ex libro, 12 descendit in domum regis ad gazofilacium scribae, et ecce: ibi omnes principes

man from his wicked way, and I will forgive their iniquity and their sin.

4 So Jeremiah called Baruch, the son of Neriah, and Baruch wrote from the mouth of Jeremiah all the words of the Lord which he spoke to him upon the roll of a book. 5 And Jeremiah commanded Baruch, saying, "I am shut up, and cannot go into the house of the Lord. 6 Go thou in therefore, and read out of the roll, which thou hast written from my mouth, the words of the Lord, in the hearing of all the people in the house of the Lord on the fasting day, and also thou shalt read them in the hearing of all Judah that come out of their cities, 7 if so be *they may present* their supplication before the Lord, and may return every one from his wicked way, for great is the wrath and indignation which the Lord hath pronounced against this people."

8 And Baruch, the son of Neriah, did according to all that Jeremiah, the prophet, had commanded him, reading out of the volume the words of the Lord in the house of the Lord. 9 And it came to pass in the fifth year of Jehoiakim, the son of Josiah, king of Judah, in the ninth month, that they proclaimed a fast before the Lord to all the people in Jerusalem and to all the people that were come together out of the cities of Judah to Jerusalem. 10 And Baruch read out of the roll the words of Jeremiah in the house of the Lord, in the treasury of Gemariah, the son of Shaphan, the scribe, in the upper court, in the entry of the new gate of the house of the Lord, in the hearing of all the people.

11 And when Micaiah, the son of Gemariah, the son of Shaphan, had heard out of the book all the words of the Lord, 12 he went down into the king's house to the secretary's chamber, and behold: all the princes sat there: El-

sedebant: Elisama, scriba, et Dalaias, filius Semeiae, et Elnathan, filius Achobor, et Gamarias, filius Saphan, et Sedecias, filius Ananiae, et universi principes. 13 Et nuntiavit eis Micheas omnia verba quae audivit legente Baruch ex volumine in auribus populi. 14 Miserunt itaque omnes principes ad Baruch Iudi, filium Nathaniae, filii Selemiae, filii Chusi, dicentes, "Volumen ex quo legisti audiente populo sume in manu tua, et veni." Tulit ergo Baruch, filius Neriae, volumen in manu sua et venit ad eos.

15 Et dixerunt ad eum, "Sede, et lege haec in auribus nostris." Et legit Baruch in auribus eorum. 16 Igitur cum audissent omnia verba, obstipuerunt unusquisque ad proximum suum, et dixerunt ad Baruch, "Nuntiare debemus regi omnes sermones istos." 17 Et interrogaverunt eum, dicentes, "Indica nobis quomodo scripsisti omnes sermones istos ex ore eius."

18 Dixit autem eis Baruch, "Ex ore suo loquebatur quasi legens ad me omnes sermones istos, et ego scribebam in volumine atramento."

19 Et dixerunt principes ad Baruch, "Vade, et abscondere, tu et Hieremias, et nemo sciat ubi sitis." 20 Et ingressi sunt ad regem, in atrium, porro volumen commendaverunt in gazofilacio Elisamae, scribae, et nuntiaverunt audiente rege omnes sermones. 21 Misitque rex Iudi ut sumeret volumen, qui tollens illud de gazofilacio Elisamae, scribae, legit audiente rege et universis principibus qui stabant circa regem. 22 Rex autem sedebat in domo hiemali in mense nono, et

ishama, the scribe, and Delaiah, the son of Shemaiah, and Elnathan, the son of Achbor, and Gemariah, the son of Shaphan, and Zedekiah, the son of Hananiah, and all the princes. 13 And Micaiah told them all the words that he had heard when Baruch read out of the book in the hearing of the people. 14 Therefore all the princes sent Jehudi, the son of Nethaniah, the son of Shelemiah, the son of Cushi, to Baruch, saying, "Take in thy hand the roll *in* which thou hast read in the hearing of the people, and come." So Baruch, the son of Neriah, took the volume in his hand and came to them.

15 And they said to him, "Sit down, and read these things in our hearing." And Baruch read in their hearing. 16 And when they had heard all the words, they looked upon one another with astonishment, and they said to Baruch, "We must tell the king all these words." 17 And they asked him, saying, "Tell us how didst thou write all these words from his mouth."

18 And Baruch said to them, "With his mouth he pronounced all these words as if he were reading to me, and I wrote them with ink in the book."

19 And the princes said to Baruch, "Go, and hide thee, both thou and Jeremiah, and let no man know where you are." 20 And they went in to the king, into the court, but they laid up the roll in the chamber of Elishama, the scribe, and they told all the words in the hearing of the king. 21 And the king sent Jehudi to fetch the roll, who, bringing it out of the chamber of Elishama, the scribe, read it in the hearing of the king and of all the princes that stood about the king. 22 Now the king sat in the winter house in the ninth month,

posita erat arula coram eo plena prunis. 23 Cumque legisset Iudi tres pagellas vel quattuor, scidit illud scalpello scribae, et proiecit in ignem qui erat super arulam donec consumeretur omne volumen igni qui erat in arula. 24 Et non timuerunt neque sciderunt vestimenta sua, rex et omnes servi eius qui audierunt universos sermones istos. 25 Verumtamen Elnathan et Dalaias et Gamarias contradixerunt regi ne conbureret librum, et non audivit eos. 26 Et praecepit rex Hieremahel, filio Ammelech, et Saraiae, filio Ezrihel, et Selemiae, filio Abdehel, ut conprehenderent Baruch, scribam, et Hieremiam, prophetam, abscondit autem eos Dominus.

27 Et factum est verbum Domini ad Hieremiam, prophetam, postquam conbuserat rex volumen et sermones quos scripserat Baruch ex ore Hieremiae, dicens, 28 "Rursum tolle volumen aliud, et scribe in eo omnes sermones priores qui erant in volumine primo quod conbusit Ioachim, rex Iuda. 29 Et ad Ioachim, regem Iuda, dices, 'Haec dicit Dominus: "Tu conbusisti volumen illud, dicens, 'Quare scripsisti in eo adnuntians, "Festinus veniet rex Babylonis et vastabit terram hanc et cessare faciet ex illa hominem et iumentum?"' 30 Propterea haec dicit Dominus contra Ioachim, regem Iuda: 'Non erit ex eo qui sedeat super solium David, et cadaver eius proicietur ad aestum per diem et ad gelu per noctem. 31 Et visitabo contra eum et contra semen eius et contra servos eius iniquitates suas, et adducam super eos et super habitatores Hierusalem et super viros Iuda omne malum quod locutus sum ad eos, et non audierunt.'"'"

and there was a hearth before him full of burning coals. 23 And when Jehudi had read three or four pages, he cut it with the penknife, and he cast it into the fire that was upon the hearth till all the roll was consumed with the fire that was on the hearth. 24 And the king and all his servants that heard all these words were not afraid nor did they rend their garments. 25 But yet Elnathan and Delaiah and Gemariah spoke to the king not to burn the book, and he heard them not. 26 And the king commanded Jerahmeel, the son of Hammelech, and Seraiah, the son of Azriel, and Shelemiah, the son of Abdeel, to take up Baruch, the scribe, and Jeremiah, the prophet, but the Lord hid them.

27 And the word of the Lord came to Jeremiah, the prophet, after that the king had burnt the roll and the words that Baruch had written from the mouth of Jeremiah, saying, 28 "Take thee again another volume, and write in it all the former words that were in the first roll which Jehoiakim, the king of Judah, hath burnt. 29 And thou shalt say to Jehoiakim, the king of Judah, 'Thus saith the Lord: "Thou hast burnt that roll, saying, 'Why hast thou written therein and said, "The king of Babylon shall come speedily and shall lay waste this land and shall cause to cease from thence man and beast?"' 30 Therefore thus saith the Lord against Jehoiakim, the king of Judah: 'He shall have none to sit upon the throne of David, and his dead body shall be cast out to the heat by day and to the frost by night. 31 And I will punish him and his seed and his servants for their iniquities, and I will bring upon them and upon the inhabitants of Jerusalem and upon the men of Judah all the evil that I have pronounced against them, *but* they have not heard.'"'"

32 Hieremias autem tulit volumen aliud et dedit illud Baruch, filio Neriae, scribae, qui scripsit in eo ex ore Hieremiae omnes sermones libri quem conbuserat Ioachim, rex Iuda, igni, et insuper additi sunt sermones multo plures quam antea fuerant.

Caput 37

Et regnavit Rex Sedecias, filius Iosiae, pro Iechonia, filio Ioachim, quem constituit regem Nabuchodonosor, rex Babylonis, in terra Iuda. 2 Et non oboedivit ipse et servi eius et populus terrae verbis Domini quae locutus est in manu Hieremia prophetae. 3 Et misit Rex Sedecias Iuchal, filium Selemiae, et Sophoniam, filium Maasiae, sacerdotem, ad Hieremiam, prophetam, dicens, "Ora pro nobis Dominum, Deum nostrum."

4 Hieremias autem libere ambulabat in medio populi, non enim miserant eum in custodiam carceris. Igitur exercitus Pharaonis egressus est de Aegypto, et audientes Chaldei qui obsidebant Hierusalem huiuscemodi nuntium recesserunt ab Hierusalem. 5 Et factum est verbum Domini ad Hieremiam, prophetam, dicens, 6 "Haec dicit Dominus, Deus

32 And Jeremiah took another roll and gave it to Baruch, the son of Neriah, the scribe, who wrote in it from the mouth of Jeremiah all the words of the book which Jehoiakim, the king of Judah, had burnt with fire, and there were added besides many more words than had been before.

Chapter 37

Jeremiah prophesies that the Chaldeans, who had departed from Jerusalem, would return and burn the city. He is cast into prison. His conference with Zedekiah.

Now King Zedekiah, the son of Josiah, reigned instead of Jeconiah, the son of Jehoiakim, whom Nebuchadnezzar, king of Babylon, made king in the land of Judah. 2 *But* neither he nor his servants nor the people of the land did obey the words of the Lord that he spoke in the hand of Jeremiah, the prophet. 3 And King Zedekiah sent Jucal, the son of Shelemiah, and Zephaniah, the son of Maaseiah, the priest, to Jeremiah, the prophet, saying, "Pray to the Lord, our God, for us.

4 Now Jeremiah walked freely in the midst of the people, for they had not *as yet* cast him into *prison*. And the army of Pharaoh was come out of Egypt, and the Chaldeans that besieged Jerusalem, hearing these tidings, departed from Jerusalem. 5 And the word of the Lord came to Jeremiah, the prophet, saying, 6 "Thus saith the Lord, the God

Israhel: 'Sic dicetis regi Iuda, qui misit vos ad me interrogandum: "Ecce: exercitus Pharaonis qui egressus est vobis in auxilium revertetur in terram suam, in Aegyptum. 7 Et redient Chaldei et bellabunt contra civitatem hanc et capient eam et incendent eam igni. 8 Haec dicit Dominus: 'Nolite decipere animas vestras, dicentes, "Euntes abibunt et recedent a nobis Chaldei," quia non abibunt. 9 Sed et si percusseritis omnem exercitum Chaldeorum qui proeliantur adversum vos, et derelicti fuerint ex eis aliqui vulnerati, singuli de tentorio suo consurgent et incendent civitatem hanc igni.'"'"

10 Ergo cum recessisset exercitus Chaldeorum ab Hierusalem propter exercitum Pharaonis, 11 egressus est Hieremias de Hierusalem ut iret in terram Beniamin et divideret ibi possessionem in conspectu civium. 12 Cumque pervenisset ad portam Beniamin, erat ibi custos portae per vices nomine Hierias, filius Selemiae, filii Ananiae, et adprehendit Hieremiam, prophetam, dicens, "Ad Chaldeos profugis."

13 Et respondit Hieremias, "Falsum est; non fugio ad Chaldeos." Et non audivit eum, sed conprehendit Hierias Hieremiam et adduxit eum ad principes, 14 quam ob rem irati principes contra Hieremiam; caesum eum miserunt in carcerem qui erat in domo Ionathan, scribae, ipse enim praepositus erat super carcerem. 15 Itaque ingressus est Hieremias in domum laci et in ergastulum, et sedit ibi Hieremias diebus multis.

16 Mittens autem, Sedecias, rex, tulit eum et interrogavit eum in domo sua abscondite, et dixit, "Putasne est sermo a Domino?"

of Israel: 'Thus shall you say to the king of Judah, who sent you to inquire of me: "Behold: the army of Pharaoh which is come forth to help you shall return into their own land, into Egypt. 7 And the Chaldeans shall come again and fight against this city and take it and burn it with fire. 8 Thus saith the Lord: 'Deceive not your souls, saying, "The Chaldeans shall surely depart and go away from us," for they shall not go away. 9 But if you should even beat all the army of the Chaldeans that fight against you, and there should be left of them some wounded men, they shall rise up, every man from his tent, and burn this city with fire.'""""

10 Now when the army of the Chaldeans was gone away from Jerusalem because of Pharaoh's army, 11 Jeremiah went forth out of Jerusalem to go into the land of Benjamin and to divide a possession there in the presence of the citizens. 12 And when he was come to the gate of Benjamin, the captain of the gate who was there in his turn was one named Irijah, the son of Shelemiah, the son of Hananiah, and he took hold of Jeremiah, the prophet, saying, "Thou art fleeing to the Chaldeans."

13 And Jeremiah answered, "It is not so; I am not fleeing to the Chaldeans." *But* he hearkened not to him, *so* Irijah took Jeremiah and brought him to the princes, 14 wherefore the princes were angry with Jeremiah, *and* they beat him, and cast him into the prison that was in the house of Jonathan, the scribe, for he was chief over the prison. 15 So Jeremiah went into the house of the prison and into the dungeon, and Jeremiah remained there many days.

16 Then Zedekiah, the king, sending, took him and asked him secretly in his house, and said, "Is there, thinkest thou, any word from the Lord?"

Et dixit Hieremias, "Est." Et ait, "In manus regis Babylonis traderis." 17 Et dixit Hieremias ad Regem Sedeciam, "Quid peccavi tibi et servis tuis et populo tuo, quia misisti me in domum carceris? 18 Ubi sunt prophetae vestri qui prophetabant vobis et dicebant, 'Non veniet rex Babylonis super vos et super terram hanc'? 19 Nunc ergo audi, obsecro, domine mi, rex, valeat deprecatio mea in conspectu tuo, et ne me remittas in domum Ionathan, scribae, ne moriar ibi."

20 Praecepit ergo Rex Sedecias ut traderetur Hieremias in vestibulo carceris et daretur ei torta panis cotidie excepto pulmento donec consumerentur omnes panes de civitate, et mansit Hieremias in vestibulo carceris.

Caput 38

Audivit autem Saphatias, filius Matthan, et Gedelias, filius Phassur, et Iuchal, filius Selemiae, et Phassur, filius Melchiae, sermones quos Hieremias loquebatur ad omnem populum, dicens, 2 "Haec dicit Dominus: 'Quicumque manserit

And Jeremiah said, "There is." And he said, "Thou shalt be delivered into the hands of the king of Babylon. 17 And Jeremiah said to King Zedekiah, "In what have I offended against thee or thy servants or thy people, that thou hast cast me into prison? 18 Where are your prophets that prophesied to you and said, 'The king of Babylon shall not come against you and against this land'? 19 Now therefore hear, I beseech thee, my lord, the king, let my petition be accepted in thy sight, and send me not back into the house of Jonathan, the scribe, lest I die there."

20 Then King Zedekiah commanded that Jeremiah should be committed into the entry of the prison and that they should give him daily a piece of bread beside broth till all the bread in the city were spent, and Jeremiah remained in the entry of the prison.

Chapter 38

The prophet at the instance of the great men is cast into a filthy dungeon. He is drawn out by Ebed-melech and has another conference with the king.

Now Shephatiah, the son of Mattan, and Gedaliah, the son of Pashhur, and Juchal, the son of Shelemiah, and Pashhur, the son of Malchiah, heard the words that Jeremiah spoke to all the people, saying, 2 "Thus saith the Lord: 'Who-

in civitate hac morietur gladio et fame et peste, qui autem profugerit ad Chaldeos vivet, et erit anima eius sospes, et vivens.' 3 Haec dicit Dominus: 'Tradendo tradetur civitas haec in manu exercitus regis Babylonis, et capiet eam.'"

4 Et dixerunt principes regi, "Rogamus ut occidatur homo iste, de industria enim dissolvit manus virorum bellantium qui remanserunt in civitate hac et manus universi populi, loquens ad eos iuxta verba haec, siquidem homo hic non quaerit pacem populi huic, sed malum."

5 Et dixit Rex Sedecias, "Ecce: ipse in manibus vestris est, nec enim fas est regem vobis quicquam negare." 6 Tulerunt ergo Hieremiam et proiecerunt eum in lacum Melchiae, filii Ammelech, qui erat in vestibulo carceris, et submiserunt Hieremiam in funibus in lacum, in quo non erat aqua sed lutum. Descendit itaque Hieremias in caenum.

7 Audivit autem Abdemelech, Aethiops vir, eunuchus qui erat in domo regis, quod misissent Hieremiam in lacum, porro rex sedebat in porta Beniamin. 8 Et egressus est Abdemelech de domo regis et locutus est ad regem, dicens, 9 "Domine mi, rex, malefecerunt viri isti omnia quaecumque perpetrarunt contra Hieremiam, prophetam, mittentes eum in lacum ut moriatur ibi fame, non sunt enim panes ultra in civitate."

10 Praecepit itaque rex Abdemelech, Aethiopi, dicens, "Tolle tecum hinc triginta viros, et leva Hieremiam, prophetam, de lacu antequam moriatur."

soever shall remain in this city shall die by the sword and by famine and by pestilence, but he that shall go forth to the Chaldeans shall live, and his life shall be safe, and he shall live.' 3 Thus saith the Lord: 'This city shall surely be delivered into the hand of the army of the king of Babylon, and he shall take it.'"

4 And the princes said to the king, "We beseech thee that this man may be put to death, for on purpose he weakeneth the hands of the men of war that remain in this city and the hands of the *people,* speaking to them according to these words, for this man seeketh not peace to this people, but evil."

5 And King Zedekiah said, "Behold: he is in your hands, for it is not lawful for the king to deny you any thing." 6 Then they took Jeremiah and cast him into the dungeon of Malchiah, the son of Hammelech, which was in the entry of the prison, and they let down Jeremiah by ropes into the dungeon, wherein there was no water but mire. And Jeremiah sunk into the mire.

7 Now Ebed-melech, the Ethiopian, an eunuch that was in the king's house, heard that they had put Jeremiah in the dungeon, but the king was sitting in the gate of Benjamin. 8 And Ebed-melech went out of the king's house and spoke to the king, saying, 9 "My lord, the king, these men have done evil in all that they have done against Jeremiah, the prophet, casting him into the dungeon to die there with hunger, for there is no more bread in the city."

10 Then the king commanded Ebed-melech, the Ethiopian, saying, "Take from hence thirty men with thee, and draw up Jeremiah, the prophet, out of the dungeon before he die."

11 Adsumptis ergo Abdemelech secum viris, ingressus est domum regis quae erat sub cellario, et tulit inde veteres pannos et antiqua quae conputruerant, et submisit ea ad Hieremiam in lacum per funiculos. 12 Dixitque Abdemelech, Aethiops, ad Hieremiam, "Pone veteres pannos et haec scissa et putrida sub cubito manuum tuarum et super funes," fecit ergo Hieremias sic. 13 Et extraxerunt Hieremiam funibus et eduxerunt eum de lacu, mansit autem Hieremias in vestibulo carceris.

14 Et misit Rex Sedecias et tulit ad se Hieremiam, prophetam, ad ostium tertium quod erat in domo Domini, et dixit rex ad Hieremiam, "Interrogo ego te sermonem; ne abscondas a me aliquid."

15 Dixit autem Hieremias ad Sedeciam, "Si adnuntiavero tibi, numquid non interficies me? Et si consilium tibi dedero, non me audies."

16 Iuravit ergo Rex Sedecias Hieremiae clam, dicens, "Vivit Dominus qui fecit nobis animam hanc, si occidero te, et si tradidero te in manus virorum istorum qui quaerunt animam tuam."

17 Et dixit Hieremias ad Sedeciam, "Haec dicit Dominus exercituum, Deus Israhel: 'Si profectus exieris ad principes regis Babylonis, vivet anima tua, et civitas haec non succendetur igni, et salvus eris tu, et domus tua. 18 Si autem non exieris ad principes regis Babylonis, tradetur civitas haec in manus Chaldeorum, et succendent eam igni, et tu non effugies de manu eorum.'"

19 Et dixit Rex Sedecias ad Hieremiam, "Sollicitus sum propter Iudaeos qui transfugerunt ad Chaldeos, ne forte tradar in manus eorum, et inludant mihi."

11 So Ebed-melech taking the men with him, went into the king's house that was under the storehouse, and he took from thence old rags and old rotten things, and he let them down by cords to Jeremiah into the dungeon. 12 And Ebed-melech, the Ethiopian, said to Jeremiah, "Put these old rags and these rent and rotten things under thy arms and upon the cords," and Jeremiah did so. 13 And they drew up Jeremiah with the cords and brought him forth out of the dungeon, and Jeremiah remained in the entry of the prison.

14 And King Zedekiah sent and took Jeremiah, the prophet, to him, to the third gate that was in the house of the Lord, and the king said to Jeremiah, "I *will* ask thee a thing; hide nothing from me."

15 Then Jeremiah said to Zedekiah, "If I shall declare it to thee, wilt thou not put me to death? And if I give thee counsel, thou wilt not hearken to me."

16 Then King Zedekiah swore to Jeremiah in private, saying, "As the Lord liveth that made us this soul, I will not put thee to death, nor will I deliver thee into the hands of these men that seek thy life."

17 And Jeremiah said to Zedekiah, "Thus saith the Lord of hosts, the God of Israel: 'If thou wilt take a resolution and go out to the princes of the king of Babylon, thy soul shall live, and this city shall not be burnt with fire, and thou shalt be safe, and thy house. 18 But if thou wilt not go out to the princes of the king of Babylon, this city shall be delivered into the hands of the Chaldeans, and they shall burn it with fire, and thou shalt not escape out of their hands.'"

19 And King Zedekiah said to Jeremiah, "I am afraid because of the Jews that are fled over to the Chaldeans, *lest* I should be delivered into their hands, and they should abuse me."

20 Respondit autem Hieremias, "Non te tradent; audi, quaeso, vocem Domini quam ego loquor ad te, et bene tibi erit, et vivet anima tua. 21 Quod si nolueris egredi, iste est sermo quem ostendit mihi Dominus: 22 'Ecce: omnes mulieres quae remanserunt in domo regis Iuda educentur ad principes regis Babylonis et ipsae dicent, "Seduxerunt te et praevaluerunt adversum te viri pacifici tui; demerserunt in caeno et in lubrico pedes tuos, et recesserunt a te." 23 Et omnes uxores tuae et filii tui educentur ad Chaldeos, et non effugies manus eorum, sed in manu regis Babylonis capieris, et civitatem hanc conburet igni.'"

24 Dixit ergo Sedecias ad Hieremiam, "Nullus sciat verba haec, et non morieris. 25 Si autem audierint principes quia locutus sum tecum et venerint ad te et dixerint tibi, 'Indica nobis quid locutus sis cum rege; ne celes nos, et non te interficiemus, et quid locutus est tecum rex,' 26 dices ad eos, 'Prostravi ego preces meas coram rege, ne me reduci iuberet in domum Ionathan et ibi morerer.'" 27 Venerunt ergo omnes principes ad Hieremiam et interrogaverunt eum, et locutus est eis iuxta omnia verba quae praeceperat ei rex, et cessaverunt ab eo, nihil enim fuerat auditum. 28 Mansit vero Hieremias in vestibulo carceris usque ad diem quo capta est Hierusalem, et factum est ut caperetur Hierusalem.

20 But Jeremiah answered, "They shall not deliver thee; hearken, I beseech thee, to the word of the Lord which I speak to thee, and it shall be well with thee, and thy soul shall live. 21 But if thou wilt not go forth, this is the word which the Lord hath shewn me: 22 'Behold: all the women that are left in the house of the king of Judah shall be brought out to the princes of the king of Babylon, and they shall say, "Thy men of peace have deceived thee and have prevailed against thee; they have plunged thy feet in the mire and in a slippery place, and they have departed from thee." 23 And all thy wives and thy children shall be brought out to the Chaldeans, and thou shalt not escape their hands, but thou shalt be taken by the hand of the king of Babylon, and he shall burn this city with fire.'"

24 Then Zedekiah said to Jeremiah, "Let no man know these words, and thou shalt not die. 25 But if the princes shall hear that I have spoken with thee and shall come to thee and say to thee, 'Tell us what thou hast said to the king; hide it not from us, and we will not kill thee, and also what the king said to thee,' 26 thou shalt say to them, 'I presented my supplication before the king, that he would not command me to be carried back into the house of Jonathan *to* die there.'" 27 So all the princes came to Jeremiah and asked him, and he spoke to them according to all the words that the king had commanded him, and they left him, for nothing had been heard. 28 But Jeremiah remained in the entry of the prison until the day that Jerusalem was taken, and it came to pass that Jerusalem was taken.

Caput 39

Anno nono Sedeciae, regis Iuda, mense decimo venit Nabuchodonosor, rex Babylonis, et omnis exercitus eius ad
Hierusalem, et obsidebant eam. 2 Undecimo autem anno
Sedeciae mense quarto, quinta mensis, aperta est civitas.
3 Et ingressi sunt omnes principes regis Babylonis et sederunt in porta media: Neregel, Sereser, Semegar Nabu, Sarsachim, Rabsares, Neregel, Sereser, Rebmag et omnes reliqui
principes regis Babylonis. 4 Cumque vidisset eos Sedecias,
rex Iuda, et omnes viri bellatores, fugerunt, et egressi sunt
nocte de civitate per viam horti regis et per portam quae
erat inter duos muros, et egressi sunt ad viam deserti. 5 Persecutus est autem eos exercitus Chaldeorum, et conprehen-
derunt Sedeciam in campo solitudinis Hiericuntinae, et
captum adduxerunt ad Nabuchodonosor, regem Babylonis,
in Reblatha, quae est in terra Emath, et locutus est ad eum
iudicia. 6 Et occidit rex Babylonis filios Sedeciae in Reblatha
in oculis eius, et omnes nobiles Iuda occidit rex Babylonis. 7 Oculos quoque Sedeciae eruit et vinxit eum conpedibus ut duceretur in Babylonem. 8 Domum quoque regis et
domum vulgi succenderunt Chaldei igni, et murum Hieru-

Chapter 39

After two years' siege Jerusalem is taken. Zedekiah is carried before Nebuchadnezzar, who kills his sons in his sight and then puts out his eyes. Jeremiah is set at liberty.

In the ninth year of Zedekiah, king of Judah, in the tenth month came Nebuchadnezzar, king of Babylon, and all his army to Jerusalem, and they besieged it. 2 And in the eleventh year of Zedekiah in the fourth month, the fifth day of the month, the city was opened. 3 And all the princes of the king of Babylon came in and sat in the middle gate: Neregel, Sereser, Semegarnabu, Sarsachim, Rabsares, Neregel, Sereser, Rebmag and all the rest of the princes of the king of Babylon. 4 And when Zedekiah, the king of Judah, and all the men of war saw them, they fled, and they went forth in the night out of the city by the way of the king's garden and by the gate that was between the two walls, and they went out to the way of the desert. 5 But the army of the Chaldeans pursued after them, and they took Zedekiah in the plain of the desert of Jericho, and when they had taken him, they brought him to Nebuchadnezzar, king of Babylon, to Riblah, which is in the land of Hamath, and he gave judgment upon him. 6 And the king of Babylon slew the sons of Zedekiah in Riblah before his eyes, and the king of Babylon slew all the nobles of Judah. 7 He also put out the eyes of Zedekiah and bound him with fetters to be carried to Babylon. 8 And the Chaldeans burnt the king's house and the houses

salem subverterunt. 9 Et reliquias populi quae remanserunt in civitate et perfugas qui transfugerant ad eum et superfluos vulgi qui remanserant transtulit Nabuzardan, magister militum, in Babylonem. 10 Et de plebe pauperum qui nihil penitus habebant dimisit Nabuzardan, magister militum, in terra Iuda, et dedit eis vineas et cisternas in die illa.

11 Praeceperat autem Nabuchodonosor, rex Babylonis, de Hieremia Nabuzardan, magistro militum, dicens, 12 "Tolle illum, et pone super eum oculos tuos, nihilque ei mali facias, sed ut voluerit, sic facias ei." 13 Misit ergo Nabuzardan, princeps militiae, et Nabusezban et Rabsares et Neregel et Sereser et Rebmag et omnes optimates regis Babylonis 14 miserunt et tulerunt Hieremiam de vestibulo carceris et tradiderunt eum Godoliae, filio Ahicam, filii Saphan, ut intraret domum et habitaret in populo.

15 Ad Hieremiam autem factus fuerat sermo Domini cum clausus esset in vestibulo carceris, dicens, 16 "Vade, et dic Abdemelech, Aethiopi, dicens, 'Haec dicit Dominus exercituum, Deus Israhel: "Ecce: ego inducam sermones meos super civitatem hanc in malum et non in bonum, et erunt in conspectu tuo in die illa. 17 Et liberabo te in die illa," ait Dominus, "et non traderis in manus virorum quos tu formidas, 18 sed eruens liberabo te, et gladio non cades, sed erit tibi anima tua in salutem, quia in me habuisti fiduciam," ait Dominus.'"

of the people with fire, and they threw down the wall of Jerusalem. 9 And Nebuzaradan, the general of the army, carried away captive to Babylon the remnant of the people that remained in the city and the fugitives that had gone over to him and the rest of the people that remained. 10 *But* Nebuzaradan, the general, left some of the poor people that had nothing at all in the land of Judah, and he gave them vineyards and cisterns at that time.

11 Now Nebuchadnezzar, king of Babylon, had given charge to Nebuzaradan, the general, concerning Jeremiah, saying, 12 "Take him, and set thy eyes upon him, and do him no harm, but as he hath a mind, so do with him." 13 Therefore Nebuzaradan, the general, sent, and Nebushazban and Rabsaris and Nergal and Sharezer and Rabmag and all the nobles of the king of Babylon 14 sent and took Jeremiah out of the court of the prison and committed him to Gedaliah, the son of Ahikam, the son of Shaphan, that he might go home and dwell among the people.

15 But the word of the Lord came to Jeremiah when he was yet shut up in the court of the prison, saying, "Go, and tell Ebed-melech, the Ethiopian, saying, 16 'Thus saith the Lord of hosts, the God of Israel: "Behold: I will bring my words upon this city unto evil and not unto good, and they shall be accomplished in thy sight in that day. 17 And I will deliver thee in that day," saith the Lord, "and thou shalt not be given into the hands of the men whom thou fearest, 18 but delivering I will deliver thee, and thou shalt not fall by the sword, but thy life shall be saved for thee, because thou hast put thy trust in me," saith the Lord.'"

Caput 40

Sermo qui factus est ad Hieremiam a Domino postquam dimissus est a Nabuzardan, magistro militiae, de Rama, quando tulit eum, vinctum catenis, in medio omnium qui migrabant de Hierusalem et Iuda et ducebantur in Babylonem. 2 Tollens ergo princeps militiae Hieremiam dixit ad eum, "Dominus, Deus tuus, locutus est malum hoc super locum istum, 3 et adduxit, et fecit Dominus sicut locutus est, quia peccastis Domino et non audistis vocem eius, et factus est vobis sermo hic. 4 Nunc ergo ecce: solvi te hodie de catenis quae sunt in manibus tuis; si placet tibi ut venias mecum in Babylonem, veni, et ponam oculos meos super te, si autem displicet tibi venire mecum in Babylonem, reside. Ecce: omnis terra in conspectu tuo est quod elegeris, et quo placuerit tibi ut vadas, illuc perge. 5 Et mecum noli venire, sed habita apud Godoliam, filium Ahicam, filii Saphan, quem praeposuit rex Babylonis civitatibus Iuda; habita ergo cum eo in medio populi, vel quocumque placuerit tibi ut vadas, vade." Dedit quoque ei magister militiae cibaria et munuscula, et dimisit eum.

6 Venit autem Hieremias ad Godoliam, filium Ahicam, in

Chapter 40

Jeremiah remains with Gedaliah the governor, who receives all the Jews that resort to him.

The word that came to Jeremiah from the Lord after that Nebuzaradan, the general, had let him go from Ramah, when he had taken him, being bound with chains, among all them that were carried away from Jerusalem and Judah and were carried to Babylon. 2 And the general of the army taking Jeremiah said to him, "The Lord, thy God, hath pronounced this evil upon this place, 3 and he hath brought it, and the Lord hath done as he hath said, because you have sinned against the Lord and have not hearkened to his voice, and this word is come upon you. 4 Now then behold: I have loosed thee this day from the chains which were upon thy hands; if it please thee to come with me to Babylon, come, and I will set my eyes upon thee, but if it do not please thee to come with me to Babylon, stay here. Behold: all the land is before thee *as* thou shalt choose, and whither it shall please thee to go, thither go. 5 And come not with me, but dwell with Gedaliah, the son of Ahikam, the son of Shaphan, whom the king of Babylon hath made governor over the cities of Judah; dwell therefore with him in the midst of the people, or whithersoever it shall please thee to go, go." And the general of the army gave him victuals and presents, and let him go.

6 And Jeremiah went to Gedaliah, the son of Ahikam, to

Masphat, et habitavit cum eo in medio populi qui relictus fuerat in terra. 7 Cumque audissent omnes principes exercitus qui dispersi fuerant per regiones, ipsi et socii eorum, quod praefecisset rex Babylonis Godoliam, filium Ahicam, terrae et quod commendasset ei viros et mulieres et parvulos et de pauperibus terrae, qui non fuerant translati in Babylonem, 8 venerunt ad Godoliam in Masphat, et Ismahel, filius Nathaniae, et Iohanan et Ionathan, filii Caree, et Sareas, filius Thanehumeth, et filii Offi qui erant de Nethophathi et Iezonias, filius Maachathi, ipsi et viri eorum. 9 Et iuravit eis Godolias, filius Ahicam, filii Saphan, et comitibus eorum dicens, "Nolite timere servire Chaldeis; habitate in terra, et servite regi Babylonis, et bene erit vobis. 10 Ecce: ego habito in Masphat ut respondeam praecepto Chaldeorum qui mittuntur ad nos, vos autem, colligite vindemiam et messem et oleum, et condite in vasis vestris, et manete in urbibus vestris quas tenetis."

11 Sed et omnes Iudaei qui erant in Moab et in filiis Ammon et in Idumea et in universis regionibus, audito quod dedisset rex Babylonis reliquias in Iudaea et quod praeposuisset super eos Godoliam, filium Ahicam, filii Saphan, 12 reversi sunt, inquam, omnes Iudaei de universis locis ad quae profugerant, et venerunt in terram Iuda ad Godoliam, in Masphat, et collegerunt vinum et messem multam nimis. 13 Iohanan autem, filius Caree, et omnes principes exercitus qui dispersi erant in regionibus venerunt ad Godoliam, in Masphat. 14 Et dixerunt ei, "Scito quia Baalis, rex filiorum

Mizpah, and dwelt with him in the midst of the people that were left in the land. 7 And when all the captains of the army that were scattered through the countries, they and their companions, had heard that the king of Babylon had made Gedaliah, the son of Ahikam, governor of the country, and that he had committed unto him men and women and children and of the poor of the land, them that had not been carried away captive to Babylon, 8 they came to Gedaliah to Mizpah, and Ishmael, the son of Nethaniah, and Johanan and Jonathan, the sons of Kareah, and Seraiah, the son of Tanhumeth, and the children of Ephai that were of Netophathi and Jezaniah, the son of Maachati, they and their men. 9 And Gedaliah, the son of Ahikam, the son of Shaphan, swore to them and to their companions, saying, "Fear not to serve the Chaldeans; dwell in the land, and serve the king of Babylon, and it shall be well with you. 10 Behold: I dwell in Mizpah that I may answer the commandment of the Chaldeans that are sent to us, but as for you, gather ye the vintage and the harvest and the oil, and lay it up in your vessels, and abide in your cities which you hold."

11 Moreover all the Jews that were in Moab and among the children of Ammon and in Edom and in all the countries, when they heard that the king of Babylon had left a remnant in Judea and that he had made Gedaliah, the son of Ahikam, the son of Shaphan, ruler over them, 12 all the Jews, I say, returned out of all the places to which they had fled, and they came into the land of Judah to Gedaliah, to Mizpah, and they gathered wine and a very great harvest. 13 Then Johanan, the son of Kareah, and all the captains of the army that had been scattered about in the countries, came to Gedaliah, to Mizpah. 14 And they said to him, "Know that

Ammon, misit Ismahel, filium Nathaniae, percutere animam tuam." Et non credidit eis Godolias, filius Ahicam.

15 Iohanan vero, filius Caree, dixit ad Godoliam seorsum in Masphat, loquens, "Ibo, et percutiam Ismahel, filium Nathaniae, nullo sciente, ne interficiat animam tuam et dissipentur omnes Iudaei qui congregati sunt ad te, et peribunt reliquiae Iuda."

16 Et ait Godolias, filius Ahicam, ad Iohanan, filium Caree, "Noli facere verbum hoc, falsum enim tu loqueris de Ismahel."

Caput 41

Et factum est in mense septimo venit Ismahel, filius Nathaniae, filii Elisama de semine regali, et optimates regis et decem viri cum eo ad Godoliam, filium Ahicam, in Masphat, et comederunt ibi panes simul in Masphat. 2 Surrexit autem Ismahel, filius Nathaniae, et decem viri qui erant cum eo, et percusserunt Godoliam, filium Ahicam, filii Saphan, gladio et interfecerunt eum quem praefecerat rex Babylonis terrae. 3 Omnes quoque Iudaeos qui erant cum

Baalis, the king of the children of Ammon, hath sent Ishmael, the son of Nethaniah, to kill thee." And Gedaliah, the son of Ahikam, believed them not.

15 But Johanan, the son of Kareah, spoke to Gedaliah privately in Mizpah, saying, "I will go, and I will kill Ishmael, the son of Nethaniah, and no man shall know it, lest he kill thee and all the Jews be scattered that are gathered unto thee, and the remnant of Judah perish."

16 And Gedaliah, the son of Ahikam, said to Johanan, the son of Kareah, "Do not this thing, for what thou sayst of Ishmael is false."

Chapter 41

Gedaliah is slain. The Jews that were with him are apprehensive of the Chaldeans.

And it came to pass in the seventh month that Ishmael, the son of Nethaniah, the son of Elishama of the royal blood, and the nobles of the king and ten men with him came to Gedaliah, the son of Ahikam, into Mizpah, and they ate bread there together in Mizpah. 2 And Ishmael, the son of Nethaniah, arose, and the ten men that were with him, and they struck Gedaliah, the son of Ahikam, the son of Shaphan, with the sword and slew him whom the king of Babylon had made governor over the land. 3 Ishmael slew

Godolia in Masphat et Chaldeos qui repperti sunt ibi et viros bellatores percussit Ismahel.

4 Secundo autem die postquam occiderat Godoliam, nullo adhuc sciente, 5 venerunt viri de Sychem et de Silo et de Samaria octoginta viri, rasi barba et scissis vestibus et squalentes, et munera et tus habebant in manu ut offerrent in domo Domini. 6 Egressus ergo Ismahel, filius Nathaniae, in occursum eorum de Masphat incedens et plorans ibat, cum autem occurrisset eis, dixit ad eos, "Venite ad Godoliam, filium Ahicam." 7 Qui cum venissent ad medium civitatis, interfecit eos Ismahel, filius Nathaniae, circa medium laci, ipse et viri qui erant cum eo.

8 Decem autem viri repperti sunt inter eos qui dixerunt ad Ismahel, "Noli occidere nos, quia habemus thesauros in agro frumenti et hordei et olei et mellis." Et cessavit et non interfecit eos cum fratribus suis.

9 Lacus autem in quem proiecerat Ismahel omnia cadavera virorum quos percussit propter Godoliam ipse est quem fecit Rex Asa propter Baasa, regem Israhel; ipsum replevit Ismahel, filius Nathaniae, occisis.

10 Et captivas duxit Ismahel omnes reliquias populi qui erant in Masphat, filias regis et universum populum qui remanserat in Masphat, quos commendarat Nabuzardan, princeps militiae, Godoliae, filio Ahicam. Et cepit eos Ismahel, filius Nathaniae, et abiit ut transiret ad filios Ammon.

also all the Jews that were with Gedaliah in Mizpah and the Chaldeans that were found there and the soldiers.

4 And on the second day after he had killed Gedaliah, no man yet knowing it, 5 there came some from Shechem and from Shiloh and from Samaria, fourscore men with their beards shaven and their clothes rent and mourning, and they had offerings and incense in their hand to offer in the house of the Lord. 6 And Ishmael, the son of Nethaniah, went forth from Mizpah to meet them, weeping all along as he went, and when he had met them, he said to them, "Come to Gedaliah, the son of Ahikam." 7 And when they were come to the midst of the city, Ishmael, the son of Nethaniah, slew them *and cast them* into the midst of the pit, he and the men that were with him.

8 But ten men were found among them that said to Ishmael, "Kill us not, for we have stores in the field of wheat and barley and oil and honey." And he forbore and slew them not with their brethren.

9 And the pit into which Ishmael cast all the dead bodies of the men whom he slew because of Gedaliah is the same that King Asa made for *fear of* Baasha, the king of Israel; the same did Ishmael, the son of Nethaniah, fill with them that were slain.

10 Then Ishmael carried away captive all the remnant of the people that were in Mizpah, the king's daughters and all the people that remained in Mizpah, whom Nebuzaradan, the general of the army, had committed to Gedaliah, the son of Ahikam. And Ishmael, the son of Nethaniah, took them, and he departed to go over to the children of Ammon.

11 Audivit autem Iohanan, filius Caree, et omnes principes bellatorum qui erant cum eo, omne malum quod fecerat
Ismahel, filius Nathaniae. 12 Et adsumptis universis viris,
profecti sunt ut bellarent adversum Ismahel, filium Nathaniae, et invenerunt eum ad aquas multas quae sunt in Gabaon. 13 Cumque vidisset omnis populus qui erat cum Ismahel Iohanan, filium Caree, et universos principes bellatorum
qui erant cum eo, laetati sunt. 14 Et reversus est omnis populus quem ceperat Ismahel in Masphat, reversusque abiit ad
Iohanan, filium Caree. 15 Ismahel autem, filius Nathaniae,
fugit cum octo viris a facie Iohanan et abiit ad filios Ammon.

16 Tulit ergo Iohanan, filius Caree, et omnes principes bellatorum qui erant cum eo universas reliquias vulgi quas reduxerat ab Ismahel, filio Nathaniae, de Masphat postquam
percussit Godoliam, filium Ahicam: fortes viros ad proelium
et mulieres et pueros et eunuchos quos reduxerat de Gabaon. 17 Et abierunt et sederunt peregrinantes in Chamaam,
quae est iuxta Bethleem, ut pergerent et introirent Aegyptum 18 a facie Chaldeorum, timebant enim eos quia percus-
serat Ismahel, filius Nathaniae, Godoliam, filium Ahicam,
quem praeposuerat rex Babylonis in terra Iuda.

11 But Johanan, the son of Kareah, and all the captains of the fighting men that were with him, heard *of* the evil that Ishmael, the son of Nethaniah, had done. 12 And taking all the men, they went out to fight against Ishmael, the son of Nethaniah, and they found him by the great waters that are in Gibeon. 13 And when all the people that were with Ishmael had seen Johanan, the son of Kareah, and all the captains of the fighting men that were with him, they rejoiced. 14 And all the people whom Ishmael had taken went back to Mizpah, and they returned and went to Johanan, the son of Kareah. 15 But Ishmael, the son of Nethaniah, fled with eight men from the face of Johanan and went to the children of Ammon.

16 Then Johanan, the son of Kareah, and all the captains of the soldiers that were with him took all the remnant of the people whom they had recovered from Ishmael, the son of Nethaniah, from Mizpah after that he had slain Gedaliah, the son of Ahikam: valiant men for war and the women and the children and the eunuchs whom he had brought back from Gibeon. 17 And they departed and sat as sojourners in Chimham, which is near Bethlehem, in order to go forward and enter into Egypt 18 from the face of the Chaldeans, for they were afraid of them because Ishmael, the son of Nethaniah, had slain Gedaliah, the son of Ahikam, whom the king of Babylon had made governor in the land of Judah.

Caput 42

Et accesserunt omnes principes bellatorum et Iohanan, filius Caree, et Iezonias, filius Osaiae, et reliquum vulgus a parvo usque ad magnum, 2 dixeruntque ad Hieremiam, prophetam, "Cadat oratio nostra in conspectu tuo, et ora pro nobis ad Dominum, Deum tuum, pro universis reliquiis, istis quia derelicti sumus pauci de pluribus, sicut oculi tui nos intuentur. 3 Et adnuntiet nobis Dominus, Deus tuus, viam per quam pergamus et verbum quod faciamus."

4 Dixit autem ad eos Hieremias, propheta, "Audivi; ecce, ego oro ad Dominum, Deum vestrum, secundum verba vestra; omne verbum quodcumque responderit mihi, indicabo vobis, nec celabo vos quicquam."

5 Et illi dixerunt ad Hieremiam, "Sit Dominus inter nos testis veritatis et fidei, si non iuxta omne verbum in quo miserit te Dominus, Deus tuus, ad nos sic faciemus. 6 Sive bonum est sive malum, voci Domini, Dei nostri, ad quem mittimus te, oboediemus, ut bene sit nobis cum audierimus vocem Domini, Dei nostri."

7 Cum autem conpleti essent decem dies, factum est verbum Domini ad Hieremiam, 8 vocavitque Iohanan, filium Caree, et omnes principes bellatorum qui erant cum eo et

Chapter 42

Jeremiah assures the remnant of the people that if they will stay in Judah, they shall be safe, but if they go down into Egypt, they shall perish.

Then all the captains of the warriors and Johanan, the son of Kareah, and Jezaniah, the son of Hoshaiah, and the rest of the people from the least to the greatest came near, 2 and they said to Jeremiah, the prophet, "Let our supplication fall before thee, and pray thou for us to the Lord, thy God, for all this remnant, for we are left but a few of many, as thy eyes do behold us. 3 And let the Lord, thy God, shew us the way by which we may walk and the thing that we must do."

4 And Jeremiah, the prophet, said to them, "I have heard you; behold, I will pray to the Lord, your God, according to your words, *and* whatsoever thing he shall answer me, I will declare it to you, and I will hide nothing from you.

5 And they said to Jeremiah, "The Lord be witness between us of truth and faithfulness, if we do not according to every thing for which the Lord, thy God, shall send thee to us. 6 Whether it be good or evil, we will obey the voice of the Lord, our God, to whom we send thee, that it may be well with us when we shall hearken to the voice of the Lord, our God."

7 Now after ten days, the word of the Lord came to Jeremiah, 8 and he called Johanan, the son of Kareah, and all the captains of the fighting men that were with him and

universum populum a minimo usque ad magnum. 9 Et dixit ad eos, "Haec dicit Dominus, Deus Israhel, ad quem misistis me ut prosternerem preces vestras in conspectu eius: 10 'Si quiescentes manseritis in terra hac, aedificabo vos et non destruam; plantabo et non evellam, iam enim placatus sum super malo quod feci vobis. 11 Nolite timere a facie regis Babylonis, quem vos pavidi formidatis; nolite eum metuere,' dicit Dominus, 'quia vobiscum sum ego ut salvos faciam vos et eruam de manu eius. 12 Et dabo vobis misericordias et miserebor vestri et habitare vos faciam in terra vestra.

13 "'Si autem dixeritis vos, "Non habitabimus in terra ista, nec audiemus vocem Domini, Dei nostri," 14 dicentes, "Nequaquam, sed ad terram Aegypti pergemus, ubi non videbimus bellum et clangorem tubae non audiemus et famem non sustinebimus, et ibi habitabimus," 15 propter hoc nunc audite verbum Domini, reliquiae Iuda.' Haec dicit Dominus exercituum, Deus Israhel: 'Si posueritis faciem vestram ut ingrediamini Aegyptum et intraveritis ut ibi habitetis, 16 gladius quem vos formidatis ibi conprehendet vos in terra Aegypti, et fames pro qua estis solliciti adherebit vobis in Aegypto, et ibi moriemini. 17 Omnesque viri qui posuerint faciem suam ut ingrediantur Aegyptum ut habitent ibi morientur gladio et fame et peste; nullus de eis remanebit nec effugiet a facie mali quod ego adferam super eos.' 18 Quia haec dicit Dominus exercituum, Deus Israhel: 'Sicut conflatus est furor meus et indignatio mea super habitatores Hierusalem, sic conflabitur indignatio mea super vos cum ingressi fueritis Aegyptum, et eritis in iusiurandum et in stuporem et in maledictum et in obprobrium, et nequaquam ultra videbitis locum istum.'

all the people from the least to the greatest. 9 And he said to them, "Thus saith the Lord, the God of Israel, to whom you sent me to present your supplications before him: 10 'If you will be quiet and remain in this land, I will build you up and not pull you down; I will plant you and not pluck you up, for now I am appeased for the evil that I have done to you. 11 Fear not *because* of the king of Babylon, of whom you are greatly afraid; fear him not,' saith the Lord, 'for I am with you to save you and to deliver you from his hand. 12 And I will shew mercies to you and will take pity on you and will cause you to dwell in your own land.

13 "'But if you say, "We will not dwell in this land, neither will we hearken to the voice of the Lord, our God," 14 saying, "No, but we will go into the land of Egypt, where we shall see no war nor hear the sound of the trumpet nor suffer hunger, and there we will dwell," 15 for this now hear the word of the Lord, ye remnant of Judah.' Thus saith the Lord of hosts, the God of Israel: 'If you set your faces to go into Egypt and enter in to dwell there, 16 the sword which you fear shall overtake you there in the land of Egypt, and the famine whereof you are afraid shall cleave to you in Egypt, and there you shall die. 17 And all the men that *set* their faces to go into Egypt to dwell there shall die by the sword and by famine and by pestilence; none of them shall remain nor escape from the face of the evil that I will bring upon them.' 18 For thus saith the Lord of hosts, the God of Israel, 'As my anger and my indignation hath been kindled against the inhabitants of Jerusalem, so shall my indignation be kindled against you when you shall enter into Egypt, and you shall be an execration and an astonishment and a curse and a reproach, and you shall see this place no more.'

19 "Verbum Domini super vos, reliquiae Iuda: 'Nolite intrare Aegyptum.' Scientes scietis quia obtestatus sum vos hodie, 20 quia decepistis animas vestras, vos enim misistis me ad Dominum, Deum nostrum, dicentes, 'Ora pro nobis ad Dominum, Deum nostrum, et iuxta omnia quaecumque dixerit tibi Dominus, Deus noster, sic adnuntia nobis, et faciemus.' 21 Et adnuntiavi vobis hodie, et non audistis vocem Domini, Dei vestri, super universis pro quibus misit me ad vos. 22 Nunc ergo scientes scietis quia gladio et fame et peste moriemini in loco ad quem voluistis intrare ut habitaretis ibi."

Caput 43

Factum est autem cum conplesset Hieremias loquens ad populum universos sermones Domini, Dei eorum, pro quibus miserat eum Dominus, Deus eorum, ad illos, omnia verba haec 2 dixit Azarias, filius Osaiae, et Iohanan, filius Caree, et omnes viri superbi, dicentes ad Hieremiam, "Mendacium tu loqueris; non misit te Dominus, Deus noster,

19 "This is the word of the Lord concerning you, O ye remnant of Judah: 'Go ye not into Egypt.' Know certainly that I have adjured you this day, 20 for you have deceived your own souls, for you sent me to the Lord, our God, saying, 'Pray for us to the Lord, our God, and according to all that the Lord, our God, shall say to thee, so declare unto us, and we will do it.' 21 And *now* I have declared it to you this day, and you have not obeyed the voice of the Lord, your God, with regard to all the things for which he hath sent me to you. 22 Now therefore know certainly that you shall die by the sword and by famine and by pestilence in the place to which you desire to go to dwell there."

Chapter 43

The Jews, contrary to the orders of God by the prophet, go into Egypt, carrying Jeremiah with them. He foretells the devastation of that land by the king of Babylon.

And it came to pass that when Jeremiah had made an end of speaking to the people all the words of the Lord, their God, for which the Lord, their God, had sent him to them, all these words 2 Azariah, the son of Hoshaiah, and Johanan, the son of Kareah, and all the proud men made answer, saying to Jeremiah, "Thou tellest a lie; the Lord, our God, hath

dicens, 'Ne ingrediamini Aegyptum ut habitetis illuc.' 3 Sed Baruch, filius Neriae, incitat te adversum nos ut tradat nos in manus Chaldeorum ut interficiat nos et transduci faciat in Babylonem." 4 Et non audivit Iohanan, filius Caree, et omnes principes bellatorum et universus populus vocem Domini ut manerent in terra Iuda. 5 Sed tollens Iohanan, filius Caree, et universi principes bellatorum universos reliquiarum Iuda qui reversi fuerant de cunctis gentibus ad quas fuerant ante dispersi ut habitarent in terra Iuda: 6 viros et mulieres et parvulos et filias regis et omnem animam quam reliquerat Nabuzardan, princeps militiae, cum Godolia, filio Ahicam, filii Saphan, et Hieremiam, prophetam, et Baruch, filium Neriae. 7 Et ingressi sunt terram Aegypti, quia non oboedierunt voci Domini, et venerunt usque ad Tafnis.

8 Et factus est sermo Domini ad Hieremiam in Tafnis, dicens, 9 "Sume in manu tua lapides grandes, et abscondes eos in crypta quae est sub muro latericio in porta domus Pharaonis in Tafnis, cernentibus viris Iudaeis. 10 Et dices ad eos, 'Haec dicit Dominus exercituum, Deus Israhel: "Ecce: ego mittam et adsumam Nabuchodonosor, regem Babylonis, servum meum, et ponam thronum eius super lapides istos quos abscondi, et statuet solium suum super eos. 11 Veniensque percutiet terram Aegypti: quos in mortem, in mortem, et quos in captivitatem, in captivitatem, et quos in gladium, in gladium. 12 Et succendet ignem in delubris deorum Aegypti, et conburet ea, et captivos ducet illos, et amicietur

not sent thee, saying, 'Go not into Egypt to dwell there.' 3 But Baruch, the son of Neriah, setteth thee on against us to deliver us into the hands of the Chaldeans to kill us and to cause us to be carried away captives to Babylon." 4 So Johanan, the son of Kareah, and all the captains of the soldiers and all the people obeyed not the voice of the Lord to remain in the land of Judah. 5 But Johanan, the son of Kareah, and all the captains of the soldiers took all the remnant of Judah that were returned out of all nations to which they had before been scattered to dwell in the land of Judah: 6 men and women and children and the king's daughters and every soul which Nebuzaradan, the general, had left with Gedaliah, the son of Ahikam, the son of Shaphan, and Jeremiah, the prophet, and Baruch, the son of Neriah. 7 And they went into the land of Egypt, for they obeyed not the voice of the Lord, and they came as far as Tahpanhes.

8 And the word of the Lord came to Jeremiah in Tahpanhes, saying, 9 "Take great stones in thy hand, and thou shalt hide them in the vault that is under the brick wall at the gate of Pharaoh's house in Tahpanhes, in the sight of the men of Judah. 10 And thou shalt say to them, 'Thus saith the Lord of hosts, the God of Israel: "Behold: I will send and take Nebuchadnezzar, the king of Babylon, my servant, and I will set his throne over these stones which I have hid, and he shall set his throne over them. 11 And he shall come and strike the land of Egypt: such as are for death, to death, and such as are for captivity, to captivity, and such as are for the sword, to the sword. 12 And he shall kindle a fire in the temples of the gods of Egypt, and he shall burn them, and he shall carry them away captives, and he shall array himself with the land

terra Aegypti sicut amicitur pastor pallio suo, et egredietur inde in pace. 13 Et conteret statuas Domus Solis quae sunt in terra Aegypti, et delubra deorum Aegypti conburet igni.

Caput 44

Verbum quod factum est ad Hieremiam ad omnes Iudaeos qui habitabant in terra Aegypti, habitantes in Magdolo et in Tafnis et in Memphis et in terra Fatures, dicens, 2 "Haec dicit Dominus exercituum, Deus Israhel: 'Vos vidistis omne malum istud quod adduxi super Hierusalem et super omnes urbes Iuda, et ecce: sunt desertae hodie, et non est in eis habitator 3 propter malitiam quam fecerunt, ut me ad iracundiam provocarent et irent et sacrificarent et colerent deos alienos quos nesciebant et illi et vos et patres vestri. 4 Et misi ad vos omnes servos meos, prophetas, de nocte consurgens mittensque et dicens, "Nolite facere verbum abominationis huiuscemodi quam odivi." 5 Et non audierunt nec inclinaverunt aurem suam ut converterentur a malis suis et non sacrificarent diis alienis. 6 Et conflata est indignatio mea et furor meus et succensa est in civitatibus Iuda et in

of Egypt as a shepherd putteth on his garment, and he shall go forth from thence in peace. 13 And he shall break the statues of the House of the Sun that are in the land of Egypt, and the temples of the gods of Egypt he shall burn with fire.

Chapter 44

The prophet's admonition to the Jews in Egypt against idolatry is not regarded. He denounces to them their destruction.

The word that came to Jeremiah concerning all the Jews that dwelt in the land of Egypt, dwelling in Migdol and in Tahpanhes and in Memphis and in the land of Pathros, saying, 2 "Thus saith the Lord of hosts, the God of Israel, 'You have seen all this evil that I have brought upon Jerusalem and upon all the cities of Judah, and behold: they are desolate this day, and there is not an inhabitant in them 3 because of the wickedness which they have committed, to provoke me to wrath and to go and offer sacrifice and worship other gods which neither they nor you nor your fathers knew. 4 And I sent to you all my servants, the prophets, rising early and sending and saying, "Do not commit *this abominable* thing *which I hate.*" 5 *But* they heard not nor inclined their ear to turn from their evil ways and not to sacrifice to strange gods. 6 *Wherefore* my indignation and my fury was poured forth and was kindled in the cities of Judah and in the streets

plateis Hierusalem, et versae sunt in solitudinem et vastitatem, secundum diem hanc.' 7 Et nunc haec dicit Dominus
exercituum, Deus Israhel: 'Quare vos facitis malum grande
hoc contra animas vestras, ut intereat ex vobis vir et mulier,
parvulus et lactens, de medio Iudae nec relinquatur vobis
quicquam residuum, 8 provocantes me in operibus manuum
vestrarum sacrificando diis alienis in terra Aegypti, in quam
ingressi estis ut habitetis ibi, et dispereatis et sitis in maledictionem et in obprobrium cunctis gentibus terrae? 9 Numquid obliti estis mala patrum vestrorum et mala regum Iuda
et mala uxorum eius et mala vestra et mala uxorum vestrarum quae fecerunt in terra Iuda et in regionibus Hierusalem? 10 Non sunt mundati usque ad diem hanc, et non timuerunt et non ambulaverunt in lege Domini et in praeceptis
meis quae dedi coram vobis et coram patribus vestris.'

11 "Ideo haec dicit Dominus exercituum, Deus Israhel:
'Ecce, ego ponam faciem meam in vobis in malum, et disperdam omnem Iudam. 12 Et adsumam reliquias Iudae qui posuerunt facies suas ut ingrederentur terram Aegypti et habitarent ibi, et consumentur omnes in terra Aegypti: cadent in
gladio et in fame, et consumentur a minimo usque ad maximum in gladio, et in fame morientur, et erunt in iusiurandum et in miraculum et in maledictionem et in obprobrium.
13 Et visitabo habitatores terrae Aegypti sicut visitavi super
Hierusalem in gladio et in fame et in peste. 14 Et non erit qui
effugiat et sit residuus de reliquiis Iudaeorum qui vadunt ut
peregrinentur in terra Aegypti et revertantur in terram

of Jerusalem, and they are turned to desolation and waste, as at this day.' 7 And now thus saith the Lord of hosts, the God of Israel: 'Why do you commit this great evil against your own souls, that there should die of you man and woman, child and suckling, out of the midst of Judah and no remnant should be left you, 8 in that you provoke me to wrath with the works of your hands by sacrificing to other gods in the land of Egypt, into which you are come to dwell there, and that you should perish and be a curse and a reproach to all the nations of the earth? 9 Have you forgotten the evils of your fathers and the evils of the kings of Judah and the evils of their wives and your evils and the evils of your wives that they have done in the land of Judah and in the *streets* of Jerusalem? 10 They are not cleansed even to this day, neither have they feared nor walked in the law of the Lord nor in my commandments which I set before you and your fathers.'

11 "Therefore thus saith the Lord of hosts, the God of Israel: 'Behold, I will set my face upon you for evil, and I will destroy all Judah. 12 And I will take the remnant of Judah that have set their faces to go into the land of Egypt and to dwell there, and they shall be all consumed in the land of Egypt: they shall fall by the sword and by the famine, and they shall be consumed from the least even to the greatest by the sword, and by the famine shall they die, and they shall be for an execration and for a wonder and for a curse and for a reproach. 13 And I will visit them that dwell in the land of Egypt as I have visited Jerusalem by the sword and by famine and by pestilence. 14 And there shall be none that shall escape and remain of the remnant of the Jews that are gone to sojourn in the land of Egypt and that shall return into the

Iuda, ad quam ipsi elevant animas suas ut revertantur et habitent ibi; non revertentur nisi qui fugerint.'"

15 Responderunt autem Hieremiae omnes viri scientes quod sacrificarent uxores eorum diis alienis et universae mulieres, quarum stabat multitudo grandis, et omnis populus habitantium in terra Aegypti in Fatures, dicentes, 16 "Sermonem quem locutus es ad nos in nomine Domini, non audiemus ex te, 17 sed facientes faciemus omne verbum quod egredietur de ore nostro, ut sacrificemus reginae caeli et libemus ei libamina sicut fecimus nos et patres nostri, reges nostri et principes nostri in urbibus Iuda et in plateis Hierusalem. Et saturati sumus panibus, et bene nobis erat, malumque non vidimus. 18 Ex eo autem tempore quo cessavimus sacrificare reginae caeli et libare ei libamina, indigemus omnibus et gladio et fame consumpti sumus. 19 Quod si nos sacrificamus reginae caeli et libamus ei libamina, numquid sine viris nostris fecimus ei placentas ad colendum eam, et libandum ei libamina?"

20 Et dixit Hieremias ad omnem populum, adversum viros et adversum mulieres et adversum universam plebem qui responderant ei verbum, dicens, 21 "Numquid non sacrificium quod sacrificastis in civitatibus Iuda et in plateis Hierusalem, vos et patres vestri, reges vestri et principes vestri et populus terrae horum recordatus est Dominus, et ascendit super cor eius? 22 Et non poterat Dominus ultra portare propter malitiam studiorum vestrorum et propter abominationes quas fecistis, et facta est terra vestra in desolationem et in stuporem et in maledictum, eo quod non sit

land of Judah, to which they *have a desire* to return *to* dwell there; there shall none return but they that shall flee.'"

15 Then all the men that knew that their wives sacrificed to other gods, and all the women, of whom there stood by a great multitude, and all the people of them that dwelt in the land of Egypt in Pathros, answered Jeremiah, saying, 16 "As for the word which thou hast spoken to us in the name of the Lord, we will not hearken to thee, 17 but we will certainly do every word that shall proceed out of our own mouth, to sacrifice to the queen of heaven and to pour out drink-offerings to her as we and our fathers have done, our kings and our princes in the cities of Judah and in the streets of Jerusalem. And we were filled with bread, and it was well with us, and we saw no evil. 18 But *since* we left off to offer sacrifice to the queen of heaven and to pour out drink-offerings to her, we have wanted all things and have been consumed by the sword and by famine. 19 And if we offer sacrifice to the queen of heaven and pour out drink offerings to her, did we make *cakes* to worship her, *to* pour out drink-offerings to her without our husbands?"

20 And Jeremiah spoke to all the people, to the men and to the women and to all the people which had given him that answer, saying, 21 "Was it not the sacrifice that you offered in the cities of Judah and in the streets of Jerusalem, you and your fathers, your kings and your princes and the people of the land which the Lord hath remembered, and hath it not entered into his heart? 22 *So that* the Lord could no longer bear because of the evil of your doings and because of the abominations which you have committed, *therefore* your land is become a desolation and an astonishment and a curse

habitator, sicut est dies haec. 23 Propterea quod sacrificaveritis idolis et peccaveritis Domino et non audieritis vocem
Domini et in lege et in praeceptis et in testimoniis eius non
ambulaveritis, idcirco evenerunt vobis mala haec, sicut est
dies haec."

24 Dixit autem Hieremias ad omnem populum et ad universas mulieres, "Audite verbum Domini, omnis Iuda, qui
estis in terra Aegypti. 25 Haec inquit Dominus exercituum,
Deus Israhel, dicens, 'Vos et uxores vestrae locuti estis ore
vestro et manibus vestris implestis, dicentes, "Faciamus vota
nostra quae vovimus, ut sacrificemus reginae caeli et libemus ei libamina." Implestis vota vestra et opere perpetrastis
ea. 26 Ideo audite verbum Domini, omnis Iuda, qui habitatis
in terra Aegypti. Ecce: ego iuravi in nomine meo magno,' ait
Dominus 'quia nequaquam ultra nomen meum vocabitur ex
ore omnis viri Iudaei, dicentis, "Vivit Dominus Deus," in
omni terra Aegypti. 27 Ecce: ego vigilabo super eos in malum
et non in bonum, et consumentur omnes viri Iuda qui sunt
in terra Aegypti gladio et fame donec penitus consumantur.
28 Et qui fugerint gladium revertentur de terra Aegypti in
terram Iuda, viri pauci, et scient, omnes reliquiae Iuda ingredientium terram Aegypti ut habitent ibi, cuius sermo
conpleatur, meus an illorum. 29 Et hoc vobis signum,' ait Dominus, 'quod visitem ego super vos in loco isto, ut sciatis
quia vere conplebuntur sermones mei contra vos in malum.' 30 Haec dicit Dominus: 'Ecce: ego tradam Pharaonem
Efree, regem Aegypti, in manu inimicorum eius et in manu

without an inhabitant, as at this day. 23 Because you have sacrificed to idols and have sinned against the Lord and have not obeyed the voice of the Lord and have not walked in his law and in his commandments and in his testimonies, therefore are these evils come upon you, as at this day."

24 And Jeremiah said to all the people and to all the women, "Hear ye the word of the Lord, all Judah, you that dwell in the land of Egypt. 25 Thus saith the Lord of hosts, the God of Israel, saying, 'You and your wives have spoken with your mouth and fulfilled with your hands, saying, "Let us perform our vows which we have made, to offer sacrifice to the queen of heaven and to pour out drink-offerings to her." You have fulfilled your vows and have performed them indeed. 26 Therefore hear ye the word of the Lord, all Judah, you that dwell in the land of Egypt. Behold: I have sworn by my great name,' saith the Lord, 'that my name shall no more be named in the mouth of any man of Judah in the land of Egypt, saying, "The Lord God liveth." 27 Behold: I will watch over them for evil and not for good, and all the men of Judah that are in the land of Egypt shall be consumed by the sword and by famine till there be an end of them. 28 And a few men that shall flee from the sword shall return out of the land of Egypt into the land of Judah, and all the remnant of Judah that are gone into the land of Egypt to dwell there shall know whose word shall stand, mine, or theirs. 29 And this shall be a sign to you,' saith the Lord, 'that I will punish you in this place, that you may know that my words shall be accomplished indeed against you for evil.' 30 Thus saith the Lord: 'Behold: I will deliver Pharaoh Hophra, king of Egypt,

quaerentium animam illius, sicut tradidi Sedeciam, regem Iuda, in manu Nabuchodonosor, regis Babylonis, inimici sui, et quaerentis animam eius.'"

Caput 45

Verbum quod locutus est Hieremias, propheta, ad Baruch, filium Neriae, cum scripsisset verba haec in libro de ore Hieremiae, anno quarto Ioachim, filii Iosiae, regis Iuda, dicens, 2 "Haec dicit Dominus, Deus Israhel, ad te, Baruch: 3 'Dixisti, "Vae misero mihi, quoniam addidit Dominus dolorem dolori meo. Laboravi in gemitu meo, et requiem non inveni." 4 Haec dices ad eum,' sic dicit Dominus: 'Ecce: quos aedificavi ego, destruo, et quos plantavi, ego evello, et universam terram hanc. 5 Et tu quaeris tibi grandia? Noli quaerere, quia ecce: ego adducam malum super omnem carnem,' ait Dominus, 'et dabo tibi animam tuam in salutem in omnibus locis ad quaecumque perrexeris.'"

into the hand of his enemies and into the hand of them that seek his life, as I delivered Zedekiah, king of Judah, into the hand of Nebuchadnezzar, the king of Babylon, his enemy, and that sought his life.'"

Chapter 45

The prophet comforts Baruch in his affliction.

The word that Jeremiah, the prophet, spoke to Baruch, the son of Neriah, when he had written these words in a book out of the mouth of Jeremiah, in the fourth year of Jehoiakim, the son of Josiah, king of Judah, saying, 2 "Thus saith the Lord, the God of Israel, to thee, Baruch: 3 'Thou hast said, "Woe is me, wretch that I am, for the Lord hath added sorrow to my sorrow. I am wearied with my groans, and I find no rest."' 4 Thus saith the Lord: 'Thus shalt thou say to him. Behold: them whom I have built, I do destroy, and them whom I have planted, I do pluck up, and all this land. 5 And dost thou seek great things for thyself? Seek not, for behold: I will bring evil upon all flesh,' saith the Lord, 'but I will give thee thy life *and save thee* in all places whithersoever thou shalt go.'"

Caput 46

Quod factum est verbum Domini ad Hieremiam, prophetam, contra Gentes, 2 ad Aegyptum, adversum exercitum Pharaonis Nechao, regis Aegypti, qui erat iuxta flumen Eufraten in Charchamis, quem percussit Nabuchodonosor, rex Babylonis, in quarto anno Ioachim, filii Iosiae, regis Iuda.

3 Praeparate scutum et clypeum, et procedite ad bellum. 4 Iungite equos, et ascendite equites; state in galeis; polite lanceas; induite vos loricis. 5 "Quid igitur? Vidi ipsos pavidos et terga vertentes, fortes eorum caesos; fugerunt conciti, nec respexerunt; terror undique," ait Dominus. 6 Non fugiat velox, nec salvari se putet fortis; ad aquilonem iuxta flumen Eufraten victi sunt et ruerunt.

7 Quis est iste qui quasi flumen ascendit, et veluti fluviorum intumescunt gurgites eius? 8 Aegyptus fluminis instar ascendit, et velut flumina movebuntur fluctus eius, et dicet, "Ascendens operiam terram; perdam civitatem et habitatores eius."

9 Ascendite equos, et exultate in curribus, et procedant fortes, Aethiopia et Lybies tenentes scutum et Lydii arripientes et iacientes sagittas. 10 Dies autem ille Domini, Dei exercituum, dies ultionis, ut sumat vindictam de inimicis

Chapter 46

A prophecy against Egypt. The Jews shall return from captivity.

The word of the Lord that came to Jeremiah, the prophet, against the Gentiles, 2 against Egypt, against the army of Pharao Neco, king of Egypt, which was by the river Euphrates in Carchemish, whom Nebuchadnezzar, the king of Babylon, defeated in the fourth year of Jehoiakim, the son of Josiah, king of Judah.

3 Prepare ye the shield and buckler, and go forth to battle. 4 Harness the horses, and get up, ye horsemen; stand forth with helmets; furbish the spears; put on coats of mail. 5 "What then? I have seen them dismayed and turning their backs, their valiant ones slain; they fled apace, and they looked not back; terror was round about," saith the Lord. 6 Let not the swift flee away, nor the strong think to escape; they are overthrown and fallen down towards the north by the river Euphrates.

7 Who is this that cometh up as a flood, and his streams swell like those of rivers? 8 Egypt riseth up like a flood, and the waves thereof shall be moved as rivers, and he shall say, "I will go up and will cover the earth; I will destroy the city and its inhabitants."

9 Get ye up on horses, and glory in chariots, and let the valiant men come forth, the Ethiopians and the Libyans that hold the shield and the Lydians that take and shoot arrows. 10 *For* this is the day of the Lord, the God of hosts, a day of

suis; devorabit gladius et saturabitur et inebriabitur sanguine eorum, victima enim Domini, Dei exercituum, in terra
aquilonis iuxta flumen Eufraten.

11 Ascende in Galaad, et tolle resinam, virgo filia Aegypti;
frustra multiplicas medicamina; sanitas non erit tibi. 12 Audierunt gentes ignominiam tuam, et ululatus tuus replevit
terram, quia fortis inpegit in fortem, et ambo pariter conciderunt.

13 Verbum quod locutus est Dominus ad Hieremiam, prophetam, super eo quod venturus esset Nabuchodonosor, rex
Babylonis, et percussurus terram Aegypti.

14 Adnuntiate Aegypto, et auditum facite in Magdolo, et
resonet in Memphis et in Tafnis; dicite, "Sta, et praepara te,
quia devorabit gladius ea quae per circuitum tuum sunt."
15 Quare conputruit fortis tuus? Non stetit, quoniam Dominus subvertit eum. 16 Multiplicavit ruentes ceciditque vir ad
proximum suum, et dicent, "Surge, et revertamur ad populum nostrum et ad terram nativitatis nostrae a facie gladii
columbae." 17 Vocate nomen Pharaonis, regis Aegypti, Tumultum Adduxit Tempus.

18 "Vivo ego," inquit Rex (Dominus exercituum nomen
eius), "quoniam sicut Thabor in montibus et sicut Carmelus
in mari, veniet." 19 Vasa transmigrationis fac tibi, habitatrix
filia Aegypti, quia Memphis in solitudinem erit et deseretur
et inhabitabilis erit.

20 Vitula eligans atque formonsa Aegyptus; stimulator ab
aquilone veniet ei. 21 Mercennarii quoque eius qui versaban-

vengeance, that he may revenge himself of his enemies; the sword shall devour and shall be filled and shall be drunk with their blood, for there is a sacrifice of the Lord, God of hosts, in the north country by the river Euphrates.

11 Go up into Gilead, and take balm, O virgin daughter of Egypt; in vain dost thou multiply medicines; there shall be no cure for thee. 12 The nations have heard of thy disgrace, and thy howling hath filled the land, for the strong hath stumbled against the strong, and both are fallen together.

13 The word that the Lord spoke to Jeremiah, the prophet, how Nebuchadnezzar, king of Babylon, should come and strike the land of Egypt.

14 Declare ye to Egypt, and publish it in Migdol, and let it be known in Memphis and in Tahpanhes; say ye, "Stand up, and prepare thyself, for the sword shall devour all round about thee." 15 Why are thy valiant men come to nothing? They stood not, because the Lord hath overthrown them. 16 He hath multiplied them that fall, and one hath fallen upon another, and they shall say, "Arise, and let us return to our own people and to the land of our nativity from the *sword* of the dove." 17 Call ye the name of Pharaoh, king of Egypt, A Tumult Time Hath Brought.

18 "As I live," saith the King (whose name is the Lord of hosts), "as Tabor is among the mountains and as Carmel by the sea, so shall he come." 19 *Furnish* thyself *to go into* captivity, thou daughter, inhabitant of Egypt, for Memphis shall be made desolate and shall be forsaken and uninhabited.

20 Egypt is like a fair and beautiful heifer; there shall come from the north one that shall goad her. 21 Her hirelings also that lived in the midst of her like fatted calves are turned

tur in medio eius quasi vituli saginati versi sunt et fugerunt simul, nec stare potuerunt, quia dies interfectionis eorum venit super eos, tempus visitationis eorum. 22 Vox eius quasi aeris sonabit, quoniam cum exercitu properabunt et cum securibus venient ei quasi ligna caedentes. 23 "Succiderunt saltum eius," ait Dominus, "qui supputari non potest; multiplicati sunt super lucustas et non est eis numerus." 24 Confusa est filia Aegypti et tradita in manu populi aquilonis.

25 Dixit Dominus exercituum, Deus Israhel, "Ecce: ego visitabo super tumultum Alexandriae et super Pharaonem et super Aegyptum et super deos eius et super reges eius et super Pharaonem et super eos qui confidunt in eo. 26 Et dabo eos in manu quaerentium animam eorum et in manu Nabuchodonosor, regis Babylonis, et in manu servorum eius, et post haec habitabitur sicut diebus pristinis," ait Dominus.

27 "Et tu ne timeas, serve meus Iacob, et ne paveas, Israhel, quia ecce: ego salvum te faciam de longinquo et semen tuum de terra captivitatis tuae, et revertetur Iacob et quiescet et prosperabitur, et non erit qui exterreat eum. 28 Et tu noli timere, serve meus Iacob," ait Dominus, "quia tecum ego sum, quia consumam ego cunctas gentes ad quas eieci te, te vero non consumam, sed castigabo te in iudicio, nec quasi innocenti parcam tibi."

back and are fled away together, and they could not stand, for the day of their slaughter is come upon them, the time of their visitation. 22 Her voice shall sound like brass, for they shall hasten with an army and with axes they shall come against her as hewers of wood. 23 "They have cut down her forest," saith the Lord, "which cannot be counted; they are multiplied above locusts and are without number." 24 The daughter of Egypt is confounded and delivered into the hand of the people of the north.

25 The Lord of hosts, the God of Israel, hath said, "Behold: I will visit upon the tumult of Alexandria and upon Pharaoh and upon Egypt and upon her gods and upon her kings and upon Pharaoh and upon them that trust in him. 26 And I will deliver them into the hand of them that seek their lives and into the hand of Nebuchadnezzar, king of Babylon, and into the hand of his servants, and afterwards it shall be inhabited as in the days of old," saith the Lord.

27 "And thou, my servant Jacob, fear not, and be not thou dismayed, O Israel, for behold: I will save thee from afar off and thy seed out of the land of thy captivity, and Jacob shall return and be at rest and prosper, and there shall be none to terrify him. 28 And thou, my servant Jacob, fear not," saith the Lord, "because I am with thee, for I will consume all the nations to which I have cast thee out, but thee I will not consume, but I will correct thee in judgment, neither will I spare thee as if thou wert innocent."

Caput 47

Quod factum est verbum Domini ad Hieremiam, prophetam, contra Palestinos antequam percuteret Pharao Gazam.

2 Haec dicit Dominus: "Ecce: aquae ascendunt ab aquilone, et erunt quasi torrens inundans, et operient terram et plenitudinem eius, urbem et habitatores eius; clamabunt homines et ululabunt omnes habitatores terrae 3 ab strepitu pompae armorum et bellatorum eius, a commotione quadrigarum eius et multitudine rotarum illius. Non respexerunt patres filios manibus dissolutis 4 pro adventu diei in quo vastabuntur omnes Philisthim et dissipabitur Tyrus et Sidon cum omnibus reliquis auxiliis suis. Depopulatus est enim Dominus Palestinos, reliquias insulae Cappadociae. 5 Venit calvitium super Gazam; conticuit Ascalon et reliquiae vallis earum; usquequo concideris?"

6 O mucro Domini, usquequo non quiesces? Ingredere in vaginam tuam; refrigerare, et sile. 7 Quomodo quiescet cum Dominus praeceperit ei adversus Ascalonem et adversus maritimas eius regiones ibique condixerit illi?

Chapter 47

A prophecy of the desolation of the Philistines, of Tyre, Sidon, Gaza and Ashkelon.

The word of the Lord that came to Jeremiah, the prophet, against the people of Palestine before Pharaoh took Gaza.

2 Thus saith the Lord: "Behold: there come up waters out of the north, and they shall be as an overflowing torrent, and they shall cover the land and all that is therein, the city and the inhabitants thereof; *then* the men shall cry and all the inhabitants of the land shall howl 3 at the noise of the marching of arms and of his soldiers, at the rushing of his chariots and the multitude of his wheels. The fathers have not looked back to the children for feebleness of hands 4 because of the coming of the day in which all the Philistines shall be laid waste and Tyre and Sidon shall be destroyed with all the rest of their helpers. For the Lord hath wasted the Philistines, the remnant of the isle of Cappadocia. 5 Baldness is come upon Gaza; Ashkelon hath held her peace with the remnant of their valley; how long shalt thou cut thyself?"

6 O thou sword of the Lord, how long wilt thou not be quiet? Go into thy scabbard; rest, and be still. 7 How shall it be quiet when the Lord hath given it a charge against Ashkelon and against the countries thereof by the sea side and there hath made an appointment for it?

Caput 48

Ad Moab haec dicit Dominus exercituum, Deus Israhel: "Vae super Nabo, quoniam vastata est et confusa; capta est Cariathaim; confusa est fortis et tremuit. 2 Non est ultra exultatio in Moab contra Esebon; cogitaverunt malum. Venite, et disperdamus eam de gente. Ergo silens conticesces, sequeturque te gladius.

3 Vox clamoris de Oronaim: vastitas et contritio magna. 4 Contrita est Moab; adnuntiate clamorem parvulis eius. 5 Per ascensum enim Luith plorans ascendet in fletu, quoniam in descensu Oronaim hostes ululatum contritionis audierunt. 6 Fugite; salvate animas vestras, et eritis quasi myricae in deserto. 7 Pro eo enim quod habuisti fiduciam in munitionibus tuis et in thesauris tuis, tu quoque capieris, et ibit Chamos in transmigrationem, sacerdotes eius et principes eius simul. 8 Et veniet praedo ad omnem urbem, et urbs nulla salvabitur, et peribunt valles, et dissipabuntur campestria, quoniam dixit Dominus: 9 "Date florem Moab, quia floriens egredietur et civitates eius desertae erunt et inhabitabiles."

10 Maledictus qui facit opus Domini fraudulenter, et maledictus qui prohibet gladium suum a sanguine.

Chapter 48

A prophecy of the desolation of Moab for their pride, but
their captivity shall at last be released.

Against Moab thus saith the Lord of hosts, the God of
Israel: "Woe to Nebo, for it is laid waste and confounded;
Kiriathaim is taken; the strong city is confounded and hath
trembled. 2 There is no more rejoicing in Moab over Heshbon; they have devised evil. Come, and let us cut it off from
being a nation. Therefore shalt thou in silence hold thy
peace, and the sword shall follow thee.

3 A voice of crying from Horonaim: waste and great destruction. 4 Moab is destroyed; proclaim a cry for her little
ones. 5 For by the ascent of Luhith shall the mourner go up
with weeping, for in the descent of Horonaim the enemies
have heard a howling of destruction. 6 Flee; save your lives,
and be as heath in the wilderness. 7 For because thou hast
trusted in thy bulwarks and in thy treasures, thou also shalt
be taken, and Chemosh shall go into captivity, his priests
and his princes together. 8 And the spoiler shall come upon
every city, and no city shall escape, and the valleys shall perish, and the plains shall be destroyed, for the Lord hath spoken: 9 "Give a flower to Moab, for in its flower it shall go out
and the cities thereof shall be desolate and uninhabited."

10 Cursed be he that doth the work of the Lord deceitfully, and cursed be he that withholdeth his sword from
blood.

11 "Fertilis fuit Moab ab adulescentia sua et requievit in fecibus suis nec transfusus est de vase in vas et in transmigrationem non abiit; idcirco permansit gustus eius in eo, et odor eius non est inmutatus. 12 Propterea ecce: dies veniunt," dicit Dominus, "et mittam ei ordinatores et stratores laguncularum, et sternent eum et vasa eius exhaurient et lagoenas eorum conlident. 13 Et confundetur Moab a Chamos sicut confusa est domus Israhel a Bethel, in qua habebat fiduciam.

14 "Quomodo dicitis, 'Fortes sumus et viri robusti ad proeliandum?' 15 Vastata est Moab, et civitates illius succiderunt, et electi iuvenes eius descenderunt in occisionem," ait Rex: Dominus exercituum nomen eius. 16 "Prope est interitus Moab ut veniat, et malum eius velociter adcurret nimis. 17 Consolamini eum, omnes qui estis in circuitu eius, et universi qui scitis nomen eius, dicite, 'Quomodo confracta est virga fortis, baculus gloriosus?' 18 Descende de gloria, et sede in siti, habitatio filiae Dibon, quoniam vastator Moab ascendet ad te, dissipabit munitiones tuas. 19 In via sta, et prospice, habitatio Aroer; interroga fugientem, et ei qui evasit dic, 'Quid accidit?' 20 Confusus est Moab quoniam victus est; ululate, et clamate; adnuntiate in Arnon quoniam vastata est Moab.

21 "Et iudicium venit ad terram campestrem, super Helon et super Iaesa et super Mefath 22 et super Dibon et super Nabo et super domum Deblathaim 23 et super Cariathaim et super Bethgamul et super Bethmaon 24 et super Carioth et super Bosra et super omnes civitates terrae Moab quae longe et quae prope sunt. 25 Abscisum est cornu Moab, et brachium eius contritum est," ait Dominus.

11 "Moab hath been fruitful from his youth and hath rested upon his lees and hath not been poured out from vessel to vessel nor hath gone into captivity; therefore his taste hath remained in him, and his scent is not changed. 12 Therefore behold: the days come," saith the Lord, "and I will send him men that shall order and overturn his bottles, and they shall cast him down and shall empty his vessels and break their bottles one against another. 13 And Moab shall be ashamed of Chemosh as the house of Israel was ashamed of Bethel, in which they trusted.

14 "How do you say, 'We are valiant and stout men in battle?' 15 Moab is laid waste, and they have cast down her cities, and her choice young men are gone down to the slaughter," saith the King, *whose* name is the Lord of hosts. 16 "The destruction of Moab is near to come; *the* calamity thereof shall come on exceeding swiftly. 17 Comfort him, all you that are round about him, and all you that know his name, say, 'How is the strong staff broken, the beautiful rod?' 18 Come down from thy glory, and sit in thirst, O dwelling of the daughter of Dibon, because the spoiler of Moab *is* come up to thee, he *hath destroyed* thy bulwarks. 19 Stand in the way, and look out, O habitation of Aroer; inquire of him that fleeth, and say to him that hath escaped, 'What is done?' 20 Moab is confounded because he is overthrown; howl ye, and cry; tell ye it in Arnon that Moab is wasted.

21 "And judgment is come upon the plain country, upon Holon and upon Jahzah and upon Mephaath 22 and upon Dibon and upon Nebo and upon the house of Diblathaim 23 and upon Kiriathaim and upon Beth-gamul and upon Beth-meon 24 and upon Kerioth and upon Bozrah and upon all the cities of the land of Moab far *or* near. 25 The horn of Moab is cut off, and his arm is broken," saith the Lord.

26 Inebriate eum quoniam contra Dominum erectus est, et adlidet manum Moab in vomitu suo, et erit in derisum etiam ipse. 27 Fuit enim in derisum tibi Israhel quasi inter fures repperisses eum; propter verba ergo tua quae adversum illum locutus es captivus duceris.

28 Relinquite civitates, et habitate in petra, habitatores Moab, et estote quasi columba nidificans in summo ore foraminis. 29 Audivimus superbiam Moab; superbus est valde — sublimitatem eius et arrogantiam et superbiam et altitudinem cordis eius. 30 "Ego scio," ait Dominus, "iactantiam eius et quod non sit iuxta eam virtus eius, nec iuxta quod poterat conata sit facere." 31 Ideo super Moab heiulabo, et ad Moab universam clamabo, ad viros muri fictilis lamentantes. 32 De planctu Iazer plorabo tibi, vinea Sobema; propagines tuae transierunt mare; usque ad mare Iazer pervenerunt; super messem tuam et vindemiam tuam praedo inruit. 33 Ablata est laetitia et exultatio de Carmelo et de terra Moab, et vinum de torcularibus sustuli; nequaquam calcator uvae solitum celeuma cantabit.

34 "De clamore Esebon usque Eleale et Iaesa dederunt vocem suam, a Segor usque ad Oronaim, vitula conternante; aquae quoque Namrim pessimae erunt. 35 Et auferam de Moab," ait Dominus, "offerentem in excelsis et sacrificantem diis eius. 36 Propterea cor meum ad Moab quasi tibiae resonabit, et cor meum ad viros muri fictilis dabit sonitum tibiarum, quia plus fecit quam potuit, idcirco perierunt.

26 Make him drunk because he lifted up himself against the Lord, and Moab shall dash his hand in his own vomit, and he also shall be in derision. 27 For Israel hath been a derision unto thee as though thou hadst found him amongst thieves; for thy words therefore which thou hast spoken against him thou shalt be led away captive.

28 Leave the cities, and dwell in the rock, you that dwell in Moab, and be ye like the dove that maketh her nest in the mouth of the hole in the highest place. 29 We have heard the pride of Moab; he is exceeding proud—his haughtiness and his arrogancy and his pride and the loftiness of his heart. 30 "I know," saith the Lord, "his boasting and that the strength thereof is not according to it, neither hath it endeavoured to do according as it was able." 31 Therefore will I lament for Moab, and I will cry out to all Moab, for the men of the brick wall that mourn. 32 O vineyard of Sibmah, I will weep for thee with the mourning of Jazer; thy branches are gone over the sea; they are come even to the sea of Jazer; the robber hath rushed in upon thy harvest and thy vintage. 33 Joy and gladness is taken away from Carmel and from the land of Moab, and I have taken away the wine out of the presses; the treader of the grapes shall not sing the accustomed cheerful tune.

34 "From the cry of Heshbon even to Elealeh and to Jahaz they have uttered their voice, from Zoar to Horonaim, as a heifer of three years old; the waters also of Nimrim shall be very bad. 35 And I will take away from Moab," saith the Lord, "him that offereth in the high places and that sacrificeth to his gods. 36 Therefore my heart shall sound for Moab like pipes, and my heart a sound *like* pipes for the men of the brick wall, because he hath done more than he could, therefore they have perished.

37 "Omne enim caput calvitium, et omnis barba rasa erit; in cunctis manibus conligatio, et super omne dorsum cilicium. 38 Super omnia tecta Moab et in plateis eius omnis planctus, quia contrivi Moab sicut vas inutile," ait Dominus 39 "Quomodo victa est, et ululaverunt? Quomodo deiecit cervicem Moab et confusus est? Eritque Moab in derisum et in exemplum omnibus in circuitu suo."

40 Haec dicit Dominus: "Ecce: quasi aquila evolabit et extendet alas suas ad Moab. 41 Capta est Carioth, et munitiones conprehensae sunt, et erit cor fortium Moab in die illa sicut cor mulieris parturientis. 42 Et cessabit Moab esse populus quoniam contra Dominum gloriatus est.

43 "Pavor et fovea et laqueus super te, O habitator Moab," ait Dominus. 44 "Qui fugerit a facie pavoris cadet in foveam, et qui conscenderit de fovea capietur laqueo, adducam enim super Moab annum visitationis eorum," dicit Dominus. 45 "In umbra Esebon steterunt de laqueo fugientes, quia ignis egressus est de Esebon, et flamma de medio Seon, et devorabit partem Moab et verticem filiorum tumultus.

46 "Vae tibi, Moab; peristi, popule Chamos, quia conprehensi sunt filii tui et filiae tuae in captivitatem. 47 Et convertam captivitatem Moab in novissimis diebus," ait Dominus.

Hucusque iudicia Moab.

37 "For every head shall be bald, and every beard shall be shaven; all hands shall be tied together, and upon every back there shall be haircloth. 38 Upon all the housetops of Moab and in the streets thereof general mourning, because I have broken Moab as an useless vessel," saith the Lord. 39 "How is it overthrown, and they have howled? How hath Moab bowed down the neck and is confounded? And Moab shall be a derision and an example to all round about him."

40 Thus saith the Lord: "Behold: he shall fly as an eagle and shall stretch forth his wings to Moab. 41 Kerioth is taken, and the strongholds are won, and the heart of the valiant men of Moab in that day shall be as the heart of a woman in labour. 42 And Moab shall cease to be a people because he hath gloried against the Lord.

43 "Fear and the pit and the snare come upon thee, O inhabitant of Moab," saith the Lord. 44 He that shall flee from the fear shall fall into the pit, and he that shall get up out of the pit shall be taken in the snare, for I will bring upon Moab the year of their visitation," saith the Lord. 45 "They that fled from the snare stood in the shadow of Heshbon, *but* there came a fire out of Heshbon, and a flame out of the midst of Sihon, and it shall devour part of Moab and the crown of the head of the children of tumult.

46 "Woe to thee, Moab; thou hast perished, O people of Chemosh, for thy sons and thy daughters are taken captives. 47 And I will bring back the captivity of Moab in the last days," saith the Lord.

Hitherto the judgments of Moab.

Caput 49

Ad filios Ammon.

Haec dicit Dominus: "Numquid filii non sunt Israhel? Aut heres non est ei? Cur igitur hereditate possedit Melchom Gad, et populus eius in urbibus eius habitavit? 2 Ideo ecce: dies veniunt," dicit Dominus, "et auditum faciam super Rabbath filiorum Ammon fremitum proelii, et erit in tumulum dissipata filiaeque eius igni succendentur, et possidebit Israhel possessores suos," dicit Dominus.

3 "Ulula, Esebon, quoniam vastata est Hai. Clamate, filiae Rabbath; accingite vos ciliciis; plangite, et circuite per sepes, quia Melchom in transmigrationem ducetur, sacerdotes eius et principes eius simul. 4 Quid gloriaris in vallibus? Defluxit vallis tua, filia delicata, quae confidebas in thesauris tuis et dicebas, 'Quis veniet ad me?' 5 Ecce: ego inducam super te terrorem," ait Dominus, Deus exercituum, "ab omnibus qui sunt in circuitu tuo, et dispergemini singuli a conspectu vestro, nec erit qui congreget fugientes. 6 Et post haec reverti faciam captivos filiorum Ammon," ait Dominus.

7 Ad Idumeam.

Haec dicit Dominus exercituum: "Numquid non est ultra

Chapter 49

The like desolation of Ammon, of Idumea, of the Syrians, of
the Agarenes and of the Elamites.

Against the children of Ammon.

Thus saith the Lord: "Hath Israel no sons? Or hath he no
heir? Why then hath Milcom inherited Gad, and his people
dwelt in his cities? 2 Therefore behold: the days come," saith
the Lord, "and I will cause the noise of war to be heard in
Rabbah of the children of Ammon, and it shall be destroyed
into a heap, and her daughters shall be burnt with fire, and
Israel shall possess them that have possessed him," saith the
Lord.

3 "Howl, O Heshbon, for Ai is wasted. Cry, ye daughters
of Rabbah; gird yourselves with haircloth; mourn, and go
about by the hedges, for Milcom shall be carried into captivity, his priests and his princes together. 4 Why gloriest thou
in the valleys? Thy valley hath flowed away, O delicate daughter, that hast trusted in thy treasures and hast said, 'Who
shall come to me?' 5 Behold: I will bring a fear upon thee,"
saith the Lord, God of hosts, "from all that are round about
thee, and you shall be scattered every one out of one another's sight, neither shall there be any to gather together them
that flee. 6 And afterwards I will cause the captives of the
children of Ammon to return," saith the Lord.

7 Against Edom.

Thus saith the Lord of hosts: "Is wisdom no more in

sapientia in Theman? Periit consilium a filiis; inutilis facta est sapientia eorum. 8 Fugite, et terga vertite; descendite in voraginem, habitatores Dedan, quoniam perditionem Esau adduxi super eum, tempus visitationis eius. 9 Si vindemiatores venissent super te, non reliquissent racemum? Si fures in nocte, rapuissent quod sufficeret sibi. 10 Ego vero discoperui Esau; revelavi abscondita eius, et celari non poterit; vastatum est semen eius et fratres eius et vicini eius, et non erit. 11 Relinque pupillos tuos; ego eos faciam vivere, et viduae tuae in me sperabunt.

12 Quia haec dicit Dominus: "Ecce: quibus non erat iudicium ut biberent calicem bibentes bibent, et tu quasi innocens relinqueris? Non eris innocens, sed bibens bibes. 13 Quia per memet ipsum iuravi," dicit Dominus, "quod in solitudinem et in obprobrium et in desertum et in maledictionem erit Bosra, et omnes civitates eius erunt in solitudines sempiternas."

14 Auditum audivi a Domino, et legatus ad gentes missus est: "Congregamini, et venite contra eam, et consurgamus in proelium."

15 "Ecce enim: parvulum dedi te in gentibus, contemptibilem inter homines. 16 Arrogantia tua decepit te et superbia cordis tui, qui habitas in cavernis petrae et adprehendere niteris altitudinem collis; cum exaltaveris quasi aquila nidum tuum, inde detraham te," dicit Dominus. 17 "Et erit Idumea deserta; omnis qui transibit per eam stupebit et sibilabit super omnes plagas eius. 18 Sicuti subversa est Sodoma et Gomorra et vicinae eius," ait Dominus, "Non habitabit ibi vir,

Teman? Counsel is perished from her children; their wisdom is become unprofitable. 8 Flee, and turn your backs; go down into the deep hole, ye inhabitants of Dedan, for I have brought the destruction of Esau upon him, the time of his visitation. 9 If grape-gatherers had come to thee, would they not have left a bunch? If thieves in the night, they would have taken what was enough for them. 10 But I have made Esau bare; I have revealed his secrets, and he cannot be hid; his seed is laid waste and his brethren and his neighbours, and he shall not be. 11 Leave thy fatherless children; I will make them live, and thy widows shall hope in me.

12 For thus saith the Lord: "Behold: they whose judgment was not to drink of the cup shall certainly drink, and shalt thou come off as innocent? Thou shalt not come off as innocent, but drinking thou shalt drink. 13 For I have sworn by myself," saith the Lord, "that Bozrah shall become a desolation and a reproach and a desert and a curse, and all her cities shall be everlasting wastes."

14 I have heard a rumour from the Lord, and an ambassador is sent to the nations: "Gather yourselves together, and come against her, and let us rise up to battle."

15 "For behold: I have made thee a little one among the nations, despicable among men. 16 Thy arrogancy hath deceived thee and the pride of thy heart, O thou that dwellest in the clefts of the rock and endeavourest to lay hold on the height of the hill; *but* though thou shouldst make thy nest as high as an eagle, I will bring thee down from thence," saith the Lord. 17 "And Edom shall be desolate; every one that shall pass by it shall be astonished and shall hiss at all its plagues. 18 As Sodom was overthrown and Gomorrah and the neighbours thereof," saith the Lord, "there shall not a

et non incolet eam filius hominis. 19 Ecce: quasi leo ascendet de superbia Iordanis ad pulchritudinem robustam, quia subito currere eum faciam ad illam, et quis erit electus quem praeponam ei? Quis enim similis mei? Et quis sustinebit me? Et quis est iste pastor qui resistat vultui meo?"

20 Propterea audite consilium Domini quod iniit de Edom et cogitationes eius quas cogitavit de habitatoribus Theman: "Si non deiecerint eos parvuli gregis; nisi dissipaverint cum eis habitaculum eorum. 21 A voce ruinae eorum commota est terra; clamor in Mari Rubro auditus est vocis eius. 22 Ecce: quasi aquila ascendet et evolabit, et expandet alas suas super Bosram, et erit cor fortium Idumeae in die illa quasi cor mulieris parturientis."

23 Ad Damascum.

Confusa est Emath et Arfad, quia auditum pessimum audierunt; turbati sunt in mari; prae sollicitudine quiescere non potuit. 24 Dissoluta est Damascus; versa est in fugam; tremor adprehendit eam; angustia et dolores tenuerunt eam quasi parturientem. 25 Quomodo dereliquerunt civitatem laudabilem, urbem laetitiae!

26 "Ideo cadent iuvenes eius in plateis eius, et omnes viri proelii conticescent in die illa," ait Dominus exercituum. 27 "Et succendam ignem in muro Damasci, et devorabit moenia Benadad."

28 Ad Cedar et ad regna Asor, quae percussit Nabuchodonosor, rex Babylonis.

Haec dicit Dominus: "Surgite, et ascendite ad Cedar, et

man dwell there, and there shall no son of man inhabit it. 19 Behold: one shall come up as a lion from the swelling of the Jordan against the strong and beautiful, for I will make him run suddenly upon her, and who shall be the chosen one whom I may appoint over her? For who is like to me? And who shall abide me? And who is that shepherd that can withstand my countenance?"

20 Therefore hear ye the counsel of the Lord which he hath taken concerning Edom and his thoughts which he hath thought concerning the inhabitants of Teman: "Surely the little ones of the flock shall cast them down; of a truth they shall destroy them with their habitation. 21 The earth is moved at the noise of their fall; the cry of their voice is heard in the Red Sea. 22 Behold: he shall come up as an eagle and fly, and he shall spread his wings over Bozrah, and in that day the heart of the valiant ones of Edom shall be as the heart of a woman in labour."

23 Against Damascus.

Hamath is confounded and Arpad, for they have heard very bad tidings; they are troubled *as* in the sea; through care they could not rest. 24 Damascus is undone; she is put to flight; trembling hath seized on her; anguish and sorrows have taken her as a woman in labour. 25 How have they forsaken the city of renown, the city of joy!

26 "Therefore her young men shall fall in her streets, and all the men of war shall be silent in that day," saith the Lord of hosts. 27 "And I will kindle a fire in the wall of Damascus, and it shall devour the strong holds of Ben-hadad."

28 Against Kedar and against the kingdoms of Hazor, which Nebuchadnezzar, king of Babylon, destroyed.

Thus saith the Lord: "Arise, and go ye up to Kedar, and

vastate filios orientis. 29 Tabernacula eorum et greges eorum capient; pelles eorum et omnia vasa eorum et camelos eorum tollent sibi, et vocabunt super eos formidinem in circuitu. 30 Fugite; abite vehementer; in voraginibus sedete, qui habitatis Asor," ait Dominus, "niit enim contra vos Nabuchodonosor, rex Babylonis, consilium et cogitavit adversum vos cogitationes.

31 "Consurgite, et ascendite ad gentem quietam et habitantem confidenter," ait Dominus. "Non ostia nec vectes eis; soli habitant. 32 Et erunt cameli eorum in direptionem, et multitudo iumentorum in praedam, et dispergam eos in omnem ventum qui sunt adtonsi in comam, et ex omni confinio eorum adducam interitum super eos," ait Dominus. 33 "Et erit Asor in habitaculum draconum, deserta usque in aeternum; non manebit ibi vir, nec incolet eam filius hominis."

34 Quod factum est verbum Domini ad Hieremiam, prophetam, adversus Aelam in principio regni Sedeciae, regis Iuda, dicens, 35 "Haec dicit Dominus exercituum: 'Ecce: ego confringam arcum Aelam et summam fortitudinem eorum. 36 Et inducam super Aelam quattuor ventos a quattuor plagis caeli, et ventilabo eos in omnes ventos istos, et non erit gens ad quam non perveniant profugi Aelam. 37 Et pavere faciam Aelam coram inimicis suis et in conspectu quaerentium animam eorum, et adducam super eos malum, iram furoris mei," dicit Dominus, "et mittam post eos gladium donec consumam eos. 38 Et ponam solium meum in Aelam et perdam inde reges et principes," ait Dominus. 39 "In novissimis autem diebus reverti faciam captivos Aelam," dicit Dominus.

waste the children of the east. 29 They shall take their tents and their flocks *and* shall carry off for themselves their curtains and all their vessels and their camels, and they shall call fear upon them round about. 30 Flee ye; get away speedily; sit in deep holes, you that inhabit Hazor," saith the Lord, "for Nebuchadnezzar, king of Babylon, hath taken counsel against you and hath conceived designs against you.

31 "Arise, and go up to a nation that is at ease and that dwelleth securely," saith the Lord. "They have neither gates nor bars; they dwell alone. 32 And their camels shall be for a spoil, and the multitude of their cattle for a booty, and I will scatter into every wind them that have their hair cut round, and I will bring destruction upon them from all their confines," saith the Lord. 33 "And Hazor shall be a habitation for dragons, desolate for ever; no man shall abide there, nor son of man inhabit it."

34 The word of the Lord that came to Jeremiah the prophet, against Elam, in the beginning of the reign of Zedekiah, king of Judah, saying, 35 "Thus saith the Lord of hosts: 'Behold: I will break the bow of Elam and their chief strength. 36 And I will bring upon Elam the four winds from the four quarters of heaven, and I will scatter them into all these winds, and there shall be no nation to which the fugitives of Elam shall not come. 37 And I will cause Elam to be afraid before their enemies and in the sight of them that seek their life, and I will bring evil upon them, *my fierce wrath*," saith the Lord, "and will send the sword after them till I consume them. 38 And I will set my throne in Elam and destroy kings and princes from thence," saith the Lord. 39 "But in the latter days I will cause the captives of Elam to return," saith the Lord.

Caput 50

Verbum quod locutus est Dominus de Babylone et de terra Chaldeorum in manu Hieremiae, prophetae.

2 Adnuntiate in gentibus, et auditum facite. Levate signum; praedicate, et nolite celare. Dicite, "Capta est Babylon; confusus est Bel; victus est Marodach. Confusa sunt sculptilia eius; superata sunt idola eorum." 3 Quoniam ascendit contra eam gens ab aquilone quae ponet terram eius in solitudinem, et non erit qui habitet in ea ab homine usque ad pecus; et moti sunt et abierunt.

4 "In diebus illis et in tempore illo," ait Dominus, "venient filii Israhel, ipsi et filii Iuda simul; ambulantes et flentes properabunt et Dominum, Deum suum, quaerent. 5 In Sion interrogabunt viam; huc facies eorum. Venient et adponentur ad Dominum foedere sempiterno quod nulla oblivione delebitur.

6 "Grex perditus factus est populus meus; pastores eorum seduxerunt eos feceruntque vagari in montibus; de monte in collem transierunt; obliti sunt cubilis sui. 7 Omnes qui invenerunt comederunt eos, et hostes eorum dixerunt, 'Non

Chapter 50

Babylon, which hath afflicted the Israelites, after their restoration shall be utterly destroyed.

The word that the Lord hath spoken against Babylon and against the land of the Chaldeans in the hand of Jeremiah, the prophet.

2 Declare ye among the nations, and publish it. Lift up a standard; proclaim, and conceal it not. Say, "Babylon is taken; Bel is confounded; Merodach is overthrown. Their graven things are confounded; their idols are overthrown." 3 For a nation is come up against her out of the north which shall make her land desolate, and there shall be none to dwell therein from man even to beast; yea they are removed and gone away.

4 "In those days and at that time," saith the Lord, "the children of Israel shall come, they and the children of Judah together; going and weeping they shall make haste and shall seek the Lord, their God. 5 They shall ask the way to Zion; their faces are hitherward. They shall come and shall be joined to the Lord by an everlasting covenant which shall never be forgotten.

6 "My people have been a lost flock; their shepherds have caused them to go astray and have made them wander in the mountains; they have gone from mountain to hill; they have forgotten their resting place. 7 All that found them have devoured them, and their enemies said, 'We have not sinned in

peccavimus pro eo quod peccaverunt Domino, decori iustitiae, et expectationi patrum eorum, Domino.'

8 "Recedite de medio Babylonis, et de terra Chaldeorum
egredimini, et estote quasi hedi ante gregem. 9 Quoniam
ecce: ego suscito et adducam in Babylonem congregationem
gentium magnarum de terra aquilonis, et praeparabuntur
adversum eam, et inde capietur; sagitta eius, quasi viri fortis,
interfectoris, non revertetur vacua. 10 Et erit Chaldea in
praedam; omnes vastantes eam replebuntur," ait Dominus.

11 Quoniam exultatis et magna loquimini, diripientes hereditatem meam, quoniam effusi estis sicut vituli super herbam et mugistis ut tauri, 12 confusa est mater vestra nimis, et
adaequata pulveri quae genuit vos; ecce: novissima erit in
gentibus, deserta invia et arens. 13 Ab ira Domini non habitabitur sed redigetur tota in solitudinem; omnis qui transibit per Babylonem stupebit et sibilabit super universis plagis
eius. 14 Praeparamini contra Babylonem per circuitum, omnes qui intenditis arcum; debellate eam; non parcatis iaculis,
quia Domino peccavit. 15 Clamate adversus eam; ubique dedit manum; ceciderunt fundamenta eius; destructi sunt muri
eius, quoniam ultio Domini est. Ultionem accipite de ea;
sicut fecit facite ei. 16 Disperdite satorem de Babylone et tenentem falcem in tempore messis; a facie gladii columbae
unusquisque ad populum suum convertetur et singuli ad terram suam fugient.

so doing because they have sinned against the Lord, the beauty of justice, and against the Lord, the hope of their fathers.'

8 "Remove out of the midst of Babylon, and go forth out of the land of the Chaldeans, and be ye as kids at the head of the flock. 9 For behold: I raise up and will bring against Babylon an assembly of great nations from the land of the north, and they shall be prepared against her, and from thence she shall be taken; their arrows, like those of a mighty man, a destroyer, shall not return in vain. 10 And Chaldea shall be made a prey; all that waste her shall be filled," saith the Lord.

11 Because you rejoice and speak great things, pillaging my inheritance, because you are spread abroad as calves upon the grass and have bellowed as bulls, 12 your mother is confounded exceedingly, and she that bore you is made even with the dust; behold: she shall be the last among the nations, a wilderness unpassable and dry. 13 Because of the wrath of the Lord it shall not be inhabited but shall be wholly desolate; every one that shall pass by Babylon shall be astonished and shall hiss at all her plagues. 14 Prepare yourselves against Babylon round about, all you that bend the bow; fight against her; spare not arrows, because she hath sinned against the Lord. 15 Shout against her; she hath everywhere given her hand; her foundations are fallen; her walls are thrown down, for it is the vengeance of the Lord. Take vengeance upon her; as she hath done so do to her. 16 Destroy the sower out of Babylon and him that holdeth the sickle in the time of harvest; *for fear* of the sword of the dove every man shall return to his people and every one shall flee to his own land.

17 Grex dispersus Israhel; leones eiecerunt eum. Primus comedit eum rex Assur; iste novissimus exossavit eum Nabuchodonosor, rex Babylonis. 18 Propterea haec dicit Dominus exercituum, Deus Israhel: "Ecce: ego visitabo regem Babylonis et terram eius sicut visitavi regem Assur. 19 Et reducam Israhel ad habitaculum suum, et pascetur Carmelum et Basan, et in Monte Ephraim et Galaad saturabitur anima eius. 20 In diebus illis et in tempore illo," ait Dominus, "quaeretur iniquitas Israhel, et non erit, et peccatum Iuda, et non invenietur, quoniam propitius ero eis quos reliquero.

21 "Super terram dominantium ascende, et super habitatores eius visita; dissipa et interfice quae post eos sunt," ait Dominus, "et fac iuxta omnia quae praecepi tibi. 22 Vox belli in terra et contritio magna. 23 Quomodo confractus est et contritus malleus universae terrae? Quomodo versa est in desertum Babylon in gentibus? 24 Inlaqueavi te, et capta es, Babylon, et nesciebas; inventa es et adprehensa quoniam Dominum provocasti."

25 Aperuit Dominus thesaurum suum et protulit vasa irae suae, quoniam opus est Domino, Deo exercituum, in terra Chaldeorum. 26 Venite ad eam ab extremis finibus; aperite ut exeant qui conculcent eam; tollite de via lapides, et redigite in acervos, et interficite eam, nec sit quicquam reliquum. 27 Dissipate universos fortes eius; descendant in occisionem; vae eis, quia venit dies eorum, tempus visitationis eorum. 28 Vox fugientium et eorum qui evaserunt de terra

17 Israel is a scattered flock; the lions have driven him away. First the king of Assyria devoured him, *and* last this Nebuchadnezzar, king of Babylon, hath broken his bones. 18 Therefore thus saith the Lord of hosts, the God of Israel: "Behold: I will visit the king of Babylon and his land as I have visited the king of Assyria. 19 And I will bring Israel again to his habitation, and he shall feed on Carmel and Bashan, and his soul shall be satisfied in Mount Ephraim and Galaad. 20 In those days and at that time," saith the Lord, "the iniquity of Israel shall be sought for, and there shall be none, and the sin of Judah, and there shall none be found, for I will be merciful to them whom I shall leave.

21 "Go up against the land of the rulers, and punish the inhabitants thereof; waste and destroy all behind them," saith the Lord, "and do according to all that I have commanded thee. 22 A noise of war in the land and a great destruction. 23 How is the hammer of the whole earth broken and destroyed? How is Babylon turned into a desert among the nations? 24 I have caused thee to fall into a snare, and thou art taken, O Babylon, and thou wast not aware of it; thou art found and caught because thou hast provoked the Lord."

25 The Lord hath opened his armoury and hath brought forth the weapons of his wrath, for the Lord, the God of hosts, hath a work to be done in the land of the Chaldeans. 26 Come ye against her from the uttermost borders; open that they may go forth that shall tread her down; take the stones out of the way, and make heaps, and destroy her, and let nothing of her be left. 27 Destroy all her valiant men; let them go down to the slaughter; woe to them, for their day is come, the time of their visitation. 28 The voice of them that

Babylonis ut adnuntient in Sion ultionem Domini, Dei nostri, ultionem templi eius.

29 Adnuntiate in Babylonem plurimis, omnibus qui tendunt arcum; consistite adversum eam per gyrum, et nullus evadat; reddite ei secundum opus suum; iuxta omnia quae fecit, facite illi, quia contra Dominum erecta est, adversum Sanctum Israhel. 30 "Idcirco cadent iuvenes eius in plateis eius, et omnes viri bellatores eius conticescent in die illa," ait Dominus.

31 "Ecce: ego ad te, superbe," dicit Dominus, Deus exercituum, "quia venit dies tuus, tempus visitationis tuae. 32 Et cadet superbus et corruet, et non erit qui suscitet eum, et succendam ignem in urbibus eius, et devorabit omnia in circuitu eius."

33 Haec dicit Dominus exercituum: "Calumniam sustinent filii Israhel et filii Iuda simul; omnes qui ceperunt eos tenent; nolunt dimittere eos. 34 Redemptor eorum fortis (Dominus exercituum nomen eius); iudicio defendet causam eorum ut exterreat terram et commoveat habitatores Babylonis.

35 "Gladius ad Chaldeos," ait Dominus, "et ad habitatores Babylonis et ad principes et ad sapientes eius. 36 Gladius ad divinos eius, qui stulti erunt; gladius ad fortes illius, qui timebunt. 37 Gladius ad equos eius et ad currus eius et ad omne vulgus quod est in medio eius, et erunt quasi mulieres; gladius ad thesauros eius, qui diripientur. 38 Siccitas super aquas eius erit, et arescent, quia terra sculptilium est et in portentis gloriantur. 39 Propterea habitabunt dracones cum

flee and of them that have escaped out of the land of Babylon to declare in Zion the revenge of the Lord, our God, the revenge of his temple.

29 Speak to many against Babylon, to all that bend the bow; stand together against her round about, and let none escape; pay her according to her work; according to all that she hath done, do ye to her, for she hath lifted up herself against the Lord, against the Holy One of Israel. 30 "Therefore shall her young men fall in her streets, and all her men of war shall hold their peace in that day," saith the Lord.

31 "Behold: I come against thee, O proud one," saith the Lord, the God of hosts, "for thy day is come, the time of thy visitation. 32 And the proud one shall fall; *he* shall fall down, and there shall be none to lift him up, and I will kindle a fire in his cities, and it shall devour all round about him."

33 Thus saith the Lord of hosts: "The children of Israel and the children of Judah are oppressed together; all that have taken them captives hold them fast; they will not let them go." 34 Their redeemer is strong (the Lord of hosts is his name); he will defend their cause in judgment to terrify the land and to disquiet the inhabitants of Babylon.

35 "A sword is upon the Chaldeans," saith the Lord, "and upon the inhabitants of Babylon and upon her princes and upon her wise men. 36 A sword upon her diviners, and they shall be foolish; a sword upon her valiant ones, and they shall be dismayed. 37 A sword upon their horses and upon their chariots and upon all the people that are in the midst of her, and they shall become as women; a sword upon her treasures, and they shall be made a spoil. 38 A drought upon her waters, and they shall be dried up, because it is a land of idols and they glory in monstrous things. 39 Therefore shall drag-

fatuis sicariis, et habitabunt in ea strutiones, et non habitabitur ultra usque in sempiternum, nec extruetur usque ad generationem et generationem. 40 Sicut subvertit Dominus Sodomam et Gomorram et vicinas eius," ait Dominus, "non habitabit ibi vir, et non incolet eam filius hominis."

41 Ecce: populus venit ab aquilone et gens magna, et reges multi consurgent a finibus terrae. 42 Arcum et scutum adprehendent; crudeles sunt et inmisericordes; vox eorum quasi mare sonabit, et super equos ascendent sicut vir paratus ad proelium contra te, filia Babylon. 43 Audivit rex Babylonis famam eorum, et dissolutae sunt manus eius; angustia adprehendit eum, dolor quasi parturientem.

44 "Ecce: quasi leo ascendet de superbia Iordanis ad pulchritudinem robustam, quia subito currere eum faciam ad illam, et quis erit electus quem praeponam ei? Quis est enim similis mei? Et quis sustinebit me? Et quis est iste pastor qui resistat vultui meo?"

45 Propterea audite consilium Domini quod mente concepit adversum Babylonem et cogitationes eius quas cogitavit super terram Chaldeorum: "Nisi detraxerint eos parvuli gregum; nisi dissipatum fuerit cum ipsis habitaculum eorum. 46 A voce captivitatis Babylonis commota est terra, et clamor inter gentes auditus est."

ons dwell there with the *fig-fauns,* and ostriches shall dwell therein, and it shall be no more inhabited for ever, neither shall it be built up *from* generation *to* generation. 40 As the Lord overthrew Sodom and Gomorrah and their neighbour cities," saith the Lord, "no man shall dwell there, neither shall the son of man inhabit it."

41 Behold: a people cometh from the north and a great nation, and many kings shall rise from the ends of the earth. 42 They shall take the bow and the shield; they are cruel and unmerciful; their voice shall roar like the sea, and they shall ride upon horses like a man prepared for battle against thee, O daughter of Babylon. 43 The king of Babylon hath heard the report of them, and his hands are grown feeble; anguish hath taken hold of him, pangs as a woman in labour.

44 "Behold: he shall come up like a lion from the swelling of the Jordan to the strong and beautiful, for I will make him run suddenly upon her, and who shall be the chosen one whom I may appoint over her? For who is like to me? And who shall bear up against me? And who is that shepherd that can withstand my countenance?"

45 Therefore hear ye the counsel of the Lord which he hath taken against Babylon and his thoughts which he hath thought against the land of the Chaldeans: "Surely the little ones of the flocks shall pull them down; of a truth their habitation shall be destroyed with them. 46 At the noise of the taking of Babylon the earth is moved, and the cry is heard amongst the nations."

Caput 51

Haec dicit Dominus: "Ecce: ego suscitabo super Babylonem et super habitatores eius qui cor suum levaverunt contra me, quasi ventum pestilentem. 2 Et mittam in Babylonem ventilatores, et ventilabunt eam et demolientur terram eius, quoniam venerunt super eam undique in die adflictionis eius. 3 Non tendat qui tendit arcum suum, et non ascendat loricatus; nolite parcere iuvenibus eius; interficite omnem militiam eius. 4 Et cadent interfecti in terra Chaldeorum, et vulnerati in regionibus eius. 5 Quoniam non fuit viduatus Israhel et Iuda a Deo suo, Domino exercituum, terra autem eorum repleta est delicto a Sancto Israhel."

6 Fugite de medio Babylonis, et salvet unusquisque animam suam; nolite tacere super iniquitatem eius, quoniam tempus ultionis est a Domino; vicissitudinem ipse retribuet ei. 7 Calix aureus Babylon in manu Domini inebrians omnem terram; de vino eius biberunt gentes, et ideo commotae sunt. 8 Subito cecidit Babylon et contrita est; ululate super eam; tollite resinam ad dolorem eius, si forte sanetur. 9 Curavimus Babylonem, et non est sanata; derelinquamus eam, et eamus unusquisque in terram suam, quoniam perve-

Chapter 51

The miseries that shall fall upon Babylon from the Medes.
The destruction of her idols.

Thus saith the Lord: "Behold: I will raise up as it were a pestilential wind against Babylon and against the inhabitants thereof who have lifted up their heart against me. 2 And I will send to Babylon fanners, and they shall fan her and shall destroy her land, for they are come upon her on every side in the day of her affliction. 3 Let not him that bendeth bend his bow, and let not him go up that is armed with a coat of mail; spare not her young men; destroy all her army. 4 And the slain shall fall in the land of the Chaldeans, and the wounded in the regions thereof. 5 For Israel and Judah have not been forsaken by their God the Lord of hosts, but their land hath been filled with sin against the Holy One of Israel."

6 Flee ye from the midst of Babylon, and let every one save his own life; be not silent upon her iniquity, for it is the time of revenge from the Lord; he will render unto her *what she hath deserved.* 7 Babylon hath been a golden cup in the hand of the Lord that made all the earth drunk; the nations have drunk of her wine, and therefore they have staggered. 8 Babylon is suddenly fallen and destroyed; howl for her; take balm for her pain, if so she may be healed. 9 We *would* have cured Babylon, *but* she is not healed; let us forsake her, and let us go every man to his own land, because her judg-

nit usque ad caelos iudicium eius et elevatum est usque ad nubes. 10 Protulit Dominus iustitias nostras; venite, et narremus in Sion opus Domini, Dei nostri.

11 Acuite sagittas; implete faretras; suscitavit Dominus spiritum regum Medorum, et contra Babylonem mens eius est ut perdat eam, quoniam ultio Domini est, ultio templi sui. 12 Super muros Babylonis levate signum; augete custodiam; levate custodes; praeparate insidias, quia cogitavit Dominus et fecit quaecumque locutus est contra habitatores Babylonis. 13 Quae habitas super aquas multas, locuples in thesauris, venit finis tuus pedalis praecisionis tuae. 14 Iuravit Dominus exercituum per animam suam, "Quoniam replebo te hominibus quasi brucho, et super te celeuma cantabitur."

15 Qui fecit terram in fortitudine sua, praeparavit orbem in sapientia sua et prudentia sua extendit caelos: 16 dante eo vocem multiplicantur aquae in caelo; qui levat nubes ab extremo terrae; fulgura in pluviam fecit et produxit ventum de thesauris suis. 17 Stultus factus est omnis homo ab scientia; confusus est omnis conflator in sculptili, quia mendax est conflatio eius nec est spiritus in eis. 18 Vana sunt opera et risu digna; in tempore visitationis suae peribunt. 19 Non sicut haec pars Iacob, quia qui fecit omnia ipse est, et Israhel sceptrum hereditatis eius; Dominus exercituum nomen eius.

20 "Conlidis tu mihi vasa belli, et ego conlidam in te gentes, et disperdam in te regna, 21 et conlidam in te equum et

ment hath reached even to the heavens and is lifted up to the clouds. 10 The Lord hath brought forth our justices; come, and let us declare in Zion the work of the Lord, our God.

11 Sharpen the arrows; fill the quivers; the Lord hath raised up the spirit of the kings of the Medes, and his mind is against Babylon to destroy it, because it is the vengeance of the Lord, the vengeance of his temple. 12 Upon the walls of Babylon set up the standard; strengthen the watch; set up the watchmen; prepare the ambushes, for the Lord hath both purposed and done all that he spoke against the inhabitants of Babylon. 13 O thou that dwellest upon many waters, rich in treasures, thy end is come for thy *entire destruction.* 14 The Lord of hosts hath sworn by himself, *saying,* "I will fill thee with men as with locusts, and they shall lift up a joyful shout against thee."

15 He that made the earth by his power, that hath prepared the world by his wisdom and stretched out the heavens by his understanding: 16 when he uttereth his voice the waters are multiplied in heaven; he lifteth up the clouds from the ends of the earth; he hath turned lightning into rain and hath brought forth the wind out of his treasures. 17 Every man is become foolish by his knowledge; every founder is confounded by his idol, for what he hath cast is a lie and there is no breath in them. 18 They are vain works, and worthy to be laughed at; in the time of their visitation they shall perish. 19 The portion of Jacob is not like them, for he is the maker of all things, and Israel is the sceptre of his inheritance; the Lord of hosts is his name.

20 "Thou dashest together for me the weapons of war, and with thee I will dash nations together, and with thee I will destroy kingdoms, 21 and with thee I will break in pieces the

equitem eius, et conlidam in te currum et ascensorem eius, 22 et conlidam in te virum et mulierem, et conlidam in te senem et puerum, et conlidam in te iuvenem et virginem, 23 et conlidam in te pastorem et gregem eius, et conlidam in te agricolam et iugales eius, et conlidam in te duces et magistratus.

24 "Et reddam Babyloni et cunctis habitatoribus Chaldeae omne malum suum quod fecerunt in Sion in oculis vestris," ait Dominus. 25 "Ecce: ego ad te, mons pestifer," ait Dominus, "qui corrumpis universam terram, et extendam manum meam super te et evolvam te de petris et dabo te in montem conbustionis. 26 Et non tollent de te lapidem in angulum et lapidem in fundamenta, sed perditus in aeternum eris," ait Dominus.

27 Levate signum in terra; clangite bucina in gentibus; sanctificate super eam gentes; adnuntiate contra illam regibus Ararat, Menni et Aschenez; numerate contra eam Thapsar; adducite equum quasi bruchum aculeatum. 28 Sanctificate contra eam gentes, reges Mediae, duces eius et universos magistratus eius cunctamque terram potestatis eius. 29 Et commovebitur terra et turbabitur, quia evigilabit contra Babylonem cogitatio Domini ut ponat terram Babylonis desertam et inhabitabilem. 30 Cessaverunt fortes Babylonis a proelio; habitaverunt in praesidiis; devoratum est robur eorum, et facti sunt quasi mulieres. Incensa sunt tabernacula eius; contriti sunt vectes eius. 31 Currens obviam currenti

horse and his rider, and with thee I will break in pieces the chariot and him that getteth up into it, 22 and with thee I will break in pieces man and woman, and with thee I will break in pieces the old man and the child, and with thee I will break in pieces the young man and the virgin, 23 and with thee I will break in pieces the shepherd and his flock, and with thee I will break in pieces the husbandman and his yoke of oxen, and with thee I will break in pieces captains and rulers.

24 "And I will render to Babylon and to all the inhabitants of Chaldea all their evil that they have done in Zion before your eyes," saith the Lord. 25 "Behold: I come against thee, thou destroying mountain," saith the Lord, "which corruptest the whole earth, and I will stretch out my hand upon thee and will roll thee down from the rocks and will make thee a burnt mountain. 26 And they shall not take of thee a stone for the corner nor a stone for foundations, but thou shalt be destroyed for ever," saith the Lord.

27 Set ye up a standard in the land; sound with the trumpet among the nations; *prepare* the nations against her; call together against her the kings of Ararat, Minni and Ashkenaz; number Taphsar against her; bring the horse as the stinging locust. 28 *Prepare* the nations against her, the kings of Media, their captains and all their rulers and all the land of their dominion. 29 And the land shall be in a commotion and shall be troubled, for the design of the Lord against Babylon shall awake to make the land of Babylon desert and uninhabitable. 30 The valiant men of Babylon have forborne to fight; they have dwelt in holds; their strength hath failed, and they are become as women. Her dwelling places are burnt; her bars are broken. 31 One running post shall meet

veniet, et nuntius obvius nuntianti ut adnuntiet regi Babylonis quia capta est civitas eius a summo usque ad summum 32 et vada praeoccupata sunt et paludes incensae sunt igni et viri bellatores conturbati sunt. 33 Quia haec dicit Dominus exercituum, Deus Israhel: "Filia Babylonis quasi area; tempus triturae eius; adhuc modicum et veniet tempus messionis eius."

34 "Comedit me, devoravit me Nabuchodonosor, rex Babylonis; reddidit me quasi vas inane; absorbuit me quasi draco; replevit ventrem suum teneritudine mea, et eiecit me. 35 Iniquitas adversum me et caro mea super Babylonem," dicit habitatio Sion, "et sanguis meus super habitatores Chaldeae," dicit Hierusalem.

36 Propterea haec dicit Dominus: "Ecce: ego iudicabo causam tuam et ulciscar ultionem tuam, et desertum faciam mare eius et siccabo venam eius. 37 Et erit Babylon in tumulos, habitatio draconum, stupor et sibilus, eo quod non sit habitator. 38 Simul ut leones rugient; excutient comas velut catuli leonum. 39 In calore eorum ponam potus eorum, et inebriabo eos ut sopiantur et dormiant somnum sempiternum et non consurgant," dicit Dominus. 40 "Deducam eos quasi agnos ad victimam et quasi arietes cum hedis."

41 Quomodo capta est Sesach, et conprehensa est inclita universae terrae? Quomodo facta est in stuporem Babylon inter gentes? 42 Ascendit super Babylonem mare; multitudine fluctuum eius operta est. 43 Factae sunt civitates eius in

another, and messenger shall meet messenger to tell the king of Babylon that his city is taken from one end to the other 32 and that the fords are taken and the marshes are burnt with fire and the men of war are affrighted. 33 For thus saith the Lord of hosts, the God of Israel: "The daughter of Babylon is like a threshingfloor; this is the time of her threshing; yet a little while and the time of her harvest shall come."

34 "Nebuchadnezzar, king of Babylon, hath eaten me up; he hath devoured me; he hath made me as an empty vessel; he hath swallowed me up like a dragon; he hath filled his belly with my delicate *meats,* and he hath cast me out. 35 The wrong done to me and my flesh be upon Babylon," saith the habitation of Zion, "and my blood upon the inhabitants of Chaldea," saith Jerusalem.

36 Therefore thus saith the Lord: "Behold: I will judge thy cause and will take vengeance for thee, and I will make her sea desolate and will dry up her spring. 37 And Babylon shall be reduced to heaps, a dwelling place for dragons, an astonishment and a hissing, because there is no inhabitant. 38 They shall roar together like lions; they shall shake their manes like young lions. 39 In their heat I will set them drink, and I will make them drunk that they may slumber and sleep an everlasting sleep and awake no more," saith the Lord. 40 "I will bring them down like lambs to the slaughter and like rams with kids."

41 How is Sheshach taken, and the renowned one of all the earth surprised? How is Babylon become an astonishment among the nations? 42 The sea is come up over Babylon; she is covered with the multitude of the waves thereof. 43 Her cities are become an astonishment, a land uninhab-

stuporem, terra inhabitabilis et deserta, terra in qua nullus
habitet nec transeat per eam filius hominis.

44 "Et visitabo super Bel in Babylone, et eiciam quod ab-
sorbuerat de ore eius, et non confluent ad eum ultra gentes,
siquidem et murus Babylonis corruet."

45 Egredimini de medio eius, populus meus, ut salvet
unusquisque animam suam ab ira furoris Domini. 46 Et ne
forte mollescat cor vestrum et timeatis auditum qui audietur in terra, et veniet in anno auditio, et post hunc annum
auditio et iniquitas in terra et dominator super dominatorem.

47 "Propterea ecce: dies veniunt, et visitabo super sculptilia Babylonis, et omnis terra eius confundetur, et universi
interfecti eius cadent in medio eius. 48 Et laudabunt super
Babylonem caeli et terra et omnia quae in eis sunt, quia ab
aquilone venient ei praedones," ait Dominus. 49 "Et quomodo fecit Babylon ut caderent occisi in Israhel, sic de Babylone cadent occisi in universa terra."

50 Qui fugistis gladium, venite; nolite stare; recordamini
procul Domini, et Hierusalem ascendat super cor vestrum.
51 Confusi sumus quoniam audivimus obprobrium; operuit
ignominia facies nostras quia venerunt alieni super sanctificationem domus Domini. 52 Propterea ecce: dies veniunt,"
ait Dominus, "et visitabo super sculptilia eius, et in omni
terra eius mugiet vulneratus. 53 Si ascenderit Babylon in caelum et firmaverit in excelso robur suum, a me venient vastatores eius," ait Dominus.

ited and desolate, a land wherein none can dwell nor son of man pass through it.

44 "And I will visit against Bel in Babylon, and I will bring forth out of his mouth that which he had swallowed down, and the nations shall no more flow together to him, for the wall also of Babylon shall fall."

45 Go out of the midst of her, my people, that every man may save his life from the *fierce* wrath of the Lord. 46 And *lest* your hearts faint and ye fear for the rumour that shall be heard in the land, and a rumour shall come in one year, and after this year *another* rumour and iniquity in the land and ruler upon ruler.

47 "Therefore behold: the days come, and I will visit the idols of Babylon, and her whole land shall be confounded, and all her slain shall fall in the midst of her. 48 And the heavens and the earth and all things that are in them shall give praise for Babylon, for spoilers shall come to her from the north," saith the Lord. 49 "And as Babylon caused that there should fall slain in Israel, so of Babylon there shall fall slain in all the earth."

50 You that have escaped the sword, come away; stand not still; remember the Lord afar off, and let Jerusalem come into your mind. 51 We are confounded because we have heard reproach; shame hath covered our faces because strangers are come upon the sanctuaries of the house of the Lord. 52 "Therefore behold: the days come," saith the Lord, "and I will visit her graven things, and in all her land the wounded shall groan. 53 If Babylon should mount up to heaven and establish her strength on high, from me there should come spoilers upon her," saith the Lord.

54 Vox clamoris de Babylone et contritio magna de terra Chaldeorum, 55 quoniam vastavit Dominus Babylonem et perdidit ex ea vocem magnam, et sonabunt fluctus eorum quasi aquae multae; dedit sonitum vox eorum. 56 Quia venit super eam, id est, super Babylonem, praedo et adprehensi sunt fortes eius et emarcuit arcus eorum, quia fortis ultor Dominus reddens retribuet.

57 "Et inebriabo principes eius et sapientes eius et duces eius et magistratus eius et fortes eius, et dormient somnum sempiternum et non expergiscentur," ait Rex; Dominus exercituum nomen eius. 58 Haec dicit Dominus exercituum: "Murus Babylonis ille latissimus suffossione suffodietur, et portae eius excelsae igni conburentur, et labores populorum ad nihilum, et gentium in ignem erunt et disperibunt."

59 Verbum quod praecepit Hieremias, propheta, Saraiae, filio Neriae, filii Maasiae, cum pergeret cum Sedecia Rege in Babylonem in anno quarto regni eius; Saraias autem erat princeps prophetiae. 60 Et scripsit Hieremias omne malum quod venturum erat super Babylonem in libro uno, omnia verba haec quae scripta sunt contra Babylonem. 61 Et dixit Hieremias ad Saraiam, "Cum veneris in Babylonem et videris et legeris omnia verba haec, 62 dices, 'Domine, tu locutus es contra locum istum ut disperderes eum ne sit qui in eo habitet ab homine usque ad pecus et ut sit perpetua solitudo.' 63 Cumque conpleveris legere librum istum, ligabis ad

54 The noise of a cry from Babylon and great destruction from the land of the Chaldeans, 55 because the Lord hath laid Babylon waste and destroyed out of her the great voice, and their wave shall roar like many waters; their voice hath made a noise. 56 Because the spoiler is come upon her, that is, upon Babylon, and her valiant men are taken and their bow is weakened, because the Lord, who is a strong revenger, will surely repay.

57 "And I will make her princes drunk and her wise men and her captains and her rulers and her valiant men, and they shall sleep an everlasting sleep and shall awake no more," saith the King, whose name is Lord of hosts. 58 Thus saith the Lord of hosts: "That *broad* wall of Babylon shall be utterly broken down, and her high gates shall be burnt with fire, and the labours of the people shall come to nothing, and of the nations shall go to the fire and shall perish."

59 The word that Jeremiah, the prophet, commanded Seraiah, the son of Neriah, the son of Maasias, when he went with King Zedekiah to Babylon in the fourth year of his reign; now Seraiah was chief over the prophecy. 60 And Jeremiah wrote in one book all the evil that was to come upon Babylon, all these words that are written against Babylon. 61 And Jeremiah said to Seraiah, "When thou shalt come into Babylon and shalt see and shalt read all these words, 62 thou shalt say, 'O Lord, thou hast spoken against this place to destroy it so that there should be *neither* man nor beast to dwell therein and that it should be desolate for ever.' 63 And when thou shalt have made an end of reading this

eum lapidem et proicies illum in medium Eufraten, 64 et dices, 'Sic submergetur Babylon, et non consurget a facie adflictionis quam ego adduco super eam, et dissolvetur.'"

Hucusque verba Hieremiae.

Caput 52

Filius viginti et unius anni erat Sedecias cum regnare coepisset, et undecim annis regnavit in Hierusalem, et nomen matris eius Amithal, filia Hieremiae de Lobna. 2 Et fecit malum in oculis Domini iuxta omnia quae fecerat Ioachim. 3 Quoniam furor Domini erat in Hierusalem et in Iuda usquequo proiceret eos a facie sua et recessit Sedecias a rege Babylonis.

4 Factum est autem in anno nono regni eius, in mense decimo, decima mensis, venit Nabuchodonosor, rex Babylonis, ipse et omnis exercitus eius, adversum Hierusalem, et obsederunt eam et aedificaverunt contra eam munitiones in circuitu. 5 Et fuit civitas obsessa usque ad undecimum annum Regis Sedeciae.

book, thou shalt tie a stone to it and shalt throw it into the midst of the Euphrates, 64 and thou shalt say, 'Thus shall Babylon sink, and she shall not rise up *from* the affliction that I will bring upon her, and she shall be utterly destroyed.'"

Thus far are the words of Jeremiah.

Chapter 52

A recapitulation of the reign of Zedekiah and the destruction of Jerusalem. The number of the captives.

Zedekiah was *one* and twenty years old when he began to reign, and he reigned eleven years in Jerusalem, and the name of his mother was Hamutal, the daughter of Jeremiah of Libnah. 2 And he did that which was evil in the eyes of the Lord according to all that Jehoiakim had done. 3 For the wrath of the Lord was against Jerusalem and against Judah till he cast them out from his presence and Zedekiah revolted from the king of Babylon.

4 And it came to pass in the ninth year of his reign, in the tenth month, the tenth day of the month, that Nebuchadnezzar, the king of Babylon, came, he and all his army, against Jerusalem, and they besieged it and built forts against it round about. 5 And the city was besieged until the eleventh year of King Zedekiah.

6 Mense autem quarto, nona mensis, obtinuit fames civitatem, et non erant alimenta populo terrae. 7 Et disrupta est civitas, et omnes viri bellatores fugerunt et exierunt de civitate nocte per viam portae quae est inter duos muros et ducit ad hortum regis (Chaldeis obsidentibus urbem in gyro), et abierunt per viam quae ducit in heremum. 8 Persecutus est autem exercitus Chaldeorum regem, et adprehenderunt Sedeciam in deserto quod est iuxta Hiericho, et omnis comitatus eius diffugit ab eo. 9 Cumque conprehendissent regem adduxerunt eum ad regem Babylonis in Reblatha, quae est in terra Emath, et locutus est ad eum iudicia. 10 Et iugulavit rex Babylonis filios Sedeciae in oculis eius, sed et omnes principes Iudae occidit in Reblatha. 11 Et oculos Sedeciae eruit et vinxit eum conpedibus, et adduxit eum rex Babylonis in Babylonem, et posuit eum in domo carceris usque ad diem mortis eius.

12 In mense autem quinto, decima mensis (ipse est annus nonusdecimus Nabuchodonosor, regis Babylonis) venit Nabuzardan, princeps militiae, qui stabat coram rege Babylonis in Hierusalem. 13 Et incendit domum Domini et domum regis et omnes domos Hierusalem, et omnem domum magnam igne conbusit. 14 Et totum murum Hierusalem per circuitum destruxit cunctus exercitus Chaldeorum qui erat cum magistro militiae. 15 De pauperibus autem populi et de reliquo vulgo quod remanserat in civitate et de perfugis qui transfugerant ad regem Babylonis et ceteros de multitudine transtulit Nabuzardan, princeps militiae. 16 De pauperibus vero terrae reliquit Nabuzardan, princeps militiae, in vinitores et agricolas.

6 And in the fourth month, the ninth day of the month, a famine overpowered the city, and there was no food for the people of the land. 7 And the city was broken up, and *the* men of war fled and went out of the city in the night by the way of the gate that is between the two walls and leadeth to the king's garden (the Chaldeans besieging the city round about), and they went by the way that leadeth to the wilderness. 8 But the army of the Chaldeans pursued after the king, and they overtook Zedekiah in the desert which is near Jericho, and all his companions were scattered from him. 9 And when they had taken the king they carried him to the king of Babylon to Riblah, which is in the land of Hamath, and he gave judgment upon him. 10 And the king of Babylon slew the sons of Zedekiah before his eyes, *and* he slew all the princes of Judah in Riblah. 11 And he put out the eyes of Zedekiah and bound him with fetters, and the king of Babylon brought him into Babylon, and he put him in prison till the day of his death.

12 And in the fifth month, the tenth day of the month (the same is the nineteenth year of Nebuchadnezzar, king of Babylon), came Nebuzaradan, the general of the army, who stood before the king of Babylon in Jerusalem. 13 And he burnt the house of the Lord and the king's house and all the houses of Jerusalem, and every great house he burnt with fire. 14 And all the army of the Chaldeans that were with the general broke down all the wall of Jerusalem round about. 15 But Nebuzaradan, the general, carried away captives some of the poor people and of the rest of the common sort who remained in the city and of the fugitives that were fled over to the king of Babylon and the rest of the multitude. 16 But of the poor of the land Nebuzaradan, the general, left some for vine-dressers and for husbandmen.

17 Columnas quoque aereas quae erant in domo Domini et bases et mare aereum quod erat in domo Domini confregerunt Chaldei, et tulerunt omne aes eorum in Babylonem. 18 Et lebetes et creagras et psalteria et fialas et mortariola et omnia vasa aerea quae in ministerio fuerant tulerunt. 19 Et hydrias et thymiamateria et urceos et pelves et candelabra et mortaria et cyatos, quotquot aurea aurea et quotquot argentea argentea tulit magister militiae 20 et columnas duas et mare unum et vitulos duodecim aereos qui erant sub basibus, quas fecerat Rex Salomon in domo Domini; non erat pondus aeris omnium vasorum horum.

21 De columnis autem: decem et octo cubiti altitudinis erant in columna una, et funiculus duodecim cubitorum circuibat eam, porro grossitudo eius quattuor digitorum, et intrinsecus cava erat. 22 Et capitella super utramque aerea; altitudo capitelli unius quinque cubitorum, et retiacula et malogranata super coronam in circuitu, omnia aerea. Similiter columnae secundae et malogranata. 23 Et fuerunt malogranata nonaginta sex dependentia, et omnia malogranata centum retiaculis circumdabantur. 24 Et tulit magister militiae Saraiam, sacerdotem primum, et Sophoniam, sacerdotem secundum, et tres custodes vestibuli. 25 Et de civitate tulit eunuchum unum qui erat praepositus super viros bellatores et septem viros de his qui videbant faciem regis qui inventi sunt in civitate et scribam, principem militum qui probabat tirones et sexaginta viros de populo terrae qui

17 The Chaldeans also broke in pieces the brazen pillars that were in the house of the Lord and the bases and the sea of brass that was in the house of the Lord, and they carried all the brass of them to Babylon. 18 And they took the cauldrons and the flesh-hooks and the psalteries and the bowls and the little mortars and all the brazen vessels that had been used in the ministry. 19 *The* general took away the pitchers and the censers and the pots and the basins and the candlesticks and the mortars and the cups, as many as were of gold in gold and as many as were of silver in silver, 20 and the two pillars and one sea and twelve oxen of brass that were under the bases, which King Solomon had made in the house of the Lord; there was no weight of the brass of all these vessels.

21 And concerning the pillars: one pillar was eighteen cubits high, and a cord of twelve cubits compassed it about, but the thickness thereof was four fingers, and it was hollow within. 22 And chapiters of brass were upon both, *and* the height of one chapiter was five cubits, and net-work and pomegranates were upon the *chapiters* round about, all of brass. The same of the second pillar and the pomegranates. 23 And there were ninety-six pomegranates hanging down, and the pomegranates, being a hundred in all, were compassed with net-work. 24 And the general took Seraiah, the chief priest, and Zephaniah, the second priest, and the three keepers of the entry. 25 He also took out of the city one eunuch that was chief over the men of war and seven men of them that were near the king's person that were found in the city and a scribe, an officer of the army who exercised the young soldiers and threescore men of the people of the land

inventi sunt in medio civitatis. 26 Tulit autem eos Nabuzardan, magister militiae, et duxit eos ad regem Babylonis in Reblatha. 27 Et percussit eos rex Babylonis et interfecit eos in Reblatha in terra Emath, et translatus est Iuda de terra sua.

28 Iste est populus quem transtulit Nabuchodonosor in anno septimo: Iudaeos tria milia et viginti tres. 29 In anno octavodecimo Nabuchodonosor: de Hierusalem animas octingentas triginta duas. 30 In anno vicesimo tertio Nabuchodonosor, transtulit Nabuzardan, magister militiae, Iudaeorum animas septingentas quadraginta quinque. Omnes ergo animae quattuor milia sescentae.

31 Et factum est in tricesimo septimo anno transmigrationis Ioachin, regis Iudae, duodecimo mense, vicesima quinta mensis, elevavit Evilmerodach, rex Babylonis, ipso anno regni sui, caput Ioachim, regis Iudae, et eduxit eum de domo carceris. 32 Et locutus est cum eo bona, et posuit thronum eius super thronos regum qui erant post se in Babylone. 33 Et mutavit vestimenta carceris eius, et comedebat panem coram eo semper cunctis diebus vitae suae. 34 Et cibaria eius cibaria perpetua dabantur ei a rege Babylonis statuta per singulos dies usque ad diem mortis suae cunctis diebus vitae eius.

that were found in the midst of the city. 26 And Nebuzara-dan, the general, took them and brought them to the king of Babylon to Riblah. 27 And the king of Babylon struck them and put them to death in Riblah in the land of Hamath, and Judah was carried away captive out of his land.

28 This is the people whom Nebuchadnezzar carried away captive in the seventh year: three thousand and twenty-three Jews. 29 In the eighteenth year of Nebuchadnezzar: eight hundred and thirty-two souls from Jerusalem. 30 In the three and twentieth year of Nebuchadnezzar, Nebuzaradan the general carried away of the Jews seven hundred and forty-five souls. So all the souls were four thousand six hundred.

31 And it came to pass in the seven and thirtieth year of the captivity of Jehoiachin, king of Judah, in the twelfth month, the five and twentieth day of the month, that Evil-merodach, king of Babylon, in the first year of his reign, lifted up the head of Jehoiachin, king of Judah, and brought him forth out of prison. 32 And he spoke *kindly* to him, and he set his throne above the thrones of the kings that were *with* him in Babylon. 33 And he changed his prison-garments, and he ate bread before him always all the days of his life. 34 And for his diet a continual provision was allowed him by the king of Babylon, every day a portion until the day of his death all the days of his life.

LAMENTATIONS

Et factum est postquam in captivitatem redactus est Israel et Hie-
rusalem deserta est sedit Hieremias propheta flens et planxit lamen-
tatione hac in Hierusalem, et amaro animo, suspirans et eiulans,
dixit:

Caput 1

ALEPH. Quomodo sedet sola civitas plena populo? Facta est quasi vidua domina gentium, princeps provinciarum facta est sub tributo?

2 BETH. Plorans ploravit in nocte, et lacrimae eius in maxillis eius. Non est qui consoletur eam ex omnibus caris eius; omnes amici eius spreverunt eam et facti sunt ei inimici.

3 GIMEL. Migravit Iuda propter adflictionem et multitudinem servitutis. Habitavit inter gentes, nec invenit requiem; omnes persecutores eius adprehenderunt eam inter angustias.

4 DELETH. Viae Sion lugent eo quod non sint qui veniant ad sollemnitatem. Omnes portae eius destructae; sacerdotes eius gementes; virgines eius squalidae, et ipsa oppressa amaritudine.

5 HE. Facti sunt hostes eius in capite; inimici illius locupletati sunt quia Dominus locutus est super eam propter

And it came to pass after Israel was carried into captivity and Je-rusalem was desolate that Jeremiah, the prophet, sat weeping and mourned with this lamentation over Jerusalem, and with a sor-rowful mind, sighing and moaning, he said:

Chapter 1

ALEPH. How doth the city sit solitary that was full of people? How is the mistress of nations become as a widow, the princess of provinces made tributary?

2 BETH. Weeping she hath wept in the night, and her tears are on her cheeks. There is none to comfort her among all them that were dear to her; all her friends have despised her and are become her enemies.

3 GHIMEL. Judah hath *removed her dwelling place* because of her affliction and the *greatness* of her bondage. She hath dwelt among the nations, and she hath found no rest; all her persecutors have taken her in the midst of straits.

4 DALETH. The ways of Zion mourn because there are none that come to the solemn *feast*. All her gates are broken down; her priests sigh; her virgins are *in affliction,* and she is oppressed with bitterness.

5 HE. Her adversaries are become *her lords;* her enemies are enriched because the Lord hath spoken against her for

multitudinem iniquitatum eius. Parvuli eius ducti sunt in captivitatem ante faciem tribulantis,

6 Vav et egressus est a filia Sion omnis decor eius. Facti sunt principes eius velut arietes non invenientes pascua, et abierunt absque fortitudine ante faciem subsequentis.

7 Zai. Recordata est Hierusalem dierum adflictionis suae et praevaricationis omnium desiderabilium suorum quae habuerat a diebus antiquis, cum caderet populus eius in manu hostili et non esset auxiliator. Viderunt eam hostes et deriserunt sabbata eius.

8 Heth. Peccatum peccavit Hierusalem; propterea instabilis facta est. Omnes qui glorificabant eam spreverunt illam quia viderunt ignominiam eius, ipsa autem gemens conversa est retrorsum.

9 Teth. Sordes eius in pedibus eius, nec recordata est finis sui; deposita est vehementer, non habens consolatorem. Vide, Domine, adflictionem meam, quoniam erectus est inimicus.

10 Ioth. Manum suam misit hostis ad omnia desiderabilia eius, quia vidit Gentes ingressas sanctuarium suum, de quibus praeceperas ne intrarent in ecclesiam tuam.

11 Caph. Omnis populus eius gemens et quaerens panem dederunt pretiosa quaeque pro cibo ad refocilandam animam. Vide, Domine, et considera, quoniam facta sum vilis.

12 Lamed. O vos omnes qui transitis per viam, adtendite, et videte si est dolor sicut dolor meus, quoniam vindemiavit me, ut locutus est Dominus in die irae furoris sui.

13 Mem. De excelso misit ignem in ossibus meis et erudi-

the multitude of her iniquities. Her children are led into captivity before the face of the oppressor,

6 VAU and from the daughter of Zion all her beauty is departed. Her princes are become like rams that find no pastures, and they are gone away without strength before the face of the pursuer.

7 ZAIN. Jerusalem hath remembered the days of her affliction and transgression of all her desirable things which she had from the days of old, when her people fell in the enemy's hand and there was no helper. The enemies have seen her and have mocked at her sabbaths.

8 HETH. Jerusalem hath grievously sinned; therefore is she become *vagabond*. All that honoured her have despised her because they have seen her shame, but she sighed and turned backward.

9 TETH. Her filthiness is on her feet, and she hath not remembered her end; she is *wonderfully* cast down, not having a comforter. Behold, O Lord, my affliction, because the enemy is lifted up.

10 JOD. The enemy hath put out his hand to all her desirable things, for she hath seen the Gentiles enter into her sanctuary, of whom thou gavest commandment that they should not enter into thy church.

11 CAPH. All her people *sigh; they seek* bread; they have given all their precious things for food to *relieve* the soul. See, O Lord, and consider, for I am become vile.

12 LAMED. O all ye that pass by the way, attend, and see if there be any sorrow like to my sorrow, for he hath made a vintage of me, as the Lord spoke in the day of his *fierce* anger.

13 MEM. From above he hath sent fire into my bones and

vit me. Expandit rete pedibus meis; convertit me retrorsum. Posuit me desolatam, tota die maerore confectam.

14 Nun. Vigilavit iugum iniquitatum mearum; in manu eius convolutae sunt et inpositae collo meo. Infirmata est virtus mea; dedit me Dominus in manu de qua non potero surgere.

15 Samech. Abstulit omnes magnificos meos Dominus de medio mei; vocavit adversum me tempus ut contereret electos meos. Torcular calcavit Dominus virgini filiae Iuda.

16 Ain. Idcirco ego plorans, et oculus meus deducens lacrimas, quia longe factus est a me consolator, convertens animam meam. Facti sunt filii mei perditi quoniam invaluit inimicus.

17 Fe. Expandit Sion manus suas; non est qui consoletur eam. Mandavit Dominus adversum Iacob; in circuitu eius hostes eius. Facta est Hierusalem quasi polluta menstruis inter eos.

18 Sade. Iustus est Dominus, quia os eius ad iracundiam provocavi. Audite, obsecro, universi populi, et videte dolorem meum. Virgines meae et iuvenes mei abierunt in captivitatem.

19 Coph. Vocavi amicos meos; ipsi deceperunt me; sacerdotes mei et senes mei in urbe consumpti sunt quia quaesierunt cibum sibi ut refocilarent animam suam.

20 Res. Vide, Domine, quoniam tribulor; venter meus conturbatus est. Subversum est cor meum in memet ipsa, quoniam amaritudine plena sum. Foris interficit gladius, et domi mors similis est.

21 Sen. Audierunt quia ingemesco ego, et non est qui consoletur me. Omnes inimici mei audierunt malum meum;

hath chastised me. He hath spread a net for my feet; he hath turned me back. He hath made me desolate *and* spent with sorrow all the day long.

14 NUN. The yoke of my iniquities hath watched *for me;* they are folded together in his hand and put upon my neck. My strength is weakened; the Lord hath delivered me into a hand out of which I am not able to rise.

15 SAMECH. The Lord hath taken away all my *mighty* men out of the midst of me; he hath called against me the time to destroy my chosen men. The Lord hath trodden the winepress for the virgin daughter of Judah.

16 AIN. Therefore do I weep, and my eyes *run down with water,* because the comforter, *the relief of* my soul, is far from me. My children are desolate because the enemy hath prevailed.

17 PHE. Zion hath spread forth her hands; there is none to comfort her. The Lord hath commanded against Jacob; his enemies are round about him. Jerusalem is as a *menstruous* woman among them.

18 SADE. The Lord is just, for I have provoked his mouth to wrath. Hear, I pray you, all ye people, and see my sorrow. My virgins and my young men are gone into captivity.

19 COPH. I called for my friends, *but* they deceived me; my priests and my ancients *pined away* in the city *while* they sought their food to *relieve* their souls.

20 RES. Behold, O Lord, for I am in distress; my bowels are troubled. My heart is turned within me, for I am full of bitterness. Abroad the sword destroyeth, and at home there is death *alike.*

21 SIN. They have heard that I sigh, and there is none to comfort me. All my enemies have heard of my evil; they have

laetati sunt quoniam tu fecisti. Adduxisti diem consolationis, et fient similes mei.

22 THAV. Ingrediatur omne malum eorum coram te, et devindemia eos sicut vindemiasti me propter omnes iniquitates meas, multi enim gemitus mei, et cor meum maerens.

Caput 2

ALEPH. Quomodo obtexit caligine in furore suo Dominus filiam Sion! Proiecit de caelo in terram inclitam Israhel
et non recordatus est scabilli pedum suorum in die furoris
sui!

2 BETH. Praecipitavit Dominus nec pepercit omnia speciosa Iacob. Destruxit in furore suo munitiones virginis Iuda
et deiecit in terram; polluit regnum et principes eius.

3 GIMEL. Confregit in ira furoris omne cornu Israhel.
Avertit retrorsum dexteram suam a facie inimici et succendit in Iacob quasi ignem flammae devorantis in gyro.

4 DELETH. Tetendit arcum suum quasi inimicus; firmavit
dexteram suam quasi hostis, et occidit omne quod pulchrum
erat visu in tabernaculo filiae Sion. Effudit quasi ignem indignationem suam.

5 HE. Factus est Dominus velut inimicus; praecipitavit Israhel; praecipitavit omnia moenia eius. Dissipavit munitiones eius et replevit in filia Iuda humiliatum et humiliatam,

rejoiced that thou hast done it. Thou hast brought a day of consolation, and they shall be like unto me.

22 THAU. Let all their evil *be present* before thee, and make vintage of them as thou hast made vintage of me for all my iniquities, for my sighs are many, and my heart is sorrowful.

Chapter 2

ALEPH. How hath the Lord covered with obscurity the daughter of Zion in his wrath! How hath he cast down from heaven to the earth the glorious one of Israel and hath not remembered *his footstool* in the day of his anger!

2 BETH. The Lord hath cast down headlong and hath not spared all that was beautiful in Jacob. He hath destroyed in his wrath the strongholds of the virgin of Judah and brought them down to the ground; he hath made the kingdom unclean and the princes thereof.

3 GHIMEL. He hath broken in *his fierce* anger all the horn of Israel. He hath *drawn* back his right hand from before the enemy and he hath kindled in Jacob as it were a flaming fire devouring round about.

4 DALETH. He hath bent his bow as an enemy; he hath fixed his right hand as an adversary, and he hath killed all that was fair to behold in the tabernacle of the daughter of Zion. He hath poured out his indignation like fire.

5 HE. The Lord is become as an enemy; he hath cast down Israel headlong; he hath overthrown all the walls thereof. He hath destroyed his strongholds and hath *multiplied* in the daughter of Judah the *afflicted, both* men and women,

6 Vav et dissipavit quasi hortum tentorium suum; demolitus est tabernaculum suum. Oblivioni tradidit Dominus in Sion festivitatem et sabbatum et in obprobrium et in indignationem furoris sui regem et sacerdotem.

7 Zai. Reppulit Dominus altare suum; maledixit sanctificationi suae. Tradidit in manu inimici muros turrium eius; vocem dederunt in domo Domini sicut in die sollemni.

8 Heth. Cogitavit Dominus dissipare murum filiae Sion. Tetendit funiculum suum et non avertit manum suam a perditione, luxitque antemurale, et murus pariter dissipatus est.

9 Teth. Defixae sunt in terra portae eius; perdidit et contrivit vectes eius. Regem eius et principes eius in Gentibus. Non est lex, et prophetae eius non invenerunt visionem a Domino.

10 Ioth. Sederunt in terra, conticuerunt senes filiae Sion. Consperserunt cinere capita sua; accincti sunt ciliciis. Abiecerunt in terram capita sua virgines Hierusalem.

11 Caph. Defecerunt prae lacrimis oculi mei; conturbata sunt viscera mea. Effusum est in terra iecur meum super contritione filiae populi mei, cum deficeret parvulus et lactens in plateis oppidi.

12 Lamed. Matribus suis dixerunt, "Ubi est triticum et vinum?" cum deficerent quasi vulnerati in plateis civitatis, cum exhalarent animas suas in sinu matrum suarum.

13 Mem. Cui conparabo te? Vel cui adsimilabo te, filia Hierusalem? Cui exaequabo te et consolabor te, virgo filia Sion?

6 VAU and he hath destroyed his tent as a garden; he hath thrown down his tabernacle. The Lord hath caused feasts and sabbaths to be forgotten in Zion and hath delivered up king and priest to reproach and to the indignation of his wrath.

7 ZAIN. The Lord hath cast off his altar; he hath cursed his sanctuary. He hath delivered the walls of the towers thereof into the hand of the enemy; they have made a noise in the house of the Lord as in the day of a solemn feast.

8 HETH. The Lord hath purposed to destroy the wall of the daughter of Zion. He hath stretched out his line and hath not withdrawn his hand from destroying, and the bulwark hath mourned, and the wall hath been destroyed together.

9 TETH. Her gates are *sunk* into the ground; he hath destroyed and broken her bars. Her king and her princes are among the Gentiles. The law is *no more,* and her prophets have found no vision from the Lord.

10 JOD. The ancients of the daughter of Zion *sit* upon the ground; they have held their peace. They have sprinkled their heads with dust; they are girded with haircloth. The virgins of Jerusalem hang down their heads to the ground.

11 CAPH. My eyes have failed with *weeping;* my bowels are troubled. My liver is poured out upon the earth for the destruction of the daughter of my people, when the children and the sucklings fainted away in the streets of the city.

12 LAMED. They said to their mothers, "Where is corn and wine?" when they fainted away as the wounded in the streets of the city, when they breathed out their souls in the bosoms of their mothers.

13 MEM. To what shall I compare thee? Or to what shall I liken thee, O daughter of Jerusalem? To what shall I equal

Magna est enim velut mare contritio tua; quis medebitur tui?

14 NUN. Prophetae tui viderunt tibi falsa et stulta, nec aperiebant iniquitatem tuam ut te ad paenitentiam provocarent, viderunt autem tibi adsumptiones falsas et eiectiones.

15 SAMECH. Plauserunt super te manibus omnes transeuntes per viam; sibilaverunt et moverunt caput suum super filiam Hierusalem, "Haecine est urbs," dicentes, "perfecti decoris, gaudium universae terrae?"

16 FE. Aperuerunt super te os suum omnes inimici tui; sibilaverunt et fremuerunt dentibus et dixerunt, "Devorabimus. En ista est dies quam expectabamus! Invenimus; vidimus."

17 AIN. Fecit Dominus quae cogitavit. Conplevit sermonem suum quem praeceperat a diebus antiquis. Destruxit et non pepercit, et laetificavit super te inimicum et exaltavit cornu hostium tuorum.

18 SADE. Clamavit cor eorum ad Dominum super muros filiae Sion. Deduc quasi torrentem lacrimas per diem et noctem! Non des requiem tibi, neque taceat pupilla oculi tui.

19 COPH. Consurge; lauda in nocte, in principio vigiliarum. Effunde sicut aquas cor tuum ante conspectum Domini. Leva ad eum manus tuas pro anima parvulorum tuorum qui defecerunt in fame in capite omnium compitorum.

20 RES. Vide, Domine, et considera quem vindemiaveris. Ita ergone comedent mulieres fructum suum, parvulos ad mensuram palmae? Si occiditur in sanctuario Domini sacerdos et propheta?

thee *that I may* comfort thee, O virgin daughter of Zion? For great as the sea is thy destruction; who shall heal thee?

14 NUN. Thy prophets have seen false and foolish things for thee, and they have not laid open thy iniquity to excite thee to penance, but they have seen for thee false revelations and banishments.

15 SAMECH. All they that passed by the way have clapped their hands at thee; they have hissed and wagged their head at the daughter of Jerusalem, saying, "Is this the city of perfect beauty, the joy of all the earth?"

16 PHE. All thy enemies have opened their mouth against thee; they have hissed and gnashed with the teeth and have said, "We will swallow her up. Lo, this is the day which we looked for! We have found it; we have seen it."

17 AIN. The Lord hath done that which he purposed. He hath fulfilled his word which he commanded *in* the days of old. He hath destroyed and hath not spared, and he hath caused the enemy to rejoice over thee and hath set up the horn of thy adversaries.

18 SADE. Their heart cried to the Lord upon the walls of the daughter of Zion. *Let* tears run down like a torrent day and night! Give thyself no rest, and let not the apple of thy eye cease.

19 COPH. Arise; give praise in the night, in the beginning of the watches. Pour out thy heart like *water* before the face of the Lord. Lift up thy hands to him for the life of thy little children that have fainted for hunger at the top of all the streets.

20 RES. Behold, O Lord, and consider whom thou hast thus dealt with. Shall women then eat their own fruit, their children of a span long? *Shall* the priest and the prophet *be* slain in the sanctuary of the Lord?

21 SEN. Iacuerunt in terra foris puer et senex; virgines meae et iuvenes mei ceciderunt in gladio. Interfecisti in die furoris tui; percussisti nec misertus es.

22 THAV. Vocasti quasi ad diem sollemnem qui terrerent me de circuitu, et non fuit in die furoris Domini qui effuge-ret et relinqueretur. Quos educavi et enutrivi, inimicus meus consumpsit eos.

Caput 3

ALEPH. Ego vir videns paupertatem meam in virga in-dignationis eius.

2 ALEPH. Me minavit et adduxit in tenebras et non in lu-cem.

3 ALEPH. Tantum in me vertit et convertit manum suam tota die.

4 BETH. Vetustam fecit pellem meam et carnem meam; contrivit ossa mea.

5 BETH. Aedificavit in gyro meo, et circumdedit me felle et labore.

6 BETH. In tenebrosis conlocavit me quasi mortuos sem-piternos.

7 GIMEL. Circumaedificavit adversum me ut non egrediar; adgravavit conpedem meam.

8 GIMEL. Sed et cum clamavero et rogavero, exclusit ora-tionem meam.

9 GIMEL. Conclusit vias meas lapidibus quadris; semitas meas subvertit.

21 SIN. The child and the old man lie without on the ground; my virgins and my young men are fallen by the sword. Thou hast slain them in the day of thy wrath; thou hast killed and shewn them no pity.

22 THAU. Thou hast called as to a *festival* those that should terrify me round about, and there was none in the day of the wrath of the Lord that escaped and was left. Those that I brought up and nourished, my enemy hath consumed them.

Chapter 3

ALEPH. I am the man that see my poverty by the rod of his indignation.

2 ALEPH. He hath led me and brought me into darkness and not into light.

3 ALEPH. Only against me he hath turned and turned again his hand all the day.

4 BETH. My skin and my flesh he hath made old; he hath broken my bones.

5 BETH. He hath built round about me, and he hath compassed me with gall and labour.

6 BETH. He hath set me in dark places as those that are dead for ever.

7 GHIMEL. He hath built against me round about that I may not get out; he hath made my fetters heavy.

8 GHIMEL. Yea, and when I cry and entreat, he hath shut out my prayer.

9 GHIMEL. He hath shut up my ways with square stones; he hath turned my paths upside down.

¹⁰ DELETH. Ursus insidians factus est mihi, leo in absconditis.

¹¹ DELETH. Semitas meas subvertit et confregit me; posuit me desolatam.

¹² DELETH. Tetendit arcum suum et posuit me quasi signum ad sagittam.

¹³ HE. Misit in renibus meis filias faretrae suae.

¹⁴ HE. Factus sum in derisum omni populo meo, canticum
eorum tota die.

¹⁵ HE. Replevit me amaritudinibus; inebriavit me absinthio

¹⁶ VAV et fregit ad numerum dentes meos; cibavit me cinere.

¹⁷ VAV. Et repulsa est a pace anima mea; oblitus sum bonorum,

¹⁸ VAV et dixi, "Periit finis meus et spes mea a Domino."

¹⁹ ZAI. Recordare paupertatis et transgressionis meae,
absinthii et fellis.

²⁰ ZAI. Memoria memor ero, et tabescet in me anima
mea.

²¹ ZAI. Hoc recolens in corde meo, ideo sperabo:

²² HETH misericordiae Domini quia non sumus consumpti, quia non defecerunt miserationes eius.

²³ HETH. Nova diluculo, multa est fides tua.

²⁴ HETH. "Pars mea Dominus," dixit anima mea. "Propterea expectabo eum."

²⁵ TETH. Bonus est Dominus sperantibus in eum, animae
quaerenti illum.

10 DALETH. He is become to me as a bear lying in wait, as a lion in secret places.

11 DALETH. He hath *turned aside* my paths and hath broken me in pieces; he hath made me desolate.

12 DALETH. He hath bent his bow and set me as a mark for *his* arrows.

13 HE. He hath shot into my reins the daughters of his quiver.

14 HE. I am made a derision to all my people, their song all the day long.

15 HE. He hath filled me with bitterness; he hath inebriated me with wormwood

16 VAU and he hath broken my teeth one by one; he hath fed me with ashes.

17 VAU. And my soul is removed far off from peace; I have forgotten good things,

18 VAU and I said, "My end and my hope is perished from the Lord."

19 ZAIN. Remember my poverty and transgression, the wormwood and the gall.

20 ZAIN. I will be mindful and remember, and my soul shall languish within me.

21 ZAIN. *These things* I shall think over in my heart; therefore will I hope:

22 HETH the mercies of the Lord that we are not consumed, because his commiserations have not failed.

23 HETH. *They are* new *every* morning; great is thy faithfulness.

24 HETH. "The Lord is my portion," said my soul. "Therefore will I wait for him."

25 TETH. The Lord is good to them that hope in him, to the soul that seeketh him.

26 TETH. Bonum est praestolari cum silentio salutare Dei.

27 TETH. Bonum est viro cum portaverit iugum ab adulescentia sua.

28 IOTH. Sedebit solitarius et tacebit quia levavit super se.

29 IOTH. Ponet in pulvere os suum, si forte sit spes.

30 IOTH. Dabit percutienti se maxillam; saturabitur obprobriis.

31 CAPH. Quia non repellet in sempiternum Dominus.

32 CAPH. Quia si abiecit, et miserebitur secundum multitudinem misericordiarum suarum.

33 CAPH. Non enim humiliavit ex corde suo et abiecit filios hominum.

34 LAMED. Ut contereret sub pedibus suis omnes vinctos terrae,

35 LAMED ut declinaret iudicium viri in conspectu vultus Altissimi,

36 LAMED ut perverteret hominem in iudicio suo, Dominus ignoravit.

37 MEM. Quis est iste qui dixit ut fieret Domino non iubente?

38 MEM. Ex ore Altissimi non egredientur nec mala nec bona?

39 MEM. Quid murmuravit homo vivens, vir pro peccatis suis?

40 NUN. Scrutemur vias nostras et quaeramus et revertamur ad Dominum.

41 NUN. Levemus corda nostra cum manibus ad Dominum in caelos.

42 NUN. Nos inique egimus et ad iracundiam provocavimus; idcirco tu inexorabilis es.

26 TETH. It is good to wait with silence for the salvation of God.

27 TETH. It is good for a man when he hath borne the yoke from his youth.

28 JOD. He shall sit solitary and hold his peace because he hath taken it up upon himself. 29 JOD. He shall put his mouth in the dust, if so be there may be hope.

30 JOD. He shall give his cheek to him that striketh him; he shall be filled with reproaches.

31 CAPH. For the Lord will not cast off for ever.

32 CAPH. For if he hath cast off, he will also have mercy according to the multitude of his mercies.

33 CAPH. For he hath not *willingly afflicted* nor cast off the children of men.

34 LAMED. To crush under his feet all the prisoners of the land,

35 LAMED to turn aside the judgment of a man before the face of the Most High,

36 LAMED to destroy a man *wrongfully* in his judgment, the Lord hath not *approved*.

37 MEM. Who is he that hath commanded a thing to be done when the Lord commandeth it not?

38 MEM. Shall not both evil and good proceed out of the mouth of the Highest?

39 MEM. Why hath a living man murmured, man *suffering* for his sins?

40 NUN. Let us search our ways and seek and return to the Lord.

41 NUN. Let us lift up our hearts with our hands to the Lord in the heavens.

42 NUN. We have done wickedly and provoked thee to wrath; therefore thou art inexorable.

⁴³ SAMECH. Operuisti in furore et percussisti nos; occidisti nec pepercisti.

⁴⁴ SAMECH. Opposuisti nubem tibi ne transeat oratio.

⁴⁵ SAMECH. Eradicationem et abiectionem posuisti me in medio populorum.

⁴⁶ FE. Aperuerunt super nos os suum omnes inimici.

⁴⁷ FE. Formido et laqueus facta est nobis vaticinatio et contritio.

⁴⁸ FE. Divisiones aquarum deduxit oculus meus in contritione filiae populi mei.

⁴⁹ AIN. Oculus meus adflictus est nec tacuit, eo quod non esset requies

⁵⁰ AIN donec respiceret et videret Dominus de caelis.

⁵¹ AIN. Oculus meus depraedatus est animam meam in cunctis filiabus urbis meae.

⁵² SADE. Venatione ceperunt me quasi avem inimici mei sine causa.

⁵³ SADE. Lapsa est in lacum vita mea, et posuerunt lapidem super me.

⁵⁴ SADE. Inundaverunt aquae super caput meum. Dixi, "Perii."

⁵⁵ COPH. Invocavi nomen tuum, Domine, de lacu novissimo.

⁵⁶ COPH. Vocem meam audisti; ne avertas aurem tuam a singultu meo et clamoribus.

⁵⁷ COPH. Adpropinquasti in die quando invocavi te; dixisti, "Ne timeas."

⁵⁸ RES. Iudicasti, Domine, causam animae meae, Redemptor vitae meae.

43 SAMECH. Thou hast covered in thy wrath and hast struck us; thou hast killed and hast not spared.

44 SAMECH. Thou hast set a cloud before thee that our prayer may not pass through.

45 SAMECH. Thou hast made me as an outcast and refuse in the midst of the people.

46 PHE. All our enemies have opened their mouths against us.

47 PHE. Prophecy is become to us a fear and a snare and destruction.

48 PHE. My eye hath *run down with* streams of water for the destruction of the daughter of my people.

49 AIN. My eye is afflicted and hath not been quiet, because there was no rest

50 AIN till the Lord regarded and looked down from the heavens.

51 AIN. My eye hath wasted my soul because of all the daughters of my city.

52 SADE. My enemies have *chased me and* caught me like a bird without cause.

53 SADE. My life is fallen into the pit, and they have laid a stone over me.

54 SADE. Waters have flowed over my head. I said, "I am *cut off.*"

55 COPH. I have called upon thy name, O Lord, from the lowest pit.

56 COPH. Thou hast heard my voice; turn not away thy ear from my sighs and cries.

57 COPH. Thou drewest near in the day when I called upon thee; thou saidst, "Fear not."

58 RES. Thou hast judged, O Lord, the cause of my soul, thou, the Redeemer of my life.

59 Res. Vidisti, Domine, iniquitatem illorum adversum me; iudica iudicium meum.

60 Res. Vidisti omnem furorem, universas cogitationes eorum adversum me.

61 Sen. Audisti opprobrium eorum, Domine, omnes cogitationes eorum adversum me,

62 Sen labia insurgentium mihi et meditationes eorum adversum me tota die.

63 Sen. Sessionem eorum et resurrectionem eorum vide; ego sum psalmus eorum.

64 Thav. Reddes eis vicem, Domine, iuxta opera manuum suarum.

65 Thav. Dabis eis scutum cordis, laborem tuum.

66 Thav. Persequeris in furore et conteres eos sub caelis, Domine.

Caput 4

Aleph. Quomodo obscuratum est aurum? Mutatus est color optimus; dispersi sunt lapides sanctuarii in capite omnium platearum.

2 Beth. Filii Sion incliti et amicti auro primo, quomodo reputati sunt in vasa testea, opus manuum figuli?

3 Gimel. Sed et lamiae nudaverunt mammam; lactaverunt catulos suos. Filia populi mei crudelis, quasi strutio in deserto.

59 RES. Thou hast seen, O Lord, their iniquity against me; judge thou my judgment.

60 RES. Thou hast seen all their fury *and* all their thoughts against me.

61 SIN. Thou hast heard their reproach, O Lord, all their imaginations against me,

62 SIN the lips of them that rise up against me and their devices against me all the day.

63 SIN. Behold their sitting down and their rising up; I am their song.

64 THAU. Thou shalt render them a recompense, O Lord, according to the works of their hands.

65 THAU. Thou shalt give them for a buckler to their heart, affliction from thee.

66 THAU. Thou shalt persecute them in anger and shalt destroy them from under the heavens, O Lord.

Chapter 4

ALEPH. How is the gold become dim? The finest colour is changed; the stones of the sanctuary are scattered in the top of every street.

2 BETH. The noble sons of Zion and they that were clothed with the best gold, how are they esteemed as earthen vessels, the work of the potter's hands?

3 GHIMEL. *Even* the sea monsters have drawn out the breast; they have given suck to their young. The daughter of my people is cruel, like the ostrich in the desert.

4 DELETH. Adhesit lingua lactentis ad palatum eius in siti; parvuli petierunt panem, et non erat qui frangeret eis.

5 HE. Qui vescebantur voluptuose interierunt in viis; qui nutriebantur in croceis amplexati sunt stercora.

6 VAV. Et maior effecta est iniquitas filiae populi mei peccato Sodomorum, quae subversa est in momento, et non ceperunt in ea manus.

7 ZAI. Candidiores Nazarei eius nive, nitidiores lacte, rubicundiores ebore antiquo, sapphyro pulchriores.

8 HETH. Denigrata est super carbones facies eorum, et non sunt cogniti in plateis. Adhesit cutis eorum ossibus; aruit et facta est quasi lignum.

9 TETH. Melius fuit occisis gladio quam interfectis fame, quoniam isti extabuerunt consumpti ab sterilitate terrae.

10 IOTH. Manus mulierum misericordium coxerunt filios suos; facti sunt cibus earum in contritione filiae populi mei.

11 CAPH. Conplevit Dominus furorem suum. Effudit iram indignationis suae et succendit ignem in Sion, et devoravit fundamenta eius.

12 LAMED. Non crediderunt reges terrae et universi habitatores orbis quoniam ingrederetur hostis et inimicus per portas Hierusalem,

13 MEM propter peccata prophetarum eius et iniquitates sacerdotum eius qui effuderunt in medio eius sanguinem iustorum.

4 DALETH. The tongue of the sucking child hath stuck to the roof of his mouth for thirst; the little ones have asked for bread, and there was none to break it unto them.

5 HE. They that were fed *delicately* have died in the streets; they that were brought up in *scarlet* have embraced the dung.

6 VAU. And the iniquity of the daughter of my people is made greater than the sin of Sodom, which was overthrown in a moment, and hands took nothing in her.

7 ZAIN. Her Nazirites were whiter than snow, purer than milk, more ruddy than the old ivory, fairer than the sapphire.

8 HETH. Their face is *now* made blacker than coals, and they are not known in the streets. Their skin hath stuck to their bones; it is withered and is become like wood.

9 TETH. It was better with them that were slain by the sword than with them that died with hunger, for these pined away being consumed *for want of the fruits* of the earth.

10 JOD. The hands of the pitiful women have sodden their own children; they were their meat in the destruction of the daughter of my people.

11 CAPH. The Lord hath accomplished his wrath. He hath poured out his *fierce* anger and he hath kindled a fire in Zion, and it hath devoured the foundations thereof.

12 LAMED. The kings of the earth and all the inhabitants of the world *would* not have believed that the adversary and the enemy should enter in by the gates of Jerusalem,

13 MEM for the sins of her prophets and the iniquities of her priests that have shed the blood of the just in the midst of her.

14 Nun. Erraverunt caeci in plateis; polluti sunt sanguine, cumque non possent tenuerunt lacinias suas.

15 Samech. "Recedite, polluti!" clamaverunt eis. "Recedite! Abite! Nolite tangere!" Iurgati quippe sunt, et commoti dixerunt inter Gentes, "Non addet ultra ut habitet in eis."

16 Fe. Facies Domini divisit eos; non addet ut respiciat eos. Facies sacerdotum non erubuerunt neque senum miserti sunt.

17 Ain. Cum adhuc subsisteremus defecerunt oculi nostri ad auxilium nostrum vanum, cum respiceremus adtenti ad gentem quae salvare non poterat.

18 Sade. Lubricaverunt vestigia nostra in itinere platearum nostrarum. Adpropinquavit finis noster; conpleti sunt dies nostri, quia venit finis noster.

19 Coph. Velociores fuerunt persecutores nostri aquilis caeli. Super montes persecuti sunt nos; in deserto insidiati sunt nobis.

20 Res. Spiritus oris nostri, Christus Dominus, captus est in peccatis nostris, cui diximus, "In umbra tua vivemus in Gentibus."

21 Sen. Gaude, et laetare, filia Edom quae habitas in terra Hus. Ad te quoque perveniet calix; inebriaberis atque nudaberis.

22 Thav. Conpleta est iniquitas tua, filia Sion; non addet ultra ut transmigret te. Visitavit iniquitatem tuam, filia Edom; discoperuit peccata tua.

14 NUN. They have wandered as blind men in the streets; they were defiled with blood, and when they could not *help walking in it* they held *up* their skirts.

15 SAMECH. "Depart, you that are defiled!" they cried out to them. "Depart! Get ye hence! Touch not!" For they quarrelled, and being removed they said among the Gentiles, "He will no more dwell among them."

16 PHE. The face of the Lord hath divided them; he will no more regard them. They respected not the persons of the priests, neither had they pity on the ancient.

17 AIN. While we were yet standing our eyes failed, *expecting* help *for us in vain,* when we looked attentively towards a nation that was not able to save.

18 SADE. Our steps have slipped in the way of our streets. Our end *draweth* near; our days are fulfilled, for our end is come.

19 COPH. Our persecutors were swifter than the eagles of the air. They pursued us upon the mountains; they lay in wait for us in the wilderness.

20 RES. The breath of our mouth, Christ the Lord, is taken in our sins, to whom we said, *"Under* thy shadow we shall live among the Gentiles."

21 SIN. Rejoice, and be glad, O daughter of Edom that dwellest in the land of Uz. To thee also shall the cup come; thou shalt be made drunk and naked.

22 THAU. Thy iniquity is accomplished, O daughter of Zion; he will no more *carry* thee *away into captivity.* He hath visited thy iniquity, O daughter of Edom; he hath discovered thy sins.

Caput 5

Recordare, Domine, quid acciderit nobis; intuere, et respice obprobrium nostrum. 2 Hereditas nostra versa est ad alienos, domus nostrae ad extraneos. 3 Pupilli facti sumus absque patre; matres nostrae quasi viduae. 4 Aquam nostram pecunia bibimus; ligna nostra pretio conparavimus. 5 Cervicibus nostris minabamur; lassis non dabatur requies. 6 Aegypto dedimus manum et Assyriis ut saturaremur pane. 7 Patres nostri peccaverunt et non sunt, et nos iniquitates eorum portavimus. 8 Servi dominati sunt nostri; non fuit qui redimeret de manu eorum. 9 In animabus nostris adferebamus panem nobis a facie gladii in deserto. 10 Pellis nostra quasi clibanus exusta est a facie tempestatum famis. 11 Mulieres in Sion humiliaverunt et virgines in civitatibus Iuda. 12 Principes manu suspensi sunt; facies senum non erubuerunt. 13 Adulescentibus inpudice abusi sunt, et pueri in ligno corruerunt. 14 Senes de portis defecerunt, iuvenes de choro psallentium. 15 Defecit gaudium cordis nostri; versus est in luctum chorus noster. 16 Cecidit corona capitis nostri; vae nobis quia peccavimus! 17 Propterea maestum factum est cor nostrum; ideo contenebrati sunt oculi nostri 18 propter Montem Sion quia disperiit; vulpes ambulaverunt in eo.

Chapter 5

Remember, O Lord, what is come upon us; consider, and behold our reproach. 2 Our inheritance is turned to aliens, our houses to strangers. 3 We are become orphans without a father; our mothers are as widows. 4 We have drunk our water for money; we have *bought* our wood. 5 We were *dragged* by the necks; *we were weary, and* no rest was given *us.* 6 We have given our hand to Egypt and to the Assyrians that we might be satisfied with bread. 7 Our fathers have sinned and are not, and we have borne their iniquities. 8 Servants have ruled over us, *and* there was none to redeem us out of their hand. 9 We fetched our bread at the peril of our lives *because* of the sword in the desert. 10 Our skin was burnt as an oven *by reason of the violence* of the famine. 11 They *oppressed* the women in Zion and the virgins in the cities of Judah. 12 The princes were hanged up by their hand; they did not respect the persons of the ancient. 13 They abused the young men indecently, and the children fell *under* the wood. 14 The ancients have ceased from the gates, the young men from the choir of the singers. 15 The joy of our heart is ceased; our dancing is turned into mourning. 16 The crown is fallen *from* our head; woe to us because we have sinned! 17 Therefore is our heart sorrowful; therefore are our eyes become dim 18 for Mount Zion because it is destroyed; foxes have walked upon it.

¹⁹ Tu autem, Domine, in aeternum permanebis, solium tuum in generatione et generationem. ²⁰ Quare in perpetuum oblivisceris nostri? Derelinques nos in longitudine dierum? ²¹ Converte nos, Domine, ad te, et convertemur; innova dies nostros sicut a principio. ²² Sed proiciens reppulisti nos; iratus es contra nos vehementer.

CHAPTER 5

19 But thou, O Lord, shalt remain for ever, thy throne *from generation* to generation. 20 Why wilt thou forget us for ever? Why wilt thou forsake us for a long time? 21 Convert us, O Lord, to thee, and we shall be converted; renew our days as from the beginning. 22 But thou hast utterly rejected us; thou art exceedingly angry against us.

BARUCH

Caput 1

Et haec verba libri quae scripsit Baruch, filius Neriae, filii Maasiae, filii Sedechiae, filii Sedei, filii Helchiae, in Babylonia 2 in anno quinto, in septima die mensis, in tempore quo ceperunt Chaldei Hierusalem et succenderunt eam igni. 3 Et legit Baruch verba libri huius ad aures Iechoniae, filii Ioachim, regis Iuda, et ad aures universi populi venientis ad librum 4 et ad aures potentium, filiorum regum, et ad aures presbyterorum et ad aures populi, a minimo usque ad maximum eorum omnium habitantium in Babylonia ad flumen Sodi, 5 qui audientes plorabant et ieiunabant et orabant in conspectu Domini. 6 Et collegerunt pecuniam secundum quod potuit uniuscuiusque manus, 7 et miserunt in Hierusalem ad Ioachim, filium Helchiae, filii Salom, sacerdotem, et ad sacerdotes et ad omnem populum qui inventi sunt cum eo in Hierusalem, 8 cum acciperet vasa templi Domini, quae ablata fuerant de templo, revocare in terram Iuda, decima

Chapter 1

The Jews of Babylon send the book of Baruch with money to Jerusalem, requesting their brethren there to offer sacrifice and to pray for the king and for them, acknowledging their manifold sins.

And these are the words of the book which Baruch, the son of Neriah, the son of Mahseiah, the son of Zedekiah, the son of Sedei, the son of Helcias, wrote in Babylonia 2 in the fifth year, in the seventh day of the month, at the time that the Chaldeans took Jerusalem and burnt it with fire. 3 And Baruch read the words of this book *in the hearing* of Jeconiah, the son of Jehoiakim, king of Judah, and *in the hearing* of all the people that came to *hear* the book 4 and *in the hearing* of the nobles, the sons of the kings, and *in the hearing* of the ancients and *in the hearing* of the people, from the least even to the greatest of *them* that dwelt in Babylonia by the river Sud, 5 and when they heard it they wept and fasted and prayed before the Lord. 6 And they made a collection of money according to every man's power, 7 and they sent it to Jerusalem to Jehoiakim, the priest, the son of Hilkiah, the son of Shallum, and to the priests and to all the people that were found with him in Jerusalem, 8 at the time when he received the vessels of the temple of the Lord, which had been taken away out of the temple, to return them into the land

die mensis Sivan, vasa argentea quae fecit Sedechias, filius Iosiae, rex Iuda, 9 posteaquam cepisset Nabuchodonosor, rex Babylonis, Iechoniam et principes et cunctos potentes et populum terrae ab Hierusalem et duxit eos vinctos in Babylonem.

10 Et dixerunt, "Ecce: misimus ad vos pecunias; de quibus emite holocaustomata et tus, et facite manna, et offerte pro peccato ad aram Domini, Dei nostri. 11 Et orate pro vita Nabuchodonosor, regis Babylonis, et pro vita Balthasar, filii eius, ut sint dies ipsorum sicut dies caeli super terram, 12 et ut det Dominus virtutem nobis et inluminet oculos nostros ut vivamus sub umbra Nabuchodonosor, regis Babylonis, et sub umbra Balthasar, filii eius, et serviamus eis multis diebus et inveniamus gratiam in conspectu eorum. 13 Et pro nobis ipsis orate ad Dominum, Deum nostrum, quia peccavimus Domino, Deo nostro, et non est aversus furor eius a nobis usque in hunc diem. 14 Et legite librum istum quem misimus ad vos recitari in templo Domini in die sollemni et in die oportuno.

15 "Et dicetis, 'Domino, Deo nostro, iustitia, nobis autem confusio faciei nostrae, sicut est dies haec omni Iuda et habitantibus in Hierusalem, 16 regibus nostris et principibus nostris et sacerdotibus nostris et prophetis nostris et patribus nostris. 17 Peccavimus ante Dominum, Deum nostrum, et non credidimus diffidentes in eum. 18 Et non fuimus subiectibiles illi, et non audivimus vocem Domini, Dei nostri, ut ambularemus in mandatis eius quae dedit nobis. 19 A die qua eduxit patres nostros de terra Aegypti usque ad diem

of Judah, the tenth day of the month Sivan, the silver vessels which Zedekiah, the son of Josiah, king of Judah, had made, 9 after that Nebuchadnezzar, the king of Babylon, had carried away Jeconiah and the princes and all the powerful men and the people of the land from Jerusalem and brought them bound to Babylon.

10 And they said, "Behold: we have sent you money; buy with it holocausts and frankincense, and make *meat offerings* and *offerings* for sin at the altar of the Lord, our God. 11 And pray ye for the life of Nebuchadnezzar, the king of Babylon, and for the life of Belshazzar, his son, that their days may be upon earth as the days of heaven, 12 and that the Lord may give us strength and enlighten our eyes that we may live under the shadow of Nebuchadnezzar, the king of Babylon, and under the shadow of Belshazzar, his son, and may serve them many days and may find favour in their sight. 13 And pray ye for us to the Lord, our God, for we have sinned against the Lord, our God, and his wrath is not turned away from us even to this day. 14 And read ye this book which we have sent to you to be read in the temple of the Lord on *feasts* and proper days.

15 "And you shall say, 'To the Lord, our God, belongeth justice, but to us confusion of our face, as it is come to pass at this day to all Judah and to the inhabitants of Jerusalem, 16 to our kings and to our princes and to our priests and to our prophets and to our fathers. 17 We have sinned before the Lord, our God, and have not believed him nor put our trust in him. 18 And we were not obedient to him, and we have not hearkened to the voice of the Lord, our God, to walk in his commandments which he hath given us. 19 From the day that he brought our fathers out of the land of Egypt even to

hanc eramus incredibiles ad Dominum, Deum nostrum, et dissipati recessimus ne audiremus vocem ipsius. 20 Et adheserunt nobis mala multa et maledictiones quae constituit Dominus Moysi, servo suo, qui eduxit patres nostros de terra Aegypti dare nobis terram fluentem lac et mel, sicut hodierna die. 21 Et non audivimus vocem Domini, Dei nostri, secundum omnia verba prophetarum quos misit ad nos, 22 et abivimus unusquisque in sensum cordis nostri maligni operari diis alienis, facientes mala ante oculos Domini, Dei nostri.'"

Caput 2

"Propter quod statuit Dominus, Deus noster, verbum suum quod locutus est ad nos et ad iudices nostros qui iudicaverunt Israhel et ad reges nostros et ad principes nostros et ad omnem Israhel et Iuda: 2 ut adduceret Dominus super nos mala magna quae non sunt facta sub caelo quemadmodum facta sunt in Hierusalem, secundum quae scripta sunt in lege Moysi, 3 ut manducaret homo carnes filii sui et carnes filiae suae. 4 Et dedit illos sub manu regum omnium qui sunt

this day we were *disobedient* to the Lord, our God, and *going astray* we *turned away from* hearing his voice. 20 And many evils have cleaved to us and the curses which the Lord *foretold by* Moses, his servant, who brought our fathers out of the land of Egypt to give us a land flowing with milk and honey, as at this day. 21 And we have not hearkened to the voice of the Lord, our God, according to all the words of the prophets whom he sent to us, 22 and we have gone away every man after the inclinations of his own wicked heart to serve strange gods and to do evil in the sight of the Lord, our God.'"

Chapter 2

A further confession of the sins of the people and of the justice of God.

"Wherefore the Lord, our God, hath *made good* his word that he spoke to us and to our judges that have judged Israel and to our kings and to our princes and to all Israel and Judah: 2 that the Lord would bring upon us great evils such as *never* happened under heaven as they have come to pass in Jerusalem, according to the things that are written in the law of Moses, 3 that a man should eat the flesh of his own son and the flesh of his own daughter. 4 And he hath delivered them up to be under the hand of all the kings that are

in circuitu nostro, in inproperium et in desolationem in omnibus populis in quibus nos dispersit Dominus. 5 Et facti sumus subtus et non supra quia peccavimus Domino, Deo nostro, non obaudiendo voci ipsius. 6 Domino, Deo nostro, iustitia, nobis autem et patribus nostris confusio faciei, sicut est dies haec, 7 quia locutus est Dominus super nos omnia mala haec quae venerunt super nos 8 et non sumus deprecati faciem Domini, Dei nostri, ut reverteremur unusquisque nostrum a viis nostris pessimis. 9 Et vigilavit Dominus in malis et adduxit ea super nos, quia iustus est Dominus in omnibus operibus suis quae mandavit nobis 10 et non audivimus vocem ipsius ut iremus in praeceptis Domini quae dedit ante faciem nostram.

11 "'Et nunc, Domine, Deus Israhel, qui eduxisti populum tuum de terra Aegypti in manu valida et in signis et in prodigiis et in virtute tua magna et in brachio excelso et fecisti tibi nomen sicut est dies iste, 12 peccavimus; impie egimus; inique gessimus, Domine, Deus noster, in omnibus iustitiis tuis. 13 Avertatur ira tua a nobis, quia derelicti sumus pauci inter gentes ubi dispersisti nos. 14 Exaudi, Domine, preces nostras et orationes nostras, et educ nos propter te, et da nobis invenire gratiam ante faciem eorum qui nos abduxerunt, 15 ut sciat omnis terra quia tu es Dominus, Deus noster, et quia nomen tuum invocatum est super Israhel et super genus ipsius. 16 Respice, Domine, de domo sancta tua in nos, et inclina aurem tuam, et exaudi nos. 17 Aperi oculos tuos, et vide, quia non mortui qui sunt in inferno, quorum spiritus acceptus est a visceribus suis, dabunt honorem et iustificationem Domino, 18 sed anima quae tristis est super

round about us, to be a reproach and desolation among all the people among whom the Lord hath scattered us. 5 And we are brought under and are not *uppermost* because we have sinned against the Lord, our God, by not obeying his voice. 6 To the Lord, our God, belongeth justice, but to us and to our fathers confusion of face, as at this day, 7 for the Lord hath pronounced against us all these evils that are come upon us 8 and we have not entreated the face of the Lord, our God, that we might return every one of us from our most wicked ways. 9 And the Lord hath watched *over us for evil* and hath brought *it* upon us, for the Lord is just in all his works which he hath commanded us 10 and we have not hearkened to his voice to walk in the commandments of the Lord which he hath set before *us*.

11 "'And now, O Lord, God of Israel, who hast brought thy people out of the land of Egypt with a strong hand and with signs and with wonders and with thy great power and with a mighty arm and hast made thee a name as at this day, 12 we have sinned; we have done wickedly; we have acted unjustly, O Lord, our God, against all thy justices. 13 Let thy wrath be turned away from us, for we are left a few among the nations where thou hast scattered us. 14 Hear, O Lord, our prayers and our petitions, and deliver us for thy own sake, and grant that we may find favour *in the sight* of them that have led us away, 15 that all the earth may know that thou art the Lord, our God, and that thy name is called upon Israel and upon his posterity. 16 Look down upon us, O Lord, from thy holy house, and incline thy ear, and hear us. 17 Open thy eyes, and behold, for the dead that are in hell, whose spirit is taken away from their bowels, shall not give glory and *justice* to the Lord, 18 but the soul that is sorrowful for the greatness of

magnitudine mali et incedit curva et infirmis et oculi deficientes et anima esuriens dat tibi gloriam et iustitiam Domino. 19 Quia non secundum iustitias patrum nostrorum nos fundimus preces et petimus misericordiam ante conspectum tuum, Domine, Deus noster, 20 sed quia misisti iram tuam et furorem tuum super nos sicut locutus es in manu puerorum tuorum, prophetarum, dicens, 21 "Sic dicit Dominus: 'Inclinate umerum vestrum et cervicem vestram, et opera facite regi Babylonis, et sedebitis in terra quam dedi patribus vestris. 22 Quod si non audieritis vocem Domini, Dei vestri, operari regi Babyloniae, defectionem vestram faciam de civitatibus Iuda et a foris Hierusalem, 23 et auferam a vobis vocem iucunditatis et vocem gaudimonii et vocem sponsi et vocem sponsae, et erit omnis terra sine vestigio ab inhabitantibus eam.

24 "'Et non audierunt vocem tuam ut operarentur regi Babylonis, et statuisti verba tua quae locutus es in manibus puerorum tuorum, prophetarum, ut transferrentur ossa regum nostrorum et ossa patrum nostrorum de loco suo. 25 Et ecce: sunt proiecta in calore solis et in gelu noctis, et mortui sunt in doloribus pessimis in fame et in gladio et in emissione. 26 Et posuisti templum, in quo invocatum est nomen tuum in ipso sicut haec dies, propter iniquitatem domus Israhel et domus Iuda.

27 "'Et fecisti in nobis, Domine, Deus noster, secundum omnem bonitatem tuam et secundum omnem miserationem tuam illam magnam 28 sicut locutus es in manu pueri tui Moysi in die qua praecepisti ei scribere legem tuam coram filiis Israhel, 29 dicens, "Si non audieritis vocem meam, multitudo haec magna convertetur in minimam inter gentes quo

evil *she hath done* and goeth bowed down and feeble and the eyes that fail and the hungry soul giveth glory and justice to thee, the Lord. 19 For it is not *for* the justices of our fathers that we pour out our prayers and beg mercy in thy sight, O Lord, our God, 20 but because thou hast sent out thy wrath and thy indignation upon us as thou hast spoken by the hand of thy servants, the prophets, saying, 21 "Thus saith the Lord: 'Bow down your shoulder and your neck, and *serve* the king of Babylon, and you shall remain in the land which I have given to your fathers. 22 But if you will not hearken to the voice of the Lord, your God, to serve the king of Babylon, I will cause you to depart out of the cities of Judah and from without Jerusalem, 23 and I will take away from you the voice of mirth and the voice of joy and the voice of the bridegroom and the voice of the bride, and all the land shall be without any footstep of inhabitants.

24 "And they hearkened not to thy voice to serve the king of Babylon, and thou hast *made good* thy words which thou spokest by the hands of thy servants, the prophets, that the bones of our kings and the bones of our fathers should be removed out of their place. 25 And behold: they are cast out to the heat of the sun and to the frost of the night, and they have died in grievous pains by famine and by the sword and in banishment. 26 And thou hast made the temple, in which thy name was called upon as it is at this day, for the iniquity of the house of Israel and the house of Judah.

27 "And thou hast dealt with us, O Lord, our God, according to all thy goodness and according to all that great mercy of thine 28 as thou spokest by the hand of thy servant Moses in the day when thou didst command him to write thy law before the children of Israel, 29 saying, "If you will not hear my voice, this great multitude shall be turned into a very

ego dispergam illos, 30 quia scio quod me non audiet populus, populus est enim dura cervice. Et convertetur ad cor suum in terra captivitatis suae, 31 et scient quoniam ego sum Dominus, Deus eorum, et dabo eis cor, et intelligent, et aures, et audient. 32 Et laudabunt me in terra captivitatis suae et memores erunt nominis mei. 33 Et avertent se a dorso suo duro et a malignitatibus suis, quia reminiscentur viam patrum suorum qui peccaverunt in me. 34 Et revocabo illos in terram quam iuravi patribus illorum, Abraham, Isaac et Iacob, et dominabuntur eius, et multiplicabo eos, et non minorabuntur. 35 Et statuam illis testamentum alterum sempiternum: ut sim illis in Deum, et ipsi erunt mihi in populum, et non movebo amplius populum meum, filios Israhel, a terra quam dedi illis.""

Caput 3

"Et nunc, Domine Omnipotens, Deus Israhel, anima in angustiis et spiritus anxius clamat ad te. 2 Audi, Domine, et miserere, quia Deus es misericors, et miserere nostri, quia

small *number* among the nations where I will scatter them, 30 for I know that the people will not hear me, for they are a people of a stiff neck. *But* they shall turn to their heart in the land of their captivity, 31 and they shall know that I am the Lord, their God, and I will give them a heart, and they shall understand, and ears, and they shall hear. 32 And they shall praise me in the land of their captivity and shall be mindful of my name. 33 And they shall turn away themselves from their stiff *neck* and from their wicked deeds, for they shall remember the way of their fathers that sinned against me. 34 And I will bring them back again into the land which I promised with an oath to their fathers, Abraham, Isaac and Jacob, and they shall be masters thereof, and I will multiply them, and they shall not be diminished. 35 And I will make with them another covenant that *shall be* everlasting: to be their God, and they shall be my people, and I will no more remove my people, the children of Israel, out of the land that I have given them.""""

Chapter 3

They pray for mercy, acknowledging that they are justly punished for forsaking true wisdom. A prophecy of Christ.

""And now, O Lord Almighty, the God of Israel, the soul in anguish and the troubled spirit crieth to thee. 2 Hear, O Lord, and have mercy, for thou art a merciful God, and

peccavimus ante te. 3 Quia tu sedes in sempiternum, et nos peribimus in aevum? 4 Domine Omnipotens, Deus Israhel, audi nunc orationem mortuorum Israhel et filiorum ipsorum qui peccaverunt ante te et non audierunt vocem Domini, Dei sui, et adglutinata sunt nobis mala. 5 Noli meminisse iniquitatum patrum nostrorum, sed memento manus tuae et nominis tui in tempore isto, 6 quia tu es Dominus, Deus noster, et laudabimus te, Domine. 7 Quia propter hoc dedisti timorem tuum in cordibus nostris et ut invocemus nomen tuum et laudemus te in captivitate nostra, quia convertimur ab iniquitate patrum nostrorum qui peccaverunt ante te. 8 Et ecce: nos hodie in captivitate nostra sumus, quo nos dispersisti in inproperium et in maledictum et in peccatum secundum omnes iniquitates patrum nostrorum qui recesserunt a te, Domine, Deus noster.

9 "Audi, Israhel, mandata vitae; auribus percipe ut scias prudentiam. 10 Quid est, Israhel, quod in terra es inimicorum? 11 Inveterasti in terra aliena; coinquinatus es cum mortuis; deputatus es cum descendentibus in infernum. 12 Dereliquisti fontem sapientiae, 13 nam si in via Dei ambulasses, habitasses utique in pace sempiterna. 14 Disce ubi sit prudentia, ubi sit virtus, ubi sit intellectus, ut scias simul ubi sit longiturnitas vitae et victus, ubi sit lumen oculorum et pax.

15 "'Quis invenit locum eius? Et quis intravit in thesauros eius? 16 Ubi sunt principes gentium et qui dominantur super bestias quae sunt super terram? 17 Qui in avibus caeli inludunt? 18 Qui argentum thesaurizant et aurum in quo confidunt homines, et non est finis adquisitionis eorum? Qui

have pity on us, for we have sinned before thee. 3 For thou remainest for ever, and shall we perish everlastingly? 4 O Lord Almighty, the God of Israel, hear now the prayer of the dead of Israel and of their children that have sinned before thee and have not hearkened to the voice of the Lord, their God, *wherefore* evils have cleaved fast to us. 5 Remember not the iniquities of our fathers, but *think* upon thy hand and upon thy name at this time, 6 for thou art the Lord, our God, and we will praise thee, O Lord. 7 Because for this end thou hast put thy fear in our hearts *to the intent* that we should call upon thy name and praise thee in our captivity, for we are converted from the iniquity of our fathers who sinned before thee. 8 And behold: we are at this day in our captivity, whereby thou hast scattered us to be a reproach and a curse and an offence according to all the iniquities of our fathers who departed from thee, O Lord, our God.

9 "Hear, O Israel, the commandments of life; give ear that thou mayst *learn* wisdom. 10 How happeneth it, O Israel, that thou art in thy enemies' land? 11 Thou art grown old in a strange country; thou art defiled with the dead; thou art counted with them that go down into hell. 12 Thou hast forsaken the fountain of wisdom, 13 for if thou hadst walked in the way of God, thou hadst surely dwelt in peace for ever. 14 Learn where is wisdom, where is strength, where is understanding, that thou mayst know also where is length of *days* and *life,* where is the light of the eyes and peace.

15 "Who hath found out her place? And who hath gone in to her treasures? 16 Where are the princes of the nations and they that rule over the beasts that are upon the earth? 17 That take their pastime with the birds of the air? 18 That hoard up silver and gold, wherein men trust, and there is no

argentum fabricant et solliciti sunt, nec est inventio operum illorum? 19 Exterminati sunt et ad inferos descenderunt, et alii loco eorum exsurrexerunt.

20 "'Iuvenes viderunt lumen et habitaverunt super terram, viam autem disciplinae ignoraverunt, 21 neque intellexerunt semitas eius, neque filii eorum susceperunt eam; a facie ipsorum longe facta est. 22 Non est audita in terra Chanaan, neque visa est in Theman. 23 Filii quoque Agar, qui exquirunt prudentiam quae de terra est, negotiatores Merrae et Theman et fabulatores et exquisitores prudentiae et intellegentiae, viam autem sapientiae nescierunt, neque commemorati sunt semitas eius.

24 "'O Israhel, quam magna est domus Dei et ingens locus possessionis eius! 25 Magnus est et non habet finem, excelsus et inmensus. 26 Ibi fuerunt gigantes, nominati illi qui ab initio fuerunt statura magna, scientes bellum. 27 Non hos elegit Dominus, neque viam disciplinae invenerunt; propterea perierunt. 28 Et quoniam non habuerunt sapientiam, interierunt propter insipientiam suam.

29 "'Quis ascendit in caelum et accepit eam et deduxit eam de nubibus? 30 Quis transfretavit mare et invenit illam et adtulit illam super aurum electum? 31 Non est qui possit scire vias eius neque qui exquirat semitas eius. 32 Sed qui scit universa novit eam et invenit eam prudentia sua, qui praeparavit terram in aeterno tempore et replevit eam pecudibus et quadrupedibus. 33 Qui emittit lumen, et vadit, et vocavit illud, et obaudit illi in tremore. 34 Stellae autem lumen dede-

end of their getting? Who work in silver and are solicitous, and *their works are unsearchable?* 19 They are cut off and are gone down to hell, and others are risen up in their place.

20 "'Young men have seen the light and dwelt upon the earth, but the way of knowledge they have not known, 21 nor have they understood the paths thereof, neither have their children received it; it is far from their face. 22 It hath not been heard of in the land of Canaan, neither hath it been seen in Teman. 23 The children of Hagar also, that search after the wisdom that is of the earth, the merchants of Merrha and of Teman and the tellers of fables and searchers of prudence and understanding, but the way of wisdom they have not known, neither have they remembered her paths.

24 "'O Israel, how great is the house of God, and how vast is the place of his possession! 25 It is great and hath no end; it is high and immense. 26 There were the giants, those renowned men that were from the beginning of great stature, expert in war. 27 The Lord chose not them, neither did they find the way of knowledge; therefore did they perish. 28 And because they had not wisdom, they perished through their folly.

29 "'Who hath gone up into heaven and taken her and brought her down from the clouds? 30 Who hath passed over the sea and found her and brought her *preferably to* chosen gold? 31 There is none that is able to know her ways nor that *can* search out her paths. 32 But he that knoweth all things knoweth her and hath found her out with his understanding, he that prepared the earth *for evermore* and filled it with cattle and four-footed beasts. 33 He that sendeth forth light, and it goeth, and hath called it, and it obeyeth him with trembling. 34 And the stars have given light in their watches

runt in custodiis suis et laetatae sunt. 35 Vocatae sunt, et dixerunt, "Adsumus!" et luxerunt ei cum iucunditate qui fecit illas. 36 Hic est Deus noster, et non aestimabitur alius adversus eum. 37 Hic adinvenit omnem viam disciplinae et tradidit illam Iacob, puero suo, et Israhel, dilecto suo. 38 Post haec in terris visus est et cum hominibus conversatus est.'"

Caput 4

"'Hic liber mandatorum Dei et lex quae est in aeternum; omnes qui tenent eam pervenient ad vitam, qui autem dereliquerunt eam in mortem. 2 Convertere, Iacob, et adprehende eam; ambula per viam ad splendorem eius contra lumen eius. 3 Ne tradas alteri gloriam tuam, et dignitatem tuam genti alienae. 4 Beati sumus, Israhel, quoniam quae Deo placent nobis manifesta sunt. 5 Animaequior esto, populus Dei, memorabilis Israhel! 6 Venundati estis Gentibus non in perditionem, sed propter quod in ira ad iracundiam provocastis Deum traditi estis adversariis, 7 exacerbastis enim eum qui fecit vos, Deum aeternum, immolantes

and rejoiced. 35 They were called, and they said, "Here we are!" and with cheerfulness they have shined forth to him that made them. 36 This is our God, and there shall no other be accounted of in comparison of him. 37 He found out all the way of knowledge and gave it to Jacob, his servant, and to Israel, his beloved. 38 Afterwards he was seen upon earth and conversed with men.'"

Chapter 4

The prophet exhorts to the keeping of the law of wisdom and encourages the people to be patient and to hope for their deliverance.

"This is the book of the commandments of God and the law that is for ever; all they that keep it shall come to life, but they that have forsaken it to death. 2 Return, O Jacob, and take hold of it; walk in the way by its brightness *in the presence of* the light thereof. 3 Give not thy honour to another, nor thy dignity to a strange nation. 4 We are happy, O Israel, because the things that are pleasing to God are made known to us. 5 Be of good comfort, O people of God, *the memorial of* Israel! 6 You have been sold to the Gentiles not for your destruction, but because *you* provoked God to wrath you are delivered to your adversaries, 7 for you have provoked him, your Maker, the eternal God, offering sacrifice

daemoniis et non Deo. 8 Obliti enim estis Deum, qui nutrivit vos, et contristastis nutricem vestram, Hierusalem.

9 "'Vidit enim iracundiam a Deo venientem vobis et dixit, "Audite, confines Sion, adduxit enim mihi Deus luctum magnum. 10 Vidi enim captivitatem populi mei, filiorum meorum et filiarum, quam superduxit illis Aeternus. 11 Nutrivi enim illos cum iucunditate, dimisi autem illos cum fletu et luctu. 12 Nemo gaudeat super me, viduam et desolatam; a multis derelicta sum propter peccata filiorum meorum quia declinaverunt a lege Dei. 13 Iustitias autem ipsius nescierunt nec ambulaverunt per vias mandatorum Dei, neque per semitas veritatis eius cum iustitia ingressi sunt. 14 Veniant confines Sion et memorentur captivitatem filiorum et filiarum mearum, quam superduxit illis Aeternus. 15 Adduxit enim super illos gentem de longinquo, gentem inprobam et alterius linguae, 16 qui non sunt reveriti senem neque puerorum miserti sunt, et abduxerunt dilectos viduae et a filiis unicam desolaverunt.

17 "'Ego autem, quid possum adiuvare vos? 18 Qui enim adduxit super vos mala, ipse vos eripiet de manibus inimicorum vestrorum. 19 Ambulate, filii, ambulate, ego enim derelicta sum sola. 20 Exui me stola pacis, indui autem me sacco obsecrationis, et clamabo ad Altissimum in diebus meis.

21 "'Animaequiores estote, filii; clamate ad Dominum, et eripiet vos de manu principum, inimicorum. 22 Ego enim speravi in Aeternum, salutem vestram, et venit mihi gaudium a Sancto super misericordia quae veniet vobis ab ae-

to devils and not to God. 8 For you have forgotten God, who brought you up, and you have grieved Jerusalem, that nursed you.

9 "For she saw the wrath of God coming upon you and she said, "Give ear, all you that dwell near Zion, for God hath brought upon me great mourning. 10 For I have seen the captivity of my people, of my sons and my daughters, which the Eternal hath brought upon them. 11 For I nourished them with joy, but I sent them away with weeping and mourning. 12 Let no man rejoice over me, a widow and desolate; I am forsaken of many for the sins of my children because they departed from the law of God. 13 And they have not known his justices nor walked by the ways of God's commandments, neither have they entered by the paths of his truth and justice. 14 Let them that dwell about Zion come and remember the captivity of my sons and daughters, which the Eternal hath brought upon them. 15 For he hath brought a nation upon them from afar, a wicked nation and of a strange tongue, 16 who have neither reverenced the ancient nor pitied children and have carried away the darlings of the widow and have left *me* all alone without children.

17 "But as for me, what help can I give you? 18 *But* he that hath brought the evils upon you, he will deliver you out of the hands of your enemies. 19 Go your way, my children, go your way, for I am left alone. 20 I have put off the robe of peace and have put upon me the sackcloth of supplication, and I will cry to the Most High in my days.

21 "Be of good comfort, my children; cry to the Lord, and he will deliver you out of the hand of the princes, your enemies. 22 For my hope *is* in the Eternal *that he will save you,* and joy is come upon me from the Holy One because of the mercy which shall come to you from our everlasting

terno salutari nostro. 23 Emisi enim vos cum luctu et ploratu, reducet autem vos mihi Dominus cum gaudio et iucunditate in sempiternum. 24 Sicut enim viderunt vicinae Sion captivitatem vestram a Deo, sic videbunt et in celeritate salutem vestram a Deo, quae superveniet vobis cum honore magno et splendore aeterno. 25 Filii, patienter sustinete iram quae supervenit vobis, persecutus est enim te inimicus tuus, sed cito videbis perditionem ipsius et super cervices ipsius ascendes. 26 Delicati mei ambulaverunt vias asperas, ducti sunt enim ut grex direptus ab inimicis. 27 Animaequiores estote, filii, et proclamate ad Dominum, erit enim memoria vestra ab eo qui duxit vos. 28 Sicut enim fuit sensus vester ut erraretis a Deo, decies tantum iterum convertentes requiretis eum, 29 qui enim induxit vobis mala ipse rursum adducet vobis sempiternam iucunditatem cum salute vestra.

30 "Animaequior esto, Hierusalem, exhortatur enim te qui te nominavit. 31 Nocentes peribunt qui te vexaverunt, et qui gratulati sunt in tua ruina punientur. 32 Civitates quibus servierunt filii tui punientur et quae accepit filios tuos. 33 Sicut enim gavisa est in tua ruina et laetata est in tuo casu, sic contristabitur in sua desolatione, 34 et amputabitur exultatio multitudinis eius, et gaudimonium eius erit in luctum. 35 Ignis enim superveniet ei ab Aeterno, in longiturnis diebus, et habitabitur a daemoniis in multitudine temporis.

36 "'Circumspice, Hierusalem, ad orientem, et vide iucunditatem a Deo tibi venientem. 37 Ecce enim veniunt filii tui quos dimisisti dispersos; veniunt collecti ab oriente usque ad occidentem in verbo Sancti gaudentes in honorem Dei.'"

saviour. 23 For I sent you forth with mourning and weeping, but the Lord will bring you back to me with joy and gladness for ever. 24 For as the neighbours of Zion have *now* seen your captivity from God, so shall they also shortly see your salvation from God, which shall come upon you with great honour and everlasting *glory.* 25 My children, suffer patiently the wrath that is come upon you, for thy enemy hath persecuted thee, but thou shalt quickly see his destruction and thou shalt get up upon his neck. 26 My delicate ones have walked rough ways, for they were taken away as a flock made a prey by the enemies. 27 Be of good comfort, my children, and cry to the Lord, for you shall be remembered by him that hath led you away. 28 For as it was your mind to go astray from God, so when you return again you shall seek him ten times as much, 29 for he that hath brought evils upon you shall bring you everlasting joy again with your salvation.

30 "Be of good heart, O Jerusalem, for he exhorteth thee that named thee. 31 The wicked that have afflicted thee shall perish, and they that have rejoiced at thy ruin shall be punished. 32 The cities which thy children have served shall be punished and she that received thy sons. 33 For as she rejoiced at thy ruin and was glad of thy fall, so shall she be grieved for her own desolation, 34 and the joy of her multitude shall be cut off, and her gladness shall be turned to mourning. 35 For fire shall come upon her from the Eternal, *long to endure,* and she shall be inhabited by devils for a great time.

36 "Look about thee, O Jerusalem, towards the east, and behold the joy that cometh to thee from God. 37 For behold: thy children come whom thou sentest away scattered; they come gathered together from the east even to the west at the word of the Holy One rejoicing for the honour of God.'"

Caput 5

Exue te, Hierusalem, stola luctus et vexationis tuae, et induce te decore et honore eius, quae a Deo tibi est, sempiternae gloriae. 2 Circumdabit te Deus deploide a Deo iustitiae et inponet mitram capiti tuo honoris aeterni, 3 Deus enim ostendet splendorem suum in te quod sub caelo est. 4 Nominabitur enim tibi nomen tuum a Deo in sempiternum: "Pax Iustitiae et Honor Pietatis." 5 Exsurge, Hierusalem, et sta in excelso, et circumspice ad orientem, et vide collectos filios tuos ab oriente sole usque ad occidentem in verbo Sancti, gaudentes Dei memoria. 6 Exierunt enim abs te pedibus ducti ab inimicis, adducet autem illos Dominus ad te sublatos in honorem sicut filios regni. 7 Constituit enim Deus humiliare omnem montem excelsum et rupes perennes et convalles replere in aequalitatem terrae ut ambulet Israhel diligenter in honorem Dei. 8 Obumbraverunt autem et silvae et omne lignum suavitatis Israhel mandato Dei, 9 adducet enim Deus Israhel cum iucunditate in lumine maiestatis suae cum misericordia et iustitia quae est ab ipso.

Chapter 5

Jerusalem is invited to rejoice and behold the return of her
children out of their captivity.

Put off, O Jerusalem, the garment of thy mourning and
affliction, and put on the beauty and honour of that everlasting glory which thou hast from God. 2 God will clothe
thee with the double garment of justice and will set a crown
on thy head of everlasting honour, 3 for God will shew his
brightness in thee *to every one* under heaven. 4 For thy name
shall be given thee by God for ever: "The Peace of Justice
and Honour of Piety." 5 Arise, O Jerusalem, and stand on
high, and look about towards the east, and behold thy children gathered together from the rising to the setting sun by
the word of the Holy One, rejoicing in the remembrance of
God. 6 For they went out from thee on foot and were led by
the enemies, but the Lord will bring them to thee exalted
with honour as children of the kingdom. 7 For God hath appointed to bring down every high mountain and the everlasting rocks and to fill up the valleys to make them even
with the ground that Israel may walk diligently to the honour of God. 8 Moreover the *woods* and every sweet-smelling
tree have overshadowed Israel by the commandment of
God, 9 for God will bring Israel with joy in the light of his
majesty with mercy and justice that cometh from him.

Caput 6

Exemplum epistulae quam misit Hieremias ad abducendos captivos in Babyloniam a rege Babyloniorum, ut nuntiaret illis secundum quod praeceptum est illi a Deo.

1 "Propter peccata quae peccastis ante Deum abducemini in Babyloniam captivi a Nabuchodonosor, rege Babylonum; 2 ingressi itaque in Babyloniam eritis illic annis plurimis et temporibus longis usque ad generationes septem, post hoc autem educam vos inde cum pace.

3 "Nunc autem videbitis in Babylonia deos aureos et argenteos et lapideos et ligneos in umeros portari, ostentantes metum Gentibus. 4 Videte ergo ne et vos similes efficiamini factis alienis et metuatis et metus vos capiat in ipsis. 5 Visa itaque turba de retro et ab ante adorantes, dicite in cordibus vestris, 'Te oportet adorari, Domine.' 6 Angelus enim meus vobiscum est, ipse autem exquiram animas vestras.

7 "Nam lingua ipsorum polita a fabro, ipsa etiam inaurata et inargentata, falsa sunt, et non possunt loqui. 8 Et sicut virgini amanti ornamenta, ita accepto auro fabricati sunt. 9 Coronas certe habent aureas super capita sua dii illorum, unde

Chapter 6

The epistle of Jeremiah to the captives as a preservative
against idolatry.

A copy of the epistle that Jeremiah sent to them that
were to be led away captives into Babylon by the king of
Babylon, to declare to them according to what was commanded him by God.

1 "For the sins that you have committed before God you
shall be carried away captives into Babylon by Nabuchodonosor, the king of Babylon, 2 *and* when you are come into
Babylon you shall be there many years and for a long *time,*
even to seven generations, and after that I will bring you
away from thence with peace.

3 "But now you shall see in Babylon gods of gold and of
silver and of stone and of wood born upon shoulders, causing fear to the Gentiles. 4 Beware therefore that *you* imitate
not the doings of others and be afraid and the fear of them
should seize upon you. 5 *But* when you see the multitude behind and before adoring them, say you in your hearts, 'Thou
oughtest to be adored, O Lord.' 6 For my angel is with you,
and I myself will demand an account of your souls.

7 "For their tongue that is polished by the craftsman and
themselves laid over with gold and silver are false things, and
they cannot speak. 8 And as if *it were* for a maiden that loveth
to go gay, so do they take gold and *make them up.* 9 Their gods
have golden crowns upon their heads, whereof the priests

subtrahunt sacerdotes ab eis aurum et argentum et erogant illud in semet ipsos. 10 Dant autem et ex ipso prostitutis et meretrices ornant, et iterum cum receperint illud a meretricibus, ornant deos suos.

11 "Hii autem non liberantur ab erugine et tinea, 12 opertis autem illis veste purpurea extergent faciem ipsorum propter pulverem domus qui est plurimus inter eos. 13 Sceptrum autem habet ut homo, sicut iudex regionis, qui in se peccantem non interficit. 14 Habet etiam gladium in manu et securem, se autem de bello et a latronibus non liberat, unde vobis notum sit quia non sunt dii. 15 Ne ergo timueritis eos.

"Sicut enim vas hominis confractum inutile efficitur, tales sunt et dii illorum. 16 Constitutis illis in domo, oculi eorum pleni sunt pulvere a pedibus introeuntium. 17 Et sicut alicui qui regem offendit circumseptae sunt ianuae aut sicut ad sepulchrum adductum mortuum, ita tutant sacerdotes ostia clusuris et seris ne a latronibus expolientur. 18 Lucernas accendunt illis et quidem multas, ex quibus nullam videre possunt, sunt autem sicut trabes in domo. 19 Corda vero eorum dicunt elingere serpentes qui de terra sunt, dum comedunt eos et vestimentum ipsorum, et non sentiunt. 20 Nigrae fiunt facies eorum a fumo qui in domo fit. 21 Supra corpus eorum et supra caput eorum volant noctuae et hirundines et aves etiam, similiter et cattae, 22 unde sciatis quia non sunt dii. Ne ergo timueritis eos.

23 "Aurum etiam quod habent ad speciem est; nisi aliquis exterserit eruginem, non fulgebunt, neque enim dum confla-

secretly convey away from them gold and silver and bestow it on themselves. 10 Yea and they give thereof to prostitutes and they dress out harlots, and again when they receive it of the harlots, they adorn their gods.

11 "And these *gods cannot defend themselves* from the rust and the moth, 12 but when they have covered them with a purple garment they wipe their face because of the dust of the house which is very much among them. 13 *This* holdeth a sceptre as a man, as a judge of the country, *but cannot* put to death one that offendeth him. 14 And *this* hath in his hand a sword *or* an ax, but cannot save himself from war *or* from robbers, whereby be it known to you that they are not gods. 15 Therefore fear them not.

"For as a vessel *that a man uses* when it is broken becometh useless, even so are their gods. 16 When they are placed in the house, their eyes are full of dust by the feet of them that go in. 17 And as the gates are made sure on every side upon one that hath offended the king or like a dead man carried to the grave, so do the priests secure the doors with bars and locks lest they be stripped by thieves. 18 They light candles to them and in great number, of which they cannot see one, but they are like beams in the house. 19 And they say that the creeping things which are of the earth gnaw their hearts, while they eat them and their garments, and they feel it not. 20 Their faces are black with the smoke that is made in the house. 21 Owls and swallows and *other birds* fly upon their bodies and upon their heads, and cats in like manner, 22 whereby you may know that they are no gods. Therefore fear them not.

23 "The gold also which they have is for shew, *but* except a man wipe off the rust, they will not shine, for neither when

rentur sentiebant. 24 Ex omni pretio empta sunt, in quibus spiritus non est in ipsis. 25 Sine pedibus in umeris portantur, ostentantes ignobilitatem suam hominibus. Confundantur etiam qui colunt ea. 26 Propterea si ceciderint in terram, a semet ipsis non surgent, neque si quis eum statuerit rectum per semet ipsum stabit, sed sicut mortuis munera eorum illis adponentur. 27 Hostias illorum sacerdotes ipsorum vendunt et abutuntur; similiter et mulieres eorum decerpentes neque infirmo neque mendicanti aliquid inpertiunt. 28 De sacrificiis eorum fetae et menstruatae contingunt. Scientes itaque ex his quia non sunt dii, ne timeatis eos.

29 "Unde enim vocantur dii? Quia mulieres adponunt diis argenteis et aureis et ligneis, 30 et in domibus eorum sacerdotes sedent, habentes tunicas scissas et capita et barbam rasam, quorum capita nuda sunt. 31 Rugiunt autem clamantes contra deos suos sicut in cena mortui. 32 Vestimenta eorum auferunt sacerdotes et vestiunt uxores suas et filios suos. 33 Neque si quid mali patiuntur ab aliquo neque si quid boni, poterunt retribuere, neque regem constituere possunt neque auferre. 34 Similiter neque divitias dare possunt neque malum retribuere. Si quis illis votum voverit et non reddiderit, nec hoc requirunt. 35 Hominem a morte non liberant neque infirmum a potentiore eripiunt. 36 Hominem caecum ad visum non restituunt; de necessitate hominem non liberabunt. 37 Viduae non miserebuntur neque orfanis benefacient. 38 Lapidibus de monte similes sunt dii illorum lignei

they were molten did they feel it. 24 Men buy them at *a high* price, whereas there is no breath in them. 25 And having not *the use of* feet they are carried upon shoulders, declaring to men *how vile they are.* Be they confounded also that worship them. 26 Therefore if they fall to the ground, they rise not up *again* of themselves, nor if a man set them upright will they stand by themselves, but their gifts shall be set before them as to the dead. 27 The things that are sacrificed to them their priests sell and abuse; in like manner also their wives take part of them *but* give nothing of it either to the sick or to the *poor.* 28 The childbearing and menstruous women touch their sacrifices. Knowing therefore by these things that they are not gods, fear them not.

29 "For *how can* they *be* called gods? Because women set offerings before the gods of silver and of gold and of wood, 30 and priests sit in their *temples,* having their garments rent and their heads and beards shaven, *and nothing upon* their heads. 31 And they roar and cry before their gods as *men do* at the feast *when one is* dead. 32 The priests *also* take away their garments and clothe their wives and their children. 33 *And whether it be evil that one doth unto them or good,* they *are* not able to recompense it, neither can they set up a king nor put him down. 34 In like manner they can neither give riches nor requite evil. If a man make a vow to them and perform it not, they cannot require it. 35 They *cannot* deliver a man from death nor save the weak from the *mighty.* 36 They *cannot* restore the blind man to his sight *nor deliver* a man from *distress.* 37 They shall not pity the widow nor do good to the fatherless. 38 Their gods of wood and of stone and of gold and

et lapidei et aurei et argentei, qui autem colunt illa confundentur. 39 Quomodo ergo aestimandum est aut dicendum illos esse deos?

40 "Adhuc enim ipsis Chaldeis non honorantibus ea, qui cum audierint mutum non posse loqui, offerunt illud ad Bel, postulantes ab eo loqui, 41 quasi possint sentire qui non habent motum, et ipsi, cum intellexerint, relinquent ea, sensum enim non habent ipsi dii illorum. 42 Mulieres autem circumdatae funibus in viis sedent, succendentes ossa olivarum, 43 cum autem aliqua ex ipsis, adtracta ab aliquo transeunte, dormierit cum eo, proximae suae exprobrat quod ea non sit digna habita sicut ipsa neque funis eius disruptus sit. 44 Omnia autem quae illis fiunt falsa sunt. Quomodo ergo aestimandum aut dicendum est esse illos deos?

45 "A fabris autem et ab aurificibus facta sunt. Nihil aliud erunt nisi id quod volunt esse sacerdotes, 46 artifices ipsi etiam qui ea faciunt non sunt multi temporis. Numquid ergo possunt ea quae ab ipsis fabricata sunt esse dii? 47 Reliquerunt autem falsa et obprobrium postea futuris, 48 nam cum supervenerit illis proelium et mala, cogitant sacerdotes apud se ubi se abscondant cum illis. 49 Quomodo ergo sentiri debeant quoniam dii sunt, qui nec de bello se liberant neque de malis se eripiunt? 50 Nam cum sint lignea et inaurata et inargentata, scietur postea quia falsa sunt ab gentibus universis et regibus, quae manifestata sunt quia non sunt dii, sed opera manuum hominum, et nullum opus Dei cum illis.

of silver are like the stones *that are hewn* out of the mountains, and they that worship them shall be confounded. 39 How then is it to be supposed or to be said that they are gods?

40 "Even the Chaldeans themselves dishonour them, who when they hear of one dumb that cannot speak, they present *him* to Bel, entreating him that he may speak, 41 as though they could be sensible that have no motion themselves, and they, when they shall perceive this, will leave them, for their gods themselves have no sense. 42 The women also with cords about them sit in the ways, burning olivestones, 43 and when any one of them, drawn away by some passenger, lieth with him, she upbraideth her neighbour that she was not thought *as* worthy as herself nor her cord broken. 44 But all things that are done about them are false. How is it then to be thought or to be said that they are gods?

45 "And they are made by workmen and by goldsmiths. They shall be nothing else but what the priests will have them to be, 46 for the artificers themselves that make them are of no long continuance. Can those things then that are made by them be gods? 47 But they have left false things and reproach to them that come after, 48 for when war cometh upon them *or* evils, the priests consult with themselves where they may hide themselves with them. 49 How then can they be thought to be gods, that *can* neither deliver themselves from war nor save themselves from evils? 50 For seeing they are *but* of wood and laid over with gold and with silver, it shall be known hereafter that they are false things by all nations and kings, and *it shall be* manifest that they are no gods, but the work of men's hands, and that there is no work of God in them.

51 "Unde ergo notum est quia non sunt dii, sed opera manuum hominum, et nullum Dei opus in ipsis est? 52 Regem regioni non suscitant neque pluviam hominibus dabunt. 53 Iudicium quoque non discernent neque regiones liberabunt ab iniuria quia nihil possunt sicut corniculae inter medium caeli et terrae. 54 Etenim cum inciderit ignis in domum deorum ligneorum et aureorum et argenteorum, sacerdotes quidem ipsorum fugient et liberabuntur, ipsi vero sicut trabes in medio conburentur. 55 Regi autem et bello non resistent. Quomodo ergo aestimandum est aut recipiendum quia dii sunt?

56 "Non a furibus neque a latronibus se liberabunt dii lignei et lapidei et inaurati et inargentati; quibus iniqui fortiores sunt 57 aurum et argentum et vestimentum quo operti sunt auferent illis et abibunt, nec sibi auxilium ferent.

58 "Itaque melius est esse regem ostentantem virtutem suam aut vas in domo utile in quo gloriabitur qui possidet illud vel ostium in domo quod custodit quae in ipsa sunt quam falsi dii. 59 Sol quidem et luna ac sidera, cum sint splendida et emissa ad utilitates, obaudiunt. 60 Similiter et fulgur cum apparuerit perspicuum est, id ipsum autem et spiritus in omni regione spirat. 61 Et nubes, quibus cum imperatum fuerit a Deo perambulare universum orbem, perficiunt quod imperatum est eis. 62 Ignis etiam missus desuper ut consumat montes et silvas facit quod praeceptum est ei. Haec autem neque speciebus neque virtutibus uni eorum similia sunt. 63 Unde neque aestimandum est neque dicendum esse illos deos, quando non possunt neque iudicium iudicare

51 "Whence therefore is it known that they are not gods, but the work of men's hands, and no work of God is in them? 52 They *cannot* set up a king over the land nor give rain to men. 53 They *determine no causes* nor *deliver* any countries from oppression because they can do nothing *and are* as daws between heaven and earth. 54 For when fire shall fall upon the house of *these* gods of wood and of silver and of gold, their priests indeed will flee away and be saved, but they themselves shall be burnt *asunder* like beams. 55 And they *cannot* withstand a king and war. How then *can* it be supposed or admitted that they are gods?

56 *"Neither are these* gods of wood and of stone and laid over with gold and with silver *able to* deliver themselves from thieves or robbers, *but they that* are stronger than them 57 shall take from them the gold and silver and the raiment wherewith they are clothed and shall go their way, neither shall they help themselves.

58 "Therefore it is better to be a king that sheweth his power or else a profitable vessel in the house with which the owner thereof will *be well satisfied* or a door in the house to keep things safe that are therein than *such* false gods. 59 The *sun* and the moon and the stars, being bright and sent forth for profitable uses, are obedient. 60 In like manner *the* lightning when it *breaketh forth* is easy to be seen, and after the same manner the *wind* bloweth in every country. 61 And the clouds, when God commandeth them to go over the whole world, do as they are bidden. 62 The fire also, being sent from above to consume mountains and woods, doth as it is commanded. But these neither in shew nor in power are like to any one of them. 63 Wherefore it is neither to be thought nor to be said that they are gods, since they are neither able

neque benefacere hominibus. 64 Scientes itaque quia non sunt dii, ne ergo timueritis eos.

65 "Neque enim regibus maledicent neque benedicent. 66 Signa etiam in caelo gentibus non ostendunt neque ut sol lucebunt neque inluminabunt ut luna. 67 Bestiae meliores sunt illis, quae possunt fugere sub tectum ac prodesse sibi. 68 Nullo itaque modo nobis est manifestum quia sunt dii, propter quod ne timeatis eos.

69 "Nam sicut in cucumerario formido nihil custodit, ita sunt dii illorum lignei et argentei et inaurati. 70 Eodem modo et in horto spina alba supra quam omnis avis sedet. Similiter et mortuo proiecto in tenebris similes sunt dii illorum lignei et inaurati et inargentati. 71 A purpura quoque et murice quae supra illos tineant scietis quia non sunt dii. Ipsi etiam postremo comeduntur et erunt obprobrium in regione. 72 Melior est homo iustus qui non habet simulacra, nam erit longe ab obprobriis."

to judge *causes* nor to do any *good* to men. 64 Knowing therefore that they are not gods, *fear* them not.

65 "For neither *can* they curse kings nor bless them. 66 Neither do they shew signs in the heaven to the nations nor *shine* as the sun nor *give light* as the moon. 67 Beasts are better than they, which can fly under a covert and help themselves. 68 Therefore there is *no manner of appearance* that they are gods, so fear them not.

69 "For as a scarecrow in a garden of cucumbers keepeth nothing, so are their gods of wood and of silver and laid over with gold. 70 *They are no better than* a white thorn in a garden upon which every bird sitteth. In like manner also their gods of wood and laid over with gold and with silver are like to a dead body cast forth in the dark. 71 By the purple also and the scarlet which are moth-eaten upon them you shall know that they are not gods. And they themselves at last are consumed and shall be a reproach in the country. 72 Better therefore is the just man that hath no idols, for he shall be far from reproach."

EZEKIEL

Caput I

Et factum est in tricesimo anno, in quarto mense, in quinta mensis, cum essem in medio captivorum iuxta fluvium Chobar, aperti sunt caeli, et vidi visiones Dei. 2 In quinta mensis (ipse est annus quintus transmigrationis Regis Ioachin) 3 factum est verbum Domini ad Hiezechielem, filium Buzi, sacerdotem, in terra Chaldeorum secus flumen Chobar, et facta est super eum ibi manus Domini.

4 Et vidi, et ecce: ventus turbinis veniebat ab aquilone et nubes magna et ignis involvens, et splendor in circuitu eius, et de medio eius quasi species electri, id est, de medio ignis, 5 et ex medio eorum similitudo quattuor animalium, et hic aspectus eorum. Similitudo hominis in eis. 6 Quattuor facies uni, et quattuor pinnae uni. 7 Pedes eorum pedes recti, et planta pedis eorum quasi planta pedis vituli, et scintillae quasi aspectus aeris candentis. 8 Et manus hominis sub pinnis eorum in quattuor partibus, et facies et pinnas per quattuor partes habebant, 9 iunctaeque erant pinnae eorum

Chapter 1

The time of Ezekiel's prophecy. He sees a glorious vision.

Now it came to pass in the thirtieth year, in the fourth month, on the fifth day of the month, when I was in the midst of the captives by the river Chebar, the heavens were opened, and I saw the visions of God. 2 On the fifth day of the month (the same was the fifth year of the captivity of King Jehoiachin) 3 the word of the Lord came to Ezekiel, the priest, the son of Buzi, in the land of the Chaldeans by the river Chebar, and the hand of the Lord was there upon him.

4 And I saw, and behold: a whirlwind came out of the north and a great cloud and a fire infolding *it,* and brightness was about it, and out of the midst thereof, that is, out of the midst of the fire, as it were the resemblance of amber, 5 and *in* the midst thereof the likeness of four living creatures, and this was their appearance. There was the likeness of a man in them. 6 *Every* one had four faces, and *every* one four wings. 7 Their feet were straight feet, and the sole of their foot was like the sole of a calf's foot, and *they sparkled* like the appearance of glowing brass. 8 And they had the hands of a man under their wings on their four sides, and they had faces and wings on the four sides, 9 and the wings of one were joined

alterius ad alterum. Non revertebantur cum incederent, sed unumquodque ante faciem suam gradiebatur. 10 Similitudo autem vultus eorum, facies hominis et facies leonis a dextris ipsorum quattuor, facies autem bovis a sinistris ipsorum quattuor, et facies aquilae desuper ipsorum quattuor. 11 Et facies eorum et pinnae eorum extentae desuper; duae pinnae singulorum iungebantur, et duae tegebant corpora eorum, 12 et unumquodque eorum coram facie sua ambulabat; ubi erat impetus spiritus, illuc gradiebantur, nec revertebantur cum ambularent. 13 Et similitudo animalium, aspectus eorum quasi carbonum ignis ardentium et quasi aspectus lampadarum. Haec erat visio discurrens in medio animalium: splendor ignis et de igne fulgor egrediens. 14 Et animalia ibant et revertebantur in similitudinem fulguris coruscantis.

15 Cumque aspicerem animalia apparuit rota una super terram iuxta animalia habens quattuor facies. 16 Et aspectus rotarum et opus earum quasi visio maris, et una similitudo ipsarum quattuor, et aspectus earum et opera quasi sit rota in medio rotae. 17 Per quattuor partes earum euntes ibant, et non revertebantur cum ambularent. 18 Statura quoque erat rotis et altitudo et horribilis aspectus, et totum corpus plenum oculis in circuitu ipsarum quattuor. 19 Cumque ambularent animalia ambulabant pariter et rotae iuxta ea, et cum elevarentur animalia de terra elevabantur simul et rotae. 20 Quocumque ibat spiritus, illuc eunte spiritu et rotae pariter levabantur sequentes eum, spiritus enim vitae erat in ro-

to the wings of another. They turned not when they went, but every one went straight forward. 10 And as for the likeness of their faces, there was the face of a man and the face of a lion on the right side of all the four, and the face of an ox on the left side of all the four, and the face of an eagle over all the four. 11 And their faces and their wings were stretched upward; two wings of every one were joined, and two covered their bodies, 12 and every one of them went straight forward; whither the impulse of the spirit was *to go,* thither they went, and they turned not when they went. 13 And as for the likeness of the living creatures, their appearance was like that of burning coals of fire and like the appearance of lamps. This was the vision running to and fro in the midst of the living creatures: a bright fire and lightning going forth from the fire. 14 And the living creatures ran and returned like flashes of lightning.

15 Now as I beheld the living creatures there appeared upon the earth by the living creatures one wheel with four faces. 16 And the appearance of the wheels and the work of them was like the appearance of the sea, and the four had all one likeness, and their appearance and their work was as it were a wheel in the midst of a wheel. 17 When they went they went by their four parts, and they turned not when they went. 18 The wheels had also a size and a height and a dreadful appearance, and the whole body was full of eyes round about all the four. 19 And when the living creatures went the wheels also went together by them, and when the living creatures were lifted up from the earth the wheels also were lifted up with them. 20 Whithersoever the spirit went, thither as the spirit went the wheels also were lifted up withal and followed it, for the spirit of life was in the wheels.

tis. 21 Cum euntibus ibant, et cum stantibus stabant, et cum elevatis a terra pariter elevabantur et rotae sequentes ea, quia spiritus vitae erat in rotis.

22 Et similitudo super capita animalium firmamenti, quasi aspectus cristalli horribilis et extenti super capita eorum desuper. 23 Sub firmamento autem pinnae eorum rectae, alterius ad alterum; unumquodque duabus alis velabat corpus suum, et alterum similiter velabatur. 24 Et audiebam sonum alarum quasi sonum aquarum multarum, quasi sonum sublimis Dei; cum ambularent quasi sonus erat multitudinis, ut sonus castrorum, cumque starent demittebantur pinnae eorum. 25 Nam cum fieret vox supra firmamentum quod erat super caput eorum, stabant et submittebant alas suas.

26 Et super firmamentum quod erat inminens capiti eorum quasi aspectus lapidis sapphyri similitudo throni, et super similitudinem throni similitudo quasi aspectus hominis desuper. 27 Et vidi quasi speciem electri velut aspectum ignis intrinsecus eius per circuitum; a lumbis eius et desuper et a lumbis eius usque deorsum vidi quasi speciem ignis splendentis in circuitu. 28 Velut aspectum arcus cum fuerit in nube in die pluviae, hic erat aspectus splendoris per gyrum.

21 When *those* went *these* went, and when *those* stood *these* stood, and when *those* were lifted up from the earth the wheels also were lifted up together and followed them, for the spirit of life was in the wheels.

22 And over the heads of the living creatures was the likeness of the firmament, as the appearance of crystal terrible *to behold* and stretched out over their heads above. 23 And under the firmament were their wings straight, the one toward the other; every one with two wings covered his body, and the other was covered in like manner. 24 And I heard the noise of their wings like the noise of many waters, as it were the voice of the *most* high God; when they walked it was like the voice of a multitude, like the noise of an army, and when they stood their wings were let down. 25 For when a voice came from above the firmament that was over their heads, they stood and let down their wings.

26 And above the firmament that was over their heads was the likeness of a throne as the appearance of the sapphire stone, and upon the likeness of the throne was a likeness as of the appearance of a man above upon it. 27 And I saw as it were the resemblance of amber as the appearance of fire within it round about; from his loins and upward and from his loins downward I saw as it were the resemblance of fire shining round about. 28 As the appearance of the rainbow when it is in a cloud on a rainy day, this was the appearance of the brightness round about.

Caput 2

Haec visio similitudinis gloriae Domini. Et vidi, et cecidi in faciem meam, et audivi vocem loquentis. Et dixit ad me, "Fili hominis, sta supra pedes tuos, et loquar tecum." 2 Et ingressus est in me spiritus postquam locutus est mihi, et statuit me supra pedes meos, et audivi loquentem ad me 3 et dicentem, "Fili hominis, mitto ego te ad filios Israhel, ad gentes apostatrices quae recesserunt a me; ipsi et patres eorum praevaricati sunt pactum meum usque ad diem hanc. 4 Et filii dura facie et indomabili corde sunt ad quos ego mitto te, et dices ad eos, 'Haec dicit Dominus Deus,' 5 si forte vel ipsi audiant et si forte quiescant, quoniam domus exasperans est, et scient quia propheta fuerit in medio eorum.

6 "Tu ergo, fili hominis, ne timeas eos, neque sermones eorum metuas, quoniam increduli et subversores sunt tecum et cum scorpionibus habitas. Verba eorum ne timeas, et vultus eorum ne formides, quia domus exasperans est. 7 Loqueris ergo verba mea ad eos, si forte audiant et quiescant, quoniam inritatores sunt.

8 "Tu autem, fili hominis, audi quaecumque loquor ad te, et noli esse exasperans sicut domus exasperatrix est; aperi os tuum, et comede quaecumque ego do tibi."

Chapter 2

The prophet receives his commission.

This was the vision of the likeness of the glory of the Lord. And I saw, and I fell upon my face, and I heard the voice of one that spoke. And he said to me, "Son of man, stand upon thy feet, and I will speak to thee." 2 And the spirit entered into me after that he spoke to me, and he set me upon my feet, and I heard him speaking to me 3 and saying, "Son of man, I send thee to the children of Israel, to a rebellious people that hath revolted from me; they and their fathers have transgressed my covenant even unto this day. 4 And they to whom I send thee are children of a hard face and of an obstinate heart, and thou shalt say to them, 'Thus saith the Lord God,' 5 if so be they at least will hear and if so be they will forbear, for they are a provoking house, and they shall know that there hath been a prophet in the midst of them.

6 "And thou, O son of man, fear not, neither be thou afraid of their words, for thou art among unbelievers and destroyers and thou dwellest with scorpions. Fear not their words, neither be thou dismayed at their looks, for they are a provoking house. 7 And thou shalt speak my words to them, if perhaps they will hear and forbear, for they provoke me to anger.

8 "But thou, O son of man, hear all that I say to thee, and do not thou provoke me as that house provoketh me; open thy mouth, and eat what I give thee."

9 Et vidi, et ecce: manus missa ad me in qua erat involutus liber, et expandit illum coram me, qui erat scriptus intus et foris, et scriptae erant in eo lamentationes et carmen et vae.

Caput 3

Et dixit ad me, "Fili hominis, quodcumque inveneris comede; comede volumen istud, et vadens loquere ad filios Israhel." 2 Et aperui os meum, et cibavit me volumine illo, 3 et dixit ad me, "Fili hominis, venter tuus comedet et viscera tua conplebuntur volumine isto quod ego do tibi." Et comedi illud, et factum est in ore meo sicut mel dulce.

4 Et dixit ad me, "Fili hominis, vade ad domum Israhel, et loqueris verba mea ad eos. 5 Non enim ad populum profundi sermonis et ignotae linguae tu mitteris, ad domum Israhel, 6 neque ad populos multos profundi sermonis et ignotae linguae quorum non possis audire sermones. Et si ad illos mittereris, ipsi audirent te. 7 Domus autem Israhel nolent audire te quia nolunt audire me, omnis quippe domus Israhel ad-

9 And I looked, and behold: a hand was sent to me wherein was a book rolled up, and he spread it before me, and it was written within and without, and there were written in it lamentations and canticles and woe.

Chapter 3

The prophet eats the book and receives further instructions. The office of a watchman.

And he said to me, "Son of man, eat all that thou shalt find; eat this book, and go speak to the children of Israel." 2 And I opened my mouth, and he caused me to eat that book, 3 and he said to me, "Son of man, thy belly shall eat and thy bowels shall be filled with this book which I give thee." And I did eat it, and it was sweet as honey in my mouth.

4 And he said to me, "Son of man, go to the house of Israel, and thou shalt speak my words to them. 5 For thou art not sent to a people of a profound speech and of an unknown tongue, *but* to the house of Israel, 6 nor to many nations of a strange speech and of an unknown tongue whose words thou canst not understand. And if thou wert sent to them, they would hearken to thee. 7 But the house of Israel will not hearken to thee because they will not hearken to me, for all the house of Israel are of a hard forehead and an obstinate

trita fronte est et duro corde. 8 Ecce: dedi faciem tuam valentiorem faciebus eorum et frontem tuam duriorem frontibus eorum. 9 Ut adamantem et ut silicem dedi faciem tuam; ne timeas eos, neque metuas a facie eorum, quia domus exasperans est."

10 Et dixit ad me, "Fili hominis, omnes sermones meos quos loquor ad te adsume in corde tuo, et auribus tuis audi. 11 Et vade; ingredere ad transmigrationem, ad filios populi tui, et loqueris ad eos et dices eis, 'Haec dicit Dominus Deus,' si forte audiant et quiescant."

12 Et adsumpsit me spiritus, et audivi post me vocem commotionis magnae: "Benedicta gloria Domini de loco suo," 13 et vocem alarum animalium percutientium altera ad alteram et vocem rotarum sequentium animalia et vocem commotionis magnae. 14 Spiritus quoque levavit me et adsumpsit me, et abii amarus in indignatione spiritus mei, manus enim Domini erat mecum, confortans me. 15 Et veni ad transmigrationem, ad acervum novarum frugum, ad eos qui habitabant iuxta flumen Chobar, et sedi ubi illi sedebant, et mansi ibi septem diebus maerens in medio eorum.

16 Cum autem pertransitssent septem dies, factum est verbum Domini ad me, dicens, 17 "Fili hominis, speculatorem dedi te domui Israhel, et audies de ore meo verbum et adnuntiabis eis ex me. 18 Si dicente me ad impium, 'Morte morieris,' non adnuntiaveris ei neque locutus fueris ut avertatur a via sua impia et vivat, ipse impius in iniquitate sua morietur, sanguinem autem eius de manu tua requiram. 19 Si

heart. 8 Behold: I have made thy face stronger than their faces and thy forehead harder than their foreheads. 9 I have made thy face like an adamant and like flint; fear them not, neither be thou dismayed at their presence, for they are a provoking house."

10 And he said to me, "Son of man, receive in thy heart, and hear with thy ears all the words that I speak to thee, 11 And go; get thee in to them of the captivity, to the children of thy people, and thou shalt speak to them and shalt say to them, 'Thus saith the *Lord,*' if so be they will hear and will forbear."

12 And the spirit took me up, and I heard behind me the voice of a great commotion, *saying,* "Blessed be the glory of the Lord from his place," 13 and the noise of the wings of the living creatures striking one against another and the noise of the wheels following the living creatures and the noise of a great commotion. 14 The spirit also lifted me and took me up, and I went away in bitterness in the indignation of my spirit, for the hand of the Lord was with me, strengthening me. 15 And I came to them of the captivity, to the heap of new corn, to them that dwelt by the river Chebar, and I sat where they sat, and I remained there seven days mourning in the midst of them.

16 And *at the end of* seven days the word of the Lord came to me, saying, 17 "Son of man, I have made thee a watchman to the house of Israel, and thou shalt hear the word out of my mouth and shalt tell it them from me. 18 If when I say to the wicked, 'Thou shalt surely die,' thou declare it not to him nor speak to him that he may be converted from his wicked way and live, the same wicked man shall die in his iniquity, but I will require his blood at thy hand. 19 But if

autem tu adnuntiaveris impio et ille non fuerit conversus ab impietate sua et a via sua impia, ipse quidem in iniquitate sua morietur, tu autem animam tuam liberasti. 20 Sed et si conversus iustus a iustitia sua fuerit et fecerit iniquitatem, ponam offendiculum coram eo. Ipse morietur quia non adnuntiasti ei; in peccato suo morietur, et non erunt in memoria iustitiae eius quas fecit, sanguinem vero eius de manu tua requiram. 21 Si autem tu adnuntiaveris iusto ut non peccet iustus et ille non peccaverit, vivens vivet quia adnuntiasti ei et tu animam tuam liberasti."

22 Et facta est super me manus Domini, et dixit ad me, "Surgens egredere in campum, et ibi loquar tecum." 23 Et surgens egressus sum in campum, et ecce: ibi gloria Domini stabat quasi gloria quam vidi iuxta fluvium Chobar, et cecidi in faciem meam.

24 Et ingressus est in me spiritus et statuit me super pedes meos, et locutus est mihi et dixit ad me, "Ingredere, et includere in medio domus tuae. 25 Et tu, fili hominis, ecce: data sunt super te vincula, et ligabunt te in eis, et non egredieris de medio eorum. 26 Et linguam tuam adherescere faciam palato tuo, et eris mutus nec quasi vir obiurgans, quia domus exasperans est. 27 Cum autem locutus fuero tibi, aperiam os tuum, et dices ad eos, 'Haec dicit Dominus Deus: "Qui audit, audiat, et qui quiescit, quiescat, quia domus exasperans est."'"

thou give warning to the wicked and he be not converted from his wickedness and from his evil way, he indeed shall die in his iniquity, but thou hast delivered thy soul. 20 Moreover if the just man shall turn away from his justice and shall commit iniquity, I will lay a stumbling block before him. He shall die because thou hast not given him warning; he shall die in his sin, and his justices which he hath done shall not be remembered, but I will require his blood at thy hand. 21 But if thou warn the just man that the just may not sin and he doth not sin, living he shall live because thou hast warned him and thou hast delivered thy soul."

22 And the hand of the Lord was upon me, and he said to me, "Rise, and go forth into the plain, and there I will speak to thee." 23 And I rose up and went forth into the plain, and behold: the glory of the Lord stood there like the glory which I saw by the river Chebar, and I fell upon my face.

24 And the spirit entered into me and set me upon my feet, and he spoke to me and said to me, "Go in, and shut thyself up in the midst of thy house. 25 And thou, O son of man, behold: they shall put bands upon thee, and they shall bind thee with them, and thou shalt not go forth from the midst of them. 26 And I will make thy tongue stick fast to the roof of thy mouth, and thou shalt be dumb and not as a man that reproveth, because they are a provoking house. 27 But when I shall speak to thee, I will open thy mouth, and thou shalt say to them, 'Thus saith the Lord God: "He that heareth, let him hear, and he that forbeareth, let him forbear, for they are a provoking house."'"

Caput 4

"Et tu, fili hominis, sume tibi laterem, et pones eum coram te, et describes in eo civitatem Hierusalem. 2 Et ordina-
bis adversus eam obsidionem, et aedificabis munitiones, et
conportabis aggerem, et dabis contra eam castra, et pones
arietes in gyro. 3 Et tu sume tibi sartaginem ferream, et pones eam in murum ferreum inter te et inter civitatem, et
obfirmabis faciem tuam ad eam, et erit in obsidionem, et
circumdabis eam; signum est domui Israhel.

4 "Et tu dormies super latus tuum sinistrum et pones iniquitates domus Israhel super eo numero dierum quibus dormies super illud, et adsumes iniquitatem eorum. 5 Ego autem dedi tibi annos iniquitatis eorum numero dierum,
trecentos et nonaginta dies, et portabis iniquitatem domus
Israhel. 6 Et cum conpleveris haec, dormies super latus tuum
dextrum secundo, et adsumes iniquitatem domus Iuda quadraginta diebus; diem pro anno, diem, inquam, pro anno
dedi tibi. 7 Et ad obsidionem Hierusalem convertes faciem
tuam, et brachium tuum erit exertum, et prophetabis adversus eam. 8 Ecce: circumdedi te vinculis, et non te convertes a
latere tuo in latus aliud donec conpleas dies obsidionis tuae.

Chapter 4

A prophetic description of the siege of Jerusalem and the famine that shall reign there.

"And thou, O son of man, take thee a tile, and *lay* it before thee, and *draw* upon it *the plan of* the city of Jerusalem. 2 And *lay* siege against it, and *build* forts, and *cast* up a mount, and *set* a camp against it, and *place* battering rams round about it. 3 And take unto thee an iron pan, and *set* it for a wall of iron between thee and the city, and *set* thy face resolutely against it, and it shall be besieged, and thou shalt lay siege against it; it is a sign to the house of Israel.

4 "And thou shalt sleep upon thy left side and shalt lay the iniquities of the house of Israel upon it according to the number of the days that thou shalt sleep upon it, and thou shalt take upon thee their iniquity. 5 And I have laid upon thee the years of their iniquity according to the number of the days, three hundred and ninety days, and thou shalt bear the iniquity of the house of Israel. 6 And when thou hast accomplished this, thou shalt sleep again upon thy right side, and thou shalt take upon thee the iniquity of the house of Judah forty days; a day for a year, yea, a day for a year I have appointed to thee. 7 And thou shalt turn thy face to the siege of Jerusalem, and thy arm shall be stretched out, and thou shalt prophesy against it. 8 Behold: I have encompassed thee with bands, and thou shalt not turn thyself from one side to the other till thou hast ended the days of thy siege.

9 "Et tu sume tibi frumentum et hordeum et fabam et lentem et milium et viciam, et mittes ea in vas unum, et facies tibi panes numero dierum quibus dormies super latus tuum; trecentis et nonaginta diebus comedes illud. 10 Cibus autem tuus quo vesceris erit in pondere viginti stateres in die; a tempore usque ad tempus comedes illud. 11 Et aquam in mensura bibes, sextam partem hin; a tempore usque ad tempus bibes illud, 12 et quasi subcinericium hordiacium comedes illud, et stercore quod egreditur de homine operies illud in oculis eorum." 13 Et dixit Dominus, "Sic comedent filii Israhel panem suum pollutum inter gentes ad quas eiciam eos."

14 Et dixi, "Ha, ha, ha, Domine Deus, ecce: anima mea non est polluta, et morticinum et laceratum a bestiis non comedi ab infantia mea usque nunc, et non est ingressa in os meum omnis caro inmunda."

15 Et dixit ad me, "Ecce: dedi tibi fimum boum pro stercoribus humanis, et facies panem tuum in eo."

16 Et dixit ad me, "Fili hominis, ecce: ego conteram baculum panis in Hierusalem, et comedent panem in pondere et in sollicitudine, et aquam in mensura et in angustia bibent, 17 ut deficientibus pane et aqua corruat unusquisque ad fratrem suum et contabescant in iniquitatibus suis."

9 "And take to thee wheat and barley and beans and lentils and millet and fitches, and put them in one vessel, and make thee bread thereof according to the number of the days that thou shalt lie upon thy side; three hundred and ninety days shalt thou eat thereof. 10 And thy meat that thou shalt eat shall be in weight twenty staters a day; from time to time thou shalt eat it. 11 And thou shalt drink water by measure, the sixth part of a hin; from time to time thou shalt drink it, 12 and thou shalt eat it as barley bread baked under the ashes, and thou shalt cover it in their sight with the dung that cometh out of a man." 13 And the Lord said, "So shall the children of Israel eat their bread all filthy among the nations whither I will cast them out."

14 And I said, "Ah, ah, ah, O Lord God, behold: my soul hath not been defiled, and from my infancy even till now I have not eaten any thing that died of itself *or* was torn by beasts, and no unclean flesh hath entered into my mouth."

15 And he said to me, "Behold: I have given thee neat's dung for man's dung, and thou shalt make thy bread therewith."

16 And he said to me, "Son of man, behold: I will break in pieces the staff of bread in Jerusalem, and they shall eat bread by weight and with care, and they shall drink water by measure and in distress, 17 so that when bread and water fail every man may fall against his brother and they may pine away in their iniquities."

Caput 5

"Et tu, fili hominis, sume tibi gladium acutum radentem pilos, et adsumes eum, et duces per caput tuum et per barbam tuam, et adsumes tibi stateram ponderis, et divides eos. 2 Tertiam partem igni conbures in medio civitatis iuxta conpletionem dierum obsidionis, et adsumes tertiam partem et concides gladio in circuitu eius, tertiam vero aliam disperges in ventum, et gladium nudabo post eos. 3 Et sumes inde parvum numerum et ligabis eos in summitate pallii tui. 4 Et ex eis rursum tolles et proicies eos in medio ignis et conbures eos igni, et ex eo egredietur ignis in omnem domum Israhel."

5 Haec dicit Dominus Deus: "Ista est Hierusalem; in medio gentium posui eam et in circuitu eius terras. 6 Et contempsit iudicia mea ut plus esset impia quam Gentes, et praecepta mea ultra quam terrae quae in circuitu eius sunt, iudicia enim mea proiecerunt et in praeceptis meis non ambulaverunt." 7 Idcirco haec dicit Dominus Deus: "Quia superastis Gentes quae in circuitu vestro sunt et in praeceptis meis non ambulastis et iudicia mea non fecistis et iuxta iudicia gentium quae in circuitu vestro sunt non estis

Chapter 5

The judgments of God upon the Jews are foreshewn under the type of the prophet's hair.

"And thou, son of man, take thee a sharp knife that shaveth the hair, *and cause* it to pass over thy head and over thy beard, and *take* thee a balance to weigh in, and *divide the hair.* 2 A third part thou shalt burn with fire in the midst of the city according to the fulfilling of the days of the siege, and thou shalt take a third part and cut it in pieces with the knife all round about, and the other third part thou shalt scatter in the wind, and I will draw out the sword after them. 3 And thou shalt take thereof a small number and shalt bind them in the skirt of thy cloak. 4 And thou shalt take of them again and shalt cast them in the midst of the fire and shalt burn them with fire, and out of it shall come forth a fire into all the house of Israel."

5 Thus saith the Lord God: "This is Jerusalem; I have set her in the midst of the nations and the countries round about her. 6 And she hath despised my judgments so as to be more wicked than the Gentiles, and my commandments more than the countries that are round about her, for they have cast off my judgments and have not walked in my commandments." 7 Therefore thus saith the Lord God: "Because you have surpassed the Gentiles that are round about you and have not walked in my commandments and have not kept my judgments and have not done according to the judg-

operati, 8 ideo haec dicit Dominus Deus: 'Ecce: ego ad te, et ipse ego faciam in medio tui iudicia in oculis Gentium. 9 Et faciam in te quae non feci et quibus similia ultra non faciam propter omnes abominationes tuas. 10 Ideo patres comedent filios in medio tui, et filii comedent patres suos, et faciam in te iudicia, et ventilabo universas reliquias tuas in omnem ventum. 11 Idcirco vivo ego,' dicit Dominus Deus, 'nisi pro eo quod sanctum meum violasti in omnibus offensionibus tuis et in omnibus abominationibus tuis, ego quoque confringam, et non parcet oculus meus, et non miserebor. 12 Tertia tui pars peste morietur et fame consumetur in medio tui, et tertia tui pars gladio cadet in circuitu tuo, tertiam vero partem tuam in omnem ventum dispergam, et gladium evaginabo post eos. 13 Et conplebo furorem meum et requiescere faciam indignationem meam in eis, et consolabor, et scient quia ego, Dominus, locutus sum in zelo meo cum implevero indignationem meam in eis. 14 Et dabo te in desertum et in obprobrium in gentibus quae in circuitu tuo sunt in conspectu omnis praetereuntis. 15 Et eris obprobrium et blasphemia, exemplum et stupor in gentibus quae in circuitu tuo sunt cum fecero in te iudicia in furore et in indignatione et in increpationibus irae. 16 Ego, Dominus, locutus sum: quando misero sagittas famis pessimas in eos, quae erunt mortiferae et quas mittam ut disperdam vos, et famem congregabo super vos, et conteram in vobis baculum

ments of the nations that are round about you, 8 therefore thus saith the Lord God: 'Behold: I come against thee, and I myself will execute judgments in the midst of thee in the sight of the Gentiles. 9 And I will do in thee that which I have not done and the like to which I will do no more because of all thy abominations. 10 Therefore the fathers shall eat the sons in the midst of thee, and the sons shall eat their fathers, and I will execute judgments in thee, and I will scatter thy whole remnant into every wind. 11 Therefore as I live,' saith the Lord God, 'because thou hast violated my sanctuary with all thy offences and with all thy abominations, I will also break thee in pieces, and my eye shall not spare, and I will not have any pity. 12 A third part of thee shall die with the pestilence and shall be consumed with famine in the midst of thee, and a third part of thee shall fall by the sword round about thee, and a third part of thee will I scatter into every wind, and I will draw out a sword after them. 13 And I will accomplish my fury and will cause my indignation to rest upon them, and I will be comforted, and they shall know that I, the Lord, have spoken it in my zeal when I shall have accomplished my indignation in them. 14 And I will make thee desolate and a reproach among the nations that are round about thee in the sight of every one that passeth by. 15 And thou shalt be a reproach and a scoff, an example and an astonishment amongst the nations that are round about thee when I shall have executed judgments in thee in anger and in indignation and in wrathful rebukes. 16 I, the Lord, have spoken it: when I shall send upon them the grievous arrows of famine, which shall bring death and which I will send to destroy you, and I will gather together famine against you, and I will break among you the staff of

panis. 17 Et inmittam in vos famem et bestias pessimas usque ad internicionem, et pestilentia et sanguis transibunt per te, et gladium inducam super te. Ego, Dominus, locutus sum.'"

Caput 6

Et factus est sermo Domini ad me, dicens, 2 "Fili hominis, pone faciem tuam ad montes Israhel, et prophetabis ad eos, 3 et dices, 'Montes Israhel, audite verbum Domini Dei! Haec dicit Dominus Deus montibus et collibus et rupibus et vallibus: "Ecce: ego inducam super vos gladium, et disperdam excelsa vestra, 4 et demoliar aras vestras, et confringentur simulacra vestra, et deiciam interfectos vestros ante idola vestra. 5 Et dabo cadavera filiorum Israhel ante faciem simulacrorum vestrorum, et dispergam ossa vestra circum aras vestras 6 in omnibus habitationibus vestris. Urbes desertae erunt, et excelsa demolientur et dissipabuntur, et interibunt arae vestrae et confringentur, et cessabunt idola vestra, et conterentur delubra vestra, et delebuntur opera vestra. 7 Et

bread. 17 And I will send in upon you famine and evil beasts unto utter destruction, and pestilence and blood shall pass through thee, and I will bring in the sword upon thee. I, the Lord, have spoken it.'"

Chapter 6

The punishment of Israel for their idolatry. A remnant shall be saved.

And the word of the Lord came to me, saying, 2 "Son of man, set thy face towards the mountains of Israel, and *prophesy* against them, 3 and *say,* 'Ye mountains of Israel, hear the word of the Lord God! Thus saith the Lord God to the mountains and to the hills and to the rocks and the valleys: "Behold: I will bring upon you the sword, and I will destroy your high places, 4 and I will throw down your altars, and your idols shall be broken in pieces, and I will cast down your slain before your idols. 5 And I will lay the dead carcasses of the children of Israel before your idols, and I will scatter your bones round about your altars 6 in all your dwelling places. The cities shall be laid waste, and the high places shall be thrown down and destroyed, and your altars shall be abolished and shall be broken in pieces, and your idols shall be no more, and your temples shall be destroyed, and your works shall be defaced. 7 And the slain

cadet interfectus in medio vestri, et scietis quia ego sum Dominus. 8 Et relinquam in vobis eos qui fugerint gladium in gentibus cum dispersero vos in terris. 9 Et recordabuntur mei liberati vestri in gentibus ad quas captivi ducti sunt, quia contrivi cor eorum fornicans et recedens a me et oculos eorum fornicantes post idola sua, et displicebunt sibimet super malis quae fecerunt in universis abominationibus suis. 10 Et scient quia ego, Dominus, non frustra locutus sum ut facerem eis malum hoc.""""

11 Haec dicit Dominus Deus: "Percute manum tuam, et adlide pedem tuum, et dic, 'Eheu ad omnes abominationes malorum domus Israhel, quia gladio, fame et peste ruituri sunt.' 12 Qui longe est peste morietur, qui autem prope gladio corruet, et qui relictus fuerit et obsessus fame morietur, et conplebo indignationem meam in eis. 13 Et scietis quia ego Dominus cum fuerint interfecti vestri in medio idolorum vestrorum, in circuitu ararum vestrarum, in omni colle excelso et in cunctis summitatibus montium et subtus omne lignum nemorosum et subtus universam quercum frondosam, locum ubi accenderunt tura redolentia universis idolis suis. 14 Et extendam manum meam super eos, et faciam terram desolatam et destitutam a deserto Deblatha in omnibus habitationibus eorum, et scient quia ego Dominus."

shall fall in the midst of you, and you shall know that I am the Lord. 8 And I will leave in you some that shall escape the sword among the nations when I shall have scattered you through the countries. 9 And they that are saved of you shall remember me amongst the nations to which they are carried captives, because I have broken their heart that was faithless and revolted from me and their eyes that went a fornicating after their idols, and they shall be displeased with themselves because of the evils which they have committed in all their abominations. 10 And they shall know that I, the Lord, have not spoken in vain that I would do this evil to them."""

11 Thus saith the Lord God: "Strike *with* thy hand, and stamp *with* thy foot, and say, 'Alas for all the abominations of the evils of the house of Israel, for they shall fall by the sword, by the famine and by the pestilence.' 12 He that is far off shall die of the pestilence, and he that is near shall fall by the sword, and he that remaineth and is besieged shall die by the famine, and I will accomplish my indignation upon them. 13 And you shall know that I am the Lord when your slain shall be amongst your idols, round about your altars, in every high hill and on all the tops of mountains and under every woody tree and under every thick oak, the place where they burnt sweet-smelling frankincense to all their idols. 14 And I will stretch forth my hand upon them, and I will make the land desolate and abandoned from the desert of Diblah in all their dwelling places, and they shall know that I am the Lord."

Caput 7

Et factus est sermo Domini ad me, dicens, 2 "Et tu, fili hominis, haec dicit Dominus Deus terrae Israhel: 'Finis venit; venit finis super quattuor plagas terrae. 3 Nunc finis super te, et inmittam furorem meum in te, et iudicabo te iuxta vias tuas, et ponam contra te omnes abominationes tuas. 4 Et non parcet oculus meus super te, et non miserebor, sed vias tuas ponam super te, et abominationes tuae in medio tui erunt, et scietis quia ego Dominus.'

5 "Haec dicit Dominus Deus: 'Adflictio una, adflictio ecce: venit. 6 Finis venit; venit finis; evigilavit adversum te; ecce: venit. 7 Venit contritio super te qui habitas in terra; venit tempus; prope est dies occisionis et non gloriae montium. 8 Nunc de propinquo effundam iram meam super te, et conplebo furorem meum in te, et iudicabo te iuxta vias tuas, et inponam tibi omnia scelera tua. 9 Et non parcet oculus meus, neque miserebor, sed vias tuas inponam tibi, et abominationes tuae in medio tui erunt, et scietis quia ego sum Dominus percutiens.'

10 "Ecce dies, ecce: venit; egressa est contractio; floruit virga; germinavit superbia. 11 Iniquitas surrexit in virga impietatis; non ex eis et non ex populo neque ex sonitu eorum,

Chapter 7

The final desolation of Israel, from which few shall escape.

And the word of the Lord came to me, saying, 2 "And thou, son of man, thus saith the Lord God to the land of Israel: 'The end is come; the end is come upon the four quarters of the land. 3 Now is an end come upon thee, and I will send my wrath upon thee, and I will judge thee according to thy ways, and I will set all thy abominations against thee. 4 And my eye shall not spare thee, and I will shew thee no pity, but I will lay thy ways upon thee, and thy abominations shall be in the midst of thee, and you shall know that I am the Lord.'

5 "Thus saith the Lord God: 'One affliction, behold: an affliction is come. 6 An end is come; the end is come; it hath awaked against thee; behold: it is come. 7 Destruction is come upon thee that dwellest in the land; the time is come; the day of slaughter is near and not of the joy of mountains. 8 Now very shortly I will pour out my wrath upon thee, and I will accomplish my anger in thee, and I will judge thee according to thy ways, and I will lay upon thee all thy crimes. 9 And my eye shall not spare, neither will I shew mercy, but I will lay thy ways upon thee, and thy abominations shall be in the midst of thee, and you shall know that I am the Lord that strike.'

10 "'Behold the day, behold: it is come; destruction is gone forth; the rod hath blossomed; pride hath budded. 11 Iniquity is risen up into a rod of impiety; nothing of them *shall*

et non erit requies in eis. 12 Venit tempus; adpropinquavit dies; qui emit non laetetur et qui vendit non lugeat, quia ira super omnem populum eius. 13 Quia qui vendit ad id quod vendidit non revertetur, et adhuc in viventibus vita eorum. Visio enim ad omnem multitudinem eius non regredietur, et vir in iniquitate vitae suae non confortabitur.

14 "Canite tuba; praeparentur omnes. Et non est qui vadat ad proelium, ira enim mea super universum populum eius: 15 gladius foris et pestis et fames intrinsecus. Qui in agro est gladio morietur, et qui in civitate pestilentia et fame devora- buntur. 16 Et salvabuntur qui fugerint ex eis, et erunt in mon- tibus quasi columbae convallium, omnes trepidi, unusquis- que in iniquitate sua. 17 Omnes manus dissolventur, et omnia genua fluent aquis. 18 Et accingent se ciliciis, et operiet eos formido, et in omni facie confusio, et in universis capitibus eorum calvitium. 19 Argentum eorum foras proicietur, et aurum eorum in sterquilinium erit. Argentum eorum et aurum eorum non valebit liberare eos in die furoris Domini. Animam suam non saturabunt, et ventres eorum non imple- buntur, quia scandalum iniquitatis eorum factum est. 20 Et ornamentum monilium suorum in superbiam posuerunt, et imagines abominationum suarum et simulacrorum fecerunt ex eo; propter hoc dedi eis illud in inmunditiam. 21 Et dabo illud in manus alienorum ad diripiendum, et impiis terrae in praedam, et contaminabunt illud. 22 Et avertam faciem meam ab eis, et violabunt arcanum meum, et introibunt in illud emissarii et contaminabunt illud.

remain nor of their people nor of the noise of them, and there shall be no rest among them. 12 The time is come; the day is at hand; let not the buyer rejoice nor the seller mourn, for wrath is upon all the people thereof. 13 For the seller shall not return to that which he hath sold, *although* their life be yet among the living. For the vision *which regardeth* all the multitude thereof shall not go back, neither shall man be strengthened in the iniquity of his life.

14 "Blow the trumpet; let all be made ready. *Yet* there is none to go to the battle, for my wrath shall be upon all the people thereof: 15 the sword without and the pestilence and the famine within. He that is in the field shall die by the sword, and they that are in the city shall be devoured by the pestilence and the famine. 16 And such of them as shall flee shall escape, and they shall be in the mountains like doves of the valleys, all of them trembling, every one for his iniquity. 17 All hands shall be made feeble, and all knees shall run with water. 18 And they shall gird themselves with haircloth, and fear shall cover them, and shame shall be upon every face, and baldness upon all their heads. 19 Their silver shall be cast forth, and their gold shall become a dunghill. Their silver and their gold shall not be able to deliver them in the day of the wrath of the Lord. They shall not satisfy their soul, and their bellies shall not be filled, because it hath been the stumbling block of their iniquity. 20 And they have turned the ornament of their jewels into pride, and have made of it the images of their abominations and idols; therefore I have made it an uncleanness to them. 21 And I will give it into the hands of strangers for spoil, and to the wicked of the earth for a prey, and they shall defile it. 22 And I will turn away my face from them, and they shall violate my secret place, and *robbers* shall enter into it and defile it.

23 "Fac conclusionem, quoniam terra plena est iudicio sanguinum et civitas plena iniquitate. 24 Et adducam pessimos de gentibus, et possidebunt domos eorum, et quiescere faciam superbiam potentium, et possidebunt sanctuaria eorum. 25 Angustia superveniente requirent pacem, et non erit. 26 Conturbatio super conturbationem veniet et auditus super auditum, et quaerent visionem de propheta, et lex peribit a sacerdote, et consilium a senioribus. 27 Rex lugebit, et princeps induetur maerore, et manus populi terrae conturbabuntur. Secundum viam eorum faciam eis et secundum iudicia eorum iudicabo eos et scient quia ego Dominus."

Caput 8

Et factum est in anno sexto, in sexto mense, in quinta mensis, ego sedebam in domo mea, et senes Iuda sedebant coram me, et cecidit super me ibi manus Domini Dei. 2 Et vidi, et ecce: similitudo quasi aspectus ignis—ab aspectu lumborum eius et deorsum ignis, et a lumbis eius et sursum

23 "Make a shutting up, for the land is full of the judgment of blood and the city is full of iniquity. 24 And I will bring the worst of the nations, and they shall possess their houses, and I will make the pride of the mighty to cease, and they shall possess their sanctuary. 25 When distress cometh upon them they will seek for peace, and there shall be none. 26 Trouble shall come upon trouble and rumour upon rumour, and they shall seek a vision of the prophet, and the law shall perish from the priest, and counsel from the ancients. 27 The king shall mourn, and the prince shall be clothed with sorrow, and the hands of the people of the land shall be troubled. I will do to them according to their way and will judge them according to their judgments, and they shall know that I am the Lord."

Chapter 8

The prophet sees in a vision the abominations committed in Jerusalem, which determine the Lord to spare them no longer.

And it came to pass in the sixth year, in the sixth month, in the fifth day of the month, as I sat in my house, and the ancients of Judah sat before me, *that* the hand of the Lord God fell there upon me. 2 And I saw, and behold: a likeness as the appearance of fire—from the appearance of his loins and downward fire, and from his loins and upward as the

quasi aspectus splendoris, ut visio electri. 3 Et emissa similitudo manus adprehendit me in cincinno capitis mei, et elevavit me spiritus inter terram et caelum et adduxit me in
Hierusalem in visione Dei iuxta ostium interius quod respiciebat ad aquilonem, ubi erat statutum idolum zeli ad pro-
vocandam aemulationem. 4 Et ecce: ibi gloria Dei Israhel
secundum visionem quam videram in campo.

5 Et dixit ad me, "Fili hominis, leva oculos tuos ad viam
aquilonis." Et levavi oculos meos ad viam aquilonis, et ecce:
ab aquilone portae altaris idolum zeli in ipso introitu. 6 Et
dixit ad me, "Fili hominis, putasne, vides tu quid isti faciunt,
abominationes magnas quas domus Israhel facit hic, ut procul recedam a sanctuario meo? Et adhuc conversus videbis
abominationes maiores."

7 Et introduxit me ad ostium atrii, et vidi, et ecce: fora-
men unum in pariete. 8 Et dixit ad me, "Fili hominis, fode
parietem." Et cum fodissem parietem, apparuit ostium
unum. 9 Et dixit ad me, "Ingredere, et vide abominationes
pessimas quas isti faciunt hic." 10 Et ingressus vidi, et ecce:
omnis similitudo reptilium et animalium, abominatio et
universa idola domus Israhel depicta erant in pariete in circuitu per totum. 11 Et septuaginta viri de senioribus domus
Israhel et Hiezonias, filius Saphan, stabat in medio eorum
stantium ante picturas, et unusquisque habebat turibulum
in manu sua, et vapor nebulae de ture consurgebat. 12 Et
dixit ad me, "Certe vides, fili hominis, quae seniores domus

appearance of brightness, as the appearance of amber. 3 And the likeness of a hand was put forth and took me by a lock of my head, and the spirit lifted me up between the earth and the heaven and brought me in the vision of God into Jerusalem near the inner gate that looked toward the north, where was set the idol of jealousy to provoke to jealousy. 4 And behold: the glory of the God of Israel was there according to the vision which I had seen in the plain.

5 And he said to me, "Son of man, lift up thy eyes towards the way of the north." And I lifted up my eyes towards the way of the north, and behold: on the north side of the gate of the altar the idol of jealousy in the very entry. 6 And he said to me, "Son of man, dost thou see, thinkest thou, what these are doing, the great abominations that the house of Israel committeth here, that I should depart far off from my sanctuary? And turn thee yet again, and thou shalt see greater abominations."

7 And he brought me in to the door of the court, and I saw, and behold: a hole in the wall. 8 And he said to me, "Son of man, dig in the wall." And when I had digged in the wall, *behold:* a door. 9 And he said to me, "Go in, and see the wicked abominations which they commit here." 10 And I went in and saw, and behold: every form of creeping things and of living creatures, the abomination and all the idols of the house of Israel were painted on the wall all round about. 11 And seventy men of the ancients of the house of Israel and Jaazaniah, the son of Shaphan, stood in the midst of them that stood before the pictures, and every one had a censer in his hand, and a cloud of smoke went up from the incense. 12 And he said to me, "Surely thou seest, O son of

Israhel faciunt in tenebris, unusquisque in abscondito cubiculi sui, dicunt enim, 'Non videt Dominus nos; dereliquit Dominus terram.'" 13 Et dixit ad me, "Adhuc conversus videbis abominationes maiores quas isti faciunt."

14 Et introduxit me per ostium portae domus Domini quod respiciebat ad aquilonem, et ecce: ibi mulieres sedebant plangentes Adonidem. 15 Et dixit ad me, "Certe vidisti, fili hominis, adhuc conversus videbis abominationes maiores his."

16 Et introduxit me in atrium domus Domini interius, et ecce: in ostio templi Domini inter vestibulum et altare quasi viginti quinque viri dorsa habentes contra templum Domini et facies ad orientem, et adorabant ad ortum solis. 17 Et dixit ad me, "Certe vidisti, fili hominis; numquid leve est hoc domui Iuda, ut facerent abominationes istas quas fecerunt hic, quia replentes terram iniquitate conversi sunt ad inritandum me? Et ecce: adplicant ramum ad nares suas. 18 Ergo et ego faciam in furore meo; non parcet oculus meus, nec miserebor, et cum clamaverint ad aures meas voce magna, non exaudiam eos."

man, what the ancients of the house of Israel do in the dark, every one in private in his chamber, for they say, 'The Lord seeth us not; the Lord hath forsaken the earth.'" 13 And he said to me, "*If* thou turn thee again thou shalt see greater abominations which these commit."

14 And he brought me in by the door of the gate of the Lord's house which looked to the north, and behold: women sat there mourning for Adonis. 15 And he said to me, "Surely thou hast seen, O son of man, but turn thee again, and thou shalt see greater abominations than these."

16 And he brought me into the inner court of the house of the Lord, and behold: at the door of the temple of the Lord between the porch and the altar were about five and twenty men having their backs towards the temple of the Lord and their faces to the east, and they adored towards the rising of the sun. 17 And he said to me, "Surely thou hast seen, O son of man; is this a light thing to the house of Judah, that they should commit these abominations which they have committed here, because they have filled the land with iniquity and have turned to provoke me to anger? And behold: they put a branch to their nose. 18 Therefore I also will deal with them in my wrath; my eye shall not spare them, neither will I shew mercy, and when they shall cry to my ears with a loud voice, I will not hear them."

Caput 9

Et clamavit in auribus meis voce magna, dicens, "Adpropinquaverunt visitationes urbis, et unusquisque vas interfectionis habet in manu sua." 2 Et ecce: sex viri veniebant de via portae superioris quae respicit ad aquilonem, et uniuscuiusque vas interitus in manu eius, vir quoque unus in medio eorum vestitus erat lineis, et atramentarium scriptoris ad renes eius, et ingressi sunt et steterunt iuxta altare aereum.

3 Et gloria Domini Israhel adsumpta est de cherub quae erat super eum ad limen domus, et vocavit virum qui indutus erat lineis et atramentarium scriptoris habebat in lumbis suis. 4 Et dixit Dominus ad eum, "Transi per mediam civitatem, in medio Hierusalem, et signa Thau super frontes virorum gementium et dolentium super cunctis abominationibus quae fiunt in medio eius." 5 Et illis dixit audiente me, "Transite per civitatem sequentes eum, et percutite; non parcat oculus vester, neque misereamini. 6 Senem, adulescentulum et virginem, parvulum et mulieres interficite usque ad internicionem, omnem autem super quem videritis Thau ne occidatis, et a sanctuario meo incipite." Coeperunt ergo a viris senioribus qui erant ante faciem domus. 7 Et dixit ad eos, "Contaminate domum, et implete atria interfectis; egredimini." Et egressi sunt et percutiebant eos qui erant in civitate.

Chapter 9

All are ordered to be destroyed that are not marked in their foreheads. God will not be entreated for them.

And he cried in my ears with a loud voice, saying, "The visitations of the city are at hand, and every one hath a destroying weapon in his hand." 2 And behold: six men came from the way of the upper gate which looketh to the north, and each one had his weapon of destruction in his hand, and there was one man in the midst of them clothed with linen with a writer's inkhorn at his reins, and they went in and stood by the brazen altar.

3 And the glory of the Lord of Israel went up from the cherub upon which he was to the threshold of the house, and he called to the man that was clothed with linen and had a writer's inkhorn at his loins. 4 And the Lord said to him, "Go through the midst of the city, *through* the midst of Jerusalem, and mark Thau upon the foreheads of the men that sigh and mourn for all the abominations that are committed in the midst thereof." 5 And to the others he said in my hearing, "Go ye after him through the city, and strike; let not your eye spare, nor be ye moved with pity. 6 *Utterly* destroy old *and* young, *maidens,* children and women, but upon whomsoever you shall see Thau, kill him not, and begin ye at my sanctuary." So they began at the ancient men who were before the house. 7 And he said to them, "Defile the house, and fill the courts with the slain; go ye forth." And they went forth and slew them that were in the city.

8 Et caede conpleta, remansi ego, ruique super faciem meam, et clamans aio, "Heu, heu, heu, Domine Deus, ergone disperdes omnes reliquias Israhel effundens furorem tuum super Hierusalem?"

9 Et dixit ad me, "Iniquitas domus Israhel et Iuda magna est nimis valde, et repleta est terra sanguinibus, et civitas repleta est aversione, dixerunt enim, 'Dereliquit Dominus terram, et Dominus non videt.' 10 Igitur et meus non parcet oculus, neque miserebor; viam eorum super caput eorum reddam."

11 Et ecce: vir qui indutus erat lineis, qui habebat atramentarium in dorso suo, respondit verbum, dicens, "Feci sicut praecepisti mihi."

Caput 10

Et vidi, et ecce: in firmamento quod erat super caput cherubin quasi lapis sapphyrus, quasi species similitudinis solii, apparuit super ea.

2 Et dixit ad virum qui indutus erat lineis et ait, "Ingredere in medio rotarum quae sunt subtus cherubim, et imple

8 And the slaughter being ended, I was left, and I fell upon my face, and crying I said, "Alas, alas, alas, O Lord God, wilt thou then destroy all the remnant of Israel by pouring out thy fury upon Jerusalem?"

9 And he said to me, "The iniquity of the house of Israel and of Judah is exceeding great, and the land is filled with blood, and the city is filled with perverseness, for they have said, 'The Lord hath forsaken the earth, and the Lord seeth not.' 10 Therefore neither shall my eye spare, nor will I have pity; I will requite their way upon their head."

11 And behold: the man that was clothed with linen, that had the inkhorn at his back, returned the word, saying, "I have done as thou hast commanded me."

Chapter 10

Fire is taken from the midst of the wheels under the cherubims and scattered over the city. A description of the cherubims.

And I saw, and behold: in the firmament that was over the heads of the cherubims there appeared over them as it were the sapphire stone, as the appearance of the likeness of a throne.

2 And he spoke to the man that was clothed with linen and said, "Go in between the wheels that are under the cher-

manum tuam prunis ignis quae sunt inter cherubin, et effunde super civitatem." Ingressusque est, in conspectu meo,
3 cherubin autem stabant a dextris domus cum ingrederetur
vir, et nubes implevit atrium interius. 4 Et elevata est gloria
Domini desuper cherub ad limen domus, et repleta est domus nube, et atrium repletum est splendore gloriae Domini.
5 Et sonitus alarum cherubin audiebatur usque ad atrium exterius quasi vox Dei Omnipotentis loquentis.

6 Cumque praecepisset viro qui indutus erat lineis, dicens,
"Sume ignem de medio rotarum quae sunt inter cherubin,"
ingressus ille stetit iuxta rotam. 7 Et extendit cherub manum
de medio cherubin ad ignem qui erat inter cherubin, et
sumpsit et dedit in manus eius qui indutus erat lineis, qui ac-
cipiens egressus est. 8 Et apparuit in cherubin similitudo
manus hominis subtus pinnas eorum.

9 Et vidi, et ecce: quattuor rotae iuxta cherubin, rota una
iuxta cherub unum et rota alia iuxta cherub unum, species
autem erat rotarum quasi visio lapidis chrysoliti, 10 et aspectus earum similitudo una quattuor, quasi sit rota in medio
rotae. 11 Cumque ambularent in quattuor partes gradiebantur, et non revertebantur ambulantes, sed ad locum ad quem
ire declinabat quae prima erat sequebantur et ceterae nec
convertebantur. 12 Et omne corpus earum et colla et manus
et pinnae et circuli plena erant oculis in circuitu quattuor rotarum. 13 Et rotas istas vocavit volubiles audiente

ubims, and fill thy hand with the coals of fire that are between the cherubims, and pour them out upon the city."
And he went in, in my sight, 3 and the cherubims stood on
the right side of the house when the man went in, and a
cloud filled the inner court. 4 And the glory of the Lord was
lifted up from above the cherub to the threshold of the
house, and the house was filled with the cloud, and the court
was filled with the brightness of the glory of the Lord. 5 And
the sound of the wings of the cherubims was heard even to
the outward court as the voice of God Almighty speaking.

6 And when he had commanded the man that was clothed
with linen, saying, "Take fire from the midst of the wheels
that are between the cherubims," he went in and stood beside the wheel. 7 And one cherub stretched out his arm from
the midst of the cherubims to the fire that was between the
cherubims, and he took and put it into the hands of him that
was clothed with linen, who took it and went forth. 8 And
there appeared in the cherubims the likeness of a man's hand
under their wings.

9 And I saw, and behold: there were four wheels by the
cherubims, one wheel by one cherub and another wheel by
another cherub, and the appearance of the wheels was to
the sight like the chrysolite stone, 10 and as to their appearance all four were alike, as if a wheel were in the midst of a
wheel. 11 And when they went they went by four ways, and
they turned not when they went, but to the place whither
the first turned the rest also followed and did not turn
back. 12 And their whole body and their necks and their
hands and their wings and the circles were full of eyes round
about the four wheels. 13 And these wheels he called voluble

me. 14 Quattuor autem facies habebat unum: facies una facies cherub, et facies secunda facies hominis, et in tertio facies leonis, et in quarto facies aquilae.

15 Et elevata sunt cherubin; ipsum est animal quod videram iuxta flumen Chobar. 16 Cumque ambularent cherubin, ibant pariter et rotae iuxta ea, et cum levarent cherubin alas suas ut exaltarentur de terra, non residebant rotae, sed et ipsae iuxta erant. 17 Stantibus illis stabant, et cum elevatis elevabantur, spiritus enim vitae erat in eis.

18 Et egressa est gloria Domini a limine templi et stetit super cherubin. 19 Et eleuantia cherubin alas suas exaltata sunt a terra coram me, et illis egredientibus rotae quoque subsecutae sunt, et stetit in introitu portae domus Domini orientalis, et gloria Dei Israhel erat super ea.

20 Ipsum est animal quod vidi subter Deum Israhel iuxta fluvium Chobar, et intellexi quia cherubin essent. 21 Quattuor vultus uni, et quattuor alae uni, et similitudo manus hominis sub alis eorum. 22 Et similitudo vultuum eorum, ipsi vultus quos videram iuxta fluvium Chobar et intuitus eorum et impetus singulorum ante faciem suam ingredi.

in my hearing. 14 And every one had four faces: one face was the face of a cherub, and the second face the face of a man, and in the third was the face of a lion, and in the fourth the face of an eagle.

15 And the cherubims were lifted up; this is the living creature that I had seen by the river Chebar. 16 And when the cherubims went, the wheels also *went* by them, and when the cherubims lifted up their wings to mount up from the earth, the wheels stayed not behind, *but* were by them. 17 When they stood these stood, and when they were lifted up these were lifted up, for the spirit of life was in them.

18 And the glory of the Lord went forth from the threshold of the temple and stood over the cherubims. 19 And the cherubims, lifting up their wings, were raised from the earth before me, and as they went out the wheels also followed, and it stood in the entry of the east gate of the house of the Lord, and the glory of the God of Israel was over them.

20 This is the living creature which I saw under the God of Israel by the river Chebar, and I understood that they were cherubims. 21 Each one had four faces, and each one had four wings, and the likeness of a man's hand was under their wings. 22 And as to the likeness of their faces, they were the same faces which I had seen by the river Chebar and their looks and the impulse of every one to go straight forward.

Caput 11

Et elevavit me spiritus et introduxit me ad portam domus Domini orientalem, quae respicit ad solis ortum, et ecce: in introitu portae viginti quinque viri, et vidi in medio eorum Hiezoniam, filium Azur, et Pheltiam, filium Banaiae, principes populi. 2 Dixitque ad me, "Fili hominis, hi sunt viri qui cogitant iniquitatem et tractant consilium pessimum in urbe ista, 3 dicentes, 'Nonne dudum aedificatae sunt domus? Haec est lebes, nos autem carnes.' 4 Idcirco vaticinare de eis; vaticinare, fili hominis."

5 Et inruit in me spiritus Domini et dixit ad me, "Loquere: 'Haec dicit Dominus: "Sic locuti estis, domus Israhel, et cogitationes cordis vestri ego novi. 6 Plurimos occidistis in urbe hac, et implestis vias eius interfectis." 7 Propterea haec dicit Dominus Deus: "Interfecti vestri quos posuistis in medio eius, hii sunt carnes, et haec est lebes, et educam vos de medio eius. 8 Gladium metuistis, et gladium inducam super vos," ait Dominus Deus. 9 "Et eiciam vos de medio eius daboque vos in manu hostium, et faciam in vobis iudicia. 10 Gladio cadetis; in finibus Israhel iudicabo vos, et scietis

Chapter 11

A prophecy against the presumptuous assurance of the great ones. A remnant shall be saved and receive a new spirit and a new heart.

And the spirit lifted me up and brought me into the east gate of the house of the Lord, which looketh towards the rising of the sun, and behold: in the entry of the gate five and twenty men, and I saw in the midst of them Jaazaniah, the son of Azzur, and Pelatiah, the son of Benaiah, princes of the people. 2 And he said to me, "Son of man, these are the men that study iniquity and frame a wicked counsel in this city, 3 saying, 'Were not houses lately built? This *city* is the cauldron, and we the flesh.' 4 Therefore prophesy against them; prophesy, thou son of man."

5 And the spirit of the Lord fell upon me and said to me, "Speak: 'Thus saith the Lord: "Thus have you spoken, O house of Israel, *for* I know the thoughts of your heart. 6 You have killed a great many in this city, and you have filled the streets thereof with the slain." 7 Therefore thus saith the Lord God: "Your slain whom you have laid in the midst thereof, they are the flesh, and this is the cauldron, and I will bring you forth out of the midst thereof. 8 You have feared the sword, and I will bring the sword upon you," saith the Lord God. 9 "And I will cast you out of the midst thereof, and I will deliver you into the hand of the enemies, and I will execute judgments upon you. 10 You shall fall by the sword; I will judge you in the borders of Israel, and you shall know

quia ego Dominus. 11 Haec non erit vobis in lebetem, et vos non eritis in medio eius in carnes; in finibus Israhel iudicabo vos. 12 Et scietis quia ego Dominus, quia in praeceptis meis non ambulastis et iudicia mea non fecistis, sed iuxta iudicia gentium quae in circuitu vestro sunt estis operati.""'

13 Et factum est cum prophetarem Pheltias, filius Banaiae, mortuus est, et cecidi in faciem meam clamans voce magna et dixi, "Heu, heu, heu, Domine Deus, consummationem tu facis reliquiarum Israhel?"

14 Et factum est verbum Domini ad me, dicens, 15 "Fili hominis, fratres tui, fratres tui, viri propinqui tui et omnis domus Israhel, universi quibus dixerunt habitatores Hieru-salem, 'Longe recedite a Domino; nobis data est terra in possessionem.' 16 Propterea haec dicit Dominus Deus: 'Quia longe feci eos in Gentibus et quia dispersi eos in terris, ero eis in sanctificationem modicam in terris ad quas venerunt.'

17 "'Propterea loquere: "Haec dicit Dominus Deus: 'Con-gregabo vos de populis et adunabo de terris in quibus dispersi estis, daboque vobis humum Israhel.'" 18 Et ingredientur il-luc et auferent omnes offensiones cunctasque abominati-ones eius de illa. 19 Et dabo eis cor unum et spiritum novum tribuam in visceribus eorum, et auferam cor lapideum de carne eorum et dabo eis cor carneum, 20 ut in praeceptis meis ambulent et iudicia mea custodiant faciantque ea et sint mihi in populum et ego sim eis in Deum. 21 Quorum cor post offendicula et abominationes suas ambulat, horum viam in capite suo ponam,' dicit Dominus Deus."

that I am the Lord. 11 This shall not be as a cauldron to you, and you shall not be as flesh in the midst thereof; I will judge you in the borders of Israel. 12 And you shall know that I am the Lord, because you have not walked in my commandments and have not done my judgments, but you have done according to the judgments of the nations that are round about you.""'

13 And it came to pass when I prophesied that Pelatiah, the son of Benaiah, died, and I fell down upon my face and cried with a loud voice and said, "Alas, alas, alas, O Lord God, wilt thou make an end of *all* the remnant of Israel?"

14 And the word of the Lord came to me, saying, 15 "Son of man, thy brethren, thy brethren, thy kinsmen and all the house of Israel, all they to whom the inhabitants of Jerusalem have said, 'Get ye far from the Lord; the land is given in possession to us.' 16 Therefore thus saith the Lord God: 'Because I have removed them far off among the Gentiles and because I have scattered them among the countries, I will be to them a little sanctuary in the countries whither they are come.

17 "'Therefore speak to them: "Thus saith the Lord God: 'I will gather you from among the peoples and assemble you out of the countries wherein you are scattered, and I will give you the land of Israel.'" 18 And they shall go in thither and shall take away all the scandals and all the abominations thereof from thence. 19 And I will give them one heart and will put a new spirit in their bowels, and I will take away the stony heart out of their flesh and will give them a heart of flesh, 20 that they may walk in my commandments and keep my judgments and do them and that they may be my people and I may be their God. 21 *But as for them* whose heart walketh after their scandals and abominations, I will lay their way upon their head,' saith the Lord God."

²² Et elevaverunt cherubin alas suas et rotae cum eis, et gloria Dei Israhel erat super ea. ²³ Et ascendit gloria Domini de medio civitatis stetitque super montem qui est ad orientem urbis. ²⁴ Et spiritus levavit me adduxitque in Chaldeam ad transmigrationem in visione in spiritu Dei, et sublata est a me visio quam videram. ²⁵ Et locutus sum ad transmigrationem omnia verba Domini quae ostenderat mihi.

Caput 12

Et factus est sermo Domini ad me, dicens, 2 "Fili hominis, in medio domus exasperantis tu habitas, qui oculos habent ad videndum et non vident, et aures ad audiendum et non audiunt, quia domus exasperans est. 3 Tu ergo, fili hominis, fac tibi vasa transmigrationis, et transmigrabis per diem coram eis, transmigrabis autem de loco tuo ad locum alterum in conspectu eorum, si forte aspiciant, quia domus exasperans est. 4 Et efferes foras vasa tua quasi vasa transmigrantis per diem in conspectu eorum, tu autem egredieris vespere

22 And the cherubims lifted up their wings and the wheels with them, and the glory of the God of Israel was over them. 23 And the glory of the Lord went up from the midst of the city and stood over the mount that is on the east side of the city. 24 And the spirit lifted me up and brought me into Chaldea to them of the captivity in vision by the spirit of God, and the vision which I had seen was taken up from me. 25 And I spoke to them of the captivity all the words of the Lord which he had shewn me.

Chapter 12

The prophet forsheweth by signs the captivity of Zedekiah and the desolation of the people, all which shall quickly come to pass.

And the word of the Lord came to me, saying, 2 "Son of man, thou dwellest in the midst of a provoking house, who have eyes to see and see not, and ears to hear and hear not, for they are a provoking house. 3 Thou therefore, O son of man, prepare thee *all necessaries* for removing, and *remove* by day in their sight, and thou shalt remove out of thy place to another place in their sight, if so be they will regard it, for they are a provoking house. 4 And thou shalt bring forth thy furniture as the furniture of one that is removing by day in their sight, and thou shalt go forth in the evening

coram eis sicut egreditur migrans. 5 Ante oculos eorum perfodi tibi parietem, et egredieris per eum. 6 In conspectu eorum in umeris portaberis; in caligine effereris; faciem tuam velabis et non videbis terram, quia portentum dedi te domui Israhel."

7 Feci ergo sicut praeceperat mihi: vasa mea protuli quasi vasa transmigrantis per diem, et vespere perfodi mihi parietem manu, et in caligine egressus sum et in umeris portatus in conspectu eorum.

8 Et factus est sermo Domini ad me mane, dicens, 9 "Fili hominis, numquid non dixerunt ad te domus Israhel, domus exasperans, 'Quid tu facis?' 10 Dic ad eos, 'Haec dicit Dominus Deus: "Super ducem onus istud qui est in Hierusalem et super omnem domum Israhel quae est in medio eorum."' 11 Dic, 'Ego portentum vestrum; quomodo feci, sic fiet illis: in transmigrationem et in captivitatem ibunt.' 12 Et dux qui est in medio eorum in umeris portabitur; in caligine egredietur; parietem perfodient ut educant eum; facies eius operietur, ut non videat oculo terram. 13 Et extendam rete meum super illum, et capietur in sagena mea, et adducam eum in Babylonem, in terram Chaldeorum, et ipsam non videbit, ibique morietur. 14 Et omnes qui circa eum sunt, praesidium eius et agmina eius, dispergam in omnem ventum, et gladium evaginabo post eos. 15 Et scient quia ego Dominus quando dispersero illos in gentibus et disseminavero eos in terris. 16 Et relinquam ex eis viros paucos a gladio et fame et

in their presence as one goeth forth that removeth his dwelling. 5 Dig thee a way through the wall before their eyes, and thou shalt go forth through it. 6 In their sight thou shalt be carried out upon men's shoulders; thou shalt be carried out in the dark; thou shalt cover thy face and shalt not see the ground, for I have set thee for a sign of things to come to the house of Israel."

7 I did therefore as he had commanded me: I brought forth my goods by day as the goods of one that removeth, and in the evening I digged through the wall with my hand, and I went forth in the dark and was carried on men's shoulders in their sight.

8 And the word of the Lord came to me in the morning, saying, 9 "Son of man, hath not the house of Israel, the provoking house, said to thee, 'What art thou doing?' 10 Say to them, 'Thus saith the Lord God: "This burden concerneth my prince that is in Jerusalem and all the house of Israel that are among them."' 11 Say, 'I am a sign of things to come to you; as I have done, so shall it be done to them: *they shall be removed from their dwellings* and go into captivity.' 12 And the prince that is in the midst of them shall be carried on shoulders; he shall go forth in the dark; they shall dig through the wall to bring him out; his face shall be covered, that he may not see the ground with his eyes. 13 And I will spread my net over him, and he shall be taken in my net, and I will bring him into Babylon, into the land of the Chaldeans, and he shall not see it, and there he shall die. 14 And all that are about him, his guards and his troops, I will scatter into every wind, and I will draw out the sword after them. 15 And they shall know that I am the Lord when I shall have dispersed them among the nations and scattered them in the countries. 16 And I will leave a few men of them from the sword

pestilentia, ut narrent omnia scelera eorum in gentibus ad quas ingredientur, et scient quia ego Dominus."

17 Et factus est sermo Domini ad me, dicens, 18 "Fili hominis, panem tuum in conturbatione comede, sed et aquam tuam in festinatione et maerore bibe. 19 Et dices ad populum terrae, 'Haec dicit Dominus Deus ad eos qui habitant in Hierusalem in terra Israhel: "Panem suum in sollicitudine comedent et aquam suam in desolatione bibent, ut desoletur terra a multitudine sua propter iniquitatem omnium qui habitant in ea. 20 Et civitates quae nunc habitantur desolatae erunt, terraque deserta, et scietis quia ego Dominus."'"

21 Et factus est sermo Domini ad me, dicens, 22 "Fili hominis, quod est proverbium istud vobis in terra Israhel, dicentium, 'In longum differentur dies, et peribit omnis visio?' 23 Ideo dic ad eos, 'Haec dicit Dominus Deus: "Quiescere faciam proverbium istud, neque vulgo dicetur ultra in Israhel."' Et loquere ad eos quod adpropinquaverint dies et sermo omnis visionis. 24 Non enim erit ultra omnis visio cassa neque divinatio ambigua in medio filiorum Israhel. 25 Quia ego, Dominus, loquar, et quodcumque locutus fuero verbum et fiet; non prolongabitur amplius, sed in diebus vestris, domus exasperans, loquar verbum et faciam illud," dicit Dominus Deus.

26 Et factus est sermo Domini ad me, dicens, 27 "Fili hominis, ecce domus Israhel, dicentium, 'Visio quam hic videt in dies multos, et in tempora longa iste prophetat.' 28 Propterea dic ad eos, 'Haec dicit Dominus Deus: "Non pro-

and from the famine and from the pestilence, that they may declare all their wicked deeds among the nations whither they shall go, and they shall know that I am the Lord."

17 And the word of the Lord came to me, saying, 18 "Son of man, eat thy bread in trouble, and drink thy water in hurry and sorrow. 19 And *say* to the people of the land, 'Thus saith the Lord God to them that dwell in Jerusalem in the land of Israel: "They shall eat their bread in care and drink their water in desolation, that the land may become desolate from the multitude that is therein for the iniquity of all that dwell therein. 20 And the cities that are now inhabited shall be laid waste, and the land shall be desolate, and you shall know that I am the Lord."'"

21 And the word of the Lord came to me, saying, 22 "Son of man, what is this proverb that you have in the land of Israel, saying, 'The days shall be prolonged, and every vision shall fail?' 23 Say to them therefore, 'Thus saith the Lord God: "I will make this proverb to cease, neither shall it be any more a common saying in Israel."' And tell them that the days are at hand and the effect of every vision. 24 For there shall be no more any vain visions nor doubtful divination in the midst of the children of Israel. 25 For I, the Lord, will speak, and what word soever I shall speak, it shall come to pass *and* shall not be prolonged any more, but in your days, ye provoking house, I will speak the word and will do it," saith the Lord God.

26 And the word of the Lord came to me, saying, 27 "Son of man, behold the house of Israel, they that say, 'The vision that this man seeth is for many days to come, and this man prophesieth of times afar off.' 28 Therefore say to them, 'Thus saith the Lord God: "Not one word of mine shall be

longabitur ultra omnis sermo meus; verbum quod locutus fuero conplebitur,"'" dicit Dominus Deus.

Caput 13

Et factus est sermo Domini ad me, dicens, 2 "Fili hominis, vaticinare ad prophetas Israhel qui prophetant, et dices prophetantibus de corde suo, 'Audite verbum Domini!' 3 Haec dicit Dominus Deus: 'Vae prophetis insipientibus qui sequuntur spiritum suum et nihil vident. 4 Quasi vulpes in desertis prophetae tui, Israhel, erant. 5 Non ascendistis ex adverso, neque opposuistis murum pro domo Israhel ut staretis in proelio in die Domini. 6 Vident vana, et divinant mendacium, dicentes, "Ait Dominus," cum Dominus non miserit eos, et perseveraverunt confirmare sermonem. 7 Numquid non visionem cassam vidistis et divinationem mendacem locuti estis, et dicitis, "Ait Dominus," cum ego non sim locutus? 8 Propterea haec dicit Dominus Deus: "Quia locuti estis vana et vidistis mendacium, ideo ecce: ego ad vos," ait Dominus Deus.

9 "'Et erit manus mea super prophetas qui vident vana et divinant mendacium; in consilio populi mei non erunt, et in

prolonged any more; the word that I shall speak shall be accomplished,"'" saith the Lord God.

Chapter 13

God declares against false prophets and prophetesses that deceive the people with lies.

And the word of the Lord came to me, saying, 2 "Son of man, prophesy thou against the prophets of Israel that prophesy, and thou shalt say to them that prophesy out of their own heart, 'Hear ye the word of the Lord!' 3 Thus saith the Lord God: 'Woe to the foolish prophets that follow their own spirit and see nothing. 4 Thy prophets, O Israel, were like foxes in the deserts. 5 You have not gone up to face the enemy, nor have you set up a wall for the house of Israel to stand in battle in the day of the Lord. 6 They see vain things, and they foretell lies, saying, "The Lord saith," whereas the Lord hath not sent them, and they have persisted to confirm what they have said. 7 Have you not seen a vain vision and spoken a lying divination, and you say, "The Lord saith," whereas I have not spoken? 8 Therefore thus saith the Lord God: "Because you have spoken vain things and have seen lies, therefore behold: I come against you," saith the Lord God.

9 "And my hand shall be upon the prophets that see vain things and that divine lies; they shall not be in the council

scriptura domus Israhel non scribentur, nec in terram Israhel ingredientur, et scietis quia ego Dominus Deus. 10 Eo quod deceperint populum meum, dicentes, "Pax," et non est pax, et ipse aedificabat parietem, illi autem liniebant eum luto absque paleis.'

11 "Dic ad eos qui liniunt absque temperatura quod casurus sit, erit enim imber inundans et dabo lapides praegrandes desuper inruentes et ventum procellae dissipantem. 12 Siquidem ecce: cecidit paries, numquid non dicetur vobis, 'Ubi est litura quam levistis?' 13 Propterea haec dicit Dominus Deus: 'Et erumpere faciam spiritum tempestatum in indignatione mea, et imber inundans in furore meo erit, et lapides grandes in ira in consumptionem. 14 Et destruam parietem quem levistis absque temperamento, et adaequabo eum terrae, et revelabitur fundamentum eius, et cadet et consumetur in medio eius, et scietis quia ego sum Dominus. 15 Et conplebo indignationem meam in pariete et in his qui linunt eum absque temperamento, dicamque vobis, "Non est paries, et non sunt qui linunt eum." 16 Prophetae Israhel qui prophetant ad Hierusalem et vident ei visionem pacis, et non est pax,' ait Dominus Deus.

17 "Et tu, fili hominis, pone faciem tuam contra filias populi tui quae prophetant de corde suo, et vaticinare super eas, 18 et dic, 'Haec ait Dominus Deus: "Vae quae consuunt pulvillos sub omni cubito manus et faciunt cervicalia sub capite universae aetatis ad capiendas animas, et cum caperent animas populi mei, vivificabant animas eorum. 19 Et viola-

of my people, nor shall they be written in the writing of the house of Israel, neither shall they enter into the land of Israel, and you shall know that I am the Lord God. 10 Because they have deceived my people, saying, "Peace," and there is no peace, and *the people* built up a wall, and they daubed it with dirt without straw.'

11 "Say to them that daub without tempering that it shall fall, for there shall be an overflowing shower and I will cause great hailstones to fall violently from above and a stormy wind to throw it down. 12 Behold: when the wall is fallen, shall it not be said to you, 'Where is the daubing wherewith you have daubed it?' 13 Therefore thus saith the Lord God: 'Lo, I will cause a stormy wind to break forth in my indignation, and there shall be an overflowing shower in my anger, and great hailstones in my wrath to consume. 14 And I will break down the wall that you have daubed with untempered mortar, and I will make it even with the ground, and the foundation thereof shall be laid bare, and it shall fall and shall be consumed in the midst thereof, and you shall know that I am the Lord. 15 And I will accomplish my wrath upon the wall and upon them that daub it without tempering the mortar, and I will say to you, "The wall is no more, and they that daub it are no more." 16 *Even* the prophets of Israel that prophesy to Jerusalem and that see visions of peace for her, and there is no peace,' saith the Lord God.

17 "And thou, son of man, set thy face against the daughters of thy people that prophesy out of their own heart, and do thou prophesy against them, 18 and say, 'Thus saith the Lord God: "Woe to them that sew cushions under every elbow and make pillows for the heads of persons of every age to catch souls, and when they caught the souls of my people, they gave life to their souls. 19 And they violated me among

bant me ad populum meum propter pugillum hordei et frag-
men panis ut interficerent animas quae non moriuntur et
vivificarent animas quae non vivunt, mentientes populo meo
credenti mendaciis."

20 "'Propter hoc haec dicit Dominus Deus: "Ecce: ego ad
pulvillos vestros quibus vos capitis animas volantes, et disrumpam eos de brachiis vestris, et dimittam animas quas vos
capitis, animas ad volandum. 21 Et disrumpam cervicalia
vestra et liberabo populum meum de manu vestra, neque
erunt ultra in manibus vestris ad praedandum, et scietis quia
ego Dominus. 22 Pro eo quod maerere fecistis cor iusti mendaciter, quem ego non contristavi, et confortastis manus impii ut non reverteretur a via sua mala et viveret, 23 propterea
vana non videbitis et divinationes non divinabitis amplius,
et eruam populum meum de manu vestra, et scietis quoniam
ego Dominus."'"

Caput 14

Et venerunt ad me viri seniorum Israhel et sederunt
coram me. 2 Et factus est sermo Domini ad me, dicens,
3 "Fili hominis, viri isti posuerunt inmunditias suas in cordi-

my people for a handful of barley and a piece of bread to kill souls which *should* not die and to save souls alive which *should* not live, telling lies to my people that believe lies."

20 "'Therefore thus saith the Lord God: "Behold: I *declare* against your cushions wherewith you catch flying souls, and I will tear them off from your arms, and I will let go the souls that you catch, the souls that should fly. 21 And I will tear your pillows and will deliver my people out of your hand, neither shall they be any more in your hands to be a prey, and you shall know that I am the Lord. 22 Because with lies you have made the heart of the just to mourn, whom I have not made sorrowful, and have strengthened the hands of the wicked that he should not return from his evil way and live, 23 therefore you shall not see vain things nor divine divinations any more, and I will deliver my people out of your hand, and you shall know that I am the Lord."'"

Chapter 14

God suffers the wicked to be deceived in punishment of their wickedness. The evils that shall come upon them for their sins, for which they shall not be delivered by the prayers of Noah, Daniel and Job. But a remnant shall be preserved.

And some of the ancients of Israel came to me and sat before me. 2 And the word of the Lord came to me, saying, 3 "Son of man, these men have placed their uncleannesses

bus suis et scandalum iniquitatis suae statuerunt contra faciem suam; numquid interrogatus respondebo eis? 4 Propter hoc loquere eis, et dices ad eos, 'Haec dicit Dominus Deus: "Homo, homo de domo Israhel qui posuerit inmunditias suas in corde suo et scandalum iniquitatis suae statuerit contra faciem suam et venerit ad prophetam interrogans per eum me, ego, Dominus, respondebo ei in multitudine inmunditiarum suarum, 5 ut capiatur domus Israhel in corde suo, quo recesserunt a me in cunctis idolis suis."'

6 "Propterea dic ad domum Israhel: 'Haec dicit Dominus Deus: "Convertimini, et recedite ab idolis vestris, et ab universis contaminationibus vestris avertite facies vestras. 7 Quia homo, homo de domo Israhel et de proselytis quicumque advena fuerit in Israhel, si alienatus fuerit a me et posuerit idola sua in corde suo et scandalum iniquitatis suae statuerit contra faciem suam et venerit ad prophetam ut interroget per eum me, ego, Dominus, respondebo ei per me. 8 Et ponam faciem meam super hominem illum et faciam eum in exemplum et in proverbium et disperdam eum de medio populi mei, et scietis quia ego Dominus.

9 ""Et propheta cum erraverit et locutus fuerit verbum, ego, Dominus, decepi prophetam illum, et extendam manum meam super eum et delebo eum de medio populi mei Israhel. 10 Et portabunt iniquitatem suam; iuxta iniquitatem interrogantis, sic iniquitas prophetae erit, 11 ut non erret ultra domus Israhel a me neque polluatur in universis praevaricationibus suis sed sit mihi in populum, et ego sim eis in Deum," ait Dominus exercituum.'"

in their hearts and have set up before their face the stumbling block of their iniquity, *and* shall I answer when they inquire of me? 4 Therefore speak to them, and *say* to them, 'Thus saith the Lord God: *"Every* man of the house of Israel that shall place his uncleannesses in his heart and set up the stumbling block of his iniquity before his face and shall come to the prophet inquiring of me by him, I, the Lord, will answer him according to the multitude of his uncleannesses, 5 that the house of Israel may be caught in their own heart, with which they have departed from me through all their idols."'

6 "Therefore say to the house of Israel: 'Thus saith the Lord God: "Be converted, and depart from your idols, and turn away your faces from all your abominations. 7 For *every* man of the house of Israel and every stranger among the proselytes in Israel, if he separate himself from me and place his idols in his heart and set the stumbling block of his iniquity before his face and come to the prophet to inquire of me by him, I, the Lord, will answer him by myself. 8 And I will set my face against that man and will make him an example and a proverb and will cut him off from the midst of my people, and you shall know that I am the Lord.

9 ""And when the prophet shall err and speak a word, I, the Lord, have deceived that prophet, and I will stretch forth my hand upon him and will cut him off from the midst of my people Israel. 10 And they shall bear their iniquity; according to the iniquity of him that inquireth, so shall the iniquity of the prophet be, 11 that the house of Israel may go no more astray from me nor be polluted with all their transgressions but may be my people, and I may be their God," saith the Lord of hosts.'"

12 Et factus est sermo Domini ad me, dicens, 13 "'Fili hominis, terra cum peccaverit mihi ut praevaricetur praevaricans, extendam manum meam super eam et conteram virgam panis eius, et inmittam in eam famem et interficiam de ea hominem et iumentum. 14 Et si fuerint tres viri isti in medio eius, Noe, Danihel et Iob, ipsi iustitia sua liberabunt animas suas,' ait Dominus exercituum. 15 'Quod si et bestias pessimas induxero super terram ut vastem eam et fuerit invia, eo quod non sit pertransitens propter bestias, 16 tres viri isti si fuerint in ea, vivo ego,' dicit Dominus, quia nec filios nec filias liberabunt, sed ipsi soli liberabuntur, terra autem desolabitur. 17 Vel si gladium induxero super terram illam et dixero gladio, "Transi per terram," et interfecero de ea hominem et iumentum, 18 et tres viri isti fuerint in medio eius, vivo ego,' dicit Dominus Deus, 'non liberabunt filios neque filias, sed ipsi soli liberabuntur. 19 Si autem et pestilentiam inmisero super terram illam et effudero indignationem meam super eam in sanguine ut auferam ex ea hominem et iumentum, 20 et Noe et Danihel et Iob fuerint in medio eius, vivo ego,' dicit Dominus Deus, 'quia filium et filiam non liberabunt, sed ipsi iustitia sua liberabunt animas suas.'

21 "Quoniam haec dicit Dominus Deus: 'Quod et si quattuor iudicia mea pessima, gladium et famem et bestias malas et pestilentiam, inmisero in Hierusalem ut interficiam de ea hominem et pecus, 22 tamen relinquetur in ea salvatio educentium filios et filias; ecce: ipsi ingredientur ad vos, et videbitis viam eorum et adinventiones eorum, et consolabimini super malo quod induxi in Hierusalem in omnibus quae

12 And the word of the Lord came to me, saying, 13 "'Son of man, when a land shall sin against me so as to transgress grievously, I will stretch forth my hand upon it and will break the staff of the bread thereof, and I will send famine upon it and will destroy man and beast out of it. 14 And if these three men, Noah, Daniel and Job, shall be in it, they shall deliver their own souls by their justice,' saith the Lord of hosts. 15 'And if I shall bring mischievous beasts also upon the land to waste it and it be desolate, *so* that there is none that can pass because of the beasts, 16 if these three men shall be in it, as I live,' saith the Lord, 'they shall deliver neither sons nor daughters, but they only shall be delivered, and the land shall be made desolate. 17 Or if I bring the sword upon that land and say to the sword, "Pass through the land," and I destroy man and beast out of it, 18 and these three men be in the midst thereof, as I live,' saith the Lord God, 'they shall deliver neither sons nor daughters, but they themselves alone shall be delivered. 19 *Or* if I also send the pestilence upon that land and pour out my indignation upon it in blood to cut off from it man and beast, 20 and Noah and Daniel and Job be in the midst thereof, as I live,' saith the Lord God, 'they shall deliver neither son nor daughter, but they shall only deliver their own souls by their justice.'

21 "For thus saith the Lord: 'Although I shall send in upon Jerusalem my four grievous judgments, the sword and the famine and the mischievous beasts and the pestilence to destroy out of it man and beast, 22 yet there shall be left in it *some* that shall be saved, who shall bring away their sons and daughters; behold: they shall come among you, and you shall see their way and their doings, and you shall be comforted concerning the evil that I have brought upon Jerusalem in

inportavi super eam. 23 Et consolabuntur vos, cum videritis viam eorum et adinventiones eorum, et cognoscetis quod non frustra fecerim omnia quae feci in ea,'" ait Dominus Deus.

Caput 15

Et factus est sermo Domini ad me dicens, 2 "Fili hominis, quid fiet de ligno vitis ex omnibus lignis nemorum quae sunt inter ligna silvarum? 3 Numquid tolletur de ea lignum ut fiat opus, aut fabricabitur de ea paxillus ut dependeat in eo quodcumque vas? 4 Ecce: igni datum est in escam; utramque partem eius consumpsit ignis, et medietas eius redacta est in favillam; numquid utile erit ad opus? 5 Etiam cum esset integrum non erat aptum ad opus; quanto magis, cum ignis illud devoraverit et conbuserit, nihil ex eo fiet operis?

6 "Propterea haec dicit Dominus Deus: 'Quomodo lignum vitis inter ligna silvarum, quod dedi igni ad devorandum, sic tradam habitatores Hierusalem. 7 Et ponam faciem meam in eos; de igne egredientur, et ignis consumet eos, et scietis

all things that I have brought upon it. 23 And they shall comfort you, when you shall see their ways and their doings, and you shall know that I have not done without cause all that I have done in it,'" saith the Lord God.

Chapter 15

As a vine cut down is fit for nothing but the fire, so it shall be with Jerusalem for her sins.

And the word of the Lord came to me, saying, 2 "Son of man, what shall be made of the wood of the vine out of all the trees of the woods that are among the trees of the forests? 3 Shall wood be taken of it to do any work, or shall a pin be made of it for any vessel to hang thereon? 4 Behold: it is cast into the fire for fuel; the fire hath consumed both ends thereof, and the midst thereof is reduced to ashes; shall it be useful for any work? 5 Even when it was whole it was not fit for work; how much *less,* when the fire hath devoured and consumed it, shall any work be made of it?

6 "Therefore thus saith the Lord God: 'As the vine tree among the trees of the forests, which I have given to the fire to be consumed, so will I deliver up the inhabitants of Jerusalem. 7 And I will set my face against them; they shall go out from fire, and fire shall consume them, and you shall

quia ego Dominus cum posuero faciem meam in eos. 8 Et dedero terram inviam et desolatam eo quod praevaricatores extiterint,' dicit Dominus Deus."

Caput 16

Et factus est sermo Domini ad me, dicens, 2 "Fili hominis, notas fac Hierusalem abominationes suas. 3 Et dices, 'Haec dicit Dominus Deus Hierusalem: "Radix tua et generatio tua de terra Chanaan; pater tuus Amorreus, et mater tua Cetthea. 4 Et quando nata es, in die ortus tui non est praecisus umbilicus tuus, et aqua non es lota in salutem nec sale salita nec involuta pannis. 5 Non pepercit super te oculus ut faceret tibi unum de his miseratus tui, sed proiecta es super faciem terrae in abiectione animae tuae in die qua nata es.

6 """Transiens autem per te vidi te conculcari in sanguine tuo, et dixi tibi cum esses in sanguine tuo, 'Vive!' Dixi, inquam, tibi, 'In sanguine tuo vive!' 7 Multiplicatam quasi

know that I am the Lord when I shall have set my face against them. 8 And I shall have made their land a wilderness and desolate because they have been transgressors,' saith the Lord God."

Chapter 16

Under the figure of an unfaithful wife God upbraids Jerusalem with her ingratitude and manifold disloyalties but promiseth mercy by a new covenant.

And the word of the Lord came to me, saying, 2 "Son of man, make known to Jerusalem her abominations. 3 And thou shalt say, 'Thus saith the Lord God to Jerusalem: "Thy root and thy nativity is of the land of Canaan; thy father was an Amorite, and thy mother a Hittite. 4 And when thou wast born, in the day of thy nativity thy navel was not cut, neither wast thou washed with water for thy health nor salted with salt nor swaddled with clouts. 5 No eye had pity on thee to do any of these things for thee out of compassion to thee, but thou wast cast out upon the face of the earth in the abjection of thy soul in the day that thou wast born.

6 ""And passing by thee I saw that thou wast trodden under foot in thy own blood, and I said to thee when thou wast in thy blood, 'Live!' I have said to *thee,* 'Live in thy blood!' 7 I caused thee to multiply as the bud of the field,

germen agri dedi te, et multiplicata es et grandis effecta et ingressa es et pervenisti ad mundum muliebrem; ubera tua intumuerunt, et pilus tuus germinavit, et eras nuda et confusionis plena. 8 Et transivi per te, et vidi te, et ecce: tempus tuum tempus amantium, et expandi amictum meum super te et operui ignominiam tuam. Et iuravi tibi, et ingressus sum pactum tecum," ait Dominus Deus, "et facta es mihi. 9 Et lavi te aqua et emundavi sanguinem tuum ex te, et unxi te oleo. 10 Et vestivi te discoloribus et calciavi te hyacinthino, et cinxi te bysso et indui te subtilibus. 11 Et ornavi te ornamento et dedi armillas in manibus tuis et torquem circa collum tuum. 12 Et dedi inaurem super os tuum et circulos auribus tuis et coronam decoris in capite tuo. 13 Et ornata es auro et argento et vestita es bysso et polymito et multis coloribus; similam et mel et oleum comedisti et decora facta es vehementer nimis et profecisti in regnum. 14 Et egressum est nomen tuum in gentes propter speciem tuam, quia perfecta eras in decore meo quem posueram super te," dicit Dominus Deus.

15 ""Et habens fiduciam in pulchritudine tua fornicata es in nomine tuo, et exposuisti fornicationem tuam omni transeunti ut eius fieres. 16 Et sumens de vestimentis tuis fecisti tibi excelsa hinc inde consuta et fornicata es super eis, sicut non est factum neque futurum est. 17 Et tulisti vasa decoris tui de auro meo et argento meo quae dedi tibi, et fecisti tibi imagines masculinas et fornicata es in eis. 18 Et sumpsisti vestimenta tua multicoloria et operuisti illas et oleum

and thou didst increase and grow great and advancedst and camest to woman's ornament; thy breasts were fashioned, and thy hair grew, and thou wast naked and full of confusion. 8 And I passed by thee and saw thee, and behold: thy time was the time of lovers, and I spread my garment over thee and covered thy ignominy. And I swore to thee, and I entered into a covenant with thee," saith the Lord God, "and thou becamest mine. 9 And I washed thee with water and cleansed away thy blood from thee, and I anointed thee with oil. 10 And I clothed thee with *embroidery* and shod thee with *violet-coloured shoes,* and I girded thee about with fine linen and clothed thee with fine garments. 11 I decked thee also with ornaments and put bracelets on thy hands and a chain about thy neck. 12 And I put a jewel upon thy forehead and earrings in thy ears and a beautiful crown upon thy head. 13 And thou wast adorned with gold and silver and wast clothed with fine linen and embroidered work and many colours; thou didst eat fine flour and honey and oil and wast made exceeding beautiful and wast advanced to be a queen. 14 And thy renown went forth among the nations for thy beauty, for thou wast perfect through my beauty which I had put upon thee," saith the Lord God.

15 ""But trusting in thy beauty thou playedst the harlot because of thy renown, and thou hast prostituted thyself to every passenger to be his. 16 And taking of thy garments thou hast made thee high places sewed together on each side and hast played the harlot upon them, as hath not been done before nor shall be hereafter. 17 And thou tookest *thy beautiful* vessels of my gold and my silver which I gave thee, and thou madest thee images of men and hast committed fornication with them. 18 And thou tookest thy garments of divers colours and coveredst them and settest my oil and my

meum et thymiama meum posuisti coram eis. 19 Et panem meum quem dedi tibi, similam et oleum et mel quibus enutrivi te, posuisti in conspectu eorum in odorem suavitatis, et factum est," ait Dominus Deus 20 "Et tulisti filios tuos et filias tuas, quas generasti mihi, et immolasti eis ad devorandum. Numquid parva est fornicatio tua? 21 Immolasti filios meos et dedisti illos, consecrans eis. 22 Et post omnes abominationes tuas et fornicationes non es recordata dierum adulescentiae tuae, quando eras nuda et confusione plena, conculcata in sanguine tuo.

23 ""Et accidit post omnem malitiam tuam ('Vae, vae tibi,' ait Dominus Deus) 24 et aedificasti tibi lupanar et fecisti tibi prostibulum in cunctis plateis. 25 Ad omne caput viae aedificasti signum prostitutionis tuae et abominabilem fecisti decorem tuum et divisisti pedes tuos omni transeunti et multiplicasti fornicationes tuas. 26 Et fornicata es cum filiis Aegypti, vicinis tuis, magnarum carnium, et multiplicasti fornicationem tuam ad inritandum me. 27 Ecce: ego extendam manum meam super te et auferam iustificationem tuam, et dabo te in animas odientium te filiarum Palestinarum, quae erubescunt in via tua scelerata. 28 Et fornicata es in filiis Assyriorum eo quod necdum fueris expleta, et postquam fornicata es, nec sic es satiata. 29 Et multiplicasti fornicationem tuam in terra Chanaan cum Chaldeis, et nec sic satiata es.

30 ""In quo mundabo cor tuum," ait Dominus Deus, "Cum facias omnia haec, opera mulieris meretricis et proca-

sweet incense before them. 19 And my bread which I gave thee, the fine flour and oil and honey wherewith I fed thee, thou hast set before them for a sweet odour, and it was done," saith the Lord God. 20 "And thou hast taken thy sons and thy daughters, whom thou hast borne to me, and hast sacrificed the same to them to be devoured. Is thy fornication small? 21 Thou hast sacrificed and given my children to them, consecrating them *by fire*. 22 And after all thy abominations and fornications thou hast not remembered the days of thy youth, when thou wast naked and full of confusion, trodden under foot in thy own blood.

23 ""And it came to pass after all thy wickedness ('Woe, woe to thee,' saith the Lord God) 24 that thou didst also build thee a common stew and madest thee a brothel house in every street. 25 At every head of the way thou hast set up a sign of thy prostitution and hast made thy beauty to be abominable and hast prostituted thyself to every one that passed by and hast multiplied thy fornications. 26 And thou hast committed fornication with the Egyptians, thy neighbours, men of large bodies, and hast multiplied thy fornications to provoke me. 27 Behold: I will stretch out my hand upon thee and will take away thy justification, and I will deliver thee up to the will of the daughters of the Philistines that hate thee, that are ashamed of thy wicked way. 28 Thou hast also committed fornication with the *Assyrians* because thou wast not yet satisfied, and after thou hadst played the harlot with them, even so thou wast not contented. 29 Thou hast also multiplied thy fornications in the land of Canaan with the Chaldeans, and neither so wast thou satisfied.

30 ""Wherein shall I cleanse thy heart," saith the Lord God, "Seeing thou dost all these, the works of a shameless

cis? 31 Quia fabricasti lupanar tuum in capite omnis viae et excelsum tuum fecisti in omni platea nec facta es quasi meretrix fastidio augens pretium 32 sed quasi mulier adultera quae super virum suum inducit alienos. 33 Omnibus meretricibus dantur mercedes, tu autem dedisti mercedes cunctis amatoribus tuis, et dona donabas eis ut intrarent ad te undique ad fornicandum tecum. 34 Factumque in te est contra consuetudinem mulierum in fornicationibus tuis, et post te non erit fornicatio, in eo enim quod dedisti mercedes et mercedes non accepisti, factum est in te contrarium.

35 """Propterea, meretrix, audi verbum Domini." 36 Haec dicit Dominus Deus: "Quia effusum est aes tuum et revelata est ignominia tua in fornicationibus tuis super amatores tuos et super idola abominationum tuarum in sanguine filiorum tuorum quos dedisti eis, 37 ecce: ego congregabo omnes amatores tuos quibus commixta es et omnes quos dilexisti cum universis quos oderas, et congregabo eos super te undique et nudabo ignominiam tuam coram eis, et videbunt omnem turpitudinem tuam. 38 Et iudicabo te iudiciis adulterarum et effundentium sanguinem, et dabo te in sanguinem furoris et zeli. 39 Et dabo te in manus eorum, et destruent lupanar tuum et demolientur prostibulum tuum, et denudabunt te vestimentis tuis et auferent vasa decoris tui et derelinquent te nudam plenamque ignominia. 40 Et adducent super te multitudinem, et lapidabunt te lapidibus et trucidabunt te gladiis suis. 41 Et conburent domos tuas igni et

prostitute? 31 Because thou hast built thy brothel house at the head of every way and thou hast made thy high place in every street and wast not as a harlot that by disdain enhanceth her price 32 but as an adulteress that bringeth in strangers over her husband. 33 Gifts are given to all harlots, but thou hast given hire to all thy lovers, and thou hast given them gifts to come to thee from every side to commit fornication with thee. 34 And it hath happened in thee contrary to the custom of women in thy fornications, and after thee there shall be no such fornication, for in that thou gavest rewards and didst not take rewards, the contrary hath been done in thee.

35 """Therefore, O harlot, hear the word of the Lord." 36 Thus saith the Lord God: "Because thy money hath been poured out and thy shame discovered through thy fornications with thy lovers and with the idols of thy abominations by the blood of thy children whom thou gavest them, 37 behold: I will gather together all thy lovers with whom thou hast taken pleasure and all whom thou hast loved with all whom thou hast hated, and I will gather them together against thee on every side and will discover thy shame in their sight, and they shall see all thy nakedness. 38 And I will judge thee as adulteresses and they that shed blood are judged, and I will give thee *blood in* fury and jealousy. 39 And I will deliver thee into their hands, and they shall destroy thy brothel house and throw down thy stews, and they shall strip thee of thy garments and shall take away the vessels of thy beauty and leave thee naked and full of disgrace. 40 And they shall bring upon thee a multitude, and they shall stone thee with stones and shall slay thee with their swords. 41 And they

facient in te iudicia in oculis mulierum plurimarum, et desines fornicari et mercedes ultra non dabis.

42 """Et requiescet indignatio mea in te, et auferetur zelus meus a te, et quiescam nec irascar amplius. 43 Eo quod non fueris recordata dierum adulescentiae tuae et provocasti me in omnibus his, quapropter et ego vias tuas in capite tuo dedi," ait Dominus Deus, "et non feci iuxta scelera tua in omnibus abominationibus tuis. 44 Ecce: omnis qui dicit vulgo proverbium in te adsumet illud, dicens, 'Sicut mater, ita et filia eius.' 45 Filia matris tuae es tu, quae proiecit virum suum et filios suos, et soror sororum tuarum es tu, quae proiecerunt viros suos et filios suos; mater vestra Cetthea, et pater vester Amorreus. 46 Et soror tua maior Samaria, ipsa et filiae eius quae habitant ad sinistram tuam, soror autem tua minor te quae habitat a dextris tuis Sodoma et filiae eius. 47 Sed nec in viis earum ambulasti, neque secundum scelera earum fecisti pauxillum minus; paene sceleratiora fecisti illis in omnibus viis tuis.

48 """Vivo ego," dicit Dominus Deus, "quia non fecit Sodoma soror tua ipsa et filiae eius sicut fecisti tu et filiae tuae. 49 Ecce: haec fuit iniquitas Sodomae, sororis tuae: superbia, saturitas panis et abundantia et otium ipsius et filiarum eius, et manum egeno et pauperi non porrigebant. 50 Et elevatae sunt et fecerunt abominationes coram me, et abstuli eas sicut vidisti. 51 Et Samaria dimidium peccatorum tuorum

shall burn thy houses with fire and shall execute judgments upon thee in the sight of many women, and thou shalt cease from fornication and shalt give no hire any more.

42 ""And my indignation shall rest in thee, and my jealousy shall depart from thee, and I will cease and be angry no more. 43 Because thou hast not remembered the days of thy youth but hast provoked me in all these things, wherefore I also have turned thy ways upon thy head," saith the Lord God, "and I have not done according to thy wicked deeds in all thy abominations. 44 Behold: every one that useth a common proverb shall use this against thee, saying, 'As the mother was, so also is her daughter.' 45 Thou art thy mother's daughter, that cast off her husband and her children, and thou art the sister of thy sisters, who cast off their husbands and their children; your mother was a Hittite, and your father an Amorite. 46 And thy elder sister is Samaria, she and her daughters that dwell at thy left hand, and thy younger sister that dwelleth at thy right hand is Sodom and her daughters. 47 But neither hast thou walked in their ways, nor hast thou done a little less than they according to their wickednesses; thou hast done almost more wicked things than they in all thy ways.

48 ""As I live," saith the Lord God, "thy sister Sodom, herself and her daughters, have not done as thou hast done and thy daughters. 49 Behold: this was the iniquity of Sodom, thy sister: pride, fulness of bread and abundance and the idleness of her and of her daughters, and they did not put forth their hand to the needy and to the poor. 50 And they were lifted up and committed abominations before me, and I took them away as thou hast seen. 51 And Samaria committed not half thy sins, but thou hast surpassed them with

non peccavit, sed vicisti eas sceleribus tuis et iustificasti sorores tuas in omnibus abominationibus tuis quas operata es. 52 Ergo et tu porta confusionem tuam, quae vicisti sorores tuas peccatis tuis, sceleratius agens ab eis, iustificatae sunt enim a te; ergo et tu confundere, et porta ignominiam tuam, quae iustificasti sorores tuas.

53 ““Et convertam restituens eas conversione Sodomorum cum filiabus suis et conversione Samariae et filiarum eius, et convertam reversionem tuam in medio earum, 54 ut portes ignominiam tuam et confundaris in omnibus quae fecisti, consolans eas. 55 Et soror tua Sodoma et filiae eius revertentur ad antiquitatem suam, et Samaria et filiae eius revertentur ad antiquitatem suam, et tu et filiae tuae revertemini ad antiquitatem vestram.

56 ““Non fuit autem Sodoma, soror tua, audita in ore tuo in die superbiae tuae, 57 antequam revelaretur malitia tua sicut hoc tempore, in obprobrium filiarum Syriae et cunctarum in circuitu tuo filiarum Palestinarum quae ambiunt te per gyrum. 58 Scelus tuum et ignominiam tuam tu portasti,” ait Dominus Deus.

59 “Quia haec dicit Dominus Deus: “Et faciam tibi sicut dispexisti iuramentum ut irritum faceres pactum, 60 et recordabor ego pacti mei tecum in diebus adulescentiae tuae, et suscitabo tibi pactum sempiternum. 61 Et recordaberis viarum tuarum et confunderis cum receperis sorores tuas, te maiores cum minoribus tuis, et dabo eas tibi in filias, sed non ex pacto tuo. 62 Et suscitabo ego pactum meum tecum, et scies quia ego Dominus, 63 ut recorderis et confundaris

thy crimes and hast justified thy sisters by all thy abominations which thou hast done. 52 Therefore do thou also bear thy confusion, thou that hast surpassed thy sisters with thy sins, doing more wickedly than they, for they are justified above thee; therefore be thou also confounded, and bear thy shame, thou that hast justified thy sisters.

53 "''And I will bring back and restore them by bringing back Sodom with her daughters and by bringing back Samaria and her daughters, and I will bring those that return of thee in the midst of them, 54 that thou mayest bear thy shame and mayest be confounded in all that thou hast done, comforting them. 55 And thy sister Sodom and her daughters shall return to their ancient state, and Samaria and her daughters shall return to their ancient state, and thou and thy daughters shall return to your ancient state.

56 "''And Sodom, thy sister, was not heard of in thy mouth in the day of thy pride, 57 before thy malice was laid open as it is at this time, making thee a reproach of the daughters of Syria and of all the daughters of Palestine round about thee that encompass thee on all sides. 58 Thou hast borne thy wickedness, and thy disgrace," saith the Lord God.

59 "'For thus saith the Lord God: "I will deal with thee as thou hast despised the oath in breaking the covenant, 60 and I will remember my covenant with thee in the days of thy youth, and I will establish with thee an everlasting covenant. 61 And thou shalt remember thy ways and be ashamed when thou shalt receive thy sisters, thy elder and thy younger, and I will give them to thee for daughters, but not by thy covenant. 62 And I will establish my covenant with thee, and thou shalt know that I am the Lord, 63 that thou mayest remem-

et non sit tibi ultra aperire os prae confusione tua, cum placatus fuero tibi in omnibus quae fecisti," ait Dominus
Deus.'"

Caput 17

Et factum est verbum Domini ad me, dicens, 2 "Fili hominis, propone enigma, et narra parabolam ad domum Israhel,
3 et dices, 'Haec dicit Dominus Deus: "Aquila grandis
magnarum alarum, longo membrorum ductu, plena plumis
et varietate, venit ad Libanum et tulit medullam cedri.
4 Summitatem frondium eius avellit et transportavit eam in
terram Chanaan; in urbe negotiatorum posuit illam. 5 Et tulit de semine terrae et posuit illud in terra pro semine, ut
firmaret radicem super aquas multas; in superficie posuit illud. 6 Cumque germinasset crevit in vineam latiorem humili
statura, respicientibus ramis eius ad eam, et radices eius sub
illa erant. Facta est ergo vinea et fructificavit in palmites et
emisit propagines.

7 ""Et facta est aquila altera grandis magnis alis multisque
plumis, et ecce: vinea ista, quasi mittens radices suas ad eam,
palmites suos extendit ad illam ut inrigaret eam de areolis

ber and be confounded and mayest no more open thy mouth because of thy confusion, when I shall be pacified toward thee for all that thou hast done," saith the Lord God.'"

Chapter 17

The parable of the two eagles and the vine. A promise of the cedar of Christ and his church.

And the word of the Lord came to me, saying, 2 "Son of man, put forth a riddle, and speak a parable to the house of Israel, 3 and *say,* 'Thus saith the Lord God: "A large eagle with great wings, long-limbed, full of feathers and of variety, came to Lebanon and took away the marrow of the cedar. 4 He cropped off the top of the twigs thereof and carried it away into the land of Canaan, *and* he set it in a city of merchants. 5 And he took of the seed of the land and put it in the ground for seed, that it might take a firm root over many waters; he planted it on the surface of the earth. 6 And *it sprung up and* grew into a spreading vine of low stature, and the branches thereof looked towards him, and the roots thereof were under him. So it became a vine and grew into branches and shot forth sprigs.

7 ""And there was another large eagle with great wings and many feathers, and behold: this vine, bending as it were her roots towards him, stretched forth her branches to him

germinis sui. 8 In terra bona super aquas multas plantata est ut faciat frondes et portet fructum, ut sit in vineam grandem."'

9 "Dic: 'Haec dicit Dominus Deus: "Ergone prosperabitur? Nonne radices eius evellet et fructus eius distringet et siccabit omnes palmites germinis eius et arescet et non in brachio grandi neque in populo multo ut evelleret eam radicitus? 10 Ecce: plantata est; ergone prosperabitur? Nonne cum tetigerit eam ventus urens siccabitur, et in areis germinis sui arescet?"'"

11 Et factum est verbum Domini ad me, dicens, 12 "Dic ad domum exasperantem, 'Nescitis quid ista significent?' Dic, 'Ecce: venit rex Babylonis in Hierusalem, et adsumet regem et principes eius et adducet eos ad semet ipsum in Babylonem. 13 Et tollet de semine regni ferietque cum eo foedus et accipiet ab eo iusiurandum. Sed et fortes terrae tollet, 14 ut sit regnum humile et non elevetur, sed custodiat pactum eius et servet illud. 15 Qui recedens ab eo misit nuntios ad Aegyptum ut daret sibi equos et populum multum. Numquid prosperabitur vel consequetur salutem qui fecit haec? Et qui dissolvit pactum numquid effugiet? 16 "Vivo ego," dicit Dominus Deus, "quoniam in loco regis qui constituit eum regem, cuius fecit irritum iuramentum et solvit pactum quod habebat cum eo, in medio Babylonis morietur. 17 Et non in exercitu grandi neque in populo multo faciet contra eum Pharao proelium in iactu aggeris et in extructione val-

that he might water it by the furrows of her plantation. 8 It was planted in a good ground upon many waters that it might bring forth branches and bear fruit, that it might become a large vine.'"

9 "Say thou: 'Thus saith the Lord God: "Shall it prosper then? Shall he not pull up the roots thereof and strip off its fruit and dry up all the branches it hath shot forth and *make* it wither, and this without a strong arm or many people to pluck it up by the root? 10 Behold: it is planted; shall it prosper then? Shall it not be dried up when the burning wind shall touch it, and shall it not wither in the furrows where it grew?"'"

11 And the word of the Lord came to me, saying, 12 "Say to the provoking house, 'Know you not what these things mean?' Tell them, 'Behold: the king of Babylon cometh to Jerusalem, and he shall take away the king and the princes thereof and carry them *with* him to Babylon. 13 And he shall take one of the king's seed and make a covenant with him and take an oath of him. Yea, and he shall take away the mighty men of the land, 14 that it may be a low kingdom and not lift itself up, but keep his covenant and observe it. 15 But he hath revolted from him and sent ambassadors to Egypt that it might give him horses and much people. And shall he that hath done thus prosper or be saved? And shall he escape that hath broken the covenant? 16 "As I live," saith the Lord God, "in the place where the king dwelleth that made him king, whose oath he hath made void and whose covenant he broke, even in the midst of Babylon shall he die. 17 And not with a great army nor with much people shall Pharaoh fight against him when he shall cast up mounts and

lorum ut interficiat animas multas. 18 Spreverat enim iuramentum ut solveret foedus, et ecce: dedit manum suam, et cum omnia haec fecerit, non effugiet." 19 Propterea haec dicit Dominus Deus: "Vivo ego quoniam iuramentum quod sprevit et foedus quod praevaricatus est ponam in caput eius. 20 Et expandam super eum rete meum, et conprehendetur in sagena mea, et adducam eum in Babylonem et iudicabo illum ibi in praevaricatione qua despexit me. 21 Et omnes profugi eius cum universo agmine suo gladio cadent, residui autem in omnem ventum dispergentur, et scietis quia ego, Dominus, locutus sum."

22 "'Haec dicit Dominus Deus: "Et sumam ego de medulla cedri sublimis et ponam; de vertice ramorum eius tenerum distringam, et plantabo super montem excelsum et eminentem. 23 In monte sublimi Israhel plantabo illud, et erumpet in germen et faciet fructum, et erit in cedrum magnam, et habitabunt sub ea omnes volucres, et universum volatile sub umbra frondium eius nidificabit. 24 Et scient omnia ligna regionis quia ego, Dominus, humiliavi lignum sublime et exaltavi lignum humile et siccavi lignum viride et frondere feci lignum aridum. Ego, Dominus, locutus sum et feci."'"

build forts to cut off many souls. 18 For he had despised the oath, *breaking* his covenant, and behold: he hath given his hand, and having done all these things, he shall not escape." 19 Therefore thus saith the Lord God: "As I live, I will lay upon his head the oath he hath despised and the covenant he hath broken. 20 And I will spread my net over him, and he shall be taken in my net, and I will bring him into Babylon and will judge him there for the transgression by which he hath despised me. 21 And all his fugitives with all his *bands* shall fall by the sword, and the residue shall be scattered into every wind, and you shall know that I, the Lord, have spoken."

22 "'Thus saith the Lord God: "I myself will take of the marrow of the high cedar and will set it; I will crop off a tender twig from the top of the branches thereof, and I will plant it on a mountain high and eminent. 23 On the high *mountains* of Israel will I plant it, and it shall shoot forth into branches and shall bear fruit, and it shall become a great cedar, and all birds shall dwell under it, and every fowl shall make its nest under the shadow of the branches thereof. 24 And all the trees of the country shall know that I, the Lord, have brought down the high tree and exalted the low tree and have dried up the green tree and have caused the dry tree to flourish. I, the Lord, have spoken and have done it.""'"

Caput 18

Et factus est sermo Domini ad me, dicens, 2 "'Quid est quod inter vos parabolam vertitis in proverbium istud in terra Israhel, dicentes, "Patres comederunt uvam acerbam, et dentes filiorum obstupescunt?" 3 Vivo ego,' dicit Dominus Deus, 'si erit vobis ultra parabola haec in proverbium in Israhel. 4 Ecce: omnes animae meae sunt; ut anima patris, ita et anima filii mea est; anima quae peccaverit, ipsa morietur. 5 Et vir si fuerit iustus et fecerit iudicium et iustitiam, 6 in montibus non comederit et oculos suos non levaverit ad idola domus Israhel et uxorem proximi sui non violaverit et ad mulierem menstruatam non accesserit 7 et hominem non contristaverit, pignus debitori reddiderit, per vim nihil rapuerit, panem suum esurienti dederit et nudum operuerit vestimento, 8 ad usuram non commodaverit et amplius non acceperit, ab iniquitate averterit manum suam et iudicium verum fecerit inter virum et virum, 9 in praeceptis meis ambulaverit et iudicia mea custodierit ut faciat veritatem, hic iustus est; vita vivet,' ait Dominus Deus. 10 'Quod si genuerit filium latronem, effundentem sanguinem et fecerit unum de istis, 11 et haec quidem omnia non facientem, sed in mon-

Chapter 18

One man shall not bear the sins of another, but every one
his own. If a wicked man truly repent, he shall be saved, and
if a just man leave his justice, he shall perish.

And the word of the Lord came to me, saying: "'What is
the meaning 2 that you use among you this parable as a proverb in the land of Israel, saying, "The fathers have eaten sour
grapes, and the teeth of the children are set on edge?" 3 As I
live,' saith the Lord God, 'this parable shall be no more to
you a proverb in Israel. 4 Behold: all souls are mine; as the
soul of the father, so also the soul of the son is mine; the soul
that sinneth, the same shall die. 5 And if a man be just and do
judgment and justice, 6 *and* hath not eaten upon the mountains nor lifted up his eyes to the idols of the house of Israel
and hath not defiled his neighbour's wife nor come near to
a menstruous woman 7 and hath not wronged any man but
hath restored the pledge to the debtor, hath taken nothing
away by violence, hath given his bread to the hungry and
hath covered the naked with a garment, 8 hath not lent upon
usury nor taken any increase, hath withdrawn his hand from
iniquity and hath executed true judgment between man and
man, 9 hath walked in my commandments and kept my judgments to do truth, he is just; he shall surely live,' saith the
Lord God. 10 'And if he beget a son that is a robber, a shed-
der of blood and that hath done some one of these things,
11 though he doth not all these things, but that eateth upon

tibus comedentem et uxorem proximi sui polluentem, 12 egenum et pauperem contristantem, rapientem rapinas, pignus non reddentem, et ad idola levantem oculos suos, abominationem facientem, 13 ad usuram dantem et amplius accipientem, numquid vivet? Non vivet. Cum universa detestanda haec fecerit, morte morietur; sanguis eius in ipso erit.

14 "'Quod si genuerit filium qui, videns omnia peccata patris sui quae fecit, timuerit et non fecerit simile eis, 15 super montes non comederit et oculos suos non levaverit ad idola domus Israhel et uxorem proximi sui non violaverit 16 et virum non contristaverit, pignus non retinuerit et rapinam non rapuerit, panem suum esurienti dederit et nudum operuerit vestimento, 17 a pauperis iniuria averterit manum suam, usuram et superabundantiam non acceperit, iudicia mea fecerit, in praeceptis meis ambulaverit, hic non morietur in iniquitate patris sui, sed vita vivet. 18 Pater eius, quia calumniatus est et vim fecit fratri et malum operatus est in medio populi sui, ecce: mortuus est in iniquitate sua.

19 "'Et dicitis, "Quare non portavit filius iniquitatem patris?" Videlicet, quia filius iudicium et iustitiam operatus est, omnia praecepta mea custodivit et fecit illa, vita vivet. 20 Anima quae peccaverit ipsa morietur; filius non portabit iniquitatem patris, et pater non portabit iniquitatem filii; iustitia iusti super eum erit, et impietas impii erit super eum.

21 "'Si autem impius egerit paenitentiam ab omnibus peccatis suis quae operatus est et custodierit universa praecepta

the mountains and that defileth his neighbour's wife, 12 that grieveth the needy and the poor, that taketh away by violence, that restoreth not the pledge and that lifteth up his eyes to idols, that committeth abomination, 13 that giveth upon usury and that taketh an increase, shall such a one live? He shall not live. Seeing he hath done all these detestable things, he shall surely die; his blood shall be upon him.

14 "But if he beget a son who, seeing all his father's sins which he hath done, is afraid and shall not do the like to them, 15 that hath not eaten upon the mountains nor lifted up his eyes to the idols of the house of Israel and hath not defiled his neighbour's wife 16 and hath not grieved any man *nor* withholden the pledge nor taken away with violence *but* hath given his bread to the hungry and covered the naked with a garment, 17 that hath turned away his hand from injuring the poor, hath not taken usury and increase, *but* hath executed my judgments *and* hath walked in my commandments, this man shall not die for the iniquity of his father, but living he shall live. 18 As for his father, because he oppressed and offered violence to his brother and wrought evil in the midst of his people, behold: he is dead in his own iniquity.

19 "And you say, "Why hath not the son borne the iniquity of his father?" Verily, because the son hath wrought judgment and justice, hath kept all my commandments and done them, living he shall live. 20 The soul that sinneth, the same shall die; the son shall not bear the iniquity of the father, and the father shall not bear the iniquity of the son; the justice of the just shall be upon him, and the wickedness of the wicked shall be upon him.

21 "But if the wicked do penance for all his sins which he hath committed and keep all my commandments and do

mea et fecerit iudicium et iustitiam, vita vivet et non morietur. 22 Omnium iniquitatum eius quas operatus est non recordabor; in iustitia sua quam operatus est vivet. 23 Numquid voluntatis meae est mors impii,' dicit Dominus Deus, 'et non ut convertatur a viis suis et vivat? 24 Si autem averterit se iustus a iustitia sua et fecerit iniquitatem secundum omnes abominationes quas operari solet impius, numquid vivet? Omnes iustitiae eius quas fecerat non recordabuntur; in praevaricatione qua praevaricatus est et in peccato suo quod peccavit, in ipsis morietur.

25 "'Et dixistis, "Non est aequa via Domini." Audite ergo, domus Israhel! Numquid via mea non est aequa, et non magis viae vestrae pravae sunt? 26 Cum enim averterit se iustus a iustitia sua et fecerit iniquitatem, morietur in eis; in iniustitia quam operatus est morietur. 27 Et cum averterit se impius ab impietate sua quam operatus est et fecerit iudicium et iustitiam, ipse animam suam vivificabit. 28 Considerans enim et avertens se ab omnibus iniquitatibus suis quas operatus est, vita vivet et non morietur. 29 Et dicunt filii Israhel, "Non est aequa via Domini." Numquid viae meae non sunt aequae, domus Israhel, et non magis viae vestrae pravae?

30 "'Idcirco unumquemque iuxta vias suas iudicabo, domus Israhel,' ait Dominus Deus. 'Convertimini, et agite paenitentiam ab omnibus iniquitatibus vestris, et non erit vobis in ruinam iniquitas. 31 Proicite a vobis omnes praevaricationes vestras in quibus praevaricati estis, et facite vobis cor novum et spiritum novum, et quare moriemini domus Israhel? 32 Quia nolo mortem morientis,' dicit Dominus Deus; 'revertimini, et vivite.'"

judgment and justice, living he shall live and shall not die. 22 I will not remember all his iniquities that he hath done; in his justice which he hath wrought he shall live. 23 Is it my will that a sinner should die,' saith the Lord God, 'and not that he should be converted from his ways and live? 24 But if the just man turn himself away from his justice and do iniquity according to all the abominations which the wicked man useth to work, shall he live? All his justices which he hath done shall not be remembered; in the prevarication by which he hath prevaricated and in his sin which he hath committed, in them he shall die.

25 "And you have said, "The way of the Lord is not right." Hear ye therefore, O house of Israel! Is it my way that is not right, and are not rather your ways perverse? 26 For when the just turneth himself away from his justice and committeth iniquity, he shall die therein; in the injustice that he hath wrought he shall die. 27 And when the wicked turneth himself away from his wickedness which he hath wrought and doeth judgment and justice, he shall save his soul alive. 28 Because he considereth and turneth away himself from all his iniquities which he hath wrought, he shall surely live and not die. 29 And the children of Israel say, "The way of the Lord is not right." Are not my ways right, O house of Israel, and are not rather your ways perverse?

30 "Therefore will I judge every man according to his ways, O house of Israel,' saith the Lord God. 'Be converted, and do penance for all your iniquities, and iniquity shall not be your ruin. 31 Cast away from you all your transgressions by which you have transgressed, and make to yourselves a new heart and a new spirit, and why will you die, O house of Israel? 32 For I desire not the death of him that dieth,' saith the Lord God; 'return ye, and live.'"

"Et tu adsume planctum super principes Israhel, 2 et dices, 'Quare mater tua, leaena, inter leones cubavit? In medio leunculorum enutrivit catulos suos? 3 Et eduxit unum de leunculis suis, et leo factus est, et didicit capere praedam hominemque comedere. 4 Et audierunt de eo gentes et non absque vulneribus suis ceperunt eum, et adduxerunt eum in catenis in terram Aegypti.

5 "'Quae cum vidisset quoniam infirmata est et periit expectatio eius, tulit unum de leunculis suis; leonem constituit eum. 6 Qui incedebat inter leones et factus est leo, et didicit praedam capere et homines devorare. 7 Didicit viduas facere et civitates eorum in desertum adducere, et desolata est terra et plenitudo eius a voce rugitus illius. 8 Et convenerunt adversum eum gentes undique de provinciis, et expanderunt super eum rete suum; in vulneribus earum captus est. 9 Et miserunt eum in caveam; in catenis adduxerunt eum ad regem Babylonis miseruntque eum in carcerem, ne audiretur vox eius ultra super montes Israhel.

10 "'Mater tua quasi vinea in sanguine tuo super aquam plantata est; fructus eius et frondes eius creverunt ex aquis multis. 11 Et factae sunt ei virgae solidae in sceptra dominan-

Chapter 19

The parable of the young lions and of the vineyard that is wasted.

"Moreover take thou up a lamentation for the princes of Israel, 2 and say, 'Why did thy mother, the lioness, lie down among the lions *and* bring up her whelps in the midst of young lions? 3 And she brought out one of her whelps, and he became a lion, and he learned to catch the prey and to devour men. 4 And the nations heard of him and took him, but not without receiving wounds, and they brought him in chains into the land of Egypt.

5 "But she, seeing herself weakened and that her hope was lost, took one of her young lions *and* set him up for a lion. 6 And he went up and down among the lions and became a lion, and he learned to catch the prey and to devour men. 7 He learned to make widows and to lay waste their cities, and the land became desolate and the fulness thereof by the noise of his roaring. 8 And the nations came together against him on every side out of the provinces, and they spread their net over him; in their wounds he was taken. 9 And they put him into a cage; they brought him in chains to the king of Babylon, and they cast him into prison, that his voice should no more be heard upon the mountains of Israel.

10 "'Thy mother is like a vine in thy blood planted by the water; her fruit and her branches have grown out of many waters. 11 And she hath strong rods to make sceptres for

tium, et exaltata est statura eius inter frondes, et vidit altitudinem suam in multitudine palmitum suorum. 12 Et evulsa est in ira in terramque proiecta, et ventus urens siccavit fructum eius; marcuerunt et arefactae sunt virgae roboris eius; ignis comedit eam. 13 Et nunc transplantata est in desertum, in terra invia et sitienti. 14 Et egressus est ignis de virga ramorum eius qui fructum eius comedit, et non fuit in ea virga fortis, sceptrum dominantium.'"

Planctus est, et erit in planctum.

Caput 20

Et factum est in anno septimo, in quinto, in decima mensis, venerunt viri de senioribus Israhel ut interrogarent Dominum, et sederunt coram me. 2 Et factus est sermo Domini ad me, dicens, 3 "Fili hominis, loquere senioribus Israhel, et dices ad eos, 'Haec dicit Dominus Deus: "Numquid ad interrogandum me vos venistis? Vivo ego quia non respondebo vobis," ait Dominus Deus.'

4 "Si iudicas eos, si iudicas, fili hominis, abominationes patrum eorum ostende eis. 5 Et dices ad eos, 'Haec dicit

them that bear rule, and her stature was exalted among the branches, and she saw her height in the multitude of her branches. 12 But she was plucked up in wrath and cast on the ground, and the burning wind dried up her fruit; her strong rods are withered and dried up; the fire hath devoured her. 13 And now she is transplanted into the desert, in a land not passable and dry. 14 And a fire is gone out from a rod of her branches which hath devoured her fruit, *so that she now hath* no strong rod to be a sceptre of rulers.'"

This is a lamentation, and it shall be for a lamentation.

Chapter 20

God refuses to answer the ancients of Israel inquiring by the prophet but by him setteth his benefits before their eyes and their heinous sins, threatening yet greater punishments but still mixed with mercy.

And it came to pass in the seventh year, in the fifth *month,* the tenth day of the month, there came men of the ancients of Israel to inquire of the Lord, and they sat before me. 2 And the word of the Lord came to me, saying, 3 "Son of man, speak to the ancients of Israel, and *say* to them: 'Thus saith the Lord God: "Are you come to inquire of me? As I live, I will not answer you," saith the Lord God.'

4 "If thou judgest them, if thou judgest, son of man, declare to them the abominations of their fathers. 5 And say to

Dominus Deus: "In die qua elegi Israhel et levavi manum meam pro stirpe domus Iacob et apparui eis in terra Aegypti et levavi manum meam pro eis, dicens, 'Ego Dominus, Deus vester,' 6 in die illa levavi manum meam pro eis ut educerem eos de terra Aegypti in terram quam provideram eis, fluentem lacte et melle, quae est egregia inter omnes terras. 7 Et dixi ad eos, 'Unusquisque offensiones oculorum suorum abiciat, et in idolis Aegypti nolite pollui; ego Dominus, Deus vester.' 8 Et inritaverunt me nolueruntque me audire; unusquisque abominationes oculorum suorum non proiecit, nec idola Aegypti reliquerunt, et dixi ut effunderem indignationem meam super eos et implerem iram meam in eis in medio terrae Aegypti.

9 ""Et feci propter nomen meum, ut non violaretur coram gentibus in quarum medio erant et inter quas apparui eis ut educerem eos de terra Aegypti. 10 Eieci ergo eos de terra Aegypti et eduxi eos in desertum 11 Et dedi eis praecepta mea, et iudicia mea ostendi eis, quae faciens homo vivet in eis. 12 Insuper et sabbata mea dedi eis ut essent signum inter me et eos et scirent quia ego Dominus sanctificans eos.

13 ""Et inritaverunt me domus Israhel in desert; in praeceptis meis non ambulaverunt, et iudicia mea proiecerunt, quae faciens homo vivet in eis, et sabbata mea violaverunt vehementer. Dixi ergo ut effunderem furorem meum super eos in deserto et consumerem eos. 14 Et feci propter nomen

them, 'Thus saith the Lord God: "In the day when I chose
Israel and lifted up my hand for the race of the house of Jacob and appeared to them in the land of Egypt and lifted up
my hand for them, saying, 'I am the Lord, your God,' 6 in
that day I lifted up my hand for them to bring them out of
the land of Egypt into a land which I had provided for them,
flowing with milk and honey, which excelleth amongst all
lands. 7 And I said to them, 'Let every man cast away the
scandals of his eyes, and defile not yourselves with the idols
of Egypt; I am the Lord, your God.' 8 But they provoked me
and would not hearken to me; they did not every man cast
away the abominations of his eyes, neither did they forsake
the idols of Egypt, and I said I would pour out my indignation upon them and accomplish my wrath against them in
the midst of the land of Egypt.

9 ""*But* I did *otherwise* for my name's sake, that it might
not be violated before the nations in the midst of whom
they were and among whom I made myself known to them
to bring them out of the land of Egypt. 10 Therefore I
brought them out from the land of Egypt and brought them
into the desert. 11 And I gave them my statutes, and I shewed
them my judgments, which if a man do, he shall live in them.
12 Moreover I gave them also my sabbaths to be a sign between me and them and that they might know that I am the
Lord that sanctify them.

13 ""*But* the house of Israel provoked me in the desert;
they walked not in my statutes, and they cast away my judgments, which if a man do he shall live in them, and they
grievously violated my sabbaths. I said therefore that I
would pour out my indignation upon them in the desert and
would consume them. 14 But I *spared them* for the sake of my

meum, ne violaretur coram gentibus de quibus eieci eos in conspectu earum. 15 Ego igitur levavi manum meam super eos in deserto ne inducerem eos in terram quam dedi eis, fluentem lacte et melle, praecipuam terrarum omnium. 16 Quia iudicia mea proiecerunt et in praeceptis meis non ambulaverunt et sabbata mea violaverunt, post idola enim cor eorum gradiebatur. 17 Et pepercit oculus meus super eos ut non interficerem eos, nec consumpsi eos in deserto.

18 ""Dixi autem ad filios eorum in solitudine, 'In praeceptis patrum vestrorum nolite incedere, nec iudicia eorum custodiatis, nec in idolis eorum polluamini. 19 Ego Dominus, Deus vester; in praeceptis meis ambulate, et iudicia mea custodite, et facite ea. 20 Et sabbata mea sanctificate ut sint signum inter me et vos et sciatis quia ego sum Dominus, Deus vester.'

21 ""Et exacerbaverunt me filii; in praeceptis meis non ambulaverunt et iudicia mea non custodierunt ut facerent ea, quae cum fecerit homo, vivet in eis, et sabbata mea violaverunt, et comminatus sum ut effunderem furorem meum super eos et implerem iram meam in eis in deserto. 22 Averti autem manum meam et feci propter nomen meum, ut non violaretur coram gentibus de quibus eieci eos in oculis earum. 23 Iterum levavi manum meam in eos in solitudine ut dispergerem illos in nationes et ventilarem in terras, 24 eo quod iudicia mea non fecissent et praecepta mea reprobassent et sabbata mea violassent et post idola patrum suorum fuissent oculi eorum. 25 Ergo et ego dedi eis praecepta non bona et iudicia in quibus non vivent. 26 Et pollui eos in

name, lest it should be profaned before the nations from which I brought them out in their sight. 15 So I lifted up my hand over them in the desert not to bring them into the land which I had given them, flowing with milk and honey, the best of all lands. 16 Because they cast off my judgments and walked not in my statutes and violated my sabbaths, for their heart went after idols. 17 Yet my eye spared them so that I destroyed them not, neither did I consume them in the desert.

18 ""And I said to their children in the wilderness, 'Walk not in the statutes of your fathers, and observe not their judgments, nor be ye defiled with their idols. 19 I am the Lord, your God; walk ye in my statutes, and observe my judgments, and do them. 20 And sanctify my sabbaths that they may be a sign between me and you and that you may know that I am the Lord, your God.'

21 ""*But* their children provoked me; they walked not in my commandments nor observed my judgments to do them, which if a man do, he shall live in them, and they violated my sabbaths, and I threatened to pour out my indignation upon them and to accomplish my wrath in them in the desert. 22 But I turned away my hand and wrought for my name's sake, that it might not be violated before the nations out of which I brought them forth in their sight. 23 Again I lifted up my hand upon them in the wilderness to disperse them among the nations and scatter them through the countries, 24 because they had not done my judgments and had cast off my statutes and had violated my sabbaths and their eyes had been after the idols of their fathers. 25 Therefore I also gave them statutes that were not good and judgments in which they shall not live. 26 And I polluted them in their own gifts,

muneribus suis, cum offerrent omne quod aperit vulvam propter delicta sua, et scient quia ego Dominus."'

27 "Quam ob rem loquere ad domum Israhel, fili hominis, et dices ad eos, 'Haec dicit Dominus Deus: "Adhuc et in hoc blasphemaverunt me patres vestri cum sprevissent me contemnentes, 28 et induxissem eos in terram super quam levavi manum meam ut darem eis; viderunt omnem collem excelsum et omne lignum nemorosum, et immolaverunt ibi victimas suas, et dederunt ibi inritationem oblationis suae, et posuerunt ibi odorem suavitatis suae et libaverunt libationes suas. 29 Et dixi ad eos, 'Quid est excelsum ad quod vos ingredimini?' Et vocatum est nomen eius Excelsum usque ad hanc diem."'

30 "Propterea dic ad domum Israhel, 'Haec dicit Dominus Deus: "Certe in via patrum vestrorum vos polluimini, et post offendicula eorum vos fornicamini. 31 Et in oblatione donorum vestrorum cum transducitis filios vestros per ignem vos polluimini in omnibus idolis vestris usque hodie, et ego respondebo vobis, domus Israhel? Vivo ego," dicit Dominus Deus, "quia non respondebo vobis. 32 Neque cogitatio mentis vestrae fiet, dicentium, 'Erimus sicut Gentes et sicut cognationes terrae, ut colamus ligna et lapides.'

33 ""Vivo ego," dicit Dominus Deus, "quoniam in manu forti et in brachio extento et in furore effuso regnabo super vos. 34 Et educam vos de populis, et congregabo vos de terris in quibus dispersi estis; in manu valida et in brachio extento et in furore effuso regnabo super vos. 35 Et adducam vos in desertum populorum, et iudicabor vobiscum ibi facie ad faciem. 36 Sicut iudicio contendi adversum patres vestros in

when they offered all that opened the womb for their offences, and they shall know that I am the Lord.'"

27 "Wherefore speak to the house of Israel, O son of man, and *say* to them, 'Thus saith the Lord God: "Moreover in this also your fathers blasphemed me when they had despised and contemned me, 28 and I had brought them into the land, for which I lifted up my hand to give it them; they saw every high hill and every shady tree, and there they sacrificed their victims, and there they presented the provocation of their offerings, and there they set their sweet odours and poured forth their libations. 29 And I said to them, 'What meaneth the high place to which you go?' And the name thereof was called High Place even to this day.'"

30 "Wherefore say to the house of Israel, 'Thus saith the Lord God: "Verily you are defiled in the way of your fathers, and you commit fornication with their abominations. 31 And you defile yourselves with all your idols unto this day in the offering of your gifts when you make your children pass through the fire, and shall I answer you, O house of Israel? As I live," saith the Lord God, "I will not answer you. 32 Neither shall the thought of your mind come to pass by which you say, 'We will be as the Gentiles and as the families of the earth, to worship stocks and stones.'

33 ""As I live," saith the Lord God, "I will reign over you with a strong hand and with a stretched out arm and with fury poured out. 34 And I will bring you out from the people, and I will gather you out of the countries in which you are scattered; I will reign over you with a strong hand, and with a stretched out arm and with fury poured out. 35 And I will bring you into the wilderness of people, and there will I plead with you face to face. 36 As I pleaded against your

deserto terrae Aegypti, sic iudicabo vos," dicit Dominus Deus. 37 "Et subiciam vos sceptro meo et inducam vos in vinculis foederis. 38 Et eligam de vobis transgressores et impios et de terra incolatus eorum educam eos, et in terram Israhel non ingredientur, et scietis quia ego Dominus.

39 "'Et vos, domus Israhel, haec dicit Dominus Deus: "Singuli post idola vestra ambulate, et servite eis. Quod si et in hoc non audieritis me et nomen meum sanctum pollueritis ultra in muneribus vestris et in idolis vestris, 40 in monte sancto meo, in monte excelso Israhel," ait Dominus Deus, "ibi serviet mihi omnis domus Israhel, omnes, inquam, in terra in qua placebunt mihi, et ibi quaeram primitias vestras et initium decimarum vestrarum in omnibus sanctificationibus vestris. 41 In odorem suavitatis suscipiam vos cum eduxero vos de populis et congregavero vos de terris in quas dispersi estis, et sanctificabor in vobis in oculis nationum. 42 Et scietis quia ego Dominus cum induxero vos ad terram Israhel, in terram pro qua levavi manum meam ut darem eam patribus vestris. 43 Et recordabimini ibi viarum vestrarum et omnium scelerum vestrorum quibus polluti estis in eis, et displicebitis vobis in conspectu vestro in omnibus malitiis vestris quas fecistis. 44 Et scietis quia ego Dominus cum benefecero vobis propter nomen meum et non secundum vias vestras malas neque secundum scelera vestra pessima, domus Israhel," ait Dominus Deus.'"

45 Et factus est sermo Domini ad me, dicens, 46 "Fili

fathers in the desert of the land of Egypt, even so will I judge you," saith the Lord God. 37 "And I will make you subject to my sceptre and will bring you into the bands of the covenant. 38 And I will pick out from among you the transgressors and the wicked and will bring them out of the land where they sojourn, and they shall not enter into the land of Israel, and you shall know that I am the Lord."

39 "'And as for you, O house of Israel, thus saith the Lord God: "Walk ye every one after your idols, and serve them. But if in this also you hear me not but defile my holy name any more with your gifts and with your idols, 40 in my holy mountain, in the high mountain of Israel," saith the Lord God, "there shall all the house of Israel serve me, all of them, I say, in the land in which they shall please me, and there will I require your firstfruits and the chief of your tithes with all your sanctifications. 41 I will accept of you for an odour of sweetness when I shall have brought you out from the people and shall have gathered you out of the lands into which you are scattered, and I will be sanctified in you in the sight of the nations. 42 And you shall know that I am the Lord when I shall have brought you into the land of Israel, into the land for which I lifted up my hand to give it to your fathers. 43 And there you shall remember your ways and all your wicked doings with which you have been defiled, and you shall be displeased with yourselves in your own sight for all your wicked deeds which you committed. 44 And you shall know that I am the Lord when I shall have done well by you for my own name's sake and not according to your evil ways nor according to your wicked deeds, O house of Israel," saith the Lord God.'"

45 And the word of the Lord came to me, saying, 46 "Son

hominis, pone faciem tuam contra viam austri, et stilla ad africum, et propheta ad saltum agri meridiani. 47 Et dices saltui meridiano, 'Audi verbum Domini: Haec dicit Dominus Deus: "Ecce: ego succendam in te ignem et conburam in te omne lignum viride et omne lignum aridum; non extinguetur flamma succensionis, et conburetur in ea omnis facies, ab austro usque ad aquilonem. 48 Et videbit universa caro quia ego, Dominus, succendi eam, nec extinguetur."'"

49 Et dixi, "Ha, ha, ha, Domine Deus! Ipsi dicunt de me, 'Numquid non per parabolas loquitur iste?'"

Caput 21

Et factus est sermo Domini ad me, dicens, 2 "Fili hominis, pone faciem tuam ad Hierusalem, et stilla ad sanctuaria, et propheta contra humum Israhel; 3 et dices terrae Israhel, 'Haec dicit Dominus Deus: "Ecce: ego ad te, et eiciam gladium meum de vagina sua et occidam in te iustum et impium. 4 Pro eo autem quod occidi in te iustum et impium, idcirco egredietur gladius meus de vagina sua ad omnem

of man, set thy face against the way of the south, and drop towards the south, and prophesy against the forest of the south field. 47 And *say* to the south forest, 'Hear the word of the Lord: Thus saith the Lord God: "Behold: I will kindle a fire in thee and will burn in thee every green tree and every dry tree; the flame of the fire shall not be quenched, and every face shall be burned in it, from the south even to the north. 48 And all flesh shall see that I the Lord have kindled it, and it shall not be quenched."'"

49 And I said, "Ah, ah, ah, O Lord God! They say of me, 'Doth not this man speak by parables?'"

Chapter 21

The destruction of Jerusalem by the sword is further described; the ruin also of the Ammonites is foreshewn. And finally Babylon, the destroyer of others, shall be destroyed.

And the word of the Lord came to me, saying, 2 "Son of man, set thy face toward Jerusalem, and let thy speech flow towards the holy places, and prophesy against the land of Israel; 3 and say to the land of Israel, 'Thus saith the Lord God: "Behold: I come against thee, and I will draw forth my sword out of its sheath and will cut off in thee the just and the wicked. 4 And forasmuch as I have cut off in thee the just and the wicked, therefore shall my sword go forth out of its

carnem ab austro usque ad aquilonem, 5 ut sciat omnis caro quia ego, Dominus, eduxi gladium meum de vagina sua inrevocabilem.'"

6 "Et tu, fili hominis, ingemesce in contritione lumborum, et in amaritudinibus ingemesce coram eis. 7 Cumque dixerint ad te, 'Quare tu gemis?' dices, 'Pro auditu, quia venit, et tabescet omne cor, et dissolventur universae manus, et infirmabitur omnis spiritus, et per cuncta genua fluent aquae; ecce: venit, et fiet,'" ait Dominus Deus.

8 Et factus est sermo Domini ad me, dicens, 9 "Fili hominis, propheta, et dices, 'Haec dicit Dominus Deus'; loquere, '"Gladius, gladius exacutus est et limatus. 10 Ut caedat victimas exacutus est; ut splendeat limatus est. Qui moves sceptrum filii mei, succidisti omne lignum. 11 Et dedi eum ad levigandum ut teneatur manu; iste exacutus est gladius, et iste limatus est, ut sit in manu interficientis.'"

12 "Clama, et ulula, fili hominis, quia hic factus est in populo meo; hic in cunctis ducibus Israhel qui fugerant; gladio traditi sunt cum populo meo. Idcirco plaude super femur, 13 quia probatus est, et hoc cum sceptrum subverterit, et non erit," dicit Dominus Deus. 14 "Tu ergo, fili hominis, propheta, et percute manu ad manum, et duplicetur gladius, ac triplicetur gladius interfectorum; hic est gladius occisionis magnae, qui obstupescere eos facit 15 et corde tabescere et multiplicat ruinas. In omnibus portis eorum dedi conturbationem gladii acuti et limati ad fulgendum, amicti ad caedem. 16 Exacuere; vade ad dextram sive ad sinistram, quo-

sheath against all flesh from the south even to the north, 5 that all flesh may know that I, the Lord, have drawn my sword out of its sheath not to be turned back.'"

6 "And thou, son of man, mourn with the breaking of thy loins, and with bitterness sigh before them. 7 And when they shall say to thee, 'Why mournest thou?' thou shalt say, 'For that which I hear, because it cometh, and every heart shall melt, and all hands shall be made feeble, and every spirit shall faint, and water shall run down every knee; behold: it cometh, and it shall be done,'" saith the Lord God.

8 And the word of the Lord came to me, saying, 9 "Son of man, prophesy, and *say,* 'Thus saith the Lord God'; say, '"The sword, the sword is sharpened and furbished. 10 It is sharpened to kill victims; it is furbished that it may glitter. Thou removest the sceptre of my son; thou hast cut down every tree. 11 And I have given it to be furbished that it may be handled; this sword is sharpened, and it is furbished, that it may be in the hand of the slayer."'

12 "Cry, and howl, O son of man, for this *sword* is upon my people; it is upon all the princes of Israel that are fled; they are delivered up to the sword with my people. Strike therefore upon thy thigh, 13 because it is tried, and that when it shall overthrow the sceptre, and it shall not be," saith the Lord God. 14 "Thou therefore, O son of man, prophesy, and strike thy hands together, and let the sword be doubled, and let the sword of the slain be tripled; this is the sword of a great slaughter, that maketh them stand amazed 15 and languish in heart and that multiplieth ruins. In all their gates I have set the dread of the sharp sword, *the sword that is* furbished to glitter, that is made ready for slaughter. 16 Be thou sharpened; go to the right hand or to

cumque faciei tuae est appetitus. 17 Quin et ego plaudam manu ad manum et implebo indignationem meam; ego, Dominus, locutus sum."

18 Et factus est sermo Domini ad me, dicens, 19 "Et tu, fili hominis, pone tibi duas vias ut veniat gladius regis Babylonis; de terra una egredientur ambae, et manu capiet coniecturam; in capite viae civitatis coniciet. 20 Viam pones ut veniat gladius ad Rabbath filiorum Ammon et ad Iudam in Hierusalem munitissimam.

21 "Stetit enim rex Babylonis in bivio in capite duarum viarum, divinationem quaerens, commiscens sagittas. Interrogavit idola et exta consuluit. 22 Ad dextram eius facta est divinatio super Hierusalem, ut ponat arietes, ut aperiat os in caede, ut elevet vocem in ululatu, ut ponat arietes contra portas, ut conportet aggerem, ut aedificet munitiones. 23 Eritque quasi consulens frustra oraculum in oculis eorum et sabbatorum otium imitans, ipse autem recordabitur iniquitatis ad capiendum.

24 "Idcirco haec dicit Dominus Deus: 'Pro eo quod recordati estis iniquitatis vestrae et revelastis praevaricationes vestras et apparuerunt peccata vestra in omnibus cogitationibus vestris, pro eo, inquam, quod recordati estis, manu capiemini.

25 "Tu autem, profane, impie dux Israhel, cuius venit dies in tempore iniquitatis praefinita, 26 haec dicit Dominus Deus: 'Aufer cidarim; tolle coronam. Nonne haec est quae humilem sublevavit et sublimem humiliavit? 27 Iniquitatem, iniquitatem, iniquitatem ponam eam; et hoc non factum est donec veniret cuius est iudicium, et tradam ei.'

the left, which way soever thou hast a mind to set thy face. 17 And I will clap my hands together and will satisfy my indignation; I, the Lord, have spoken."

18 And the word of the Lord came to me, saying, 19 "And thou, son of man, set thee two ways for the sword of the king of Babylon to come; both shall come forth out of one land, and with his hand he shall draw lots; he shall consult at the head of the way of the city. 20 Thou shalt make a way that the sword may come to Rabbah of the children of Ammon and to Judah unto Jerusalem, the strong city.

21 "For the king of Babylon stood in the highway at the head of two ways, seeking divination, shuffling arrows; he inquired of the idols and consulted entrails. 22 On his right hand was the divination for Jerusalem, to set battering rams, to open the mouth in slaughter, to lift up the voice in howling, to set engines against the gates, to cast up a mount, to build forts. 23 And he shall be in their eyes as one consulting the oracle in vain and imitating the leisure of sabbaths, but he will call to remembrance the iniquity that they may be taken.

24 "Therefore thus saith the Lord God: 'Because you have remembered your iniquity and have discovered your prevarications and your sins have appeared in all your devices: because, I say, you have remembered, you shall be taken with the hand.'

25 "But thou, profane wicked prince of Israel, whose day is come that hath been appointed in the time of iniquity, 26 thus saith the Lord God: 'Remove the diadem; take off the crown. Is it not this that hath exalted the low one and brought down him that was high? 27 I will shew it to be iniquity, iniquity, iniquity; *but* this was not done till he came to whom judgment belongeth, and I will give it him.'

28 "Et tu, fili hominis, propheta, et dic, 'Haec dicit Dominus Deus ad filios Ammon et ad obprobrium eorum,' et dices, 'Mucro, mucro, evaginate ad occidendum, limate ut interficias et fulgeas, 29 cum tibi viderentur vana et divinarentur mendacia ut dareris super colla vulneratorum impiorum, quorum venit dies in tempore iniquitatis praefinita. 30 Revertere ad vaginam tuam. In loco in quo creatus es, in terra nativitatis tuae, iudicabo te. 31 Et effundam super te indignationem meam; in igne furoris mei sufflabo in te daboque te in manus hominum insipientium et fabricantium interitum. 32 Igni eris cibus; sanguis tuus erit in medio terrae; oblivioni traderis, quia ego, Dominus, locutus sum.'"

Caput 22

Et factum est verbum Domini ad me, dicens, 2 "Et tu, fili hominis, nonne iudicas, nonne iudicas civitatem sanguinum? 3 Et ostendes ei omnes abominationes suas et dices, 'Haec dicit Dominus Deus: "Civitas effundens sanguinem in medio sui, ut veniat tempus eius, et quae fecit idola contra

28 "And thou, son of man, prophesy, and say, 'Thus saith the Lord God concerning the children of Ammon and concerning their reproach,' and thou shalt say, 'O sword, O sword, come out of the scabbard to kill; be furbished to destroy and to glitter, 29 whilst they see vain things in thy regard and they divine lies to bring thee upon the necks of the wicked that are wounded, whose appointed day is come in the time of iniquity. 30 Return into thy sheath. I will judge thee in the place wherein thou wast created, in the land of thy nativity. 31 And I will pour out upon thee my indignation; in the fire of my rage will I blow upon thee and will give thee into the hands of men that are brutish and contrive thy destruction. 32 Thou shalt be fuel for the fire; thy blood shall be in the midst of the land; thou shalt be forgotten, for I, the Lord, have spoken it.'"

Chapter 22

The general corruption of the inhabitants of Jerusalem, for which God will consume them as dross in his furnace.

And the word of the Lord came to me, saying, 2 "And thou, son of man, dost thou not judge, dost thou not judge the city of blood? 3 And thou shalt shew her all her abominations and shalt say, 'Thus saith the Lord God: "This is the city that sheddeth blood in the midst of her, that her time

semet ipsam, ut pollueretur. 4 In sanguine tuo qui a te effusus est deliquisti, et in idolis tuis quae fecisti polluta es, et
adpropinquare fecisti dies tuos, et adduxisti tempus annorum tuorum; propterea dedi te obprobrium Gentibus et in-
risionem universis terris. 5 Quae iuxta sunt et quae procul a
te triumphabunt de te, sordida, nobilis, grandis interitu.

6 ““Ecce: principes Israhel singuli in brachio suo fuerunt
in te ad effundendum sanguinem. 7 Patrem et matrem contu-
meliis adfecerunt in te; advenam calumniati sunt in medio
tui; pupillum et viduam contristaverunt apud te. 8 Sanctuaria mea sprevistis et sabbata mea polluistis. 9 Viri detracto-
res fuerunt in te ad effundendum sanguinem, et super montes comederunt in te; scelus operati sunt in medio tui.
10 Verecundiora patris discoperuerunt in te; inmunditiam
menstruatae humiliaverunt in te. 11 Et unusquisque in uxorem proximi sui operatus est abominationem, et socer nu-
rum suam polluit nefarie; frater sororem suam, filiam patris
sui oppressit in te. 12 Munera acceperunt apud te ad effundendum sanguinem; usuram et superabundantiam accepisti
et avare proximos tuos calumniabaris meique oblita es,” ait
Dominus Deus.

13 ““Ecce: conplosi manus meas super avaritiam tuam
quam fecisti et super sanguinem qui effusus est in medio tui.
14 Numquid sustinebit cor tuum aut praevalebunt manus

may come, and that hath made idols against herself, to defile herself. 4 Thou art become guilty in thy blood which thou hast shed, and thou art defiled in thy idols which thou hast made, and thou hast made thy days to draw near and hast brought on the time of thy years; therefore have I made thee a reproach to the Gentiles and a mockery to all countries. 5 Those that are near and those that are far from thee shall triumph over thee, thou filthy one, infamous, great in destruction.

6 ""Behold: the princes of Israel, every one hath employed his arm in thee to shed blood. 7 They have abused father and mother in thee; they have oppressed the stranger in the midst of thee; they have grieved the fatherless and widow in thee. 8 Thou hast despised my sanctuaries and profaned my sabbaths. 9 Slanderers have been in thee to shed blood, and they have eaten upon the mountains in thee; they have committed wickedness in the midst of thee. 10 They have discovered the nakedness of their father in thee; they have humbled the uncleanness of the menstruous woman in thee.

11 ""And every one hath committed abomination with his neighbour's wife, and the father-in-law hath wickedly defiled his daughter-in-law; the brother hath oppressed his sister, the daughter of his father in thee. 12 They have taken gifts in thee to shed blood; thou hast taken usury and increase and hast covetously oppressed thy neighbours, and thou hast forgotten me," saith the Lord God.

13 ""Behold: I have clapped my hands at thy covetousness which thou hast exercised and at the blood that hath been shed in the midst of thee. 14 Shall thy heart endure or shall thy hands prevail in the days which I will bring upon thee? I,

tuae in diebus quos ego faciam tibi? Ego, Dominus, locutus sum et faciam. 15 Et dispergam te in nationes et ventilabo te in terras, et deficere faciam inmunditiam tuam a te. 16 Et possidebo te in conspectu Gentium, et scies quia ego Dominus.'""

17 Et factum est verbum Domini ad me, dicens, 18 "Fili hominis, versa est mihi domus Israhel in scoriam; omnes isti aes et stagnum et ferrum et plumbum in medio fornacis; scoria argenti facti sunt. 19 Propterea haec dicit Dominus Deus: 'Eo quod versi estis omnes in scoriam, propterea ecce: ego congregabo vos in medium Hierusalem. 20 Congregatione argenti et aeris et ferri et stagni et plumbi in medium fornacis ut succendam in ea ignem ad conflandum, sic congregabo in furore meo et in ira mea et requiescam, et conflabo vos. 21 Et congregabo vos et succendam vos in igne furoris mei, et conflabimini in medio eius. 22 Ut conflatur argentum in medio fornacis, sic eritis in medio eius, et scietis quia ego Dominus cum effuderim indignationem meam super vos.'"

23 Et factum est verbum Domini ad me, dicens, 24 "Fili hominis, dic ei, 'Tu es terra inmunda et non conpluta in die furoris. 25 Coniuratio prophetarum in medio eius; sicut leo rugiens rapiensque praedam animas devoraverunt, opes et pretium acceperunt, viduas eius multiplicaverunt in medio illius. 26 Sacerdotes eius contempserunt legem meam et polluerunt sanctuaria mea; inter sanctum et profanum non habuere distantiam et inter pollutum et mundum non intellexerunt, et a sabbatis meis averterunt oculos suos, et coin-

the Lord, have spoken and will do it. 15 And I will disperse thee in the nations and will scatter thee among the countries, and I will put an end to thy uncleanness in thee. 16 And I will possess thee in the sight of the Gentiles, and thou shalt know that I am the Lord.""'

17 And the word of the Lord came to me, saying, 18 "Son of man, the house of Israel is become dross to me; all these are brass and tin and iron and lead in the midst of the furnace; they are become the dross of silver. 19 Therefore thus saith the Lord God: 'Because you are all turned into dross, therefore behold: I will gather you together in the midst of Jerusalem. 20 As they gather silver and brass and tin and iron and lead in the midst of the furnace that I may kindle a fire in it to melt it, so will I gather you together in my fury and in my wrath and will take my rest, and I will melt you down. 21 And I will gather you together and will burn you in the fire of my wrath, and you shall be melted in the midst thereof. 22 As silver is melted in the midst of the furnace, so shall you be in the midst thereof, and you shall know that I am the Lord when I have poured out my indignation upon you.'"

23 And the word of the Lord came to me, saying, 24 "Son of man, say to her, 'Thou art a land that is unclean and not rained upon in the day of wrath. 25 There is a conspiracy of prophets in the midst thereof; like a lion that roareth and catcheth the prey they have devoured souls, they have taken riches and hire, they have made many widows in the midst thereof. 26 Her priests have despised my law and have defiled my sanctuaries; they have put no difference between holy and profane nor have distinguished between the polluted and the clean, and they have turned away their eyes from my

quinabar in medio eorum. 27 Principes eius in medio illius quasi lupi rapientes praedam ad effundendum sanguinem et ad perdendas animas et avare ad sectanda lucra. 28 Prophetae autem eius liniebant eos absque temperamento, videntes vana et divinantes eis mendacium, dicentes, "Haec dicit Dominus Deus," cum Dominus non sit locutus. 29 Populi terrae calumniabantur calumniam et rapiebant violenter; egenum et pauperem adfligebant, et advenam opprimebant calumnia absque iudicio. 30 Et quaesivi de eis virum qui interponeret sepem et staret oppositus contra me pro terra, ne dissiparem eam, et non inveni. 31 Et effudi super eos indignationem meam; in igne irae meae consumpsi eos; viam eorum in caput eorum reddidi,' ait Dominus Deus."

Caput 23

Et factus est sermo Domini ad me, dicens, 2 "Fili hominis, duae mulieres, filiae matris unius, fuerunt. 3 Et fornicatae sunt in Aegypto; in adulescentia sua fornicatae sunt; ibi sub-

sabbaths, and I was profaned in the midst of them. 27 Her princes in the midst of her are like wolves ravening the prey to shed blood and to destroy souls, and to run after gains through covetousness. 28 And her prophets have daubed them without tempering *the morter,* seeing vain things and divining lies unto them, saying, "Thus saith the Lord God," when the Lord hath not spoken. 29 The people of the land have used oppression and committed robbery; they afflicted the needy and poor, and they oppressed the stranger by calumny without judgment. 30 And I sought among them for a man that might set up a hedge and stand in the gap before me in favour of the land, that I might not destroy it, and I found none. 31 And I poured out my indignation upon them; in the fire of my wrath I consumed them; I have rendered their way upon their own head,' saith the Lord God."

Chapter 23

Under the names of the two harlots Oholah and Oholibah are described the manifold disloyalties of Samaria and Jerusalem with the punishment of them both.

And the word of the Lord came to me, saying, 2 "Son of man, there were two women, daughters of one mother. 3 And they committed fornication in Egypt; in their youth they committed fornication; there were their breasts pressed

acta sunt ubera earum, et fractae sunt mammae pubertatis earum. 4 Nomina autem earum Oolla, maior, et Ooliba, soror eius minor; et habui eas, et pepererunt filios et filias. Porro earum nomina: Samaria Oolla, et Hierusalem Ooliba.

5 "Fornicata est igitur Oolla super me et insanivit in amatores suos, in Assyrios propinquantes, 6 vestitos hyacintho, principes et magistratus, iuvenes cupidinis, universos equites, ascensores equorum. 7 Et dedit fornicationes suas super eos electos, filios Assyriorum universos, et in omnibus in quos insanivit in inmunditiis eorum polluta est. 8 Insuper et fornicationes suas quas habuerat in Aegypto non reliquit, nam et illi dormierunt cum ea in adulescentia eius, et illi confregerunt ubera pubertatis eius et effuderunt fornicationem suam super eam. 9 Propterea tradidi eam in manus amatorum suorum, in manus filiorum Assur, super quorum insanivit libidinem. 10 Ipsi discoperuerunt ignominiam eius, filios et filias eius tulerunt et ipsam occiderunt gladio, et factae sunt famosae mulieres, et iudicia perpetrarunt in ea.

11 "Quod cum vidisset soror eius Ooliba, plus quam illa insanivit libidine, et fornicationem suam super fornicationem sororis suae, 12 ad filios Assyriorum praebuit inpudenter, ducibus et magistratibus ad se venientibus, indutis veste varia, equitibus qui vectabantur equis et adulescentibus forma cunctis egregia. 13 Et vidi quod polluta esset, via una ambarum. 14 Et auxit fornicationes suas cumque vidisset viros depictos in pariete, imagines Chaldeorum expressas coloribus 15 et accinctos balteis renes et tiaras tinctas in capiti-

down, and the teats of their virginity were bruised. 4 And their names were Oholah, the elder, and Oholibah, her younger sister; and I took them, and they bore sons and daughters. Now for their names: Samaria is Oholah, and Jerusalem is Oholibah.

5 "And Oholah committed fornication against me and doted on her lovers, on the Assyrians that came to her, 6 who were clothed with blue, princes and rulers, *beautiful* youths, all horsemen, mounted upon horses. 7 And she committed her fornications with those chosen men, all sons of the Assyrians, and she defiled herself with the uncleanness of all them on whom she doted. 8 Moreover also she did not forsake her fornications which she had committed in Egypt, for they also lay with her in her youth, and they bruised the breasts of her virginity and poured out their fornication upon her. 9 Therefore have I delivered her into the hands of her lovers, into the hands of the sons of the Assyrians, upon whose lust she doted. 10 They discovered her disgrace, took away her sons and daughters and slew her with the sword, and they became infamous women, and they executed judgments in her.

11 "And when her sister Oholibah saw this, she was mad with lust more than she, and she carried her fornication beyond the fornication of her sister, 12 impudently *prostituting herself* to the children of the Assyrians, the princes and rulers that came to her, clothed with divers colours, to the horsemen that rode upon horses and to young men all of great beauty. 13 And I saw that she was defiled *and that they* both *took* one way. 14 And she increased her fornications, and when she had seen men painted on the wall, the images of the Chaldeans set forth in colours 15 and girded with girdles

bus eorum, formam ducum omnium, similitudinem filiorum Babylonis terraeque Chaldeorum, in qua orti sunt, 16 et insanivit super eos concupiscentia oculorum suorum, et misit nuntios ad eos in Chaldeam. 17 Cumque venissent ad eam filii Babylonis ad cubile mammarum, polluerunt eam stupris suis, et polluta est ab eis, et saturata est anima eius ab illis. 18 Denudavit quoque fornicationes suas et discoperuit ignominiam suam, et recessit anima mea ab ea sicut recesserat anima mea a sorore eius. 19 Multiplicavit enim fornicationes suas, recordans dies adulescentiae suae, quibus fornicata est in terra Aegypti. 20 Et insanivit libidine super concubitu eorum quorum carnes sunt ut carnes asinorum et sicut fluxus equorum fluxus eorum. 21 Et visitasti scelus adulescentiae tuae, quando subacta sunt in Aegypto ubera tua, et confractae mammae pubertatis tuae.

22 "Propterea, Ooliba, haec dicit Dominus Deus: 'Ecce: ego suscitabo omnes amatores tuos contra te de quibus satiata est anima tua, et congregabo eos adversum te in circuitu, 23 filios Babylonis et universos Chaldeos, nobiles tyrannosque et principes, omnes filios Assyriorum, iuvenes forma egregia, duces et magistratus universos, principes principum et nominatos ascensores equorum. 24 Et venient super te instructi curru et rota, multitudo populorum; lorica et clypeo et galea armabuntur contra te undique, et dabo coram eis iudicium, et iudicabunt te iudiciis suis. 25 Et ponam zelum meum in te, quem exercent tecum in furore; nasum tuum et aures tuas praecident, et quae remanserint gladio

about their reins and with dyed turbans on their heads, the resemblance of all the captains, the likeness of the sons of Babylon and of the land of the Chaldeans wherein they were born, 16 she doted upon them with the lust of her eyes, and she sent messengers to them into Chaldea. 17 And when the sons of Babylon were come to her to the bed of love, they defiled her with their fornications, and she was polluted by them, and her soul was glutted with them. 18 And she discovered her fornications and discovered her disgrace, and my soul was alienated from her as my soul was alienated from her sister. 19 For she multiplied her fornications, remembering the days of her youth, in which she played the harlot in the land of Egypt. 20 And she was mad with lust after lying with them whose flesh is as the flesh of asses and whose issue as the issue of horses. 21 And thou hast renewed the wickedness of thy youth, when thy breasts were pressed in Egypt, and the paps of thy virginity broken.

22 "Therefore, Oholibah, thus saith the Lord God: 'Behold: I will raise up against thee all thy lovers with whom thy soul hath been glutted, and I will gather them together against thee round about, 23 the children of Babylon and all the Chaldeans, the nobles and the kings and princes, all the sons of the Assyrians, beautiful young men, all the captains and rulers, the princes of princes and the renowned horsemen. 24 And they shall come upon thee well appointed with chariot and wheel, a multitude of people; they shall be armed against thee on every side with breastplate and buckler and helmet, and I will set judgment before them, and they shall judge thee by their judgments. 25 And I will set my jealousy against thee, which they shall execute upon thee with fury; they shall cut off thy nose and thy ears, and what remains

concident; ipsi filios tuos et filias tuas capient, et novissimum tuum devorabitur igni. 26 Et denudabunt te vestimentis tuis et tollent vasa gloriae tuae. 27 Et requiescere faciam scelus tuum de te et fornicationem tuam de terra Aegypti, nec levabis oculos tuos ad eos et Aegypti non recordaberis amplius.'

28 "Quia haec dicit Dominus Deus: 'Ecce: ego tradam te in manus eorum quos odisti, in manus de quibus satiata est anima tua. 29 Et agent tecum in odio, et tollent omnes labores tuos et dimittent te nudam et ignominia plenam, et revelabitur ignominia fornicationum tuarum, scelus tuum et fornicationes tuae. 30 Fecerunt haec tibi quia fornicata es post gentes inter quas polluta es in idolis eorum. 31 In via sororis tuae ambulasti, et dabo calicem eius in manu tua.' 32 Haec dicit Dominus Deus: 'Calicem sororis tuae bibes profundum et latum eris in derisum et in subsannationem, quae est capacissima. 33 Ebrietate et dolore repleberis, calice maeroris et tristitiae, calice sororis tuae Samariae. 34 Et bibes illum et epotabis usque ad feces, et fragmenta eius devorabis; ubera tua lacerabis, quia ego locutus sum,' ait Dominus Deus.

35 "Propterea haec dicit Dominus Deus: 'Quia oblita es mei et proiecisti me post corpus tuum, tu quoque porta scelus tuum et fornicationes tuas.'"

36 Et ait Dominus ad me, dicens, "Fili hominis, numquid iudicas Oollam et Oolibam, et adnuntias eis scelera ea-

shall fall by the sword; they shall take thy sons and thy daughters, and thy residue shall be devoured by fire. 26 And they shall strip thee of thy garments and take away the instruments of thy glory. 27 And I will put an end to thy wickedness in thee and thy fornication brought out of the land of Egypt, neither shalt thou lift up thy eyes to them nor remember Egypt any more.'

28 "For thus saith the Lord God: 'Behold: I will deliver thee into the hands of them whom thou hatest, into their hands with whom thy soul hath been glutted. 29 And they shall deal with thee in hatred, and they shall take away all thy labours and shall let thee go naked and full of disgrace, and the disgrace of thy whoredoms shall be discovered, thy wickedness and thy fornications. 30 They have done these things to thee because thou hast played the harlot with the nations among which thou wast defiled with their idols. 31 Thou hast walked in the way of thy sister, and I will give her cup into thy hand.' 32 Thus saith the Lord God: 'Thou shalt drink thy sister's cup deep and wide; thou shalt be had in derision and scorn, which containeth very much. 33 Thou shalt be filled with drunkenness and sorrow, with the cup of grief and sadness, with the cup of thy sister Samaria. 34 And thou shalt drink it and shalt drink it up even to the dregs, and thou shalt devour the fragments thereof; thou shalt rend thy breasts, because I have spoken it,' saith the Lord God.

35 "Therefore thus saith the Lord God: 'Because thou hast forgotten me and hast cast me off behind thy back, bear thou also thy wickedness and thy fornications.'"

36 And the Lord spoke to me, saying, "Son of man, dost thou judge Oholah and Oholibah, and dost thou declare to

rum? ³⁷ Quia adulteratae sunt, et sanguis in manibus earum, et cum idolis suis fornicatae sunt; insuper et filios suos quos genuerunt mihi obtulerunt eis ad devorandum. ³⁸ Sed et hoc fecerunt mihi. Polluerunt sanctuarium meum in die illa et sabbata mea profanaverunt. ³⁹ Cumque immolarent filios suos idolis suis et ingrederentur sanctuarium meum in die illa ut polluerent illud, etiam haec fecerunt in medio domus meae. ⁴⁰ Miserunt ad viros venientes de longe, ad quos nuntium miserant, itaque ecce: venerunt, quibus te lavisti et circumlevisti stibio oculos tuos et ornata es mundo muliebri. ⁴¹ Sedisti in lecto pulcherrimo, et mensa ornata est ante te; thymiama meum et unguentum meum posuisti super eam. ⁴² Et vox multitudinis exultantis erat in ea, et in viris qui de multitudine hominum adducebantur et veniebant de deserto posuerunt armillas in manibus eorum et coronas speciosas in capitibus eorum.

⁴³ "Et dixi ei quae adtrita est in adulteriis, 'Nunc fornicabitur in fornicatione sua etiam haec.' ⁴⁴ Et ingressi sunt ad eam quasi ad mulierem meretricem; sic ingrediebantur ad Oollam et Oolibam, mulieres nefarias. ⁴⁵ Viri ergo iusti sunt; hii iudicabunt eas iudicio adulterarum et iudicio effundentium sanguinem, quia adulterae sunt et sanguis in manibus earum.

⁴⁶ Haec enim dicit Dominus Deus: 'Adduc ad eas multitudinem, et trade eas in tumultum et in rapinam, ⁴⁷ et lapidentur lapidibus populorum, et confodiantur gladiis eorum; filios et filias earum interficient, et domos earum igne succendent. ⁴⁸ Et auferam scelus de terra, et discent omnes

them their wicked deeds? 37 Because they have committed adultery, and blood is in their hands, and they have committed fornication with their idols; moreover also their children whom they bore to me they have offered to them to be devoured. 38 Yea, and they have done this to me. They polluted my sanctuary on the same day and profaned my sabbaths. 39 And when they sacrificed their children to their idols and went into my sanctuary the same day to profane it, they did these things even in the midst of my house. 40 They sent for men coming from afar, to whom they had sent a messenger, and behold: they came, for whom thou didst wash thyself and didst paint thy eyes and wast adorned with women's ornaments. 41 Thou sattest on a very fine bed, and a table was decked before thee whereupon thou didst set my incense and my ointment. 42 And there was in her the voice of a multitude rejoicing, and to some that were brought of the multitude of men and that came from the desert, they put bracelets on their hands and beautiful crowns on their heads.

43 "And I said to her that was worn out in her adulteries, 'Now will this woman still continue in her fornication.' 44 And they went in to her as to a harlot; so went they in unto Oholah and Oholibah, wicked women. 45 They therefore are just men; these shall judge them as adulteresses are judged and as shedders of blood are judged, because they are adulteresses and blood is in their hands.

46 "For thus saith the Lord God: 'Bring a multitude upon them, and deliver them over to tumult and rapine, 47 and let the people stone them with stones, and let them be stabbed with their swords; they shall kill their sons and daughters, and their houses they shall burn with fire. 48 And I will take away wickedness out of the land, and all women shall learn

mulieres ne faciant secundum scelus earum. 49 Et dabunt scelus vestrum super vos, et peccata idolorum vestrorum portabitis, et scietis quia ego Dominus Deus.'"

Caput 24

Et factum est verbum Domini ad me in anno nono, in mense decimo, decima die mensis, dicens, 2 "Fili hominis, scribe tibi nomen diei huius, in qua confirmatus est rex Babylonis adversum Hierusalem hodie. 3 Et dices per proverbium ad domum inritatricem parabolam et loqueris ad eos, 'Haec dicit Dominus Deus: "Pone ollam, pone, inquam et mitte in eam aquam. 4 Congere frusta eius in eam omnem partem bonam, femur et armum, electa et ossibus plena. 5 Pinguissimum pecus adsume, conpone quoque strues ossuum sub ea; efferbuit coctio eius, et discocta sunt ossa illius in medio eius. 6 Propterea haec dicit Dominus Deus: "Vae civitati sanguinum ollae cuius rubigo in ea est et rubigo eius non exivit de ea: per partes et per partes suas eice eam; non cecidit super eam sors. 7 Sanguis enim eius in medio eius est

not to do according to the wickedness of them. 49 And they shall render your wickedness upon you, and you shall bear the sins of your idols, and you shall know that I am the Lord God.'"

Chapter 24

Under the parable of a boiling pot is shewn the utter destruction of Jerusalem, for which the Jews at Babylon shall not dare to mourn.

And the word of the Lord came to me in the ninth year, in the tenth month, the tenth day of the month, saying, 2 "Son of man, write thee the name of this day, on which the king of Babylon hath set himself against Jerusalem today. 3 And thou shalt speak by a figure a parable to the provoking house and say to them, 'Thus saith the Lord God: "Set on a pot, set it on, I say, and put water into it. 4 Heap together into it the pieces thereof, every good piece, the thigh and the shoulder, choice pieces and full of bones. 5 Take the fattest of the flock, and lay together piles of bones under it; the seething thereof is boiling hot, and the bones thereof are thoroughly sodden in the midst of it." 6 "'Therefore thus saith the Lord God: "Woe to the bloody city, to the pot whose rust is in it and its rust is not gone out of it: cast it out piece by piece; there hath no lot fallen upon it. 7 For her blood is in the midst of her; she hath shed it upon the

super limpidissimam petram; effudit illum; non effudit illum super terram ut possit operiri pulvere. 8 Ut superinducerem indignationem meam et vindicta ulciscerer, dedi sanguinem eius super petram limpidissimam, ne operiretur."

9 "'Propterea haec dicit Dominus Deus: "Vae civitati sanguinum, cuius ego grandem faciam pyram. 10 Congere ossa, quae igne succendam; consumentur carnes, et concoquetur universa conpositio, et ossa tabescent. 11 Pone quoque eam super prunas vacuam, ut incalescat et liquefiat aes eius, et confletur in medio eius inquinamentum eius, et consumatur rubigo eius. 12 Multo labore sudatum est, et non exivit de ea nimia rubigo eius, neque per ignem. 13 Inmunditia tua execrabilis; quia mundare te volui et non es mundata a sordibus tuis, sed nec mundaberis prius donec quiescere faciam indignationem meam in te. 14 Ego, Dominus, locutus sum; veniet, et faciam; non transeam nec parcam nec placabor; iuxta vias tuas et iuxta adinventiones tuas iudicabo te," dicit Dominus.'"

15 Et factum est verbum Domini ad me, dicens, 16 "Fili hominis, ecce: ego tollo a te desiderabile oculorum tuorum in plaga, et non planges neque plorabis, neque fluent lacrimae tuae. 17 Ingemesce tacens; mortuorum luctum non facies; corona tua circumligata sit tibi, et calciamenta tua erunt in pedibus tuis, nec amictu ora velabis, nec cibos lugentium comedes." 18 Locutus sum ergo ad populum mane, et mortua est uxor mea vesperi, fecique mane sicut praeceperat mihi.

smooth rock; she hath not shed it upon the ground that it might be covered with dust. 8 *And* that I might bring my indignation upon her and take my vengeance, I have shed her blood upon the *smooth* rock, that it should not be covered."

9 "'Therefore thus saith the Lord God: "Woe to the bloody city, of which I will make a great bonfire. 10 Heap together the bones, which I will burn with fire; the flesh shall be consumed, and the whole composition shall be sodden, and the bones shall be consumed. 11 Then set it empty upon burning coals, that it may be hot and the brass thereof may be melted, and let the filth of it be melted in the midst thereof, and let the rust of it be consumed. 12 Great pains have been taken, and the great rust thereof is not gone out, not even by fire. 13 Thy uncleanness is execrable; because I desired to cleanse thee and thou art not cleansed from thy filthiness, neither shalt thou be cleansed before I cause my indignation to rest in thee. 14 I, the Lord, have spoken; it shall come to pass, and I will do it; I will not pass by nor spare nor be pacified; I will judge thee according to thy ways and according to thy doings," saith the Lord.'"

15 And the word of the Lord came to me, saying, 16 "Son of man, behold: I take from thee the desire of thy eyes with a stroke, and thou shalt not lament nor weep, neither shall thy tears run down. 17 Sigh in silence; make no mourning for the dead; let the tire of thy head be upon thee, and thy shoes on thy feet, and cover not thy face, nor eat the meat of mourners." 18 So I spoke to the people in the morning, and my wife died in the evening, and I did in the morning as he had commanded me.

19 Et dixit ad me populus, "Quare non indicas nobis quid ista significent quae tu facis?"

20 Et dixi ad eos, "Sermo Domini factus est ad me, dicens, 21 'Loquere domui Israhel: "Haec dicit Dominus Deus: 'Ecce: ego polluam sanctuarium meum, superbiam imperii vestri et desiderabile oculorum vestrorum et super quo pavet anima vestra; filii vestri et filiae vestrae quas reliquistis gladio cadent.' 22 Et facietis sicut feci; ora amictu non velabitis, et cibos lugentium non comedetis. 23 Coronas habebitis in capitibus vestris et calciamenta in pedibus; non plangetis neque flebitis, sed tabescetis in iniquitatibus vestris, et unusquisque gemet ad fratrem suum. 24 'Eritque Hiezechiel vobis in portentum; iuxta omnia quae fecit, facietis cum venerit istud, et scietis quia ego Dominus Deus."'

25 "'Et tu, fili hominis, ecce: in die quo tollam ab eis fortitudinem eorum et gaudium dignitatis et desiderium oculorum eorum super quo requiescunt animae eorum, filios et filias eorum, 26 in die illa, cum venerit fugiens ad te ut adnuntiet tibi, 27 in die, inquam, illa aperietur os tuum cum eo qui fugit, et loqueris et non silebis ultra erisque eis in portentum, et scietis quia ego Dominus."'

19 And the people said to me, Why dost thou not tell us what these things mean that thou doest?

20 And I said to them, "The word of the Lord came to me, saying, 21 'Speak to the house of Israel: "Thus saith the Lord God: 'Behold: I will profane my sanctuary, the glory of your realm and the thing that your eyes desire and for which your soul feareth; your sons and your daughters whom you have left shall fall by the sword.' 22 And you shall do as I have done; you shall not cover your faces, nor shall you eat the meat of mourners. 23 You shall have crowns on your heads and shoes on your feet; you shall not lament nor weep, but you shall pine away for your iniquities, and every one shall sigh with his brother. 24 'And Ezekiel shall be unto you for a sign of things to come; according to all that he hath done, so shall you do when this shall come to pass, and you shall know that I am the Lord God.'"

25 "'And thou, O son of man, behold: in the day wherein I will take away from them their strength, and the joy of their glory, and the desire of their eyes upon which their souls rest, their sons and their daughters, 26 in that day, when he that escapeth shall come to thee to tell thee, 27 in that day, I say, shall thy mouth be opened *to* him that hath escaped, and thou shalt speak and shalt be silent no more, and thou shalt be unto them for a sign of things to come, and you shall know that I am the Lord.'"

Caput 25

Et factus est sermo Domini ad me, dicens, 2 "Fili hominis, pone faciem tuam contra filios Ammon, et prophetabis de eis. 3 Et dices filiis Ammon, 'Audite verbum Domini Dei: "Haec dicit Dominus Deus: 'Pro eo quod dixisti, "Euge, euge!" super sanctuarium meum quia pollutum est, et super terram Israhel quoniam desolata est, et super domum Iuda quoniam ducti sunt in captivitatem, 4 idcirco ego tradam te filiis orientalibus in hereditatem, et conlocabunt caulas suas in te et ponent in te tentoria sua; ipsi comedent fruges tuas, et ipsi bibent lac tuum. 5 Daboque Rabbath in habitaculum camelorum, et filios Ammon in cubile pecorum, et scietis quia ego Dominus.' 6 Quia haec dicit Dominus Deus: 'Pro eo quod plausisti manu et percussisti pede et gavisa es ex toto affectu super terram Israhel, 7 idcirco ecce ego: extendam manum meam super te et tradam te in direptionem gentium et interficiam te de populis et perdam de terris et conteram, et scies quia ego Dominus.'

8 ""Haec dicit Dominus Deus: 'Pro eo quod dixerunt Moab et Seir, "Ecce: sicut omnes gentes domus Iuda, 9 idcirco ecce: ego aperiam umerum Moab de civitatibus, de

Chapter 25

A prophecy against the Ammonites, Moabites, Edomites and Philistines for their malice against the Israelites.

And the word of the Lord came to me, saying, 2 "Son of man, set thy face against the children of Ammon, and thou shalt prophesy of them. 3 And thou shalt say to the children of Ammon, 'Hear ye the word of the Lord God: "Thus saith the Lord God: 'Because thou hast said, "Ha, ha!" upon my sanctuary because it was profaned, and upon the land of Israel because it was laid waste, and upon the house of Judah, because they are led into captivity, 4 therefore will I deliver thee to the men of the east for an inheritance, and they shall place their sheepcotes in thee and shall set up their tents in thee; they shall eat thy fruits, and they shall drink thy milk. 5 And I will make Rabbah a stable for camels, and the children of Ammon a couching place for flocks, and you shall know that I am the Lord.' 6 For thus saith the Lord God: 'Because thou hast clapped thy hands and stamped with thy foot and hast rejoiced with all thy heart against the land of Israel, 7 therefore behold: I will stretch forth my hand upon thee and will deliver thee to be the spoil of nations and will cut thee off from among the people and destroy thee out of the lands and break thee in pieces, and thou shalt know that I am the Lord.'

8 """Thus saith the Lord God: 'Because Moab and Seir have said, "Behold: the house of Judah is like all *other* nations," 9 therefore behold: I will open the shoulder of Moab

civitatibus, inquam, eius, et de finibus eius, inclitas terrae Bethiesimoth et Beelmeon et Cariathaim, 10 filiis orientis cum filiis Ammon, et dabo eam in hereditatem, ut non sit memoria ultra filiorum Ammon in gentibus. 11 Et in Moab faciam iudicia, et scient quia ego Dominus.'

12 """Haec dicit Dominus Deus: 'Pro eo quod fecit Idumea ultionem ut se vindicaret de filiis Iuda peccavitque delinquens et vindictam expetivit de eis, 13 idcirco haec dicit Dominus Deus: extendam manum meam super Idumeam et auferam de ea hominem et iumentum et faciam eam desertam ab austro, et qui sunt in Daedan gladio cadent. 14 Et dabo ultionem meam super Idumeam per manum populi mei Israhel, et facient in Edom iuxta iram meam et furorem meum, et scient vindictam meam," dicit Dominus Deus.'

15 """Haec dicit Dominus Deus: 'Pro eo quod fecerunt Palestini vindictam et ulti se sunt toto animo, interficientes et implentes inimicitias veteres, 16 propterea haec dicit Dominus Deus: "Ecce: ego extendam manum meam super Palestinos et interficiam interfectores et perdam reliquias maritimae regionis. 17 Faciamque in eis ultiones magnas, arguens in furore, et scient quia ego Dominus cum dedero vindictam meam super eos."""""

from the cities, from his cities, I say, and his borders, the noble cities of the land of Beth-jeshimoth and Baal-meon and Kiriathaim, 10 to the people of the east with the children of Ammon, and I will give it them for an inheritance, that there may be no more any remembrance of the children of Ammon among the nations. 11 And I will execute judgments in Moab, and they shall know that I am the Lord.'

12 """Thus saith the Lord God: 'Because Edom hath taken vengeance to revenge herself of the children of Judah and hath greatly offended, and hath sought revenge of them, 13 therefore thus saith the Lord God: "I will stretch forth my hand upon Edom and will take away out of it man and beast and will make it desolate from the south, and they that are in Dedan shall fall by the sword. 14 And I will lay my vengeance upon Edom by the hand of my people Israel, and they shall do in Edom according to my wrath and my fury, and they shall know my vengeance," saith the Lord God.'

15 """Thus saith the Lord God: 'Because the Philistines have taken vengeance and have revenged themselves with all their mind, destroying and satisfying old enmities, 16 therefore thus saith the Lord God: "Behold: I will stretch forth my hand upon the Philistines and will kill the killers and will destroy the remnant of the sea coast. 17 And I will execute great vengeance upon them, rebuking them in fury, and they shall know that I am the Lord when I shall lay my vengeance upon them.""""

Caput 26

Et factum est in undecimo anno, prima mensis, factus est sermo Domini ad me, dicens, 2 "Fili hominis, pro eo quod dixit Tyrus de Hierusalem, 'Euge, confractae sunt portae populorum; conversa est ad me: implebor; deserta est,' 3 propterea haec dicit Dominus Deus: 'Ecce: ego super te, Tyre, et ascendere faciam ad te gentes multas, sicut ascendit mare fluctuans. 4 Et dissipabunt muros Tyri et destruent turres eius, et radam pulverem eius de ea et dabo eam in limpidissimam petram. 5 Siccatio sagenarum erit in medio maris, quia ego locutus sum,' ait Dominus Deus, 'et erit in direptionem gentibus. 6 Filiae quoque eius quae sunt in agro gladio interficientur, et scient quia ego Dominus.'

7 "Quia haec dicit Dominus Deus: 'Ecce: ego adducam ad Tyrum Nabuchodonosor, regem Babylonis, ab aquilone, regem regum, cum equis et curribus et equitibus et coetu populoque magno. 8 Filias tuas quae sunt in agro gladio interficiet, et circumdabit te munitionibus et conportabit aggerem in gyro, et levabit contra te clypeum. 9 Et vineas et arietes temperabit in muros tuos et turres tuas destruet in armatura

Chapter 26

A prophecy of the destruction of the famous city of Tyre by Nebuchadnezzar.

And it came to pass in the eleventh year, the first day of the month, that the word of the Lord came to me, saying, 2 "Son of man, because Tyre hath said of Jerusalem, 'Aha, the gates of the people are broken; she is turned to me: I shall be filled; *now* she is laid waste,' 3 therefore thus saith the Lord God: 'Behold: I come against thee, O Tyre, and I will cause many nations to come up to thee, as the waves of the sea rise up. 4 And they shall break down the walls of Tyre and destroy the towers thereof, and I will scrape her dust from her and make her like a *smooth* rock. 5 She shall be a drying place for nets in the midst of the sea, because I have spoken it,' saith the Lord God, 'and she shall be a spoil to the nations. 6 Her daughters also that are in the field shall be slain by the sword, and they shall know that I am the Lord.'

7 "For thus saith the Lord God: 'Behold: I will bring against Tyre Nebuchadnezzar, king of Babylon, the king of kings, from the north with horses and chariots and horsemen and companies and much people. 8 Thy daughters that are in the field he shall kill with the sword, and he shall compass thee with forts and shall cast up a mount round about, and he shall lift up the buckler against thee. 9 And he shall set engines of war and battering rams against thy walls and

sua. 10 Inundatione equorum eius operiet te pulvis eorum; a sonitu equitum et rotarum et curruum movebuntur muri tui cum ingressus fuerit portas tuas quasi per introitum urbis dissipatae. 11 Ungulis equorum suorum conculcabit omnes plateas tuas; populum tuum gladio caedet, et statuae tuae nobiles in terram corruent. 12 Vastabunt opes tuas; diripient negotiationes tuas, et destruent muros tuos et domos tuas praeclaras subvertent, et lapides tuos et ligna tua et pulverem tuum in medio aquarum ponent. 13 Et quiescere faciam multitudinem canticorum tuorum, et sonitus cithararum tuarum non audietur amplius. 14 Et dabo te in limpidissimam petram; siccatio sagenarum eris, nec aedificaberis ultra, quia ego locutus sum,' dicit Dominus Deus.

15 "Haec dicit Dominus Deus: 'Tyro numquid non a sonitu ruinae tuae et gemitu interfectorum tuorum cum occisi fuerint in medio tui commovebuntur insulae? 16 Et descendent de sedibus suis omnes principes maris et auferent exuvias suas et vestimenta sua varia abicient et induentur stupore; in terra sedebunt et adtoniti super repentino casu tuo admirabuntur. 17 Et adsumentes super te lamentum dicent, "Tibi quomodo peristi quae habitas in mari, urbs inclita quae fuisti fortis in mari cum habitatoribus tuis, quos formidabant universi? 18 Nunc stupebunt naves in die pavoris tui, et turbabuntur insulae in mari eo quod nullus egrediatur ex te."'

19 "Quia haec dicit Dominus Deus: 'Cum dedero te urbem desolatam sicut civitates quae non habitantur et ad-

shall destroy thy towers with his arms. 10 By reason of the multitude of his horses their dust shall cover thee; thy walls shall shake at the noise of the horsemen and wheels and chariots when they shall go in at thy gates as by the entrance of a city that is destroyed. 11 With the hoofs of his horses he shall tread down all thy streets; thy people he shall kill with the sword, and thy famous statues shall fall to the ground. 12 They shall waste thy riches; they shall make a spoil of thy merchandise, and they shall destroy thy walls and pull down thy fine houses, and they shall lay thy stones and thy timber and thy dust in the midst of the waters. 13 And I will make the multitude of thy songs to cease, and the sound of thy harps shall be heard no more. 14 And I will make thee like a naked rock; thou shalt be a drying place for nets, neither shalt thou be built any more, for I have spoken it,' saith the Lord God.

15 "Thus saith the Lord God to Tyre: 'Shall not the islands shake at the sound of thy fall and the groans of thy slain when they shall be killed in the midst of thee? 16 Then all the princes of the sea shall come down from their thrones and take off their robes and cast away their broidered garments and be clothed with astonishment; they shall sit on the ground and with amazement shall wonder at thy sudden fall. 17 And taking up a lamentation over thee they shall say to thee, "How art thou fallen that dwellest in the sea, renowned city that wast strong in the sea with thy inhabitants, whom all did dread? 18 Now shall the ships be astonished in the day of thy terror, and the islands in the sea shall be troubled because no one cometh out of thee."'

19 "For thus saith the Lord God: 'When I shall make thee a desolate city like the cities that are not inhabited and shall

duxero super te abyssum et operuerint te aquae multae 20 et detraxero te cum his qui descendunt in lacum ad populum sempiternum et conlocavero te in terra novissima sicut solitudines veteres cum his qui deducuntur in lacum, ut non habiteris, porro dedero gloriam in terra viventium; 21 in nihilum redigam te, et non eris, et requisita non invenieris ultra in sempiternum,' dicit Dominus Deus."

Caput 27

Et factum est verbum Domini ad me, dicens, 2 "Tu ergo, fili hominis, adsume super Tyrum lamentum, 3 et dices Tyro, quae habitat in introitu maris, negotiationi populorum ad insulas multas, 'Haec dicit Dominus Deus: "O Tyre, tu dixisti, 'Perfecti decoris ego sum 4 et in corde maris sita.' Finitimi tui qui te aedificaverunt impleverunt decorem tuum; 5 abietibus de Sanir extruxerunt te cum omnibus tabulatis maris; cedrum de Libano tulerunt ut facerent tibi malum. 6 Quercus de Basan dolaverunt in remos tuos, et transtra tua fecerunt tibi ex ebore Indico et praetoriola de

bring the deep upon thee and many waters shall cover thee, 20 and when I shall bring thee down with those that descend into the pit to the everlasting people and shall set thee in the lowest parts of the earth as places desolate of old with them that are brought down into the pit, that thou be not inhabited, and when I shall give glory in the land of the living, 21 I will bring thee to nothing, and thou shalt not be, and if thou be sought for, thou shalt not be found any more for ever,' saith the Lord God."

Chapter 27

A description of the glory and riches of Tyre and of her irrecoverable fall.

And the word of the Lord came to me, saying: 2 Thou therefore, O son of man, take up a lamentation for Tyre, 3 and say to Tyre, that dwelleth at the entry of the sea, being the mart of the people for many islands, 'Thus saith the Lord God: "O Tyre, thou hast said, 'I am of perfect beauty 4 and situate in the heart of the sea.' Thy neighbours that built thee have perfected thy beauty: 5 with fir trees of Senir they have built thee with all sea planks; they have taken cedars from Lebanon to make thee masts. 6 They have *cut thy oars out of the oaks* of Bashan, and they have made thee benches of Indian ivory and cabins *with things brought* from

insulis Italiae. 7 Byssus varia de Aegypto texta est tibi in velum ut poneretur in malo; hyacinthus et purpura de insulis Elisa facta sunt operimentum tuum.

8 """Habitatores Sidonis et Aradii fuerunt remiges tui; sapientes tui, Tyre, facti sunt gubernatores tui. 9 Senes Giblii et prudentes eius habuerunt nautas ad ministerium variae supellectilis tuae; omnes naves maris et nautae earum fuerunt in populo negotiationis tuae. 10 Persae et Lydi et Lybies erant in exercitu tuo viri bellatores tui; clypeum et galeam suspenderunt in te pro ornatu tuo. 11 Filii Aradii cum exercitu tuo erant super muros tuos in circuitu sed et Pigmei qui erant in turribus tuis faretras suas suspenderunt in muris tuis per gyrum ipsi conpleverunt pulchritudinem tuam 12 Carthaginienses, negotiatores tui, a multitudine cunctarum divitiarum, argento, ferro, stagno plumboque, repleverunt nundinas tuas. 13 Graecia, Thubal et Mosoch, ipsi institores tui; mancipia et vasa aerea adduxerunt populo tuo. 14 De domo Thogorma equos et equites et mulos adduxerunt ad forum tuum. 15 Filii Dadan negotiatores tui; insulae multae negotiatio manus tuae; dentes eburneos et hebeninos commutaverunt in pretio tuo. 16 Syrus negotiator tuus; propter multitudinem operum tuorum gemmam et purpuram et scutulata et byssum et sericum et chodchod proposuerunt in mercatu tuo. 17 Iuda et terra Israhel, ipsi institores tui in frumento primo; balsamum et mel et oleum et resinam proposuerunt in nundinis tuis. 18 Damascenus negotiator tuus in multitudine operum tuorum, in multitudine diversarum opum, in vino pingui, in lanis coloris optimi. 19 Dan et Graecia et Mozel in nundinis tuis proposuerunt

the islands of Italy. 7 Fine broidered linen from Egypt was woven for thy sail to be spread on thy mast; blue and purple from the islands of Elishah were made thy covering.

8 """The inhabitants of Sidon and the Arvadians were thy rowers; thy wise men, O Tyre, were thy pilots. 9 The ancients of Gebal and the wise men thereof furnished mariners for the service of thy various furniture; all the ships of the sea and their mariners were thy factors. 10 The Persians and Lydians and the Libyans were thy soldiers in thy army; they hung up the buckler and the helmet in thee for thy ornament. 11 The men of Arvad were with thy army upon thy walls round about; the Pygmeans also that were in thy towers hung up their quivers on thy walls round about; they perfected thy beauty.

12 """The Carthaginians, thy merchants, supplied thy fairs with a multitude of all kinds of riches, with silver, iron, tin and lead. 13 Greece, Tubal, and Meshech, they were thy merchants; they brought to thy people slaves and vessels of brass. 14 From the house of Togarmah they brought horses and horsemen and mules to thy market. 15 The men of Dedan were thy merchants: many islands were the traffic of thy hand, they exchanged for thy price teeth of ivory and ebony. 16 The Syrian was thy merchant; by reason of the multitude of thy works they set forth precious stones and purple and broidered works and fine linen and silk and chodchod in thy market. 17 Judah and the land of Israel, they were thy merchants with the best corn; they set forth balm and honey and oil and rosin in thy fairs. 18 The *men* of Damascus were thy *merchants* in the multitude of thy works, in the multitude of divers riches, in rich wine, in wool of the best colour. 19 Dan and Greece and Mosel have set forth in thy marts

EZEKIEL

ferrum fabrefactum; stacte et calamus in negotiatione tua.
20 Dadan institores tui in tapetibus ad sedendum; 21 Arabia
et universi principes Cedar, ipsi negotiatores manus tuae;
cum agnis et arietibus et hedis venerunt ad te negotiatores
tui. 22 Venditores Saba et Reema, ipsi negotiatores tui cum
universis primis aromatibus et lapide pretioso et auro quod
proposuerunt in mercatu tuo. 23 Aran et Chenne et Eden
negotiatores tui; Saba, Assur et Chelmad venditores tui.
24 Ipsi negotiatores tui multifariam, involucris hyacinthi et
polymitorum gazarumque pretiosarum quae obvolutae et
adstrictae erant funibus; cedros quoque habebant in nego-
tiationibus tuis.

25 """Naves maris principes tuae in negotiatione tua, et repleta es et glorificata nimis in corde maris. 26 In aquis multis
adduxerunt te remiges tui; ventus auster contrivit te in corde
maris. 27 Divitiae tuae et thesauri tui et multiplex instru-
mentum tuum, nautae tui et gubernatores tui qui tenebant
supellectilem tuam et populo tuo praeerant, viri quoque bellatores tui qui erant in te, cum universa multitudine tua quae
est in medio tui, cadent in corde maris in die ruinae tuae.
28 A sonitu clamoris gubernatorum tuorum conturbabuntur
classes. 29 Et descendent de navibus suis omnes qui tenebant
remum; nautae et universi gubernatores maris in terra stabunt, 30 et heiulabunt super te voce magna et clamabunt
amare, et superiacient pulverem capitibus suis et cinere
conspergentur. 31 Et radent super te calvitium et accingentur ciliciis, et plorabunt te in amaritudine animae ploratu
amarissimo.

32 """Et adsument super te carmen lugubre et plangent te:

wrought iron; stacte and calamus were in thy market. 20 *The men of* Dedan were thy merchants in tapestry for seats; 21 Arabia and all the princes of Kedar, they were the merchants of thy hand; thy merchants came to thee with lambs and rams and kids. 22 The sellers of Sheba and Raamah, they were thy merchants with all the best spices and precious stones and gold which they set forth in thy market. 23 Haran and Canneh and Eden were thy merchants; Sheba, Asshur and Chilmad sold to thee. 24 They were thy merchants in divers manners, with bales of blue cloth and of embroidered work and of precious riches which were wrapped up and bound with cords; they had cedars also in thy merchandise.

25 """The ships of the sea were thy chief in thy merchandise, and thou wast replenished and glorified exceedingly in the heart of the sea. 26 Thy rowers have brought thee into great waters; the south wind hath broken thee in the heart of the sea. 27 Thy riches and thy treasures and thy manifold furniture, thy mariners and thy pilots who kept thy goods and were chief over thy people, thy men of war also that were in thee, with all thy multitude that is in the midst of thee, shall fall in the heart of the sea in the day of thy ruin. 28 Thy fleets shall be troubled at the sound of the cry of thy pilots. 29 And all that handled the oar shall come down from their ships; the mariners and all the pilots of the sea shall stand upon the land, 30 and they shall mourn over thee with a loud voice and shall cry bitterly, and they shall cast up dust upon their heads and shall be sprinkled with ashes. 31 And they shall shave themselves bald for thee and shall be girded with haircloth, and they shall weep for thee with bitterness of soul, with most bitter weeping.

32 """And they shall take up a mournful song for thee and

"Quae est ut Tyrus, quae obmutuit in medio maris? 33 Quae
in exitu negotiationum tuarum de mari implesti populos
multos, in multitudine divitiarum tuarum et populorum
tuorum ditasti reges terrae. 34 Nunc contrita es a mari, in
profundis aquarum opes tuae et omnis multitudo tua quae
erat in medio tui ceciderunt. 35 Universi habitatores insularum obstipuerunt super te, et reges earum omnes tempestate perculsi mutaverunt vultus. 36 Negotiatores populorum
sibilaverunt super te; ad nihilum deducta es, et non eris usque in perpetuum.'""""

Caput 28

Et factus est sermo Domini ad me, dicens, 2 "Fili hominis,
dic principi Tyri, 'Haec dicit Dominus Deus: "Eo quod elevatum est cor tuum et dixisti, 'Deus ego sum, et in cathedra
Dei sedi in corde maris,' cum sis homo et non Deus et dedisti cor tuum quasi cor Dei.

3 """Ecce: sapientior es tu Danihele; omne secretum non

shall lament thee: 'What *city* is like Tyre, which is become silent in the midst of the sea? 33 Which by thy merchandise that went *from thee by* sea didst fill many people, which by the multitude of thy riches and of thy people didst enrich the kings of the earth. 34 Now thou art destroyed by the sea, thy riches are in the bottom of the waters and all the multitude that was in the midst of thee is fallen. 35 All the inhabitants of the islands are astonished at thee, and all their kings being struck with the storm have changed their countenance. 36 The merchants of people have hissed at thee; thou art brought to nothing, and thou shalt never be any more.""""

Chapter 28

The king of Tyre, who affected to be like to God, shall fall under the like sentence with Lucifer. The judgment of Sidon. The restoration of Israel.

And the word of the Lord came to me, saying, 2 "Son of man, say to the prince of Tyre, 'Thus saith the Lord God: "Because thy heart is lifted up and thou hast said, 'I am God, and I sit in the chair of God in the heart of the sea,' whereas thou art a man and not God and hast set thy heart as if it were the heart of God.

3 """Behold thou art wiser than Daniel; no secret is hid

est absconditum a te. 4 In sapientia et prudentia tua fecisti tibi fortitudinem et adquisisti aurum et argentum in thesauris tuis. 5 In multitudine sapientiae tuae et in negotiatione tua multiplicasti tibi fortitudinem, et elevatum est cor tuum in robore tuo."

6 "'Propterea haec dicit Dominus Deus: "Eo quod elevatum est cor tuum quasi cor Dei, 7 idcirco ecce: ego adducam super te alienos, robustissimos gentium, et nudabunt gladios suos super pulchritudinem sapientiae tuae, et polluent decorem tuum. 8 Interficient et detrahent te, et morieris in interitu occisorum in corde maris. 9 Numquid dicens loqueris, 'Deus ego sum,' coram interficientibus te, cum sis homo et non Deus, in manu occidentium te? 10 Morte incircumcisorum morieris in manu alienorum, quia ego locutus sum," ait Dominus Deus.'"

11 Et factus est sermo Domini ad me, dicens, "Fili hominis, leva planctum super regem Tyri, 12 et dices ei, 'Haec dicit Dominus Deus: "Tu signaculum similitudinis, plenus sapientia et perfectus decore. 13 In deliciis paradisi Dei fuisti; omnis lapis pretiosus operimentum tuum, sardius, topazius et iaspis, chrysolitus et onyx et berillus, sapphyrus et carbunculus et zmaragdus; aurum opus decoris tui, et foramina tua in die qua conditus es praeparata sunt. 14 Tu cherub extentus et protegens, et posui te in monte sancto Dei; in medio lapidum ignitorum ambulasti. 15 Perfectus in viis tuis a die conditionis tuae donec inventa est iniquitas in te.

16 ""In multitudine negotiationis tuae repleta sunt inter-

from thee. 4 In thy wisdom and thy understanding thou hast made thyself strong and hast gotten gold and silver into thy treasures. 5 By the greatness of thy wisdom and by thy traffic thou hast increased thy strength, and thy heart is lifted up with thy strength."

6 "'Therefore thus saith the Lord God: 'Because thy heart is lifted up as the heart of God, 7 therefore behold: I will bring upon thee strangers, the strongest of the nations, and they shall draw their swords against the beauty of thy wisdom, and they shall defile thy beauty. 8 They shall kill thee and bring thee down, and thou shalt die the death of them that are slain in the heart of the sea. 9 Wilt thou yet say before them that slay thee, "I am God," whereas thou art a man and not God, in the hand of them that slay thee? 10 Thou shalt die the death of the uncircumcised by the hand of strangers, for I have spoken it," saith the Lord God.'"

11 And the word of the Lord came to me, saying, "Son of man, take up a lamentation upon the king of Tyre, 12 and *say* to him, 'Thus saith the Lord God: "Thou wast the seal of resemblance, full of wisdom and perfect in beauty. 13 Thou wast in the pleasures of the paradise of God; every precious stone was thy covering, the sardius, the topaz and the jasper, the chrysolite and the onyx and the beryl, the sapphire and the carbuncle and the emerald, gold the work of thy beauty, and thy pipes were prepared in the day that thou wast created. 14 Thou a cherub stretched out and protecting, and I set thee in the holy mountain of God; thou hast walked in the midst of the stones of fire. 15 Thou wast perfect in thy ways from the day of thy creation until iniquity was found in thee.

16 "'"By the multitude of thy merchandise thy inner parts

iora tua iniquitate, et peccasti; et eieci te de monte Dei et perdidi te, O cherub protegens, de medio lapidum ignitorum. 17 Et elevatum est cor tuum in decore tuo; perdidisti sapientiam tuam in decore tuo: in terram proieci te; ante faciem regum dedi te, ut cernerent te. 18 In multitudine iniquitatum tuarum et iniquitate negotiationis tuae polluisti sanctificationem tuam; producam ergo ignem de medio tui qui comedat te, et dabo te in cinerem super terram in conspectu omnium videntium te. 19 Omnes qui viderint te in gentibus obstupescent super te; nihili factus es, et non eris in perpetuum."""

20 Et factus est sermo Domini ad me, dicens, 21 "Fili hominis, pone faciem tuam contra Sidonem, et prophetabis de ea 22 et dices, 'Haec dicit Dominus Deus: "Ecce: ego ad te, Sidon, et glorificabor in medio tui, et scient quia ego Dominus cum fecero in ea iudicia et sanctificatus fuero in ea. 23 Et inmittam ei pestilentiam, et sanguinem in plateis eius, et corruent interfecti in medio eius gladio per circuitum, et scient quia ego Dominus.

24 Et non erit ultra domui Israhel offendiculum amaritudinis et spina dolorem inferens undique per circuitum eorum qui adversantur eis, et scient quia ego Dominus Deus."

25 '"Haec dicit Dominus Deus: "Quando congregavero domum Israhel de populis in quibus dispersi sunt, sanctificabor in eis coram Gentibus, et habitabunt in terra sua quam dedi servo meo Iacob. 26 Et habitabunt in ea securi, et aedi-

were filled with iniquity, and thou hast sinned; and I cast thee out from the mountain of God and destroyed thee, O covering cherub, out of the midst of the stones of fire. 17 And thy heart was lifted up with thy beauty; thou hast lost thy wisdom in thy beauty: I have cast thee to the ground; I have set thee before the face of kings, that they might behold thee. 18 Thou hast defiled thy sanctuaries by the multitude of thy iniquities and by the iniquity of thy traffic; therefore I will bring forth a fire from the midst of thee to devour thee, and I will make thee as ashes upon the earth in the sight of all that see thee. 19 All that shall see thee among the nations shall be astonished at thee; thou art brought to nothing, and thou shalt never be any more."'"

20 And the word of the Lord came to me, saying, 21 "Son of man, set thy face against Sidon, and thou shalt prophesy of it 22 and shalt say, 'Thus saith the Lord God: "Behold: I come against thee, Sidon, and I will be glorified in the midst of thee, and they shall know that I am the Lord when I shall execute judgments in her and shall be sanctified in her. 23 And I will send into her pestilence, and blood in her streets: and they shall fall being slain by the sword on all sides in the midst thereof, and they shall know that I am the Lord.

24 ""And the house of Israel shall have no more a stumbling block of bitterness nor a thorn causing pain on every side round about them of them that are against them: and they shall know that I am the Lord God."

25 "'Thus saith the Lord God: "When I shall have gathered together the house of Israel out of the people among whom they are scattered, I will be sanctified in them before the Gentiles: and they shall dwell in their own land, which I gave to my servant Jacob. 26 And they shall dwell therein

ficabunt domos plantabuntque vineas et habitabunt confidenter, cum fecero iudicia in omnibus qui adversantur eis per circuitum; et scient quia ego Dominus, Deus eorum.""

Caput 29

In anno decimo, decimo mense, undecima die mensis, factum est verbum Domini ad me, dicens, 2 "Fili hominis, pone faciem tuam contra Pharaonem, regem Aegypti, et prophetabis de eo et de Aegypto universa; 3 loquere, et dices, 'Haec dicit Dominus Deus: "Ecce: ego ad te, Pharao, rex Aegypti, draco magne qui cubas in medio fluminum tuorum et dicis, 'Meus est fluvius, et ego feci memet ipsum.'

4 ""Et ponam frenum in maxillis tuis, et adglutinabo pisces fluminum tuorum squamis tuis, et extraham te de medio fluminum tuorum, et universi pisces tui squamis tuis adherebunt. 5 Et proiciam te in desertum, et omnes pisces fluminis tui; super faciem terrae cades; non colligeris neque congregaberis; bestiis terrae et volatilibus caeli dedi te ad devorandum.

6 ""Et scient omnes habitatores Aegypti quia ego Domi-

secure, and they shall build houses and shall plant vineyards and shall dwell with confidence, when I shall have executed judgments upon all that are their enemies round about; and they shall know that I am the Lord, their God.""""

Chapter 29

The king of Egypt shall be overthrown, and his kingdom wasted; it shall be given to Nebuchadnezzar for his service against Tyre.

In the tenth year, the tenth month, the eleventh day of the month, the word of the Lord came to me, saying, 2 "Son of man, set thy face against Pharaoh, king of Egypt, and thou shalt prophesy of him and of all Egypt; 3 speak, and say, 'Thus saith the Lord God: "Behold: I come against thee, Pharaoh, king of Egypt, thou great dragon that liest in the midst of thy rivers and sayest, 'The river is mine, and I made myself.'

4 ""But I will put a bridle in thy jaws, and I will cause the fish of thy rivers to stick to thy scales, and I will draw thee out of the midst of thy rivers, and all thy fish shall stick to thy scales. 5 And I will cast thee forth into the desert and all the fish of thy river; thou shalt fall upon the face of the earth; thou shalt not be taken up nor gathered together; I have given thee for meat to the beasts of the earth and to the fowls of the air.

6 ""And all the inhabitants of Egypt shall know that I am

nus pro eo quod fuisti baculus harundineus domui Israhel.
7 Quando adprehenderunt te manu et confractus es et lace-
rasti omnem umerum eorum, et innitentibus eis super te
comminutus es et dissolvisti omnes renes eorum."

8 "'Propterea haec dicit Dominus Deus: "Ecce: ego adducam super te gladium et interficiam de te hominem et iumentum. 9 Et erit terra Aegypti in desertum et in solitudinem, et scient quia ego Dominus, pro eo quod dixeris,
'Fluvius meus est, et ego feci eum.'

10 ""'Idcirco ecce: ego ad te et ad flumina tua daboque terram Aegypti in solitudines, gladio dissipatam, a turre Syenes
usque ad terminos Aethiopiae. 11 Non pertransitbit eam pes
hominis, neque pes iumenti gradietur in ea, et non habitabitur quadraginta annis. 12 Daboque terram Aegypti desertam
in medio terrarum desertarum, et civitates eius in medio ur-
bium subversarum, et erunt desolatae quadraginta annis, et
dispergam Aegyptios in nationes et ventilabo eos in terras."

13 "'Quia haec dicit Dominus Deus: "Post finem quadraginta annorum congregabo Aegyptum de populis in quibus
dispersi fuerant. 14 Et reducam captivitatem Aegypti et
conlocabo eos in terra Fatures, in terra nativitatis suae, et
erunt ibi in regnum humile; 15 inter regna cetera erit humil-
lima, et non elevabitur ultra super nationes, et inminuam
eos ne imperent gentibus. 16 Neque erunt ultra domui Israhel in confidentia, docentes iniquitatem, ut fugiant et se-
quantur eos; et scient quia ego Dominus Deus.""'

the Lord because thou hast been a staff of a reed to the house of Israel. 7 When they took hold of thee with the hand thou didst break and rent all their shoulder, and when they leaned upon thee thou brokest and weakenest all their loins."

8 "'Therefore thus saith the Lord God: "Behold: I will bring the sword upon thee and cut off man and beast out of thee. 9 And the land of Egypt shall become a desert and a wilderness, and they shall know that I am the Lord, because thou hast said, 'The river is mine, and I made it.'

10 ""'Therefore behold: I come against thee and thy rivers, and I will make the land of Egypt *utterly* desolate *and* wasted by the sword from the tower of Syene even to the borders of Ethiopia. 11 The foot of man shall not pass through it, neither shall the foot of beasts go through it, nor shall it be inhabited during forty years. 12 And I will make the land of Egypt desolate in the midst of the lands that are desolate, and the cities thereof in the midst of the cities that are destroyed, and they shall be desolate for forty years, and I will scatter the Egyptians among the nations and will disperse them through the countries."

13 "'For thus saith the Lord God: At the end of forty years I will gather the Egyptians from the people among whom they had been scattered. 14 And I will bring back the captivity of Egypt and will place them in the land of Pathros, in the land of their nativity, and they shall be there a low kingdom; 15 it shall be the lowest among other kingdoms, and it shall no more be exalted over the nations, and I will diminish them that they shall rule no more over the nations. 16 And they shall be no more a confidence to the house of Israel, teaching iniquity, that they may flee and follow them; and they shall know that I am the Lord God.""'

17 Et factum est in vicesimo et septimo anno, in primo, in una mensis, factum est verbum Domini ad me, dicens, 18 "Fili hominis, Nabuchodonosor, rex Babylonis, servire fecit exercitum suum servitute magna adversum Tyrum; omne caput decalvatum, et omnis umerus depilatus est, et merces non est reddita ei neque exercitui eius de Tyro pro servitute qua servivit mihi adversum eam. 19 Propterea haec dicit Dominus Deus: 'Ecce: ego dabo Nabuchodonosor, regem Babylonis, in terra Aegypti, et accipiet multitudinem eius et depraedabitur manubias eius et diripiet spolia eius, et erit merces exercitui illius. 20 Et operi quo servivit adversum eam dedi ei terram Aegypti pro eo quod laboraverunt mihi,' ait Dominus Deus.

21 "'In die illo pullulabit cornu domui Israhel, et tibi dabo apertum os in medio eorum, et scient quoniam ego Dominus.'"

Caput 30

Et factum est verbum Domini ad me, dicens, 2 "Fili hominis, propheta, et dic, 'Haec dicit Dominus Deus: "Ululate, 'Vae, vae diei!' 3 Quia iuxta est dies, et adpropinquat dies

17 And it came to pass in the seven and twentieth year, in the first month, in the first of the month, that the word of the Lord came to me, saying, 18 "Son of man, Nebuchadnezzar, king of Babylon, hath made his army to undergo hard service against Tyre; every head was made bald, and every shoulder was peeled, and there hath been no reward given him nor his army for Tyre for the service that he rendered me against it. 19 Therefore thus saith the Lord God: 'Behold: I will set Nabuchodonosor, the king of Babylon, in the land of Egypt, and he shall take her multitude and take the booty thereof for a prey and rifle the spoils thereof, and it shall be wages for his army. 20 And for the service that he hath done me against it I have given him the land of Egypt because he hath laboured for me,' saith the Lord God.

21 "'In that day a horn shall bud forth to the house of Israel, and I will give thee an open mouth in the midst of them, and they shall know that I am the Lord.'"

Chapter 30

The desolation of Egypt and her helpers; all her cities shall be wasted.

And the word of the Lord came to me, saying, 2 "Son of man, prophesy, and say, 'Thus saith the Lord God: "Howl ye, 'Woe, woe to the day!' 3 For the day is near, yea the day of the

Domini; dies nubis, tempus gentium erit. 4 Et veniet gladius in Aegyptum, et erit pavor in Aethiopia cum ceciderint vulnerati in Aegypto et ablata fuerit multitudo illius et destructa fundamenta eius. 5 Aethiopia et Lybia et Lydii et omne reliquum vulgus et Chub et filii terrae foederis cum eis gladio cadent."

6 "'Haec dicit Dominus Deus: "Et corruent fulcientes Aegyptum, et destruetur superbia imperii eius; a turre Syenes gladio cadent in ea," ait Dominus, Deus exercituum. 7 "Et dissipabuntur in medio terrarum desolatarum, et urbes eius in medio civitatum desertarum erunt. 8 Et scient quoniam ego Dominus cum dedero ignem in Aegypto et adtriti fuerint omnes auxiliatores eius.

9 ""In die illa egredientur nuntii a facie mea in trieribus ad conterendam Aethiopiae confidentiam, et erit pavor in eis in die Aegypti, quia absque dubio veniet."

10 "Haec dicit Dominus Deus: "Cessare faciam multitudinem Aegypti in manu Nabuchodonosor, regis Babylonis. 11 Ipse et populus eius cum eo, fortissimi gentium, adducentur ad disperdendam terram, et evaginabunt gladios suos super Aegyptum et implebunt terram interfectis. 12 Et faciam alveos fluminum aridos et tradam terram in manus pessimorum et dissipabo terram et plenitudinem eius in manibus alienorum. Ego, Dominus, locutus sum."

13 "'Haec dicit Dominus Deus: "Et disperdam simulacra,

Lord is near; a cloudy day, it shall be the time of the nations. 4 And the sword shall come upon Egypt, and there shall be dread in Ethiopia when the wounded shall fall in Egypt and the multitude thereof shall be taken away and the foundations thereof shall be destroyed. 5 Ethiopia and Libya and Lydia and all the rest of the crowd, and Cub and the children of the land of the covenant shall fall with them by the sword."

6 "Thus saith the Lord God: "They also that uphold Egypt shall fall, and the pride of her empire shall be brought down; from the tower of Syene shall they fall in it by the sword," saith the Lord, the God of hosts. 7 "And they shall be desolate in the midst of the lands that are desolate, and the cities thereof shall be in the midst of the cities that are wasted. 8 And they shall know that I am the Lord when I shall have set a fire in Egypt and all the helpers thereof shall be destroyed.

9 """In that day shall messengers go forth from my face in ships to destroy the confidence of Ethiopia, and there shall be dread among them in the day of Egypt, because it shall certainly come."

10 "Thus saith the Lord God: "I will make the multitude of Egypt to cease by the hand of Nebuchadnezzar, the king of Babylon. 11 He and his people with him, the strongest of nations, shall be brought to destroy the land, and they shall draw their swords upon Egypt and shall fill the land with the slain. 12 And I will make the channels of the rivers dry and will deliver the land into the hand of the *wicked* and will lay waste the land and all that is therein by the hands of strangers. I, the Lord, have spoken it."

13 "Thus saith the Lord God: "I will also destroy the

et cessare faciam idola de Memphis, et dux de terra Aegypti non erit amplius, et dabo terrorem in terra Aegypti. 14 Et disperdam terram Fatures et dabo ignem in Tafnis et faciam iudicia in Alexandria. 15 Et effundam indignationem meam super Pelusium, robur Aegypti, et interficiam multitudinem Alexandriae. 16 Et dabo ignem in Aegypto; quasi parturiens dolebit Pelusium, et Alexandria erit dissipata, et in Memphis angustiae cotidianae. 17 Iuvenes Eliupoleos et Bubasti gladio cadent, et ipsae captivae ducentur. 18 Et in Tafnis nigrescet dies cum contrivero ibi sceptra Aegypti et defecerit in ea superbia potentiae eius; ipsam nubes operiet, filiae autem eius in captivitatem ducentur. 19 Et faciam iudicia in Aegypto, et scient quia ego Dominus.""'"

20 Et factum est in undecimo anno, in primo mense, in septima mensis, factum est verbum Domini ad me, dicens, 21 "Fili hominis, brachium Pharaonis, regis Aegypti, confregi, et ecce: non est obvolutum ut restitueretur ei sanitas, ut ligaretur pannis et fasciaretur linteolis, ut recepto robore posset tenere gladium. 22 Propterea haec dicit Dominus Deus: 'Ecce: ego ad Pharaonem, regem Aegypti, et comminuam brachium eius forte, iam confractum, et deiciam gladium de manu eius, 23 et dispergam Aegyptum in gentibus et ventilabo eos in terris. 24 Et confortabo brachia regis Babylonis daboque gladium meum in manu eius, et confringam brachia Pharaonis, et gement gemitibus, interfecti coram fa-

idols, and I will make an end of the idols of Memphis, and there shall be no more a prince of the land of Egypt, and I will cause a terror in the land of Egypt. 14 And I will destroy the land of Pathros and will make a fire in Tahpanhes and will execute judgments in Alexandria. 15 And I will pour out my indignation upon Pelusium, the strength of Egypt, and will cut off the multitude of Alexandria. 16 And I will make a fire in Egypt; Pelusium shall be in pain like a woman in labour, and Alexandria shall be laid waste, and in Memphis there shall be daily distresses. 17 The young men of Heliopolis and of Bubastis shall fall by the sword, and they themselves shall go into captivity. 18 And in Tahpanhes the day shall be darkened when I shall break there the sceptres of Egypt and the pride of her power shall cease in her; a cloud shall cover her, and her daughters shall be led into captivity. 19 And I will execute judgments in Egypt, and they shall know that I am the Lord.""'

20 And it came to pass in the eleventh year, in the first month, in the seventh day of the month, that the word of the Lord came to me, saying, 21 "Son of man, I have broken the arm of Pharaoh, king of Egypt, and behold: it is not bound up to be healed, to be tied up with clothes and swathed with linen, that it might recover strength and hold the sword. 22 Therefore thus saith the Lord God: 'Behold: I come against Pharaoh, king of Egypt, and I will break into pieces his strong arm, which is *already* broken, and I will cause the sword to fall out of his hand, 23 and I will disperse Egypt among the nations and scatter them through the countries. 24 And I will strengthen the arms of the king of Babylon and will put my sword in his hand, and I will break the arms of Pharaoh, and they shall groan bitterly, being

cie eius. 25 Et confortabo brachia regis Babylonis, et brachia Pharaonis concident, et scient quia ego Dominus cum dedero gladium meum in manu regis Babylonis et extenderit eum super terram Aegypti. 26 Et dispergam Aegyptum in nationes et ventilabo eos in terras, et scient quia ego Dominus.'"

Caput 31

Et factum est in undecimo anno, tertio mense, una mensis, factum est verbum Domini ad me, dicens, 2 "Fili hominis, dic Pharaoni, regi Aegypti, et populo eius: 'Cui similis factus es in magnitudine tua? 3 Ecce: Assur quasi cedrus in Libano, pulcher ramis et frondibus nemorosus excelsusque altitudine, et inter condensas frondes elevatum est cacumen eius. 4 Aquae nutrierunt illum; abyssus exaltavit eum; flumina eius manabant in circuitu radicum eius, et rivos suos emisit ad universa ligna regionis. 5 Propterea elevata est altitudo eius super omnia ligna regionis, et multiplicata sunt arbusta eius, et elevati sunt rami eius prae aquis multis. 6 Cumque extendisset umbram suam, in ramis eius fecerunt

slain before his face. 25 And I will strengthen the arms of the king of Babylon, and the arms of Pharaoh shall fall, and they shall know that I am the Lord when I shall have given my sword into the hand of the king of Babylon and he shall have stretched it forth upon the land of Egypt. 26 And I will disperse Egypt among the nations, and will scatter them through the countries, and they shall know that I am the Lord.'"

Chapter 31

The Assyrian empire fell for their pride; the Egyptian shall fall in like manner.

And it came to pass in the eleventh year, the third month, the first day of the month, that the word of the Lord came to me, saying, 2 "Son of man, speak to Pharaoh, king of Egypt, and to his people: 'To whom art thou like in thy greatness? 3 Behold: the Assyrian was like a cedar in Lebanon with fair branches and full of leaves, *of* a high stature, and his top was elevated among the thick boughs. 4 The waters nourished him; the deep set him up on high; the streams thereof ran round about his roots, and it sent forth its rivulets to all the trees of the country. 5 Therefore was his height exalted above all the trees of the country, and his branches were multiplied, and his boughs were elevated because of many waters. 6 And when he had spread forth his shadow, all the

nidos omnia volatilia caeli, et sub frondibus eius genuerunt omnes bestiae saltuum, et sub umbraculo illius habitabat coetus gentium plurimarum. 7 Eratque pulcherrimus in magnitudine sua et in dilatatione arbustorum suorum, erat enim radix illius iuxta aquas multas. 8 Cedri non fuerunt altiores illo in paradiso Dei; abietes non adaequaverunt summitatem eius, et platani non fuerunt aequae frondibus illius; omne lignum paradisi Dei non est adsimilatum illi et pulchritudini eius. 9 Quoniam speciosum feci eum et multis condensisque frondibus, et aemulata sunt eum omnia ligna voluptatis quae erant in paradiso Dei.'

10 "Propterea haec dicit Dominus Deus: 'Pro eo quod sublimatus est in altitudine et dedit summitatem suam virentem atque condensam et elevatum est cor eius in altitudine sua, 11 tradidi eum in manus fortissimi gentium; faciens faciet ei; iuxta impietatem eius eieci eum. 12 Et succident illum alieni et crudelissimi nationum et proicient eum super montes, et in cunctis convallibus corruent rami eius, et confringentur arbusta eius in universis rupibus terrae, et recedent de umbraculo eius omnes populi terrae et relinquent eum. 13 In ruina eius habitaverunt omnia volatilia caeli, et in ramis eius fuerunt universae bestiae regionis.

14 "'Quam ob rem non elevabuntur in altitudine sua omnia ligna aquarum neque ponent sublimitatem suam inter nemorosa atque frondosa, nec stabunt in sublimitate sua omnia quae inrigantur aquis, quia omnes traditi sunt in mortem ad terram ultimam in medio filiorum hominum, ad eos qui descendunt in lacum.'

fowls of the air made their nests in his boughs, and all the beasts of the forest brought forth their young under his branches, and the assembly of many nations dwelt under his shadow. 7 And he was most beautiful for his greatness and for the spreading of his branches, for his root was near great waters. 8 The cedars in the paradise of God were not higher than he; the fir trees did not equal his top, neither were the plane trees to be compared with him for branches; no tree in the paradise of God was like him *in* his beauty. 9 For I made him beautiful and thick set with many branches, and all the trees of pleasure that were in the paradise of God envied him.'

10 "Therefore thus saith the Lord God: 'Because he was exalted in height and shot up his top green and thick and his heart was lifted up in his height, 11 I have delivered him into the hands of the mighty one of the nations; *he* shall deal with him; I have cast him out according to his wickedness. 12 And strangers and the most cruel of the nations shall cut him down and cast him away upon the mountains, and his boughs shall fall in every valley, and his branches shall be broken on every rock of the country, and all the people of the earth shall depart from his shadow and leave him. 13 All the fowls of the air dwelt upon his ruins, and all the beasts of the field were among his branches.

14 "'For which cause none of the trees *by* the waters shall exalt themselves for their height nor shoot up their tops among the thick branches and leaves, neither shall any of them that are *watered* stand up in their height, for they are all delivered unto death to the lowest parts of the earth in the midst of the children of men, *with* them that go down into the pit.'

15 "Haec dicit Dominus Deus: 'In die quando descendit ad inferos, induxi luctum; operui eum abysso, et prohibui flumina eius et coercui aquas multas; contristatus est super eum Libanus, et omnia ligna agri concussa sunt. 16 A sonitu ruinae eius commovi gentes cum deducerem eum ad infernum cum his qui descendebant in lacum, et consolata sunt in terra infima omnia ligna voluptatis, egregia atque praeclara in Libano, universa quae inrigabantur aquis. 17 Nam et ipsi cum eo descendent ad infernum, ad interfectos gladio, et brachium uniuscuiusque sedebit sub umbraculo eius in medio nationum.

18 "'Cui adsimilatus es, O inclite atque sublimis inter ligna voluptatis? Ecce: deductus es cum lignis voluptatis ad terram ultimam; in medio incircumcisorum dormies, cum eis qui interfecti sunt gladio: ipse est Pharao et omnis multitudo eius,' dicit Dominus Deus."

Caput 32

Et factum est duodecimo anno, in mense duodecimo, in una mensis, factum est verbum Domini ad me, dicens, 2 "Fili hominis, adsume lamentum super Pharaonem, regem Aegypti, et dices ad eum, 'Leoni gentium adsimilatus es

15 "Thus saith the Lord God: 'In the day when he went down to hell, I brought in mourning; I covered him with the deep, and I withheld its rivers and restrained the many waters; Lebanon grieved for him, and all the trees of the field trembled. 16 I shook the nations with the sound of his fall when I brought him down to hell with them that descend into the pit, and all the trees of pleasure, the choice and best in Lebanon, all that were moistened with waters, were comforted in the lowest parts of the earth. 17 For they also shall go down with him to hell, to them that are slain by the sword, and the arm of every one shall sit down under his shadow in the midst of the nations.

18 "'To whom art thou like, O thou that art famous and lofty among the trees of pleasure? Behold: thou art brought down with the trees of pleasure to the lowest parts of the earth; thou shalt sleep in the midst of the uncircumcised, with them that are slain by the sword: this is Pharaoh and all his multitude,' saith the Lord God."

Chapter 32

The prophet's lamentation for the king of Egypt.

And it came to pass in the twelfth year, in the twelfth month, in the first day of the month, that the word of the Lord came to me, saying, 2 "Son of man, take up a lamentation for Pharaoh, the king of Egypt, and say to him, 'Thou

et draconi qui est in mari, et ventilabas cornu in fluminibus tuis et conturbabas aquas pedibus tuis et conculcabas flumina earum. 3 Propterea haec dicit Dominus Deus: "Expandam super te rete meum in multitudine populorum multorum, et extraham te in sagena mea. 4 Et proiciam te in terram; super faciem agri abiciam te, et habitare faciam super te omnia volatilia caeli, et saturabo de te bestias universae terrae. 5 Et dabo carnes tuas super montes et implebo colles tuos sanie tua. 6 Et inrigabo terram pedore sanguinis tui super montes, et valles implebuntur ex te. 7 Et operiam cum extinctus fueris caelos, et nigrescere faciam stellas eius; solem nube tegam, et luna non dabit lumen suum. 8 Omnia luminaria caeli maerere faciam super te, et dabo tenebras super terram tuam," dicit Dominus Deus, "cum ceciderint vulnerati tui in medio terrae," ait Dominus Deus.

9 ""Et inritabo cor populorum multorum cum induxero contritionem tuam in gentibus super terras quas nescis. 10 Et stupescere faciam super te populos multos, et reges eorum horrore nimio formidabunt super te, cum volare coeperit gladius meus super facies eorum, et obstupescent repente singuli pro anima sua in die ruinae tuae."

11 "'Quia haec dicit Dominus Deus: "Gladius regis Babylonis veniet tibi. 12 In gladiis fortium deiciam multitudinem tuam; inexpugnabiles gentes omnes hae, et vastabunt superbiam Aegypti, et dissipabitur multitudo eius. 13 Et perdam

art like the lion of the nations and the dragon that is in the sea, and thou didst push with the horn in thy rivers and didst trouble the waters with thy feet and didst trample upon their streams. 3 Therefore thus saith the Lord God: "I will spread out my net over thee with the multitude of many people, and I will draw thee up in my net. 4 And I will throw thee out on the land; I will cast thee away into the *open* field, and I will cause all the fowls of the air to dwell upon thee, and I will fill the beasts of all the earth with thee. 5 And I will lay thy flesh upon the mountains and will fill thy hills with thy corruption. 6 And I will water the earth with thy stinking blood upon the mountains, and the valleys shall be filled with thee. 7 And I will cover the heavens when thou shalt be put out, and I will make the stars thereof dark; I will cover the sun with a cloud, and the moon shall not give her light. 8 I will make all the lights of heaven to mourn over thee, and I will cause darkness upon thy land," saith the Lord God, "when thy wounded shall fall in the midst of the land," saith the Lord God.

9 ""And I shall provoke to anger the heart of many people when I shall have brought in thy destruction among the nations upon the lands which thou knowest not. 10 And I will make many people to be amazed at thee, and their kings shall be horribly afraid for thee, when my sword shall begin to fly upon their faces, and they shall be astonished on a sudden every one for his own life in the day of thy ruin."

11 "For thus saith the Lord God: "The sword of the king of Babylon shall come upon thee. 12 By the swords of the mighty I will overthrow thy multitude; all these nations are invincible, and they shall waste the pride of Egypt, and the multitude thereof shall be destroyed. 13 I will destroy also all

omnia iumenta eius quae erant super aquas plurimas, et non conturbabit eas pes hominis ultra, neque ungula iumentorum turbabit eas. 14 Tunc purissimas reddam aquas eorum et flumina eorum quasi oleum adducam," ait Dominus Deus, 15 "cum dedero terram Aegypti desolatam, deseretur autem terra a plenitudine sua quando percussero omnes habitatores eius, et scient quia ego Dominus.

16 """Planctus est, et plangent eum; filiae gentium plangent eum; super Aegypto et super multitudine eius plangent eum," ait Dominus Deus.'"

17 Et factum est in duodecimo anno, in quintadecima mensis, factum est verbum Domini ad me, dicens, 18 "Fili hominis, cane lugubre super multitudine Aegypti, et detrahe eam, ipsam et filias gentium robustarum, ad terram ultimam cum his qui descendunt in lacum. 19 Quo pulchrior es? Descende, et dormi cum incircumcisis. 20 In medio interfectorum gladio cadent. Gladius datus est; adtraxerunt eam et omnes populos eius.

21 "Loquentur ei potentissimi robustorum de medio inferni, qui cum auxiliatoribus eius descenderunt et dormierunt incircumcisi, interfecti gladio. 22 Ibi Assur et omnis multitudo eius; in circuitu illius sepulchra eius, omnes interfecti et qui ceciderunt gladio. 23 Quorum data sunt sepulchra in novissimis laci, et facta est multitudo eius per gyrum sepulchri eius, universi interfecti cadentesque gladio, qui dederant quondam formidinem in terra viventium. 24 Ibi Aelam et omnis multitudo eius per gyrum sepulchri sui, om-

the beasts thereof that were beside the great waters, and the foot of man shall trouble them no more, neither shall the hoof of beasts trouble them. 14 Then will I make their waters clear and cause their rivers to run like oil," saith the Lord God, 15 "when I shall have made the land of Egypt desolate, and the land shall be destitute of her fulness when I shall have struck all the inhabitants thereof, and they shall know that I am the Lord.

16 """This is the lamentation, and they shall lament therewith; the daughters of the nations shall lament therewith; for Egypt and for the multitude thereof they shall lament therewith," saith the Lord God.'"

17 And it came to pass in the twelfth year, in the fifteenth day of the month, that the word of the Lord came to me, saying, 18 "Son of man, sing a mournful song for the multitude of Egypt, and cast her down, *both* her and the daughters of the mighty nations, to the lowest part of the earth with them that go down into the pit. 19 Whom dost thou excel in beauty? Go down, and sleep with the uncircumcised. 20 They shall fall in the midst of them that are slain with the sword. The sword is given; they have drawn her down and all her people.

21 "The most mighty among the strong ones shall speak to him from the midst of hell, they that went down with his helpers and slept uncircumcised, slain by the sword. 22 Asshur is there and all his multitude; their graves are round about him, all of them slain and that fell by the sword. 23 Whose graves are set in the lowest parts of the pit, and his multitude lay round about his grave, all of them slain and fallen by the sword, they that heretofore *spread* terror in the land of the living. 24 There is Elam and all his multitude round about his grave, all of them slain and fallen by the

nes hii interfecti ruentesque gladio, qui descenderunt incircumcisi ad terram ultimam, qui posuerunt terrorem suum in terra viventium, et portaverunt ignominiam suam cum his qui descendunt in lacum. 25 In medio interfectorum posuerunt cubile eius in universis populis eius; in circuitu eius sepulchrum illius; omnes hii incircumcisi interfectique gladio, dederunt enim terrorem suum in terra viventium et portaverunt ignominiam suam cum his qui descendunt in lacum; in medio interfectorum positi sunt. 26 Ibi Mosoch et Thubal et omnis multitudo eius; in circuitu illius sepulchra eius, omnes hii incircumcisi interfectique et cadentes gladio, quia dederunt formidinem suam in terra viventium. 27 Et non dormient cum fortibus cadentibusque et incircumcisis, qui descenderunt ad infernum cum armis suis et posuerunt gladios suos sub capitibus suis et fuerunt iniquitates eorum in ossibus eorum, quia terror fortium facti sunt in terra viventium. 28 Et tu ergo in medio incircumcisorum contereris et dormies cum interfectis gladio. 29 Ibi Idumea et reges eius et omnes duces eius, qui dati sunt cum exercitu suo cum interfectis gladio et qui cum incircumcisis dormierunt et cum his qui descendunt in lacum. 30 Ibi principes aquilonis omnes et universi venatores qui deducti sunt cum interfectis, paventes et in sua fortitudine confusi, qui dormierunt incircumcisi cum interfectis gladio et portaverunt confusionem suam cum his qui descendunt in lacum.

31 "Vidit eos Pharao, et consolatus est super universa multitudine sua quae interfecta est gladio, Pharao et omnis exercitus eius," ait Dominus Deus, 32 "quia dedi terrorem

sword, that went down uncircumcised to the lowest parts of the earth, that caused their terror in the land of the living, and they have borne their shame with them that go down into the pit. 25 In the midst of the slain they have set *him* a bed among all *his* people; their graves are round about *him;* all these are uncircumcised and slain by the sword, for they spread their terror in the land of the living and have borne their shame with them that descend into the pit; they are laid in the midst of the slain. 26 There is Meshech and Tubal and all their multitude; their graves are round about him, all of them uncircumcised and slain and falling by the sword, *though* they spread their terror in the land of the living. 27 And they shall not sleep with the brave and with them that fell *uncircumcised,* that went down to hell with their weapons and laid their swords under their heads and their iniquities were in their bones, because they were the terror of the mighty in the land of the living. 28 So thou also shalt be broken in the midst of the uncircumcised and shalt sleep with them that are slain by the sword. 29 There is Edom and her kings and all her princes, who with their army are joined with them that are slain by the sword and have slept with the uncircumcised and with them that go down into the pit. 30 There are all the princes of the north and all the hunters who were brought down with the slain, fearing and confounded in their strength, who slept uncircumcised with them that are slain by the sword and have borne their shame with them that go down into the pit.

31 "Pharaoh saw them, and he was comforted concerning all his multitude which was slain by the sword, Pharaoh and all his army," saith the Lord God, 32 "because I have spread

meum in terra viventium et dormivit in medio incircumcisorum cum interfectis gladio, Pharao et omnis multitudo
eius," ait Dominus Deus.

Caput 33

Et factum est verbum Domini ad me, dicens, 2 "Fili hominis, loquere ad filios populi tui, et dices ad eos, 'Terra cum
induxero super eam gladium et tulerit populus terrae virum,
unum de novissimis suis, et constituerit eum super se speculatorem, 3 et ille viderit gladium venientem super terram et
cecinerit bucina et adnuntiaverit populo, 4 audiens autem,
quisquis ille est, sonum bucinae et non se observaverit, veneritque gladius et tulerit eum, sanguis ipsius super caput
eius erit. 5 Sonum bucinae audivit et non se observavit; sanguis eius in ipso erit. Si autem se custodierit, animam suam
salvabit. 6 Quod si speculator viderit gladium venientem et
non insonuerit bucina, et populus non se custodierit veneritque gladius et tulerit de eis animam, ille quidem in iniqui

my terror in the land of the living and he hath slept in the midst of the uncircumcised with them that are slain by the sword, Pharaoh and all his multitude," saith the Lord God.

Chapter 33

The duty of the watchman appointed by God. The justice of God's ways. His judgments upon the Jews.

And the word of the Lord came to me, saying, 2 "Son of man, speak to the children of thy people, and *say* to them, 'When I bring the sword upon a land, *if* the people of the land take a man, one of their meanest, and make him a watchman over them, 3 and he see the sword coming upon the land and sound the trumpet and tell the people, 4 *then* he that heareth the sound of the trumpet, whosoever he be, and doth not look to himself, *if* the sword come and cut him off, his blood shall be upon his own head. 5 He heard the sound of the trumpet and did not look to himself; his blood shall be upon him. But if he look to himself, he shall save his life. 6 And if the watchman see the sword coming and sound not the trumpet, and the people look not to themselves, and the sword come and cut off a soul from among them, he in-

tate sua captus est, sanguinem autem eius de manu specula-
toris requiram.'

7 "Et tu, fili hominis, speculatorem dedi te domui Israhel;
audiens ergo ex ore meo sermonem adnuntiabis eis ex me.
8 Si me dicente ad impium, 'Impie, morte morieris,' non fueris locutus ut se custodiat impius a via sua, ipse impius in iniquitate sua morietur, sanguinem autem eius de manu tua requiram. 9 Si autem adnuntiante te ad impium ut a viis suis
convertatur non fuerit conversus a via sua, ipse in iniquitate
sua morietur, porro tu animam tuam liberasti.

10 "Tu ergo, fili hominis, dic ad domum Israhel, 'Sic locuti
estis, dicentes, "Iniquitates nostrae et peccata nostra super
nos sunt, et in ipsis nos tabescimus; quomodo ergo vivere
poterimus?"'

11 "Dic ad eos, '"Vivo ego," dicit Dominus Deus, "Nolo
mortem impii sed ut convertatur impius a via sua et vivat.
Convertimini, convertimini a viis vestris pessimis, et quare
moriemini, domus Israhel?"' 12 Tu itaque, fili hominis, dic ad
filios populi tui, 'Iustitia iusti non liberabit eum in quacumque die peccaverit, et impietas impii non nocebit ei in quacumque die conversus fuerit ab impietate sua, et iustus non
poterit vivere in iustitia sua in quacumque die peccaverit.

13 "'Etiam si dixero iusto quod vita vivat, et confisus in
iustitia sua, fecerit iniquitatem, omnes iustitiae eius oblivioni tradentur, et in iniquitate sua quam operatus est, in
ipsa morietur. 14 Si autem dixero impio, "Morte morieris," et

deed is taken away in his iniquity, but I will require his blood at the hand of the watchman.'

7 "So thou, O son of man, I have made thee a watchman to the house of Israel; therefore thou shalt hear the word from my mouth and shalt tell it them from me. 8 When I say to the wicked, 'O wicked man, thou shalt surely die,' if thou dost not speak to warn the wicked man from his way, that wicked man shall die in his iniquity, but I will require his blood at thy hand. 9 But if thou tell the wicked man that he may be converted from his ways *and* he be not converted from his way, he shall die in his iniquity, but thou hast delivered thy soul.

10 "Thou therefore, O son of man, say to the house of Israel, 'Thus you have spoken, saying, "Our iniquities and our sins are upon us, and we pine away in them; how then can we live?"'

11 "Say to them, "'As I live," saith the Lord God, "I desire not the death of the wicked but that the wicked turn from his way and live. Turn ye, turn ye from your evil ways, and why will you die, O house of Israel?"' 12 Thou therefore, O son of man, say to the children of thy people, 'The justice of the just shall not deliver him in what day soever he shall sin, and the wickedness of the wicked shall not hurt him in what day soever he shall turn from his wickedness, and the just shall not be able to live in his justice in what day soever he shall sin.

13 "'Yea, if I shall say to the just that he shall surely live, and he, trusting in his justice, commit iniquity, all his justices shall be forgotten, and in his iniquity which he hath committed, in the same shall he die. 14 And if I shall say to the wicked, "Thou shalt surely die," and he do penance for his

egerit paenitentiam a peccato suo feceritque iudicium et iustitiam, 15 et pignus restituerit ille impius rapinamque reddiderit, in mandatis vitae ambulaverit nec fecerit quicquam iniustum, vita vivet et non morietur. 16 Omnia peccata eius quae peccavit non inputabuntur ei: iudicium et iustitiam fecit; vita vivet.

17 "'Et dixerunt filii populi tui, "Non est aequi ponderis via Domini," et ipsorum via iniusta est. 18 Cum enim recesserit iustus a iustitia sua feceritque iniquitates, morietur in eis. 19 Et cum recesserit impius ab impietate sua feceritque iudicium et iustitiam, vivet in eis. 20 Et dicitis, "Non est recta via Domini." Unumquemque iuxta vias suas iudicabo de vobis, domus Israhel.'"

21 Et factum est in duodecimo anno, in decimo mense, in quinta mensis transmigrationis nostrae, venit ad me qui fugerat de Hierusalem, dicens, "Vastata est civitas." 22 Manus autem Domini facta fuerat ad me vespere antequam veniret qui fugerat, aperuitque os meum donec veniret ad me mane, et aperto ore meo, non silui amplius.

23 Et factum est verbum Domini ad me, dicens, 24 "Fili hominis, qui habitant in ruinosis his super humum Israhel loquentes aiunt, 'Unus erat Abraham, et hereditate possedit terram, nos autem multi sumus; nobis data est terra in possessionem.'

25 "Idcirco dices ad eos, 'Haec dicit Dominus Deus: "Qui in sanguine comeditis et oculos vestros levatis ad inmunditias vestras et sanguinem funditis, numquid terram here-

sin and do judgment and justice, 15 and *if* that wicked man restore the pledge and render what he had robbed *and* walk in the commandments of life and do no unjust thing, he shall surely live and shall not die. 16 None of his sins which he hath committed shall be imputed to him: he hath done judgment and justice; he shall surely live.

17 "And the children of thy people have said, "The way of the Lord is not *equitable,*" whereas their own way is unjust. 18 For when the just shall depart from his justice and commit iniquities, he shall die in them. 19 And when the wicked shall depart from his wickedness and shall do judgments and justice, he shall live in them. 20 And you say, "The way of the Lord is not right." I will judge every one of you according to his ways, O house of Israel.'"

21 And it came to pass in the twelfth year of our captivity, in the tenth month, in the fifth day of the month, that there came to me one that was fled from Jerusalem, saying, "The city is laid waste." 22 And the hand of the Lord had been upon me in the evening before he that was fled came, and he opened my mouth till he came to me in the morning, and my mouth being opened, I was silent no more.

23 And the word of the Lord came to me, saying, 24 "Son of man, they that dwell in these ruinous places in the land of Israel speak, saying, 'Abraham was one, and he inherited the land, but we are many; the land is given us in possession.'

25 "Therefore say to them, 'Thus saith the Lord God: "You that eat with the blood and lift up your eyes to your uncleannesses and that shed blood, shall you possess the

ditate possidebitis? 26 Stetistis in gladiis vestris, fecistis abominationes et unusquisque uxorem proximi sui polluit; et
terram hereditate possidebitis?'" 27 Haec dices ad eos: 'Sic
dicit Dominus Deus: "Vivo ego quia qui in ruinosis habitant
gladio cadent, et qui in agro est bestiis tradetur ad devorandum, qui autem in praesidiis et speluncis sunt peste morientur. 28 Et dabo terram in solitudinem et in desertum, et deficiet superba fortitudo eius, et desolabuntur montes Israhel
eo quod nullus sit qui per eos transeat. 29 Et scient quia ego
Dominus cum dedero terram eorum desolatam et desertam
propter universas abominationes suas quas operati sunt."'

30 "Et tu, fili hominis, filii populi tui qui loquuntur de te
iuxta muros et in ostiis domorum et dicunt unus ad alterum,
vir ad proximum suum, loquentes, 'Venite, et audiamus qui
sit sermo egrediens a Domino.' 31 Et veniunt ad te quasi si
ingrediatur populus, et sedent coram te populus meus et
audiunt sermones tuos et non faciunt eos, quia in canticum
oris sui vertunt illos et avaritiam suam sequitur cor eorum.
32 Et es eis quasi carmen musicum quod suavi dulcique sono

land by inheritance? 26 You stood on your swords, you have committed abominations and every one hath defiled his neighbour's wife; and shall you possess the land by inheritance?"' 27 Say thou thus to them: 'Thus saith the Lord God: "As I live, they that dwell in the ruinous places shall fall by the sword, and he that is in the field shall be given to the beasts to be devoured, and they that are in holds and caves shall die of the pestilence. 28 And I will make the land a wilderness and a desert, and the proud strength thereof shall fail, and the mountains of Israel shall be desolate because there is none to pass by them. 29 And they shall know that I am the Lord when I shall have made their land waste and desolate for all their abominations which they have committed."'

30 "And thou, son of man, the children of thy people that talk of thee by the walls and in the doors of the houses and speak one to another, each man to his neighbour, saying, 'Come, and let us hear what is the word that cometh forth from the Lord.' 31 And they come to thee as if a people were coming in, and my people sit before thee and hear thy words and do them not, for they turn them into a song of their mouth and their heart goeth after their covetousness. 32 And thou art to them as a musical song which is sung with a sweet and agreeable voice, and they hear thy words

canitur, et audiunt verba tua et non faciunt ea. 33 Et cum venerit quod praedictum est (ecce enim: venit), tunc scient quod prophetes fuerit inter eos."

Caput 34

Et factum est verbum Domini ad me, dicens, 2 "Fili hominis, propheta de pastoribus Israhel; propheta, et dices pastoribus, 'Haec dicit Dominus Deus: "Vae pastoribus Israhel qui pascebant semet ipsos! Nonne greges pascuntur a pastoribus? 3 Lac comedebatis, et lanis operiebamini, et quod crassum erat occidebatis, gregem autem meum non pascebatis. 4 Quod infirmum fuit non consolidastis, et quod aegrotum non sanastis; quod fractum est non alligastis, et quod abiectum est non reduxistis, et quod perierat non quaesistis, sed cum austeritate imperabatis eis et cum potentia. 5 Et dispersae sunt oves meae eo quod non esset pastor, et factae sunt in devorationem omnium bestiarum agri et dispersae sunt. 6 Erraverunt greges mei in cunctis montibus et in universo colle excelso, et super omnem

and do them not. 33 And when that which was foretold shall come to pass (for behold: it is coming), then shall they know that a prophet hath been among them."

Chapter 34

Evil pastors are reproved. Christ, the true pastor, shall come and gather together his flock from all parts of the earth and preserve it for ever.

And the word of the Lord came to me, saying, 2 "Son of man, prophesy concerning the shepherds of Israel; prophesy, and *say* to the shepherds, 'Thus saith the Lord God: "Woe to the shepherds of Israel that fed themselves! Should not the flocks be fed by the shepherds? 3 You ate the milk, and you clothed yourselves with the wool, and you killed that which was fat, but my flock you did not feed. 4 The weak you have not strengthened, and that which was sick you have not healed; that which was broken you have not bound up, and that which was driven away you have not brought again, neither have you sought that which was lost, but you ruled over them with rigour and with *a high hand*. 5 And my sheep were scattered because there was no shepherd, and they became the prey of all the beasts of the field and were scattered. 6 My sheep have wandered in every mountain and in every high hill, and my flocks were scat-

faciem terrae dispersi sunt greges mei, et non erat qui requireret, non erat, inquam, qui requireret."

7 "'Propterea, pastores, audite verbum Domini: 8 "Vivo ego," dicit Dominus Deus, "quia pro eo quod facti sunt greges mei in rapinam et oves meae in devorationem omnium bestiarum agri eo quod non esset pastor, neque enim quaesierunt pastores mei gregem meum, sed pascebant pastores semet ipsos et greges meos non pascebant." 9 Propterea, pastores, audite verbum Domini: 10 "Haec dicit Dominus Deus: 'Ecce: ego ipse super pastores; requiram gregem meum de manu eorum, et cessare eos faciam ut ultra non pascant gregem, nec pascant amplius pastores semet ipsos, et liberabo gregem meum de ore eorum, et non erit ultra eis in escam.'"

11 "'Quia haec dicit Dominus Deus: "Ecce: ego ipse requiram oves meas et visitabo eas. 12 Sicut visitat pastor gregem suum in die quando fuerit in medio ovium suarum dissipatarum, sic visitabo oves meas et liberabo eas de omnibus locis in quibus dispersae fuerant in die nubis et caliginis. 13 Et educam eas de populis et congregabo eas de terris et inducam eas in terram suam, et pascam eas in montibus Israhel, in rivis et in cunctis sedibus terrae. 14 In pascuis uberrimis pascam eas, et in montibus excelsis Israhel erunt pascua earum; ibi requiescent in herbis virentibus et in pascuis pinguibus pascentur super montes Israhel. 15 Ego pascam oves meas, et ego eas accubare faciam," dicit Dominus Deus. 16 "Quod perierat requiram, et quod abiectum erat reducam, et quod confractum fuerat alligabo, et quod infirmum erat

tered upon the face of the earth, and there was none that sought them, there was none, I say, that sought them."

7 "'Therefore, ye shepherds, hear the word of the Lord: 8 "As I live," saith the Lord God, "forasmuch as my flocks have been made a spoil and my sheep are become a prey to all the beasts of the field because there was no shepherd, for my shepherds did not seek after my flock, but the shepherds fed themselves and fed not my flocks." 9 Therefore, ye shepherds, hear the word of the Lord: 10 "Thus saith the Lord God: 'Behold: I myself come upon the shepherds; I will require my flock at their hand, and I will cause them to cease from feeding the flock any more, neither shall the shepherds feed themselves any more, and I will deliver my flock from their mouth, and it shall no more be meat for them.'"

11 "'For thus saith the Lord God: "Behold: I myself will seek my sheep and will visit them. 12 As the shepherd visiteth his flock in the day when he shall be in the midst of his sheep that were scattered, so will I visit my sheep and will deliver them out of all the places where they have been scattered in the cloudy and dark day. 13 And I will bring them out from the peoples and will gather them out of the countries and will bring them to their own land, and I will feed them in the mountains of Israel, by the rivers and in all the habitations of the land. 14 I will feed them in the most fruitful pastures, and their pastures shall be in the high mountains of Israel; there shall they rest on the green grass and be fed in fat pastures upon the mountains of Israel. 15 I will feed my sheep, and I will cause them to lie down," saith the Lord God. 16 "I will seek that which was lost, and that which was driven away I will bring again, and I will bind up that which was broken, and I will strengthen that which was weak, and

consolidabo, et quod pingue et forte custodiam, et pascam illas in iudicio.

17 """Vos autem, greges mei, haec dicit Dominus Deus: 'Ecce: ego iudico inter pecus et pecus, arietum et hircorum. 18 Nonne satis vobis erat pascua bona depasci? Insuper et reliquias pascuarum vestrarum conculcastis pedibus vestris, et cum purissimam aquam biberetis reliquam pedibus vestris turbabatis. 19 Et oves meae his quae conculcata pedibus vestris fuerant pascebantur, et quae pedes vestri turbaverant, haec bibebant.'

20 """Propterea haec dicit Dominus Deus ad vos: 'Ecce: ego ipse iudico inter pecus pingue et macilentum. 21 Pro eo quod lateribus et umeris inpingebatis et cornibus vestris ventilabatis omnia infirma pecora donec dispergerentur foras, 22 salvabo gregem meum, et non erit ultra in rapinam, et iudicabo inter pecus et pecus.'

23 """Et suscitabo super ea pastorem unum, qui pascat ea, servum meum David; ipse pascet ea, et ipse erit eis in pastorem. 24 Ego autem, Dominus, ero eis in Deum, et servus meus David princeps in medio eorum; ego, Dominus, locutus sum.

25 """Et faciam cum eis pactum pacis et cessare faciam bestias pessimas de terra, et qui habitant in deserto securi dormient in saltibus. 26 Et ponam eos in circuitu collis mei benedictionem, et deducam imbrem in tempore suo; pluviae benedictionis erunt. 27 Et dabit lignum agri fructum suum, et terra dabit germen suum, et erunt in terra sua absque timore, et scient quia ego Dominus, cum contrivero catenas iugi eorum et eruero eos de manu imperantium

that which was fat and strong I will preserve, and I will feed them in judgment.

17 ""And as for you, O my flocks, thus saith the Lord God: 'Behold: I judge between cattle and cattle, of rams and of he-goats. 18 Was it not enough for you to feed upon good pastures? But you must also tread down with your feet the residue of your pastures, and when you drank the clearest water, you troubled the rest with your feet. 19 And my sheep were fed with that which you had trodden with your feet, and they drank what your feet had troubled.'

20 ""Therefore thus saith the Lord God to you: 'Behold: I myself will judge between the fat cattle and the lean. 21 Because you thrusted with sides and shoulders and struck all the weak cattle with your horns till they were scattered abroad, 22 I will save my flock, and it shall be no more a spoil, and I will judge between cattle and cattle.'

23 ""And I will set up one shepherd over them, and he shall feed them, *even* my servant David; he shall feed them, and he shall be their shepherd. 24 And I, the Lord, will be their God, and my servant David the prince in the midst of them; I, the Lord, have spoken it.

25 ""And I will make a covenant of peace with them and will cause the evil beasts to cease out of the land, and they that dwell in the wilderness shall sleep secure in the forests. 26 And I will make them a blessing round about my hill, and I will send down the rain in its season; there shall be showers of blessing. 27 And the tree of the field shall yield its fruit, and the earth shall yield her increase, and they shall be in their land without fear, and they shall know that I am the Lord, when I shall have broken the bonds of their yoke and shall have delivered them out of the hand of those that rule

sibi. 28 Et non erunt ultra in rapinam in gentibus, neque bestiae terrae devorabunt eos, sed habitabunt confidenter absque ullo terrore. 29 Et suscitabo eis germen nominatum, et non erunt amplius inminuti fame in terra, neque portabunt amplius obprobrium Gentium. 30 Et scient quia ego, Dominus, Deus eorum, cum eis et ipsi populus meus, domus Israhel," ait Dominus Deus. 31 "Vos autem, greges mei, greges pascuae meae, homines estis, et ego Dominus, Deus vester," dicit Dominus Deus.'"

Caput 35

Et factus est sermo Domini ad me, dicens, 2 "Fili hominis, pone faciem tuam adversum Montem Seir, et prophetabis de eo, et dices illi, 3 'Haec dicit Dominus Deus: "Ecce: ego ad te, Mons Seir, et extendam manum meam super te, et dabo te desolatum atque desertum. 4 Urbes tuas demoliar, et tu desertus eris, et scies quia ego Dominus.

5 """Eo quod fueris inimicus sempiternus et concluseris filios Israhel in manus gladii in tempore adflictionis eorum, in tempore iniquitatis extremae, 6 propterea vivo ego," dicit Dominus Deus, "quoniam sanguini tradam te, et sanguis te

over them. 28 And they shall be no more for a spoil to the nations, neither shall the beasts of the earth devour them, but they shall dwell securely without any terror. 29 And I will raise up for them a bud of renown, and they shall be no more consumed with famine in the land, neither shall they bear any more the reproach of the Gentiles. 30 And they shall know that I, the Lord, their God, am with them and that they are my people, the house of Israel," saith the Lord God. 31 "And you, my flocks, the flocks of my pasture, are men, and I am the Lord, your God," saith the Lord God.'"

Chapter 35

The judgment of Mount Seir for their hatred of Israel.

And the word of the Lord came to me, saying, 2 "Son of man, set thy face against Mount Seir, and *prophesy* concerning it, and *say* to it, 3 'Thus saith the Lord God: "Behold: I come against thee, Mount Seir, and I will stretch forth my hand upon thee, and I will make thee desolate and waste. 4 I will destroy thy cities, and thou shalt be desolate, and thou shalt know that I am the Lord.

5 ""Because thou hast been an everlasting enemy and hast shut up the children of Israel in the hands of the sword in the time of their affliction, in the time of their last iniquity, 6 therefore as I live," saith the Lord God, "I will deliver thee

persequetur, et cum sanguinem oderis, sanguis persequetur te. 7 Et dabo Montem Seir desolatum et desertum, et auferam de eo euntem et redeuntem. 8 Et implebo montes eius occisorum suorum; in collibus tuis et in vallibus tuis atque in torrentibus interfecti gladio cadent. 9 In solitudines sempiternas tradam te, et civitates tuae non habitabuntur, et scietis quoniam ego Dominus Deus.

10 """Eo quod dixeris, 'Duae gentes et duae terrae meae erunt, et hereditate possidebo eas,' cum Dominus esset ibi, 11 propterea vivo ego," dicit Dominus Deus, "quia faciam iuxta iram tuam et secundum zelum tuum quem fecisti odio habens eos, et notus efficiar per eos cum te iudicavero. 12 Et scies quia ego, Dominus, audivi universa obprobria tua quae locutus es de montibus Israhel, dicens, 'Deserti; nobis dati sunt ad devorandum.' 13 Et insurrexistis super me ore vestro et derogastis adversum me verba vestra; ego audivi." 14 Haec dicit Dominus Deus: "Laetante universa terra in solitudinem te redigam. 15 Sicuti gavisus es super hereditatem domus Israhel eo quod fuerit dissipata, sic faciam tibi: dissipatus eris, Mons Seir, et Idumea omnis, et scient quia ego Dominus.""""

up to blood, and blood shall pursue thee, and whereas thou hast hated blood, blood shall pursue thee. 7 And I will make Mount Seir waste and desolate, and I will take away from it him that goeth and him that returneth. 8 And I will fill his mountains with his men that are slain; in thy hills and in thy valleys and in thy torrents they shall fall that are slain with the sword. 9 I will make thee everlasting desolations, and thy cities shall not be inhabited, and thou shalt know that I am the Lord God.

10 ““Because thou hast said, 'The two nations and the two lands shall be mine, and I will possess them by inheritance,' whereas the Lord was there, 11 therefore as I live," saith the Lord God, "I will do according to thy wrath and according to thy envy which thou hast exercised in hatred to them, and I will be made known by them when I shall have judged thee. 12 And thou shalt know that I, the Lord, have heard all thy reproaches that thou hast spoken against the mountains of Israel, saying, 'They are desolate; they are given to us to consume.' 13 And you rose up against me with your mouth and have derogated from me by your words; I have heard them." 14 Thus saith the Lord God: "When the whole earth shall rejoice I will make thee a wilderness. 15 As thou hast rejoiced over the inheritance of the house of Israel because it was laid waste, so will I do to thee: thou shalt be laid waste, O Mount Seir, and all Edom, and they shall know that I am the Lord."”"

Caput 36

"Tu autem, fili hominis, propheta super montes Israhel, et dices, 'Montes Israhel, audite verbum Domini. 2 Haec dicit Dominus Deus: "Eo quod dixerit inimicus de vobis, 'Euge, altitudines sempiternae in hereditatem datae sunt nobis,' 3 propterea vaticinare, et dic, 'Haec dicit Dominus Deus: "Pro eo quod desolati estis et conculcati per circuitum et facti in hereditatem reliquis gentibus et ascendistis super labium linguae et obprobrium populi, 4 propterea, montes Israhel, audite verbum Domini Dei. Haec dicit Dominus Deus montibus et collibus, torrentibus vallibusque et desertis et parietinis et urbibus derelictis, quae depopulatae sunt et subsannatae a reliquis gentibus per circuitum—5 propterea haec dicit Dominus Deus: 'Quoniam in igne zeli mei locutus sum de reliquis gentibus et de Idumea universa, qui dederunt terram meam sibi in hereditatem cum gaudio et toto corde et ex animo et eiecerunt eam ut vastarent.'" 6 Idcirco vaticinare super humum Israhel, et dices montibus et collibus, iugis et vallibus, "Haec dicit Dominus Deus: 'Ecce: ego in zelo meo et in furore meo locutus sum, eo quod confusionem Gentium sustinueritis.' 7 Idcirco haec dicit Dominus Deus: 'Ego levavi manum meam, ut

Chapter 36

The restoration of Israel, not for their merits but by God's special grace. Christ's baptism.

"And thou, son of man, prophesy to the mountains of Israel, and *say,* 'Ye mountains of Israel, hear the word of the Lord. 2 Thus saith the Lord God: "Because the enemy hath said of you, 'Aha, the everlasting heights are given to us for an inheritance,' 3 therefore prophesy, and say, 'Thus saith the Lord God: "Because you have been desolate and trodden under foot on every side and made an inheritance to the rest of the nations and *are become the subject of the talk* and the reproach of the people, 4 therefore, ye mountains of Israel, hear the word of the Lord God. Thus saith the Lord God to the mountains and to the hills, to the brooks and to the valleys and to desolate places and ruinous walls and to the cities that are forsaken, that are spoiled and derided by the rest of the nations round about—5 therefore thus saith the Lord God: *'In* the fire of my zeal I have spoken of the rest of the nations and of all Edom, who have taken my land to themselves for an inheritance with joy and with all the heart and with the mind and have cast it out to lay it waste.'" 6 Prophesy therefore concerning the land of Israel, and *say* to the mountains and to the hills, to the ridges and to the valleys: "Thus saith the Lord God: 'Behold: I have spoken in my zeal and in my indignation, because you have borne the shame of the Gentiles.' 7 Therefore thus saith the Lord God: 'I have

847

Gentes quae in circuitu vestro sunt ipsae confusionem suam portent.'"

8 """"Vos autem, montes Israhel, ramos vestros germinetis, et fructum vestrum adferatis populo meo Israhel, prope est enim ut veniat. 9 Quia ecce: ego ad vos, et convertar ad vos, et arabimini, et accipietis sementem. 10 Et multiplicabo in vobis homines omnemque domum Israhel, et habitabuntur civitates, et ruinosa instaurabuntur. 11 Et replebo vos hominibus et iumentis, et multiplicabuntur et crescent, et habitare vos faciam sicut a principio bonisque donabo maioribus quam habuistis ab initio, et scietis quia ego Dominus. 12 Et adducam super vos homines, populum meum Israhel, et hereditate possidebunt te, et eris eis in hereditatem et non addes ultra ut absque eis sis.'"

13 "'Haec dicit Dominus Deus: "Pro eo quod dicunt de vobis, 'Devoratrix hominum es et suffocans gentem tuam,' 14 propterea homines non comedes amplius et gentem tuam non necabis ultra," ait Dominus Deus, 15 "nec auditam faciam in te amplius confusionem gentium, et obprobrium populorum nequaquam portabis et gentem tuam non amittes amplius," ait Dominus Deus.'"

16 Et factum est verbum Domini ad me, dicens, 17 "Fili hominis, domus Israhel habitaverunt in humo sua, et polluerunt eam in viis suis et in studiis suis; iuxta inmunditiam menstruatae facta est via eorum coram me. 18 Et effudi indignationem meam super eos pro sanguine quem fuderunt

lifted up my hand, that the Gentiles who are round about you shall themselves bear their shame.'"

8 """But as for you, O mountains of Israel, shoot ye forth your branches, and yield your fruit to my people of Israel, for they are at hand to come. 9 For lo: I am for you, and I will turn to you, and you shall be ploughed and sown. 10 And I will multiply men upon you and all the house of Israel, and the cities shall be inhabited, and the ruinous places shall be repaired. 11 And I will make you abound with men and with beasts, and they shall be multiplied and increased, and I will settle you as from the beginning and will give you greater gifts than you had from the beginning, and you shall know that I am the Lord. 12 And I will bring men upon you, my people Israel, and they shall possess thee for their inheritance, and thou shalt be their inheritance and shalt no more henceforth be without them.'"

13 "'Thus saith the Lord God: "Because they say of you, 'Thou art a devourer of men and one that suffocatest thy nation,' 14 therefore thou shalt devour men no more, nor destroy thy nation any more," saith the Lord God, 15 "neither will I cause men to hear in thee the shame of the nations any more, nor shalt thou bear the reproach of the people nor lose thy nation any more," saith the Lord God.'"

16 And the word of the Lord came to me, saying, 17 "Son of man, *when* the house of Israel dwelt in their own land, *they* defiled it with their ways and with their doings; their way was before me like the uncleanness of a menstruous woman. 18 And I poured out my indignation upon them for the blood which they had shed upon the land, and with their idols

super terram, et in idolis suis polluerunt eam. 19 Et dispersi eos in gentes, et ventilati sunt in terras; iuxta vias eorum et adinventiones eorum iudicavi eos. 20 Et ingressi sunt ad gentes ad quas introierunt, et polluerunt nomen sanctum meum, cum diceretur de eis, 'Populus Domini iste est, et de terra eius egressi sunt.' 21 Et peperci nomini meo sancto, quod polluerat domus Israhel in gentibus ad quas ingressi sunt.

22 "Idcirco dices domui Israhel, 'Haec dicit Dominus Deus: "Non propter vos ego faciam, domus Israhel, sed propter nomen sanctum meum, quod polluistis in gentibus ad quas intrastis. 23 Et sanctificabo nomen meum magnum, quod pollutum est inter Gentes, quod polluistis in medio earum, ut sciant Gentes quia ego Dominus," ait Dominus exercituum, "cum sanctificatus fuero in vobis coram eis. 24 Tollam quippe vos de Gentibus et congregabo vos de universis terris et adducam vos in terram vestram. 25 Et effundam super vos aquam mundam, et mundabimini ab omnibus inquinamentis vestris, et ab universis idolis vestris mundabo vos. 26 Et dabo vobis cor novum et spiritum novum ponam in medio vestri, et auferam cor lapideum de carne vestra et dabo vobis cor carneum. 27 Et spiritum meum ponam in medio vestri, et faciam ut in praeceptis meis ambuletis et iudicia mea custodiatis et operemini. 28 Et habitabitis in terra quam dedi patribus vestris, et eritis mihi in populum, et ego

they defiled it. 19 And I scattered them among the nations, and they are dispersed through the countries; I have judged them according to their ways and their devices. 20 And *when* they entered among the nations whither they went, *they* profaned my holy name, when it was said of them, 'This is the people of the Lord, and they are come forth out of his land.' 21 And I have *regarded* my own holy name, which the house of Israel hath profaned among the nations to which they went in.

22 "Therefore thou shalt say to the house of Israel, 'Thus saith the Lord God: "It is not for your sake that I will do this, O house of Israel, but for my holy name's sake, which you have profaned among the nations whither you went. 23 And I will sanctify my great name, which was profaned among the Gentiles, which you have profaned in the midst of them, that the Gentiles may know that I am the Lord," saith the Lord of hosts, "when I shall be sanctified in you before their eyes. 24 For I will take you from among the Gentiles and will gather you together out of all the countries and will bring you into your own land. 25 And I will pour upon you clean water, and you shall be cleansed from all your filthiness, and I will cleanse you from all your idols. 26 And I will give you a new heart and put a new spirit within you, and I will take away the stony heart out of your flesh and will give you a heart of flesh. 27 And I will put my spirit in the midst of you, and I will cause you to walk in my commandments and to keep my judgments and do them. 28 And you shall dwell in the land which I gave to your fathers, and you shall

ero vobis in Deum. 29 Et salvabo vos ex universis inquinamentis vestris, et vocabo frumentum et multiplicabo illud et non inponam in vobis famem. 30 Et multiplicabo fructum ligni et genimina agri, ut non portetis ultra obprobrium famis in gentibus. 31 Et recordabimini viarum vestrarum pessimarum studiorumque non bonorum, et displicebunt vobis iniquitates vestrae et scelera vestra.

32 """Non propter vos ego faciam," ait Dominus Deus. "Notum sit vobis; confundimini et erubescite super viis vestris, domus Israhel."

33 "Haec dicit Dominus Deus: "In die qua mundavero vos ex omnibus iniquitatibus vestris et habitari fecero urbes et instauravero ruinosa 34 et terra deserta fuerit exculta quae quondam erat desolata in oculis omnis viatoris, 35 dicent, 'Terra illa inculta facta est ut hortus voluptatis, et civitates desertae et destitutae atque suffossae munitae sederunt.' 36 Et scient gentes quaecumque derelictae fuerint in circuitu vestro quia ego, Dominus, aedificavi dissipata plantavique inculta, ego, Dominus, locutus sim et fecerim."

37 "Haec dicit Dominus Deus: "Adhuc in hoc invenient me domus Israhel ut faciam eis; multiplicabo eos sicut gregem hominum, 38 ut gregem sanctum, ut gregem Hierusalem in sollemnitatibus eius; sic erunt civitates desertae plenae gregibus hominum, et scient quia ego Dominus.""""

be my people, and I will be your God. 29 And I will save you from all your uncleannesses, and I will call for corn and will multiply it and will lay no famine upon you. 30 And I will multiply the fruit of the tree and the increase of the field, that you bear no more the reproach of famine among the nations. 31 And you shall remember your wicked ways and your doings that were not good, and your iniquities and your wicked deeds shall displease you.

32 """It is not for your sakes that I will do this," saith the Lord God. "Be it known to you; be confounded and ashamed at your own ways, O house of Israel."

33 "'Thus saith the Lord God: "In the day that I shall cleanse you from all your iniquities and shall cause the cities to be inhabited and shall repair the ruinous places 34 and the desolate land shall be tilled which before was waste in the sight of all that passed by, 35 they shall say, 'This land that was untilled is become as a garden of pleasure, and the cities that were abandoned and desolate and destroyed are peopled and fenced.' 36 And the nations that shall be left round about you shall know that I, the Lord, have built up what was destroyed and planted what was desolate, that I, the Lord, have spoken and done it."

37 "'Thus saith the Lord God: "Moreover in this shall the house of Israel find me that I will do it for them; I will multiply them as a flock of men, 38 as a holy flock, as the flock of Jerusalem in her solemn feasts; so shall the waste cities be full of flocks of men, and they shall know that I am the Lord."""

Caput 37

Facta est super me manus Domini et eduxit me in spiritu Domini et dimisit me in medio campi qui erat plenus ossibus. 2 Et circumduxit me per ea in gyro; erant autem multa valde super faciem campi siccaque vehementer. 3 Et dixit ad me, "Fili hominis, putasne vivent ossa ista?"

Et dixi, "Domine Deus, tu nosti."

4 Et dixit ad me, "Vaticinare de ossibus istis, et dices eis, 'Ossa arida, audite verbum Domini. 5 Haec dicit Dominus Deus ossibus his: "Ecce: ego intromittam in vos spiritum, et vivetis. 6 Et dabo super vos nervos et succrescere faciam super vos carnes et superextendam in vobis cutem, et dabo vobis spiritum, et vivetis, et scietis quia ego Dominus."'"

7 Et prophetavi sicut praeceperat mihi, factus est autem sonitus prophetante me, et ecce: commotio, et accesserunt ossa ad ossa, unumquodque ad iuncturam suam. 8 Et vidi, et ecce: super ea nervi et carnes ascenderunt, et extenta est in eis cutis desuper, et spiritum non habebant.

9 Et dixit ad me, "Vaticinare ad spiritum; vaticinare, fili hominis, et dices ad spiritum, 'Haec dicit Dominus Deus:

Chapter 37

A vision of the resurrection of dry bones, foreshewing the
deliverance of the people from their captivity. Judah and Israel shall be all one kingdom under Christ. God's everlasting
covenant with the church.

The hand of the Lord was upon me and brought me forth
in the spirit of the Lord and set me down in the midst of a
plain that was full of bones. 2 And he led me about through
them on every side; now they were very many upon the face
of the plain, and they were exceeding dry. 3 And he said to
me, "Son of man, dost thou think these bones shall live?"

And I answered, "O Lord God, thou knowest."

4 And he said to me, "Prophesy concerning these bones,
and *say* to them, 'Ye dry bones, hear the word of the Lord.
5 Thus saith the Lord God to these bones: "Behold: I will
send spirit into you, and you shall live. 6 And I will lay sinews
upon you and will cause flesh to grow over you and will cover
you with skin, and I will give you spirit, and you shall live,
and you shall know that I am the Lord."'"

7 And I prophesied as he had commanded me, and as I
prophesied there was a noise, and behold: a commotion, and
the bones came together, each one to its joint. 8 And I saw,
and behold: the sinews and the flesh came up upon them,
and the skin was stretched out over them, *but* there was no
spirit in them.

9 And he said to me, "Prophesy to the spirit; prophesy, O
son of man, and *say* to the spirit, 'Thus saith the Lord God:

"A quattuor ventis veni, spiritus, et insufla super interfectos istos, et revivescant."'" 10 Et prophetavi sicut praeceperat mihi, et ingressus est in ea spiritus, et vixerunt, steteruntque super pedes suos, exercitus grandis nimis valde.

11 Et dixit ad me, "Fili hominis, ossa haec universa domus Israhel est; ipsi dicunt, 'Aruerunt ossa nostra, et periit spes nostra, et abscisi sumus.' 12 Propterea vaticinare, et dices ad eos, 'Haec dicit Dominus Deus: "Ecce: ego aperiam tumulos vestros et educam vos de sepulchris vestris, populus meus, et inducam vos in terram Israhel. 13 Et scietis quia ego Dominus cum aperuero sepulchra vestra et eduxero vos de tumulis vestris, popule meus, 14 et dedero spiritum meum in vobis, et vixeritis, et requiescere vos faciam super humum vestram, et scietis quia ego, Dominus, locutus sum et feci," ait Dominus Deus.'"

15 Et factus est sermo Domini ad me, dicens, 16 "Et tu, fili hominis, sume tibi lignum unum, et scribe super illud, 'Iudae et filiorum Israhel, sociorum eius,' et tolle lignum alterum, et scribe super eum, 'Ioseph, ligno Ephraim, et cunctae domui Israhel sociorumque eius.' 17 Et adiunge illa unum ad alterum tibi in lignum unum, et erunt in unionem in manu tua.

18 "Cum autem dixerint ad te filii populi tui, loquentes, 'Nonne indicas nobis quid in his tibi velis?' 19 loqueris ad eos, 'Haec dicit Dominus Deus: "Ecce: ego adsumam lignum Ioseph, quod est in manu Ephraim, et tribus Israhel quae sunt ei adiunctae, et dabo eas pariter cum ligno Iuda, et faciam eas in lignum unum, et erunt unum in manu eius."' 20 Erunt

"Come, spirit, from the four winds, and blow upon these slain, and let them live again."'" 10 And I prophesied as he had commanded me, and the spirit came into them, and they lived, and they stood up upon their feet, an exceeding great army.

11 And he said to me, "Son of man, all these bones are the house of Israel; they say, 'Our bones are dried up, and our hope is lost, and we are cut off.' 12 Therefore prophesy, and *say* to them, 'Thus saith the Lord God: "Behold: I will open your graves, and will bring you out of your sepulchres, O my people, and will bring you into the land of Israel. 13 And you shall know that I am the Lord when I shall have opened your sepulchres and shall have brought you out of your graves, O my people, 14 and shall have put my spirit in you, and you shall live, and I shall make you rest upon your own land, and you shall know that I, the Lord, have spoken and done it," saith the Lord God.'"

15 And the word of the Lord came to me, saying, 16 "And thou, son of man, take thee a stick, and write upon it, 'Of Judah and of the children of Israel, his associates,' and take another stick, and write upon it, 'For Joseph, the stick of Ephraim, and for all the house of Israel and of his associates.' 17 And join them one to the *other* into one stick, and they shall become one in thy hand.

18 "And when the children of thy people shall speak to thee, saying, 'Wilt thou not tell us what thou meanest by this?' 19 say to them, 'Thus saith the Lord God: "Behold: I will take the stick of Joseph, which is in the hand of Ephraim, and the tribes of Israel that are associated with him, and I will put them together with the stick of Judah, and will make them one stick, and they shall be one in his hand."'" 20 And

autem ligna super quae scripseris in manu tua in oculis eorum.

21 "Et dices ad eos, 'Haec dicit Dominus Deus: "Ecce: ego adsumam filios Israhel de medio nationum ad quas abierunt, et congregabo eos undique et adducam eos ad humum suam. 22 Et faciam eos in gentem unam in terra in montibus Israhel, et rex unus erit omnibus imperans, et non erunt ultra duae gentes, nec dividentur amplius in duo regna. 23 Neque polluentur ultra in idolis suis et abominationibus suis et cunctis iniquitatibus suis, et salvos eos faciam de universis sedibus suis in quibus peccaverunt, et mundabo eos, et erunt mihi populus, et ego ero eis Deus.

24 ""Et servus meus David rex super eos, et pastor unus erit omnium eorum; in iudiciis meis ambulabunt et mandata mea custodient et facient ea. 25 Et habitabunt super terram quam dedi servo meo Iacob, in qua habitaverunt patres vestri, et habitabunt super eam, ipsi et filii eorum et filii filiorum eorum, usque in sempiternum, et David, servus meus, princeps eorum in perpetuum. 26 Et percutiam illis foedus pacis; pactum sempiternum erit eis, et fundabo eos et multiplicabo et dabo sanctificationem meam in medio eorum in perpetuum. 27 Et erit tabernaculum meum in eis, et ero eis Deus, et ipsi erunt mihi populus. 28 Et scient gentes quia ego Dominus, sanctificator Israhel, cum fuerit sanctificatio mea in medio eorum in perpetuum.""""

the sticks whereon thou hast written shall be in thy hand before their eyes.

21 "And thou shalt say to them, 'Thus saith the Lord God: "Behold: I will take the children of Israel from the midst of the nations whither they are gone, and I will gather them on every side and will bring them to their own land. 22 And I will make them one nation in the land on the mountains of Israel, and one king shall be king over them all, and they shall no more be two nations, neither shall they be divided any more into two kingdoms. 23 Nor shall they be defiled any more with their idols nor with their abominations nor with all their iniquities, and I will save them out of all the places in which they have sinned, and I will cleanse them, and they shall be my people, and I will be their God.

24 ""And my servant David shall be king over them, and they shall have one *shepherd;* they shall walk in my judgments and shall keep my commandments and shall do them. 25 And they shall dwell in the land which I gave to my servant Jacob, wherein your fathers dwelt, and they shall dwell in it, they and their children and their children's children, for ever, and David, my servant, shall be their prince for ever. 26 And I will make a covenant of peace with them; it shall be an everlasting covenant with them, and I will establish them and will multiply them and will set my sanctuary in the midst of them for ever. 27 And my tabernacle shall be with them, and I will be their God, and they shall be my people. 28 And the nations shall know that I am the Lord, the sanctifier of Israel, when my sanctuary shall be in the midst of them for ever.""""

Caput 38

Et factus est sermo Domini ad me, dicens, 2 "Fili hominis, pone faciem tuam contra Gog, terram Magog, principem capitis Mosoch et Thubal, et vaticinare de eo, 3 et dices ad eum, 'Haec dicit Dominus Deus: "Ecce: ego ad te, Gog, principem capitis Mosoch et Thubal. 4 Et circumagam te, et ponam frenum in maxillis tuis, et educam te et omnem exercitum tuum, equos et equites vestitos loricis universos, multitudinem magnam hastam et clypeum arripientium et gladium, 5 persae, Aethiopes et Lybies cum eis, omnes scutati et galeati, 6 Gomer et universa agmina eius, domus Thogorma, latera aquilonis et totum robur eius populique multi tecum.

7 """Praepara, et instrue te et omnem multitudinem tuam quae coacervata est ad te, et esto eis in praeceptum. 8 Post dies multos visitaberis; in novissimo annorum venies ad terram quae reversa est a gladio et congregata est de populis multis ad montes Israhel, qui fuerunt deserti iugiter; haec de populis educta est, et habitabunt in ea confidenter universi. 9 Ascendens autem quasi tempestas venies et quasi nubes ut operias terram, tu et omnia agmina tua et populi multi tecum."

Chapter 38

Gog shall persecute the church in the latter days. He shall be overthrown.

And the word of the Lord came to me, saying, 2 "Son of man, set thy face against Gog, the land of Magog, the chief prince of Meshech and Tubal, and prophesy of him, 3 and *say* to him, 'Thus saith the Lord God: "Behold: I come against thee, O Gog, the chief prince of Meshech and Tubal. 4 And I will turn thee about, and I will put a bit in thy jaws, and I will bring thee forth and all thy army, horses and horsemen all clothed with coats of mail, a great multitude armed with spears and shields and swords, 5 the Persians, Ethiopians and Libyans with them, all with shields and helmets, 6 Gomer and all his bands, the house of Togarmah, the northern parts and all his strength and many peoples with thee.

7 """Prepare, and make thyself ready and all thy multitude that is assembled about thee, and be thou commander over them. 8 After many days thou shalt be visited; at the end of years thou shalt come to the land that is returned from the sword and is gathered out of many nations to the mountains of Israel, which have been continually waste; *but* it hath been brought forth out of the nations, and they shall all of them dwell securely in it. 9 And thou shalt go up and come like a storm and like a cloud to cover the land, thou and all thy bands and many people with thee."

10 "'Haec dicit Dominus Deus: "In die illa ascendent sermones super cor tuum, et cogitabis cogitationem pessimam. 11 Et dices, 'Ascendam ad terram absque muro; veniam ad quiescentes habitantesque secure; hi omnes habitant sine muro; vectes et portae non sunt eis,' 12 ut diripias spolia et invadas praedam, ut inferas manum tuam super eos qui deserti fuerant et postea restituti et super populum qui est congregatus ex gentibus, qui possidere coepit et esse habitator umbilici terrae. 13 Saba et Dedan et negotiatores Tharsis et omnes leones eius dicent tibi, "Numquid ad sumenda spolia tu venis? Ecce: ad diripiendam praedam congregasti multitudinem tuam, ut tollas argentum et aurum et auferas supellectilem atque substantiam et diripias manubias infinitas.'"''

14 "Propterea vaticinare, fili hominis, et dices ad Gog, 'Haec ait Dominus Deus: "Numquid non in die illo cum habitaverit populus meus Israhel confidenter scies? 15 Et venies de loco tuo a lateribus aquilonis, tu et populi multi tecum, ascensores equorum universi, coetus magnus et exercitus vehemens. 16 Et ascendes super populum meum Israhel quasi nubes ut operias terram. In novissimis diebus eris, et adducam te super terram meam, ut sciant gentes me cum sanctificatus fuero in te in oculis eorum, O Gog."

17 "'Haec dicit Dominus Deus: "Tu ergo ille es de quo locutus sum in diebus antiquis in manu servorum meorum, prophetarum Israhel, qui prophetaverunt in diebus illorum temporum ut adducerem te super eos. 18 Et erit in die illa, in die adventus Gog super terram Israhel," ait Dominus Deus, "ascendet indignatio mea in furore meo."

10 "'Thus saith the Lord God: "In that day *projects* shall *enter into* thy heart, and thou shalt conceive a mischievous design. 11 And thou shalt say, 'I will go up to the land which is without a wall; I will come to them that are at rest and dwell securely; all these dwell without a wall; they have no bars nor gates,' 12 to take spoils and lay hold on the prey, to lay thy hand upon them that had been wasted and afterwards restored and upon the people that is gathered together out of the nations, which hath begun to possess and to dwell in the midst of the earth. 13 Sheba and Dedan and the merchants of Tarshish and all the lions thereof shall say to thee, 'Art thou come to take spoils? Behold: thou hast gathered thy multitude to take a prey, to take silver and gold and to carry away goods and substance and to take rich spoils.'"'"

14 "Therefore, thou son of man, prophesy, and *say* to Gog: 'Thus saith the Lord God: "Shalt thou not know in that day when my people of Israel shall dwell securely? 15 And thou shalt come out of thy place from the northern parts, thou and many people with thee, all of them riding upon horses, a great company and a mighty army. 16 And thou shalt come upon my people of Israel like a cloud to cover the earth. Thou shalt be in the latter days, and I will bring thee upon my land, that the nations may know me when I shall be sanctified in thee, O Gog, before their eyes."

17 "'Thus saith the Lord God: "Thou then art he of whom I have spoken in the days of old *by* my servants, the prophets of Israel, who prophesied in the days of those times that I would bring thee upon them. 18 And it shall come to pass in that day, in the day of the coming of Gog upon the land of Israel," saith the Lord God, "that my indignation shall come up in my wrath."

19 """Et in zelo meo et in igne irae meae locutus sum quia in die illa erit commotio magna super terram Israhel, 20 et commovebuntur a facie mea, pisces maris et volucres caeli et bestiae agri et omne reptile quod movetur super humum cunctique homines qui sunt super faciem terrae, et subvertentur montes, et cadent sepes, et omnis murus corruet in terram. 21 Et convocabo adversum eum in cunctis montibus meis gladium," ait Dominus Deus. "Gladius uniuscuiusque in fratrem suum dirigetur. 22 Et iudicabo eum peste et sanguine et imbre vehementi et lapidibus inmensis; ignem et sulphur pluam super eum et super exercitum eius et super populos multos qui sunt cum eo. 23 Et magnificabor, et sanctificabor, et notus ero in oculis gentium multarum, et scient quia ego Dominus.""

Caput 39

"Tu autem, fili hominis, vaticinare adversum Gog, et dices, 'Haec dicit Dominus Deus: "Ecce: ego super te, Gog, principem capitis Mosoch et Thubal. 2 Et circumagam te, et reducam te et ascendere te faciam de lateribus aquilonis et

19 ""And I have spoken in my zeal and in the fire of my anger that in that day there shall be a great commotion upon the land of Israel, 20 *so that* the fishes of the sea and the birds of the air and the beasts of the field and every creeping thing that *creepeth* upon the ground and all men that are upon the face of the earth shall be moved at my presence, and the mountains shall be thrown down, and the hedges shall fall, and every wall shall fall to the ground. 21 And I will call in the sword against him in all my mountains," saith the Lord God. "Every man's sword shall be pointed against his brother. 22 And I will judge him with pestilence and with blood and with violent rain and vast hailstones; I will rain fire and brimstone upon him and upon his army and upon the many nations that are with him. 23 And I will be magnified, and I will be sanctified, and I will be known in the eyes of many nations, and they shall know that I am the Lord.""

Chapter 39

God's judgments upon Gog. God's people were punished
for their sins but shall be favoured with everlasting kindness.

"And thou, son of man, prophesy against Gog, and *say,* 'Thus saith the Lord God: "Behold: I come against thee, O Gog, the chief prince of Meshech and Tubal. 2 And I will turn thee round, and I will lead thee *out* and will make thee

adducam te super montes Israhel. 3 Et percutiam arcum tuum in manu sinistra tua, et sagittas tuas de manu dextera tua deiciam. 4 Super montes Israhel cades, tu et omnia agmina tua et populi tui qui sunt tecum; feris, avibus omnique volatili et bestiis terrae dedi te ad devorandum 5 Super faciem agri cades, quia ego locutus sum," ait Dominus Deus. 6 "Et inmittam ignem in Magog et in his qui habitant in insulis confidenter, et scient quia ego Dominus.

7 ""Et nomen sanctum meum notum faciam in medio populi mei Israhel, et non polluam nomen sanctum meum amplius, et scient Gentes quia ego Dominus, Sanctus Israhel. 8 Ecce: venit, et factum est," ait Dominus Deus. "Haec est dies de qua locutus sum.

9 ""Et egredientur habitatores de civitatibus Israhel et succendent et conburent arma, clypeum et hastas, arcum et sagittas et baculos manuum et contos, et succendent ea igne septem annis. 10 Et non portabunt ligna de regionibus neque succident de saltibus, quoniam arma succendent igne et depraedabuntur eos quibus praedae fuerant, et diripient vastatores suos," ait Dominus Deus.

11 ""Et erit in die illa dabo Gog locum nominatum sepulchrum in Israhel, vallem viatorum ad orientem maris, quae obstupescere faciet praetereuntes; et sepelient ibi Gog et omnem multitudinem eius, et vocabitur vallis multitudinis Gog. 12 Et sepelient eos domus Israhel ut mundent terram

go up from the northern parts and will bring thee upon the mountains of Israel. 3 And I will break thy bow in thy left hand, and I will cause thy arrows to fall out of thy right hand. 4 Thou shalt fall upon the mountains of Israel, thou and all thy bands and thy nations that are with thee; I have given thee to the wild beasts, to the birds and to every fowl and to the beasts of the earth to be devoured. 5 Thou shalt fall upon the face of the field, for I have spoken it," saith the Lord God. 6 "And I will send a fire on Magog and on them that dwell confidently in the islands, and they shall know that I am the Lord.

7 ""And I will make my holy name known in the midst of my people Israel, and my holy name shall be profaned no more, and the Gentiles shall know that I am the Lord, the Holy One of Israel. 8 Behold: it cometh, and it is done," saith the Lord God. "This is the day whereof I have spoken.

9 ""And the inhabitants shall go forth of the cities of Israel and shall set on fire and burn the weapons, the shields and the spears, the bows and the arrows and the handstaves and the pikes, and they shall burn them with fire seven years. 10 And they shall not bring wood out of the countries nor cut down out of the forests, for they shall burn the weapons with fire and shall make a prey of them to whom they had been a prey, and they shall rob those that robbed them," saith the Lord God.

11 ""And it shall come to pass in that day that I will give Gog a noted place for a sepulchre in Israel, the valley of the passengers on the east of the sea, which shall cause astonishment in them that pass by; and there shall they bury Gog and all his multitude, and it shall be called the valley of the multitude of Gog. 12 And the house of Israel shall bury them

septem mensibus. 13 Sepeliet autem eum omnis populus terrae, et erit eis nominata dies in qua glorificatus sum," ait Dominus Deus. 14 "Et viros iugiter constituent lustrantes terram qui sepeliant et requirant eos qui remanserant super faciem terrae, ut emundent eam, post menses autem septem quaerere incipient. 15 Et circumibunt peragrantes terram cumque viderint os hominis statuent iuxta illud titulum donec sepeliant illud pollinctores in valle multitudinis Gog. 16 Nomen autem civitatis Amona, et mundabunt terram.'"

17 "Tu ergo, fili hominis" (haec dicit Dominus Deus), "dic omni volucri et universis avibus cunctisque bestiis agri, 'Convenite; properate; concurrite undique ad victimam meam quam ego immolo vobis, victimam grandem super montes Israhel, ut comedatis, carnem et bibatis sanguinem. 18 Carnes fortium comedetis, et sanguinem principum terrae bibetis, arietum, agnorum et hircorum taurorumque et altilium et pinguium omnium. 19 Et comedetis adipem in saturitatem et bibetis sanguinem in ebrietatem de victima quam ego immolabo vobis. 20 Et saturabimini super mensam meam de equo et equite forti et de universis viris bellatoribus,'" ait Dominus Deus.

21 "'Et ponam gloriam meam in gentibus, et videbunt omnes gentes iudicium meum quod fecerim et manum meam quam posuerim super eos. 22 Et scient domus Israhel quia ego Dominus, Deus eorum, a die illa et deinceps. 23 Et scient gentes quoniam in iniquitate sua capta sit domus Israhel eo quod reliquerint me et absconderim faciem meam ab

for seven months to cleanse the land. 13 And all the people of the land shall bury him, and it shall be unto them a noted day wherein I was glorified," saith the Lord God. 14 "And they shall appoint men to go continually about the land to bury and to seek out them that were remaining upon the face of the earth, that they may cleanse it, and after seven months they shall begin to seek. 15 And they shall go about passing through the land, and when they shall see the bone of a man they shall set up a sign by it till the buriers bury it in the valley of the multitude of Gog. 16 And the name of the city shall be Hamonah, and they shall cleanse the land."'

17 "And thou, O son of man" (*saith* the Lord God), "say to every fowl and to all the birds and to all the beasts of the field, 'Assemble yourselves; make haste; come together from every side to my victim which I slay for you, a great victim upon the mountains of Israel, to eat flesh and drink blood. 18 You shall eat the flesh of the mighty, and you shall drink the blood of the princes of the earth, of rams *and* of lambs and of he-goats and bullocks and of all that are well fed and fat. 19 And you shall eat the fat till you be full and shall drink blood till you be drunk of the victim which I shall slay for you. 20 And you shall be filled at my table with horses and mighty horsemen and all the men of war,'" saith the Lord God.

21 "'And I will set my glory among the nations, and all nations shall see my judgment that I have executed and my hand that I have laid upon them. 22 And the house of Israel shall know that I am the Lord, their God, from that day and forward. 23 And the nations shall know that the house of Israel were made captives for their iniquity because they forsook me and I hid my face from them and I delivered them

eis et tradiderim eos in manus hostium et ceciderint in gladio universi. 24 Iuxta inmunditiam eorum et scelus feci eis et abscondi faciem meam ab illis.

25 "'Propterea haec dicit Dominus Deus: "Nunc reducam captivitatem Iacob et miserebor omnis domus Israhel, et adsumam zelum pro nomine sancto meo. 26 Et portabunt confusionem suam et omnem praevaricationem qua praevaricati sunt in me cum habitaverint in terra sua confidenter, neminem formidantes, 27 et reduxero eos de populis et congregavero de terris inimicorum suorum et sanctificatus fuero in eis in oculis gentium plurimarum. 28 Et scient quia ego Dominus, Deus eorum, eo quod transtulerim eos in nationes et congregaverim eos super terram suam et non dereliquerim quemquam ex eis ibi. 29 Et non abscondam ultra faciem meam ab eis, eo quod effuderim spiritum meum super omnem domum Israhel," ait Dominus Deus.'"

Caput 40

In vicesimo et quinto anno transmigrationis nostrae, in exordio anni, decima mensis, quartodecimo anno postquam percussa est civitas, in ipsa hac die facta est super me manus

into the hands of their enemies and they fell all by the sword. 24 I have dealt with them according to their uncleanness and wickedness and hid my face from them.

25 "'Therefore thus saith the Lord God: "Now will I bring back the captivity of Jacob and will have mercy on all the house of Israel, and I will be jealous for my holy name. 26 And they shall bear their confusion and all the transgressions wherewith they have transgressed against me when they shall dwell in their land securely, fearing no man, 27 and I shall have brought them back from among the nations and shall have gathered them together out of the lands of their enemies and shall be sanctified in them in the sight of many nations. 28 And they shall know that I am the Lord, their God, because I caused them to be carried away among the nations and I have gathered them together unto their own land and have not left any of them there. 29 And I will hide my face no more from them, for I have poured out my spirit upon all the house of Israel," saith the Lord God.'"

Chapter 40

The prophet sees in a vision the rebuilding of the temple;
the dimensions of several parts thereof.

In the five and twentieth year of our captivity, in the beginning of the year, the tenth day of the month, the fourteenth year after the city was destroyed, in the selfsame day

Domini, et adduxit me illuc. 2 In visionibus Dei adduxit me in terram Israhel et dimisit me super montem excelsum nimis, super quem erat quasi aedificium civitatis vergentis ad austrum. 3 Et introduxit me illuc, et ecce: vir, cuius erat species quasi species aeris et funiculus lineus in manu eius et calamus mensurae in manu eius, stabat autem in porta.

4 Et locutus est ad me idem vir, "Fili hominis, vide oculis tuis, et auribus tuis audi, et pone cor tuum in omnia quae ego ostendam tibi, quia ut ostendantur tibi adductus es huc; adnuntia omnia quae tu vides domui Israhel."

5 Et ecce: murus forinsecus in circuitu domus undique, et in manu viri calamus mensurae sex cubitorum et palmo, et mensus est latitudinem aedificii calamo uno, altitudinem quoque calamo uno.

6 Et venit ad portam quae respiciebat viam orientalem, et ascendit per gradus eius, et mensus est limen portae calamo uno latitudinem, id est, limen unum calamo uno in latitudine. 7 Et thalamum uno calamo in longum et uno calamo in latum, et inter thalamos quinque cubitos, 8 et limen portae iuxta vestibulum portae intrinsecus calamo uno. 9 Et mensus est vestibulum portae octo cubitorum et frontem eius duobus cubitis, vestibulum autem portae erat intrinsecus. 10 Porro thalami portae ad viam orientalem tres hinc et tres inde; mensura una trium et mensura una frontium ex utraque parte. 11 Et mensus est latitudinem liminis portae decem cubitorum, et longitudinem portae tredecim cubito-

the hand of the Lord was upon me, and he brought me thither. 2 In the visions of God he brought me into the land of Israel and set me upon a very high mountain, upon which there was as the building of a city bending towards the south. 3 And he brought me in thither, and behold: a man, whose appearance was like the appearance of brass with a line of flax in his hand and a measuring reed in his hand, and he stood in the gate.

4 And this man said to me, "Son of man, see with thy eyes, and hear with thy ears, and set thy heart upon all that I shall shew thee, for thou art brought hither that they may be shewn to thee; declare all that thou seest to the house of Israel."

5 And behold: there was a wall on the outside of the house round about, and in the man's hand a measuring reed of six cubits and a handbreadth, and he measured the breadth of the building one reed and the height one reed.

6 And he came to the gate that looked toward the east, and he went up the steps thereof, and he measured the breadth of the threshold of the gate one reed, that is, one threshold was one reed broad. 7 And every little chamber was one reed long and one reed broad, and between the little chambers were five cubits, 8 and the threshold of the gate by the porch of the gate within was one reed. 9 And he measured the porch of the gate eight cubits and the front thereof two cubits, and the porch of the gate was inward. 10 And the little chambers of the gate that looked eastward were three on this side and three on that side; all three were of one measure and the fronts of one measure on both parts. 11 And he measured the breadth of the threshold of the gate ten cubits, and the length of the gate thirteen cu-

rum. 12 Et marginem ante thalamos cubiti unius, et cubitus unus finis utrimque, thalami autem sex cubitorum erant hinc et inde. 13 Et mensus est portam a tecto thalami usque ad tectum eius, latitudinem viginti et quinque cubitorum, ostium contra ostium. 14 Et fecit frontes per sexaginta cubitos, et ad frontem atrium portae undique per circuitum. 15 Et ante faciem portae quae pertingebat usque ad faciem vestibuli portae interioris quinquaginta cubitos. 16 Et fenestras obliquas in thalamis et in frontibus eorum, quae erant intra portam undique per circuitum, similiter autem erant et in vestibulis fenestrae per gyrum intrinsecus et ante frontes pictura palmarum.

17 Et eduxit me ad atrium exterius, et ecce: gazofilacia, et pavimentum stratum lapide in atrio per circuitum; triginta gazofilacia in circuitu pavimenti. 18 Et pavimentum in fronte portarum secundum longitudinem portarum erat inferius. 19 Et mensus est latitudinem a facie portae inferioris usque ad frontem atrii interioris extrinsecus, centum cubitos ad orientem et ad aquilonem.

20 Portam quoque quae respiciebat viam aquilonis atrii exterioris mensus est, tam in longitudine quam in latitudine, 21 et thalamos eius, tres hinc et tres inde, et frontem eius et vestibulum eius secundum mensuram portae prioris: quinquaginta cubitorum longitudinem eius et latitudinem viginti quinque cubitorum. 22 Fenestrae autem eius et vestibulum et scalpturae secundum mensuram portae quae respiciebat ad orientem, et septem graduum erat ascensus

bits. 12 And the border before the little chambers one cubit, and one cubit was the border on both sides, and the little chambers were six cubits on this side and that side. 13 And he measured the gate from the roof of one little chamber to the roof of another, in breadth five and twenty cubits, door against door. 14 He made also fronts of sixty cubits, and to the front the court of the gate on every side round about. 15 And before the face of the gate which reached even to the face of the porch of the inner gate fifty cubits. 16 And slanting windows in the little chambers and in their fronts, which were within the gate on every side round about, and in like manner there were also in the porches windows round about within and before the fronts the representation of palm trees.

17 And he brought me into the outward court, and behold: there were chambers, and a pavement of stone in the court round about; thirty chambers encompassed the pavement. 18 And the pavement in the front of the gates according to the length of the gates was lower. 19 And he measured the breadth from the face of the lower gate to the front of the inner court without, a hundred cubits to the east and to the north.

20 He measured also both the length and the breadth of the gate of the outward court, which looked northward, 21 and the little chambers thereof, three on this side and three on that side, and the front thereof and the porch thereof according to the measure of the former gate: fifty cubits long and five and twenty cubits broad. 22 And the windows thereof and the porch and the gravings according to the measure of the gate that looked to the east, and they went up to it by seven steps, and a porch was be-

eius, et vestibulum ante eam. 23 Et porta atrii interioris contra portam aquilonis et orientalem, et mensus est a porta usque ad portam centum cubitos.

24 Et eduxit me ad viam australem, et ecce: porta quae respiciebat ad austrum, et mensus est frontem eius et vestibulum eius iuxta mensuras superiores. 25 Et fenestras eius et vestibula in circuitu, sicut fenestras ceteras: quinquaginta cubitorum longitudine et latitudine viginti quinque cubitorum. 26 Et in gradibus septem ascendebatur ad eam et vestibulum ante fores eius, et celatae palmae erant, una hinc et altera inde in fronte eius. 27 Et porta atrii interioris in via australi, et mensus est a porta usque ad portam in via australi centum cubitos.

28 Et introduxit me in atrium interius ad portam australem, et mensus est portam iuxta mensuras superiores. 29 Thalamum eius et frontem eius et vestibulum eius eisdem mensuris, et fenestras eius et vestibulorum eius in circuitu: quinquaginta cubitos longitudinis et latitudinis viginti quinque cubitos. 30 Et vestibulum per gyrum longitudine viginti quinque cubitorum et latitudine quinque cubitorum. 31 Et vestibulum eius ad atrium exterius, et palmas eius in fronte, et octo gradus erant quibus ascendebatur per eam.

32 Et introduxit me in atrium interius per viam orientalem, et mensus est portam secundum mensuras superiores. 33 Thalamum eius et frontem eius et vestibulum eius sicut supra, et fenestras eius et vestibula eius in circuitu: longitudine quinquaginta cubitorum et latitudine viginti quinque

fore it. 23 And the gate of the inner court was over against the gate of the north and that of the east, and he measured from gate to gate a hundred cubits.

24 And he brought me out to the way of the south, and behold: the gate that looked to the south, and he measured the front thereof and the porch thereof according to the former measures. 25 And the windows thereof and the porches round about, as the other windows: the length was fifty cubits and the breadth five and twenty cubits. 26 And there were seven steps to go up to it and a porch before the doors thereof, and there were graven palm trees, one on this side and another on that side in the front thereof. 27 And there was a gate of the inner court towards the south, and he measured from gate to gate towards the south a hundred cubits.

28 And he brought me into the inner court at the south gate, and he measured the gate according to the former measures. 29 The little chamber thereof and the front thereof and the porch thereof with the same measures, and the windows thereof and the porch thereof round about: it was fifty cubits in length and five and twenty cubits in breadth. 30 And the porch round about was five and twenty cubits long and five cubits broad. 31 And the porch thereof to the outward court, and the palm trees thereof in the front, and there were eight steps to go up to it.

32 And he brought me into the inner court by the way of the east, and he measured the gate according to the former measures. 33 The little chamber thereof and the front thereof and the porch thereof as before, and the windows thereof and the porches thereof round about: it was fifty cu-

cubitorum. 34 Et vestibulum eius, id est, atrii exterioris, et palmae celatae in fronte eius hinc et inde, et in octo gradibus ascensus eius. 35 Et introduxit me ad portam quae respiciebat ad aquilonem, et mensus est secundum mensuras superiores. 36 Thalamum eius et frontem eius et vestibulum eius et fenestras eius per circuitum: longitudine quinquaginta cubitorum et latitudine viginti quinque cubitorum. 37 Et vestibulum eius respiciebat ad atrium exterius, et celatura palmarum in fronte illius hinc et inde, et in octo gradibus ascensus eius.

38 Et per singula gazofilacia ostium in frontibus portarum; ibi lavabant holocaustum. 39 Et in vestibulo portae duae mensae hinc et duae mensae inde, ut immoletur super eas holocaustum et pro peccato et pro delicto. 40 Et ad latus exterius, quod ascendit ad ostium portae quae pergit ad aquilonem, duae mensae, et ad latus alterum ante vestibulum portae duae mensae. 41 Quattuor mensae hinc, et quattuor mensae inde; per latera portae octo mensae erant, super quas immolabant. 42 Quattuor autem mensae ad holocaustum de lapidibus quadris extructae, longitudine cubiti unius et dimidii et latitudine cubiti unius et dimidii et altitudine cubiti unius, super quas ponant vasa in quibus immolatur holocaustum et victima. 43 Et labia earum palmi unius, reflexa intrinsecus per circuitum, super mensas autem carnes oblationis.

44 Et extra portam interiorem gazofilacia cantorum in atrio interiori, quod erat in latere portae respicientis ad

bits long and five and twenty cubits broad. 34 And the porch thereof, that is, of the outward court, and the graven palm trees in the front thereof on this side and on that side, and the going up thereof was by eight steps. 35 And he brought me into the gate that looked to the north, and he measured according to the former measures. 36 The little chamber thereof and the front thereof and the porch thereof and the windows thereof round about: it was fifty cubits long and five and twenty cubits broad. 37 And the porch thereof looked to the outward court, and the graving of palm trees in the front thereof was on this side and on that side, and the going up to it was by eight steps.

38 And at every chamber was a door in the forefronts of the gates; there they washed the holocaust. 39 And in the porch of the gate were two tables on this side and two tables on that side, that the holocaust and the sin-offering and the trespass-offering might be slain thereon. 40 And on the outward side, which goeth up to the entry of the gate that looketh toward the north, were two tables, and at the other side before the porch of the gate were two tables. 41 Four tables were on this side, and four tables on that side; at the sides of the gate were eight tables, upon which they slew the victims. 42 And the four tables for the holocausts were made of square stones, one cubit and a half long and one cubit and a half broad and one cubit high, to lay the vessels upon in which the holocaust and the victim is slain. 43 And the borders of them were of one handbreadth, turned inwards round about, and upon the tables was the flesh of the offering.

44 And without the inner gate were the chambers of the singing men in the inner court, which was on the side of the

aquilonem, et facies eorum contra viam australem, una ex latere portae orientalis, quae respiciebat ad viam aquilonis.

45 Et dixit ad me, "Hoc est gazofilacium quod respicit viam meridianam; sacerdotum erit qui excubant in custodiis templi. 46 Porro gazofilacium quod respicit ad viam aquilonis sacerdotum erit qui excubant ad ministerium altaris. Isti sunt filii Sadoc, qui accedunt de filiis Levi ad Dominum ut ministrent ei." 47 Et mensus est atrium longitudine centum cubitorum et latitudine centum cubitorum per quadrum et altare ante faciem templi.

48 Et introduxit me in vestibulum templi, et mensus est vestibulum quinque cubitis hinc et quinque cubitis inde, et latitudinem portae trium cubitorum hinc et trium cubitorum inde. 49 Longitudinem autem vestibuli viginti cubitorum et latitudinem undecim cubitorum, et octo gradibus ascendebatur ad eam. Et columnae erant in frontibus, una hinc et altera inde.

Caput 41

Et introduxit me in templum, et mensus est frontes sex cubitos latitudinis hinc et sex cubitos latitudinis inde, latitudinem tabernaculi. 2 Et latitudo portae decem cubito-

gate that looketh to the north, and their prospect was towards the south, one at the side of the east gate, which looketh toward the north.

45 And he said to me, "This chamber, which looketh toward the south, shall be for the priests that watch in the wards of the temple. 46 But the chamber that looketh towards the north shall be for the priests that watch over the ministry of the altar. These are the sons of Zadok, who among the sons of Levi come near to the Lord to minister to him." 47 And he measured the court a hundred cubits long and a hundred cubits broad foursquare and the altar that was before the face of the temple.

48 And he brought me into the porch of the temple, and he measured the porch five cubits on this side and five cubits on that side, and the breadth of the gate three cubits on this side and three cubits on that side. 49 And the length of the porch was twenty cubits, and the breadth eleven cubits, and there were eight steps to go up to it. And there were pillars in the fronts, one on this side and another on that side.

Chapter 41

A description of the temple and of all the parts of it.

And he brought me into the temple, and he measured the fronts six cubits broad on this side and six cubits on that side, the breadth of the tabernacle. 2 And the breadth of the

rum erat, et latera portae quinque cubitis hinc et quinque cubitis inde, et mensus est longitudinem eius quadraginta cubitorum et latitudinem viginti cubitorum. 3 Et introgressus intrinsecus mensus est in fronte portae duos cubitos et portam sex cubitorum et latitudinem portae septem cubitorum. 4 Et mensus est longitudinem eius viginti cubitorum et latitudinem viginti cubitorum ante faciem templi, et dixit ad me, "Hoc est sanctum sanctorum." 5 Et mensus est parietem domus sex cubitorum et latitudinem lateris quattuor cubitorum undique per circuitum domus. 6 Latera autem latus ad latus bis triginta tria, et erant eminentia, quae ingrederentur per parietem domus in lateribus per circuitum ut continerent et non adtingerent parietem templi.

7 Et platea erat in rotundum ascendens sursum per cocleam, et in cenaculum templi deferebat per gyrum; idcirco latius erat templum in superioribus, et sic de inferioribus ascendebatur ad superiora in medium. 8 Et vidi in domo altitudinem per circuitum, fundata latera ad mensuram calami sex cubitorum spatio. 9 Et latitudinem per parietem lateris forinsecus quinque cubitorum, et erat interior domus in lateribus domus. 10 Et inter gazofilacia latitudinem viginti cubitorum in circuitu domus undique. 11 Et ostium lateris ad orationem; ostium unum ad viam aquilonis, et ostium unum ad viam australem, et latitudinem loci ad orationem quinque cubitorum in circuitu.

12 Et aedificium quod erat separatum versumque ad viam

gate was ten cubits, and the sides of the gate five cubits on this side and five cubits on that side, and he measured the length thereof forty cubits and the breadth twenty cubits. 3 Then going inward he measured the front of the gate two cubits and the gate six cubits and the breadth of the gate seven cubits. 4 And he measured the length thereof twenty cubits and the breadth twenty cubits before the face of the temple, and he said to me, "This is the holy of holies." 5 And he measured the wall of the house six cubits and the breadth of every side chamber four cubits round about the house on every side. 6 And the side chambers one by another were twice thirty-three, and they bore outwards, that they might enter in through the wall of the house in the sides round about to hold in and not to touch the wall of the temple.

7 And there was a broad passage round about going up by winding stairs, and it led into the upper loft of the temple all round; therefore was the temple broader in the higher parts, and so from the lower parts they went to the higher by the midst. 8 And I saw in the house the height round about, the foundations of the side chambers, which were the measure of a reed, the space of six cubits, 9 And the thickness of the wall for the side chamber without, which was five cubits, and the inner house was within the side chambers of the house. 10 And between the chambers was the breadth of twenty cubits round about the house on every side. 11 And the door of the side chambers was turned towards the place of prayer; one door was toward the north, and another door was toward the south, and the breadth of the place for prayer was five cubits round about.

12 And the building that was separate and turned to the

respicientem ad mare latitudinis septuaginta cubitorum, paries autem aedificii quinque cubitorum latitudinis per circuitum, et longitudo eius nonaginta cubitorum.

13 Et mensus est domus longitudinem centum cubitorum, et quod separatum erat aedificium et parietes eius longitudinis centum cubitorum. 14 Latitudo autem ante faciem domus et eius quod erat separatum contra orientem centum cubitorum.

15 Et mensus est longitudinem aedificii contra faciem eius, quod erat separatum ad dorsum, ethecas ex utraque parte centum cubitorum, et templum interius et vestibula atrii. 16 Limina et fenestras obliquas et ethecas in circuitu per tres partes contra uniuscuiusque limen stratumque ligno per gyrum in circuitu; terra autem usque ad fenestras, et fenestrae clausae super ostia. 17 Et usque ad domum interiorem et forinsecus per omnem parietem in circuitu intrinsecus et forinsecus ad mensuram. 18 Et fabrefacta cherubin et palmae, et palma inter cherub et cherub, duasque facies habebat cherub. 19 Faciem hominis iuxta palmam ex hac parte, et faciem leonis iuxta palmam ex alia parte, expressam per omnem domum in circuitu. 20 De terra usque ad superiora portae cherubin et palmae celatae erant in pariete templi. 21 Limen quadrangulum, et facies sanctuarii aspectus contra aspectum. 22 Altaris lignei trium cubitorum altitudo, et longitudo eius duorum cubitorum, et anguli eius et longitudo eius et parietes eius lignei. Et locutus est ad me, "Haec est mensa coram Domino."

way that looked toward the sea was seventy cubits broad, and the wall of the building five cubits thick round about and ninety cubits long.

13 And he measured the length of the house a hundred cubits and the separate building and the walls thereof a hundred cubits in length. 14 And the breadth before the face of the house and of the separate place toward the east a hundred cubits.

15 And he measured the length of the building over against it, which was separated at the back of it, and the galleries on both sides a hundred cubits, and the inner temple and the porches of the court. 16 The thresholds and the oblique windows and the galleries round about on three sides over against the threshold of every one and floored with wood all round about; and the ground was up to the windows, and the windows were shut over the doors. 17 And even to the inner house and without all the wall round about within and without by measure. 18 And there were cherubims and palm trees wrought, *so that* a palm tree was between a cherub and a cherub, and *every* cherub had two faces. 19 The face of a man was toward the palm tree on one side, and the face of a lion was toward the palm tree on the other side, set forth through all the house round about. 20 From the ground even to the upper parts of the gate were cherubims and palm trees wrought in the wall of the temple. 21 The threshold was foursquare, and the face of the sanctuary sight to sight. 22 The altar of wood was three cubits high, and the length thereof was two cubits, and the corners thereof and the length thereof and the walls thereof were of wood. And he said to me, "This is the table before the Lord."

23 Et duo ostia erant in templo et in sanctuario. 24 Et in duobus ostiis ex utraque parte bina erant ostiola quae in se invicem plicabantur, bina enim ostia erant ex utraque parte ostiorum. 25 Et celata erant in ipsis ostiis templi cherubin et scalptura palmarum, sicut in parietibus quoque expressae erant, quam ob rem erant et grossiora ligna in vestibuli fronte forinsecus. 26 Super quae fenestrae obliquae et similitudo palmarum hinc atque inde in umerulis vestibuli secundum latera domus latitudinemque parietum.

Caput 42

Et eduxit me in atrium exterius per viam ducentem ad aquilonem, et introduxit me in gazofilacium quod erat contra separatum aedificium et contra aedem vergentem ad aquilonem. 2 In facie longitudinis centum cubitos ostii aquilonis et latitudinis quinquaginta cubitos. 3 Contra viginti cubitos atrii interioris et contra pavimentum stratum lapide

23 And there were two doors in the temple and in the sanctuary. 24 And in the two doors on both sides were two little doors which were folded within each other, for there were two wickets on both sides of the doors. 25 And there were cherubims also wrought in the doors of the temple and the figures of palm trees, like as were made on the walls, for which cause also the planks were thicker in the front of the porch without. 26 Upon which were the oblique windows and the representation of palm trees on this side and on that side in the sides of the porch according to the sides of the house and the breadth of the walls.

Chapter 42

A description of the courts, chambers and other places belonging to the temple.

And he brought me forth into the outward court by the way that leadeth to the north, and he brought me into the chamber that was over against the separate building and over against the house toward the north. 2 In the face of the north door was the length of a hundred cubits and the breadth of fifty cubits. 3 Over against the twenty cubits of the inner court and over against the pavement of the out-

atrii exterioris, ubi erat porticus iuncta porticui triplici, 4 et ante gazofilacia deambulatio decem cubitorum latitudinis ad interiora respiciens viae cubiti unius. Et ostia earum ad aquilonem, 5 ubi erant gazofilacia in superioribus humiliora, quia subportabant porticus, quae ex illis eminebant de inferioribus et de mediis aedificii. 6 Tristega enim erant, et non habebant columnas sicut erant columnae atriorum; propterea eminebant de inferioribus et de mediis a terra cubitis quinquaginta. 7 Et peribolus exterior secundum gazofilacia quae erant in via atrii exterioris ante gazofilacia, longitudo eius quinquaginta cubitorum. 8 Quia longitudo erat gazofilaciorum atrii exterioris quinquaginta cubitorum, et longitudo ante faciem templi centum cubitorum. 9 Et erat subter gazofilacia haec introitus ab oriente ingredientium in ea de atrio exteriori.

10 In latitudine periboli atrii quod erat contra viam orientalem, in faciem aedificii separati, et erant ante aedificium gazofilacia. 11 Et via ante faciem eorum iuxta similitudinem gazofilaciorum quae erant in via aquilonis; secundum longitudinem eorum sic et latitudo eorum, et omnis introitus eorum et similitudines et ostia eorum. 12 Secundum ostia gazofilaciorum quae erant in via respiciente ad notum ostium in capite viae, quae via erat ante vestibulum, separatum per viam orientalem ingredientibus.

ward court that was paved with stone, where there was a gallery joined to a triple gallery, 4 and before the chambers was a walk ten cubits broad looking to the inner parts of a way of one cubit. And their doors were toward the north, 5 where were the store-chambers lower above, because they bore up the galleries, which appeared above out of them from the lower parts and from the midst of the building. 6 For they were of three stories, and had not pillars as the pillars of the courts; therefore did they appear above out of the lower places and out of the middle places fifty cubits from the ground. 7 And the outward wall that went about by the chambers which were towards the outward court on the forepart of the chambers was fifty cubits long. 8 For the length of the chambers of the outward court was fifty cubits, and the length before the face of the temple a hundred cubits. 9 And there was under these chambers an entrance from the east for them that went into them out of the outward court.

10 In the breadth of the outward wall of the court that was toward the east, over against the separate building, and there were chambers before the building. 11 And the way before them was like the chambers which were toward the north; they were as long as they and as broad as they, and all the going in to them and their fashions and their doors were alike. 12 According to the doors of the chambers that were *towards* the south there was a door in the head of the way, which way was before the porch, separated towards the east as one entereth in.

13 Et dixit ad me, "Gazofilacia aquilonis et gazofilacia austri quae sunt ante aedificium separatum, haec sunt gazofilacia sancta in quibus vescuntur sacerdotes qui adpropinquant
ad Dominum in sancta sanctorum; ibi ponent sancta sanctorum et oblationem pro peccato et pro delicto, locus enim
sanctus est. 14 Cum autem ingressi fuerint sacerdotes, non
egredientur de sanctis in atrium exterius, et ibi reponent
vestimenta sua in quibus ministrant, quia sancta sunt, ves-
tienturque vestimentis aliis, et sic procedent ad populum."

15 Cumque conplesset mensuras domus interioris, eduxit
me per viam portae quae respiciebat ad viam orientalem, et
mensus est eam undique per circuitum. 16 Mensus autem est
contra ventum orientalem calamo mensurae quingentos
calamos in calamo mensurae per circuitum. 17 Et mensus est
contra ventum aquilonem quingentos calamos in calamo
mensurae per gyrum. 18 Et ad ventum australem mensus est
quingentos calamos in calamo mensurae per circuitum. 19 Et
ad ventum occidentalem mensus est quingentos calamos in
calamo mensurae. 20 Per quattuor ventos mensus est murum
eius undique per circuitum longitudinem quingentorum
cubitorum et latitudinem quingentorum cubitorum, divi-
dentem inter sanctuarium et vulgi locum.

13 And he said to me, "The chambers of the north and the chambers of the south which are before the separate building, they are holy chambers in which the priests shall eat that approach to the Lord into the holy of holies; there they shall lay the most holy things and the offering for sin and for trespass, for it is a holy place. 14 And when the priests shall have entered in, they shall not go out of the holy places into the outward court, but there they shall lay their vestments wherein they minister, for they are holy, and they shall put on other garments, and so they shall go forth to the people."

15 Now when he had made an end of measuring the inner house, he brought me out by the way of the gate that looked toward the east, and he measured it on every side round about. 16 And he measured toward the east with the measuring reed five hundred reeds with the measuring reed round about. 17 And he measured toward the north five hundred reeds with the measuring reed round about. 18 And towards the south he measured five hundred reeds with the measuring reed round about. 19 And toward the west he measured five hundred reeds with the measuring reed. 20 By the four winds he measured the wall thereof on every side round about five hundred cubits long and five hundred cubits broad, making a separation between the sanctuary and the place of the people.

Caput 43

Et duxit me ad portam quae respiciebat ad viam orientalem. 2 Et ecce: gloria Dei Israhel ingrediebatur per viam orientalem, et vox erat ei quasi vox aquarum multarum, et terra splendebat a maiestate eius. 3 Et vidi visionem secundum speciem quam videram quando venit ut disperderet civitatem, et species secundum aspectum quem videram iuxta fluvium Chobar, et cecidi super faciem meam. 4 Et maiestas Domini ingressa est templum per viam portae quae respiciebat ad orientem. 5 Et levavit me spiritus et introduxit me in atrium interius, et ecce: repleta erat gloria Domini domus.

6 Et audivi loquentem ad me de domo, et vir qui stabat iuxta me 7 dixit ad me, "Fili hominis, locus solii mei et locus vestigiorum pedum meorum, ubi habito in medio filiorum Israhel in aeternum, et non polluent ultra domus Israhel nomen sanctum meum, ipsi et reges eorum, in fornicationibus suis et in ruinis regum suorum et in excelsis. 8 Qui fabricati sunt limen suum iuxta limen meum, et postes suos iuxta

Chapter 43

The glory of God returns to the new temple. The Israelites shall no more profane God's name by idolatry. The prophet is commanded to shew them the dimensions and form of the temple and of the altar, with the sacrifices to be offered thereon.

And he brought me to the gate that looked towards the east. 2 And behold: the glory of the God of Israel came in by the way of the east, and his voice was like the noise of many waters, and the earth shone with his majesty. 3 And I saw the vision according to the appearance which I had seen when he came to destroy the city, and the appearance was according to the vision which I had seen by the river Chebar, and I fell upon my face. 4 And the majesty of the Lord went into the temple by the way of the gate that looked to the east. 5 And the spirit lifted me up and brought me into the inner court, and behold: the house was filled with the glory of the Lord.

6 And I heard one speaking to me out of the house, and the man that stood by me 7 said to me, "Son of man, the place of my throne and the place of the soles of my feet, where I dwell in the midst of the children of Israel for ever, and the house of Israel shall no more profane my holy name, they and their kings, by their fornications and by the carcasses of their kings and by the high places. 8 They who have set their threshold by my threshold, and their posts by my

postes meos, et murus erat inter me et eos, et polluerunt nomen sanctum meum in abominationibus quas fecerunt, propter quod consumpsi eos in ira mea. 9 Nunc ergo repellant procul fornicationem suam et ruinas regum suorum a me, et habitabo in medio eorum semper.

10 "Tu autem, fili hominis, ostende domui Israhel templum, et confundantur ab iniquitatibus suis, et metiantur fabricam, 11 et erubescant ex omnibus quae fecerunt. Figuram domus et fabricae eius, exitus et introitus et omnem descriptionem eius et universa praecepta eius cunctumque ordinem eius et omnes leges eius ostende eis, et scribes in oculis eorum ut custodiant omnes descriptiones eius et praecepta illius et faciant ea.

12 "Ista est lex domus in summitate montis: omnis finis eius in circuitu sanctum sanctorum est. Haec ergo est lex domus.

13 "Istae autem mensurae altaris in cubito verissimo, qui habebat cubitum et palmum: in sinu eius erat cubitus, et cubitus in latitudine, et definitio eius usque ad labium eius et in circuitu palmus unus, haec quoque erat fossa altaris. 14 Et de sinu terrae usque ad crepidinem novissimam duo cubiti, et latitudo cubiti unius, et a crepidine minore usque ad crepidinem maiorem quattuor cubiti, et latitudo unius cubiti. 15 Ipse autem Arihel quattuor cubitorum, et ab Arihel usque sursum cornua quattuor. 16 Et Arihel duodecim cubitorum in longitudine per duodecim cubitos latitudinis, quadrangulatum aequis lateribus. 17 Et crepido quattuordecim cubitorum longitudinis per quattuordecim cubitos latitudinis in quattuor angulis eius, et corona in circuitu eius dimidii

posts, and there was but a wall between me and them, and they profaned my holy name by the abominations which they committed, for which reason I consumed them in my wrath. 9 Now therefore let them put away their fornications and the *carcasses* of their kings far from me, and I will dwell in the midst of them for ever.

10 "But thou, son of man, shew to the house of Israel the temple, and let them be ashamed of their iniquities, and let them measure the building, 11 and be ashamed of all that they have done. Shew them the form of the house and of the fashion thereof, the goings out and the comings in and the whole plan thereof and all its ordinances and all its order and all its laws, and thou shalt write it in their sight that they may keep the whole form thereof and its ordinances and do them.

12 "This is the law of the house upon the top of the mountain: all its border round about is most holy. This then is the law of the house.

13 "And these are the measures of the altar by the truest cubit, which is a cubit and a handbreadth: the bottom thereof was a cubit, and the breadth a cubit, and the border thereof unto its edge and round about one handbreadth, and this was the trench of the altar. 14 And from the bottom of the ground to the lowest brim two cubits, and the breadth of one cubit, and from the lesser brim to the greater brim four cubits, and the breadth of one cubit. 15 And the Ariel itself was four cubits, and from the Ariel upward were four horns. 16 And the Ariel was twelve cubits long *and* twelve cubits broad, foursquare with equal sides. 17 And the brim was fourteen cubits long *and* fourteen cubits broad in the four corners thereof, and the crown round about it was half a

cubiti, et sinus eius unius cubiti per circuitum, gradus autem eius versi ad orientem."

18 Et dixit ad me, "Fili hominis, haec dicit Dominus Deus: 'Hii sunt ritus altaris, in quacumque die fuerit fabricatum, ut offeratur super illud holocaustum et effundatur sanguis. 19 Et dabis sacerdotibus et Levitis qui sunt de semine Sadoc qui accedunt ad me,' ait Dominus Deus, 'ut offerant mihi vitulum de armento pro peccato. 20 Et adsumens de sanguine eius pones super quattuor cornua eius et super quattuor angulos crepidinis et super coronam in circuitu, et mundabis illud et expiabis. 21 Et tolles vitulum qui oblatus fuerit pro peccato, et conbures illum in separato loco domus extra sanctuarium.

22 "'Et in die secunda offeres hircum caprarum inmaculatum pro peccato, et expiabunt altare sicut expiaverunt in vitulo. 23 Cumque conpleveris expians illud, offeres vitulum de armento inmaculatum et arietem de grege inmaculatum. 24 Et offeres eos in conspectu Domini, et mittent sacerdotes super eos sal et offerent eos holocaustum Domino. 25 Septem diebus facies hircum pro peccato cotidie; et vitulum de armento et arietem de pecoribus inmaculatos offerent. 26 Septem diebus expiabunt altare et mundabunt illud, et implebunt manum eius. 27 Expletis autem diebus, in die octava et ultra facient sacerdotes super altare holocausta vestra et quae pro pace offerunt, et placatus ero vobis,' ait Dominus Deus."

cubit, and the bottom of it one cubit round about, and its steps turned toward the east.

18 And he said to me, "Son of man, thus saith the Lord God: 'These are the ceremonies of the altar, in what day soever it shall be made, that holocausts may be offered upon it and blood poured out. 19 And thou shalt give to the priests and the Levites that are of the race of Zadok who approach to me,' saith the Lord God, 'to offer to me a calf of the herd for sin. 20 And thou shalt take of his blood and shalt put it upon the four horns thereof and upon the four corners of the brim and upon the crown round about, and thou shalt cleanse and expiate it. 21 And thou shalt take the calf that is offered for sin, and thou shalt burn him in a separate place of the house without the sanctuary.

22 "'And in the second day thou shalt offer a he-goat without blemish for sin, and they shall expiate the altar as they expiated it with the calf. 23 And when thou shalt have made an end of the expiation thereof, thou shalt offer a calf of the herd without blemish and a ram of the flock without blemish. 24 And thou shalt offer them in the sight of the Lord, and the priests shall put salt upon them and shall offer them a holocaust to the Lord. 25 Seven days shalt thou offer a he-goat for sin daily; they shall offer also a calf of the herd and a ram of the flock without blemish. 26 Seven days shall they expiate the altar and shall cleanse it, and they shall *consecrate it*. 27 And the days being expired, on the eighth day and thenceforward the priests shall offer your holocausts upon the altar and the peace offerings, and I will be pacified towards you,' saith the Lord God."

Caput 44

Et convertit me ad viam portae sanctuarii exterioris, quae respiciebat ad orientem, et erat clausa. 2 Et dixit Dominus ad me, "Porta haec clausa erit; non aperietur, et vir non transiet per eam, quoniam Dominus, Deus Israhel, ingressus est per eam, eritque clausa 3 principi. Princeps ipse sedebit in ea ut comedat panem coram Domino; per viam vestibuli portae ingredietur et per viam eius egredietur."

4 Et adduxit me per viam portae aquilonis in conspectu domus, et vidi, et ecce: implevit gloria Domini domum Domini, et cecidi in faciem meam.

5 Et dixit ad me Dominus, "Fili hominis, pone cor tuum, et vide oculis tuis, et auribus tuis audi omnia quae ego loquor ad te de universis caerimoniis domus Domini et de cunctis legibus eius, et pones cor tuum in viis templi per omnes exitus sanctuarii.

6 "Et dices ad exasperantem me domum Israhel, 'Haec dicit Dominus Deus: "Sufficiant vobis omnia scelera vestra, domus Israhel, 7 eo quod inducitis filios alienos incircumci-

Chapter 44

The east gate of the sanctuary shall be always shut. The uncircumcised shall not enter into the sanctuary nor the Levites that have served idols, but the sons of Zadok shall do the priestly functions, who stood firm in the worst of times.

And he brought me back to the way of the gate of the outward sanctuary, which looked towards the east, and it was shut. 2 And the Lord said to me, "This gate shall be shut; it shall not be opened, and no man shall pass through it, because the Lord, the God of Israel, hath entered in by it, and it shall be shut 3 for the prince. The prince himself shall sit in it to eat bread before the Lord; he shall enter in by the way of the porch of the gate and shall go out by the same way."

4 And he brought me by the way of the north gate in the sight of the house, and I saw, and behold: the glory of the Lord filled the house of the Lord, and I fell on my face.

5 And the Lord said to me, "Son of man, attend with thy heart, and behold with thy eyes, and hear with thy ears all that I say to thee concerning all the ceremonies of the house of the Lord and concerning all the laws thereof, and *mark well* the ways of the temple with all the goings out of the sanctuary.

6 "And thou shalt say to the house of Israel that provoketh me, 'Thus saith the Lord God: "Let all your wicked doings suffice you, O house of Israel, 7 in that you have brought in

sos corde et incircumcisos carne ut sint in sanctuario meo et polluant domum meam, et offertis panes meos, adipem et sanguinem, et dissolvitis pactum meum in omnibus sceleribus vestris. 8 Et non servastis praecepta sanctuarii mei, et posuistis custodes observationum mearum in sanctuario meo vobismet ipsis."

9 "Haec dicit Dominus Deus: "Omnis alienigena incircumcisus corde et incircumcisus carne non ingredietur sanctuarium meum, omnis filius alienus qui est in medio filiorum Israhel. 10 Sed et Levitae, qui longe recesserunt a me in errore filiorum Israhel et erraverunt a me post idola sua et portaverunt iniquitatem suam, 11 erunt in sanctuario meo aeditui et ianitores portarum domus et ministri domus; ipsi mactabunt holocausta et victimas populi, et ipsi stabunt in conspectu eorum ut ministrent eis. 12 Pro eo quod ministraverunt illis in conspectu idolorum suorum et facti sunt domui Israhel in offendiculum iniquitatis, idcirco levavi manum meam super eos," dicit Dominus Deus, "et portabunt iniquitatem suam, 13 et non adpropinquabunt ad me ut sacerdotio fungantur mihi, neque accedent ad omne sanctuarium meum iuxta sancta sanctorum, sed portabunt confusionem suam et scelera sua quae fecerunt. 14 Et dabo eos ianitores domus in omni ministerio eius et in universis quae fient in ea.

15 ""Sacerdotes autem et Levitae, filii Sadoc, qui custodierunt caerimonias sanctuarii mei cum errarent filii Israhel a me, ipsi accedent ad me ut ministrent mihi, et stabunt in conspectu meo ut offerant mihi adipem et sanguinem," ait

strangers uncircumcised in heart and uncircumcised in flesh to be in my sanctuary and to defile my house, and you offer my bread, the fat and the blood, and you have broken my covenant by all your wicked doings. 8 And you have not kept the ordinances of my sanctuary, *but* you have set keepers of my charge in my sanctuary for yourselves."

9 "'Thus saith the Lord God: "No stranger uncircumcised in heart and uncircumcised in flesh shall enter into my sanctuary, no stranger that is in the midst of the children of Israel. 10 Moreover the Levites, that went away far from me when the children of Israel went astray and have wandered from me after their idols and have borne their iniquity, 11 they shall be officers in my sanctuary and doorkeepers of the gates of the house and ministers to the house; they shall slay the holocausts and the victims of the people, and they shall stand in their sight to minister to them. 12 Because they ministered to them before their idols and were a stumbling block of iniquity to the house of Israel, therefore have I lifted up my hand against them," saith the Lord God, "and they shall bear their iniquity, 13 and they shall not come near to me to do the office of priest to me, neither shall they come near to any of my holy things that are by the holy of holies, but they shall bear their shame and their wickednesses which they have committed. 14 And I will make them doorkeepers of the house for all the service thereof and for all that shall be done therein.

15 "'"But the priests and Levites, the sons of Zadok, who kept the ceremonies of my sanctuary when the children of Israel went astray from me, they shall come near to me to minister to me, and they shall stand before me to offer me

Dominus Deus. 16 "Ipsi ingredientur sanctuarium meum, et ipsi accedent ad mensam meam ut ministrent mihi et custodiant caerimonias meas. 17 Cumque ingredientur portas atrii interioris, vestibus lineis induentur, nec ascendet super eos quicquam laneum quando ministrant in portis atrii interioris et intrinsecus. 18 Vittae lineae erunt in capitibus eorum et feminalia linea erunt in lumbis eorum, et non accingentur in sudore. 19 Cumque egredientur atrium exterius ad populum, exuent se vestimenta sua in quibus ministraverant et reponent ea in gazofilacio sanctuarii, et vestient se vestimentis aliis, et non sanctificabunt populum in vestibus suis. 20 Caput autem suum non radent neque comam nutrient, sed tondentes adtondent capita sua. 21 Et vinum non bibet omnis sacerdos quando ingressurus est atrium interius. 22 Et viduam et repudiatam non accipient uxores, sed virgines de semine domus Israhel; sed et viduam quae fuerit vidua a sacerdote accipient. 23 Et populum meum docebunt quid sit inter sanctum et pollutum et inter mundum et inmundum ostendent eis. 24 Et cum fuerit controversia, stabunt in iudiciis meis et iudicabunt; leges meas et praecepta mea in omnibus sollemnitatibus meis custodient et sabbata mea sanctificabunt. 25 Et ad mortuum hominem non ingredientur ne polluantur, nisi ad patrem et matrem et filium et filiam et fratrem et sororem quae alterum virum non habuit, in quibus contaminabuntur.

26 """Et postquam fuerit emundatus, septem dies numerabuntur ei. 27 Et in die introitus sui in sanctuarium, ad atrium

the fat and the blood," saith the Lord God. 16 "They shall enter into my sanctuary, and they shall come near to my table to minister unto me and to keep my ceremonies. 17 And when they shall enter in at the gates of the inner court, they shall be clothed with linen garments, neither shall any woollen come upon them when they minister in the gates of the inner court and within. 18 They shall have linen mitres on their heads and linen breeches on their loins, and they shall not be girded with *any thing that causeth* sweat. 19 And when they shall go forth to the outward court to the people, they shall put off their garments wherein they *ministered* and lay them up in the store-chamber of the sanctuary, and they shall clothe themselves with other garments, and they shall not sanctify the people with their vestments. 20 Neither shall they shave their heads nor wear long hair, but they shall only poll their heads. 21 And no priest shall drink wine when he is to go into the inner court. 22 Neither shall they take to wife a widow nor one that is divorced, but they shall take virgins of the seed of the house of Israel; but they may take a widow also that is the widow of a priest. 23 And they shall teach my people the difference between holy and profane and shew them how to discern between clean and unclean. 24 And when there shall be a controversy, they shall stand in my judgments and shall judge; they shall keep my laws and my ordinances in all my solemnities and sanctify my sabbaths. 25 And they shall come near no dead person lest they be defiled, only their father and mother and son and daughter and brother and sister that hath not had another husband, for whom they may become unclean.

26 """And after one is cleansed, they shall reckon unto him seven days. 27 And in the day that he goeth into the sanctu-

interius, ut ministret mihi in sanctuario, offeret pro peccato suo," ait Dominus Deus. 28 "Non erit autem eis hereditas; ego hereditas eorum: et possessionem non dabitis eis in Israhel, ego enim possessio eorum. 29 Victimam et pro peccato et pro delicto ipsi comedent, et omne votum in Israhel ipsorum erit. 30 Et primitiva omnium primogenitorum et omnia libamenta ex omnibus quae offeruntur sacerdotum erunt, et primitiva ciborum vestrorum dabitis sacerdoti, ut reponat benedictionem domui tuae. 31 Omne morticinum et captum a bestia de avibus et de pecoribus non comedent sacerdotes."""

Caput 45

""""Cumque coeperitis terram dividere sortito, separate primitias Domino, sanctificatum de terra, longitudine viginti quinque milia et latitudine decem milia; sanctificatum erit in omni termino eius per circuitum. 2 Et erit ex omni parte sanctificatum quingentos per quingentos quadrifariam per circuitum, et quinquaginta cubitis in suburbana eius per gyrum. 3 Et a mensura ista mensurabis longitudinem viginti quinque milium et latitudinem decem milium,

ary, to the inner court, to minister unto me in the sanctuary, he shall offer for his sin," saith the Lord God. 28 "And they shall have no inheritance; I am their inheritance: neither shall you give them any possession in Israel, for I am their possession. 29 They shall eat the victim both for sin and for trespass, and every vowed thing in Israel shall be theirs. 30 And the firstfruits of all the firstborn and all the libations of all things that are offered shall be the priests', and you shall give the firstfruits of your meats to the priest, that he may return a blessing upon thy house. 31 The priests shall not eat of any thing that is dead of itself or caught by a beast, whether it be fowl or cattle.""""

Chapter 45

Portions of land for the sanctuary, for the city and for the prince. Ordinances for the prince.

"""" And when you shall begin to divide the land by lot, separate ye firstfruits to the Lord, a portion of the land to be holy, in length twenty-five thousand and in breadth ten thousand; it shall be holy in all the borders thereof round about. 2 And there shall be for the sanctuary on every side five hundred by five hundred foursquare round about, and fifty cubits for the suburbs thereof round about. 3 And with this measure thou shalt measure the length of five and twenty thousand and the breadth of ten thousand, and in it

et in ipso erit templum sanctumque sanctorum. 4 Sanctificatum de terra erit sacerdotibus, ministris sanctuarii, qui accedunt ad ministerium Domini, et erit eis locus in domos et in sanctuarium sanctitatis. 5 Viginti quinque autem milia longitudinis et decem milia latitudinis erunt Levitis qui ministrant domui; ipsi possidebunt viginti gazofilacia.

6 """Et possessionem civitatis dabitis quinque milia latitudinis et longitudinis viginti quinque milia secundum separationem sanctuarii omni domui Israhel.

7 """Principi quoque hinc et inde in separationem sanctuarii et in possessionem civitatis contra faciem separationis sanctuarii et contra faciem possessionis urbis a latere maris usque ad mare et a latere orientis usque ad orientem. Longitudinem autem iuxta unamquamque partem a termino occidentali usque ad terminum orientalem. 8 De terra erit ei possessio in Israhel, et non depopulabuntur ultra principes populum meum, sed terram dabunt domui Israhel secundum tribus eorum."

9 "Haec dicit Dominus Deus: "Sufficiat vobis, principes Israhel; iniquitatem et rapinas intermittite, et iudicium et iustitiam facite; separate confinia vestra a populo meo," ait Dominus Deus.

10 """Statera iusta et oephi iustum et batus iustus erit vobis. 11 Oephi et batus aequalia et unius mensurae erunt, ut capiat decimam partem chori batus, et decimam partem chori oephi; iuxta mensuram chori erit aequa libratio eorum. 12 Siclus autem viginti obolos habet. Porro viginti sicli et viginti quinque sicli et quindecim sicli minam facient.

shall be the temple and the holy of holies. 4 The holy portion of the land shall be for the priests, the ministers of the sanctuary, who come near to the ministry of the Lord, and it shall be a place for their houses and for the holy place of the sanctuary. 5 And five and twenty thousand of length and ten thousand of breadth shall be for the Levites that minister in the house; they shall possess twenty store-chambers.

6 ""And you shall appoint the possession of the city five thousand broad and five and twenty thousand long according to the separation of the sanctuary for the whole house of Israel.

7 ""For the prince also on the one side and on the other side according to the separation of the sanctuary and according to the possession of the city over against the separation of the sanctuary and over against the possession of the city from the side of the sea even to the sea and from the side of the east even to the east. And the length according to every part from the west border to the east border. 8 He shall have a portion of the land in Israel, and the princes shall no more rob my people, but they shall give the land to the house of Israel according to their tribes."

9 "'Thus saith the Lord God: "Let it suffice you, O princes of Israel; cease from iniquity and robberies, and execute judgment and justice; separate your confines from my people," saith the Lord God.

10 ""You shall have just balances and a just ephi and a just bate. 11 The ephi and the bate shall be equal and of one measure, that the bate may contain the tenth part of a core, and the ephi the tenth part of a core; their weight shall be equal according to the measure of a core. 12 And the sicle hath twenty obols. Now twenty sicles and five and twenty sicles and fifteen sicles make a mna.

13 """Et haec sunt primitiae quas tolletis: sextam partem oephi de choro frumenti et sextam partem oephi de choro hordei. 14 Mensura quoque olei: batus olei decima pars chori est, et decem bati chorum faciunt, quia decem bati implent chorum. 15 Et arietem unum de grege ducentorum de his quae nutriunt Israhel in sacrificium et in holocaustum et in pacifica ad expiandum pro eis," ait Dominus Deus. 16 "Omnis populus terrae tenebitur primitiis his principi in Israhel. 17 Et super principem erunt holocausta et sacrificium et libamina in sollemnitatibus et in kalendis et in sabbatis et in universis sollemnitatibus domus Israhel; ipse faciet pro peccato sacrificium et holocaustum et pacifica ad expiandum pro domo Israhel."

18 "Haec dicit Dominus Deus: "In primo mense, una mensis, sumes vitulum de armento inmaculatum, et expiabis sanctuarium. 19 Et tollet sacerdos de sanguine quod erit pro peccato, et ponet in postibus domus et in quattuor angulis crepidinis altaris et in postibus portae atrii interioris. 20 Et sic facies in septima mensis pro unoquoque qui ignoravit et errore deceptus est, et expiabitis pro domo.

21 """In primo mense, quartadecima die mensis, erit vobis paschae sollemnitas; septem diebus azyma comedentur. 22 Et faciet princeps in die illa pro se et pro universo populo terrae vitulum pro peccato. 23 Et in septem dierum sollemnitate faciet holocaustum Domino septem vitulos et septem arietes inmaculatos cotidie septem diebus, et pro peccato

13 ""And these are the firstfruits which you shall take: the sixth part of an ephi of a core of wheat and the sixth part of an ephi of a core of barley. 14 The measure of oil also: a bate of oil is the tenth part of a core, and ten bates make a core, for ten bates fill a core. 15 And one ram out of a flock of two hundred of those that Israel feedeth for sacrifice and for holocausts and for peace offerings to make atonement for them," saith the Lord God. 16 "All the people of the land shall be bound to these firstfruits for the prince in Israel. 17 And the prince shall give the holocaust and the sacrifice and the libations on the feasts and on the new moons and on the sabbaths and on all the solemnities of the house of Israel; he shall offer the sacrifice for sin and the holocaust and the peace offerings to make expiation for the house of Israel."

18 "'Thus saith the Lord God: "In the first month, the first of the month, thou shalt take a calf of the herd without blemish, and thou shalt expiate the sanctuary. 19 And the priest shall take of the blood of the sin offering, and he shall put it on the posts of the house and on the four corners of the brim of the altar and on the posts of the gate of the inner court. 20 And so shalt thou do in the seventh day of the month for every one that hath been ignorant and hath been deceived by error, and thou shalt make expiation for the house.

21 ""In the first month, the fourteenth day of the month, you shall observe the solemnity of the pasch; seven days unleavened bread shall be eaten. 22 And the prince on that day shall offer for himself and for all the people of the land a calf for sin. 23 And in the solemnity of the seven days he shall offer for a holocaust to the Lord seven calves and seven rams

hircum caprarum cotidie. 24 Et sacrificium oephi per vitulum et oephi per arietem faciet et olei hin per singula oephi.
25 Septimo mense, quintadecima die mensis, in sollemnitate
faciet sicut supra dicta sunt per septem dies, tam pro peccato quam pro holocausto et in sacrificio et in oleo.""""

Caput 46

""Haec dicit Dominus Deus: "Porta atrii interioris
quae respicit ad orientem erit clausa sex diebus in quibus
opus fit, die autem sabbati aperietur, sed et in die kalendarum aperietur. 2 Et intrabit princeps per viam vestibuli portae de foris, et stabit in limine portae, et facient sacerdotes
holocaustum eius et pacifica eius, et adorabit super limen
portae et egredietur porta autem non claudetur usque ad
vesperam. 3 Et adorabit populus terrae ad ostium portae illius in sabbatis et in kalendis coram Domino.

4 """Holocaustum autem hoc offeret princeps Domino
in die sabbati: sex agnos inmaculatos et arietem inmacula-

without blemish daily for seven days, and for sin a he-goat daily. 24 And he shall offer the sacrifice of an ephi for every calf and an ephi for every ram and a hin of oil for every ephi. 25 In the seventh month, in the fifteenth day of the month, in the solemn feast he shall do the like for the seven days, as well in regard to the sin offering as to the holocaust and the sacrifice and the oil.""""

Chapter 46

Other ordinances for the prince and for the sacrifices.

""Thus saith the Lord God: "The gate of the inner court that looketh toward the east shall be shut the six days on which work is done, but on the sabbath day it shall be opened, yea and on the day of the new moon it shall be opened. 2 And the prince shall enter by the way of the porch of the gate from without, and he shall stand at the threshold of the gate, and the priests shall offer his holocaust and his peace offerings, and he shall adore upon the threshold of the gate and shall go out, but the gate shall not be shut till the evening. 3 And the people of the land shall adore at the door of that gate before the Lord on the sabbaths and on the new moons.

4 """"And the holocaust that the prince shall offer to the Lord on the sabbath day shall be six lambs without blemish

tum. 5 Et sacrificium oephi per arietem, in agnis autem sacrificium quod dederit manus eius, et olei hin per singula oephi. 6 In die autem kalendarum vitulum de armento inmaculatum, et sex agni et arietes inmaculati erunt. 7 Et oephi per vitulum, oephi quoque per arietem faciet sacrificium, de agnis autem sicut invenerit manus eius, et olei hin per singula oephi. 8 Cumque ingressurus est princeps, per viam vestibuli portae ingrediatur, et per eandem viam exeat.

9 """Et cum intrabit populus terrae in conspectu Domini in sollemnitatibus, qui ingreditur per portam aquilonis ut adoret egrediatur per viam portae meridianae, porro qui ingreditur per viam portae meridianae egrediatur per viam portae aquilonis; non revertetur per viam portae per quam ingressus est sed e regione illius egredietur. 10 Princeps autem in medio eorum cum ingredientibus ingredietur et cum egredientibus egredietur.

11 """Et in nundinis et in sollemnitatibus erit sacrificium oephi per vitulum et oephi per arietem, agnis autem erit sacrificium sicut invenerit manus eius, et olei hin per singula oephi. 12 Cum autem fecerit princeps spontaneum holocaustum aut pacifica voluntaria Domino, aperietur ei porta quae respicit ad orientem, et faciet holocaustum suum et pacifica sua sicut fieri solet in die sabbati, et egredietur claudeturque porta postquam exierit.

13 """Et agnum eiusdem anni inmaculatum faciet holocaustum cotidie Domino; semper mane faciet illud. 14 Et sacrificium faciet super eo cata mane mane, sextam partem oephi et de oleo tertiam partem hin ut misceatur similae,

and a ram without blemish. 5 And the sacrifice of an ephi for a ram, but for the lambs what sacrifice his hand shall allow, and a hin of oil for every ephi. 6 And on the day of the new moon a calf of the herd without blemish, and the six lambs and the rams shall be without blemish. 7 And he shall offer in sacrifice an ephi for a calf, an ephi also for a ram, but for the lambs as his hand shall find, and a hin of oil for every ephi. 8 And when the prince is to go in, let him go in by the way of the porch of the gate, and let him go out the same way.

9 ""*But* when the people of the land shall go in before the Lord in the solemn feasts, he that goeth in by the north gate to adore shall go out by the way of the south gate, and he that goeth in by the way of the south gate shall go out by the way of the north gate; he shall not return by the way of the gate whereby he came in but shall go out at that over against it. 10 And the prince in the midst of them shall go in when they go in and go out when they go out.

11 ""And in the fairs and in the solemnities there shall be the sacrifice of an ephi to a calf and an ephi to a ram, and to the lambs the sacrifice shall be as his hand shall find, and a hin of oil to every ephi. 12 But when the prince shall offer a voluntary holocaust or voluntary peace offerings to the Lord, the gate that looketh towards the east shall be opened to him, and he shall offer his holocaust and his peace offerings as it is wont to be done on the sabbath day, and he shall go out, and the gate shall be shut after he is gone forth.

13 ""And he shall offer every day for a holocaust to the Lord a lamb of the same year without blemish; he shall offer it always in the morning. 14 And he shall offer the sacrifice

sacrificium Domino legitimum iuge atque perpetuum. 15 Faciet agnum et sacrificium et oleum cata mane mane, holocaustum sempiternum."

16 "'Haec dicit Dominus Deus: "Si dederit princeps donum alicui de filiis suis, hereditas eius filiorum suorum erit; possidebunt eam hereditarie. 17 Si autem dederit legatum de hereditate sua uni servorum suorum, erit illius usque ad annum remissionis, et revertetur ad principem, hereditas autem eius filiis eius erit. 18 Et non accipiet princeps de hereditate populi per violentiam et de possessione eorum, sed de possessione sua hereditatem dabit filiis suis, ut non dispergatur populus meus unusquisque a possessione sua."'"

19 Et introduxit me per ingressum qui erat ex latere portae in gazofilacia sanctuarii ad sacerdotes, quae respiciebant ad aquilonem. Et erat ibi locus vergens ad occidentem. 20 Et dixit ad me, "Iste est locus ubi coquent sacerdotes pro peccato et pro delicto, ubi coquent sacrificium, ut non efferant in atrium exterius et sanctificetur populus."

21 Et eduxit me in atrium exterius, et circumduxit me per quattuor angulos atrii, et ecce: atriolum erat in angulo atrii; atriola singula per angulos atrii. 22 In quattuor angulos atrii atriola disposita quadraginta cubitorum per longum et triginta per latum; mensurae unius quattuor erant. 23 Et paries per circuitum ambiens quattuor atriola, et culinae fabrica-

for it morning by morning, the sixth part of an ephi and the third part of a hin of oil to be mingled with the fine flour, a sacrifice to the Lord by ordinance continual and everlasting. 15 He shall offer the lamb and the sacrifice and the oil morning by morning, an everlasting holocaust."

16 "'Thus saith the Lord God: "If the prince give a gift to any of his sons, the inheritance of it shall go to his children; they shall possess it by inheritance. 17 But if he give a legacy out of his inheritance to one of his servants, it shall be his until the year of release, and it shall return to the prince, but his inheritance shall go to his sons. 18 And the prince shall not take of the people's inheritance by violence nor of their possession, but out of his own possession he shall give an inheritance to his sons, that my people be not dispersed every man from his possession."'"

19 And he brought me in by the entry that was at the side of the gate into the chambers of the sanctuary that were for the priests, which looked toward the north. And there was a place bending to the west. 20 And he said to me, "This is the place where the priests shall boil the sin offering and the trespass offering, where they shall dress the sacrifice, that they may not bring it out into the outward court and the people be sanctified."

21 And he brought me into the outward court, and he led me about by the four corners of the court, and behold: there was a little court in the corner of the court; to every corner of the court there was a little court. 22 In the four corners of the court were little courts disposed forty cubits long and thirty broad, all the four were of one measure. 23 And there was a wall round about compassing the four little courts, and there were kitchens built under the rows

tae erant subter porticus per gyrum. 24 Et dixit ad me, "Haec est domus culinarum in qua coquent ministri domus Domini victimas populi."

Caput 47

Et convertit me ad portam domus, et ecce: aquae egrediebantur subter limen domus ad orientem, facies enim domus respiciebat ad orientem, aquae autem descendebant in latus templi dextrum ad meridiem altaris. 2 Et eduxit me per viam portae aquilonis, et convertit me ad viam foras portam exteriorem viam quae respiciebat ad orientem, et ecce: aquae redundantes a latere dextro.

3 Cum egrederetur vir ad orientem qui habebat funiculum in manu sua, et mensus est mille cubitos, et transduxit me per aquam usque ad talos. 4 Rursumque mensus est mille, et transduxit me per aquam usque ad genua. 5 Et mensus est mille, et transduxit me per aquam usque ad renes. Et mensus est mille: torrentem quem non potui pertransitre, quoniam intumuerant aquae profundi torrentis qui non potest transvadari.

round about. 24 And he said to me, "This is the house of the kitchens wherein the ministers of the house of the Lord shall boil the victims of the people."

Chapter 47

The vision of the holy waters issuing out from under the temple. The borders of the land to be divided among the twelve tribes.

And he brought me again to the gate of the house, and behold: waters issued out from under the threshold of the house toward the east, for the forefront of the house looked toward the east, but the waters came down to the right side of the temple to the south part of the altar. 2 And he led me out by the way of the north gate, and he caused me to turn to the way without the outward gate to the way that looked toward the east, and behold: there ran out waters on the right side.

3 And when the man that had the line in his hand went out towards the east, he measured a thousand cubits, and he brought me through the water up to the ankles. 4 And again he measured a thousand, and he brought me through the water up to the knees. 5 And he measured a thousand, and he brought me through the water up to the loins. And he measured a thousand, and it was a torrent which I could not pass over, for the waters were risen so as to make a deep torrent which could not be passed over.

6 Et dixit ad me, "Certe vidisti, fili hominis." Et eduxit me et convertit ad ripam torrentis. 7 Cumque me convertissem, ecce: in ripa torrentis ligna multa nimis ex utraque parte. 8 Et ait ad me, "Aquae istae quae egrediuntur ad tumulos sabuli orientalis et descendunt ad plana deserti intrabunt mare et exibunt, et sanabuntur aquae. 9 Et omnis anima vivens quae serpit quocumque venerit torrens vivet, et erunt pisces multi satis postquam venerint illuc aquae istae, et sanabuntur, et vivent omnia ad quae venerit torrens. 10 Et stabunt super illa piscatores; ab Engaddi usque ad Engallim siccatio sagenarum erit; plurimae species erunt piscium eius, sicut pisces maris magni, multitudinis nimiae; 11 in litoribus autem eius et in palustribus non sanabuntur quia in salinas dabuntur. 12 Et super torrentem orietur in ripis eius ex utraque parte omne lignum pomiferum; non defluet folium ex eo, et non deficiet fructus eius; per singulos menses adferet primitiva, quia aquae eius de sanctuario egredientur; et erunt fructus eius in cibum, et folia eius ad medicinam."

13 "Haec dicit Dominus Deus: 'Hic est terminus in quo possidebitis terram in duodecim tribubus Israhel, quia Ioseph duplicem funiculum habet. 14 Possidebitis autem eam singuli aeque ut frater suus, super quam levavi manum meam ut darem patribus vestris, et cadet terra haec vobis in possessionem.

15 "'Hic est autem terminus terrae: ad plagam septen-

6 And he said to me, "Surely thou hast seen, O son of man." And he brought me out, and he caused me to turn to the bank of the torrent. 7 And when I had turned myself, behold: on the bank of the torrent were very many trees on both sides. 8 And he said to me, "These waters that issue forth toward the hillocks of sand to the east and go down to the plains of the desert shall go into the sea and shall go out, and the waters shall be healed. 9 And every living creature that creepeth whithersoever the torrent shall come shall live, and there shall be fishes in abundance after these waters shall come thither, and they shall be healed, and all things shall live to which the torrent shall come. 10 And the fishers shall stand over these *waters;* from En-gedi even to En-eglaim there shall be drying of nets: there shall be many sorts of the fishes thereof, as the fishes of the great sea, a very great multitude; 11 but on the shore thereof and in the fenny places they shall not be healed, because they shall be turned into saltpits. 12 And by the torrent on the banks thereof on both sides shall grow all trees that bear fruit; their leaf shall not fall off, and their fruit shall not fail; every month shall they bring forth firstfruits, because the waters thereof shall issue out of the sanctuary; and the fruits thereof shall be for food, and the leaves thereof for medicine."

13 "Thus saith the Lord God: 'This is the border by which you shall possess the land according to the twelve tribes of Israel, for Joseph hath a double portion. 14 And you shall possess it every man in like manner as his brother, concerning which I lifted up my hand to give it to your fathers, and this land shall fall unto you for a possession.

15 "'And this is the border of the land: toward the north

trionalem a mari magno via Hethalon venientibus Sadada, 16 Emath, Berotha, Sabarim, quae est inter terminum Damasci et confinium Emath, domus Tichon, quae est iuxta terminum Auran. 17 Et erit terminus a mari usque ad atrium Aenon terminus Damasci, et ab aquilone ad aquilonem terminus Emath, plaga septentrionalis.

18 "'Porro plaga orientalis de medio Auran et de medio Damasci et de medio Galaad et de medio terrae Israhel; Iordanis disterminans ad mare orientale. Metiemini etiam plagam orientalem.

19 "'Plaga autem australis meridiana a Thamar usque ad Aquas Contradictionis Cades et torrens usque ad mare magnum, et haec est plaga ad meridiem australis.

20 "'Et plaga maris mare magnum a confinio per directum donec venias Emath; haec est plaga maris

21 "'Et dividetis terram istam vobis per tribus Israhel, 22 et mittetis eam in hereditatem vobis et advenis qui accesserint ad vos qui genuerint filios in medio vestrum, et erunt vobis sicut indigenae inter filios Israhel; vobiscum divident possessionem in medio tribuum Israhel. 23 In tribu autem quacumque fuerit advena, ibi dabitis possessionem illi,' ait Dominus Deus."

side from the great sea by the way of Hethlon as men go to Zedad, 16 Hamath, Berothah, Sibraim, which is between the border of Damascus and the border of Hamath, the house of Ticon, which is by the border of Hauran. 17 And the border from the sea even to the court of Enon, shall be the border of Damascus, and from the north to the north, the border of Hamath; this is the north side.

18 "'And the east side is from the midst of Hauran and from the midst of Damascus and from the midst of Gilead and from the midst of the land of Israel, Jordan making the bound to the east sea; and thus you shall measure the east side.

19 "'And the south side southward is from Tamar even to the waters of contradiction of Kadesh and the torrent even to the great sea, and this is the south side southward.

20 "'And the side toward the sea is the great sea from the borders straight on till thou come to Hamath; this is the side of the sea.

21 "'And you shall divide this land unto you by the tribes of Israel, 22 and you shall divide it by lot for an inheritance to you and to the strangers that shall come over to you that shall beget children among you, and they shall be unto you as men of the same country born among the children of Israel; they shall divide the possession with you in the midst of the tribes of Israel. 23 And in what tribe soever the stranger shall be, there shall you give him possession,' saith the Lord God."

Caput 48

"'Et haec nomina tribuum a finibus aquilonis iuxta viam Aethlon pergentibus Emath:

"'Atrium Aenon, terminus Damasci ad aquilonem, iuxta viam Emath. Et erit ei plaga orientalis mare Dan una.

2 "'Et ad terminum Dan a plaga orientali usque ad plagam maris Aser una, 3 et super terminum Aser a plaga orientali usque ad plagam maris Nepthalim una.

4 "'Et super terminum Nepthalim a plaga orientali usque ad plagam maris Manasse una.

5 "'Et super terminum Manasse a plaga orientali usque ad plagam maris Ephraim una.

6 "'Et super terminum Ephraim a plaga orientali usque ad plagam maris Ruben una.

7 "'Et super terminum Ruben a plaga orientali usque ad plagam maris Iuda una.

8 "'Et super terminum Iuda a plaga orientali usque ad plagam maris erunt primitiae quas separabitis, viginti quinque milibus latitudinis et longitudinis sicuti singulae partes a

Chapter 48

The portions of the twelve tribes, of the sanctuary, of the
city and of the prince. The dimensions and gates of the city.

"'And these are the names of the tribes from the borders of the north by the way of Hethlon as they go to
Hamath:

"'The court of Enon, the border of Damascus northward,
by the way of Hamath. And from the east side thereof to the
sea shall be one portion for Dan.

2 "And by the border of Dan from the east side even to
the side of the sea one portion for Asher, 3 and by the border
of Asher from the east side even to the side of the sea one
portion for Naphtali.

4 "And by the border of Naphtali from the east side even
to the side of the sea one portion for Manasseh.

5 "And by the border of Manasseh from the east side even
to the side of the sea one portion for Ephraim.

6 "And by the border of Ephraim from the east side even
to the side of the sea one portion for Reuben.

7 "And by the border of Reuben, from the east side even
to the side of the sea, one portion for Judah.

8 "And by the border of Judah from the east side even to
the side of the sea shall be the firstfruits which you shall set
apart, five and twenty thousand in breadth and in length as
every one of the portions from the east side to the side of

plaga orientali usque ad plagam maris, et erit sanctuarium in medio eius. ⁹ Primitiae quas separastis Domino longitudo viginti quinque milibus et latitudo decem milibus.

¹⁰ "'Hae autem erunt primitiae sanctuarii sacerdotum: ad aquilonem longitudinis viginti quinque milia et ad mare latitudinis decem milia sed et ad orientem latitudinis decem milia et ad meridiem longitudinis viginti quinque milia, et erit sanctuarium Domini in medio eius.

¹¹ "'Sacerdotibus sanctuarium erit de filiis Sadoc, qui custodierunt caerimonias meas et non erraverunt cum errarent filii Israhel, sicut erraverunt et Levitae. ¹² Et erunt eis primitiae de primitiis terrae sanctum sanctorum iuxta terminum Levitarum.

¹³ "'Sed et Levitis similiter iuxta fines sacerdotum viginti quinque milia longitudinis et latitudinis decem milia. Omnis longitudo viginti et quinque milium, et latitudo decem milium. ¹⁴ Et non venundabunt ex eo neque mutabunt, nec transferentur primitiae terrae, quia sanctificatae sunt Domino. ¹⁵ Quinque milia autem quae supersunt in latitudine per viginti quinque milia profana erunt urbis in habitaculum et in suburbana, et erit civitas in medio eius.

¹⁶ "'Et heae mensurae eius: ad plagam septentrionalem quingenti et quattuor milia et ad plagam meridianam quingenti et quattuor milia et ad plagam orientalem quingenti et quattuor milia et ad plagam occidentalem quingenti et quattuor milia. ¹⁷ Erunt autem suburbana civitatis ad aquilonem ducenti quinquaginta et in meridie ducenti quinquaginta et

the sea, and the sanctuary shall be in the midst thereof. 9 The firstfruits which you shall set apart for the Lord shall be the length of five and twenty thousand and the breadth of ten thousand.

10 "And these shall be the firstfruits of the sanctuary for the priests: toward the north five and twenty thousand in length and toward the sea ten thousand in breadth and toward the east also ten thousand in breadth and toward the south five and twenty thousand in length, and the sanctuary of the Lord shall be in the midst thereof.

11 "'The sanctuary shall be for the priests of the sons of Zadok, who kept my ceremonies and went not astray when the children of Israel went astray, as the Levites also went astray. 12 And for them shall be the firstfruits of the firstfruits of the land holy of holies by the border of the Levites.

13 "And the Levites in like manner shall have by the borders of the priests five and twenty thousand in length and ten thousand in breadth. All the length shall be five and twenty thousand, and the breadth ten thousand. 14 And they shall not sell thereof nor exchange, neither shall the firstfruits of the land be alienated, because they are sanctified to the Lord. 15 But the five thousand that remain in the breadth over against the five and twenty thousand shall be a profane place for the city for dwelling and for suburbs, and the city shall be in the midst thereof.

16 "And these are the measures thereof: on the north side four thousand and five hundred and on the south side four thousand and five hundred and on the east side four thousand and five hundred and on the west side four thousand and five hundred. 17 And the suburbs of the city shall be to the north two hundred and fifty and to the south two hun-

ad orientem ducenti quinquaginta et ad mare ducenti quinquaginta. 18 Quod autem reliquum fuerit in longitudine secundum primitias sanctuarii, decem milia in orientem et decem milia ad occidentem, erunt sicut primitiae sanctuarii, et erunt fruges eius in panes his qui serviunt civitati. 19 Servientes autem civitati operabuntur ex omnibus tribubus Israhel.

20 "'Omnes primitiae viginti quinque milium per viginti quinque milia in quadrum separabuntur in primitias sanctuarii et in possessionem civitatis. 21 Quod autem reliquum fuerit principis erit ex omni parte primitiarum sanctuarii et possessionis civitatis e regione viginti quinque milium primitiarum usque ad terminum orientalem; sed et ad mare e regione viginti quinque milium usque ad terminum maris similiter in partibus principis erit, et erunt primitiae sanctuarii et sanctuarium templi in medio eius. 22 De possessione autem Levitarum et de possessione civitatis in medio partium principis, erit inter terminum Iuda et inter terminum Beniamin et ad principem pertinebit.

23 "'Et reliquis tribubus:

"'A plaga orientali usque ad plagam occidentalem Beniamin una.

24 "'Et contra terminum Beniamin a plaga orientali usque ad plagam occidentalem Symeon una.

25 "'Et super terminum Symeonis a plaga orientali usque ad plagam occidentis Isachar una.

26 "'Et super terminum Isachar a plaga orientali usque ad plagam occidentalem Zabulon una.

27 "'Et super terminum Zabulon a plaga orientali usque ad plagam maris Gad una.

dred and fifty and to the east two hundred and fifty and to the sea two hundred and fifty. 18 And the residue in length by the firstfruits of the sanctuary, ten thousand toward the east and ten thousand toward the west, shall be as the firstfruits of the sanctuary, and the fruits thereof shall be for bread to them that serve the city. 19 And they that serve the city shall serve it out of all the tribes of Israel.

20 "All the firstfruits of five and twenty thousand by five and twenty thousand foursquare shall be set apart for the firstfruits of the sanctuary and for the possession of the city. 21 And the residue shall be for the prince on every side of the firstfruits of the sanctuary and of the possession of the city over against the five and twenty thousand of the firstfruits unto the east border; toward the sea also over against the five and twenty thousand unto the border of the sea shall likewise be the portion of the prince, and the firstfruits of the sanctuary and the sanctuary of the temple shall be in the midst thereof. 22 And from the possession of the Levites and from the possession of the city which are in the midst of the prince's portions, what shall be to the border of Judah and to the border of Benjamin shall also belong to the prince.

23 "And for the rest of the tribes:

"From the east side to the west side one portion for Benjamin.

24 "And over against the border of Benjamin from the east side to the west side one portion for Simeon.

25 "And by the border of Simeon from the east side to the west side one portion for Issachar.

26 "And by the border of Issachar from the east side to the west side one portion for Zabulun.

27 "And by the border of Zabulun from the east side to the side of the sea one portion for Gad.

28 "'Et super terminum Gad ad plagam austri in meridiem; et erit finis de Thamar usque ad Aquas Contradictionis Cades, hereditas contra mare magnum. 29 Haec est terra quam mittetis in sortem tribubus Israhel, et hae partitiones earum,' ait Dominus Deus.

30 "Et hii egressus civitatis:

A plaga septentrionali quingentos et quattuor milia mensurabis. 31 Et portae civitatis in nominibus tribuum Israhel; portae tres a septentrione, porta Ruben una, porta Iudae una, porta Levi una. 32 Et ad plagam orientalem quingentos et quattuor milia, et portae tres: porta Ioseph una, porta Beniamin una, porta Dan una. 33 Et ad plagam meridianam quingentos et quattuor milia metieris; et portae tres: portam Symeonis unam, portam Isachar unam, portam Zabulon unam. 34 Et ad plagam occidentalem quingenti et quattuor milia et portae eorum tres: porta Gad una, porta Aser una, porta Nepthalim una. 35 Per circuitum decem et octo milia, et nomen civitatis ex illa die: Dominus Ibidem."

28 "'And by the border of Gad the south side southward; and the border shall be from Taamar even to the Waters of Contradiction of Kadesh, the inheritance over against the great sea. 29 This is the land which you shall divide by lot to the tribes of Israel, and these are the portions of them,' saith the Lord God.

30 "And these are the goings out of the city:

On the north side thou shalt measure four thousand and five hundred. 31 And the gates of the city according to the names of the tribes of Israel; three gates on the north side: the gate of Reuben one, the gate of Judah one, the gate of Levi one. 32 And at the east side four thousand and five hundred and three gates: the gate of Joseph one, the gate of Benjamin one, the gate of Dan one. 33 And at the south side thou shalt measure four thousand and five hundred; and three gates: the gate of Simeon one, the gate of Issachar one, the gate of Zabulun one. 34 And at the west side four thousand and five hundred and their three gates: the gate of Gad one, the gate of Asher one, the gate of Naphtali one. 35 Its circumference was eighteen thousand, and the name of the city from that day: The Lord is There."

DANIEL

Caput 1

Anno tertio regni Ioachim, regis Iuda, venit Nabuchodonosor, rex Babylonis, in Hierusalem et obsedit eam. 2 Et tradidit Dominus in manu eius Ioachim, regem Iudae, et partem vasorum domus Dei, et asportavit ea in terram Sennaar
in domum dei sui, et vasa intulit in domum thesauri dei sui.

3 Et ait rex Asfanaz, praeposito eunuchorum, ut introdu-
ceret de filiis Israhel et de semine regio et tyrannorum,
4 pueros in quibus nulla esset macula, decoros forma et eru-
ditos omni sapientia, cautos scientia et doctos disciplina et
qui possent stare in palatio regis, ut doceret eos litteras et
linguam Chaldeorum. 5 Et constituit eis rex annonam per
singulos dies de cibis suis et de vino unde bibebat ipse, ut
enutriti tribus annis, postea starent in conspectu regis.
6 Fuerunt ergo inter eos de filiis Iuda Danihel, Ananias, Misahel et Azarias. 7 Et inposuit eis praepositus eunuchorum

Chapter 1

Daniel and his companions are taken into the palace of the
king of Babylon. They abstain from his meat and wine and
succeed better with pulse and water. Their excellence and
wisdom.

In the third year of the reign of Jehoiakim, king of Judah,
Nebuchadnezzar, king of Babylon, came to Jerusalem and
besieged it. 2 And the Lord delivered into his hands Jehoiakim, the king of Judah, and part of the vessels of the house
of God, and he carried them away into the land of Shinar to
the house of his god, and the vessels he brought into the
treasure house of his god.

3 And the king spoke to Ashpenaz, the master of the eunuchs, that he should bring in *some* of the children of Israel
and of the king's seed and of the princes, 4 children in whom
there was no blemish, well favoured and skillful in all wisdom, cunning in knowledge and instructed in science and
such as might stand in the king's palace, that he might teach
them the learning and the tongue of the Chaldeans. 5 And
the king appointed them a daily provision of his own meat
and of the wine of which he drank himself, that being nourished three years, afterwards they might stand before the
king. 6 Now there were among them of the children of Judah
Daniel, Hananiah, Mishael and Azariah. 7 And the master of

nomina: Daniheli, Balthasar; Ananiae, Sedrac; Misaheli, Misac; et Azariae, Abdenago.

8 Proposuit autem Danihel in corde suo ne pollueretur de mensa regis neque de vino potus eius, et rogavit eunuchorum praepositum ne contaminaretur. 9 Dedit autem Deus Daniheli gratiam et misericordiam in conspectu principis eunuchorum.

10 Et ait princeps eunuchorum ad Danihel, "Timeo ego dominum meum, regem, qui constituit vobis cibum et potum, qui si viderit vultus vestros macilentiores prae ceteris adulescentibus, coaevis vestris, condemnabitis caput meum regi."

11 Et dixit Danihel ad Malassar, quem constituerat princeps eunuchorum super Danihel, Ananiam, Misahel et Azariam, 12 "Tempta, obsecro, servos tuos diebus decem, et dentur nobis legumina ad vescendum et aqua ad bibendum, 13 et contemplare vultus nostros et vultus puerorum qui vescuntur cibo regio, et sicut videris, facies cum servis tuis." 14 Qui audito sermone huiuscemodi temptavit eos diebus decem. 15 Post dies autem decem apparuerunt vultus eorum meliores et corpulentiores prae omnibus pueris qui vescebantur cibo regio. 16 Porro Malassar tollebat cibaria et vinum, potus eorum, dabatque eis legumina. 17 Pueris autem his dedit Deus scientiam et disciplinam in omni libro et sapientiam, Daniheli autem intellegentiam omnium visionum et somniorum.

18 Conpletis itaque diebus post quos dixerat rex ut introducerentur, introduxit eos praepositus eunuchorum in conspectu Nabuchodonosor. 19 Cumque locutus eis fuisset rex,

the eunuchs gave them names: to Daniel, Belteshazzar; to Hananiah, Shadrach; to Mishael, Meshach; and to Azariah, Abednego.

8 But Daniel purposed in his heart that he would not be defiled with the king's table nor with the wine which he drank, and he requested the master of the eunuchs that he might not be defiled. 9 And God gave to Daniel grace and mercy in the sight of the prince of the eunuchs.

10 And the prince of the eunuchs said to Daniel, "I fear my lord, the king, who hath appointed you meat and drink, who if he should see your faces leaner than those of the other youths, your equals, you shall endanger my head to the king."

11 And Daniel said to Melzar, whom the prince of the eunuchs had appointed over Daniel, Hananiah, Mishael and Azariah, 12 "Try, I beseech thee, thy servants for ten days, and let pulse be given us to eat and water to drink, 13 and look upon our faces and the faces of the children that eat of the king's meat, and as thou shalt see, *deal* with thy servants." 14 And when he had heard these words he tried them for ten days. 15 And after ten days their faces appeared fairer and fatter than all the children that ate of the king's meat. 16 So Melzar took their portions and the wine *that they should* drink, and he gave them pulse. 17 And to these children God gave knowledge and understanding in every book and wisdom, but to Daniel the understanding *also* of all visions and dreams.

18 And when the days were ended after which the king had ordered they should be brought in, the prince of the eunuchs brought them in before Nebuchadnezzar. 19 And when the king had spoken to them, there were not found

non sunt inventi de universis tales ut Danihel, Ananias, Misahel et Azarias, et steterunt in conspectu regis. 20 Et omne verbum sapientiae et intellectus quod sciscitatus est ab eis rex invenit in eis decuplum super cunctos ariolos et magos qui erant in universo regno eius. 21 Fuit autem Danihel usque ad annum primum Cyri Regis.

Caput 2

In anno secundo regni Nabuchodonosor, vidit Nabuchodonosor somnium, et conterritus est spiritus eius, et somnium eius fugit ab eo. 2 Praecepit autem rex ut convocarentur arioli et magi et malefici et Chaldei ut indicarent regi somnia sua, qui cum venissent steterunt coram rege.

3 Et dixit ad eos rex, "Vidi somnium, et mente confusus ignoro quid viderim."

4 Responderuntque Chaldei regi Syriace, "Rex, in sempiternum vive. Dic somnium servis tuis, et interpretationem eius indicabimus."

5 Et respondens rex ait Chaldeis, "Sermo recessit a me; nisi indicaveritis mihi somnium et coniecturam eius, peribi-

among them all such as Daniel, Hananiah, Mishael and Azariah, and they stood in the king's presence. 20 And in all matters of wisdom and understanding that the king inquired of
them he found them ten times better than all the diviners
and wise men that were in all his kingdom. 21 And Daniel
continued even to the first year of King Cyrus.

Chapter 2

Daniel by divine revelation declares the dream of Nebuchadnezzar and the interpretation of it. He is highly honoured by the king.

In the second year of the reign of Nebuchadnezzar, Nebuchadnezzar had a dream, and his spirit was terrified, and his
dream went out of *his mind*. 2 Then the king commanded to
call together the diviners and the wise men and the magi-
cians and the Chaldeans to declare to the king his dreams, *so
they came and* stood before the king.

3 And the king said to them, "I saw a dream, and being
troubled in mind I know not what I saw."

4 And the Chaldeans answered the king in Syriac, "O king,
live for ever. Tell to thy servants thy dream, and we will declare the interpretation thereof."

5 And the king, answering, said to the Chaldeans, "The
thing is gone out of *my mind;* unless you tell me the dream
and the meaning thereof, you shall be put to death, and your

tis vos, et domus vestrae publicabuntur. 6 Si autem somnium et coniecturam eius narraveritis, praemia et dona et honorem multum accipietis a me; somnium igitur et interpretationem eius indicate mihi."

7 Responderunt secundo atque dixerunt, "Rex somnium dicat servis suis, et interpretationem illius indicabimus."

8 Respondit rex et ait, "Certo novi quia tempus redimitis, scientes quod recesserit a me sermo. 9 Si ergo somnium non indicaveritis mihi, una est de vobis sententia: quod interpretationem quoque fallacem et deceptione plenam conposueritis, ut loquamini mihi donec tempus pertranseat. Somnium itaque dicite mihi ut sciam quod interpretationem quoque eius veram loquamini."

10 Respondentes ergo Chaldei coram rege dixerunt, "Non est homo super terram qui sermonem tuum, rex, possit implere, sed neque regum quisquam, magnus et potens, verbum huiuscemodi sciscitatur ab omni ariolo et mago et Chaldeo. 11 Sermo enim quem tu, rex, quaeris gravis est, nec repperietur quisquam qui indicet illum in conspectu regis exceptis dii, quorum non est cum hominibus conversatio."

12 Quo audito rex in furore et in ira magna praecepit ut perirent omnes sapientes Babylonis. 13 Et egressa sententia, sapientes interficiebantur quaerebanturque Danihel et socii eius ut perirent. 14 Tunc Danihel requisivit de lege atque sententia ab Arioch, principe militiae regis, qui egressus fuerat ad interficiendos sapientes Babylonis. 15 Et interrogavit eum qui a rege acceperat potestatem quam ob causam tam crudelis sententia a facie esset regis egressa. Cum ergo rem indi-

houses shall be confiscated. 6 But if you tell the dream and the meaning of it, you shall receive of me rewards and gifts and great honour; therefore tell me the dream and the interpretation thereof."

7 They answered again and said, "Let the king tell his servants the dream, and we will declare the interpretation of it."

8 The king answered and said, "I know for certain that you *seek to* gain time, since you know that the thing is gone from me. 9 If therefore you tell me not the dream, there is one sentence concerning you: that you have also framed a lying interpretation and full of deceit, to speak before me till the time pass away. Tell me therefore the dream that I may know that you also give a true interpretation thereof."

10 Then the Chaldeans answered before the king and said, "There is no man upon earth that can accomplish thy word, O king, *neither* doth any king, though great and mighty, ask such a thing of any diviner *or* wise man *or* Chaldean. 11 For the thing that thou askest, O king, is difficult, nor *can* any one be found that can shew it before the king except the gods, whose conversation is not with men."

12 Upon hearing this the king in fury and in great wrath commanded that all the wise men of Babylon should be put to death. 13 And the decree being gone forth, the wise men were slain, and Daniel and his companions were sought for to be put to death. 14 Then Daniel inquired concerning the law and the sentence of Arioch, the general of the king's army, who was gone forth to kill the wise men of Babylon. 15 And he asked him that had received the orders of the king why so cruel a sentence was gone forth from the face of the king. And when Arioch had told the matter to

casset Arioch Daniheli, 16 Danihel ingressus rogavit regem ut tempus daret sibi ad solutionem indicandam regi.

17 At ingressus est domum suam Ananiaeque et Misaheli et Azariae, sociis suis, indicavit negotium 18 ut quaererent misericordiam a facie Dei caeli super sacramento isto et non perirent Danihel et socii eius cum ceteris sapientibus Babylonis. 19 Tunc Daniheli per visionem nocte mysterium revelatum est, et Danihel benedixit Deo caeli, 20 et locutus ait, "Sit nomen Domini benedictum a saeculo et usque in saeculum, quia sapientia et fortitudo eius sunt. 21 Et ipse mutat tempora et aetates, transfert regna atque constituit, dat sapientiam sapientibus et scientiam intellegentibus disciplinam. 22 Ipse revelat profunda et abscondita et novit in tenebris constituta, et lux cum eo est. 23 Tibi, Deus patrum nostrorum, confiteor, teque laudo, quia sapientiam et fortitudinem dedisti mihi et nunc ostendisti mihi quae rogavimus te, quia sermonem regis aperuisti nobis."

24 Post haec Danihel ingressus ad Arioch, quem constituerat rex ut perderet sapientes Babylonis, sic ei locutus est: "Sapientes Babylonis ne perdas; introduc me in conspectu regis, et solutionem regi enarrabo."

25 Tunc Arioch festinus introduxit Danihelem ad regem et dixit ei, "Inveni hominem de filiis transmigrationis Iudae qui solutionem regi adnuntiet."

26 Respondit rex et dixit Daniheli, cuius nomen erat Balthasar, "Putasne vere potes indicare mihi somnium quod vidi et interpretationem eius?"

Daniel, 16 Daniel went in and desired of the king that he would give him time to *resolve the question and* declare it to the king.

17 And he went into his house and told the matter to Hananiah and Mishael and Azariah, his companions 18 to the end that they should ask mercy at the face of the God of heaven concerning this secret and that Daniel and his companions might not perish with the rest of the wise men of Babylon. 19 Then was the mystery revealed to Daniel by a vision in the night, and Daniel blessed the God of heaven, 20 and speaking he said, "Blessed be the name of the Lord from eternity and for evermore, for wisdom and fortitude are his. 21 And he changeth times and ages, taketh away kingdoms and establisheth them, giveth wisdom to the wise and knowledge to them that have understanding. 22 He revealeth deep and hidden things and knoweth what is in darkness, and light is with him. 23 To thee, O God of our fathers, I give thanks, and I praise thee, because thou hast given me wisdom and strength and now thou hast shewn me what we desired of thee, for thou hast made known to us the king's discourse."

24 After this Daniel went in to Arioch, to whom the king had given orders to destroy the wise men of Babylon, and he spoke thus to him: "Destroy not the wise men of Babylon; bring me in before the king, and I will tell the solution to the king."

25 Then Arioch in haste brought in Daniel to the king and said to him, "I have found a man of the children of the captivity of Judah that will resolve the question to the king."

26 The king answered and said to Daniel, whose name was Belteshazzar, "Thinkest thou indeed that thou canst tell me the dream that I saw and the interpretation thereof?"

27 Et respondens Danihel coram rege ait, "Mysterium quod rex interrogat sapientes magi et arioli et aruspices non queunt indicare regi. 28 Sed est Deus in caelo revelans mysteria, qui indicavit tibi, Rex Nabuchodonosor, quae ventura sunt novissimis temporibus. Somnium tuum et visiones capitis tui in cubili tuo huiuscemodi sunt: 29 tu, rex, cogitare coepisti in stratu tuo quid esset futurum post haec, et qui revelat mysteria ostendit tibi quae ventura sunt. 30 Mihi quoque non in sapientia quae est in me plus quam in cunctis viventibus sacramentum hoc revelatum est sed ut interpretatio regi manifesta fieret et cogitationes mentis tuae scires.

31 "Tu, rex, videbas, et ecce: quasi statua una grandis; statua illa, magna et statura sublimis, stabat contra te, et intuitus eius erat terribilis. 32 Huius statuae caput ex auro optimo erat, pectus autem et brachia de argento, porro venter et femora ex aere, 33 tibiae autem ferreae; pedum quaedam pars erat ferrea, quaedam autem fictilis. 34 Videbas ita donec abscisus est lapis de monte sine manibus et percussit statuam in pedibus eius ferreis et fictilibus et comminuit eos. 35 Tunc contrita sunt pariter ferrum, testa, aes, argentum et aurum et redacta quasi in favillam aestivae areae, quae rapta sunt vento, nullusque locus inventus est eis, lapis autem qui percussit statuam factus est mons magnus et implevit universam terram.

36 "Hoc est somnium; interpretationem quoque eius dicemus coram te, rex. 37 Tu rex regum es, et Deus caeli regnum

27 And Daniel made answer before the king and said, "The secret that the king desireth to know none of the wise men or the philosophers or the diviners or the soothsayers can declare to the king. 28 But there is a God in heaven that revealeth mysteries, who hath shewn to thee, O King Nebuchadnezzar, what is to come to pass in the latter times. Thy dream and the visions of thy head upon thy bed are these: 29 thou, O king, didst begin to think in thy bed what should come to pass hereafter, and he that revealeth mysteries shewed thee what shall come to pass. 30 To me also this secret is revealed, not by any wisdom that I have more than all men alive but that the interpretation might be made manifest to the king and thou mightest know the thoughts of thy mind.

31 "Thou, O king, sawest, and behold: there was as it were a great statue; this statue, which was great and high, *tall* of stature, stood before thee, and the look thereof was terrible. 32 The head of this statue was of fine gold, but the breast and the arms of silver, and the belly and the thighs of brass, 33 and the legs of iron, the feet part of iron and part of clay. 34 Thus thou sawest till a stone was cut out of a mountain without hands and it struck the statue upon the feet thereof that were of iron and of clay and broke them in pieces. 35 Then was the iron, the clay, the brass, the silver and the gold broken to pieces together and became like the chaff of a summer's threshingfloor, and they were carried away by the wind, and there was no place found for them, but the stone that struck the statue became a great mountain and filled the whole earth.

36 "This is the dream; we will also tell the interpretation thereof before thee, O king. 37 Thou art a king of kings, and

et fortitudinem et imperium et gloriam dedit tibi 38 et omnia in quibus habitant filii hominum et bestiae agri; volucres quoque caeli dedit in manu tua et sub dicione tua universa constituit; tu es ergo caput aureum. 39 Et post te consurget regnum aliud, minus te, argenteum et regnum tertium aliud aereum, quod imperabit universae terrae. 40 Et regnum quartum erit velut ferrum. Quomodo ferrum comminuit et domat omnia, sic comminuet omnia haec et conteret. 41 Porro quia vidisti pedum et digitorum, partem testae figuli et partem ferream, regnum divisum erit, quod tamen de plantario ferri orietur secundum quod vidisti ferrum mixtum testae ex luto. 42 Et digitos pedum ex parte ferreos et ex parte fictiles; ex parte regnum erit solidum et ex parte contritum. 43 Quia autem vidisti ferrum mixtum testae ex luto, commiscebuntur quidem humano semine, sed non adherebunt sibi sicuti ferrum misceri non potest testae. 44 In diebus autem regnorum illorum suscitabit Deus caeli regnum quod in aeternum non dissipabitur, et regnum eius populo alteri non tradetur, comminuet autem et consumet universa regna haec et ipsum stabit in aeternum. 45 Secundum quod vidisti quod de monte abscisus est lapis sine manibus et comminuit testam et ferrum et aes et argentum et aurum, Deus magnus ostendit regi quae ventura sunt postea, et verum est somnium, et fidelis interpretatio eius."

46 Tunc Rex Nabuchodonosor cecidit in faciem suam et Danihelum adoravit et hostias et incensum praecepit ut sa-

the God of heaven hath given thee a kingdom and strength and power and glory 38 and all places wherein the children of men and the beasts of the field do dwell; he hath also given the birds of the air into thy hand and hath put all things under thy power; thou therefore art the head of gold. 39 And after thee shall rise up another kingdom, inferior to thee, of silver, and another third kingdom of brass, which shall rule over all the world. 40 And the fourth kingdom shall be as iron. As iron breaketh into pieces and subdueth all things, so shall that break and destroy all these. 41 And whereas thou sawest the feet and the toes, part of potter's clay and part of iron, the kingdom shall be divided, but yet it shall take its origin from the *iron* according as thou sawest the iron mixed with the miry clay. 42 And *as* the toes of the feet *were* part of iron and part of clay, the kingdom shall be partly strong and partly broken. 43 And whereas thou sawest the iron mixed with miry clay, they shall be mingled indeed together with the seed of man, but they shall not stick fast one to another as iron cannot be mixed with clay. 44 But in the days of those kingdoms the God of heaven will set up a kingdom that shall never be destroyed, and his kingdom shall not be delivered up to another people, and it shall break in pieces and shall consume all these kingdoms and itself shall stand for ever. 45 According as thou sawest that the stone was cut out of the mountain without hands and broke in pieces the clay and the iron and the brass and the silver and the gold, the great God hath shewn the king what shall come to pass hereafter, and the dream is true, and the interpretation thereof is faithful."

46 Then King Nebuchadnezzar fell on his face and worshipped Daniel and commanded that they should offer in

crificarent ei. [47] Loquens ergo rex ait Daniheli, "Vere Deus vester Deus deorum est et Dominus regum et revelans mysteria, quoniam potuisti aperire sacramentum hoc." [48] Tunc rex Danihelum in sublime extulit et munera multa et magna dedit ei, et constituit eum principem super omnes provincias Babylonis et praefectum magistratuum super cunctos sapientes Babylonis. [49] Danihel autem postulavit a rege, et constituit super opera provinciae Babylonis Sedrac, Misac et Abdenago, ipse autem Danihel erat in foribus regis.

Caput 3

Nabuchodonosor Rex fecit statuam auream altitudine cubitorum sexaginta, latitudine cubitorum sex, et statuit eam in campo Dura provinciae Babylonis. [2] Itaque Nabuchodonosor, rex, misit ad congregandos satrapas, magistratus et iudices, duces et tyrannos et praefectos omnesque principes regionum ut convenirent ad dedicationem statuae quam erexerat Nabuchodonosor Rex. [3] Tunc congregati sunt

sacrifice to him victims and incense. 47 And the king spoke to Daniel and said, "Verily your God is the God of gods and Lord of kings and a revealer of hidden things, seeing thou couldst discover this secret." 48 Then the king advanced Daniel to a high station and gave him many and great gifts, and he made him governor over all the provinces of Babylon and chief of the magistrates over all the wise men of Babylon. 49 And Daniel requested of the king, and he appointed Shadrach, Meshach and Abednego over the works of the province of Babylon, but Daniel himself was in the king's palace.

Chapter 3

Nebuchadnezzar set up a golden statue, which he commands all to adore. The three children for refusing to do it are cast into the fiery furnace, but are not hurt by the flames. Their prayer and canticle of praise.

King Nebuchadnezzar made a statue of gold of sixty cubits high *and* six cubits broad, and he set it up in the plain of Dura of the province of Babylon. 2 Then Nebuchadnezzar, the king, sent to call together the nobles, the magistrates and the judges, the captains, *the* rulers and governors and all the chief men of the provinces to come to the dedication of the statue which King Nebuchadnezzar had set up. 3 Then

satrapae, magistratus et iudices, duces et tyranni et optimates qui erant in potestatibus constituti et universi principes
regionum ut convenirent ad dedicationem statuae quam
erexerat Nabuchodonosor Rex. Stabant autem in conspectu
statuae quam posuerat Nabuchodonosor Rex.

4 Et praeco clamabat valenter, "Vobis dicitur, populis, tribubus et linguis, 5 in hora qua audieritis sonitum tubae et
fistulae et citharae, sambucae et psalterii et symphoniae et
universi generis musicorum, cadentes adorate statuam
auream quam constituit Nabuchodonosor Rex. 6 Si quis autem non prostratus adoraverit, eadem hora mittetur in fornacem ignis ardentis." 7 Post haec igitur, statim ut audierunt
omnes populi sonitum tubae, fistulae et citharae, sambucae
et psalterii, symphoniae et omnis generis musicorum, cadentes omnes populi, tribus et linguae adoraverunt statuam
auream quam constituerat Nabuchodonosor Rex.

8 Statimque in ipso tempore accedentes viri Chaldei
accusaverunt Iudaeos 9 dixeruntque Nabuchodonosor Regi,
"Rex, in aeternum vive. 10 Tu, rex, posuisti decretum ut omnis homo qui audierit sonitum tubae, fistulae et citharae,
sambucae et psalterii et symphoniae et universi generis musicorum, prosternat se et adoret statuam auream, 11 si quis
autem non procidens adoraverit, mittatur in fornacem ignis
ardentis. 12 Sunt ergo viri Iudaei quos constituisti super
opera regionis Babylonis: Sedrac, Misac et Abdenago; viri

the nobles, the magistrates and the judges, the captains and rulers and the great men that were placed in authority and all the princes of the provinces were gathered together to come to the dedication of the statue which King Nebuchadnezzar had set up. And they stood before the statue which King Nebuchadnezzar had set up.

4 Then a herald cried with a strong voice, "To you it is commanded, O nations, tribes and languages, 5 that in the hour that you shall hear the sound of the trumpet and of the flute and of the harp, of the sackbut and of the psaltery and of the symphony and of all kind of music, ye fall down and adore the golden statue which King Nebuchadnezzar hath set up. 6 But if any man shall not fall down and adore, he shall the same hour be cast into a furnace of burning fire." 7 Upon this therefore, at the time when all the people heard the sound of the trumpet, the flute and the harp, of the sackbut and the psaltery, of the symphony and of all kind of music, all the nations, tribes and languages fell down and adored the golden statue which King Nebuchadnezzar had set up.

8 And presently at that very time some Chaldeans came and accused the Jews 9 and said to King Nebuchadnezzar, "O king, live for ever. 10 Thou, O king, hast made a decree that every man that shall hear the sound of the trumpet, the flute and the harp, of the sackbut and the psaltery, *of* the symphony and of all kind of music, shall prostrate himself and adore the golden statue, 11 and that if any man shall not fall down and adore, he should be cast into a furnace of burning fire. 12 Now there are certain Jews whom thou hast set over the works of the province of Babylon: Shadrach, Meshach and Abednego; these men, O king, have slighted thy

isti contempserunt, rex, decretum tuum: deos tuos non colunt, et statuam auream quam erexisti non adorant."

13 Tunc Nabuchodonosor in furore et in ira praecepit ut adducerentur Sedrac, Misac et Abdenago, qui confestim adducti sunt in conspectu regis. 14 Pronuntiansque Nabuchodonosor, rex, ait eis, "Verene, Sedrac, Misac et Abdenago, deos meos non colitis et statuam auream quam constitui non adoratis? 15 Nunc ergo si estis parati quacumque hora audieritis sonitum tubae, fistulae, citharae, sambucae et psalterii et symphoniae omnisque generis musicorum, prosternite vos et adorate statuam quam feci; quod si non adoraveritis, eadem hora mittemini in fornacem ignis ardentis, et quis est Deus qui eripiet vos de manu mea?"

16 Respondentes Sedrac, Misac et Abdenago dixerunt Regi Nabuchodonosor, "Non oportet nos de hac re respondere tibi. 17 Ecce enim: Deus noster quem colimus potest eripere nos de camino ignis ardentis et de manibus tuis, rex, liberare. 18 Quod si noluerit, notum tibi sit, rex, quia deos tuos non colimus et statuam auream quam erexisti non adoramus."

19 Tunc Nabuchodonosor repletus est furore, et aspectus faciei illius inmutatus est super Sedrac, Misac et Abdenago, et praecepit ut succenderetur fornax septuplum quam succendi consuerat. 20 Et viris fortissimis de exercitu suo iussit ut ligatis pedibus Sedrac, Misac et Abdenago mitterent eos in fornacem ignis ardentis. 21 Et confestim viri illi vincti cum

decree: they worship not thy gods, nor do they adore the golden statue which thou hast set up."

13 Then Nebuchadnezzar in fury and in wrath commanded that Shadrach, Meshach and Abednego should be brought, who immediately were brought before the king. 14 And Nebuchadnezzar, the king, spoke to them, and said, "Is it true, O Shadrach, Meshach and Abednego, that you do not worship my gods nor adore the golden statue that I have set up? 15 Now therefore if you be ready at what hour soever you shall hear the sound of the trumpet, flute, harp, sackbut and psaltery and symphony and of all kind of music, prostrate yourselves and adore the statue which I have made; but if you do not adore, you shall be cast the same hour into the furnace of burning fire, and who is the God that shall deliver you out of my hand?"

16 Shadrach, Meshach and Abednego answered and said to King Nebuchadnezzar, "We have no occasion to answer thee concerning this matter. 17 For behold: our God whom we worship is able to save us from the furnace of burning fire and to deliver us out of thy hands, O king. 18 But if he will not, be it known to thee, O king, that we will not worship thy gods nor adore the golden statue which thou hast set up."

19 Then was Nebuchadnezzar filled with fury, and the countenance of his face was changed against Shadrach, Meshach and Abednego, and he commanded that the furnace should be heated seven times more than it had been accustomed to be heated. 20 And he commanded the strongest men that were in his army to bind the feet of Shadrach, Meshach and Abednego and to cast them into the furnace of burning fire. 21 And immediately these men were bound and

bracis suis et tiaris et calciamentis et vestibus missi sunt in fornacem ignis ardentis. 22 Nam iussio regis urguebat, fornax autem succensa erat nimis. Porro viros illos qui miserant Sedrac, Misac et Abdenago interfecit flamma ignis. 23 Viri autem hii tres, id est, Sedrac, Misac et Abdenago, ceciderunt in medio camini ignis ardentis conligati.

Quae sequuntur in Hebraicis voluminibus non repperi.

24 Et ambulabant in medio flammae laudantes Deum et benedicentes Domino. 25 Stans autem Azarias oravit sic, aperiensque os suum in medio ignis ait, 26 "Benedictus es, Domine, Deus patrum nostrorum, et laudabilis et gloriosum nomen tuum in saecula, 27 quia iustus es in omnibus quae fecisti nobis et universa opera tua vera et viae tuae rectae et omnia iudicia tua vera. 28 Iudicia enim vera fecisti iuxta omnia quae induxisti super nos et super civitatem sanctam patrum nostrorum, Hierusalem, quia in veritate et in iudicio induxisti omnia haec propter peccata nostra. 29 Peccavimus enim et inique egimus recedentes a te, et deliquimus in omnibus, 30 et praecepta tua non audivimus, nec observavimus nec fecimus sicut praeceperas nobis ut bene nobis esset. 31 Omnia ergo quae induxisti super nos et universa quae fecisti nobis vero iudicio fecisti, 32 et tradidisti nos in manibus inimicorum nostrorum iniquorum et pessimorum praevaricatorumque et regi iniusto et pessimo ultra omnem terram. 33 Et nunc non possumus aperire os; confusio et obprobrium facti sumus servis tuis et his qui colunt te.

were cast into the furnace of burning fire with their coats and their caps and their shoes and their garments. 22 For the king's commandment was urgent, and the furnace was heated exceedingly. And the flame of the fire slew those men that had cast in Shadrach, Meshach and Abednego. 23 But these three men, that is, Shadrach, Meshach and Abednego, fell down bound in the midst of the furnace of burning fire.

That which followeth I found not in the Hebrew volumes.

24 And they walked in the midst of the flame praising God and blessing the Lord. 25 Then Azariah standing up prayed in this manner, and opening his mouth in the midst of the fire he said, 26 "Blessed art thou, O Lord, the God of our fathers, and thy name is worthy of praise and glorious for ever, 27 for thou art just in all that thou hast done to us and all thy works are true and thy ways right and all thy judgments true. 28 For thou hast executed true judgments in all the things that thou hast brought upon us and upon Jerusalem, the holy city of our fathers, for according to truth and judgment thou hast brought all these things upon us for our sins. 29 For we have sinned and committed iniquity departing from thee, and we have trespassed in all things, 30 and we have not hearkened to thy commandments, nor have we observed nor done as thou hadst commanded us that it might go well with us. 31 Wherefore all that thou hast brought upon us and every thing that thou hast done to us thou hast done in true judgment, 32 and thou hast delivered us into the hands of our enemies that are unjust and most wicked and prevaricators and to a king unjust and most wicked beyond all *that are upon* the earth. 33 And now we cannot open our mouths; we are become a shame and reproach to thy servants and to them that worship thee.

34 "Ne, quaesumus, tradas nos in perpetuum propter nomen tuum, et ne dissipes testamentum tuum. 35 Neque auferas misericordiam tuam a nobis propter Abraham, dilectum tuum, et Isaac, servum tuum, et Israhel, sanctum tuum, 36 quibus locutus es, pollicens quod multiplicares semen eorum sicut stellas caeli et sicut harenam quae est in litore maris. 37 Quia, Domine, inminuti sumus plus quam omnes gentes sumusque humiles in universa terra hodie propter peccata nostra. 38 Et non est in tempore hoc princeps et propheta et dux neque holocaustum neque sacrificium neque oblatio neque incensum neque locus primitiarum coram te 39 ut possimus invenire misericordiam tuam; sed in anima contrita et spiritu humilitatis suscipiamur. 40 Sicut in holocausto arietum et taurorum et sicut in milibus agnorum pinguium, sic fiat sacrificium nostrum in conspectu tuo hodie ut placeat tibi, quoniam non est confusio confidentibus in te.

41 "Et nunc sequimur te in toto corde, et timemus te et quaerimus faciem tuam. 42 Ne confundas nos, sed fac nobiscum iuxta mansuetudinem tuam et secundum multitudinem misericordiae tuae. 43 Et erue nos in mirabilibus tuis, et da gloriam nomini tuo, Domine, 44 et confundantur omnes qui ostendunt servis tuis mala; confundantur in omni potentia tua, et robur eorum conteratur. 45 Et sciant quia tu es Domine, Deus solus, et gloriosus super orbem terrarum."

46 Et non cessabant qui inmiserant eos ministri regis succendere fornacem naptha et stuppa et pice et malleolis, 47 et effundebatur flamma super fornacem cubitis quadraginta novem, 48 et erupit et incendit quos repperit iuxta fornacem

34 "Deliver us not up for ever, we beseech thee, for thy name's sake, and abolish not thy covenant. 35 And take not away thy mercy from us for the sake of Abraham, thy beloved, and Isaac, thy servant, and Israel, thy holy one, 36 to whom thou hast spoken, promising that thou wouldst multiply their seed as the stars of heaven and as the sand that is on the sea shore. 37 For we, O Lord, are diminished more than any nation and are brought low in all the earth this day for our sins. 38 Neither is there at this time prince *or* leader *or* prophet *or* holocaust *or* sacrifice *or* oblation *or* incense *or* place of firstfruits before thee 39 that we may find thy mercy; nevertheless in a contrite heart and humble spirit let us be accepted. 40 As in holocausts of rams and bullocks and as in thousands of fat lambs, so let our sacrifice be made in thy sight this day that it may please thee, for there is no confusion to them that trust in thee.

41 "And now we follow thee with all our heart, and we fear thee and seek thy face. 42 Put us not to confusion, but deal with us according to thy meekness and according to the multitude of thy mercies. 43 And deliver us *according to* thy wonderful works, and give glory to thy name, O Lord, 44 and let all them be confounded that shew evils to thy servants; let them be confounded in all thy might, and let their strength be broken. 45 And let them know that thou art the Lord, the only God, and glorious over all the world."

46 Now the king's servants that had cast them in ceased not to heat the furnace with brimstone and tow and pitch and dry sticks, 47 and the flame mounted up above the furnace nine and forty cubits, 48 and it broke forth and burnt

de Chaldeis. 49 Angelus autem Domini descendit cum Azaria et sociis eius in fornacem, et excussit flammam ignis de
fornace, 50 et fecit medium fornacis quasi ventum roris flan-
tem, et non tetigit eos omnino ignis neque contristavit nec
quicquam molestiae intulit.

51 Tunc hii tres quasi ex uno ore laudabant et glorificabant
et benedicebant Deo in fornace, dicentes, 52 "Benedictus es,
Domine, Deus patrum nostrorum, et laudabilis et gloriosus
et superexaltatus in saecula, et benedictum nomen gloriae
tuae sanctum et laudabile et superexaltatum in omnibus saeculis. 53 Benedictus es in templo sancto gloriae tuae et superlaudabilis et supergloriosus in saecula. 54 Benedictus es in
throno regni tui et superlaudabilis et superexaltatus in saecula. 55 Benedictus es qui intueris abyssos et sedes super
cherubin et laudabilis et superexaltatus in saecula. 56 Benedictus es in firmamento caeli et laudabilis et gloriosus in saecula.

57 "Benedicite, omnia opera Domini, Domino; laudate et
superexaltate eum in saecula. 58 Benedicite, angeli Domini,
Domino; laudate et superexaltate eum in saecula. 59 Benedicite, caeli, Domino; laudate et superexaltate eum in saecula.
60 Benedicite, aquae omnes quae super caelos sunt, Domino;
laudate et superexaltate eum in saecula. 61 Benedicite, omnes virtutes Domini, Domino; laudate et superexaltate eum
in saecula. 62 Benedicite, sol et luna, Domino; laudate et superexaltate eum in saecula. 63 Benedicite, stellae caeli, Do-

such of the Chaldeans as it found near the furnace. 49 But the angel of the Lord went down with Azariah and his companions into the furnace, and he drove the flame of the fire out of the furnace, 50 and made the midst of the furnace like the blowing of a wind bringing dew, and the fire touched them not at all nor troubled them nor did them any harm.

51 Then these three as with one mouth praised and glorified and blessed God in the furnace, saying, 52 "Blessed art thou, O Lord, the God of our fathers, and worthy to be praised and glorified and exalted above all for ever, and blessed is the holy name of thy glory and worthy to be praised and exalted above all in all ages. 53 Blessed art thou in the holy temple of thy glory and exceedingly to be praised and exceeding glorious for ever. 54 Blessed art thou on the throne of thy kingdom and exceedingly to be praised and exalted above all for ever. 55 Blessed art thou that beholdest the depths and sittest upon the cherubims and worthy to be praised and exalted above all for ever. 56 Blessed art thou in the firmament of heaven and worthy of praise and glorious for ever.

57 "All ye works of the Lord, bless the Lord; praise and exalt him above all for ever. 58 O ye angels of the Lord, bless the Lord; praise and exalt him above all for ever. 59 O ye heavens, bless the Lord; praise and exalt him above all for ever. 60 O all ye waters that are above the heavens, bless the Lord; praise and exalt him above all for ever. 61 O all ye powers of the Lord, bless the Lord; praise and exalt him above all for ever. 62 O ye sun and moon, bless the Lord; praise and exalt him above all for ever. 63 O ye stars of heaven, bless

mino; laudate et superexaltate eum in saecula. 64 Benedicite, omnis imber et ros, Domino; laudate et superexaltate eum in saecula. 65 Benedicite, omnis spiritus Dei, Domino; laudate et superexaltate eum in saecula. 66 Benedicite, ignis et aestus, Domino; laudate et superexaltate eum in saecula. 67 Benedicite, frigus et aestus, Domino; laudate et superexaltate eum in saecula. 68 Benedicite, rores et pruina, Domino; laudate et superexaltate eum in saecula. 69 Benedicite, gelu et frigus, Domino; laudate et superexaltate eum in saecula. 70 Benedicite, glacies et nives, Domino; laudate et superexaltate eum in saecula. 71 Benedicite, noctes et dies, Domino; laudate et superexaltate eum in saecula. 72 Benedicite, lux et tenebrae, Domino; laudate et superexaltate eum in saecula. 73 Benedicite, fulgura et nubes, Domino; laudate et superexaltate eum in saecula.

74 "Benedicat terra Dominum; laudet et superexaltet eum in saecula. 75 Benedicite, montes et colles, Domino; laudate et superexaltate eum in saecula. 76 Benedicite, universa germinantia in terra, Domino; laudate et superexaltate eum in saecula. 77 Benedicite, fontes, Domino; laudate et superexaltate eum in saecula. 78 Benedicite, maria et flumina, Domino; laudate et superexaltate eum in saecula. 79 Benedicite, cete et omnia quae moventur in aquis, Domino; laudate et superexaltate eum in saecula. 80 Benedicite, omnes volucres caeli, Domino; laudate et superexaltate eum in saecula. 81 Benedicite, omnes bestiae et pecora, Domino; laudate et superexaltate eum in saecula.

82 "Benedicite, filii hominum, Domino; laudate et superexaltate eum in saecula. 83 Benedicat Israhel Dominum; laudet et superexaltet eum in saecula. 84 Benedicite, sacerdotes

the Lord; praise and exalt him above all for ever. 64 O every shower and dew, bless ye the Lord; praise and exalt him above all for ever. 65 O all ye spirits of God, bless the Lord; praise and exalt him above all for ever. 66 O ye fire and heat, bless the Lord; praise and exalt him above all for ever. 67 O ye cold and heat, bless the Lord; praise and exalt him above all for ever. 68 O ye dews and hoar frosts, bless the Lord; praise and exalt him above all for ever. 69 O ye frost and cold, bless the Lord; praise and exalt him above all for ever. 70 O ye ice and snow, bless the Lord; praise and exalt him above all for ever. 71 O ye nights and days, bless the Lord; praise and exalt him above all for ever. 72 O ye light and darkness, bless the Lord; praise and exalt him above all for ever. 73 O ye lightnings and clouds, bless the Lord; praise and exalt him above all for ever.

74 "O let the earth bless the Lord; let it praise and exalt him above all for ever. 75 O ye mountains and hills, bless the Lord; praise and exalt him above all for ever. 76 O all ye things that spring up in the earth, bless the Lord; praise and exalt him above all for ever. 77 O ye fountains, bless the Lord; praise and exalt him above all for ever. 78 O ye seas and rivers, bless the Lord; praise and exalt him above all for ever. 79 O ye whales and all that move in the waters, bless the Lord; praise and exalt him above all for ever. 80 O all ye fowls of the air, bless the Lord; praise and exalt him above all for ever. 81 O all ye beasts and cattle, bless the Lord; praise and exalt him above all for ever.

82 "O ye sons of men, bless the Lord; praise and exalt him above all for ever. 83 O let Israel bless the Lord; let them praise and exalt him above all for ever. 84 O ye priests of the

Domini, Domino; laudate et superexaltate eum in saecula.
85 Benedicite, servi Domini, Domino; laudate et superexaltate eum in saecula. 86 Benedicite, spiritus et animae iustorum, Domino; laudate et superexaltate eum in saecula. 87 Benedicite, sancti et humiles corde, Domino; laudate et superexaltate eum in saecula. 88 Benedicite, Anania, Azaria et Misahel, Domino; laudate et superexaltate eum in saecula. Quia eruit nos de inferno et salvos fecit de manu mortis et liberavit nos de medio ardentis flammae et de medio ignis eruit nos. 89 Confitemini Domino quoniam bonus, quoniam in saeculum misericordia eius. 90 Benedicite, omnes religiosi, Domino, Deo deorum; laudate, et confitemini ei quia in omnia saecula misericordia eius."

Hucusque non habetur in Hebraeo, et quae posuimus de Theodotionis editione translata sunt.

91 Tunc Nabuchodonosor, rex, obstipuit et surrexit propere et ait optimatibus suis, "Nonne tres viros misimus in medium ignis conpeditos?"

Qui respondentes dixerunt regi, "Vere, rex."

92 Respondit et ait, "Ecce: ego video viros quattuor solutos et ambulantes in medio ignis, et nihil corruptionis in eis est, et species quarti similis filio Dei." 93 Tunc accessit Nabuchodonosor ad ostium fornacis ignis ardentis et ait, "Sedrac, Misac et Abdenago, servi Dei excelsi, egredimini, et venite." Statimque egressi sunt Sedrac, Misac et Abdenago de medio ignis. 94 Et congregati satrapae et magistra-

Lord, bless the Lord; praise and exalt him above all for ever. 85 O ye servants of the Lord, bless the Lord; praise and exalt him above all for ever. 86 O ye spirits and souls of the just, bless the Lord; praise and exalt him above all for ever. 87 O ye holy and humble of heart, bless the Lord; praise and exalt him above all for ever. 88 O Hananiah, Azariah and Mishael, bless ye the Lord; praise and exalt him above all for ever. For he hath delivered us from hell and saved us out of the hand of death and delivered us out of the midst of the burning flame and saved us out of the midst of the fire. 89 O give thanks to the Lord because he is good, because his mercy endureth for ever and ever. 90 O all ye religious, bless the Lord, the God of gods; praise him, and give him thanks because his mercy endureth for ever and ever."

Hitherto it is not in the Hebrew, and that which we have put is translated out of the edition of Theodotion.

91 Then Nebuchadnezzar, the king, was astonished and rose up in haste and said to his nobles, "Did we not cast three men bound into the midst of the fire?"

They answered the king and said, "True, O king."

92 He answered and said, "Behold: I see four men loose and walking in the midst of the fire, and there is no hurt in them, and the form of the fourth is like the son of God." 93 Then Nebuchadnezzar came to the door of the burning fiery furnace and said, "Shadrach, Meshach and Abednego, ye servants of the most high God, go ye forth, and come." And immediately Shadrach, Meshach and Abednego went out from the midst of the fire. 94 And the nobles and the

tus et iudices et potentes regis contemplabantur viros illos, quoniam nihil potestatis habuisset ignis in corporibus eorum et capillus capitis eorum non esset adustus et sarabara eorum non fuissent inmutata et odor ignis non transisset per eos.

95 Et erumpens Nabuchodonosor ait, "Benedictus Deus eorum, Sedrac, videlicet, Misac et Abdenago, qui misit angelum suum et eruit servos suos qui crediderunt in eo, et verbum regis inmutaverunt et tradiderunt corpora sua ne servirent et ne adorarent omnem deum excepto Deo suo. 96 A me ergo positum est hoc decretum ut omnis populus, tribus et lingua quaecumque locuta fuerit blasphemiam contra Deum Sedrac, Misac et Abdenago dispereat et domus eius vastetur, neque enim est Deus alius qui possit ita salvare." 97 Tunc rex promovit Sedrac, Misac et Abdenago in provincia Babylonis.

98 "Nabuchodonosor, rex omnibus populis, gentibus et linguis quae habitant in universa terra: pax vobis multiplicetur.

99 "Signa et mirabilia fecit apud me Deus excelsus. Placuit ergo mihi praedicare 100 signa eius quia magna sunt et mirabilia eius quia fortia, et regnum eius regnum sempiternum, et potestas eius in generatione et generationem."

magistrates and the judges and the great men of the king being gathered together considered these men, that the fire had no power on their bodies and that not a hair of their head had been singed nor their garments altered nor the smell of the fire had passed on them.

95 Then Nebuchadnezzar breaking forth said, "Blessed be the God of them, to wit, of Shadrach, Meshach and Abednego, who hath sent his angel and delivered his servants that believed in him, and they changed the king's word and delivered up their bodies that they might not serve nor adore any god except their own God. 96 By me therefore this decree is made that every people, tribe and tongue which shall speak blasphemy against the God of Shadrach, Meshach and Abednego shall be destroyed and their houses laid waste, for there is no other God that can save in this manner." 97 Then the king promoted Shadrach, Meshach and Abednego in the province of Babylon.

98 "Nebuchadnezzar, the king to all peoples, nations and tongues that dwell in all the earth: peace be multiplied unto you.

99 "The most high God hath wrought signs and wonders toward me. It hath seemed good to me therefore to publish 100 his signs because they are great and his wonders because they are mighty, and his kingdom is an everlasting kingdom, and his power to all generations."

Caput 4 ˚

"Ego, Nabuchodonosor, quietus eram in domo mea et florens in palatio meo; 2 somnium vidi quod perterruit me, et cogitationes meae in stratu meo et visiones capitis mei conturbaverunt me. 3 Et per me propositum est decretum ut introducerentur in conspectu meo cuncti sapientes Babylonis et ut solutionem somnii indicarent mihi. 4 Tunc ingrediebantur arioli, magi, Chaldei et aruspices, et somnium narravi in conspectu eorum, et solutionem eius non indicaverunt mihi 5 donec collega ingressus est in conspectu meo, Danihel, cuius nomen Balthasar secundum nomen dei mei, qui habet spiritum deorum sanctorum in semet ipso, et somnium coram eo locutus sum.

6 "'Balthasar, princeps ariolorum, quoniam ego scio quod spiritum deorum sanctorum habeas in te et omne sacramentum non est inpossibile tibi, visiones somniorum meorum quas vidi et solutionem eorum narra.

7 "'Visio capitis mei in cubili meo: videbam, et ecce: arbor in medio terrae, et altitudo eius nimia. 8 Magna arbor et fortis, et proceritas eius contingens caelum; aspectus illius erat usque ad terminos universae terrae. 9 Folia eius pulcherrima, et fructus eius nimius, et esca universorum in ea; subter eam

Chapter 4

Nebuchadnezzar's dream, by which the judgments of God are denounced against him for his pride, is interpreted by Daniel and verified by the event.

"I, Nebuchadnezzar, was at rest in my house and flourishing in my palace; 2 I saw a dream that affrighted me, and my thoughts in my bed and the visions of my head troubled me. 3 Then I set forth a decree that all the wise men of Babylon should be brought in before me and that they should shew me the interpretation of the dream. 4 Then came in the diviners, the wise men, the Chaldeans and the soothsayers, and I told the dream before them, *but* they did not shew me the interpretation thereof 5 till their colleague, Daniel, came in before me, whose name is Belteshazzar according to the name of my god, who hath in him the spirit of the holy gods, and I told the dream before him.

6 "Belteshazzar, prince of the diviners, because I know that thou hast in thee the spirit of the holy gods and that no secret is impossible to thee, tell me the visions of my dreams that I have seen and the interpretation of them.

7 "This was the vision of my head in my bed: I saw, and behold: a tree in the midst of the earth, and the height thereof was exceeding great. 8 The tree was great and strong, and the height thereof reached unto heaven; the sight thereof was even to the ends of all the earth. 9 Its leaves were most beautiful, and its fruit exceeding much, and in it was

habitabant animalia et bestiae, et in ramis eius conversabantur volucres caeli, et ex ea vescebatur omnis caro. 10 Videbam in visione capitis mei super stratum meum, et ecce: vigil et sanctus de caelo descendit. 11 Clamavit fortiter et sic ait: "Succidite arborem, et praecidite ramos eius; excutite folia eius, et dispergite fructus eius; fugiant bestiae quae subter eam sunt, et volucres de ramis eius. 12 Verumtamen germen radicum eius in terra sinite, et alligetur vinculo ferreo et aereo in herbis quae foris sunt, et rore caeli tinguatur, et cum feris pars eius in herba terrae. 13 Cor eius ab humano commutetur, et cor ferae detur ei, et septem tempora mutentur super eum. 14 In sententia vigilum decretum est et sermo sanctorum et petitio, donec cognoscant viventes quoniam dominatur Excelsus in regno hominum, et cuicumque voluerit dabit illud, et humillimum hominem constituet super eo."

15 "'Hoc somnium vidi ego, Rex Nabuchodonosor; tu ergo, Balthasar, interpretationem narra festinus, quia omnes sapientes regni mei non queunt solutionem edicere mihi, tu autem potes quia spiritus deorum sanctorum in te est.'

16 "Tunc Danihel, cuius nomen Balthasar, coepit intra semet ipsum tacitus cogitare quasi hora una, et cogitationes eius conturbabant eum. Respondens autem rex ait, 'Balthasar, somnium et interpretatio eius non conturbent te.' Respondit Balthasar et dixit, 'Domine mi, somnium his qui te oderunt, et interpretatio eius hostibus tuis sit. 17 Arborem

food for all; under it dwelt cattle and beasts, and in the branches thereof the fowls of the air had their abode, and all flesh did eat of it. 10 I saw in the vision of my head upon my bed, and behold: a watcher and a holy one came down from heaven. 11 He cried aloud and said thus: "Cut down the tree, and chop off the branches thereof; shake off its leaves, and scatter its fruits; let the beasts fly away that are under it, and the birds from its branches. 12 Nevertheless leave the stump of its roots in the earth, and let it be tied with a band of iron and of brass among the grass that is without, and let it be wet with the dew of heaven, and let its portion be with the wild beasts in the grass of the earth. 13 Let his heart be changed from man's, and let a beast's heart be given him, and let seven times pass over him. 14 This is the decree by the sentence of the watchers and the word and demand of the holy ones, till the living know that the Most High ruleth in the kingdom of men, and he will give it to whomsoever it shall please him, and he will appoint the basest man over it."

15 "'I, King Nebuchadnezzar, saw this dream; thou therefore, O Belteshazzar, tell me quickly the interpretation, for all the wise men of my kingdom are not able to declare the meaning of it to me, but thou art able because the spirit of the holy gods is in thee.'

16 "Then Daniel, whose name was Belteshazzar, began silently to think within himself for about one hour, and his thoughts troubled him. But the king answering said, 'Belteshazzar, let not the dream and the interpretation thereof trouble thee.' Belteshazzar answered and said, 'My lord, the dream be to them that hate thee, and the interpretation thereof to thy enemies. 17 The tree which thou sawest which

quam vidisti sublimem atque robustam, cuius altitudo pertingit ad caelum et aspectus illius in omnem terram, 18 et rami eius pulcherrimi, et fructus eius nimius, et esca omnium in ea, subter eam habitantes bestiae agri, et in ramis eius commorantes aves caeli: 19 tu es, rex, qui magnificatus es et invaluisti, et magnitudo tua crevit et pervenit usque ad caelum, et potestas tua in terminos universae terrae. 20 Quod autem vidit rex vigilem et sanctum descendere de caelo et dicere, "Succidite arborem, et dissipate illam, attamen germen radicum eius in terra dimittite, et vinciatur ferro et aere in herbis foris, et rore caeli conspergatur, et cum feris sit pabulum eius donec septem tempora commutentur super eum," 21 haec est interpretatio sententiae Altissimi quae pervenit super dominum meum, regem. 22 Eicient te ab hominibus, et cum bestiis ferisque erit habitatio tua, et faenum ut bos comedes et rore caeli infunderis, septem quoque tempora mutabuntur super te donec scias quod dominetur Excelsus super regnum hominum et cuicumque voluerit det illud. 23 Quod autem praecepit ut relinqueretur germen radicum eius, id est, arboris, regnum tuum tibi manebit postquam cognoveris potestatem esse caelestem. 24 Quam ob rem, rex, consilium meum placeat tibi, et peccata tua elemosynis redime, et iniquitates tuas misericordiis pauperum; forsitan ignoscet delictis tuis.'"

25 Omnia haec venerunt super Nabuchodonosor Regem. 26 Post finem mensuum duodecim in aula Babylonis deam-

was high and strong, whose height reached to the skies and the sight thereof into all the earth, 18 and the branches thereof were most beautiful, and its fruit exceeding much, and in it was food for all, under which the beasts of the field dwelt, and the birds of the air had their abode in its branches: 19 it is thou, O king, who art grown great and become mighty, *for* thy greatness hath grown and hath reached to heaven, and thy power unto the ends of the earth. 20 And whereas the king saw a watcher and a holy one come down from heaven and say, "Cut down the tree, and destroy it, but leave the stump of the roots thereof in the earth, and let it be bound with iron and brass among the grass without, and let it be sprinkled with the dew of heaven, and let his feeding be with the wild beasts till seven times pass over him," 21 this is the interpretation of the sentence of the Most High which is come upon my lord, the king. 22 They shall cast thee out from among men, and thy dwelling shall be with cattle and with wild beasts, and thou shalt eat grass as an ox and shalt be wet with the dew of heaven, and seven times shall pass over thee till thou know that the Most High ruleth over the kingdom of men and giveth it to whomsoever he will. 23 But whereas he commanded that the stump of the roots thereof, that is, of the tree, should be left, thy kingdom shall remain to thee after thou shalt have known that power is from heaven. 24 Wherefore, O king, let my counsel be acceptable to thee, and redeem thou thy sins with alms, and thy iniquities with works of mercy to the poor; perhaps he will forgive thy offences.'"

25 All these things came upon King Nebuchadnezzar. 26 At the end of twelve months he was walking in the palace

bulabat. 27 Responditque rex et ait, "Nonne haec est Babylon magna, quam ego aedificavi in domum regni in robore fortitudinis meae et in gloria decoris mei?"

28 Cumque adhuc sermo esset in ore regis, vox de caelo ruit: "Tibi dicitur, Nabuchodonosor Rex, 'Regnum tuum transiit a te, 29 et ab hominibus te eicient, et cum bestiis et feris erit habitatio tua; faenum quasi bos comedes, et septem tempora mutabuntur super te donec scias quod dominetur Excelsus in regno hominum et cuicumque voluerit det illud.'" 30 Eadem hora sermo conpletus est super Nabuchodonosor, et ex hominibus abiectus est et faenum ut bos comedit, et rore caeli corpus eius infectum est donec capilli eius in similitudinem aquilarum crescerent et ungues eius quasi avium.

31 "Igitur post finem dierum ego, Nabuchodonosor, oculos meos ad caelum levavi, et sensus meus redditus est mihi, et Altissimo benedixi, et viventem in sempiternum laudavi et glorificavi, quia potestas eius potestas sempiterna et regnum eius in generationem et generationem. 32 Et omnes habitatores terrae apud eum in nihilum reputati sunt, iuxta voluntatem enim suam facit tam in virtutibus caeli quam in habitatoribus terrae, et non est qui resistat manui eius et dicat ei, 'Quare fecisti?' 33 In ipso tempore sensus meus reversus est ad me, et ad honorem regni mei decoremque perveni, et figura mea reversa est ad me, et optimates mei et magistratus mei requisierunt me, et in regno meo restitutus sum, et magnificentia amplior addita est mihi. 34 Nunc igitur ego, Nabuchodonosor, laudo et magnifico et glorifico Regem

of Babylon. 27 And the king answered and said, "Is not this the great Babylon, which I have built to be the seat of the kingdom by the strength of my power and in the glory of my excellence?"

28 And while the word was yet in the king's mouth, a voice came down from heaven: "To thee, O King Nebuchadnezzar, it is said, 'Thy kingdom shall pass from thee, 29 and they shall cast thee out from among men, and thy dwelling shall be with cattle and wild beasts; thou shalt eat grass like an ox, and seven times shall pass over thee till thou know that the Most High ruleth in the kingdom of men and giveth it to whomsoever he will.'" 30 The same hour the word was fulfilled upon Nebuchadnezzar, and he was driven away from among men and did eat grass like an ox, and his body was wet with the dew of heaven till his hairs grew like *the feathers* of eagles and his nails like birds' *claws.*

31 "Now at the end of the days I, Nebuchadnezzar, lifted up my eyes to heaven, and my sense was restored to me, and I blessed the Most High, and I praised and glorified him that liveth for ever, for his power is an everlasting power and his kingdom is to all generations. 32 And all the inhabitants of the earth are reputed as nothing before him, for he doth according to his will as well with the powers of heaven as among the inhabitants of the earth, and there is none that can resist his hand and say to him, 'Why hast thou done it?' 33 At the same time my sense returned to me, and I came to the honour and glory of my kingdom, and my shape returned to me, and my nobles and my magistrates sought for me, and I was restored to my kingdom, and greater majesty was added to me. 34 Therefore I, Nebuchadnezzar, do now praise and magnify and glorify the King of heaven because

caeli quia omnia opera eius vera, et viae eius iudicia, et gradientes in superbia potest humiliare."

Caput 5

Balthasar, rex, fecit grande convivium optimatibus suis mille, et unusquisque secundum suam bibebat aetatem. 2 Praecepit ergo iam temulentus ut adferrentur vasa aurea et argentea quae asportaverat Nabuchodonosor, pater eius, de templo quod fuit in Hierusalem, ut biberent in eis rex et optimates eius uxoresque eius et concubinae. 3 Tunc adlata sunt vasa aurea et argenta quae asportaverat de templo quod fuerat in Hierusalem, et biberunt in eis rex et optimates eius, uxores et concubinae illius. 4 Bibebant vinum et laudabant deos suos aureos et argenteos, aereos, ferreos ligneosque et lapideos.

5 In eadem hora apparuerunt digiti quasi manus hominis scribentis contra candelabrum in superficie parietis aulae regiae, et rex aspiciebat articulos manus scribentis. 6 Tunc regis facies commutata est, et cogitationes eius conturbabant eum, et conpages renum eius solvebantur, et genua eius

all his works are true, and his ways judgments, and them that walk in pride he is able to abase."

Chapter 5

Belshazzar's profane banquet. His sentence is denounced by a handwriting on the wall, which Daniel reads and interprets.

Belshazzar, the king, made a great feast for a thousand of his nobles, and every one drank according to his age. 2 And being now drunk he commanded that they should bring the vessels of gold and silver which Nebuchadnezzar, his father, had brought away out of the temple that was in Jerusalem, that the king and his nobles and his wives and his concubines might drink in them. 3 Then were the golden and silver vessels brought which he had brought away out of the temple that was in Jerusalem, and the king and his nobles, his wives and his concubines, drank in them. 4 They drank wine and praised their gods of gold and of silver, of brass, of iron and of wood and of stone.

5 In the same hour there appeared fingers as it were of the hand of a man writing over against the candlestick upon the surface of the wall of the king's palace, and the king beheld the joints of the hand that wrote. 6 Then was the king's countenance changed, and his thoughts troubled him, and the joints of his loins were loosed, and his knees struck one

ad se invicem conlidebantur. 7 Exclamavit itaque rex fortiter ut introducerent magos, Chaldeos et aruspices. Et proloquens rex ait sapientibus Babylonis, "Quicumque legerit scripturam hanc et interpretationem eius manifestam mihi fecerit purpura vestietur et torquem auream habebit in collo et tertius in regno meo erit." 8 Tunc ingressi omnes sapientes regis non potuerunt nec scripturam legere nec interpretationem indicare regi. 9 Unde Rex Balthasar satis conturbatus est et vultus illius inmutatus est, sed et optimates eius turbabantur.

10 Regina autem pro re quae acciderat regi et optimatibus eius domum convivii ingressa est, et proloquens ait, "Rex, in aeternum vive. Non te conturbent cogitationes tuae, neque facies tua inmutetur. 11 Est vir in regno tuo qui spiritum deorum sanctorum habet in se, et in diebus patris tui scientia et sapientia inventae sunt in eo, nam et Rex Nabuchodonosor, pater tuus, principem magorum, incantatorum, Chaldeorum et aruspicum constituit eum; pater, inquam, tuus, O rex, 12 quia spiritus amplior et prudentia intellegentiaque et interpretatio somniorum et ostensio secretorum ac solutio ligatorum inventae sunt in eo, hoc est, in Danihele, cui rex posuit nomen Balthasar. Nunc itaque Danihel vocetur, et interpretationem narrabit."

13 Igitur introductus est Danihel coram rege. Ad quem praefatus rex ait, "Tu es Danihel, de filiis captivitatis Iudae, quam adduxit rex, pater meus, de Iudaea? 14 Audivi de te quoniam spiritum deorum habeas et scientia intellegentiaque ac sapientia ampliores inventae sint in te. 15 Et nunc in-

against the other. 7 And the king cried out aloud to bring in the wise men, the Chaldeans and the soothsayers. And the king spoke and said to the wise men of Babylon, "Whosoever shall read this writing and shall make known to me the interpretation thereof shall be clothed with purple and shall have a golden chain on his neck and shall be the third man in my kingdom." 8 Then came in all the king's wise men, *but* they could neither read the writing nor declare the interpretation to the king. 9 Wherewith King Belshazzar was much troubled and his countenance was changed, and his nobles also were troubled.

10 Then the queen on occasion of what had happened to the king and his nobles came into the banquet house, and she spoke and said, "O king, live for ever. Let not thy thoughts trouble thee, neither let thy countenance be changed. 11 There is a man in thy kingdom that hath the spirit of the holy gods in him, and in the days of thy father knowledge and wisdom were found in him, *for* King Nebuchadnezzar, thy father, appointed him prince of the wise men, enchanters, Chaldeans and soothsayers; thy father, I say, O king, 12 because a greater spirit and knowledge and understanding and interpretation of dreams and shewing of secrets and resolving of difficult things were found in him, that is, in Daniel, whom the king named Belteshazzar. Now therefore let Daniel be called for, and he will tell the interpretation."

13 Then Daniel was brought in before the king. *And* the king spoke and said to him, "Art thou Daniel, of the children of the captivity of Judah, whom my father, the king, brought out of Judea? 14 I have heard of thee that thou hast the spirit of the gods and *excellent* knowledge and understanding and wisdom are found in thee. 15 And now the wise men, the ma-

trogressi sunt in conspectu meo sapientes, magi, ut scripturam hanc legerent et interpretationem eius indicarent mihi, et nequiverunt sensum sermonis huius edicere mihi. 16 Porro ego audivi de te quod possis obscura interpretari et ligata dissolvere; si ergo vales scripturam legere et interpretationem eius indicare mihi, purpura vestieris et torquem auream circa collum tuum habebis et tertius in regno meo princeps eris."

17 Ad quae respondens Danihel ait coram rege, "Munera tua sint tibi, et dona domus tuae alteri da, scripturam autem legam tibi, rex, et interpretationem eius ostendam tibi. 18 O rex, Deus altissimus regnum et magnificentiam, gloriam et honorem dedit Nabuchodonosor, patri tuo. 19 Et propter magnificentiam quam dederat ei, universi populi, tribus et linguae tremebant et metuebant eum; quos volebat interficiebat, et quos volebat percutiebat, et quos volebat exaltabat, et quos volebat humiliabat. 20 Quando autem elevatum est cor eius et spiritus illius obfirmatus est ad superbiam, depositus est de solio regni sui, et gloria eius ablata est. 21 Et a filiis hominum eiectus est, sed et cor eius cum bestiis positum est, et cum onagris erat habitatio eius, faenum quoque ut bos comedebat, et rore caeli corpus eius infectum est donec cognosceret quod potestatem haberet Altissimus in regno hominum et quemcumque voluerit suscitabit super illud. 22 Tu quoque, filius eius, Balthasar, non humiliasti cor tuum, cum scires haec omnia 23 sed adversum Dominatorem caeli elevatus es, et vasa domus eius adlata sunt coram te, et tu et optimates tui et uxores tuae et concubinae tuae vinum bibistis in eis, deos quoque argenteos et aureos et aereos,

gicians, have come in before me to read this writing and shew me the interpretation thereof, and they could not declare to me the meaning of this writing. 16 But I have heard of thee that thou canst interpret obscure things and resolve difficult things; now if thou art able to read the writing and to shew me the interpretation thereof, thou shalt be clothed with purple and shalt have a chain of gold about thy neck and shalt be the third prince in my kingdom."

17 To which Daniel made answer and said before the king, "Thy rewards be to thyself, and the gifts of thy house give to another, but the writing I will read to thee, O king, and shew thee the interpretation thereof. 18 O king, the most high God gave to Nebuchadnezzar, thy father, a kingdom and greatness *and* glory and honour. 19 And for the greatness that he gave to him, all people, tribes and languages trembled and were afraid of him; whom he would he slew, and whom he would he destroyed, and whom he would he set up, and whom he would he brought down. 20 But when his heart was lifted up and his spirit hardened unto pride, he was put down from the throne of his kingdom, and his glory was taken away. 21 And he was driven out from the sons of men, and his heart was made like the beasts, and his dwelling was with the wild asses, and he did eat grass like an ox, and his body was wet with the dew of heaven till he knew that the Most High ruled in the kingdom of men and that he will set over it whomsoever it shall please him. 22 Thou also, his son, O Belshazzar, hast not humbled thy heart, whereas thou knewest all these things 23 but hast lifted thyself up against the Lord of heaven, and the vessels of his house have been brought before thee, and thou and thy nobles and thy wives and thy concubines have drunk wine in them, and thou hast praised the gods of silver and of gold and of brass,

ferreos ligneosque et lapideos, qui non vident neque audiunt neque sentiunt laudasti, porro Deum qui habet flatum tuum in manu sua et omnes vias tuas non glorificasti.

24 "Idcirco ab eo missus est articulus manus quae scripsit hoc quod exaratum est. 25 Haec est autem scriptura quae digesta est: 'Mane,' 'Thecel,' 'Fares.' 26 Et haec interpretatio sermonis 'Mane': numeravit Deus regnum tuum et conplevit illud. 27 'Thecel': adpensum est in statera et inventus es minus habens. 28 'Fares': divisum est regnum tuum et datum est Medis et Persis."

29 Tunc iubente rege indutus est Danihel purpura, et circumdata est torques aurea collo eius, et praedicatum est de eo quod haberet potestatem tertius in regno.

30 Eadem nocte interfectus est Balthasar, rex Chaldeus. 31 Et Darius, Medus, successit in regnum, annos natus sexaginta duo.

Caput 6

Placuit Dario, et constituit supra regnum satrapas centum viginti ut essent in toto regno suo 2 et super eos principes tres, ex quibus Danihel unus erat, ut satrapae illis red-

of iron and of wood and of stone, that neither see nor hear nor feel, but the God who hath thy breath in his hand and all thy ways thou hast not glorified.

24 "Wherefore he hath sent the part of the hand which hath written this that is set down. 25 And this is the writing that is written: 'Mane,' 'Thecel,' 'Phares.' 26 And this is the interpretation of the word 'Mane': God hath numbered thy kingdom and hath finished it. 27 'Thecel': thou art weighed in the balance and art found wanting. 28 'Phares': thy kingdom is divided and is given to the Medes and Persians."

29 Then by the king's command Daniel was clothed with purple, and a chain of gold was put about his neck, and it was proclaimed of him that he had power as the third man in the kingdom.

30 The same night Belshazzar, the Chaldean king, was slain. 31 And Darius, the Mede, succeeded to the kingdom, being threescore and two years old.

Chapter 6

Daniel is promoted by Darius. His enemies procure a law forbidding prayer. For the transgression of this law Daniel is cast into the lions' den but miraculously delivered.

It seemed good to Darius, and he appointed over the kingdom a hundred and twenty governors to be over his whole kingdom 2 and three princes over them, of whom Daniel

derent rationem et rex non sustineret molestiam. 3 Igitur Danihel superabat omnes principes et satrapas quia spiritus Dei amplior erat in eo. 4 Porro rex cogitabat constituere eum super omne regnum, unde principes et satrapae quaerebant occasionem ut invenirent Daniheli ex latere regni, nullamque causam et suspicionem repperire potuerunt eo quod fidelis esset, et omnis culpa et suspicio non inveniretur in eo. 5 Dixerunt ergo viri illi, "Non inveniemus Daniheli huic aliquam occasionem nisi forte in lege Dei sui."

6 Tunc principes et satrapae subripuerunt regi et sic locuti sunt ei: "Darie Rex, in aeternum vive. 7 Consilium inierunt cuncti principes regni, magistratus et satrapae, senatores et iudices, ut decretum imperatorium exeat et edictum ut omnis qui petierit aliquam petitionem a quocumque deo et homine usque ad dies triginta nisi a te, rex, mittatur in lacum leonum. 8 Nunc itaque, rex, confirma sententiam, et scribe decretum, ut non inmutetur quod statutum est a Medis atque Persis, nec praevaricari cuiquam liceat." 9 Porro rex Darius proposuit edictum et statuit.

10 Quod cum Danihel conperisset, id est, constitutam legem, ingressus est domum suam, et fenestris apertis in cenaculo suo contra Hierusalem, tribus temporibus in die flectebat genua sua et adorabat confitebaturque coram Deo suo sicut et ante facere consuerat. 11 Viri igitur illi curiosius inquirentes invenerunt Danihel orantem et obsecrantem Deum suum. 12 Et accedentes locuti sunt regi super edicto: "Rex, numquid non constituisti ut omnis homo qui rogaret

was one, that the governors might give an account to them and the king might have no trouble. 3 And Daniel excelled all the princes and governors because a greater spirit of God was in him. 4 And the king thought to set him over all the kingdom, whereupon the princes and the governors sought to find occasion against Daniel with regard to the king, and they could find no cause nor suspicion because he was faithful, and no fault nor suspicion was found in him. 5 Then these men said, "We shall not find any occasion against this Daniel unless perhaps concerning the law of his God."

6 Then the princes and the governors craftily suggested to the king and spoke thus unto him: "King Darius, live for ever. 7 All the princes of the kingdom, the magistrates and governors, the senators and judges, have consulted together that an imperial decree and an edict be published that whosoever shall ask any petition of any god or man for thirty days but of thee, O king, shall be cast into the den of lions. 8 Now therefore, O king, confirm the sentence, and sign the decree, that what is decreed by the Medes and Persians may not be altered, nor any man be allowed to transgress it." 9 So king Darius set forth the decree and established it.

10 Now when Daniel knew this, that is to say, that the law was made, he went into his house, and opening the windows in his upper chamber towards Jerusalem, he knelt down three times a day and adored and gave thanks before his God as he had been accustomed to do before. 11 Wherefore those men carefully watching him found Daniel praying and making supplication to his God. 12 And they came and spoke to the king concerning the edict: "O king, hast thou not decreed that every man that should make a request to

quemquam de diis et hominibus usque ad dies triginta nisi te, rex, mitteretur in lacum leonum?"

Ad quos respondens rex ait, "Verus sermo iuxta decretum Medorum atque Persarum, quod praevaricari non licet."

13 Tunc respondentes dixerunt coram rege, "Danihel, de filiis captivitatis Iudae, non curavit de lege tua et de edicto quod constituisti, sed tribus temporibus per diem orat obsecratione sua."

14 Quod verbum cum audisset rex satis contristatus est, et pro Danihel posuit cor ut liberaret eum, et usque ad occasum solis laborabat ut erueret illum. 15 Viri autem illi, intellegentes regem, dixerunt ei, "Scito, rex, quia lex Medorum est atque Persarum ut omne decretum quod constituerit rex non liceat inmutari."

16 Tunc rex praecepit, et adduxerunt Danihelem et miserunt eum in lacum leonum. Dixitque rex Daniheli, "Deus tuus, quem colis semper, ipse liberabit te." 17 Adlatusque est lapis unus et positus est super os laci, quem obsignavit rex anulo suo et anulo optimatum suorum, ne quid fieret contra Danihel. 18 Et abiit rex in domum suam et dormivit incenatus, cibique non sunt adlati coram eo, insuper et somnus recessit ab eo.

19 Tunc rex primo diluculo consurgens festinus ad lacum leonum perrexit 20 adpropinquansque laci Danihelem voce lacrimabili inclamavit et affatus est eum, "Danihel, serve Dei viventis, Deus tuus, cui tu servis semper, putasne, valuit

any of the gods or men for thirty days but to thyself, O king, should be cast into the den of the lions?"

And the king answered them, saying, "The word is true according to the decree of the Medes and Persians, which it is not lawful to violate."

13 Then they answered and said before the king, "Daniel, who is of the children of the captivity of Judah, hath not regarded thy law nor the decree that thou hast made, but three times a day he maketh his prayer."

14 Now when the king had heard these words he was very much grieved, and in behalf of Daniel he set his heart to deliver him, and even till sunset he laboured to save him. 15 But those men, perceiving the *king's design,* said to him, "Know thou, O king, that the law of the Medes and Persians is that no decree which the king hath made may be altered."

16 Then the king commanded, and they brought Daniel and cast him into the den of the lions. And the king said to Daniel, "Thy God, whom thou always servest, he will deliver thee." 17 And a stone was brought and laid upon the mouth of the den, which the king sealed with his own ring and with the ring of his nobles, that nothing should be done against Daniel. 18 And the king went away to his house and laid himself down without taking supper, and meat was not set before him, and even sleep departed from him.

19 Then the king rising very early in the morning went in haste to the lions' den 20 and coming near to the den cried with a lamentable voice to Daniel and said to him, "Daniel, servant of the living God, hath thy God, whom thou servest

liberare te a leonibus?" 21 Et Danihel regi respondens ait, "Rex, in aeternum vive. 22 Deus meus misit angelum suum et conclusit ora leonum, et non nocuerunt mihi, quia coram eo iustitia inventa est in me, sed et coram te, rex, delictum non feci." 23 Tunc rex vehementer gavisus est super eo, et Danihelem praecepit educi de lacu eductusque est Danihel de lacu, et nulla laesio inventa est in eo, quia credidit Deo suo. 24 Iubente autem rege adducti sunt viri illi qui accusaverant Danihelem, et in lacum leonum missi sunt, ipsi et filii et uxores eorum, et non pervenerunt usque ad pavimentum laci donec arriperent eos leones et omnia ossa eorum comminuerunt.

25 Tunc Darius Rex scripsit universis populis, tribubus et linguis habitantibus in universa terra, "Pax vobis multiplicetur. 26 A me constitutum est decretum ut in universo imperio et regno meo tremescant et paveant Deum Danihelis. Ipse est enim Deus vivens et aeternus in saecula, et regnum eius non dissipabitur, et potestas eius usque in aeternum. 27 Ipse liberator atque salvator, faciens signa et mirabilia in caelo et in terra, qui liberavit Danihelem de lacu leonum." 28 Porro Danihel perseveravit usque ad regnum Darii regnumque Cyri, Persae.

always, been able, thinkest thou, to deliver thee from the lions?" 21 And Daniel answering the king said, "O king, live for ever. 22 My God hath sent his angel and hath shut up the mouths of the lions, and they have not hurt me, forasmuch as before him justice hath been found in me, yea, and before thee, O king, I have done no offence." 23 Then was the king exceeding glad for him, and he commanded that Daniel should be taken out of the den, and Daniel was taken out of the den, and no hurt was found in him, because he believed in his God. 24 And by the king's commandment those men were brought that had accused Daniel, and they were cast into the lions' den, they and their children and their wives, and they did not reach the bottom of the den before the lions caught them and broke all their bones in pieces.

25 Then King Darius wrote to all people, tribes and languages dwelling in the whole earth, "Peace be multiplied unto you. 26 It is decreed by me that in all my empire and my kingdom *all men* dread and fear the God of Daniel. For he is the living and eternal God for ever, and his kingdom shall not be destroyed, and his power shall be for ever. 27 He is the deliverer and saviour, doing signs and wonders in heaven and in earth, who hath delivered Daniel out of the lions' den." 28 Now Daniel continued unto the reign of Darius and the reign of Cyrus, the Persian.

Caput 7

Anno primo Balthasar, regis Babylonis, Danihel somnium vidit, visio autem capitis eius in cubili suo, et somnium scribens, brevi sermone conprehendit, summatimque perstringens ait, 2 "Videbam in visione mea nocte, et ecce: quattuor venti caeli pugnabant in mari magno. 3 Et quattuor bestiae grandes ascendebant de mari, diversae inter se. 4 Prima quasi leaena et alas habebat aquilae; aspiciebam donec evulsae sunt alae eius et sublata est de terra et super pedes quasi homo stetit, et cor hominis datum est ei. 5 Et ecce: bestia alia similis urso in parte stetit, et tres ordines erant in ore eius et in dentibus eius, et sic dicebant ei: 'Surge; comede carnes plurimas.' 6 Post hoc aspiciebam, et ecce: alia quasi pardus, et alas habebat quasi avis quattuor super se, et quattuor capita erant in bestia, et potestas data est ei. 7 Post hoc aspiciebam in visione noctis, et ecce: bestia quarta, terribilis atque mirabilis et fortis nimis; dentes ferreos habebat magnos comedens atque comminuens et reliqua pedibus suis conculcans, dissimilis autem erat ceteris bestiis quas videram ante

Chapter 7

Daniel's vision of the four beasts, signifying four kingdoms,
of God sitting on his throne and of the opposite kingdoms
of Christ and Antichrist.

In the first year of Belshazzar, king of Babylon, Daniel saw
a dream, and the vision of his head was upon his bed, and
writing the dream, he comprehended it in few words, and
relating the sum of it in short he said, 2 "I saw in my vision
by night, and behold: the four winds of the heaven strove
upon the great sea. 3 And four great beasts, different one
from another, came up out of the sea. 4 The first was like a
lioness and had the wings of an eagle; I beheld till her wings
were plucked off and she was lifted up from the earth and
stood upon her feet as a man, and the heart of a man was
given to her. 5 And behold: another beast like a bear stood
up on one side, and there were three rows in the mouth
thereof and in the teeth thereof, and thus they said to it:
'Arise; devour much flesh.' 6 After this I beheld, and lo: another like a leopard, and it had upon it four wings as of a
fowl, and the beast had four heads, and power was given to
it. 7 After this I beheld in the vision of the night, and lo: a
fourth beast, terrible and wonderful and exceeding strong; it
had great iron teeth eating and breaking in pieces and treading down the rest with its feet, and it was unlike to the other

eam et habebat cornua decem. 8 Considerabam cornua, et ecce: cornu aliud parvulum ortum est de medio eorum, et tria de cornibus primis evulsa sunt a facie eius, et ecce: oculi quasi oculi hominis erant in cornu isto, et os loquens ingentia.

9 "Aspiciebam donec throni positi sunt et Antiquus Dierum sedit; vestimentum eius quasi nix candidum, et capilli capitis eius quasi lana munda; thronus eius flammae ignis; rotae eius ignis accensus. 10 Fluvius igneus rapidusque egrediebatur a facie eius; milia milium ministrabant ei, et decies milies centena milia adsistebant ei; iudicium sedit, et libri aperti sunt. 11 Aspiciebam propter vocem sermonum grandium quos cornu illud loquebatur, et vidi quoniam interfecta esset bestia et perisset corpus eius et traditum esset ad conburendum igni 12 aliarum quoque bestiarum ablata esset potestas et tempora vitae constituta essent eis usque ad tempus et tempus. 13 Aspiciebam ergo in visione noctis, et ecce: cum nubibus caeli quasi filius hominis veniebat, et usque ad Antiquum Dierum pervenit, et in conspectu eius obtulerunt eum. 14 Et dedit ei potestatem et honorem et regnum, et omnes populi, tribus ac linguae ipsi servient; potestas eius potestas aeterna quae non auferetur, et regnum eius, quod non corrumpetur.

15 "Horruit spiritus meus; ego, Danihel, territus sum in his, et visiones capitis mei conturbaverunt me. 16 Accessi ad unum de adsistentibus et veritatem quaerebam ab eo de omnibus his, qui dixit mihi interpretationem sermonum et edocuit me: 17 'Hae quattuor bestiae magnae quattuor sunt

beasts which I had seen before it and had ten horns. 8 I considered the horns, and behold: another little horn sprung
out of the midst of them, and three of the first horns were
plucked up at the presence thereof, and behold: eyes like the
eyes of a man were in this horn, and a mouth speaking great
things.

9 "I beheld till thrones were placed and the Ancient of
Days sat; his garment was white as snow, and the hair of his
head like clean wool, his throne *like* flames of fire, the wheels
of it *like* a burning fire. 10 A swift stream of fire issued forth
from before him; thousands of thousands ministered to him,
and ten thousand times a hundred thousand stood before
him; the judgment sat, and the books were opened. 11 I
beheld because of the voice of the great words which that
horn spoke, and I saw that the beast was slain and the body
thereof was destroyed and given to the fire to be burnt 12 and
that the power of the other beasts was taken away and that
times of life were appointed them for a time and a time. 13 I
beheld therefore in the vision of the night, and lo: one like
the son of man came with the clouds of heaven, and he came
even to the Ancient of Days, and they presented him before
him. 14 And he gave him power and glory and a kingdom,
and all peoples, tribes and tongues shall serve him; his power
is an everlasting power that shall not be taken away, and his
kingdom, that shall not be destroyed.

15 "My spirit trembled; I, Daniel, was affrighted at these
things, and the visions of my head troubled me. 16 I went
near to one of them that stood by and asked the truth of
him concerning all these things, and he told me the interpretation of the words and instructed me: 17 'These four
great beasts are four kingdoms which shall arise out of the

regna quae consurgent de terra. 18 Suscipient autem regnum sancti Dei altissimi, et obtinebunt regnum usque in saeculum et saeculum saeculorum.' 19 Post hoc volui diligenter discere de bestia quarta, quae erat dissimilis valde ab omnibus et terribilis nimis—dentes et ungues eius ferrei; comedebat et comminuebat, et reliquias pedibus suis conculcabat— 20 et de cornibus decem quae habebat in capite et de alio quod ortum fuerat, ante quod ceciderant tria cornua, et de cornu illo quod habebat oculos et os loquens grandia et maius erat ceteris. 21 Aspiciebam, et ecce: cornu illud faciebat bellum adversus sanctos et praevalebat eis 22 donec venit Antiquus Dierum et iudicium dedit sanctis Excelsi, et tempus advenit, et regnum obtinuerunt sancti.

23 "Et sic ait: 'Bestia quarta regnum quartum erit in terra, quod maius erit omnibus regnis et devorabit universam terram et conculcabit et comminuet eam. 24 Porro cornua decem ipsius regni decem reges erunt, et alius consurget post eos, et ipse potentior erit prioribus, et tres reges humiliabit. 25 Et sermones contra Excelsum loquetur et sanctos Altissimi conteret, et putabit quod possit mutare tempora et leges, et tradentur in manu eius usque ad tempus et tempora et dimidium temporis. 26 Et iudicium sedebit ut auferatur potentia et conteratur et dispereat usque in finem. 27 Regnum autem et potestas et magnitudo regni quae est subter omne caelum detur populo sanctorum Altissimi, cuius regnum regnum sempiternum est, et omnes reges servient ei et oboedient.'

earth. 18 But the saints of the most high God shall take the kingdom, and they shall possess the kingdom for ever and ever.' 19 After this I would diligently learn concerning the fourth beast, which was very different from all and exceeding terrible—his teeth and claws were of iron; he devoured and broke in pieces, and the rest he stamped upon with his feet— 20 and concerning the ten horns that he had on his head and concerning the other that came up, before which three horns fell, and of that horn that had eyes and a mouth speaking great things and was greater than the rest. 21 I beheld, and lo: that horn made war against the saints and prevailed over them 22 till the Ancient of Days came and gave judgment to the saints of the Most High, and the time came, and the saints obtained the kingdom.

23 "And thus he said: 'The fourth beast shall be the fourth kingdom upon earth, which shall be greater than all the kingdoms and shall devour the whole earth and shall tread it down and break it in pieces. 24 And the ten horns of the same kingdom shall be ten kings, and another shall rise up after them, and he shall be mightier than the former, and he shall bring down three kings. 25 And he shall speak words against the High One and shall crush the saints of the Most High, and he shall think himself able to change times and laws, and they shall be delivered into his hand until a time and times and half a time. 26 And judgment shall sit that his power may be taken away and be broken in pieces and perish even to the end. 27 And that the kingdom and power and the greatness of the kingdom under the whole heaven may be given to the people of the saints of the Most High, whose kingdom is an everlasting kingdom, and all kings shall serve him and shall obey him.'

28 "Hucusque finis verbi. Ego, Danihel, multum cogitationibus meis conturbabar, et facies mea mutata est in me,
verbum autem in corde meo conservavi."

Caput 8

"Anno tertio regni Balthasar Regis, visio apparuit mihi.
Ego, Danihel, post id quod videram in principio, 2 vidi in visione mea cum essem in Susis castro, quod est in Aelam regione, vidi autem in visione esse me super portam Ulai. 3 Et
levavi oculos meos et vidi, et ecce: aries unus stabat ante pa-
ludem habens cornua excelsa, et unum excelsius altero atque
succrescens. 4 Postea vidi arietem cornibus ventilantem
contra occidentem et contra aquilonem et contra meridiem,
et omnes bestiae non poterant resistere ei neque liberari de
manu eius, fecitque secundum voluntatem suam et magnificatus est.

5 "Et ego intellegebam, ecce autem: hircus caprarum veniebat ab occidente super faciem totius terrae et non tange-
bat terram, porro hircus habebat cornu insigne inter oculos
suos. 6 Et venit usque ad arietem illum cornutum quem videram stantem ante portam, et cucurrit ad eum in impetu fortitudinis suae. 7 Cumque adpropinquasset prope arietem ef-

28 "Hitherto is the end of the word. I, Daniel, was much troubled with my thoughts, and my countenance was changed in me, but I kept the word in my heart."

Chapter 8

Daniel's vision of the ram and he-goat, interpreted by the angel Gabriel.

"In the third year of the reign of King Belshazzar, a vision appeared to me. I, Daniel, after what I had seen in the beginning, 2 saw in my vision when I was in the castle of Susa, which is in the province of Elam, and I saw in the vision that I was over the gate of Ulai. 3 And I lifted up my eyes and saw, and behold: a ram stood before the water having *two* high horns, and one higher than the other and growing up. 4 Afterward I saw the ram pushing with his horns against the west and against the north and against the south, and no beasts could withstand him nor be delivered out of his hand, and he did according to his own will and became great.

5 "And I understood, and behold: a he-goat came from the west on the face of the whole earth, and he touched not the ground, and the he-goat had a notable horn between his eyes. 6 And he went up to the ram that had the horns which I had seen standing before the gate, and he ran towards him in the force of his strength. 7 And when he was come near

feratus est in eum et percussit arietem et comminuit duo cornua eius, et non poterat aries resistere ei, cumque eum misisset in terram conculcavit, et nemo quibat liberare arietem de manu eius. 8 Hircus autem caprarum magnus factus est nimis, cumque crevisset fractum est cornu magnum, et orta sunt cornua quattuor subter illud per quattuor ventos caeli. 9 De uno autem ex eis egressum est cornu unum modicum, et factum est grande contra meridiem et contra orientem et contra fortitudinem. 10 Et magnificatum est usque ad fortitudinem caeli, et deiecit de fortitudine et de stellis et conculcavit eas. 11 Et usque ad principem fortitudinis magnificatum est, et ab eo tulit iuge sacrificium et deiecit locum sanctificationis eius. 12 Robur autem datum est contra iuge sacrificium propter peccata, et prosternetur veritas in terra, et faciet et prosperabitur. 13 Et audivi unum de sanctis loquentem, et dixit unus sanctus alteri, nescio cui, loquenti, 'Usquequo visio et iuge sacrificium et peccatum desolationis quae facta est, et sanctuarium et fortitudo conculcabitur?' 14 Et dixit ei, 'Usque ad vesperam et mane duo milia trecenti, et mundabitur sanctuarium.'

15 "Factum est autem cum viderem ego, Danihel, visionem et quaererem intellegentiam, ecce: stetit in conspectu meo quasi species viri. 16 Et audivi vocem viri inter Ulai, et clamavit et ait, 'Gabrihel, fac intellegere istum visionem.' 17 Et venit et stetit iuxta ubi ego stabam, cumque venisset pavens corrui in faciem meam, et ait ad me, 'Intellege, fili

the ram he was enraged against him and struck the ram and broke his two horns, and the ram could not withstand him, and when he had cast him down on the ground he stamped upon him, and none could deliver the ram out of his hand. 8 And the he-goat became exceeding great, and when he was grown the great horn was broken, and there came up four horns under it towards the four winds of heaven. 9 And out of one of them came forth a little horn, and it became great against the south and against the east and against the strength. 10 And it was magnified even unto the strength of heaven, and it threw down of the strength and of the stars and trod upon them. 11 And it was magnified even to the prince of the strength and it took away from him the continual sacrifice and cast down the place of his sanctuary. 12 And strength was given him against the continual sacrifice because of sins, and truth shall be cast down on the ground, and he shall do and shall prosper. 13 And I heard one of the saints speaking, and one saint said to another, I know not to whom, that was speaking, 'How long shall be the vision concerning the continual sacrifice and the sin of the desolation that is made, and the sanctuary and the strength be trodden under foot?' 14 And he said to him, 'Unto evening and morning two thousand three hundred *days,* and the sanctuary shall be cleansed.'

15 "And it came to pass when I, Daniel, saw the vision and sought the meaning, that behold: there stood before me as it were the appearance of a man. 16 And I heard the voice of a man between Ulai, and he called and said, 'Gabriel, make this man to understand the vision.' 17 And he came and stood near where I stood, and when he was come I fell on my face trembling, and he said to me, 'Understand, O son of man,

hominis, quoniam in tempore finis conplebitur visio.' ¹⁸ Cumque loqueretur ad me conlapsus sum pronus in terram, et tetigit me et statuit me in gradu meo ¹⁹ dixitque mihi, 'Ego ostendam tibi quae futura sint in novissimo maledictionis, quoniam habet tempus finem suum.

²⁰ "'Aries quem vidisti habere cornua rex Medorum est atque Persarum. ²¹ Porro hircus caprarum rex Graecorum est, et cornu grande quod erat inter oculos eius, ipse est rex primus. ²² Quod autem fracto illo surrexerunt quattuor pro eo, quattuor reges de gente eius consurgent, sed non in fortitudine eius. ²³ Et post regnum eorum cum creverint iniquitates, consurget rex inpudens facie et intellegens propositiones. ²⁴ Et roborabitur fortitudo eius, sed non in viribus suis, et supra quam credi potest universa vastabit et prosperabitur et faciet. Et interficiet robustos et populum sanctorum ²⁵ secundum voluntatem suam, et dirigetur dolus in manu eius, et cor suum magnificabit, et in copia rerum omnium occidet plurimos, et contra principem principum consurget et sine manu conteretur. ²⁶ Et visio vespere et mane quae dicta est vera est; tu ergo signa visionem quia post dies multos erit.'

²⁷ "Et ego, Danihel, langui et aegrotavi per dies, cumque surrexissem faciebam opera regis, et stupebam ad visionem, et non erat qui interpretaretur."

for in the time of the end the vision shall be fulfilled.' 18 And when he spoke to me I fell flat on the ground, and he touched me and set me upright, 19 and he said to me, 'I will shew thee what things are to come to pass in the end of the malediction, for the time hath its end.

20 "'The ram which thou sawest with horns is the king of the Medes and Persians. 21 And the he-goat is the king of the Greeks, and the great horn that was between his eyes, the same is the first king. 22 But whereas when that was broken there arose up four for it, four kings shall rise up of his nation, but not with his strength. 23 And after their reign when iniquities shall be grown up, there shall arise a king of a shameless face and understanding *dark* sentences. 24 And his power shall be strengthened, but not by his own force, and he shall lay all things waste and shall prosper and do more than can be believed. And he shall destroy the mighty and the people of the saints 25 according to his will, and craft shall be successful in his hand, and his heart shall be puffed up, and in the abundance of all things he shall kill many, and he shall rise up against the prince of princes and shall be broken without hand. 26 And the vision of the evening and the morning which was told is true; thou therefore seal up the vision because it shall come to pass after many days.'

27 "And I, Daniel, languished and was sick for some days, and when I was risen up I did the king's business, and I was astonished at the vision, and there was none that could interpret it."

Caput 9

"In anno primo Darii, filii Asueri, de semine Medorum, qui imperavit super regnum Chaldeorum, 2 anno uno regni eius, ego, Danihel, intellexi in libris numerum annorum de quo factus est sermo Domini ad Hieremiam prophetam, ut conplerentur desolationes Hierusalem septuaginta anni.

3 "Et posui faciem meam ad Dominum, Deum meum, rogare et deprecari in ieiuniis, sacco et cinere. 4 Et oravi Dominum, Deum meum, et confessus sum et dixi, 'Obsecro, Domine Deus, magne et terribilis, custodiens pactum et misericordiam diligentibus te et custodientibus mandata tua. 5 Peccavimus; iniquitatem fecimus; impie egimus et recessimus, et declinavimus a mandatis tuis ac iudiciis. 6 Non oboedivimus servis tuis, prophetis, qui locuti sunt in nomine tuo regibus nostris, principibus nostris, patribus nostris omnique populo terrae.

7 "'Tibi, Domine, iustitia, nobis autem confusio faciei, sicut est hodie viro Iuda et habitatoribus Hierusalem et omni Israhel, his qui prope sunt et his qui procul in universis

Chapter 9

Daniel's confession and prayer. Gabriel informs him concerning the seventy weeks to the coming of Christ.

"In the first year of Darius, the son of Ahasuerus, of the seed of the Medes, who reigned over the kingdom of the Chaldeans, 2 the first year of his reign, I, Daniel, understood by books the number of the years concerning which the word of the Lord came to Jeremiah the prophet, that seventy years should be accomplished of the desolation of Jerusalem.

3 "And I set my face to the Lord, my God, to pray and make supplication with fasting *and* sackcloth and ashes. 4 And I prayed to the Lord, my God, and I made my confession and said, 'I beseech thee, O Lord God, great and terrible, who keepest the covenant and mercy to them that love thee and keep thy commandments. 5 We have sinned; we have committed iniquity; we have done wickedly and have revolted, and we have gone aside from thy commandments and thy judgments. 6 We have not hearkened to thy servants, the prophets, that have spoken in thy name to our kings, to our princes, to our fathers and to all the people of the land.

7 "'To thee, O Lord, justice, but to us confusion of face, as at this day to the men of Judah and to the inhabitants of Jerusalem and to all Israel, to them that are near and to them that are far off in all the countries whither thou hast driven

terris ad quas eiecisti eos propter iniquitates eorum in quibus peccaverunt in te. 8 Domine, nobis confusio faciei, regibus nostris, principibus nostris et patribus nostris qui peccaverunt. 9 Tibi autem, Domino, Deo nostro, misericordia et propitiatio quia recessimus a te, 10 et non audivimus vocem Domini, Dei nostri, ut ambularemus in lege eius, quam posuit nobis per servos suos, prophetas.

11 "'Et omnis Israhel praevaricati sunt legem tuam et declinaverunt ne audirent vocem tuam, et stillavit super nos maledictio et detestatio quae scripta est in libro Mosi, servi Dei, quia peccavimus ei. 12 Et statuit sermones suos quos locutus est super nos et super principes nostros qui iudicaverunt nos, ut superinduceret in nos malum magnum quale numquam fuit sub omni caelo secundum quod factum est in Hierusalem. 13 Sicut scriptum est in lege Mosi, omne malum hoc venit super nos, et non rogavimus faciem tuam, Domine, Deus noster, ut reverteremur ab iniquitatibus nostris et cogitaremus veritatem tuam. 14 Et vigilavit Dominus super malitiam et adduxit eam super nos; iustus Dominus, Deus noster, in omnibus operibus suis quae fecit, non enim audivimus vocem eius.

15 "'Et nunc, Domine, Deus noster, qui eduxisti populum tuum de terra Aegypti in manu forti et fecisti tibi nomen secundum diem hanc, peccavimus, iniquitatem fecimus, 16 Domine, in omnem iustitiam tuam; avertatur, obsecro, ira tua et furor tuus a civitate tua Hierusalem et monte sancto tuo. Propter peccata enim nostra et iniquitates patrum nostrorum, Hierusalem et populus tuus in obprobrium sunt omnibus per circuitum nostrum. 17 Nunc ergo exaudi, Deus

them for their iniquities by which they have sinned against thee. 8 O Lord, to us belongeth confusion of face, *to* our princes and to our fathers that have sinned. 9 But to thee, the Lord, our God, mercy and forgiveness for we have departed from thee, 10 and we have not hearkened to the voice of the Lord, our God, to walk in his law, which he set before us by his servants, the prophets.

11 "And all Israel have transgressed thy law and have turned away from hearing thy voice, and the malediction and the curse which is written in the book of Moses, the servant of God, is fallen upon us because we have sinned against him. 12 And he hath confirmed his words which he spoke against us and against our princes that judged us, that he would bring in upon us a great evil such as never was under all the heaven according to that which hath been done in Jerusalem. 13 As it is written in the law of Moses, all this evil is come upon us, and we entreated not thy face, O Lord, our God, that we might turn from our iniquities and think on thy truth. 14 And the Lord hath watched upon the evil and hath brought it upon us; the Lord, our God, is just in all his works which he hath done, for we have not hearkened to his voice.

15 "And now, O Lord, our God, who hast brought forth thy people out of the land of Egypt with a strong hand and hast made thee a name as at this day, we have sinned, we have committed iniquity, 16 O Lord, against all thy justice; let thy wrath and thy indignation be turned away, I beseech thee, from thy city Jerusalem and from thy holy mountain. For by reason of our sins and the iniquities of our fathers, Jerusalem and thy people are a reproach to all that are round about us. 17 Now therefore, O our God, hear the supplica-

noster, orationem servi tui et preces eius, et ostende faciem tuam super sanctuarium tuum, quod desertum est, propter temet ipsum. 18 Inclina, Deus meus, aurem tuam, et audi; aperi oculos tuos, et vide desolationem nostram et civitatem super quam invocatum est nomen tuum, neque enim in iustificationibus nostris prosternimus preces ante faciem tuam sed in miserationibus tuis multis. 19 Exaudi, Domine; placare, Domine; adtende, et fac; ne moreris: propter temet ipsum, Deus meus, quia nomen tuum invocatum est super civitatem et super populum tuum.'

20 "Cumque adhuc loquerer et orarem et confiterer peccata mea et peccata populi mei Israhel et prosternerem preces meas in conspectu Dei mei pro monte sancto Dei mei, 21 adhuc me loquente in oratione, ecce: vir, Gabrihel, quem videram in visione a principio, cito volans tetigit me in tempore sacrificii vespertini. 22 Et docuit me et locutus est mihi dixitque, 'Danihel, nunc egressus sum ut docerem te et intellegeres. 23 Ab exordio precum tuarum egressus est sermo, ego autem veni ut indicarem tibi quia vir desideriorum es tu; ergo animadverte sermonem, et intellege visionem.

24 "'Septuaginta ebdomades adbreviatae sunt super populum tuum et super urbem sanctam tuam ut consummetur praevaricatio et finem accipiat peccatum et deleatur iniquitas et adducatur iustitia sempiterna et impleatur visio et prophetia et unguatur sanctus sanctorum. 25 Scito ergo, et animadverte: ab exitu sermonis ut iterum aedificetur Hierusalem usque ad Christum, ducem, ebdomades septem et ebdomades sexaginta duae erunt, et rursum aedificabitur platea, et muri in angustia temporum. 26 Et post ebdomades sexaginta duas occidetur Christus, et non erit eius popu-

tion of thy servant and his prayers, and shew thy face upon thy sanctuary, which is desolate, for thy own sake. 18 Incline, O my God, thy ear, and hear; open thy eyes, and see our desolation and the city upon which thy name is called, for it is not for our justifications that we present our prayers before thy face but for the multitude of thy tender mercies. 19 O Lord, hear; O Lord, be appeased; hearken, and do; delay not: for thy own sake, O my God, because thy name is invocated upon thy city and upon thy people.'

20 "Now while I was yet speaking and praying and confessing my sins and the sins of my people of Israel and presenting my supplications in the sight of my God for the holy mountain of my God, 21 as I was yet speaking in prayer, behold: the man, Gabriel, whom I had seen in the vision at the beginning, flying swiftly touched me at the time of the evening sacrifice. 22 And he instructed me and spoke to me and said, 'O Daniel, I am now come forth to teach thee and that thou mightest understand. 23 From the beginning of thy prayers the word came forth, and I am come to shew it to thee because thou art a man of desires; therefore do thou mark the word, and understand the vision.

24 "'Seventy weeks are shortened upon thy people and upon thy holy city that transgression may be finished and sin may have an end and iniquity may be abolished and everlasting justice may be brought and vision and prophecy may be fulfilled and the saint of saints may be anointed. 25 Know thou therefore, and take notice *that* from the going forth of the word to build up Jerusalem again unto Christ, the prince, there shall be seven weeks and sixty-two weeks, and the street shall be built again, and the walls in straitness of times. 26 And after sixty-two weeks Christ shall be slain, and

lus qui eum negaturus est. Et civitatem et sanctuarium dissipabit populus cum duce venturo, et finis eius vastitas, et
post finem belli statuta desolatio. 27 Confirmabit autem pactum multis ebdomada una, et in dimidio ebdomadis deficiet
hostia et sacrificium, et in templo erit abominatio desolationis, et usque ad consummationem et finem perseverabit desolatio.'"

Caput 10

Anno tertio Cyri, regis Persarum, verbum revelatum est
Daniheli, cognomento Balthasar, et verum verbum et fortitudo magna, intellexitque sermonem, intellegentia est enim
opus in visione.

2 "In diebus illis ego, Danihel, lugebam trium ebdomadarum diebus. 3 Panem desiderabilem non comedi, et caro et
vinum non introierunt in os meum, sed neque unguento
unctus sum donec conplerentur trium ebdomadarum dies.
4 Die autem vicesima et quarta mensis primi eram iuxta fluvium magnum, qui est Tigris. 5 Et levavi oculos meos, et vidi,

the people that shall deny him shall not be his. And a people with their leader that shall come shall destroy the city and the sanctuary, and the end thereof shall be waste, and after the end of the war the appointed desolation. 27 And he shall confirm the covenant with many in one week, and in the half of the week the victim and the sacrifice shall fall, and there shall be in the temple the abomination of desolation, and the desolation shall continue even to the consummation and to the end.'"

Chapter 10

Daniel, having humbled himself by fasting and penance, seeth a vision with which he is much terrified, but he is comforted by an angel.

In the third year of Cyrus, king of the Persians, a word was revealed to Daniel, surnamed Belteshazzar, and a true word and great strength, and he understood the word, for there is need of understanding in a vision.

2 "In those days I, Daniel, mourned the days of three weeks. 3 I ate no desirable bread, and neither flesh nor wine entered into my mouth, *neither* was I anointed with ointment till the days of three weeks were accomplished. 4 And in the four and twentieth day of the first month I was by the great river, which is the Tigris. 5 And I lifted up my eyes, and

et ecce: vir unus vestitus lineis, et renes eius accincti auro obrizo, 6 et corpus eius quasi chrysolitus, et facies eius velut species fulgoris, et oculi eius ut lampas ardens, et brachia eius et quae deorsum sunt usque ad pedes quasi species aeris candentis, et vox sermonum eius ut vox multitudinis. 7 Vidi autem ego, Danihel, solus visionem, porro viri qui erant mecum non viderunt, sed terror nimius inruit super eos, et fugerunt in absconditum. 8 Ego autem relictus solus vidi visionem grandem hanc, et non remansit in me fortitudo, sed et species mea inmutata est in me, et emarcui nec habui quicquam virium. 9 Et audivi vocem sermonum eius, et audiens iacebam consternatus super faciem meam vultusque meus herebat terrae.

10 "Et ecce: manus tetigit me et erexit me super genua mea et super articulos manuum mearum. 11 Et dixit ad me, 'Danihel, vir desideriorum, intellege verba quae ego loquor ad te, et sta in gradu tuo, nunc enim sum missus ad te.' Cumque dixisset mihi sermonem istum, steti tremens. 12 Et ait ad me, 'Noli metuere, Danihel, quia ex die primo quo posuisti cor tuum ad intellegendum, ut te adfligeres in conspectu Dei tui, exaudita sunt verba tua, et ego veni propter sermones tuos. 13 Princeps autem regni Persarum restitit mihi viginti et uno diebus, et ecce: Michahel, unus de principibus primis, venit in adiutorium meum, et ego remansi ibi iuxta regem Persarum. 14 Veni autem ut docerem te quae ventura sunt populo tuo in novissimis diebus, quoniam adhuc visio in dies.'

15 "Cumque loqueretur mihi huiuscemodi verbis, deieci vultum meum ad terram et tacui. 16 Et ecce: quasi similitudo filii hominis tetigit labia mea, et aperiens os meum locutus

I saw, and behold: a man clothed in linen, and his loins were girded with the finest gold, 6 and his body was like the chrysolite, and his face as the appearance of lightning, and his eyes as a burning lamp, and his arms and all downward even to the feet like in appearance to glittering brass, and the voice of his word like the voice of a multitude. 7 And I, Daniel, alone saw the vision, for the men that were with me saw it not, but an exceeding great terror fell upon them, and they fled away and hid themselves. 8 And I being left alone saw this great vision, and there remained no strength in me, and the appearance of my countenance was changed in me, and I fainted away and retained no strength. 9 And I heard the voice of his words, and when I heard I lay in a consternation upon my face, and my face was close to the ground.

10 "And behold: a hand touched me and lifted me up upon my knees and upon the joints of my hands. 11 And he said to me, 'Daniel, thou man of desires, understand the words that I speak to thee, and stand upright, for I am sent now to thee.' And when he had said this word to me, I stood trembling. 12 And he said to me, 'Fear not, Daniel, for from the first day that thou didst set thy heart to understand, to afflict thyself in the sight of thy God, thy words have been heard, and I am come for thy words. 13 But the prince of the kingdom of the Persians resisted me one and twenty days, and behold: Michael, one of the chief princes, came to help me, and I remained there by the king of the Persians. 14 But I am come to teach thee what things shall befall thy people in the latter days, for as yet the vision is for days.'

15 "And when he was speaking such words to me, I cast down my countenance to the ground and held my peace. 16 And behold: as it were the likeness of a son of man touched

sum et dixi ad eum qui stabat contra me, 'Domine mi, in visione tua dissolutae sunt conpages meae, et nihil in me remansit virium. 17 Et quomodo poterit servus domini mei loqui cum domino meo? Nihil enim in me remansit virium, sed et halitus meus intercluditur.'

18 "Rursum ergo tetigit me quasi visio hominis et confortavit me. 19 Et dixit, 'Noli timere, vir desideriorum; pax tibi; confortare, et esto robustus.' Cumque loqueretur mecum, convalui, et dixi, 'Loquere, domine mi, quia confortasti me.'

20 "Et ait, 'Numquid scis quare venerim ad te? Et nunc revertar ut proelier adversum principem Persarum. Cum ergo egrederer apparuit princeps Graecorum veniens. 21 Verumtamen adnuntiabo tibi quod expressum est in scriptura veritatis, et nemo est adiutor meus in omnibus his nisi Michahel, princeps vester.'"

Caput 11

"Ego autem ab anno primo Darii, Medi, stabam ut confortaretur et roboraretur.

2 "'Et nunc veritatem adnuntiabo tibi. Ecce: adhuc tres

my lips, then I opened my mouth and spoke and said to him that stood before me, 'O my Lord, at the sight of thee my joints are loosed, and no strength hath remained in me. 17 And how can the servant of my lord speak with my lord? For no strength remaineth in me; moreover my breath is stopped.'

18 "Therefore he that looked like a man touched me again and strengthened me. 19 And he said, 'Fear not, O man of desires; peace be to thee; take courage, and be strong.' And when he spoke to me, I grew strong, and I said, 'Speak, O my lord, for thou hast strengthened me.'

20 "And he said, 'Dost thou know wherefore I am come to thee? And now I will return to fight against the prince of the Persians. When *I* went forth there appeared the prince of the Greeks coming. 21 But I will tell thee what is set down in the scripture of truth, and none is my helper in all these things but Michael, your prince.'"

Chapter 11

The angel declares to Daniel many things to come with regard to the Persian and Grecian kings, more especially with regard to Antiochus as a figure of Antichrist.

"And from the first year of Darius, the Mede, I stood up that he might be strengthened and confirmed.

2 "And now I will shew thee the truth. Behold: there shall

reges stabunt in Perside, et quartus ditabitur opibus nimiis super omnes, et cum invaluerit divitiis suis concitabit omnes adversum regnum Graeciae. 3 Surget vero rex fortis et dominabitur potestate multa, et faciet quod placuerit ei. 4 Et cum steterit, conteretur regnum eius, et dividetur in quattuor ventos caeli, sed non in posteros eius neque secundum potentiam illius qua dominatus est. Lacerabitur enim regnum eius etiam in externos exceptis his.

5 "Et confortabitur rex austri, et de principibus eius praevalebit super eum, et dominabitur dicione, multa enim dominatio eius. 6 Et post finem annorum foederabuntur filiaque regis austri veniet ad regem aquilonis facere amicitiam, et non obtinebit fortitudinem brachii, nec stabit semen eius, et tradetur ipsa et qui adduxerunt eam adulescentes eius et qui confortabant eam in temporibus.

7 "Et stabit de germine radicum eius plantatio, et veniet cum exercitu et ingredietur provinciam regis aquilonis, et abutetur eis et obtinebit. 8 Insuper et deos eorum et sculptilia, vasa quoque pretiosa argenti et auri captiva ducet in Aegyptum; ipse praevalebit adversum regem aquilonis. 9 Et intrabit in regnum rex austri et revertetur ad terram suam.

10 "Filii autem eius provocabuntur, et congregabunt multitudinem exercituum plurimorum, et veniet properans et inundans, et revertetur et concitabitur, et congredietur cum robore eius. 11 Et provocatus rex austri egredietur et pugna-

stand yet three kings in Persia, and the fourth shall be enriched exceedingly above them all, and when he shall be grown mighty by his riches he shall stir up all against the kingdom of Greece. 3 But there shall rise up a strong king and shall rule with great power, and he shall do what he pleaseth. 4 And when he shall *come to his height,* his kingdom shall be broken, and it shall be divided towards the four winds of the heaven, but not to his posterity nor according to his power with which he ruled. For his kingdom shall be rent in pieces even for strangers beside these.

5 "And the king of the south shall be strengthened, and *one* of his princes shall prevail over him, and he shall rule with *great* power, for his dominion shall be great. 6 And after the end of years they shall be in league together, and the daughter of the king of the south shall come to the king of the north to make friendship, *but* she shall not obtain the strength of the arm, neither shall her seed stand, and she shall be given up and her young men that brought her and they that strengthened her in *these* times.

7 "And a plant of the bud of her roots shall stand up, and he shall come with an army and shall enter into the province of the king of the north, and he shall abuse them and shall prevail. 8 And he shall also carry away captive into Egypt their gods and their graven things and their precious vessels of gold and silver; he shall prevail against the king of the north. 9 And the king of the south shall enter into the kingdom and shall return to his own land.

10 "And his sons shall be provoked, and they shall assemble a multitude of great forces, and he shall come with haste *like a flood,* and he shall return and be stirred up, and he shall join battle with his forces. 11 And the king of the south

bit adversum regem aquilonis et praeparabit multitudinem nimiam, et dabitur multitudo in manu eius. 12 Et capiet multitudinem, et exaltabitur cor eius, et deiciet multa milia, sed non praevalebit. 13 Convertetur enim rex aquilonis et praeparabit multitudinem multo maiorem quam prius, et in fine temporum annorumque veniet properans cum exercitu magno et opibus nimiis.

14 "Et in temporibus illis multi consurgent adversum regem austri, filii quoque praevaricatorum populi tui extollentur ut impleant visionem, et corruent. 15 Et veniet rex aquilonis et conportabit aggerem et capiet urbes munitissimas, et brachia austri non sustinebunt, et consurgent electi eius ad resistendum, et non erit fortitudo. 16 Et faciet veniens super eum iuxta placitum suum, et non erit qui stet contra faciem eius, et stabit in terra inclita, et consumetur in manu eius. 17 Et ponet faciem suam ut veniat ad tenendum universum regnum eius, et recta faciet cum eo, et filiam feminarum dabit ei ut evertat illud, et non stabit, nec illius erit. 18 Et convertet faciem suam ad insulas et capiet multas, et cessare faciet principem obprobrii sui, et obprobrium eius convertetur in eum. 19 Et convertet faciem suam ad imperium terrae suae, et inpinget et corruet et non invenietur.

20 "Et stabit in loco eius vilissimus et indignus decore regio, et in paucis diebus contertur, non in furore nec in proelio. 21 Et stabit in loco eius despectus, et non tribuetur ei

being provoked shall go forth and shall fight against the king of the north and shall prepare an exceeding great multitude, and a multitude shall be given into his hand. 12 And he shall take a multitude, and his heart shall be lifted up, and he shall cast down many thousands, but he shall not prevail. 13 For the king of the north shall return and shall prepare a multitude much greater than before, and in the end of times and years he shall come in haste with a great army and much riches.

14 "'And in those times many shall rise up against the king of the south, and the children of prevaricators of thy people shall lift up themselves to fulfill the vision, and they shall fall. 15 And the king of the north shall come and shall cast up a mount and shall take the best fenced cities, and the arms of the south shall not withstand, and his chosen ones shall rise up to resist, and they shall not have strength. 16 And he shall come upon him and do according to his pleasure, and there shall be none to stand against his face, and he shall stand in the glorious land, and it shall be consumed by his hand. 17 And he shall set his face to come to possess all his kingdom, and he shall make upright conditions with him, and he shall give him a daughter of women to overthrow it, and she shall not stand, neither shall she be for him. 18 And he shall turn his face to the islands and shall take many, and he shall cause the prince of his reproach to cease, and his reproach shall be turned upon him. 19 And he shall turn his face to the empire of his own land, and he shall stumble and fall and shall not be found.

20 "'And there shall stand up in his place one most vile and unworthy of kingly honour, and in a few days he shall be destroyed, not in rage nor in battle. 21 And there shall stand up

honor regius, et veniet clam et obtinebit regnum in fraudulentia. 22 Et brachia pugnantis expugnabuntur a facie eius et conterentur, insuper et dux foederis. 23 Et post amicitias cum eo faciet dolum, et ascendet et superabit in modico populo. 24 Et abundantes et uberes urbes ingredietur et faciet quae non fecerunt patres eius et patres patrum eius: rapinas et praedam et divitias eorum dissipabit et contra firmissimas cogitationes iniet, et hoc usque ad tempus. 25 Et concitabitur fortitudo eius et cor eius adversum regem austri in exercitu magno, et rex austri provocabitur ad bellum multis auxiliis et fortibus nimis, et non stabunt, quia inibunt adversum eum consilia. 26 Et comedentes panem cum eo conterent illum exercitusque eius opprimetur, et cadent interfecti plurimi. 27 Duorum quoque regum cor erit ut malefaciant, et ad mensam unam mendacium loquentur, et non proficient, quia adhuc finis in aliud tempus. 28 Et revertetur in terram suam cum opibus multis, et cor eius adversus testamentum sanctum, et faciet et revertetur in terram suam.

29 "'Statuto tempore revertetur, et veniet ad austrum, et non erit priori simile novissimum. 30 Et venient super eum trieres et Romani, et percutietur et revertetur et indignabitur contra testamentum sanctuarii, et faciet reverteturque et cogitabit adversum eos qui dereliquerunt testamentum sanctuarii. 31 Et brachia ex eo stabunt, et polluent sanctua-

in his place one despised, and the kingly honour shall not be given him, and he shall come privately and shall obtain the kingdom by fraud. 22 And the arms of the fighter shall be overcome before his face and shall be broken, yea also the prince of the covenant. 23 And after friendships he will deal deceitfully with him, and he shall go up and shall overcome with a small people. 24 And he shall enter into rich and plentiful cities and he shall do that which his fathers never did nor his fathers' fathers: he shall scatter their spoils and their prey and their riches and shall forecast devices against the best fenced places, and this until a time. 25 And his strength and his heart shall be stirred up against the king of the south with a great army, and the king of the south shall be stirred up to battle with many and very strong succours, and they shall not stand, for they shall form designs against him. 26 And they that eat bread with him shall destroy him, and his army shall be overthrown, and many shall fall down slain. 27 And the heart of the two kings shall be to do evil, and they shall speak lies at one table, and they shall not prosper, because as yet the end is unto another time. 28 And he shall return into his land with much riches, and his heart shall be against the holy covenant, and he shall succeed and shall return into his own land.

29 "At the time appointed he shall return, and he shall come to the south, *but* the latter time shall not be like the former. 30 And the galleys and the Romans shall come upon him, and he shall be struck and shall return and shall have indignation against the covenant of the sanctuary, and he shall succeed, and he shall return and shall devise against them that have forsaken the covenant of the sanctuary. 31 And arms shall stand on his part, and they shall defile the

rium fortitudinis et auferent iuge sacrificium, et dabunt abominationem in desolationem. 32 Et impii in testamentum simulabunt fraudulenter, populus autem sciens Deum suum obtinebit et faciet. 33 Et docti in populo docebunt plurimos, et ruent in gladio et in flamma et in captivitate et in rapina dierum. 34 Cumque corruerint sublevabuntur auxilio parvulo, et adplicabuntur eis plurimi fraudulenter. 35 Et de eruditis ruent ut conflentur et eligantur et dealbentur usque ad tempus praefinitum, quia adhuc aliud tempus erit.

36 "Et faciet iuxta voluntatem suam rex, et elevabitur et magnificabitur adversum omnem deum, et adversum Deum deorum loquetur magnifica et dirigetur donec conpleatur iracundia, perpetrata est quippe definitio. 37 Et Deum patrum suorum non reputabit, et erit in concupiscentiis feminarum, nec quemquam deorum curabit, quia adversum universa consurget. 38 Deum autem Maozim in loco suo venerabitur, et deum quem ignoraverunt patres eius colet auro et argento et lapide pretioso rebusque pretiosis. 39 Et faciet ut muniat Maozim cum deo alieno quem cognovit, et multiplicabit gloriam et dabit eis potestatem in multis et terram dividet gratuito.

40 "Et in tempore praefinito proeliabitur adversum eum rex austri, et quasi tempestas veniet contra illum rex aquilonis in curribus et in equitibus et in classe magna, et ingredietur terras et conteret et pertransitet. 41 Et introibit in

sanctuary of strength and shall take away the continual sacrifice, and they shall place there the abomination unto desolation. 32 And such as deal wickedly against the covenant shall deceitfully dissemble, but the people that know their God shall prevail and succeed. 33 And they that are learned among the people shall teach many, and they shall fall by the sword and by fire and by captivity and by spoil for many days. 34 And when they shall have fallen they shall be relieved with a small help, and many shall be joined to them deceitfully. 35 And some of the learned shall fall that they may be tried and may be chosen and made white even to the appointed time, because yet there shall be another time.

36 "And the king shall do according to his will, and he shall be lifted up and shall magnify himself against every god, and he shall speak great things against the God of gods and shall prosper till the wrath be accomplished, for the determination is made. 37 And he shall make no account of the God of his fathers, and he shall follow the lust of women, and he shall not regard any gods, for he shall rise up against all things. 38 But he shall worship the god Mauzzim in his place, and a god whom his fathers knew not he shall worship with gold and silver and precious stones and things of great price. 39 And he shall do this to fortify Mauzzim with a strange god whom he hath acknowledged, and he shall increase glory and shall give them power over many and shall divide the land gratis.

40 "And at the time prefixed the king of the south shall fight against him, and the king of the north shall come against him like a tempest with chariots and with horsemen and with a great navy, and he shall enter into the countries and shall destroy and pass through. 41 And he shall enter into

terram gloriosam, et multae corruent, hae autem solae salvabuntur de manu eius: Edom et Moab et principium filiorum
Ammon. 42 Et mittet manum suam in terras, et terra Aegypti
non effugiet. 43 Et dominabitur thesaurorum auri et argenti
et in omnibus pretiosis Aegypti, per Lybiam quoque et Aethiopiam transibit. 44 Et fama turbabit eum ab oriente et ab
aquilone, et veniet in multitudine magna ut conterat et
interficiat plurimos. 45 Et figet tabernaculum suum Apadno
inter maria super montem inclitum et sanctum, et veniet usque ad summitatem eius, et nemo auxiliabitur ei.'"

Caput 12

"'In tempore autem illo consurget Michahel, princeps
magnus qui stat pro filiis populi tui, et veniet tempus quale
non fuit ab eo ex quo gentes esse coeperunt usque ad tempus illud. Et in tempore illo salvabitur populus tuus, omnis
qui inventus fuerit scriptus in libro. 2 Et multi de his qui dormiunt in terrae pulvere evigilabunt, alii in vitam aeternam et
alii in obprobrium ut videant semper. 3 Qui autem docti fue-

the glorious land, and many shall fall, and these only shall be saved out of his hand: Edom and Moab and the principality of the children of Ammon. 42 And he shall lay his hand upon the lands, and the land of Egypt shall not escape. 43 And he shall have power over the treasures of gold and of silver and all the precious things of Egypt, and he shall pass through Libya and Ethiopia. 44 And tidings out of the east and out of the north shall trouble him, and he shall come with a great multitude to destroy and slay many. 45 And he shall fix his tabernacle Apadno between the seas upon a glorious and holy mountain, and he shall come even to the top thereof, and none shall help him.'"

Chapter 12

Michael shall stand up for the people of God, with other things relating to Antichrist and the end of the world.

"But at that time shall Michael rise up, the great prince who standeth for the children of thy people, and a time shall come such as never was from the time that nations began even until that time. And at that time shall thy people be saved, every one that shall be found written in the book. 2 And many of those that sleep in the dust of the earth shall awake, some unto life everlasting and others unto reproach to see it always. 3 But they that are learned shall shine as the

rint fulgebunt quasi splendor firmamenti, et qui ad iustitiam erudiunt multos quasi stellae in perpetuas aeternitates. 4 Tu autem, Danihel, clude sermones, et signa librum, usque ad tempus statutum; pertransibunt plurimi, et multiplex erit scientia.'

5 "Et vidi ego, Danihel, et ecce: quasi duo alii stabant, unus hinc super ripam fluminis et alius inde ex altera ripa fluminis. 6 Et dixi viro qui indutus erat lineis qui stabat super aquas fluminis, 'Usquequo finis horum mirabilium?'

7 "Et audivi virum qui indutus erat lineis qui stabat super aquas fluminis, cum levasset dexteram et sinistram suam in caelum et iurasset per viventem in aeternum quia in tempus et tempora et dimidium temporis. Et cum conpleta fuerit dispersio manus populi sancti, conplebuntur universa haec. 8 Et ego audivi, et non intellexi.

"Et dixi, 'Domine mi, quid erit post haec?'

9 "Et ait, 'Vade, Danihel, quia clausi sunt signatique sermones usque ad tempus praefinitum. 10 Eligentur et dealbabuntur et quasi ignis probabuntur multi, et impie agent impii, neque intellegent omnes impii, porro docti intellegent. 11 Et a tempore cum ablatum fuerit iuge sacrificium et posita fuerit abominatio in desolatione, dies mille ducenti nonaginta. 12 Beatus qui expectat et pervenit ad dies mille trecentos triginta quinque. 13 Tu autem vade ad praefinitum, et requiesces et stabis in sorte tua in finem dierum.'"

brightness of the firmament, and they that instruct many to justice as stars for all eternity. 4 But thou, O Daniel, shut up the words, and seal the book, even to the time appointed; many shall pass over, and knowledge shall be manifold.'

5 "And I, Daniel, looked, and behold: as it were two others stood, one on this side upon the bank of the river and another on that side on the other bank of the river. 6 And I said to the man that was clothed in linen that stood upon the waters of the river, 'How long shall it be to the end of these wonders?'

7 "And I heard the man that was clothed in linen that stood upon the waters of the river, when he had lifted up his right hand and his left hand to heaven and had sworn by him that liveth for ever that it should be unto a time and times and half a time. And when the scattering of the band of the holy people shall be accomplished, all these things shall be finished. 8 And I heard, and understood not.

"And I said, 'O my lord, what shall be after these things?'

9 "And he said, 'Go, Daniel, because the words are shut up and sealed until the appointed time. 10 Many shall be chosen and made white and shall be tried as fire, and the wicked shall deal wickedly, and none of the wicked shall understand, but the learned shall understand. 11 And from the time when the continual sacrifice shall be taken away and the abomination unto desolation shall be set up, there shall be a thousand two hundred ninety days. 12 Blessed is he that waiteth and cometh unto a thousand three hundred thirty-five days. 13 But go thou thy ways until the time appointed, and thou shalt rest and stand in thy lot unto the end of the days.'"

Caput 13

Et erat vir habitans in Babylone, et nomen eius Ioachim, 2 et accepit uxorem, nomine Susannam, filiam Chelciae, pulchram nimis et timentem Deum. 3 Parentes enim illius cum essent iusti erudierunt filiam suam secundum legem Mosi. 4 Erat autem Ioachim dives valde et erat ei pomarium vicinum domui suae, et ad ipsum confluebant Iudaei eo quod esset honorabilior omnium.

5 Et constituti sunt duo senes iudices in anno illo, de quibus locutus est Dominus, quia "Egressa est iniquitas de Babylone a senioribus iudicibus qui videbantur regere populum." 6 Isti frequentabant domum Ioachim, et veniebant ad eos omnes qui habebant iudicia.

7 Cum autem populus revertisset per meridiem ingrediebatur Susanna et deambulabat in pomario viri sui. 8 Et videbant eam senes cotidie ingredientem et deambulantem, et exarserunt in concupiscentiam eius, 9 et everterunt sensum suum et declinaverunt oculos suos ut non viderent caelum neque recordarentur iudiciorum iustorum. 10 Erant ergo ambo vulnerati amore eius, nec indicaverunt sibi vicissim dolorem suum, 11 erubescebant enim indicare sibi concupiscentiam suam, volentes concumbere cum ea.

Chapter 13

Now there was a man that dwelt in Babylon, and his name was Joakim, 2 and he took a wife, whose name was Susanna, the daughter of Hilkiah, a very beautiful woman and one that feared God. 3 For her parents being just had instructed their daughter according to the law of Moses. 4 Now Joakim was very rich and had an orchard near his house, and the Jews resorted to him because he was the most honourable of them all.

5 And there were two of the ancients of the people appointed judges that year, of whom the Lord said, "Iniquity came out from Babylon from the ancient judges that seemed to govern the people." 6 These men frequented the house of Joakim, and all that had any matters of judgment came to them.

7 And when the people departed away at noon Susanna went in and walked in her husband's orchard. 8 And the old men saw her going in every day and walking, and they were inflamed with lust towards her, 9 and they perverted their own mind and turned away their eyes that they might not look unto heaven nor remember just judgments. 10 So they were both wounded with the love of her, yet they did not make known their grief one to the other, 11 for they were ashamed to declare to one another their lust, being desirous to *have to do* with her.

12 Et observabant cotidie sollicitius videre eam. Dixitque alter ad alterum, 13 "Eamus domum, quia prandii hora est." Et egressi recesserunt a se. 14 Cumque revertissent venerunt in unum, et sciscitantes ab invicem causam, confessi sunt concupiscentiam suam, et tunc in commune statuerunt tempus quando eam possent invenire solam.

15 Factum est autem, cum observarent diem aptum, ingressa est aliquando sicut heri et nudius tertius cum duabus solis puellis voluitque lavari in pomerio, aestus quippe erat. 16 Et non erat ibi quisquam praeter duos senes absconditos et contemplantes eam. 17 Dixit ergo puellis, "Adferte mihi oleum et smegmata, et ostia pomerii claudite ut laver." 18 Et fecerunt sicut praeceperat, clauseruntque ostia pomerii et egressae sunt per posticum ut adferrent quae iusserat, nesciebantque senes intus esse absconditos.

19 Cum autem egressae essent puellae, surrexerunt duo senes et adcurrerunt ad eam et dixerunt, 20 "Ecce: ostia pomerii clausa sunt, et nemo nos videt, et nos in concupiscentia tui sumus, quam ob rem adsentire nobis et commiscere nobiscum. 21 Quod si nolueris, dicemus testimonium contra te quod fuerit tecum iuvenis et ob hanc causam emiseris puellas a te."

22 Ingemuit Susanna et ait, "Angustiae sunt mihi undique, si enim hoc egero, mors mihi est, si autem non egero, non effugiam manus vestras. 23 Sed melius mihi est absque opere incidere in manus vestras quam peccare in conspectu Domini."

24 Et exclamavit voce magna Susanna, exclamaverunt au-

12 And they watched carefully every day to see her. And one said to the other, 13 "Let us now go home, for it is dinner time." So going out they departed one from another. 14 And turning back again they came both to the same place, and asking one another the cause, they acknowledged their lust, and then they agreed upon a time when they might find her alone.

15 And it fell out, as they watched a fit day, she went in on a time as yesterday and the day before with two maids only and was desirous to wash herself in the orchard, for it was hot weather. 16 And there was nobody there but the two old men that had hid themselves and were beholding her. 17 So she said to the maids, "Bring me oil and washing balls, and shut the doors of the orchard that I may wash me." 18 And they did as she bade them, and they shut the doors of the orchard and went out by a back door to fetch what she had commanded them, and they knew not that the elders were hid within.

19 Now when the maids were gone forth, the two elders arose and ran to her and said, 20 "Behold: the doors of the orchard are shut, and nobody seeth us, and we are in love with thee, wherefore consent to us and lie with us. 21 But if thou wilt not, we will bear witness against thee that a young man was with thee and therefore thou didst send away thy maids from thee."

22 Susanna sighed and said, "I am straitened on every side, for if I do this thing, it is death to me, and if I do it not, I shall not escape your hands. 23 But it is better for me to fall into your hands without doing it than to sin in the sight of the Lord."

24 *With that* Susanna cried out with a loud voice, and the

tem et senes adversus eam. 25 Et cucurrit unus et aperuit ostia pomerii. 26 Cum ergo audissent clamorem in pomerio famuli domus, inruerunt per posticam ut viderent quidnam esset. 27 Postquam autem senes locuti sunt, erubuerunt servi vehementer, quia numquam dictus fuerat sermo huiuscemodi de Susanna.

Et facta est dies crastina. 28 Cumque venisset populus ad virum eius, Ioachim, venerunt, et duo presbyteri pleni iniqua cogitatione adversum Susannam ut interficerent eam. 29 Et dixerunt coram populo, "Mittite ad Susannam, filiam Chelciae, uxorem Ioachim." Et statim miserunt. 30 Et venit cum parentibus et filiis et universis cognatis suis.

31 Porro Susanna erat delicata nimis et pulchra specie. 32 At iniqui illi iusserunt ut discoperiretur erat (enim cooperta), ut vel sic satiarentur decore eius. 33 Flebant igitur sui et omnes qui noverant eam. 34 Consurgentes autem duo presbyteri in medio populi posuerunt manus super caput eius. 35 Quae flens suspexit ad caelum, erat enim cor eius fiduciam habens in Domino.

36 Et dixerunt presbyteri, "Cum deambularemus in pomerio soli, ingressa est haec cum duabus puellis et clausit ostia pomerii et dimisit puellas. 37 Venitque ad eam adulescens qui erat absconditus et concubuit cum ea. 38 Porro nos cum essemus in angulo pomerii, videntes iniquitatem, cucurrimus ad eos, et vidimus eos pariter commisceri. 39 Et illum quidem non quivimus conprehendere quia fortior nobis erat, et apertis ostiis exilivit, 40 hanc autem cum adprehendissemus interrogavimus quisnam esset adulescens, et noluit indicare nobis; huius rei testes sumus."

elders also cried out against her. 25 And one *of them* ran to the door of the orchard and opened it. 26 So when the servants of the house heard the cry in the orchard, they rushed in by the back door to see what was the matter. 27 But after the old men had spoken, the servants were greatly ashamed, for never had there been any such word said of Susanna.

And *on* the next day, 28 *when* the people were come to Joakim, her husband, the two elders also came full of wicked device against Susanna to put her to death. 29 And they said before the people, "Send to Susanna, daughter of Hilkiah, the wife of Joakim." And presently they sent. 30 And she came with her parents and children and all her kindred.

31 Now Susanna was exceeding delicate and beautiful to behold. 32 But those wicked men commanded that *her face* should be uncovered (for she was covered), that so at least they might be satisfied with her beauty. 33 Therefore her friends and all her acquaintance wept. 34 But the two elders rising up in the midst of the people laid their hands upon her head. 35 And she weeping looked up to heaven, for her heart had confidence in the Lord.

36 And the elders said, "As we walked in the orchard alone, this woman came in with two maids and shut the doors of the orchard and sent away the maids from her. 37 Then a young man that was there hid came to her and lay with her. 38 But we that were in a corner of the orchard, seeing this wickedness, ran up to them, and we saw them lie together. 39 And him indeed we could not take because he was stronger than us, and opening the doors he leaped out, 40 but having taken this woman we asked who the young man was, *but* she would not tell us; of this thing we are witnesses."

41 Credidit eis multitudo quasi senibus populi et iudicibus, et condemnaverunt eam ad mortem.

42 Exclamavit autem voce magna Susanna et dixit, "Deus aeterne, qui absconditorum es cognitor, qui nosti omnia antequam fiant, 43 tu scis quoniam falsum contra me tulerunt testimonium, et ecce: morior, cum nihil horum fecerim quae isti malitiose conposuerunt adversum me."

44 Exaudivit autem Dominus vocem eius. 45 Cumque duceretur ad mortem, suscitavit Deus spiritum sanctum pueri iunioris cuius nomen Danihel, 46 et exclamavit voce magna, "Mundus ego sum a sanguine huius."

47 Et conversus omnis populus ad eum dixit, "Quis est sermo iste quem tu locutus es?"

48 Qui cum staret in medio eorum ait, "Sic fatui, filii Israhel, non iudicantes neque quod verum est cognoscentes condemnastis filiam Israhel? 49 Revertimini ad iudicium, quia falsum testimonium locuti sunt adversum eam."

50 Reversus est ergo populus cum festinatione, et dixerunt ei senes, "Veni, et sede in medio nostrum, et indica nobis, quia tibi dedit Deus honorem senectutis."

51 Et dixit ad populum Danihel, "Separate illos ab invicem procul, et diiudicabo eos."

52 Cum ergo divisi essent alter ab altero, vocavit unum de eis et dixit ad eum, "Inveterate dierum malorum, nunc venerunt peccata tua quae operabaris prius 53 iudicans iudicia iniusta, innocentes opprimens et dimittens noxios, dicente Domino, 'Innocentem et iustum non interficies.' 54 Nunc ergo, si vidisti eam, dic sub qua arbore videris eos loquentes sibi."

41 The multitude believed them as being the elders and the judges of the people, and they condemned her to death.

42 Then Susanna cried out with a loud voice and said, "O eternal God, who knowest hidden things, who knowest all things before they come to pass, 43 thou knowest that they have borne false witness against me, and behold: I *must* die, whereas I have done none of these things which these men have maliciously forged against me."

44 And the Lord heard her voice. 45 And when she was led to be put to death, the Lord raised up the holy spirit of a young boy whose name was Daniel, 46 and he cried out with a loud voice, "I am clear from the blood of this woman."

47 Then all the people turning themselves towards him said, "What meaneth this word that thou hast spoken?"

48 But he standing in the midst of them said, "Are ye so foolish, ye children of Israel, that without examination *or* knowledge *of* the truth you have condemned a daughter of Israel? 49 Return to judgment, for they have borne false witness against her."

50 So all the people turned again in haste, and the old men said to him, "Come, and sit thou down among us, and shew it us, seeing God hath given thee the honour of old age."

51 And Daniel said to the people, "Separate *these two* far from one another, and I will examine them."

52 So when they were put asunder one from the other, he called one of them and said to him, "O thou that art grown old in evil days, now are thy sins come out which thou hast committed before 53 in judging unjust judgments, oppressing the innocent and letting the guilty to go free, whereas the Lord saith, 'The innocent and the just thou shalt not kill.' 54 Now then, if thou sawest her, tell me under what tree thou sawest them conversing together."

Qui ait, "Sub scino."

⁵⁵ Dixit autem Danihel, "Recte mentitus es in caput tuum, ecce enim: angelus Dei, accepta sententia ab eo, scindet te medium."

⁵⁶ Et amoto eo, iussit venire alium, et dixit ei, "Semen Chanaan et non Iuda, species decepit te, et concupiscentia subvertit cor tuum; ⁵⁷ sic faciebatis filiabus Israhel, et illae timentes loquebantur vobis, sed non filia Iuda sustinuit iniquitatem vestram. ⁵⁸ Nunc ergo dic mihi sub qua arbore conprehenderis eos loquentes sibi."

Qui ait, "Sub prino."

⁵⁹ Dixit autem ei Danihel, "Recte mentitus es et tu in caput tuum, manet enim angelus Dei gladium habens ut secet te medium et interficiat vos."

⁶⁰ Exclamavit itaque omnis coetus voce magna, et benedixerunt Deum, qui salvat sperantes in se. ⁶¹ Et consurrexerunt adversum duos presbyteros, convicerat enim eos Danihel ex ore suo falsum dixisse testimonium, feceruntque eis sicuti male egerant adversum proximum ⁶² ut facerent secundum legem Mosi, et interfecerunt eos, et salvatus est sanguis innoxius in die illa.

⁶³ Chelcias autem et uxor eius laudaverunt Deum pro filia sua Susanna cum Ioachim, marito eius, et cognatis omnibus, quia non esset inventa in ea res turpis. ⁶⁴ Danihel autem factus est magnus in conspectu populi a die illa et deinceps.

⁶⁵ Et Rex Astyages adpositus est ad patres suos, et suscepit Cyrus, Perses, regnum eius.

He said, "Under a mastic tree."

55 And Daniel said, "Well hast thou lied against thy own head, for behold: the angel of God, having received the sentence of him, shall cut thee in two."

56 And having put him aside, he commanded that the other should come, and he said to him, "O thou seed of Canaan and not of Judah, beauty hath deceived thee, and lust hath perverted thy heart; 57 thus did you do to the daughters of Israel, and they for fear conversed with you, but a daughter of Judah *would* not abide your wickedness. 58 Now therefore tell me under what tree didst thou take them conversing together."

And he *answered,* "Under a holm tree."

59 And Daniel said to him, "Well hast thou also lied against thy own head, for the angel of the Lord waiteth with a sword to cut thee in two and to destroy you."

60 *With that* all the assembly cried out with a loud voice, and they blessed God, who saveth them that trust in him. 61 And they rose up against the two elders, for Daniel had convicted them of false witness by their own mouth, and they did to them as they had maliciously dealt against their neighbour 62 to fulfill the law of Moses, and they put them to death, and innocent blood was saved in that day.

63 But Hilkiah and his wife praised God for their daughter Susanna with Joakim, her husband, and all her kindred, because there was no dishonesty found in her. 64 And Daniel became great in the sight of the people from that day and thenceforward.

65 And King Astyages was gathered to his fathers, and Cyrus, the Persian, received his kingdom.

Caput 14

Erat autem Danihel conviva regis et honoratus super omnes amicos eius. 2 Erat quoque idolum nomine Bel apud Babylonios, et inpendebantur in eo per dies singulos similae artabae duodecim et oves quadraginta vinique amphorae sex.

3 Rex quoque colebat eum et ibat per singulos dies adorare eum, porro Danihel adorabat Deum suum. Dixitque ei rex, "Quare non adoras Bel?"

4 Qui respondens ait ei, "Quia non colo idola manufacta, sed viventem Deum qui creavit caelum et terram et habet potestatem omnis carnis."

5 Et dixit ad eum rex, "Non tibi videtur esse Bel vivens deus? An non vides quanta comedat et bibat cotidie?"

6 Et ait Danihel adridens, "Ne erres, rex, iste enim intrinsecus luteus est et forinsecus aereus, neque comedit aliquando."

7 Et iratus rex vocavit sacerdotes eius et ait eis, "Nisi dixeritis mihi quis est qui comedat inpensas has, moriemini. 8 Si autem ostenderitis quoniam Bel comedat haec, morietur Danihel quia blasphemavit in Bel."

Et dixit Danihel regi, "Fiat iuxta verbum tuum."

Chapter 14

The history of Bel and of the great serpent worshipped by the Babylonians.

And Daniel was the king's guest and was honoured above all his friends. 2 Now the Babylonians had an idol called Bel, and there were spent upon him every day twelve great measures of fine flour and forty sheep and six vessels of wine.

3 The king also worshipped him and went every day to adore him, but Daniel adored his God. And the king said to him, "Why dost thou not adore Bel?"

4 And he answered and said to him, "Because I do not worship idols made with hands, but the living God that created heaven and earth and hath power over all flesh."

5 And the king said to him, "Doth not Bel seem to thee to be a living god? Seest thou not how much he eateth and drinketh every day?"

6 Then Daniel smiled and said, "O king, be not deceived, for this is but clay within and brass without, neither hath he eaten at any time."

7 And the king being angry called for his priests and said to them, "If you tell me not who it is that eateth up these expenses, you shall die. 8 But if you can shew that Bel eateth these things, Daniel shall die because he hath blasphemed against Bel."

And Daniel said to the king, "Be it done according to thy word."

9 Erant autem sacerdotes Bel septuaginta exceptis uxoribus et parvulis et filiis. Et venit rex cum Danihele in templum Belis. 10 Et dixerunt sacerdotes Belis, "Ecce: nos egredimur foras; et tu, rex, pone escas, et vinum misce, et claude ostium, et signa anulo tuo, 11 et cum ingressus fueris mane nisi inveneris omnia comesta a Bel, moriemur, vel Danihel, qui mentitus est adversum nos." 12 Contemnebant autem, quia fecerant sub mensa absconditum introitum, et per illum ingrediebantur semper et devorabant ea.

13 Factum est igitur postquam egressi sunt illi, rex posuit cibos ante Bel, praecepit Danihel pueris suis, et adtulerunt cinerem, et cribravit per totum templum coram rege, et egressi clauserunt ostium, et signantes anulo regis abierunt. 14 Sacerdotes autem ingressi sunt nocte iuxta consuetudinem suam et uxores et filii eorum, et comederunt omnia et biberunt.

15 Surrexit autem rex primo diluculo et Danihel cum eo. 16 Et ait rex, "Salvane sunt signa, Danihel?"

Qui respondit, "Salva, rex."

17 Statimque cum aperuisset ostium, intuitus rex mensam exclamavit voce magna, "Magnus es, Bel, et non est apud te dolus quisquam."

18 Et risit Danihel, et tenuit regem ne ingrederetur intro, et dixit, "Ecce pavimentum; animadverte cuius vestigia sunt haec."

19 Et dixit rex, "Video vestigia virorum et mulierum et infantium." Et iratus est rex.

20 Tunc adprehendit sacerdotes et uxores et filios eorum,

9 Now the priests of Bel were seventy besides their wives and little ones and children. And the king went with Daniel into the temple of Bel. 10 And the priests of Bel said, "Behold: we go out; and do thou, O king, set on the meats, and make ready the wine, and shut the door fast, and seal it with thy own ring, 11 and when thou comest in the morning if thou findest not that Bel hath eaten up all, we will suffer death, or else Daniel, that hath lied against us." 12 And they little regarded it, because they had made under the table a secret entrance, and they always came in by it and consumed those things.

13 So it came to pass after they were gone out, the king set the meats before Bel, *and* Daniel commanded his servants, and they brought ashes, and he sifted them all over the temple before the king, and going forth they shut the door, and having sealed it with the king's ring they departed. 14 But the priests went in by night according to their custom with their wives and their children, and they ate and drank up all.

15 And the king arose early in the morning and Daniel with him. 16 And the king said, "Are the seals whole, Daniel?"

And he answered, "They are whole, O king."

17 And as soon as he had opened the door, the king looked upon the table and cried out with a loud voice, "Great art thou, O Bel, and there is not any deceit with thee."

18 And Daniel laughed, and he held the king that he should not go in, and he said, "Behold the pavement; mark whose footsteps these are."

19 And the king said, "I see the footsteps of men and women and children." And the king was angry.

20 Then he took the priests and their wives and their chil-

et ostenderunt ei abscondita ostiola per quae ingrediebantur et consumebant quae erant super mensam. 21 Occidit ergo illos rex et tradidit Bel in potestatem Danihelis, qui subvertit eum et templum eius.

22 Et erat draco magnus in loco illo, et colebant eum Babylonii. 23 Et dixit rex Daniheli, "Ecce: nunc non potes dicere quia non sit iste deus vivens; adora ergo eum."

24 Dixitque Danihel, "Dominum, Deum meum, adoro, quia ipse est Deus vivens. 25 Tu autem, rex, da mihi potestatem, et interficiam draconem absque gladio et fuste."

Et ait rex, "Do tibi."

26 Tulit ergo Danihel picem et adipem et pilos et coxit pariter, fecitque massas et dedit in os draconis, et disruptus est draco. Et dixit, "Ecce quem colebatis."

27 Quod cum audissent Babylonii indignati sunt vehementer, et congregati adversum regem dixerunt, "Iudaeus factus est rex. Bel destruxit, draconem interfecit, et sacerdotes occidit." 28 Et dixerunt cum venissent ad regem, "Trade nobis Danihelem, alioquin interficiemus te et domum tuam." 29 Vidit ergo rex quod inruerent in eum vehementer, et necessitate conpulsus tradidit eis Danihelem.

30 Qui miserunt eum in lacum leonum, et erat ibi diebus sex. 31 Porro in lacu erant septem leones, et dabantur eis cotidie duo corpora et duae oves, et tunc non data sunt eis, ut devorarent Danihelem.

32 Erat autem Abacuc propheta in Iudaea, et ipse coxerat

dren, and they shewed him the private doors by which they came in and consumed the things that were on the table. 21 The king therefore put them to death and delivered Bel into the power of Daniel, who destroyed him and his temple.

22 And there was a great dragon in that place, and the Babylonians worshipped him. 23 And the king said to Daniel, "Behold: thou canst not say now that this is not a living god; adore him therefore."

24 And Daniel said, "I adore the Lord, my God, for he is the living God, *but that is no living god.* 25 But give me leave, O king, and I will kill this dragon without sword or club."

And the king said, "I give thee *leave.*"

26 Then Daniel took pitch and fat and hair and boiled them together, and he made lumps and put them into the dragon's mouth, and the dragon burst asunder. And he said, "Behold him whom you worshipped."

27 And when the Babylonians had heard this they took great indignation, and being gathered together against the king they said, "The king is become a Jew. He hath destroyed Bel, he hath killed the dragon, and he hath put the priests to death." 28 And they came to the king and said, "Deliver us Daniel, or else we will destroy thee and thy house." 29 And the king saw that they pressed upon him violently, and being constrained by necessity he delivered Daniel to them.

30 And they cast him into the den of lions, and he was there six days. 31 And in the den there were seven lions, and they had given to them two carcasses every day and two sheep, *but* then they were not given unto them, that they might devour Daniel.

32 Now there was in Judea a prophet *called* Habakkuk,

pulmentum et intriverat panes in alveolo et ibat in campum ut ferret messoribus.

33 Dixitque angelus Domini ad Abacuc, "Fer prandium quod habes in Babylonem Daniheli, qui est in lacu leonum."

34 Et dixit Abacuc, "Domine, Babylonem non vidi, et lacum nescio."

35 Et adprehendit eum angelus Domini in vertice eius et portavit eum capillo capitis sui posuitque eum in Babylone supra lacum in impetu spiritus sui.

36 Et clamavit Abacuc, dicens, "Danihel, tolle prandium quod misit tibi Deus."

37 Et ait Danihel, "Recordatus es mei, Deus, et non dereliquisti diligentes te." 38 Surgensque Danihel comedit. Porro angelus Domini restituit Abacuc confestim in loco suo.

39 Venit ergo rex die septima ut lugeret Danihelem, et venit ad lacum et introspexit, et ecce: Danihel sedens in medio leonum. 40 Et exclamavit rex voce magna, dicens, "Magnus es, Domine, Deus Danihelis." Et extraxit eum de lacu leonum.

41 Porro illos qui perditionis eius causa fuerant intromisit in lacum, et devorati sunt in momento coram eo. 42 Tunc rex ait, "Paveant omnes habitantes in universa terra Deum Danihelis, quia ipse est salvator, faciens signa et mirabilia in terra, qui liberavit Danihelem de lacu leonum."

and he had boiled pottage and had broken bread in a bowl and was going into the field to carry it to the reapers.

33 And the angel of the Lord said to Habakkuk, "Carry the dinner which thou hast into Babylon to Daniel, who is in the lions' den."

34 And Habakkuk said, "Lord, I never saw Babylon, nor do I know the den."

35 And the angel of the Lord took him by the top of his head and carried him by the hair of his head and set him in Babylon over the den in the force of his spirit.

36 And Habakkuk cried, saying, "O Daniel, thou *servant of God,* take the dinner that God hath sent thee."

37 And Daniel said, "Thou hast remembered me, O God, and thou hast not forsaken them that love thee." 38 And Daniel arose and ate. And the angel of the Lord presently set Habakkuk again in his own place.

39 And upon the seventh day the king came to bewail Daniel, and he came to the den and looked in, and behold: Daniel was sitting in the midst of the lions. 40 And the king cried out with a loud voice, saying, "Great art thou, O Lord, the God of Daniel." And he drew him out of the lions' den.

41 But those that had been the cause of his destruction he cast into the den, and they were devoured in a moment before him. 42 Then the king said, "Let all the inhabitants of the whole earth fear the God of Daniel, for he is the saviour, working signs and wonders in the earth, who hath delivered Daniel out of the lions' den."

Note on the Text

This edition is meant to present a Latin text close to what the Douay-Rheims translators saw. Therefore the readings in this edition are not necessarily preferred in the sense that they are thought to be "original"; instead, they represent the Latin Bible as it was read by many from the eighth through the sixteenth century. Furthermore, in the service of economy, sources for the text are cited according to a hierarchy and consequently the lists of sources following the lemmas and alternate readings are not necessarily comprehensive. If a reading appears in Weber's text or apparatus, no other sources are cited; if it is not in Weber but is in Quentin, only the sources cited by Quentin are reproduced. The complete list of sources for the Latin text, in their hierarchical order, is Weber, the Sixto-Clementine edition, Weber's apparatus, Quentin, his apparatus, the Vetus Latina edition of Pierre Sabatier (1682–1742), the *Glossa Ordinaria* attributed (wrongly) to Walafrid Strabo in the Patrologia Latina, and the database of the Beuroner Vetus Latina-Institut.

When no source can be found for what seems to be the correct Latin, a reconstruction is proposed in the Notes to the Text but the Weber text is generally printed in the edition. Trivial differences between the Weber and Sixto-Clementine editions in word order and orthography, alternative spellings and inflections of proper names, and synco-

pation of verbs have not been noted, nor have many differences that do not affect translation, such as the omission or inclusion of forms of *esse,* variant forms of personal pronouns, conjunctions treated by the Douay-Rheims translators as synonymous, and the omission or inclusion of certain pronouns or possessive adjectives.

Whenever it has been necessary to stray from Weber's text (about one thousand times in the first volume), the departures are recorded in the Notes to the Text. These notes by no means constitute a true *apparatus criticus,* but they enable interested readers to see both the deviations from Weber (whose text is preferable for people wanting to get as close as possible to the earliest versions of the many Latin texts which, combined, form the Vulgate Bible) and significant differences among the Weber, Sixto-Clementine, and Douay-Rheims texts.

When the translation reflects a reading closer to Weber's than to the Sixto-Clementine edition, the Sixto-Clementine variation is printed in the Notes to the Text. Less frequently, there are two readings that would translate the same way but that differ sufficiently to warrant noting, as at Gen 19:6, where Weber reads "umbraculum tegminis" while the Sixto-Clementine version has "umbra culminis."

Often the punctuation of the Douay-Rheims edition reflects an understanding of the Latin different from that of the Weber, Sixto-Clementine, or both editions. The Weber edition has no punctuation marks in most books; rather, the editors inserted line breaks to mark new clauses or sentences, a punctuation style known as *per cola et commata,* which is meant to assist readers without inserting anachronistic markings. These line breaks have been represented in

the notes by slashes (/). In general, differences in punctuation among this edition, the Sixto-Clementine Bible, and Weber's edition have been cited only when they demonstrate considerably different understandings of the Latin. Often Weber's presentation is too equivocal to shed light on his understanding; in these cases, his edition is not cited.

While the Douay-Rheims translation belongs to a tradition of exceptionally literal renderings of the Latin Bible, Challoner's revision contains some divergences from the Latin. Any English that does not square with the text *en face* is italicized, and where possible, Challoner's source has been indicated in the Notes to the Text. When Challoner's source is given, it is not necessarily quoted word for word in the lemma; indeed, the Septuagint is cited as a source, yet almost no Greek is quoted in the notes. Whenever there can be doubt of a source based on a slight difference between its reading and Challoner's, the difference has been recorded following the lemma, either in parentheses or in brackets when containing explanatory material that is not a quotation from the source. Sources for the English text are cited in a hierarchical fashion similar to that of the Latin, in the following order: Douay-Rheims, Sixto-Clementine, King James, Septuagint, Hebrew text; this means that if an English reading is found in the King James Version that may also be in the Septuagint, only the King James Version is cited. Also, if Challoner's translation seems to approximate a source that is cited, the distance between source and translation is indicated by a question mark following the siglum.

Words cited from biblical sources are in italics in the notes, and the sigla and any comments are in roman type. Lemmas precede colons; other readings follow them. Occa-

sionally Challoner indicated that he was adding words to his revision that did not appear in the Latin text; he did this by italicizing the relevant words, much as the authors of the King James Version printed occasional words in roman as opposed to black-letter type to indicate an addition. Bracketed explanations or underlinings draw attention to these typographical variations in the Notes to the Text where necessary.

Notes to the Text

Sigla

*D-R = Latin text that seems to give rise to the D-R translation but that is not represented in S-C, Weber, or in any of the manuscripts cited in those editions.

D-R = *The Holie Bible: Faithfully Translated into English out of the Authentical Latin* (The English Colleges of Douay and Rheims, OT 1609–10, NT 1582)

D-Rn = marginalia in D-R

D-R/C = *The Holy Bible: Translated from the Latin Vulgat* (Challoner's 1750 revision, Dublin?)

Heb = Hebrew sources for the text

KJV = *The Holy Bible, Conteyning the Old Testament, and the New: Newly Translated out of the Originall tongues: & with the former Translations diligently compared and reuised: by his Maiesties speciall Comandement Appointed to be read in Churches* (London: Robert Barker, Printer to the Kings most Excellent Maiestie, 1611, rpr. Thomas Nelson Publishers, 1990)

KJVn = marginalia in KJV

PG = J.-P. Migne, ed., *Patrologiae Graecae* (Paris, 1857–1866)

PL = J.-P. Migne, ed., *Patrologia Latina* (Paris, 1844–1864)

Quentin = *Biblia sacra iuxta Vulgatam versionem* (Typis Polyglottis Vaticanis, 1926–[1995])

S = A. Rahlfs, ed., R. Hanhart, rev., *Septuaginta,* 2nd ed. (Deutsche Bibelgesellschaft, 2006)

S-C = *Biblia Sacra: Vulgatae Editionis Sixti V Pont. Max. iussu recognita et Clementis VIII auctoritate edita* (Vatican City: Marietti, 1959)

Sabatier: P. Sabatier, *Bibliorum Sacrorum Latinae versiones antiquae, seu Vetus Italica.* 3 vols. (Rheims: Apud Reginaldum Florentain, Regis Typographicum & Bibliopolam, sub signo Bibliorum aureorum, 1743–1749)

Smyth = H. W. Smyth, ed., G. M. Messing, rev., *Greek Grammar* (Cambridge, MA: Harvard University Press, 1956)

Weber = R. Weber, ed., *Biblia Sacra Vulgata,* 5th ed. (Deutsche Bibelgesellschaft, 2007); in the Psalms this siglum refers to Weber's Psalmi Iuxta LXX

Weber Iuxta Hebr. = Psalmi Iuxta Hebr. in R. Weber, ed., *Biblia Sacra Vulgata,* 5th ed. (Deutsche Bibelgesellschaft, 2007)

The use of sigla from Weber and Quentin's critical apparatus is indicated in brackets following the sigla; Weber's practice of adding a full stop after certain entries to indicate that a citation is limited to the sources referenced has not been followed.

Other abbreviations follow those found in H. J. Frede, *Kirchenschriftsteller: Verzeichnis und Sigel* (Freiburg: Verlag Herder, 1995), and R. Gryson, *Altlateinische Handschriften.* 2 vols. (Freiburg: Verlag Herder, 1999).

Isaiah

1:1   *et Ezechiae*: *Ezechiae* Weber
1:3   *autem me non*: *non* Weber; *et populus*: *populus* Weber
<1:6   *dressed* D-R/C: *cured with medicine* D-R>
1:8   *cucumerario et*: *cucumerario* Weber
<1:11   *do you offer me* D-R (in italics in D-R/C): literally, *for me is*>

1:12 *veniretis: veneritis* Weber

<1:12 *to appear* KJV: omitted in D-R>

1:13 *offeratis: adferatis* Weber

<1:14 *new moons* KJV: *Calendes* D-R>

1:15 *manus enim: manus* Weber

<1:18 *then* KJV (*now*): omitted in D-R>

1:18 *lana alba: lana* Weber

1:19 *audieritis me: audieritis* Weber

1:24 *Dominus, Deus: Dominus* Weber

<1:25 *clean purge away thy dross* KJV (*purely* for *clean*): *boyle out thy drosse til it be pure* D-R>

2:1 *Iudam: Iuda* S-C

2:10 *petram, et abscondere in: petram abscondere* Weber

<2:10 *pit* D-R/C: *pitte, in the ground* D-R>

2:11 *sublimes: sublimis* Weber

2:15 *omnem murum* Frede HI Is 1 p. 36.1 [siglum W in Gryson's Esaias]: *super omnem murum* Weber, S-C

2:21 *fissuras: scissuras* S-C; *et in: et* Weber

2:22 *eius est: eius* Weber

3:1 *Dominus: Deus* Weber

<3:2 *cunning man* D-R/C: *southsayer* D-R>

3:3 *consiliarium et: consiliarium* Weber

<3:3 *architect* KJV (*cunning artificer*): *wise of workemasters* D-R; *eloquent* KJV: *mystical* D-R>

3:5 *virum, et: virum* Weber

<3:6 *saying* KJV (in roman type in KJV and italics in D-R/C): omitted in D-R>

<3:9 *shew* KJV: *knowlege* D-R; *abroad* D-R/C: omitted in D-R>

3:9 *Sodoma: Sodomae* Weber

<3:10 *doings* KJV: *inuentions* D-R>

3:12 *eis: eius* Weber

3:14 *vineam, et: vineam* Weber

<3:16 *wanton* KJV *glances* D-R/C: *went with twinglings* D-R; *made a noise as they* D-R/C: *clapped their handes* D-R>

3:16 *pedibus suis et: et in pedibus suis* Weber

3:18 *ornatum: ornamentum* S-C

3:20   *et discriminalia*: *discriminalia* Weber

3:22   *palliola*: *pallia* Weber

<3:22   *crisping pins* KJV: *nedles* D-R>

<3:23   *fine* D-R/C: omitted in D-R>

4:1   *invocetur*: *vocetur* Weber

4:2   *et gloria*: *et in gloria* Weber

4:4   *sordes*: *sordem* Weber; *eius in*: *eius* Weber

<5:1   *on a hill in a fruitful place* S [glossed as *in the horn, the son of oil* in D-R/C]: *in horne the sonne of oile* D-R>

<5:2   *with choicest vines* KJV (*vine* for *vines*): *elect* D-R>

<5:3   *And* KJV: *therfore* D-R>

5:3   *habitatores*: *habitator* Weber; *viri*: *vir* Weber; *vineam*: *inter vineam* Weber

<5:4   *that* KJV: *and* D-R>

<5:6   *but* KJV: *and* D-R; *come up* S-C: *ouergrowe it* D-R>

5:6   *super eam vepres* ΘΨ^DΩagre cum HI [Quentin's sigla]: *vepres* Weber, S-C

5:7   *Israhel est*: *Israhel* Weber

5:9   *dicit Dominus*: *Domini* Weber

5:10   *iugera*: *iuga* Weber

<5:10   *measure* D-R/C: *flagon* D-R>

5:19   *et veniat* PG 57.195: *et adpropiet et veniat* Weber, S-C

<5:19   *come that* KJV: *come, and* D-R>

<5:20   *for light and light for* KJV (*for . . . for* in italics in D-R/C): *light, and light* D-R>

5:25   *populum suum*: *populo suo* Weber

5:26   *levabit*: *elevabit* S-C; *signum in*: *signum* Weber

<5:29   *roar* KJV: *gnash* D-R>

<6:1   *his train* KJV: *those thinges that were vnder him* D-R>

6:1   *implebant*: *replebant* S-C

6:3   *Dominus, Deus*: *Dominus* Weber

6:4   *impleta*: *repleta* S-C

6:6   *carbonem* Sabatier: *calculus* Weber, S-C

<6:7   *iniquities* S: *iniquitie* D-R>

6:8   *ego sum*: *ego* S-C

<7:1   *but* KJV: *and* D-R>

<7:2 *with* KJV: *at the face of* D-R>

7:3 *extremum aquaeductus*: *aquaeductum* *D-R

7:4 *duabus*: *duobus* Weber; *regis*: *et* Weber

7:5 *in malum*: *malum* Weber

<7:8 *Ephraim* KJV: *and Ephraim* D-R>

<7:11 *either* KJV: omitted in D-R>

7:14 *vocabitur*: *vocabitis* Weber

7:19 *in cavernis*: *cavernis* Weber

7:23 *in spinas*: *et in spinas* Weber

<7:25 *but* KJV: *and* D-R>

8:1 *cito*: *Cito* Weber

<8:13 *and let . . . let* KJV (*let . . . let* in roman type in KJV): omitted in D-R>

8:18 *pueri mei*: *pueri* Weber; *Israhel*: *Israhelis* Weber

8:19 *stridunt*: *strident* S-C; *requiret*: *requirit* Weber

<8:19 *Should* KJV: *shal* D-R>

8:22 *et angustia*: *angustia* Weber

9:3 *et non*: *non* Weber; *sicut qui*: *sicut* Weber; *victores capta praeda quando*: *quando* Weber

9:6 *et filius*: *filius* Weber

9:7 *eius sedebit*: *eius* Weber

<9:9 *haughtiness* S: *greatnes* D-R>

<9:11 *bring on* D-R/C: *turne* D-R; *in a crowd* D-R/C: *into tumult* D-R>

<9:12 *the Syrians* KJV: *Syria* D-R; *open* KJV: *ful* D-R>

<9:16 *shall* D-R/C: omitted in D-R>

<9:20 *and* KJV (in roman type in KJV and italics in D-R/C): omitted in D-R>

<10:1 *write* KJV: *haue written* D-R>

10:3 *fugietis*: *confugietis* S-C

10:5 *ipse est*: *ipse* Weber

<10:5 *and* KJV: omitted in D-R>

10:7 *aestimabit*: *existimabit* S-C

<10:9 *as so many* D-R/C: *with al* D-R>

<10:14 *or . . . or* KJV: *and . . . and* D-R>

10:15 *levantem*: *elevantem* S-C

10:16 *Dominus*: *Deus* Weber

10:18   *carmeli*: *Carmeli* Weber

10:19   *pro*: *prae* S-C

<10:19   *shall be so few that they* KJV (without *so* or *they*): *for the fewnes* D-R;
              easily D-R/C: omitted in D-R>

<10:22   *overflow with justice* KJV (*righteousnesse* for *justice*): *make iustice ouer-*
              flow D-R>

10:29   *Gaba*: *Gabee* Weber

<10:30   *Lift up* KJV: *Neay with* D-R>

10:32   *Nobe*: *Nob* Weber

11:5   *renum*: *renis* Weber

<11:8   *sucking child* KJV: *infant from the brest* D-R>

11:15   *flumen*: *Flumen* Weber

11:16   *Israheli*: *Israhel* Weber; *die*: *die illa* S-C

12:2   *Dominus*: *Dominus Deus* Weber

<12:5   *great things* KJV (*excellent* for *great*): *magnifically* D-R>

13:7   *tabescet*: *contabescet* S-C

13:8   *Torsiones*: *tortiones* Weber

13:9   *veniet*: *venit* Weber; *solitudine*: *solitudinem* S-C

<13:12   *finest of* D-R/C: *pure fine* D-R>

<13:13   *his fierce wrath* KJV (*anger* for *wrath*): *the wrath of his furie* D-R>

13:16   *adlidentur*: *adlident* Weber

13:18   *interficiant*: *interficient* S-C; *uteri*: *uteris* S-C; *misereantur*: *miserebun-*
              tur S-C; *parcat*: *parcet* S-C

13:19   *in superbia*: *superbia* S-C; *Dominus*: *Deus* Weber

<13:19   *pride* S-C: *in the pride* D-R>

13:22   *sirenae*: *sirenes* S-C

<14:1   *and* KJV: omitted in D-R>

<14:8   *saying* KJV (in roman type in KJV and italics in D-R/C): omitted in
              D-R>

14:8   *ascendit*: *ascendet* S-C

14:9   *gigantas*: *gigantes* S-C

14:10   *et nos*: *nos* Weber

14:19   *obvolutus cum his*: *obvolutus* Weber

14:20   *terram tuam*: *terram* Weber; *populum tuum*: *populum* Weber

14:21   *suorum*: *eorum* Weber

14:22   *ait*: *dicit* S-C

14:31 *veniet*: *venit* Weber; *effugiat*: *effugiet* S-C

14:32 *gentium* Q [Quentin's siglum]: *gentis* Weber, S-C; *ipso*: *ipsa* Weber

15:2 *ululabit*: *ululavit* S-C; *et omnis*: *omnis* Weber

<15:2 *Moab hath howled* S-C: *shal Moab howle* D-R>

15:3 *ululatus*: *ululat* Weber

<15:3 *shall howl* KJV: *howling* D-R>

15:4 *Clamabit*: *clamavit* Weber

16:1 *agnum, Domine*: *agnum* Weber

16:5 *illud*: *eum* Weber

16:7 *muros*: *muro* Weber

<16:7 *brick* D-R/C: *baqued bricke* D-R>

16:8 *vineam*: *vinea* Weber

<16:11 *brick* D-R/C: *baqued bricke* D-R>

17:4 *pinguedo*: *pingue* Weber

<17:6 *berries* KJV: *oliues* D-R>

17:9 *eris*: *erit* Weber

17:12 *multitudini*: *multitudo* Weber

<17:13 *but* KJV: *and* D-R>

<17:14 *behold*: D-R/C *there shall be* S: *and behold* D-R; *The morning shall come* D-R/C: *in the morning* D-R>

18:2 *mare*: *mari* Weber; *ad gentem*: *expectantem*: *gentem expectantem ex-pectantem* Weber

18:5 *abscidentur et*: *abscidentur* Weber, *abscindentur et* S-C

19:1 *movebuntur*: *commovebuntur* S-C

<19:7 *by the water* KJV (*brooks* for *water*): *that is watered* D-R>

19:8 *aquae*: *aquarum* S-C; *marcescent*: *emarcescent* S-C

<19:8 *waters* KJV: *face of the water* D-R>

<19:10 *shall mourn* S (in italics in D-R/C): omitted in D-R>

19:11 *Pharaonis*: *Pharao* Weber

<19:13 *gone astray* KJV (*deceiued*): *withered away* D-R>

<19:16 *because of* KJV [properly a Hebraism]: *at the face of* D-R>

19:17 *pavorem*: *festivitatem* Weber

<19:17 *because of* KJV [properly a Hebraism]: *at the face of* D-R>

19:18 *civitas solis*: *civitas Solis* Weber, *Civitas solis* S-C

19:20 *Erit*: *et erit* Weber

<19:20 *because of* KJV [properly a Hebraism]: *at the presence of* D-R>

19:21 *et in*: *et* Weber

20:4 *natibus ad*: *natibus* Weber

20:6 *liberarent*: *liberaret* Weber

21:3 *parturientis*: *parientis* Weber

21:5 *et bibentes*: *bibentes* Weber

21:8 *speculam*: *specula* Weber

21:10 *filii*: *fili* Weber

21:13 *Dedanim*: *Dodanim* Weber

<21:16 *hireling* S: *hyred man, and* D-R>

22:1 *visionis*: *Visionis* Weber

22:11 *ad aquam*: *et aquam* Weber

22:12 *vocabit*: *vocavit* Weber

22:14 *meis vox*: *meis* Weber

22:15 *templi, et dices ad eum*: *templi* Weber

22:16 *memoriam*: *memoriale* S-C

<22:18 *He will crown thee with a crown of tribulation* D-R/C: *Crowning he wil crowne thee with tribulation* D-R>

22:21 *tunica tua*: *tunicam tuam* Weber

22:23 *sui*: *eius* S-C

22:25 *illa*: *illo* Weber

23:2 *negotiatores*: *negotiatio* Weber

<23:4 *even* KJV (in roman type in KJV): omitted in D-R>

23:7 *haec civitas* X² [Quentin's siglum]: *haec* Weber, S-C

<23:8 *and* D-R/C: omitted in D-R>

23:18 *negotiationes*: *negotiatio* Weber

24:5 *infecta*: *interfecta* Weber

<24:13 *or* D-R/C: *and* D-R>

<24:14 *make a joyful noise* D-R: literally, *neigh*>

24:22 *congregationem*: *congregatione* S-C; *carcere*: *carcerem* Weber

25:1 *te et*: *te* Weber

<25:4 *refuge from* KJV: *hope against* D-R>

25:5 *aestum*: *aestus* S-C

25:7 *universas*: *omnes* S-C

<25:9 *they* S: *he* D-R>

26:1 *nostrae, Sion*: *nostrae* Weber

<26:10 *but* KJV (*yet*; in roman type in KJV): *and* D-R>

26:10 *iniqua*: *inique* Weber

26:21 *egredietur*: *egreditur* Weber

27:1 *illa*: *illo* Weber

<27:2 *there shall be singing to the vineyard* D-R/C: *the vineyard . . . shal sing to it* D-R>

<27:6 *When they* D-R/C: *They that* D-R; *shall* KJV: omitted in D-R>

27:6 *ingrediuntur*: *egrediuntur* Weber

27:8 *Meditatus*: *meditata* Weber

<27:10 *branches* KJV: *toppes* D-R>

27:11 *messes*: *messis* Weber

<28:1 *fat* KJV: *most fatte* D-R>

28:2 *Dominus*: *Domini* Weber

<28:4 *flower, the glory* D-R/C [cf. Is 28:1]: *flowre of the glorie* D-R; *fat valley* KJV: *valley of fatte ones* D-R>

28:9 *avulsos*: *apulsos* Weber

28:12 *est requies mea*: *requies* Weber

28:21 *Gabaon*: *Gabao* Weber; *est opus eius*: *est opus* Weber

<28:22 *lest* KJV: *lest perhaps* D-R>

28:26 *illum* [both times]: *eum illud* Weber

28:28 *nec in*: *nec* S-C

29:1 *expugnavit*: *circumdedit* Weber

<29:3 *a* D-R/C: *as a* D-R>

29:6 *flamma* $\Sigma^T \Delta^L$grel [Quentin's sigla]: *flammae* Weber, S-C

29:8 *expergefactus*: *expertus* Weber

29:9 *non ab*: *non* Weber

29:16 *quasi*: *quasi si* S-C; *aut* Sabatier: *et* Weber, S-C

29:17 *Chermel* [both times]: *charmel* S-C

<29:17 *charmel, and charmel* S-C: *Charmel, & Charmel* D-R>

30:1 *adderetis*: *adderetur* Weber

30:2 *Pharaonis*: *Pharao* Weber

30:4 *Tani*: *Tanis* Weber; *Hanes*: *Anes* Weber

30:5 *in obprobrium*: *obprobrium* Weber

30:8 *Nunc ergo*: *nunc* Weber; *ei*: *eis* Weber; *usque in*: *usque ad* Weber

30:9 *Dei*: *Domini* Weber

30:12 *calumniam et tumultum*: *calumnia et in tumultu* S-C

<30:16 *but* KJV: *and* D-R>

30:16 *velociores*: *veloces* Weber

30:21 *est via*: *via* Weber; *ea, et non declinetis*: *ea* Weber

30:24 *sicut in area*: *sic in area ut* Weber

30:32 *citharis*: *in citharis* Weber

31:3 *Deus*: *deus* Weber

31:4 *et cum*: *cum* Weber

<32:5 *great* D-R/C: *the greater man* D-R>

32:6 *vacuefaciat*: *vacuam faciat* S-C

32:7 *mendacii*: *mendaci* S-C [1593 and 1598 editions, according to Weber]

<32:7 *lying words* S-C [1593 and 1598 editions, according to Weber]: *the word of lying* D-R>

32:8 *cogitabit*: *cogitavit* Weber

32:10 *enim et annum, vos*: *et annum et vos* Weber

32:13 *spinae*: *spina* Weber

32:15 *charmel* [both times]: *Chermel* Weber

32:16 *charmel*: *Chermel* Weber

33:2 *te enim*: *te* Weber; *nostrum*: *eorum* Weber

33:3 *et ab*: *ab* Weber

33:6 *ipse est*: *ipse* Weber

33:15 *veritatem*: *veritates* Weber

33:21 *magnificus est*: *magnificus* Weber

33:23 *et*: *sed* Weber

34:3 *sanguine*: *a sanguine* S-C

34:10 *saeculum*: *saecula* S-C

34:11 *Et possidebunt*: *Possidebunt* *D-R; *et ibis*: *ibis* S-C

34:16 *alter*: *alter ad* Weber

34:17 *generatione* [both times]: *generationem* S-C

<34:17 *from generation* KJV *to generation* S-C: *in generation & generation* D-R>

35:4 *et nolite*: *nolite* Weber

35:7 *erit in*: *in* Weber

35:8 *vobis*: *nobis* Weber

<35:9 *but* KJV: *and* D-R; *there* KJV (in roman type in KJV and italics in D-R/C): omitted in D-R>

36:6 *manum*: *manu* Weber

<36:9 *least* KJV: *lesser* D-R>

36:9 *quadrigis*: *quadriga* Weber

<36:12 *their urine* KJV (*their owne pisse*): *vrine of their feete* D-R>

<36:15 *and* S (in italics in D-R/C): omitted in D-R>

36:18 *Nec*: *ne* Weber

37:3 *pariendi*: *parienti* Weber

37:4 *Rabsacis*: *Rabsaces* Weber; *obprobrandum*: *exprobrandum* S-C

37:8 *Lobnam*: *Lobna* Weber

37:13 *Ana*: *Anahe* Weber

37:22 *te et*: *te* Weber

37:24 *eius et*: *eius* Weber

<37:25 *shut up in banks* KJVn? (*of the fenced and closed places*): *of the rampiers* D-R>

<37:27 *were weak of* KJV (*were of small power*; *were* in roman type in KJV): *with shortened* D-R>

37:29 *viam*: *via* Weber

37:33 *introibit*: *intrabit* S-C

<37:33 *into it* S: *there* D-R; *nor come before it with shield* KJV (*shields* for *shield*): *and shilde shal not occupie it* D-R>

<37:35 *and will* D-R/C: *that I may* D-R>

37:38 *Nesroch*: *Nesrach* Weber; *Asarhaddon*: *Asorhaddon* Weber

<38:3 *how* KJV: *I pray thee how* D-R>

38:5 *et vidi*: *vidi* Weber; *lacrimas tuas*: *lacrimam tuam* Weber

38:11 *Deum*: *Dominum* Weber; *quietis*: *quievit* Weber

<38:14 *I will* D-R/C: *so wil I* D-R>

38:14 *responde*: *sponde* Weber

38:15 *tibi omnes*: *omnes* Weber

38:16 *si sic*: *sic* Weber

<38:18 *nor shall they* S: *they . . . shal not* D-R>

<38:19 *do* KJV (in roman type in KJV): *also* D-R>

<38:21 *had* KJV: omitted in D-R>

<38:22 *had* KJV: omitted in D-R>

38:22 *domum*: *domo* Weber

39:1 *Merodach*: *Marodach* Weber

<39:2 *at their coming* D-R/C [cf. 4 Kings 20:13]: *vpon them* D-R; *precious* KJV: *best* D-R>

<39:6 *that* KJV: *and* D-R>

40:1 *popule*: *populus* Weber

40:2 *advocate*: *avocate* Weber

40:8 *et cecidit*: *cecidit* Weber; *Domini*: *Dei* Weber; *manet*: *stabit* Weber

40:9 *qui* [both times]: *quae* Weber; *Iudae*: *Iuda* S-C

40:10 *illo*: *eo* Weber

40:11 *et fetas* Sabatier: *fetas* Weber, S-C

40:21 *scitis*: *scietis* Weber; *audistis*: *audietis* Weber

<40:21 *Hath it not been* D-R/C: *why, haue you not* D-R>

<40:22 *globe* D-R/C: *compasse* D-R>

<40:23 *bringeth* KJV: *maketh* D-R; *to nothing* KJV: *as if they were not* D-R>

40:24 *plantatus neque satus neque radicatus*: *plantatos neque satos neque radicato* Weber; *truncus*: *trunco* Weber

<40:26 *greatness* KJV: *multitude* D-R>

40:27 *transivit*: *transibit* Weber

<41:1 *take new* KJV (*renew*): *change* D-R>

41:6 *auxiliabitur*: *auxiliatur* Weber; *dicet*: *dicit* Weber

41:7 *Confortavit*: *confortabit* Weber; *eum in*: *eum* S-C; *moveretur*: *moveatur* Weber

41:10 *tibi*: *tui* Weber; *suscepit*: *suscepi* Weber

41:14 *tibi*: *tui* Weber

41:18 *supernis* Π^{L} [Quentin's siglum]: *supinis* Weber, S-C

<41:19 *plant in* KJV: *geue into* D-R>

41:19 *solitudinem*: *solitudine* Weber

<41:21 *if* D-R/C: *if perhaps* D-R; *to allege* D-R/C (in italics): omitted in D-R>

41:22 *fuerunt*: *fuerint* Weber

41:25 *veniet*: *venit* Weber

<41:28 *or* D-R/C: *and* D-R>

42:6 *servavi te*: *servavi* Weber

42:7 *et de* CΣΛ [Weber's sigla]: *de* Weber, S-C

42:9 *fuerunt*: *fuerant* Weber

42:14 *parturiens*: *pariens* Weber

42:16 *viam*: *via* Weber; *et in*: *in* Weber

<42:19 *Or deaf* KJV: *and deafe* D-R; *Or who* D-R/C: *and who* D-R>

42:19 *Et quis*: *quis* Weber

42:22 *direptionem, nec*: *direptionem et non* Weber

43:1   *vocavi te*: *vocavi* Weber

<43:4   *thou art* KJV (*hast bene* for *art*): *and* D-R>

43:5   *quoniam*: *quia* S-C

43:7   *formavi*: *et formavi* Weber

43:9   *faciet*: *faciat* Weber; *eorum et*: *eorum* S-C

<43:9   *let them* S-C: *and* D-R>

43:14   *misi in*: *emisi* Weber

<43:22   *But* KJV (in italics in D-R/C): omitted in D-R>

44:6   *Deus*: *deus* Weber

<44:7   *And* KJV: omitted in D-R>

44:8   *Deus*: *deus* Weber

<44:8   *a maker* D-R/C: *and a maker* D-R>

<44:12   *strength of his arm* KJV (*armes* for *arm*): *arme of his strength* D-R>

44:16   *conbusit* *D-R: *eius conbusit* Weber, S-C; *carnes* *D-R: *eius carnes* Weber, S-C; *coxit et comedit* $\Sigma^{\mathrm{T}}\Omega$e [Quentin's sigla]: *comedit* Weber, S-C

<44:16   *Part* KJV *of it* S-C: *Halfe* D-R; *part* KJV *of it* S-C: *the halfe* D-R; *his meat* D-R/C: *flesh & eate it* D-R>

44:17   *fecit et*: *fecit* Weber

44:18   *obliti*: *lutati* Weber

44:21   *ne obliviscaris*: *non oblivisceris* Weber

44:23   *misericordiam fecit*: *fecit* Weber

45:4   *nomine*: *in nomine* Weber

45:5   *Deus*: *deus* Weber

45:11   *mandate*: *mandastis* Weber

45:14   *te Deus*: *te deus* Weber

45:16   *confusionem*: *confusione* Weber

45:18   *habitaretur*: *habitetur* Weber

45:23   *curvabitur omne*: *curvabunt omnia* Weber

46:1   *Confractus*: *conflatus* Weber

46:3   *et omne*: *omne* *D-R; *gestamini* Π^{L} [Quentin's siglum]: *qui gestamini* Weber, S-C

46:4   *feram*: *feram et* Weber

46:7   *illum*: *illud* Weber

46:8   *confundamini*: *fundamini* Weber

46:13   *Israheli*: *in Israhel* S-C

47:1   *pulvere*: *pulverem* Weber

47:2   *crura*: *crus* Weber

47:5   *tacens*: *tace* Weber

48:1   *haec*: *hoc* Weber

<48:1   *but* KJV (in roman type in KJV and italics in D-R/C): omitted in D-R>

<48:5   *lest* KJV: *lest perhaps* D-R>

<48:6   *now* D-R/C: omitted in D-R>

48:6   *num*: *non* Weber; *tunc*: *nunc* Weber; *sunt quae*: *quae* Weber

<48:7   *when* KJV: *and* D-R; *lest* KJV: *lest perhaps* D-R>

48:8   *praevaricabis*: *praevaricaberis* S-C; *utero*: *ventre* Weber

48:20   *et efferte*: *efferte* Weber

49:6   *Ecce: dedi*: *dedi* Weber

49:10   *qui miseretur* Sabatier: *miserator* Weber, S-C; *ad fontes aquarum potabit*: *ad fontes aquarum portabit* Weber

<49:21   *begotten* D-R/C: *begot me* D-R>

49:21   *ubi*: *ubi hic* Weber

49:22   *levabo*: *levo* Weber

49:23   *terram demisso*: *terra dimisso* Weber

50:6   *conspuentibus*: *conspuentibus in me* S-C

<50:6   *them that ... spit upon me* S-C: *spitters* D-R>

51:3   *Sion et consolabitur*: *et Sion consolabitur* Weber

51:4   *popule*: *populus* Weber

51:7   *populus meus*: *populus* Weber; *cuius lex* Sabatier: *lex* Weber, S-C

<51:8   *from generation to generation* KJV: *vnto generations of generations* D-R>

<51:9   *and* KJV (in roman type in KJV and italics in D-R/C): omitted in D-R>

<51:11   *singing praises* KJV (without *praises*): *praysing* D-R>

<51:14   *unto you* D-R/C (in italics): omitted in D-R>

51:17   *et epotasti usque*: *et potasti usque* S-C

51:20   *oryx inlaqueatus*: *bestia inlaqueata* Weber

51:22   *pugnavit*: *pugnabit* S-C; *illum*: *illud* Weber

<51:22   *will fight* S-C: *hath fought* D-R; *dregs* KJV: *botome* D-R>

51:23   *illum*: *illud* Weber

52:5   *nunc quid*: *numquid* S-C

52:7   *Regnabit*: *regnavit* Weber

52:8   *oculo*: *oculum* Weber

<53:2   *that we should be* KJV: *and we were* D-R>

53:7   *tondente*: *tondente se* S-C

53:8   *abscisus*: *abscissus* S-C; *percussi eum*: *percussit eos* Weber

53:12   *mortem*: *morte* Weber; *peccata*: *peccatum* Weber

<54:1   *make a joyful noise* D-R: literally, *neigh*>

54:1   *habet*: *habebat* Weber

54:4   *erubesces*: *erubescas* Weber

<54:7   *but* KJV: *&* D-R>

<54:8   *but* KJV: *and* D-R>

54:10   *recedet a te*: *recedet* Weber

54:17   *Haec est*: *haec* Weber

<54:17   *This is*: verse 18 begins here D-R>

55:1   *Omnes*: *o omnes* Weber

55:3   *vobiscum*: *vobis* Weber

56:2   *adprehendet*: *adprehendit* Weber

<56:3   *and separate* D-R/C: *By seperation* D-R>

56:4   *quae*: *quae ego* S-C

57:1   *nemo*: *non* S-C

57:5   *eminentes*: *inminentes* Weber

57:8   *eis foedus*: *eis* Weber

<57:9   *perfumes* KJV: *gay payntings* D-R>

<57:10   *ways* S: *way* D-R; *yet* KJV (in roman type in KJV and italics in D-R/C): omitted in D-R>

<57:13   *but* KJV: *and* D-R>

57:17   *abscondi a te faciem meam*: *abscondi* Weber

57:18   *sanavi*: *dimisi* Weber

<57:20   *cast up dirt* KJV: *ouerflowe vnto conculcation* D-R>

57:21   *impiis," dicit Dominus Deus*: *dixit Deus meus impiis* Weber

58:2   *fecerit et*: *fecerit et quae* Weber; *reliquerit*: *dereliquerit* S-C

58:3   *animas nostras*: *animam nostram* Weber; *voluntas vestra*: *voluntas* Weber

<58:7   *Deal* KJV: *Breake* D-R>

<58:12   *repairer* KJV: *builder* D-R>

58:13   *ne facias* O^2 [Quentin's siglum]: *facere* Weber, S-C

59:4   *nihili*: *nihilo* S-C

<59:5 *brought out* D-R/C: *nourished* D-R>

59:8 *in eis*: *in ea* Weber

<59:10 *and* D-R/C: omitted in D-R; *we* D-R/C: *and* D-R>

<59:13 *but* D-R/C: *that* D-R>

59:15 *oblivionem*: *oblivione* Weber

59:21 *tui," dicit*: *tui dixit* Weber

60:1 *inluminare, Hierusalem*: *inluminare* Weber

60:4 *de latere surgent*: *in latere sugent* Weber

60:20 *erit tibi Dominus*: *Dominus erit* Weber

61:2 *Domino*: *Domini* Weber

<61:6 *riches* KJV: *strength* D-R>

61:7 *suam*: *eorum* Weber

61:8 *et odio*: *odio* Weber

61:9 *scient*: *scietur* Weber

62:4 *Inhabitata*: *inhabitabitur* S-C

62:5 *sponsam, et*: *sponsam* Weber

62:6 *perpetuo*: *in perpetuum* S-C

62:9 *congregabunt*: *congregant* S-C

<62:9 *gather* S-C: *shal gather* D-R>

62:10 *et eligite*: *eligite* S-C; *lapides, et*: *lapides* Weber

<62:10 *pick* S-C: *& picke* D-R>

63:6 *terram*: *terra* Weber

<63:8 *Surely* KJV: *But yet* D-R; *will not deny* KJV (*lie* for *deny*): *denie not* D-R; *so* KJV: *and* D-R>

63:9 *levavit*: *elevavit* S-C

63:11 *Mosi et*: *Mosi* Weber

63:13 *eduxit*: *duxit* Weber

<63:15 *the place* D-R/C: omitted in D-R>

64:6 *nos et*: *nos* Weber

64:8 *fictor noster es tu* Ψ^D cum $\tau^{56\ 69}$ [Π^LR has *fictor noster es*; Quentin's sigla]: *fictor noster tu* S-C, *fictor noster* Weber

64:9 *iniquitatis nostrae*: *iniquitatis* Weber

64:10 *desolata est*: *desolata* Weber

<65:1 *for me* KJV (in roman type in KJV and italics in D-R/C): omitted in D-R>

65:1 *invocabat*: *vocabat* Weber

65:6 *sinum*: *sinu* Weber

65:16 *meis*: *nostris* Weber

65:21 *fructus*: *fructum* Weber

65:23 *Electi mei*: *electis meis* Weber

65:25 *leo*: *et leo* Weber

66:1 *et terra*: *terra autem* S-C; *Quae est*: *quae* Weber; *quis est*: *quis* Weber

66:5 *tremitis*: *tremetis* Weber

66:16 *diiudicabit*: *diiudicatur* Weber

66:17 *ianuam*: *unam* Weber

66:18 *eorum novi* Sabatier: *eorum* Weber, S-C

66:19 *mare*: *mari* Weber; *Africam et Lydiam*: *Africa in Lydia* Weber; *tenentes*: *tendentes* S-C

<66:19 *draw* S-C: *hold* D-R; *bow* KJV: *arrow* D-R>

66:21 *et*: *et in* Weber

<66:23 *and* D-R/C (in italics): omitted in D-R>

JEREMIAH

<1:3 *to him* D-R/C (in italics): omitted in D-R>

<1:4 *carrying away of Jerusalem captive* KJV: *transmigration of Ierusalem* D-R>

<1:5 *bowels of thy mother* D-R/C: *wombe* D-R>

1:5 *te et*: *te* Weber; *in gentibus*: *gentibus* Weber

<1:7 *whatsoever* KJV: *al thinges whatsoeuer* D-R>

1:16 *omni malitia*: *omnem malitiam* S-C

<1:18 *behold* KJV: omitted in D-R>

<2:2 *espousals* KJV: *despousing* D-R>

2:11 *deos suos*: *deos* Weber

2:13 *et foderunt*: *ut foderent* Weber

<2:13 *water* KJV: *waters* D-R>

2:21 *es mihi*: *es* Weber

<2:21 *good for nothing* D-R/C: *depraued* D-R>

<2:23 *and* S: omitted in D-R; *as* D-R/C (in italics): omitted in D-R>

2:23 *suas*: *tuas* Weber

<2:24 *filth* D-R/C: *flowres* D-R>

<2:25 *But* KJV: *And* D-R>

2:30   *generatio*: verse 31 begins here Weber, S-C

2:32   *obliviscetur*: *obliviscitur* Weber; *sui aut*: *sui* Weber

<2:33   also D-R/C: *moreouer also* D-R>

<2:34   skirts KJV: *winges* D-R>

<2:36   ashamed [both times] KJV: *confounded* D-R>

2:37   *prosperum in ea*: *prosperum* Weber

3:1   *Dominus, "et ego suscipiam te*: *Dominus* Weber

<3:2   on high KJV: *direct* D-R>

3:3   *meretricis* Sabatier, *mulieris meretricis* Weber, S-C

3:6   *omni ligno frondoso*: *omne lignum frondosum* Weber

3:7   *revertere*: *convertere* Weber

<3:8   yet KJV: *and* D-R>

3:9   *ligno*: *cum ligno* Weber

<3:9   with stones and with stocks KJV: *with stone and wood* D-R>

<3:10   after D-R/C: *in* D-R>

3:13   *Verumtamen*: *tamen* Weber

<3:13   acknowledge KJV: *know* D-R>

3:19   *filiis*: *filios* S-C

<3:19   lovely KJV? (*pleasant*): *worthie to be desired* D-R>

3:23   *colles et*: *colles* Weber

4:1   *converteris*: *reverteris* S-C

<4:3   men KJV: *man* D-R>

4:4   *viri*: *vir* Weber

<4:4   lest KJV: *lest perhapes* D-R>

4:5   *et dicite*: *dicite* Weber

<4:5   aloud D-R/C: *strongly* D-R>

4:7   *desolationem*: *solitudinem* S-C

<4:9   that KJV: omitted in D-R>

4:12   *ego*: *ego sed* Weber

4:16   *Dicite gentibus*: *concitate gentes* Weber

<4:20   and KJV (in roman type in KJV): omitted in D-R>

<4:23   nothing S: *a thing of nothing* D-R>

<4:25   lo: KJV: omitted in D-R>

4:31   *inter morientes* ACΣSΦ [Weber's sigla]: *intermorientis* Weber, S-C;
         expandentesque AΣSΦ [Weber's sigla]: *expandentisque* Weber, S-C

<4:31 *dying away* S-C: *amongst them that dye* D-R; *spreading her* KJV: *and stretch forth their* D-R>

<5:1 *about through* KJV: *round about*: D-R>

5:1 *ei*: *eius* Weber

5:3 *supra*: *super* Weber; *et noluerunt*: *noluerunt* Weber

<5:5 *and* KJV (in roman type in KJV and italics in D-R/C): omitted in D-R>

<5:7 *How* KJV: *Wherupon* D-R>

5:8 *admissarii*: *emissarii* S-C

<5:10 *utterly destroy* D-R/C: *make . . . a consummation* D-R>

<5:11 *greatly* KJV? (*very treacherously*): *by preuarication* D-R>

5:13 *ventum locuti*: *ventum* Weber

<5:13 *word* KJV: *answer* D-R; *of God* S (in italics in D-R/C): omitted in D-R>

5:14 *in ligna*: *ligna* Weber

5:18 *in diebus*: *et diebus* Weber

<5:18 *utter destruction* D-R/C: *consummation* D-R>

<5:20 *and without understanding* KJV: *that hast no hart* D-R>

5:21 *popule*: *populus* Weber

<5:22 *repent* D-R/C: *be sorie* D-R; *they* D-R/C: *and the waues* D-R>

5:25 *vestrae*: *nostrae* Weber; *vestra*: *nostra* Weber; *vobis*: *nobis* Weber

<5:25 *things* KJV: omitted in D-R>

5:28 *viduae non*: *non* Weber

6:6 *effundite* ST [Weber's sigla]: *et fundite* Weber, S-C

6:7 *facit*: *fecit* S-C

<6:8 *lest* [both times] KJV: *lest perhaps* D-R>

6:10 *audiat*: *audiant* Weber

6:11 *concilium*: *consilium* S-C

<6:13 *least* KJV: *lesser* D-R; *greatest* KJV: *greater* D-R; *are given to* KJV: *studie* D-R; *are guilty of* D-R/C: *commit* D-R>

<6:14 *breach* KJVn: *destruction* D-R>

<6:16 *for* KJV: *of* D-R>

<6:17 *saying* KJV (in roman type in KJV): omitted in D-R>

6:21 *et peribunt*: *peribunt* S-C

<6:21 *kinsman shall* S-C: *neighbour, and they shal* D-R>

<6:23   *men* KJV: *a man* D-R>

<6:25   *and* KJV (in roman type in KJV and italics in D-R/C): omitted in
           D-R>

6:28   *declinantes*: *declinantum* Weber

<6:28   *they are* KJV (in roman type in KJV and italics in D-R/C): omitted
           in D-R>

<7:6   *the* KJV: *& . . . the* D-R>

7:7   *saeculo et*: *saeculo* Weber

7:9   *adulturare*: *adulturari* Weber

7:11   *Numquid ergo*: *ergo* Weber

7:17   *faciant*: *faciunt* S-C

<7:24   *But* KJV: *And* D-R>

7:24   *et in*: *et* Weber

<7:25   *from day to day* D-R/C: *by day* D-R>

7:26   *suam et*: *et* Weber

<7:27   *but . . . but* KJV: *& . . . and* D-R>

7:31   *qui*: *quae* S-C

<7:32   *nor* KJV: *and* D-R>

7:33   *cibum*: *cibos* S-C

7:34   *desolatione*: *desolationem* S-C

8:1   *regum*: *regis* Weber

8:2   *expandent*: *pandent* Weber

<8:3   *death shall be chosen rather than life by all* KJV: *they shal choose rather
           death then life, al* D-R>

8:4   *cadit*: *cadet* Weber

8:6   *ad proelium*: *in proelio* Weber

<8:10   *others for an inheritance* S?: *inheritours* D-R>

<8:11   *breach* KJVn [Jer 6:14]: *destruction* D-R>

8:14   *Deus noster*: *noster* Weber

<8:15   *no good came* KJV (*came* in roman type in KJV): *there was no good*
           D-R>

<8:17   *among* KJV: omitted in D-R>

8:21   *contritione*: *contritionem* Weber

<9:4   *utterly* KJV: *supplanting* D-R>

<9:7   *before* KJV? (*for*): *at the face of* D-R>

9:9   *gentem*: *gente* S-C

9:12 *terra et: terra* Weber

<9:12 *which* KJV: *because* D-R>

<9:14 *But* KJV: *And* D-R>

9:14 *quod: quos* Weber

9:15 *cibabo: cibabo eos* Weber

9:17 *exercituum, Deus Israhel: exercituum* Weber

9:20 *adsumant aures vestrae: adsumat auris vestra* Weber

<9:26 *are uncircumcised* KJV *in the flesh* D-Rn: *haue the prepuce* D-R>

10:3 *manus: manuum* Weber

<10:5 *must be carried* KJV: *being* D-R; *to be* D-R/C: *they shal be* D-R>

10:6 *es tu: tu* Weber

<10:9 *spread into plates* KJV: *wrapped vp* D-R>

<10:10 *be able to* KJV: omitted in D-R>

10:11 *caelo: caelis* Weber

<10:12 *that* D-R/C: omitted in D-R>

<10:19 *evil* D-R/C: *infirmitie* D-R>

<10:24 *lest* KJV: *lest perhappes* D-R>

11:2 *et ad: et* Weber

11:7 *surgens: consurgens* S-C

11:13 *posuisti: posuistis* Weber

<11:16 *and* KJV: omitted in D-R>

11:19 *consilia, dicentes: consilia* Weber

11:20 *corda: cor* Weber

<12:3 *prepare* KJV: *sanctifie* D-R>

12:5 *secura: securus* S-C

<12:5 *swelling* KJV: *pride* D-R>

12:12 *devorabit: devoravit* Weber

<12:13 *fierce wrath* KJV (*anger* for *wrath*): *wrath of the furie* D-R>

12:15 *evellero: evulsero* S-C

<12:17 *utterly pluck out and destroy* KJV: *plucke out . . . with plucking vp and with destruction* D-R>

13:5 *Eufrate: Eufraten* Weber

<13:5 *by* KJV: *in* D-R>

13:11 *essent: esset* Weber

<13:11 *but they would not hear* KJV: *and they heard not* D-R>

<13:14 *but* KJV: *not* D-R>

\<13:17   *for* KJV [properly a Hebraism]: *because of* D-R\>
\<13:19   *entire* KJV (*wholly*): *perfect* D-R\>
\<13:22   *nakedness* D-R/C: *more shamelie partes* D-R\>
\<13:27   *and* KJV (in roman type in KJV): omitted in D-R\>
  14:4   *terram: terra* Weber
  14:7   *responderint: responderunt* Weber
\<14:7   *testified against* KJV: *answered* D-R\>
  14:17   *lacrimas* ACO [Weber's sigla]: *lacrimam* Weber, S-C
\<14:19   *for us* KJV: omitted in D-R\>
  14:20   *iniquitates: iniquitatem* Weber
  14:22   *Dominus: Domine* Weber
  15:7   *perdidi: disperdidi* S-C
  15:14   *quam: qua* Weber
  15:15   *pro: propter* S-C
\<15:18   *so as to refuse* D-R/C: *refuseth* D-R\>
  15:20   *eruam te: eruam* Weber
  16:8   *ingrediaris: ingredieris* Weber
\<16:13   *So* KJV (*Therefore*): *And* D-R\>
  16:17   *occulta: occultata* S-C
\<16:19   *lies* KJV: *lying* D-R\>
  17:2   *lucorum suorum: lucorum* Weber
\<17:3   *and* KJV (in roman type in KJV and italics in D-R/C): omitted in
        D-R\>
  17:6   *myricae: myrice* Weber
  17:9   *hominis: omnium* Weber
\<17:9   *heart . . . above all things* KJV: *hart of man* D-R\>
  17:10   *suam et: et* Weber
\<17:11   *As . . . so* KJV (in roman type in KJV and italics in D-R/C): omitted
        in D-R; *hatched eggs* KJV (*sitteth on* for *hatched*; *eggs* in roman type
        in KJV and italics in D-R/C): *nourished* D-R\>
  17:13   *a te in: in* Weber
  17:20   *omnis Iuda: omnis Iudaea* Weber
  17:24   *ea: eo* S-C
  17:25   *viri: vir* Weber
\<17:25   *then* KJV: omitted in D-R; *riding in* KJV: *mounting on* D-R\>
  17:26   *civitatibus: civitate* Weber

<18:4   *made* D-R/C: *made it* D-R>

18:9   *et de*: *et* Weber; *plantem*: *ut plantem* Weber

18:11   *Iudae*: *Iuda* S-C

<18:11   *make . . . good* KJV: *direct* D-R>

18:16   *praeterierit*: *praeterit* Weber

<19:1   *and take* KJV (in italics in D-R/C): omitted in D-R>

19:2   *fictilis*: *Fictilis* Weber

<19:4   *profaned this place* D-R/C: *made this place strange* D-R>

19:4   *libaverint*: *libaverunt* S-C

19:5   *Baalim* [both times]: *Baali* Weber

<19:6   *that* KJV: *and* D-R>

<19:8   *plagues* KJV: *plague* D-R>

19:9   *carnes*: *carnem* S-C

<19:11   *Even* KJV: omitted in D-R>

19:12   *et ponam*: *ut ponam* Weber

20:4   *manum*: *manu* Weber

<20:5   *precious thing thereof* KJV: *price* D-R>

<20:8   *against* D-R/C (in italics): omitted in D-R>

<20:9   *Then* KJV: *And* D-R; *burning fire shut* KJV: *fire boyling, and shut* D-R>

<20:10   *familiars* KJV: *peaceables* D-R; *continued at* D-R/C: *garding* D-R>

<20:15   *greatly* KJV (*very*): *as it were with ioy* D-R>

<21:2   *that* KJV: *and* D-R>

<21:4   *with which* KJV (*wherewith*): *and wherewith* D-R>

21:5   *in brachio*: *brachio* Weber

21:7   *movebitur*: *flectetur* S-C

<21:7   *to pity* KJV: omitted in D-R>

<21:12   *lest* KJV: *lest perhaps* D-R>

<21:13   *in a valley upon a rock above a plain* D-R/C [KJV has *rocke* and *plaine*]: *of the firme & champaine valley* D-R>

<21:14   *But* KJV: *And* D-R>

<22:3   *oppressed* D-R/C: *oppressed by violence* D-R; *the fatherless* KJV: *and pupil* D-R>

<22:4   *then* KJV: omitted in D-R; *riding in* KJV: *mounting vpon* D-R>

<22:6   *yet . . . and* KJV (in roman type in KJV and italics in D-R/C): omitted in D-R>

<22:7 *prepare against thee the destroyer* KJV: *sanctifie vpon thee a killing man* D-R>

22:7 *electas cedros tuas*: *electam cedrum tuam* Weber

<22:10 *your tears* D-R/C: *weeping* D-R>

<22:11 *his father* D-R/C: *Iosias his father* D-R>

<22:13 *that* KJV: *he* D-R>

<22:15 *and it was then* KJV (*and* and *it was* in roman type in KJV): *then when it was* D-R>

22:18 *soror*: *fratres* Weber

22:21 *et dixisti*: *dixisti* Weber

22:24 *avellam*: *evellam* S-C

23:2 *meum et*: *meum* Weber

<23:2 *for* S: omitted in D-R>

23:6 *illis*: *illius* Weber

<23:10 *by reason of* D-R [properly a Hebraism]: literally, *from the face of*>

23:10 *et factus* Gryson 177 E p. 299: *factus* Weber, S-C

23:14 *adulterantium*: *adulterium* Weber; *omnes ut*: *omnes* Weber

<23:14 *wicked* KJV (*euill doers*): *most wicked* D-R>

<23:16 *and* KJV (in roman type in KJV): omitted in D-R>

<23:21 *yet* [both times] KJV: *and* D-R>

<23:22 *should have* KJV: *had verely* D-R>

23:24 *Occultabitur* Φ^E [Quentin's siglum]: *si occultabitur* Weber, S-C

<23:26 *shall this be* KJV: *is this* D-R>

23:27 *narrat*: *narrant* Weber

<23:32 *tell* KJV: *haue told* D-R; *cause . . . to err* KJV: *haue seduced* D-R>

23:33 *Vos estis*: *ut quid vobis* Weber

23:34 *propheta*: *prophetes* Weber

<23:34 *shall* KJV: omitted in D-R>

23:36 *pervertistis*: *pervertitis* Weber; *viventis*: *videntis* S-C [1598 edition, according to Weber]

<23:36 *for* KJV: *&* D-R>

<23:40 *forgotten* KJV: *put away by obliuion* D-R>

<24:1 *craftsmen and engravers* KJV (*carpenters and smiths*): *craftesman, and incloser* D-R>

<24:2 *season* KJV (*ripe*): *time are wont to be* D-R>

<24:5 *captives* KJV: *transmigration* D-R; *their* KJV (in roman type in KJV): omitted in D-R>

24:9 *quos*: *quae* S-C

25:2 *quod*: *quae* Weber

25:3 *iste est*: *iste* S-C

25:5 *terra*: *terram* Weber

25:9 *Nabuchodonosor*: *ad Nabuchodonosor* Weber

25:11 *haec*: *eius* Weber

<25:12 *for* KJV: omitted in D-R>

<25:16 *because of* KJV [properly a Hebraism]: *at the face of* D-R>

<25:18 *to wit* KJV (in roman type in KJV): *to* D-R>

25:18 *et in sibilum*: *in sibilum* Weber

25:21 *et Idumeae*: *Idumeae* Weber

25:22 *Tyri et cunctis*: *Tyri et universis* S-C

25:26 *et cunctis*: *cunctis quoque* S-C

<25:27 *because of* KJV [properly a Hebraism]: *at the face of* D-R>

25:28 *manu tua*: *manu* Weber

25:29 *incipiam*: *incipio* Weber; *et inmunes*: *inmunes* Weber

<25:29 *I begin to bring evil* KJV: *wil I beginne to afflict* D-R>

<25:30 *the place of* D-R/C: omitted in D-R>

25:31 *tradidi*: *tradidit* Weber

<25:34 *the days of your slaughter* KJV: *your daies . . . to be slaine* D-R>

<25:35 *the shepherds shall have no way to flee, nor the leaders of the flock to save* KJV (*principall* for *leaders* and *escape* for *save*): *flight shal faile from the pastours, and saluation from the principals of the flocke* D-R; *themselves* D-R/C: omitted in D-R>

25:36 *pascua*: *pascuam* Weber

<25:37 *because of* KJV [properly a Hebraism]: *at the presence of* D-R>

25:38 *quia facta*: *facta* Weber

<25:38 *because of* [both times] KJV [properly a Hebraism]: *at the presence of* D-R; *fierce anger* KJV: *wrath of the furie* D-R>

26:1 *regni*: *regis* Weber

<26:3 *that* KJV: *and* D-R>

26:3 *malitia*: *malitias* Weber

26:8 *moriatur*: *morietur* Weber

<26:9   *without an inhabitant* KJV: *for that there is no inhabitant* D-R>

26:9   *domo*: *domum* Weber

26:10   *portae domus*: *portae* Weber

<26:12   *Then* KJV: *And* D-R>

26:14   *quod*: *ut* Weber

26:15   *tradetis*: *traditis* Weber

<26:15   *shed* D-R/C: *betray* D-R>

<26:16   *Then* KJV: *And* D-R>

26:16   *et ad*: *et* Weber

<26:17   *And* S: *therefore* D-R; *some* KJV (*certaine*): *Men* D-R>

26:18   *Micheas*: *Michas* Weber

26:20   *universa*: *omnia* S-C

<26:23   *common people* KJV: *base vulgar people* D-R>

26:24   *in manus*: *in manu* Weber

<26:24   *to put him to death* KJV: *and they kil him* D-R>

27:5   *homines*: *hominem* Weber

27:10   *eiciant*: *eiciam* Weber

27:13   *et fame*: *fame* Weber

<27:16   *should this city be* KJV: *is this citie* D-R>

27:18   *domo* [both times]: *domum* Weber

27:21   *domo* [both times]: *domum* Weber

28:3   *vasa domus*: *vasa* Weber

<28:4   *captives* KJV: *transmigration* D-R>

28:5   *oculis* [both times]: *conspectu* *D-R; *stabat*: *stabant* Weber

28:6   *domum*: *domo* Weber

<28:6   *captives* KJV: *transmigration* D-R>

28:8   *ante te*: *te* Weber

<28:11   *Even* KJV: omitted in D-R; *full years* KJV: *yeares of dayes* D-R>

28:12   *propheta, in*: *prophetes in* Weber

<28:12   *had broken* KJV: *brake* D-R>

<28:13   *tell* KJV: *thou shalt tel* D-R>

<28:15   *now* KJV: omitted in D-R>

28:16   *emittam*: *mittam* S-C

29:1   *quem misit*: *quae misit* Weber

<29:1   *that were carried into* KJV (*which were caried away*): *of the* D-R>

JEREMIAH

<29:2 *craftsmen and the engravers* KJV (*carpenters and the smithes*): *craftes man, and the incloser* D-R>

29:3 *Gamariae*: *Gamaliae* Weber

<29:4 *that are carried away captives* KJV: *the transmigration* D-R; *caused to be* KJV: omitted in D-R>

29:5 *pomaria* Sabatier: *hortos* Weber, S-C

29:6 *et date*: *date* Weber

<29:6 *take wives for* KJV: *geue wiues to* D-R>

29:8 *inducant*: *seducant* S-C

<29:10 *in your favour* D-R/C: *vpon you* D-R>

<29:14 *bring you* KJV: *make you to returne* D-R>

29:17 *in eos*: *in eis* Weber

29:18 *gladio et*: *gladio* Weber

29:21 *Coliae*: *Culia* Weber; *manus*: *manu* Weber

<29:23 *words* KJV: *the word* D-R>

<29:28 *For* D-R/C: *Because vpon this* D-R>

29:28 *fructus*: *fructum* Weber

<29:32 *to sit* KJV (*to dwell*): *sitting* D-R>

<30:3 *captivity* KJV: *conuersion* D-R>

<30:6 *hands* KJV: *hand* D-R; *loins* KJV: *loyne* D-R>

30:6 *parturientis*: *parientis* Weber

<30:7 *but* KJV: *and* D-R>

30:10 *salvabo*: *salvo* Weber; *bonis, et*: *et* Weber

<30:11 *utterly consume* D-R/C: *make a consumation* D-R; *utterly consume* D-R/C: *make into consummation* D-R>

<30:12 *bruise* KJV: *wound* D-R>

30:14 *teque*: *te* Weber

30:15 *et propter*: *et* Weber

<30:18 *captivity* KJV: *conuersion* D-R>

30:19 *inminuentur*: *minuentur* S-C

31:2 *a gladio*: *gladio* Weber

<31:4 *dances* KJV: *quyre* D-R>

31:7 *et canite*: *canite* Weber

31:8 *claudus*: *claudus et* Weber

31:9 *misericordia reducam*: *precibus deducam* Weber

31:10 *in insulis*: *insulis* Weber

<31:18 *unaccustomed to the yoke* KJV (*to the yoke* in roman type in KJV): *not tamed* D-R>

31:18 *convertar*: *revertar* Weber

31:21 *rectam*: *directam* Weber

31:27 *hominum*: *hominis* Weber

31:31 *venient*: *veniunt* Weber

31:32 *patribus eorum*: *patribus vestris* Weber

31:34 *docebit*: *docebunt* Weber; *Cognoscite*: *Cognosce* S-C; *memorabor*: *ero memor* Weber

<31:38 *that* KJV: *and* D-R>

32:1 *octavusdecimus*: *decimus octavus* S-C

32:3 *manu*: *manus* S-C

32:4 *manus*: *manu* Weber; *loquetur*: *loquetur cum illo* *D-R

<32:4 *he shall speak to him mouth to mouth* D-R: literally, *his mouth shall speak with his* [i.e., the king's] *mouth*>

<32:8 *Buy* KJV: *Possesse* D-R; *this* KJV: *it* D-R>

32:8 *es ut*: *ut* Weber

32:11 *et stipulationes*: *stipulationes* Weber

32:12 *et in oculis testium*: *in oculis testium* S-C; *emptionis et*: *emptionis* Weber

<32:12 *in* S-C: *and in* D-R>

32:14 *pone*: *pones* Weber

<32:16 *had* KJV: omitted in D-R>

32:18 *reddis*: *reddes* Weber; *sinum*: *sinu* Weber; *magne et*: *magne* Weber

<32:23 *but* KJV: *and* D-R; *and* D-R/C: omitted in D-R>

32:24 *manus*: *manu* Weber

<32:24 *by* D-R/C: *at the presence of* D-R>

32:25 *manus*: *manu* Weber

32:28 *manus* [both times]: *manu* Weber; *capient*: *capiet* Weber

32:31 *auferetur*: *aufertur* Weber

32:32 *sacerdotes eorum*: *sacerdotes* Weber; *viri*: *vir* Weber

32:36 *tradatur*: *tradetur* S-C; *manus*: *manu* Weber

<32:36 *shall be* S-C: *is* D-R>

32:43 *manus*: *manu* Weber

<32:44 *deeds shall be written* D-R/C: *shal be written in a booke* D-R>

33:2 *est*: *est Dominus* Weber

33:4   *ad gladium*: *gladium* Weber

33:5   *quos*: *quas* Weber

33:6   *eis*: *ei* Weber

<33:7   *captivity* [both times] KJV: *conuersion* D-R>

33:9   *faciam eis*: *faciam ei* Weber

33:10   *nec*: *et* Weber

<33:11   *shall* [both times] KJV: omitted in D-R; *captivity* KJV: *conuersion* D-R>

<33:13   *And* D-R/C: omitted in D-R>

<33:14   *that* KJV: *and* D-R>

33:16   *est nomen*: *est* Weber; *vocabunt eum*: *vocabit eam* Weber

33:18   *et Levitis*: *et de Levitis* S-C

33:22   *numerari*: *enumerari* S-C

<33:24   *so that* KJV (without *so*): *because* D-R>

33:26   *Isaac*: *et Isaac* Weber

<33:26   *captivity* KJV: *conuersion* D-R>

34:2   *manus*: *manu* Weber

<34:5   *saying* KJV (in roman type in KJV): omitted in D-R>

<34:9   *Jews, their brethren* KJV (*Iew his brother*): *Iewe and his brother* D-R>

34:10   *eis*: *in eis* Weber

<34:11   *But* KJV: *And* D-R>

34:11   *famulas*: *in famulas* Weber

34:17   *praedico vobis*: *praedico* Weber; *ad pestem*: *et pestem* Weber; *et ad*: *et* Weber

34:18   *conciderunt*: *ceciderunt* Weber

34:20   *manus* [both times]: *manu* Weber; *volatilibus*: *volucribus* Weber

34:21   *manus* [all three times]: *manu* Weber; *animas*: *animam* Weber

<35:8   *nor* S: omitted in D-R>

35:10   *fuimus*: *fecimus* Weber

<35:11   *let* D-R/C: *and let* D-R>

35:17   *adducam*: *adduco* Weber; *Iudam*: *Iuda* S-C; *adversum illos*: *adversum eos* Weber

<36:7   *they may present their supplication* KJV (*will* for *may*): *their prayer may fal* D-R>

36:7   *est quam*: *quam* Weber

<36:14   *in* KJV: *out of* D-R>

36:23 *ignem*: *igne* Weber

36:27 *Hieremiam, prophetam*: *Hieremiam* Weber

<36:31 *but* KJV: *and* D-R>

36:32 *antea*: *ante* Weber

<37:2 *But* KJV: *And* D-R>

<37:4 *as yet* D-R/C: omitted in D-R; *prison* KJV: *ward in prison* D-R>

37:4 *Pharaonis*: *Pharao* Weber; *de Aegypto*: *Aegyptum* Weber

37:6 *me*: *me ad* Weber

37:7 *incendent*: *succendent* S-C; *eam igni*: *igni* Weber

<37:13 *But* KJV: *And* D-R; *so* KJV: *but* D-R>

<37:14 *and* KJV: omitted in D-R>

37:15 *ergastulum*: *ergastula* Weber

37:16 *eum in*: *in* Weber; *manus*: *manu* Weber

38:3 *Tradendo*: *tradenda* Weber

38:4 *universi populi*: *populi* *D-R; *hic*: *iste* S-C; *huic*: *huius* Weber

38:6 *lacum Melchiae*: *lacu Melchiae* Weber; *in funibus*: *funibus* S-C; *in lacum, in quo*: *et in lacum* Weber

38:12 *cubito*: *cubitu* Weber; *super*: *subter* Weber

<38:14 *will* KJV: omitted in D-R>

38:16 *manus*: *manu* Weber

38:18 *manus*: *manu* Weber

<38:19 *lest* KJV: *lest perhaps* D-R>

38:22 *in lubrico*: *lubrico* Weber

<38:26 *to* KJV: *&* D-R>

39:9 *quae*: *qui* S-C; *remanserunt*: *remanserant* S-C

<39:10 *But* KJV: *And* D-R>

39:11 *militum*: *militiae* Weber

39:12 *facias ei*: *facies ei* Weber

39:13 *Nabusezban*: *Nabu et Sesban* Weber

39:14 *domum*: *in domum* S-C

40:4 *tuo est*: *tuo* Weber

<40:4 *as* D-R/C: omitted in D-R>

40:5 *Iuda*: *Iudaeae* Weber

40:7 *Cumque*: *Cum ergo* Weber

40:8 *Thanehumeth*: *Thenoemeth* Weber; *erant*: *erat* Weber

40:11 *Iudaea*: *Iudaeam* Weber

40:14 *quia*: *quod* S-C

40:15 *vero*: *autem* S-C

41:5 *barba*: *barbam* Weber; *et munera*: *munera* Weber

<41:7 *and cast them* KJV (in roman type in KJV and italics in D-R/C): omitted in D-R>

<41:9 *fear of* KJV: omitted in D-R>

<41:11 *of* D-R/C: *al* D-R>

<42:4 *and whatsoever thing* KJV: *euerie word whatsoeuer* D-R>

<42:11 *because of* S [properly a Hebraism]: *at the face of* D-R>

42:12 *misericordias*: *misericordiam* Weber

42:16 *gladius*: *gladium* Weber

42:17 *posuerint*: *posuerunt* S-C; *ut habitent*: *et habitent* Weber; *effugiet*: *effugient* Weber

<42:17 *set* S-C: *shal set* D-R>

42:19 *sum vos*: *sum vobis* Weber

<42:21 *now* KJV (in roman type in KJV): omitted in D-R>

43:3 *manus*: *manibus* Weber

43:4 *manerent*: *maneret* Weber

43:7 *Tafnis*: *Tafnas* Weber

43:9 *abscondes*: *absconde* Weber

43:11 *mortem, in mortem*: *morte in morte* Weber; *captivitatem, in captivitatem*: *captivitate in captivitate* Weber; *gladium, in gladium*: *gladio in gladio* Weber

44:1 *est ad*: *est per* S-C; *habitabant*: *habitant* Weber

44:3 *irent et*: *irent ut* S-C

44:4 *huiuscemodi quam odivi*: *huius quam odi* Weber

<44:4 *this abominable thing which I hate* KJV: *the word of this manner of abomination, which I hated* D-R>

<44:5 *But* KJV: *And* D-R>

<44:6 *Wherefore* KJV: *And* D-R>

44:7 *grande hoc*: *grande* Weber; *lactens*: *lactans* Weber

<44:9 *streets* KJV: *countries* D-R>

44:10 *Domini et*: *et* Weber

44:11 *ponam*: *pono* Weber

44:12 *in fame, et*: *in fame* Weber

44:13 *visitabo*: *visitabo super* S-C; *in fame et in*: *fame et* S-C

<44:14 *have a desire* KJV: *eleuate their soules* D-R; *to* KJV: *and* D-R>

44:15 *dicentes: dicens* Weber

44:17 *egredietur: egreditur* Weber

44:18 *tempore quo: quo* Weber

<44:18 *since* KJV: *from that time, since* D-R>

<44:19 *cakes* D-R/C: *her cakes* D-R; *to* D-R/C: *and to* D-R>

44:19 *libandum ei libamina: liba libandi* Weber

<44:22 *So that* KJV: *And* D-R; *therefore* KJV: *and* D-R; *without* KJV: *for that
        there is not* D-R>

45:1 *Neriae: Neri* Weber; *de: ex* S-C

<45:5 *but* KJV: *and* D-R: *and save thee* D-R/C: *into safetie* D-R>

46:2 *flumen: fluvium* S-C

46:8 *ascendit: ascendet* Weber

<46:10 *For* KJV: *And* D-R>

46:10 *Domini Dei: Domini* Weber

46:12 *et ambo: ambo* Weber

46:14 *facite in: facite* Weber; *devorabit: devoravit* Weber

<46:16 *sword* KJV?: *face of the sword* D-R>

46:17 *Pharaonis: Pharao* Weber

<46:19 *Furnish thyself to go into captivity* KJV: *Make ye vessels of transmigra-
        tion* D-R>

46:19 *et inhabitabilis erit: inhabitabilis* Weber

46:25 *Pharaonem* [both times]: *Pharao* Weber

46:26 *manu servorum: manus servorum* S-C

46:27 *tuae: suae* Weber; *quiescet: requiescet* S-C

<47:2 *then* KJV: omitted in D-R>

47:2 *ululabunt omnes habitatores: ululabit omnis habitator* Weber

47:6 *quiesces: quiescis* Weber

48:5 *Luith: Luaith* Weber

48:6 *myricae: myrice* Weber

48:8 *peribunt valles: peribit vallis* Weber

48:12 *lagoenas: lagunculas* S-C

48:15 *succiderunt: ascenderunt* Weber; *nomen eius: nomen ei* Weber

<48:15 *whose* KJV: *his* D-R>

48:16 *et malum: malum* *D-R

48:18 *ascendet: ascendit* S-C; *dissipabit: dissipavit* S-C

<48:18 *is come up* S-C: *shal come up* D-R; *hath destroyed* S-C: *shal destroy* D-R>

48:19 *ei: eum* Weber

<48:24 *or* KJV: *and* D-R>

48:25 *Abscisum: Abscissum* S-C

<48:36 *like* KJV: *of* D-R>

48:38 *quia: quoniam* S-C

48:40 *evolabit: volabit* S-C

48:44 *fugerit: fugit* Weber

<48:45 *but* KJV: *because* D-R>

49:3 *Hai: Ahi* Weber; *quia: quoniam* S-C; *transmigrationem: transmigratione* Weber

49:5 *fugientes: fugientem* Weber

49:8 *et terga: terga* Weber; *voraginem: voragine* Weber

<49:16 *but* KJV: omitted in D-R>

49:22 *evolabit: avolabit* S-C

<49:23 *as* KJVn (in italics in D-R/C): omitted in D-R>

49:23 *prae sollicitudine: sollicitudine* Weber

49:24 *est in: in* Weber

49:28 *et ascendite: ascendite* Weber

<49:29 *and* D-R/C: omitted in D-R>

49:31 *nec: non* Weber; *eis: ei* Weber

49:35 *Aelam et: Aelam* Weber

<49:37 *my fierce wrath* KJV (*anger* for *wrath*): *the wrath of my furie* D-R>

49:37 *mittam: emittam* Weber

50:8 *gregem: greges* Weber

50:11 *vituli: vitulus* Weber; *ut: sicut* S-C

50:13 *transibit: transit* Weber

50:14 *intenditis: tenditis* S-C

<50:16 *for fear of* KJV: *at the face of* D-R>

<50:17 *and* KJV: omitted in D-R>

50:23 *malleus: malleus est* Weber

50:29 *eam: eum* S-C [an error, according to Weber]

<50:32 *he shall* D-R/C: *and* D-R>

50:39 *fatuis: faunis* S-C; *sicariis* CΣT [Weber's sigla]: *ficariis* Weber, S-C; *habitabitur: inhabitabitur* S-C; *usque in: usque ad* Weber

<50:39 *fig-fawns* S-C: *foolish murderers* D-R; *from . . . to* KJV (*fro* [sic] for *from*): *to . . . and* D-R>

50:40 *subvertit Dominus*: *subvertit Deus* Weber; *et non*: *nec* Weber

50:44 *est enim*: *enim* Weber

51:6 *est a*: *est* Weber

<51:6 *what she hath deserved* D-R/C: *the like* D-R>

<51:9 *would* KJV: omitted in D-R; *but* KJV: *and* D-R>

51:11 *est ut*: *ut* Weber

<51:13 *for thy entire destruction* D-R/C: *with in a foote of thy cutting of* D-R>

<51:14 *saying* KJV (in roman type in KJV): *that* D-R>

51:17 *mendax est*: *mendax* Weber; *eius*: *eorum* S-C

<51:27 *prepare* KJV: *sanctifie* D-R>

<51:28 *Prepare* KJV: *Sanctifie* D-R>

51:29 *turbabitur*: *conturbabitur* S-C; *evigilabit*: *evigilavit* Weber

51:33 *Babylonis*: *Babylon* Weber

51:34 *quasi draco*: *sicut draco* Weber

<51:34 *delicate meats* D-R/C: *tendernes* D-R>

51:40 *et quasi*: *quasi* Weber

51:44 *corruet*: *corruit* Weber

<51:45 *fierce wrath* KJV (*anger* for *wrath*): *wrath of the furie* D-R>

<51:46 *lest* KJV: *lest perhaps* D-R; *another* KJV (in roman type in KJV and italics in D-R/C): omitted in D-R>

51:57 *et duces*: *duces* Weber

<51:58 *broad* KJV: *most brode* D-R>

51:58 *ignem*: *igne* Weber

51:59 *propheta*: *prophetes* Weber

51:61 *veneris in*: *veneris* Weber

<51:62 *neither man nor* KJV: *none . . . from man euen vnto* D-R>

51:63 *medium*: *medio* Weber

<51:64 *from* KJV: *from the face of* D-R>

51:64 *dissolvetur*: *dissolventur* Weber

<52:1 *one* KJV: *A Child of one* D-R>

52:1 *anni erat*: *anni* Weber

52:6 *civitatem*: *in civitate* Weber

<52:7 *the* D-R/C: *al the* D-R>

52:7 *bellatores*: *bellatores eius* S-C

<52:10 *and* KJV (*also*): *yea and* D-R>

52:16 *in vinitores: vinitores* S-C; *et: et in* Weber

52:17 *aereum: aeneum* S-C

52:18 *lebetes: lebetas* Weber

<52:19 *The* D-R/C: *and the* D-R>

52:20 *et columnas: columnas* Weber; *et vitulos: vitulos* Weber

<52:22 *and* KJV: omitted in D-R; *chapiters* KJV: *crowne* D-R>

52:22 *retiacula et malogranata super coronam in circuitu, omnia aerea. Similiter columnae secundae et malogranata: retiacula* Weber

52:23 *fuerunt malogranata: mala granata* Weber; *et omnia malogranata: omnia mala granata* Weber

52:31 *Ioachin: Ioachim* Weber

<52:32 *kindly* KJV: *good thinges* D-R; *with him* KJV: *after himself* D-R>

LAMENTATIONS

1:1 *sedet: sedit* Weber

<1:3 *hath removed her dwelling place* D-R/C: *is gone into transmigration*
D-R; *greatness* KJVn: *multitude* D-R>

<1:4 *solemn feast* KJV: *solemnitie* D-R; *are in affliction* KJV: *lothsome* D-R>

<1:5 *her lords* D-R/C: *in the head* D-R>

1:5 *in captivitatem: captivi* Weber

1:6 *pascua: pascuam* Weber

<1:8 *vagabond* KJVn (*a removing or wandering* for *vagabond*): *unstable*
D-R>

1:8 *conversa est: et conversa* Weber

<1:9 *wonderfully* KJV: *exceedingly* D-R>

<1:11 *sigh; they seek* KJV: *sighing, and seeking* D-R; *relieve* KJV: *refresh*
D-R>

1:11 *et considera: considera* Weber

<1:12 *his fierce anger* KJV: *the wrath of his furie* D-R>

<1:13 *and* KJV (in roman type in KJV and italics in D-R/C): omitted in
D-R>

<1:14 *for me* D-R/C (in italics): omitted in D-R>

<1:15 *mighty men* KJV: *magnifical ones* D-R>

1:16 *lacrimas* Frede RES-R 7473 p. 366: *aquam* Weber, *aquas* S-C

<1:16   *run down with water* KJV: *shedding tears* D-R; *the relief of* KJV (*that should relieue*): *conuerting* D-R>

<1:17   *menstruous woman* KJV: *woman polluted with menstrous floores* D-R>

1:19   *ipsi* relv [Quentin's sigla]: *et ipsi* Weber, S-C

<1:19   *but* KJV (in roman type in KJV): omitted in D-R; *pined away* D-R/C: *are consumed* D-R; *while* KJV: *because* D-R; *relieve* KJV: *refresh* D-R>

<1:20   *death alike* D-R/C: *lyke death* D-R>

1:20   *interficit: interfecit* Weber

<1:22   *be present* D-R/C: *enter in* D-R>

1:22   *devindemia: vindemia* S-C

2:1   *in terram: terram* Weber

<2:1   *his footstool* KJV: *the footestoole of his feete* D-R>

2:2   *et deiecit: deiecit* Weber

2:3   *furoris: furoris sui* S-C

<2:3   *his* S-C *fierce anger* KJV: *the wrath of furie* D-R; *drawn* KJV: *turned away* D-R>

<2:5   *multiplied* S? [also similar to KJV *increased*]: *replenished* D-R; *afflicted, both men and women* D-R/C: *humbled man and humbled woman* D-R>

2:6   *in obprobrium et in indignationem: obprobrio in indignatione* Weber

<2:9   *sunk* KJV: *fastened* D-R; *The law is no more:* KJV (*is* and *more* in roman type in KJV): *there is no law* D-R>

<2:10   *sit* KJV: *haue sitten* D-R>

2:10   *terram capita: terra capita* Weber

<2:11   *weeping* D-R/C: *teares* D-R>

2:11   *lactens: lactans* Weber

<2:13   *that I may comfort* KJV: *and comfort* D-R>

2:13   *magna est: magna* Weber

2:16   *dentibus et: dentibus* Weber; *Devorabimus: devoravimus* Weber

<2:17   *in* KJV: *from* D-R>

<2:18   *Let tears run down* KJV: *Shede teares* D-R>

2:18   *noctem: per noctem* Weber

2:19   *aquas* PL 85.306B: *aquam* S-C, *aqua* Weber; *compitorum: conpetorum* Weber

<2:19   *water* S-C: *waters* D-R>

<2:20   *Shall . . . be slain* KJV: *is . . . slaine* D-R>

2:20   *occiditur: occidetur* Weber

<2:22   *festival* S: *solemne day* D-R>

3:2   *tenebras: tenebris* Weber

<3:11   *turned aside* KJV: *subverted* D-R>

<3:12   *his arrows* D-R/C: *the arrow* D-R>

3:14   *derisum: derisu* Weber

3:21   *Hoc: haec* S-C

<3:21   *These things* S-C: *This thing* D-R>

3:23   *Nova* R* cum 177 [Quentin's sigla, without capitalization]: *novae* Weber, *novi* S-C

<3:23   *They are new every* KJV, D-Rn? (*They are* and *new* in roman type in KJV and italics in D-R/C): *New in the* D-R>

3:26   *Dei: Domini* Weber

<3:33   *willingly afflicted* KJV: *humbled from his hart* D-R>

3:33   *hominum: hominis* Weber

<3:36   *wrongfully* D-R/C: omitted in D-R; *approved* KJV: *known* D-R>

<3:39   *suffering* D-R/C (in italics): omitted in D-R>

<3:48   *run down with* KJV: *shed* D-R>

<3:52   *chased me* KJV and D-R/C: *in hunting* D-R>

3:52   *sine causa* Frede ANT-M 161v p. 116, PL 86.583D: *gratis* S-C, Weber

3:53   *lacum: lacu* Weber

<3:54   *cut off* KJV: *vndone* D-R>

3:55   *lacu novissimo: lacis novissimis* Weber

3:59   *iniquitatem illorum: iniquitatem* Weber

<3:60   *and* KJV (in roman type in KJV and italics in D-R/C): omitted in D-R>

3:61   *obprobrium: obprobria* Weber

<4:3   *Even* KJV: *Yea euen* D-R>

4:4   *lactentis: lactantis* Weber

<4:5   *delicately* KJV: *voluptuously* D-R; *scarlet* D-R: literally, *saffron*>

<4:8   *now* D-R/C (in italics): omitted in D-R>

<4:9   *for want of the fruits of the earth* KJV (*want* in roman type in KJV): *by the barrennes of the countrie* D-R>

<4:10   *sodden* D-R: colloquially, *boiled*>

<4:11   *his fierce anger* KJV: *the wrath of his indignation* D-R>

<4:12   *would not have believed* KJV: *did not beleue* D-R>

4:13   *eius et: eius* Weber

<4:14   *help walking in it* D-R/C (in italics): omitted in D-R; *up* D-R/C:
    omitted in D-R>

4:14   *sunt: sunt in* S-C

<4:17   *expecting help for us in vain* D-R/C: *towards our vaine helpe* D-R>

4:18   *adpropinquavit: adpropinquat* *D-R

<4:20   *Under* KJV: *In* D-R>

<4:22   *carry thee away into captivity* KJV: *transport thee* D-R>

4:22   *Oratio Hieremiae, prophetae:* omitted in Weber

<5:4   *bought* D-R/C: *bought for a price* D-R>

5:5   *nostris minabamur: minabamur* Weber

<5:5   *dragged* D-R/C: *led* D-R; *we were weary* S *and* KJV *no rest was given
    us* D-R/C: *no rest was given to the wearie* D-R>

<5:8   *and* D-R/C (in italics): omitted in D-R>

<5:9   *because of* KJV [properly a Hebraism]: *at the face of* D-R>

<5:10   *by reason of* D-R [properly a Hebraism]: literally, *at the face of*; *the
    violence* D-R/C: *the tempests* D-R>

5:11   *humiliaverunt et: humiliaverunt* Weber

<5:11   *oppressed* D-R/C: *humbled* D-R>

<5:13   *under* KJV: *in* D-R>

5:15   *luctum: luctu* Weber

<5:16   *is fallen from our head* KJV: *of our head is fallen* D-R>

<5:19   *from generation* KJV: *in generation and* D-R>

5:19   *generatione: generationem* S-C; *generationem: generatione* Weber

5:20   *longitudine: longitudinem* Weber

BARUCH

1:1   *Neriae, filii Maasiae: Neeri filius Maasei* Weber

<1:3   *in the hearing of Jeconiah* KJV: *vnto the eares of Jechonias* D-R; *in* KJV
    the hearing of all D-R/C: *to the eares of al* D-R; *hear* KJV (in brack-
    ets in KJV and italics in D-R/C): omitted in D-R>

<1:4   *in the hearing* [first two times] KJV: *to the eares* D-R; *in the hearing*
    [third time] D-R/C: *to the eares* D-R>

1:4   *maximum: magnum* Weber; *eorum omnium: eorum* *D-R; *Sodi: Sudi*
    Weber

1:8   *mensis: illius* Weber

1:9   *Babylonis: Babylonum* Weber; *cunctos: vinctos et* Weber; *eos vinctos: eos* Weber; *Babylonem: Babyloniam* Weber

<1:10   *meat offerings* KJVn: *manna* D-R; *offerings* KJV: *offer* D-R>

1:11   *Babylonis: Babyloniae* Weber

1:12   *et ut: et* Weber; *Babylonis: Babyloniae* Weber

<1:14   *feasts* KJV: *a solemn day* D-R>

1:15   *sicut est: sicut* Weber

1:16   *et sacerdotibus: sacerdotibus* Weber

1:17   *Deum nostrum: nostrum* Weber

1:18   *audivimus: obaudivimus* Weber; *quae: quibus* Weber

1:19   *ad diem hanc: in hunc diem* Weber

<1:19   *were disobedient to* KJV: *would not be brought to beleue* D-R, literally, *were unbelieving toward*; *going astray* D-R/C: *dissipated* D-R; *turned away from hearing* D-R/C: *reuolted, that we might not heare* D-R>

<1:20   *foretold* D-R/C: *appoynted* D-R; *by* KJV: *to* D-R>

<2:1   *made good* KJV: *established* D-R>

2:1   *Israhel: in Israhel* Weber

<2:2   *never happened* KJV: *were not done* D-R>

2:2   *in Hierusalem: Hierusalem* Weber

2:4   *manu: manus* Weber; *in omnibus: et in omnibus* Weber; *in quibus: quo* Weber

<2:5   *uppermost* D-R/C: *aboue* D-R>

2:5   *voci: vocem* Weber

2:6   *est dies: dies* Weber

2:7   *quia: quae* Weber; *venerunt: evenerunt* Weber

<2:9   *over us for evil* KJV: *in euils* D-R; *it* KJV: *them* D-R>

<2:10   *set before us* KJV: *geuen before our face* D-R>

2:11   *populum tuum: plebem tuam* Weber; *sicut est: sicut* Weber

<2:14   *in the sight of them* KJV: *before their face* D-R>

2:16   *exaudi nos: audi* Weber

2:17   *spiritus acceptus: spiritum acceptum* Weber

<2:17   *justice* KJV (*righteousnesse*): *iustification* D-R>

2:18   *magnitudine mali: magnitudine* Weber; *infirmis: infirma* S-C

<2:18   *she hath done* D-R/C (in italics): omitted in D-R>

<2:19   *for* KJV: *according to* D-R>

2:19   *fundimus preces et petimus: fundimus* Weber

2:20   *manu*: *manus* Weber

2:21   *opera*: *operam* Weber

<2:21   *serve* KJV: *doe workes* D-R>

2:22   *si*: *si autem* Weber; *defectionem vestram*: *defectionem* Weber

2:23   *gaudimonii*: *gaudii* S-C

2:24   *Babylonis*: *Babyloniae* Weber; *transferrentur*: *proferrentur* Weber

<2:24   *made good* KJV: *established* D-R>

2:27   *bonitatem*: *benignitatem* Weber

2:29   *audieritis*: *obaudieritis* Weber; *multitudo*: *ambitio* Weber; *magna*: *magna et multa* Weber; *minimam*: *minimo* Weber

<2:29   *number* KJV (in brackets in KJV): *one* D-R>

<2:30   *But* KJV: *and* D-R>

2:31   *quoniam*: *quia* S-C; *intelligent, et aures, et audient* Ω^{SJ}agrel [without punctuation; Quentin's sigla]: *intelligent, aures et audient* S-C, *audient aures* Weber

<2:33   *stiff neck* KJV: *hard backe* D-R>

2:34   *Isaac*: *et Isaac* Weber; *eius*: *eis* S-C

<2:35   *that shall be* D-R/C (*shall be* in italics): omitted in D-R>

<3:4   *wherefore* KJV (*for the which*): *and* D-R>

3:5   *iniquitatum*: *iniquitates* Weber

<3:5   *think upon* KJV: *remember* D-R>

<3:7   *to the intent* KJV: *and* D-R>

3:7   *convertimur ab iniquitate*: *convertemus iniquitatem* Weber

3:8   *recesserunt*: *discesserunt* Weber

3:9   *percipe*: *percipite* Weber

<3:9   *learn* D-R/C: *know* D-R>

3:10   *quod*: *quid est quod* Weber

3:13   *nam si*: *si* Weber; *utique in*: *in* Weber

<3:14   *days and life* KJV: *life and liuing* D-R>

3:17   *inludunt*: *ludunt* S-C

3:18   *confidunt*: *confidebant* Weber

<3:18   *their works are unsearchable* KJV: *is there invention of their workes* D-R>

3:19   *exsurrexerunt*: *surrexerunt* S-C

3:23   *exquisitores prudentiae et*: *exquisitores* Weber

3:25   *est et*: *et* Weber

3:27   *Dominus: Deus* Weber; *invenerunt: dedit illis* Weber; *propterea: et* Weber

3:28   *Et quoniam non habuerunt: eo quod non haberent* Weber; *interierunt: et perierunt* Weber

3:29   *deduxit: eduxit* S-C

<3:30   *preferably to* D-R/C: *aboue* D-R>

3:31   *vias: viam* Weber; *exquirat: possit exquirere* *D-R

3:32   *invenit: adinvenit* S-C

<3:32   *for evermore* KJV: *in time euerlasting* D-R>

3:33   *obaudit: obedit* S-C

3:36   *est Deus: Deus* Weber; *et non: non* Weber

4:1   *pervenient ad: ad* Weber; *dereliquerunt: dereliquerint* Weber

<4:2   *in the presence of* KJV: *against* D-R>

4:3   *alteri: altero* Weber

4:4   *quoniam: quia* S-C

<4:5   *the memorial of* KJV: *memorable* D-R>

<4:6   *you* KJV: *in anger you* D-R>

4:8   *enim: autem* Weber; *Deum: eum* Weber

4:13   *iustitia: iustitias* Weber

<4:16   *me all alone* D-R/C (*me* in italics): *the sole woman* D-R>

<4:18   *But* D-R/C: *For* D-R>

<4:22   *my hope is* KJV: *I haue hoped* D-R; *that he will save you* KJV: *for your saluation* D-R>

4:23   *Dominus: Deus* Weber

<4:24   *now* KJV: omitted in D-R; *glory* D-R/C: *brightnes* D-R>

4:24   *vestram a Deo: vestram* Weber

4:27   *Dominum: Deum* Weber; *duxit: ducit* Weber

4:31   *peribunt: parebunt* Weber

4:32   *punientur et: punietur* Weber

<4:35   *long to endure* KJV: *in long during dayes*>

4:35   *multitudine: multitudinem* Weber

5:1   *sempiternae gloriae: in sempiterna gloriae* Weber

5:2   *Circumdabit: circumdato* Weber; *te Deus: te* Weber; *inponet: inpone* Weber; *capiti tuo: capiti* S-C

5:3   *quod* θ [Weber's siglum]: *omni quod* Weber, *omni qui* S-C

<5:3   *to every one* S-C: *which is* D-R>

5:6   *sublatos* C [Quentin's siglum]: *portatos* Weber, S-C; *honorem*: *honore*
       S-C

<5:6   *with honour* S-C: *into honour* D-R>

<5:8   *the woods* D-R/C: *the woods also* D-R>

5:8   *mandato*: *ex mandato* S-C

5:9   *ab*: *ex* S-C

6:0   (introductory text) *Exemplum*: *exemplar* S-C; *abducendos*: *abductos*
       Weber; *nuntiaret*: *adnuntiaret* S-C

6:1   *Babylonum*: *Babyloniorum* S-C

<6:2   *and* D-R/C: *therfore* D-R; *a long time* KJV (*season* for *time*): *long times*
       D-R>

6:2   *illic*: *ibi* S-C; *temporibus longis*: *tempus longum* Weber

6:3   *umeros*: *humeris* S-C

<6:4   *you* KJV: *you also* D-R>

<6:5   *But* D-R/C: *therefore* D-R>

6:5   *Te*: *tibi* Weber

6:6   *enim*: *autem* Weber

<6:8   *it were* KJV: omitted in D-R; *to go gay* KJV: *ornaments* D-R; *make
       them up* D-R/C: *their goddes are forged*>

6:8   *ornamenta*: *ornamenti* Weber; *fabricati*: *dii illorum fabricati* *D-R

<6:9   *gods have* D-R/C: *goddes certes haue* D-R>

6:9   *subtrahunt*: *subtrahent* Weber; *ipsos*: *ipsis* Weber

<6:11 *gods cannot defend themselves* KJV (*saue* for *defend*): *are not deliuered*
       D-R>

6:12   *extergent*: *extergunt* S-C

<6:13 *This* D-R/C: *And he* D-R; *but* D-R/C: *that* D-R; *cannot put to death*
       KJV: *killeth . . . not* D-R>

<6:14 *this* D-R/C: *He* D-R; *or* [both times] D-R/C: *and* D-R>

6:15   *Ne*: *non* S-C

<6:15 *a vessel that a man uses* KJV: *a mans vessel* D-R>

6:17   *tutant*: *tutantur* S-C

6:19   *comedunt*: *comedent* Weber

<6:21 *other birds* D-R/C: *the birds also* D-R>

6:21   *caput eorum*: *caput* Weber

6:22   *sciatis*: *scietis* Weber

<6:23 *but* D-R/C: omitted in D-R>

<6:24 *a high price* KJV (*most hie* for *high*): *al price* D-R>

6:24 *est in*: *inest* S-C

<6:25 *the use of* D-R/C: omitted in D-R; *how vile they are* D-R/C: *their basenes* D-R>

6:26 *surgent*: *consurgunt* S-C

<6:26 *again* KJV: omitted in D-R>

<6:27 *but* KJV: omitted in D-R; *poor* KJV: *begger* D-R>

<6:29 *how can they be called* KJV: *whence are they called* D-R>

<6:30 *temples* KJV: *houses* D-R; *and nothing upon their heads* KJV: *whose heades be bare* D-R>

6:30 *barbam rasam*: *barbas rasa* Weber

<6:31 *men do* KJV: omitted in D-R; *when one is dead* KJV: *of the dead* D-R>

6:32 *Vestimenta*: *a vestimento* Weber; *auferunt*: *auferent* Weber

<6:32 *also* KJV (in italics in D-R/C): omitted in D-R>

<6:33 *And whether it be evil that one doth unto them or good* KJV: *Neither if they suffer anie euil, nor if anie good of anie man* D-R>

6:33 *patiuntur*: *patiantur* Weber; *boni*: *bonum* Weber; *poterunt*: *possunt* *D-R

6:34 *requirunt*: *requirent* Weber

<6:35 *cannot deliver* KJV (*can saue no*): *deliuer not* D-R; *mighty* KJV: *mightier* D-R>

6:35 *infirmum*: *infimum* Weber; *eripiunt*: *eripient* Weber

6:36 *restituunt*: *restituent* Weber

<6:36 *cannot restore* KJV: *restore not* D-R; *nor deliver* KJV (*helpe* for *deliver*): *they shal not deliuer* D-R; *distress* KJV: *necessitie* D-R>

<6:38 *that are hewn out* KJV: omitted in D-R>

6:38 *et aurei*: *aurei* Weber

6:40 *offerunt illud*: *offerent illum* Weber

<6:40 *him* KJV: *it* D-R>

6:42 *circumdatae*: *circumdatis* Weber

6:43 *dormierit cum eo*: *dormierit* Weber

<6:43 *as* KJV: omitted in D-R>

6:44 *Quomodo ergo*: *quomodo* S-C

6:45 *erunt*: *erint* Weber

6:46 *artifices*: *aurifices* Weber; *ea quae*: *quae* Weber

<6:48   *or* KJV: *and* D-R>

  6:48   *sacerdotes apud se*: *post se sacerdotes* Weber

<6:49   *can* KJV: omitted in D-R>

<6:50   *but* KJV: omitted in D-R; *it shall be* KJV: *Which are* D-R>

  6:50   *lignea et*: *lignea* S-C; *sunt ab*: *sunt* Weber; *manifestata*: *manifesta* S-C;
          cum illis: *in illis* Weber

<6:52   *cannot set up* KJV: *raise not up* D-R>

<6:53   *They determine no* D-R/C *causes* KJV: *Iudgement also they shal not de-*
          cerne D-R; *deliver* D-R/C: *shal they deliuer* D-R; *and* D-R/C:
          omitted in D-R; *are* KJV: omitted in D-R>

  6:53   *regiones*: *regionem* Weber

<6:54   *these* D-R/C (in italics): omitted in D-R; *asunder* KJV: *in the middes*
          D-R>

  6:54   *ligneorum et* Ω^J*agrelv* [Quentin's sigla]: *ligneorum* Weber, S-C

<6:55   *cannot* KJV: *shal not* D-R; *can it be* KJV: *is it . . . to be* D-R>

<6:56   *Neither are these gods . . . able to* KJV: *Not . . . shal the goddes* D-R; *but*
          D-R/C (in italics): omitted in D-R; *they that* S-C: *the wicked men*
          D-R>

  6:56   *inargentati*: *argentati* Weber; *iniqui* Ω^S*arels* [Quentin's sigla]: *hii qui*
          Weber, S-C

  6:57   *quo*: *quod* Weber; *ferent*: *ferunt* Weber

<6:58   *be well satisfied* D-R/C: *glorie* D-R; *such* KJV: omitted in D-R>

  6:58   *illud*: *illud / quam falsi dii* Weber

<6:59   *The sun* D-R/C: *The sunne certes* D-R>

  6:59   *ac sidera*: *sidera* Weber

<6:60   *the lightning* KJV: *also the lightning* D-R; *breaketh forth* KJV: *shal ap-*
          peare D-R; *wind* KJV: *winde also* D-R>

  6:63   *aestimandum*: *existimandum* S-C; *possunt*: *possint* Weber; *quidquam*
          facere: *benefacere* Weber

<6:63   *causes* KJV: *iudgment* D-R; *good* KJV: *thing* D-R>

<6:64   *fear* KJV: *then feare* D-R>

<6:65   *can* KJV: *shal* D-R>

<6:66   *shine . . . nor give light* KJV: *shal they shine . . . nor geue light* D-R>

<6:68   *there is no manner of appearance* D-R/C: *By no meanes . . . is it manifest*
          vnto vs D-R>

6:69   *cucumerario*: *cucumeraria* Weber

<6:70   *They are no better than* D-R/C: *After the same sorte also* D-R>

6:71   *murice*: *marmore* Weber; *illos*: *illud* Weber; *quia* CΔΛ^LΩ^S grel [Quentin's sigla]: *quia itaque* Weber, S-C; *erunt*: *erit* Weber

EZEKIEL

1:2   *Hiezechielem*: *Hiezechiel* Weber

<1:4   *it* KJV? (in italics in D-R/C): omitted in D-R>

1:5   *ex medio eorum*: *in medio eius* S-C

<1:5   *in* S-C: *out of* D-R>

1:6   *Quattuor*: *et quattuor* Weber

<1:6   *Every . . . every* KJV: omitted in D-R>

1:7   *Pedes*: *et pedes* Weber

<1:7   *they sparkled* KJV: *sparkes* D-R>

1:10   *aquilae desuper*: *aquilae* Weber

1:11   *Et facies*: *Facies* S-C

1:12   *unumquodque eorum*: *unumquodque* Weber

<1:12   *to go* KJV: omitted in D-R>

1:13   *fulgor*: *fulgur* S-C

1:20   *levabantur*: *elevabantur* S-C

<1:21   *those* [all three times] KJV: *them* D-R; *these* [both times] KJV (in roman type in KJV): *they* D-R>

<1:22   *to behold* D-R/C: omitted in D-R>

1:22   *capita*: *caput* Weber

<1:24   *most high* KJV (*Almightie*): *high* D-R>

1:24   *demittebantur* S-C [1592 and 1593 editions, according to Weber]: *dimittebantur* Weber

1:25   *supra*: *super* S-C

2:1   *supra*: *super* S-C

2:3   *me; ipsi et*: *me* Weber

<3:5   *but* KJV (in roman type in KJV and italics in D-R/C): omitted in D-R>

3:7   *nolent*: *nolunt* S-C

3:10   *quos*: *quos ego* S-C

<3:11 *Lord* S: *Lord God* D-R>

<3:12 *saying* KJV (in roman type in KJV and italics in D-R/C): omitted in D-R>

3:13 *altera*: *alteram* S-C

3:15 *transmigrationem, ad*: *transmigrationem* Weber

<3:16 *at the end of seven days* KJV: *when seuen dayes, were passed* D-R>

3:19 *et a*: *et* Weber

3:20 *sua fuerit et*: *sua* Weber

3:25 *de*: *in* Weber

3:26 *adherescere*: *adherere* S-C

<4:1 *lay* KJV: *thou shalt put* D-R; *draw* KJV (*pourtray*): *thou shalt draw* D-R; *the plan of* D-R/C: omitted in D-R>

<4:2 *lay* KJV: *thou shalt lay* D-R; *build* KJV: *shalt build* D-R; *cast* KJV: *shalt . . . cast* D-R; *set* KJV: *shalt . . . pitch* D-R; *place* KJV (*set*): *shalt . . . place* D-R>

<4:3 *set* [both times] KJV: *thou shalt set* D-R>

4:3 *eam in*: *eam* Weber

4:7 *exertum*: *extentum* S-C

4:12 *egreditur*: *egredietur* Weber

<4:14 *or* KJV: *and* D-R>

4:14 *ingressa in*: *ingressa* Weber

5:1 *pilos, et*: *pilos* Weber

<5:1 *and* D-R/C *cause* KJV: *and thou shalt take it and draw* D-R; *take* KJV: *thou shalt take* D-R; *divide the hair* KJV (*hair* in roman type in KJV and italics in D-R/C): *shalt diuide them* D-R>

5:2 *adsumes*: *adsumens* Weber: *partem et*: *partem* Weber

5:4 *proicies eos*: *proicies* Weber; *igni, et*: *igni* Weber

5:7 *sunt et*: *sunt* Weber

5:9 *quae*: *quod* S-C

5:12 *gladio*: *in gladio* S-C

5:13 *conplebo*: *conpleam* Weber

5:14 *in gentibus*: *gentibus* S-C

5:16 *conteram in*: *conteram* Weber

<6:2 *prophesy* KJV: *thou shalt prophecie* D-R>

<6:3 *say* KJV: *shalt say* D-R>

6:3   *et rupibus* Frede HI Ez 2 58B and 63C (*rupesque*): *rupibus* Weber, S-C

6:7   *quia ego sum: quoniam ego* Weber

6:11   *manum tuam: manu tua* Weber; *Eheu: Heu* S-C; *quia: qui* Weber; *fame et: fame* Weber

<6:11   *with* [both times] KJV: omitted in D-R>

6:12   *conplebo: conpleam* Weber

6:13   *excelso et: excelso* Weber

7:2   *venit; venit: venit* Weber

7:3   *inmittam: emittam* Weber

7:7   *contritio: contractio* Weber

7:8   *conplebo: conpleam* Weber

<7:11   *shall remain* KJV (in roman type in KJV and italics in D-R/C): omitted in D-R>

<7:13   *although* KJV: *and* D-R; *which regardeth* D-R/C: *to* D-R>

<7:14   *Yet* KJV (*but*): *and* D-R>

7:15   *foris et: foris* Weber

7:19   *foras: foris* Weber

<7:22   *robbers* D-R (*spoylers*): literally, *emissaries* or *attendants*>

<8:1   *that* KJV: *and* D-R>

8:3   *adduxit me: adduxit* Weber; *ad aquilonem: aquilonem* Weber

8:6   *faciunt: faciant* Weber

8:8   *fodissem: perfodissem* Weber

<8:8   *behold* KJV: *there appered* D-R>

<8:13   *If* D-R/C: omitted in D-R>

8:18   *furore meo* $\Theta^S Q^2$ cum G [Quentin's sigla]: *furore* Weber, S-C

9:2   *vestitus erat: vestitus* Weber

<9:4   *through* KJV: *in* D-R>

<9:6   *Utterly* KJV: *to vtter destruction* D-R; *and* KJV (in roman type in KJV): omitted in D-R; *maidens* D-R/C: *and the virgin* D-R>

10:2   *cherubim: cherub* Weber

10:11   *gradiebantur, et: gradiebantur* Weber

10:15   *flumen: fluvium* S-C

<10:16   *went* KJV: *went together* D-R; *but* D-R/C: *but also* D-R>

10:16   *levarent: elevarent* Weber

10:21   *Quattuor*: *quattuor per quattuor* Weber

11:1   *respicit ad*: *respicit* Weber

11:2   *hi sunt*: *hi* Weber

<11:3   *city* KJV (in roman type in KJV and italics in D-R/C): omitted in D-R>

<11:5   *for* KJV: *and* D-R>

11:12   *quia*: *qui* Weber

<11:13   *all* D-R/C: omitted in D-R>

<11:21   *But as for them* KJV (in italics in D-R/C; *as for them* in roman type in KJV): omitted in D-R>

<12:3   *all necessaries* D-R/C: *vessels* D-R; *remove* KJV: *thou shalt flitte* D-R>

12:5   *perfodi*: *perfode* S-C

12:7   *mihi*: *mihi Dominus* S-C; *manu, et*: *manu* Weber; *et in umeris*: *in umeris* S-C

<12:11   *they shall be removed from their dwellings* D-R/C [KJV has *they shall remooue*]: *into transmigration* D-R>

12:11   *in captivitatem*: *captivitatem* Weber

12:16   *narrent*: *enarrent* S-C

<12:19   *say* KJV: *thou shalt say* D-R>

12:25   *loquar, et*: *loquar* Weber; *et fiet*: *fiet et* S-C

<12:25   *come to pass and* S-C: *also be done* D-R>

13:9   *consilio*: *concilio* Weber; *terram*: *terra* Weber

<13:10   *the people* D-R/C: *he* D-R>

13:13   *consumptionem*: *consummationem* Weber

13:15   *pariete*: *parietem* Weber

<13:16   *Even* D-R/C: omitted in D-R>

13:18   *animas, et*: *animas* Weber

<13:19   *should not die* KJV: *dye not* D-R; *should not live* KJV: *liue not*>

<13:20   *declare* D-R/C (in italics): omitted in D-R>

<14:3   *and* D-R/C: omitted in D-R>

<14:4   *say* KJV: *thou shalt say* D-R; *Every* KJV (in italics in D-R/C): *Man* D-R>

<14:7   *every* KJV: *man* D-R>

14:11   *sit*: *sint* S-C

<14:15   *so that* KJV: *for that* D-R>

14:16   *si*: *qui* Weber; *Dominus* Θ^S^E*T*HI [Quentin's sigla]: *Dominus Deus* Weber, S-C

<14:19   *Or* KJV: *And* D-R>

14:21   *inmisero*: *misero* Weber

14:22   *salvatio*: *salvatio aliquorum* *D-R; *ingredientur*: *egredientur* Weber

15:2   *de ligno*: *ligno* Weber

<15:5   *less* KJV: *more* D-R>

15:6   *tradam*: *tradidi* Weber

16:3   *Chanaan*: *chananea* Weber

16:4   *aqua*: *in aqua* Weber

16:5   *faceret*: *facerem* Weber; *miseratus*: *misertus* S-C

<16:6   *thee* KJV: *thee, I say* D-R>

16:7   *confusionis*: *confusione* S-C

<16:10   *embroidery* KJV (*broidred worke*): *diuers colours* D-R; *violet-coloured* S-C *shoes* D-R/C: *hyacinth* D-R>

16:10   *hyacinthino* ACΣΛOSTMΦ [Weber's sigla]: *ianthino* Weber, S-C

16:13   *multis coloribus* ACΣΛOSTMΦ [Weber's sigla]: *multicoloribus* Weber, S-C

16:16   *tuis*: *meis* Weber

<16:17   *thy beautiful vessels* KJV (*thy faire iewels*): *vessels of thy beautie* D-R>

16:18   *operuisti illas*: *vestita es eis* Weber

16:21   *Immolasti*: *immolantis* Weber

<16:21   *by* D-R/C (in italics): omitted in D-R; *fire* KJV (in roman type in KJV and italics in D-R): omitted in D-R>

16:27   *extendam*: *extendi* Weber; *iustificationem tuam*: *ius tuum* Weber; *animas*: *animam* Weber

<16:28   *Assyrians* KJV: *sonnes of the Assyrians* D-R>

16:33   *dona donabas*: *donabas* Weber

<16:38   *blood in* KJV: *into bloud of* D-R>

16:45   *tuarum es*: *tuarum* Weber

16:46   *habitant*: *habitat* Weber

<17:3   *say* KJV: *thou shalt say* D-R>

17:4   *avellit*: *avulsit* S-C; *urbe*: *urbem* Weber

<17:4   *and* D-R/C: omitted in D-R>

17:5   *semine*: *semente* Weber

<17:6 *it sprung up and* KJV (*grew* for *sprung up*): *when it had budded, it* D-R>

17:6 *erant*: *erunt* Weber

17:8 *ut sit*: *et* Weber

17:9 *fructus*: *fructum* Weber

<17:9 *make it* KJV? (*that* for *make*): *it shal* D-R>

17:12 *in Hierusalem*: *Hierusalem* Weber

<17:12 *with* KJV: *to* D-R>

<17:18 *breaking* KJV: *that he might breake* D-R>

17:20 *in sagena*: *sagena* Weber

17:21 *agmine suo*: *agmine* Weber

<17:21 *bands* KJV: *troupe* D-R>

17:23 *monte sublimi*: *montibus sublimibus* *D-R; *volucres, et*: *volucres* Weber; *ea*: *eo* Weber

<18:6 *and* KJV: omitted in D-R>

18:8 *suam et*: *suam* Weber

<18:16 *nor withholden* S: *hath not withheld* D-R; *but* KJV (in roman type in KJV and italics in D-R/C): omitted in D-R>

<18:17 *but* D-R/C (in italics): omitted in D-R; *and* S (in italics in D-R/C): omitted in D-R>

18:21 *universa*: *omnia* S-C; *vivet et*: *vivet* Weber

18:25 *Audite ergo*: *audite* Weber

<19:2 *and* D-R/C (in italics): omitted in D-R>

19:3 *suis, et*: *suis* Weber

<19:5 *and* KJV (in roman type in KJV and italics in D-R/C): omitted in D-R>

19:6 *leo, et*: *leo* Weber

19:10 *plantata est*: *plantata* Weber

<19:14 *so that she now hath* KJV (without *now*): *and there was* D-R>

<20:1 *month* KJV (in roman type in KJV and italics in D-R/C): omitted in D-R>

<20:3 *say* KJV: *thou shalt say* D-R>

<20:5 *say* KJV: *thou shalt say* D-R>

20:8 *nolueruntque me*: *nolueruntque* Weber

<20:9 *But* KJV: *And* D-R; *otherwise* D-R/C (in italics): omitted in D-R>

20:10 *eduxi eos*: *eduxi* Weber

20:11 *faciens homo vivet*: *faciat homo et vivat* Weber

20:12 *essent*: *esset* Weber

<20:13 *But* KJV: *And* D-R>

<20:14 *spared them* D-R/C: *did* D-R>

20:20 *sint*: *sit* Weber; *sciatis*: *sciatur* Weber; *ego sum*: *ego* Weber

<20:21 *But* KJV (*Notwithstanding*): *And* D-R>

<20:27 *say* KJV: *thou shalt say* D-R>

20:33 *in brachio*: *brachio* Weber

20:34 *in brachio*: *brachio* Weber

20:38 *in terram*: *terram* Weber

20:44 *meum et*: *meum* Weber

<20:47 *say* KJV: *thou shalt say* D-R>

21:4 *usque ad*: *ad* Weber

<21:9 *say* KJV: *thou shalt say* D-R>

21:11 *limatus est*: *limatus* Weber

<21:12 *sword* D-R/C (in italics): *same* D-R>

<21:15 *the sword that is* D-R/C: *and* D-R>

21:19 *ambae*: *ambo* Weber

21:21 *idola et* Fragmenta Sangallensia p. 241 [Dold, 1923] (*sculptilibus et*): *idola* Weber, S-C

21:26 *humilem*: *humiles* S-C

<21:27 *but* S: *and* D-R>

21:27 *non*: *nunc* Weber

22:2 *nonne* [both times]: *num* Weber

22:20 *ea*: *eam* Weber

22:22 *Dominus cum*: *Dominus* Weber

22:25 *rapiensque*: *rapiens* Weber; *animas*: *animam* Weber

22:27 *ad perdendas*: *perdendas* Weber; *ad sectanda*: *sectanda* Weber

<22:28 *the morter* KJV (in roman type in KJV and italics in D-R/C): omitted in D-R>

23:4 *eius minor*: *eius* Weber

<23:6 *beautiful youths* KJV? (*desireable yong men*): *youngmen of concupiscences* D-R>

23:8 *dormierunt*: *dormierant* Weber; *confregerunt*: *confregerant* Weber; *effuderunt*: *effuderant* Weber

23:9 *manus*: *manu* Weber; *libidinem*: *libidine* S-C

<23:12   *prostituting herself* D-R/C: omitted in D-R>

<23:13   *and* D-R/C (in italics): omitted in D-R; *that they both took* KJV (*took* in roman type in KJV): *both* D-R>

23:20   *concubitu*: *concubitum* S-C

23:28   *manus* [second time]: *manu* Weber

23:29   *plenam, et*: *plenam* Weber

23:30   *eorum*: *earum* S-C

23:32   *est*: *es* Weber

23:34   *ubera* elv [Quentin's sigla]: *et ubera* Weber, S-C

23:37   *adulteratae*: *adulterae* Weber

23:40   *circumlevisti*: *circumlinisti* S-C

23:41   *ornata*: *ordinata* Weber

23:44   *Oolibam*: *et Oolibam* Weber

24:1   *decima die*: *decima* Weber

24:3   *eam*: *ea* Weber

24:4   *eam*: *ea* Weber; *strues*: *struices* Weber

<24:8   *And* D-R/C: omitted in D-R; *smooth* S: *most clere* D-R>

24:10   *concoquetur*: *coquetur* S-C

24:12   *exivit*: *exibit* Weber

24:14   *veniet*: *venit* Weber; *iudicabo*: *iudicavi* Weber

24:21   *filii*: *et filii* Weber; *filiae vestrae*: *filiae* Weber

24:25   *quo* [first time]: *qua* S-C

<24:27   *to him* KJV: *with him* D-R>

<25:8   *other* D-R/C: omitted in D-R>

25:13   *desertam*: *desertum* Weber

25:15   *vindictam*: *in vindictam* Weber

<26:2   *now* KJV (in roman type in KJV and italics in D-R/C): omitted in D-R>

<26:4   *smooth* S: *most cleare* D-R>

26:8   *levabit*: *elevabit* Weber

26:10   *cum*: *dum* Weber; *introitum*: *introitus* Weber

26:20   *porro cum*: *porro* Weber

<27:6   *They have cut thy oars out of the oaks* KJV (*made* for *cut*): *Okes . . . they haue hewed for thine ores* D-R; *with things* D-R/C *brought* KJV (*brought* in roman type in KJV): omitted in D-R>

27:6   *tuos, et: tuos* Weber

27:9   *Giblii: Bibli* Weber

27:14 *adduxerunt: advexerunt* S-C

27:16 *gemmam et: gemmam* Weber

<27:18 *men of Damascus* D-R/C: *Damacene* D-R; *merchants* S: *merchant* D-R>

<27:20 *The men of* D-R/C: omitted in D-R>

27:23 *negotiatores tui: negotiatores* Weber; *Assur et: Assur* Weber

27:25 *tuae: tui* S-C

<27:32 *city* D-R (in italics in D-R/C): literally would be omitted>

<27:33 *from thee by sea* D-R/C: *from the sea* D-R>

28:8   *in interitu: interitu* Weber

<28:11 *say* KJV: *thou shalt say* D-R>

28:17 *Et elevatum: elevatum* Weber

28:26 *plantabuntque: et plantabunt* Weber

29:1   *decimo* [second time]: *in decimo* Weber; *undecima die: undecima* Weber

29:9   *in solitudinem: solitudinem* Weber; *pro eo: eo* Weber; *dixeris: dixerit* Weber; *feci eum: feci* Weber

<29:10 *utterly* KJV: omitted in D-R; *and* KJV (in italics in D-R/C): omitted in D-R>

29:12 *et erunt: erunt* Weber

29:13 *fuerant: fuerunt* Weber

29:20 *quo: pro quo* Weber

30:3   *adpropinquat: adpropinquavit* Weber

30:6   *Dominus, Deus: Dominus* Weber

30:8   *Aegypto: Aegyptum* Weber

30:10 *Cessare: et cessare* Weber

30:12 *manus: manu* Weber; *in manibus* Sabatier: *in manu* Weber, *manu* S-C

<30:12 *hand of the wicked* KJV: *handes of the most wicked* D-R>

30:14 *Alexandria: Alexandriam* Weber

30:20 *primo mense: primo* Weber

30:21 *Pharaonis: Pharao* Weber; *fasciaretur: farciretur* Weber; *ut recepto: et recepto* Weber

30:22 *Pharaonem*: *Pharao* Weber; *iam* *D-R: *sed* Weber, S-C

30:26 *terras*: *terris* Weber

31:1 *tertio mense*: *tertio* Weber

<31:3 *of a high* D-R/C: *and high of* D-R>

<31:8 *in* KJV: *and to* D-R>

31:11 *manus* $\Lambda^L\Omega$arel cum G [Quentin's sigla]: *manu* Weber, S-C

<31:11 *he shall deal* S?: *doing he shal doe* D-R>

31:14 *sua*: *eorum* Weber

<31:14 *by* KJV: *of* D-R; *are watered* KJV (*drinke water*): *are watered with waters* D-R; *with* KJV: *to* D-R>

31:15 *induxi*: *indixi* Weber

31:17 *eo*: *ea* Weber; *ad infernum*: *in infernum* S-C

31:18 *eis*: *his* Weber

32:2 *Pharaonem*: *Pharao* Weber; *earum*: *eorum* Weber

32:3 *extraham*: *extrahent* Weber

<32:4 *into the open* KJV (*vpon* for *into*): *vpon the face of the* D-R>

32:6 *pedore*: *fetore* S-C

32:7 *caelos*: *caelum* S-C

32:8 *Deus, "cum ceciderint vulnerati tui in medio terrae," ait Dominus Deus*: *Deus* Weber

32:10 *tuae*: *suae* Weber

32:12 *hae*: *heae* Weber

32:16 *Aegypto*: *Aegyptum* S-C; *multitudine*: *multitudinem* S-C

32:18 *multitudine*: *multitudinem* S-C

<32:18 *both* KJV (*euen*; in roman type in KJV and italics in D-R/C): omitted in D-R>

<32:23 *spread* KJV (*caused*): *had geuen* D-R>

32:25 *dederunt*: *dederant* Weber; *terrorem suum*: *terrorem* Weber

<32:25 *him a bed* KJV (*her* for *him*): *her couche* D-R; *him . . . his . . . him*: the Latin does not indicate a gender for these pronouns, but the sense requires that they be considered feminine (as D-R and KJV translate). D-R/C alone treats them as masculine>

<32:26 *though* KJV: *because* D-R>

<32:27 *uncircumcised* KJV: *and the vncircumcised* D-R>

32:29 *eius et*: *eius* Weber; *descendunt*: *descenderunt* Weber

<33:2   *say* KJV: *thou shalt say* D-R; *if* KJV: *and* D-R>
<33:4   *then* KJV: *and* D-R; *if* KJV: *and* D-R>
  33:4   *sonum*: *sonitum* S-C; *et non*: *non* Weber
  33:5   *autem se*: *autem* Weber; *salvabit*: *salvavit* Weber
<33:9   *and* S: omitted in D-R>
  33:11   *convertatur*: *revertatur* Weber; *convertimini, convertimini*: *con-
          vertimini* Weber
  33:14   *Si*: *sin* Weber
  33:15   *et pignus*: *pignus* Weber; *et non*: *non* Weber
<33:15   *if* KJV (in roman type in KJV): omitted in D-R; *and* D-R/C (in ital-
          ics): omitted in D-R>
<33:17   *equitable* KJV (*equall*): *of equal weight* D-R>
  33:18   *iniquitates*: *iniquitatem* Weber
  33:20   *Non est*: *non* Weber
  33:21   *decimo*: *duodecimo* Weber
  33:27   *speluncis*: *in speluncis* Weber
  33:28   *in desertum*: *desertum* Weber
  33:29   *terram eorum*: *terram* Weber
  33:30   *qui* [second time]: *quis* S-C
  33:32   *audiunt*: *audient* Weber; *faciunt*: *facient* Weber
<34:1   *say* KJV: *thou shalt say* D-R>
  34:4   *fractum*: *confractum* S-C; *reduxistis, et*: *reduxistis* Weber; *pastores mei*:
          pastores Weber
<34:4   *a high hand* D-R/C: *might* D-R>
  34:8   *pastores mei*: *pastores* Weber
  34:10   *erit*: *erunt* Weber
  34:12   *in quibus*: *quo* Weber
  34:14   *pascua earum*: *pascuae eorum* Weber
  34:16   *fuerat*: *erat* Weber
  34:18   *pascua bona*: *pascuam bonam* Weber
  34:20   *vos*: *eos* Weber
  34:23   *ea* [all three times]: *eas* S-C
<34:23   *even* KJV (in roman type in KJV): omitted in D-R>
  34:26   *benedictionis*: *benedictiones* S-C
  34:28   *rapinam in*: *rapinam* Weber

34:29   *amplius*: *ultra* S-C; *obprobrium*: *obprobria* Weber

<34:29   *prophesy* KJV: *thou shalt prophecie* D-R; *say* KJV: *shalt say* D-R>

35:9   *Dominus Deus*: *Dominus* Weber

35:13   *derogastis*: *rogastis* Weber

<36:1   *say* KJV: *thou shalt say* D-R>

<36:3   *are become the subject of the talk* D-R/C: *haue ascended vpon the lippe of the tongue* D-R>

36:4   *desertis et parietinis* Frede HI Ez 11 339D (*desertis Ecclesiis, et parietinis*) and 338A (*desertis atque vastatis*): *desertis, parietinis* S-C, Weber [without punctuation]

<36:5   *In* KJV (*Surely in*): *Because in* D-R>

36:5   *qui*: *quae* S-C; *corde et*: *corde* Weber

<36:6   *say* KJV: *thou shalt say* D-R>

36:11   *habitare*: *habitari* Weber

<36:17   *when* KJV: omitted in D-R; *they defiled* KJV: *and polluted* D-R>

36:19   *terras*: *terris* Weber; *adinventiones eorum*: *adinventiones* Weber

<36:20   *when* KJV: omitted in D-R; *they profaned* KJV: *and haue polluted* D-R>

<36:21   *regarded* S?: *spared* D-R>

36:24   *congregabo vos*: *congregabo* Weber

36:29   *in vobis*: *vobis* S-C

36:33   *habitari*: *inhabitari* S-C

36:36   *sim*: *sum* Weber

36:38   *plenae*: *plenaeque* Weber

<37:4   *say* KJV: *thou shalt say* D-R>

<37:8   *but* KJV: *and* D-R>

<37:9   *say* KJV: *thou shalt say* D-R>

37:11   *abscisi*: *abscissi* S-C

<37:12   *say* KJV: *thou shalt say* D-R>

37:13   *popule*: *populus* Weber

37:16   *sociorum*: *sociis* Weber; *ligno*: *lignum* Weber

<37:17   *the other* KJV (*another*): *the other for thee* D-R>

37:19   *sunt ei adiunctae*: *iunctae sunt ei* Weber

37:22   *eos in*: *eos* Weber

37:23   *abominationibus suis*: *abominationibus* Weber; *cunctis*: *in cunctis* Weber; *mundabo*: *emundabo* S-C

<37:24   *shepherd* D-R/C: *pastour of them al* D-R>

<38:3   *say* KJV: *thou shalt say* D-R>

38:8   *gladio et*: *gladio* Weber; *habitabunt*: *habitaverunt* Weber

<38:8   *but* KJV: omitted in D-R>

<38:10   *projects shall enter into* KJV (*shall things come into*): *shal wordes ascend vpon* D-R>

38:11   *hi omnes*: *omnes* Weber

38:13   *Saba*: *Seba* Weber; *aurum et*: *aurum* Weber

<38:14   *say* KJV: *thou shalt say* D-R>

<38:17   *by* KJV: *in the hand of* D-R>

38:19   *et in igne* Γ^A [Quentin's siglum]: *in igne* Weber, S-C

<38:20   *so that* KJV: *and* D-R; *creepeth* KJV: *moueth* D-R>

38:20   *corruet in terram*: *in terra corruet* Weber

<39:1   *say* KJV: *thou shalt say* D-R>

39:2   *reducam* $C\Sigma\Phi$ [Weber's sigla]: *seducam* Weber, *educam* S-C; *ascendere te*: *ascendere* Weber

<39:2   *lead thee out* S-C: *reduce thee* D-R>

39:4   *populi tui*: *populi* Weber; *te ad*: *te* Weber

39:6   *inmittam*: *emittam* Weber

39:9   *manuum*: *manus* Weber

39:11   *faciet*: *facit* Weber

39:13   *autem eum*: *autem* Weber

39:17   *haec dicit*: *dicit* *D-R; *carnem*: *carnes* Weber

39:18   *arietum*: *arietum et* S-C; *taurorumque et*: *taurorumque* Weber

<39:18   *and* S-C: omitted in D-R>

39:19   *saturitatem*: *saturitate* Weber; *ebrietatem*: *ebrietate* Weber

39:20   *equite*: *de equite* Weber

39:23   *reliquerint*: *dereliquerint* S-C; *manus*: *manu* Weber

39:26   *qua*: *quam* Weber

39:28   *congregaverim*: *congregavero* Weber

40:1   *vicesimo et*: *vicesimo* S-C

40:13   *viginti et*: *viginti* S-C

40:22   *scalpturae*: *sculpturae* S-C

40:24   *eduxit*: *duxit* Weber

40:29   *eisdem*: *hisdem* Weber

40:33   *vestibulum*: *vestibula* Weber; *vestibula*: *vestibuli* Weber

40:36 *et frontem: frontem* Weber; *et vestibulum: vestibulum* Weber

40:37 *Et vestibulum eius respiciebat ad: vestibulum eius in* Weber

40:38 *lavabant: lavabunt* Weber

40:41 *erant: erunt* Weber; *immolabant: immolabunt* Weber

40:45 *sacerdotum erit: sacerdotum* Weber

41:4 *latitudinem: latitudinem eius* S-C

41:9 *et erat: et* Weber

41:15 *ethecas: ekthetas* Weber

41:16 *ethecas: ekthetas* Weber

<41:18 *so that* KJV: *and* D-R; *every* KJV (in roman type in KJV and italics
in D-R/C): *a* D-R>

41:22 *duorum: duo* Weber

41:25 *scalptura: sculpturae* S-C; *expressae erant: expressa erat* Weber

42:1 *introduxit: eduxit* Weber

42:4 *earum: eorum* S-C

42:6 *terra cubitis quinquaginta: terra* Weber

42:10 *faciem: facie* Weber

<42:12 *towards* KJV: *in the way looking to* D-R>

42:17 *aquilonem: aquilonis* S-C

42:20 *murum: illud murum* Weber; *longitudinem: longitudine* Weber; *latitudinem: latitudine* Weber

43:5 *levavit: elevavit* S-C

<43:9 *carcasses* KJV: *ruins* D-R>

43:11 *ut: et* Weber

43:12 *omnis finis: omnes fines* Weber

43:13 *definitio eius: definitio* Weber; *eius et: eius* Weber

43:14 *minore: maiori* Weber; *maiorem: minorem* Weber

43:15 *usque: usque ad* S-C

<43:16 *and* D-R/C: *by* D-R>

<43:17 *and* KJV: *by* D-R>

43:17 *quattuordecim cubitos: quattuordecim* Weber; *dimidii cubiti: dimidii cubiti* Weber

43:19 *sacerdotibus et: sacerdotibus* Weber

<43:26 *consecrate it* KJV (glossed by D-R/C as *fill its hand*): *fil his hand*
D-R>

44:2 *transiet: transibit* S-C

<44:5 *mark well* KJV: *thou shalt set thy hart* D-R>

<44:8 *but* KJV: *and* D-R>

44:11 *holocausta*: *holocaustosin* Weber

44:12 *portabunt*: *portaverunt* Weber

44:14 *et in*: *et* Weber; *fient*: *fiunt* Weber

44:15 *autem et*: *autem* Weber

<44:18 *any thing that causeth* KJV (in italics in D-R/C): omitted in D-R>

44:19 *vestimenta sua*: *vestimentis suis* S-C; *ministraverant*: *ministraverunt* Weber

<44:19 *ministered* KJV: *had ministered* D-R>

44:25 *habuit*: *habuerit* S-C

44:28 *Non erit*: *erit* Weber

44:30 *tuae*: *suae* Weber

45:7 *Longitudinem*: *longitudinis* S-C; *partem*: *partium* Weber

45:12 *habet*: *habeat* Weber; *faciunt*: *facient* Weber

45:13 *haec*: *hae* S-C

45:17 *sabbatis et*: *sabbatis* Weber; *faciet*: *faciat* Weber

46:5 *arietem, in*: *arietem* Weber

46:6 *arietes*: *aries* Weber

46:7 *de agnis*: *agnis* Weber

<46:9 *But* KJV: *And* D-R>

46:16 *eam*: *ea* Weber

46:20 *peccato et pro delicto*: *delicto et pro peccato* Weber; *atrium exterius*: *atrio exteriori* Weber

46:22 *angulis*: *angulos* Weber

47:5 *profundi*: *profundae* Weber

47:6 *eduxit*: *duxit* Weber

47:10 *Et*: *vivent et* Weber; *illa*: *illas* S-C; *erit*: *erunt* Weber

<47:10 *waters* D-R/C (in italics): omitted in D-R>

47:14 *suus, super*: *suus* Weber

47:15 *Hethalon*: *Bethalon* Weber

47:16 *Tichon*: *Atticon* Weber; *terminum*: *terminos* Weber

47:17 *aquilonem*: *aquilonem et* Weber; *plaga*: *plaga autem* Weber

47:19 *et haec est*: *et* Weber

48:1 *iuxta viam* [second time]: *iuxta* Weber

48:8 *separabitis*: *separastis* Weber

48:10 *aquilonem longitudinis*: *aquilonem* Weber

48:16 *quingenti* [all four times]: *quingenta* S-C

48:17 *ducenti* [all four times]: *ducenta* S-C

48:20 *et in*: *et* Weber

48:25 *occidentalem*: *occidentis* Weber

48:28 *meridiem*: *meridie* S-C

48:31 *in*: *ex* S-C

48:33 *metieris; et portae tres*: *metieris* Weber; *portam* [all three times]: *porta* S-C; *unam* [all three times]: *una* S-C

48:34 *quingenti*: *quingentos* S-C; *milia et*: *milia* Weber

DANIEL

1:1 *in Hierusalem*: *Hierusalem* Weber

1:3 *eunuchorum*: *eunuchorum suorum* Weber

<1:3 *some* KJV (*certaine*; in roman type in KJV and italics in D-R): omitted in D-R>

1:7 *Ananiae*: *et Ananiae* Weber

1:12 *Tempta* HI ep 100.7 p. 220.29: *Tempta nos* S-C, Weber [without capitalization]

<1:13 *deal* KJV: *thou shalt doe* D-R>

<1:16 *that they should drink* KJV: *of their drinke* D-R>

1:17 *sapientiam*: *sapientia* Weber

<1:17 *also* D-R/C (in italics): omitted in D-R>

<2:1 *his mind* D-R/C: *him* D-R>

2:2 *autem*: *ergo* Weber; *ut*: *et* Weber

<2:2 *so they came and* KJV: *who when they were come* D-R>

<2:5 *my mind* D-R/C: *me* D-R>

<2:8 *seek to gain* D-R/C [KJV has *would gaine*]: *redeme* D-R>

<2:10 *neither* D-R/C: *yea neither* D-R; *or . . . or* KJV: *&. . . and* D-R>

<2:11 *can* KJV: *shal* D-R>

2:13 *quaerebanturque*: *quaerebaturque* Weber

<2:16 *resolve the question* D-R/C: *the solution* D-R; *and* KJV: omitted in D-R>

2:17 *et Misaheli*: *Misaheli* Weber

2:19   *Deo*: *Deum* S-C

2:23   *nostrorum*: *meorum* Weber

2:27   *non queunt*: *nequeunt* S-C

2:28   *sunt*: *sunt in* S-C

<2:31   *tall* D-R/C: omitted in D-R>

2:33   *quaedam autem*: *quaedam* Weber

2:34   *abscisus*: *abscissus* S-C; *lapis de monte*: *lapis* Weber

2:35   *areae quae*: *areae* Weber; *percussit* U†Q cum CY te, FIRM et QU
       pro [Quentin's sigla]: *percusserat* Weber, S-C

2:37   *regnum et*: *regnum* Weber

2:38   *volucres quoque*: *volucresque* Weber

2:39   *te, argenteum*: *te* Weber

<2:41   *iron* D-R/C: *ground of yron* D-R>

<2:42   *as . . . were* KJV (in roman type in KJV): omitted in D-R>

2:44   *comminuet autem*: *comminuet* Weber

2:45   *ventura*: *futura* Weber

2:47   *quoniam*: *quoniam tu* S-C

<3:1   *and* KJV (in roman type in KJV): omitted in D-R>

3:1   *Dura*: *Duram* Weber

<3:2   *the* KJV: *and* D-R>

3:3   *Nabuchadonosor Rex*: *Nabuchodonosor* Weber

3:7   *psalterii* ΛSMΦr [Weber's sigla]: *psalterii et* Weber; *populi, tribus*:
       populi et tribus Weber

3:8   *Statimque*: *statimque et* Weber

3:10   *psalterii et*: *psalterii* *D-R

3:11   *ardentis*: *ardentem* Weber

3:12   *Babylonis*: *Babyloniae* Weber

3:13   *adducerentur*: *adducerent* Weber

3:15   *sambucae et*: *sambucae* Weber; *ardentis*: *ardentem* Weber; *eripiet*: *erip-
       iat* Weber

3:17   *rex*: *o rex* S-C

3:20   *ardentis*: *ardentem* Weber

3:21   *fornacem* OΘ^{H}Ψ^{D}Ω^M cum G [Quentin's sigla]: *medium fornacis*
       Weber, S-C

3:23   *tres, id est*: *id est tres* Weber; *camino*: *camini* Weber

<3:23 *That—volumes* D-R (with my revisions): omitted in D-R/C>

3:31 *nobis*: *nobis in* S-C

3:32 *inimicorum nostrorum*: *inimicorum* Weber

<3:32 *that are upon* D-R/C: omitted in D-R>

3:33 *colunt*: *colebant* Weber

<3:38 *or leader or* KJV: *& duke, and* D-R; *or* [remaining five times] KJV: *nor* D-R>

3:39 *misericordiam tuam*: *misericordiam* Weber; *anima contrita*: *animo contrito* S-C

3:40 *holocausto*: *holocaustum* Weber

3:41 *sequimur te*: *sequimur* Weber

<3:43 *according to* KJV: *in* D-R>

3:44 *potentia tua*: *potentia* Weber

3:45 *Et sciant*: *sciant* Weber; *tu es Dominus*: *tu Domine* Weber

3:49 *autem Domini*: *autem* Weber

3:51 *hii tres*: *tres* Weber; *Deo*: *Deum* S-C

3:52 *laudabilis et gloriosus*: *laudabilis* Weber

3:58 *angeli Domini*: *angeli* Weber

3:65 *omnes spiritus Dei*: *omnis spiritus* Weber

3:82 *Benedicat Israhel Dominum; laudet et superexaltet*: *benedic Israhel Dominum laudate et superexaltate* Weber

3:88 *liberavit nos*: *liberavit* Weber

3:90 *confitemini ei*: *confitemini* Weber

<3:90 *Hitherto—Theodotion*: D-R (with my revisions): omitted in D-R/C>

3:91 *medium*: *medio* Weber

3:94 *satrapae et*: *satrapae* Weber; *sarabara*: *sarabala* S-C

3:95 *qui*: *quia* Weber; *eo*: *eum* S-C

3:96 *populus*: *populus et* Weber

3:98 *quae*: *qui* S-C

3:100 *generatione*: *generationem* S-C

<4:4 *but* KJV: *&* D-R>

4:5 *cuius*: *cui* S-C

4:6 *quoniam*: *quem* Weber; *eorum*: *earum* S-C

4:11 *fructus*: *fructum* Weber

4:14 *eo*: *eum* Weber

<4:19 *for* KJV: *&* D-R>

4:20   *commutentur*: *mutentur* S-C

4:22   *ferisque*: *feris* Weber

4:24   *ignoscet*: *ignoscat* Weber

4:25   *"Omnia haec*: *omnia* Weber

4:28   *Cumque*: *cum* Weber

4:29   *Regnum tuum*: *regnum* Weber; *bestiis et*: *bestiis* Weber

4:30   *et ex*: *ex* Weber

<4:30   like the feathers KJV (*feathers* in roman type in KJV): *into the simili-
           tude* D-R; claws KJV (in roman type in KJV): omitted in D-R>

4:33   *restitutus*: *constitutus* Weber

5:3   *aurea et argenta*: *aurea* Weber

5:4   *argenteos et*: *argenteos* Weber

5:6   *conturbabant*: *perturbabant* S-C

<5:8   but they KJV: omitted in D-R>

<5:11   for D-R/C: *for . . . also* D-R>

5:12   *intellegentiaque et*: *intellegentiaque* Weber; *Danihele*: *Danihelo* Weber

<5:13   And KJV (in roman type in KJV): omitted in D-R>

5:13   *quam*: *quem* S-C

<5:14   excellent KJV: *more ample* D-R>

5:14   *sint*: *sunt* S-C

5:15   *edicere mihi* Φ^{ERG}Θ^{H2}EUΓ^AΩ^{SJ} cum Theodotion [Quentin's sigla]:
           edicere Weber, S-C

5:16   *interpretationem eius*: *interpretationem* Weber

<5:18   and KJV: omitted in D-R>

5:19   *et quos*: *quos* Weber

5:21   *haberet*: *habeat* Weber

5:23   *concubinae tuae*: *concubinae* Weber

5:26   *haec*: *haec est* S-C

5:31   *duo*: *duos* S-C

6:1   *supra*: *super* S-C

6:4   *regis*: *regni* Weber

6:6   *cuncti*: *omnes* S-C

6:11   *igitur*: *ergo* S-C

6:12   *te*: *a te* Weber; *quos*: *quod* Weber; *Verus*: *verus est* S-C

<6:15   king's design D-R/C: *king* D-R>

6:15   *constituerit*: *constituit* Weber

6:18   *adlati*: *inlati* Weber

<6:26   *all* D-R/C *men* KJV: *they* D-R>

6:27   *lacu*: *manu* Weber

7:4   *hominis*: *eius* Weber

7:6   *hoc*: *haec* S-C; *habebat quasi*: *habebat* Weber; *hoc*: *haec* S-C

<7:9   *like flames* KJV (*like* in roman type in KJV): *flames* D-R; *like a burn-ing fire* KJV (*as* for *like a*): *fire kindled* D-R>

7:17   *edocuit*: *docuit* S-C; *quattuor bestiae magnae quattuor sunt regna quae*: *bestiae magnae quattuor / quattuor regna* Weber

7:19   *quae*: *quia* Weber; *reliquias*: *reliqua* S-C

7:20   *cornua, et*: *cornua* Weber

8:2   *castro*: *castrorum* S-C; *regione*: *civitate* Weber

<8:3   *two* KJV: omitted in D-R>

8:11   *magnificatum*: *magnificatus* Weber

8:14   *mane*: *mane dies* S-C

<8:14   *days* S-C: omitted in D-R>

8:19   *sint*: *sunt* S-C

<8:23   *dark sentences* KJV: *propositions* D-R>

9:3   *Deum meum*: *Deum* Weber

<9:3   *and* KJV: omitted in D-R>

9:5   *iniquitatem*: *inique* Weber

9:8   *regibus nostris principibus*: *principibus* *D-R

9:12   *superinduceret*: *superducerent* Weber

9:14   *Dominus super malitiam*: *Dominus* Weber

9:20   *et prosternerem*: *ut prosternerem* Weber

9:21   *visione a*: *visione* Weber

9:24   *prophetia*: *prophetes* Weber

<9:25   *that* KJV (in roman type in KJV and italics in D-R/C): omitted in D-R>

9:26   *eius populus qui eum negaturus est*: *eius* Weber

9:27   *Confirmabit*: *confirmavit* Weber; *ebdomada*: *ebdomas* Weber

<10:3   *neither* KJV: *yea neither* D-R>

10:6   *fulgoris*: *fulguris* S-C; *deorsum sunt*: *deorsum* Weber

10:16   *visione tua*: *visione* Weber

10:20   *ergo* Φ [Weber's siglum]: *enim* Weber, *ego* S-C

<10:20   *I* S-C: *I therfore* D-R>

<11:4   *come to his height* D-Rn: *stand* D-R>

<11:5   *one* KJV (in roman type in KJV): omitted in D-R; *great* D-R/C: omitted in D-R>

<11:6   *but* KJV: *and* D-R; *these* KJV (in italics in D-R/C): omitted in D-R>

11:6   *fortitudinem*: *fortitudine* Weber

<11:10   *like a flood* D-R/C: *and ouerflowing* D-R>

11:24   *Et abundantes*: *abundantes* Weber; *iniet*: *inibit* S-C

<11:29   *but* KJV: *and* D-R>

11:33   *flamma et*: *flamma* Weber; *in rapina*: *rapina* Weber

11:36   *dirigetur*: *diriget* Weber

11:43   *Lybiam*: *Lybias* Weber; *Aethiopiam*: *Aethiopias* Weber

11:45   *Apadno*: *Apedno* Weber

12:1   *eo ex*: *eo* Weber

12:6   *dixi*: *dixit* Weber

12:7   *levasset*: *elevasset* S-C; *et tempora*: *temporum* Weber

12:11   *desolationem*: *desolatione* Weber

12:13   *requiesces*: *requiesce* Weber; *finem*: *fine* Weber

13:2   *Deum*: *Dominum* Weber

13:4   *pomarium*: *pomerium* Weber; *domui*: *domus* Weber

13:5   *sunt*: *sunt de populo* S-C; *senioribus*: *senibus* Weber

13:7   *pomario*: *pomerio* Weber

13:8   *concupiscentiam*: *concupiscentia* Weber

13:11   *indicare sibi*: *indicare* Weber

<13:11   *have to do* KJV: *lie* D-R>

13:14   *commune*: *communi* S-C

13:17   *laver*: *lavem* Weber

13:18   *posticum*: *posticium* Weber

13:20   *et nos*: *et* Weber

13:22   *sunt mihi*: *mihi* Weber

<13:24   *With that* KJV: *And* D-R>

<13:25   *of them* D-R/C (in italics): omitted in D-R>

13:26   *posticam*: *posticum* S-C

<13:27   *on the next day* KJV? (*it came to pass the next day*): *the morrow came* D-R>

<13:28   *when* KJV: *And when* D-R>

<13:32 *her face* KJV: *she* D-R>

13:34 *manus suas*: *manus* Weber

13:36 *a se puellas*: *puellas* Weber

<13:40 *but* KJV: *and* D-R>

<13:43 *must* KJV: omitted in D-R>

13:44 *Dominus*: *Deus* Weber

<13:48 *or knowledge of* KJV: *nor discerning that which is* D-R>

13:51 *populum* Frede LUC Ath 2.10, p. 165.29: *eos* Weber, S-C

<13:51 *these two* KJV: *them* D-R>

<13:57 *would* KJV: *did* D-R>

<13:58 *answered* KJV: *said* D-R>

13:59 *Domini*: *Dei* Weber

<13:60 *With that* KJV: *Therfore* D-R>

13:60 *Deum*: *Deo* Weber

14:11 *morte moriemur*: *moriemur* Weber

14:13 *rex*: *et rex* Weber; *praecepit*: *et praecepit* *D-R

14:16 *signa*: *signacula* S-C

14:17 *aperuisset*: *aperuissent* Weber

14:18 *sunt*: *sint* S-C

14:19 *est rex*: *rex* Weber

14:21 *potestatem*: *potestate* Weber; *Danihelis*: *Daniheli* Weber

14:24 *vivens*: *vivens iste autem non est Deus vivens* S-C

<14:24 *but that is no living god* S-C: omitted in D-R>

14:25 *tibi*: *tibi potestatem* *D-R

14:26 *draconis*: *draconi* Weber; *quem*: *quae* Weber

<14:31 *but* S: *and* D-R>

<14:32 *called* KJV: omitted in D-R>

14:35 *supra*: *super* Weber

14:36 *Danihel*: *Danihel, serve Dei* S-C

<14:36 *thou servant of God* S-C: omitted in D-R>

14:37 *es*: *es enim* Weber

14:38 *Domini*: *Dei* Weber

14:39 *sedens in medio leonum*: *sedens* Weber

14:40 *eum de lacu leonum*: *eum* Weber

14:41 *intromisit in lacum*: *intromisit* Weber

14:42 verse omitted in Weber

Alternate Spellings

In general, the translators of the Douay-Rheims edition of the Bible preserved the transliterations of Hebrew names (and words based on those names) found throughout the textual tradition of the Sixto-Clementine edition of the Vulgate Bible. While these transliterations do reflect the Latin sources for the English presented in this edition, they do not represent what is currently thought to be the likely pronunciation of the Hebrew words or, in some books, words from other ancient languages: for example, the name we see in the New Revised Standard Version (NRSV) as "Ahuzzath" (Gen 26:26) was transliterated by the authors and revisers of the Latin text as "Ochozath." This sort of transliteration renders a few well-known characters harder to recognize, such as Noah, or "Noe" in the Latin tradition. Furthermore, there are frequent inconsistencies in the Douay-Rheims translation as to the spellings of names.

Another quirk of the Douay-Rheims and Vulgate Bibles is that they often identify locations by the names they were understood to have had at the time of the Vulgate's composition rather than the names found in Hebrew scripture. For example, "Mesopotamia of Syria" (Gen 28:2) represents a place referred to in the NRSV as "Paddan-aram."

In presenting the Latin text and the Douay-Rheims transla-

tion, the transliterations in the English have been updated for the sake of accuracy and ease of reference. The Latin has been preserved to reflect its own textual tradition in accordance with the principles stated in the Introduction. However, when names given are not simply a matter of representing vowel and consonant sounds, the Douay-Rheims translation has been left intact so that it remains a genuine translation of the facing text.

There are moments in the Bible where the anachronistic place-names are of significance: at the end of Balaam's last prophetic blessing of Israel, he declares, "They shall come in galleys from Italy; they shall overcome the Assyrians and shall waste the Hebrews, and at the last they themselves also shall perish" (Nm 24:24). The Hebrew word rendered as "Italy" is transliterated in the NRSV as "Kittim," and though the meaning is obscure, it is almost certainly not Italy, for reasons outlined by Milgrom (1990), ad loc. Nevertheless, it is fascinating and important to realize that in the Western European tradition from the fourth century CE until the twentieth century, many read, wrote, and learned that Italians would "waste the Hebrews." Because of this and other instances in which the place-names, however unrepresentative of the Hebrew tradition they may be, are important in terms of what readers of these versions of the Bible may have believed, the Vulgate words have been retained.

Below is a list of the names in the English translation of the Major Prophetical Books (Volume IV) and the Minor Prophetical Books and Maccabees (Volume V). The names are followed by an alternate spelling (or, in some cases, an alternate word) if there is one. An entry presented in italic text signifies a word retained from the Douay-Rheims translation; all other words are the spellings given by the NRSV. An entry in roman text

with no alternative spelling means that the spellings are identical in the two editions; one in italic text with no alternative spelling means that the name is in the Douay-Rheims translation but no parallel was found in the NRSV. In a few cases, words have been based on the spellings of the NRSV and the form in the Douay-Rheims text. For example, the Douay-Rheims text reads "the Sichemites" (Gen 33:18), where the NRSV has "Shechem." To illustrate the translation of the Douay-Rheims while providing an up-to-date transliteration of the Hebrew word, "the Shechemites" has been printed; similarly, in cases where Jerome translated parts of a Hebrew place-name into Latin where the NRSV left the whole name in Hebrew (such as the "temple of Phogor," as opposed to "Beth-peor" at Dt 3:29), the transliterated part of the name has been updated in this edition, but the Latin and English translations have not been changed, yielding "temple of Peor."

Aaron
Abdeel
Abednego [Abdenago]
Abraham
Absalom
Absalom [Abesalom]
Abubus [Abobus]
Achbor [Achobor]
Achor
Adam
Adam, children of [mortals]
Adar
Adasa [Adarsa]
Adasa [Adazer]

Adida [Addus]
Adida [Adiada]
Admah [Adama]
Adonis [Tammuz]
Adora [Ador]
Adrammelech [Adramelech]
Adullam [Odollam]
Africa [Put]
Agarenes
Ahab [Achab]
Ahasuerus [Assuerus]
Ahaz [Achaz]
Ahikam [Ahicam]
Ai

Aiath

Akrabattene [Acrabathane]

Alcimus

Alema [Alima]

Alexander

Alexandria

Alexandria [Thebes]

Almighty [Sovereign]

Amariah [Amarias]

Amaziah [Amasias]

Amittai [Amathi]

Ammon

*Ammon, children of [Ammo-
    nites]*

Ammonites

*Ammonites, country of the [Am-
    mon]*

Amon

Amon [Ammon]

Amorite [Amorrhite]

Amos

Amoz [Amos]

Anathoth

Anathothite [of Anathoth]

Ancient of days [Ancient One]

Andronicus

Antichrist

Antioch

*Antiochians [citizens of Anti-
    och]*

Antiochis

Antiochus

Antipater

*Apadno, tabernacle [palatial
    tents]*

Aphairema [Apherema]

Apollonius

Apollophanes

Apphus

Ar

Arabia

Arabian [Arab]

Arabian [Arabs]

Arabians [Arabs]

Arabians [nomads]

Aradus

Ararat

Arbatta [Arbatis]

Arbela [Arbella]

Arcturus [Pleiades]

Aretas

Ariarathes

Ariel

Ariel [altar hearth]

Arioch

Aristobulus [Aristobolus]

Arius

Arnon

Aroer

Arpad

Arpad [Arphad]

Arsaces

*Arvadians [inhabitants of Ar-
    vad]*

Asa
Asaph
Asaramel
Ashdod [Azotus]
Asher [Aser]
Ashkelon [Ascalon]
Ashkenaz [Ascenez]
Ashpenaz [Asphenez]
Asia
Askalon [Ascalon]
Asphar
Asshur [Assur]
Asshur [Assyria]
Assyria
Assyrian
Assyrians
Astyages
Athenians [citizens of Athens]
Athenobius
Attalus
Ausitis [Uz]
Avaran [Abaron]
Azariah [Azarias]
Azekah [Azecha]
Azotus
Azriel [Ezriel]
Azzur [Azur]

Baal
Baal, house of him that judged [Beth-arbel]

Baali [my Baal]
Baalim [Baal]
Baalim [Baals]
Baalis
Baal-meon [Beelmeon]
Baal-peor [Beelphegor]
Baasha [Baasa]
Babylon
Babylonia
Babylonia [Babylon]
Babylonians
Bacchides
Bacchus [Dionysus]
Bacenor
Baean [Bean]
Balaam
Baladan
Balak [Balach]
Balas [Bales]
Baruch
Bashan [Basan]
Baskama [Bascama]
Beautiful place [Shaphir]
Beeri
Beer-sheba [Bersabee]
Bel
Belial
Belshazzar [Baltasar]
Belshazzar [Baltassar]
Belteshazzar [Baltassar]
Benaiah [Banaias]
Ben-hadad [Benadad]

Ben-hadad [Benadad]
Benjamin
Beor
Berea
Berechiah [Barachias]
Berothah [Berotha]
Beth-aven [Bethaven]
Bethbasi [Bethbessen]
Beth-dagon [Bethdagon]
Bethel
Beth-gamul [Bethgamul]
Beth-haccherem [Bethaca-
    rem]
Beth-horon [Bethoron]
Beth-horon [Beth-zur]
Beth-jeshimoth [Bethiesim-
    oth]
Bethlehem
Beth-meon [Bethmaon]
Beth-shan [Bethsan]
Beth-zaith [Bethzecha]
Beth-zechariah
    [Bethzecharam]
Beth-zur [Bethsura]
Bosor
Bosor [Bozrah]
Bosphorus [Sepharad]
Bozrah [Barasa]
Bozrah [Bosra]
Bubastis [Pi-beseth]
Buz
Buzi

Caleb
Callisthenes
Calneh [Chalane]
Calno [Calano]
Canaan [a trader]
Canaan [Chanaan]
Canaanites [Chanaanites]
Canneh [Chene]
Caphar-salama
    [Capharsalama]
Cappadocia [Caphtor]
Carchemish [Charcamis]
Caria
Carmel
Carnaim
Carnaim [Carnion]
Carthaginians [Tarshish]
Caspin [Casphin]
Cendebeus
Chaereas
Chaldea
Chaldeans
Chalphi [Calphi]
Chaphenatha [Caphetetha]
Charax [Characa]
Chaspho [Casphor]
Chebar [Chobar]
Chemosh [Chamos]
Chilmad [Chelmad]
Chimham [Chamaam]
Chislev [Casleu]
Christ

Cilicia

Cnidus [Gnidus]

Coelesyria [Celesyria]

Coelesyria [Celesyria]

Cos

Cub [Chub]

Cushi [Chusi]

Cyprians [Cyprian troops]

Cyprus

Cyrene

Cyrene [Kir]

Cyrus

Dagon

Damascus

Damascus [men of Damascus]

Dan

Dan [Vedan]

Daniel

Daphne

Darius

Dathema [Datheman]

David

Dedan

Dedan, men of [Dedanites]

Dedanim [Dedanites]

Delaiah [Dalaias]

Delos [Delus]

Demetrius

Demophon

Dessau

Diblah [Riblah]

Diblaim [Debelaim]

Diblathaim, house of [Beth-
    diblathaim]

Dibon

Dioscorus [Dioscorinthius]

Dok [Doch]

Dor [Dora]

Dorymenes [Dorymenus]

Dositheus

Dumah [Duma]

Dura

Dust, house of [Beth-leaphrah]

Ebed-melech [Abdemelech]

Ecbatana

Eden

Edom

Edomites

Eglaim [Gallim]

Egypt

Egyptians

Ekron [Accaron]

Elam

Elamites

Elasa [Laisa]

Elealeh [Eleale]

Eleazar

Eleutherus

Eliakim [Eliacim]

Elijah [Elias]

Elim, well of [Beer-elim]

Elishah [Elisa]

Elishama [Elisama]

Elkoshite [of Elkosh]

Elnathan

Elul

Elymais

Emmaus

Emmaus [Ammaus]

En-eglaim [Engallim]

En-gedi [Engaddi]

Enon, the court of [Hazar-enon]

Ephah [Epha]

Ephai [Ophi]

Ephraim

Ephrathah [Ephrata]

Ephron

Esar-haddon [Asarhaddon]

Esau

Esdris [Esdrin]

Ethiopia

Ethiopia [Cushan]

Ethiopia [Ethiopians]

Ethiopian

Ethiopians [Ethiopia]

Eumenes

Eupator

Euphrates

Eupolemus

Evil-merodach

Ezekiel

Ezra [Esdras]

Gabriel

Gad

Gaddi [Gaddis]

Galatia [the Gauls]

Galatians

Galilee

Gallim

Gareb

Gath [Geth]

Gaza

Gazara

Gazara [Gezeron]

Geba [Gaba]

Gebal

Gebim [Gabim]

Gedaliah [Gedelias]

Gedaliah [Godolias]

Gemariah [Gamarias]

Gennaeus [Genneus]

Gennesaret [Genesar]

Gentiles

Gerizim [Garizim]

Gerrenians [Gerar]

Gibeah [Gabaa]

Gibeah [Gabaath]

Gibeon [Gabaon]

Gilead [Galaad]

Gilgal [Galgal]

Goatha

Gog

Gomer

Gomer

Gomorrah [Gomorrha]

Gorgias

Gortyna

Gozan [Gozam]

Grecian

Grecians [Greeks]

Greece

Greece [Javan]

Greece [the Greeks]

Habakkuk [Habacuc]

Habazziniah [Habsanias]

Hadad-rimmon [Adadrem-
mon]

Hadrach

Hagar [Agar]

Haggai [Aggeus]

Halicarnassus [Alicarnassus]

Hamath [Amath]

Hamath [Emath]

Hamath [Emath]

*Hamath, as they go to [Lebo-
hamath]*

*Hamath, till thou come to [Lebo-
hamath]*

Hammelech [the king]

Hamonah [Amona]

Hamutal [Amital]

Hanan

Hananel [Hanameel]

Hananel [Hananeel]

Hananiah [Ananias]

Hananiah [Hananias]

Hanes

Haran

Haran [Haram]

Harmon [Armon]

Hasideans [Assideans]

Hauran [Auran]

Hazael [Azael]

Hazor [Asor]

Hebrew

Hebrews

Hebron [Chebron]

Heldai [Holdai]

Helem

Heliodorus

Heliopolis [On]

Hen [Hem]

Hena [Ana]

Hercules

Heshbon [Hesebon]

Hethlon [Hethalon]

Hezekiah [Ezechias]

Hieronymus

High-place [Bamah]

Hilkiah [Helcias]

Hinnom [Ennom]

Hittite [Cethite]

Holon [Helon]

Hophra [Ephree]

Horonaim [Oronaim]

Hosea [Osee]

Hoshaiah [Osaias]

House adjoining [Beth-ezel]

Iddo [Addo]

Idumea

Idumea [Edom]

Idumeans

Igdaliah [Jegedelias]

Illustrious [Epiphanes]

Imalkue [Emalchuel]

Immanuel [Emmanuel]

Immer [Emmer]

Indian

Indians [India]

Irijah [Jerias]

Isaac

Isaiah [Isaias]

Ishmael [Ismahel]

Israel

Israel, children of [Israelites]

Issachar

Italy [Tubal]

Ivvah [Ava]

Jaazaniah [Jezonias]

Jacob

Jacob [Accos]

Jahaz [Jasa]

Jahzah [Jasa]

Jambri

Jamnia

Jamnites

Jashub . . . that is left [Shear-jashub]

Jason

Jazer

Jazer [Gazer]

Jeberechiah [Barachias]

Jebusite

Jeconiah [Coniah]

Jeconiah [Conias]

Jeconiah [Jechonias]

Jedaiah [Idaias]

Jehoahaz [Joachaz]

Jehoiachin [Joachin]

Jehoiada [Joiada]

Jehoiakim [Joakim]

Jehoiakim [Joakim]

Jehoshaphat [Josaphat]

Jehozadak [Josedec]

Jehu

Jehudi [Judi]

Jerahmeel [Jeremiel]

Jeremiah [Jeremias]

Jericho

Jeroboam

Jerusalem

Jesse

Jew

Jews

Jews [Judeans]
Jezaniah [Jezonias]
Jezreel [Jezrahel]
Joah [Joahe]
Joakim
Joarib
Joarib [Jarib]
Joash [Joas]
Job
Joel
Johanan
John
Jonadab
Jonah [Jonas]
Jonathan
Joppa [Joppe]
Joppites [community of
 Joppa]
Jordan
Joseph
Josephus
Joshua [Jesus]
Joshua [Josue]
Josiah [Josias]
Jotham [Joathan]
Jucal [Juchal]
Judah [Juda]
Judah [Judea]
Judas
Judea
Judea [Judah]

Jupiter Hospitalis [Zeus-the-
 Friend-of-Strangers]
Jupiter Olympius [Olympian
 Zeus]

Kadesh [Cades]
Kadesh, Waters of Contradiction
 of [Meribath-kadesh]
Kareah [Caree]
Kedar [Cedar]
Kedron [Cedron]
Kedron [Gedor]
Kerioth [Carioth]
Kerioth [Carioth]
Kethim [Cyprus]
Kidron, the torrent [the Wadi
 Kidron]
Kiriathaim [Cariathaim]
Kiriath-jearim [Cariathiarim]
Kitteans [Ceteans]
Kittim [Cethim]
Kolaiah [Colias]

Lacedaemon [Lacedaemonians]
Lacedaemonians [Lacedemoni-
 ans]
Lachish [Lachis]
Laishah [Laisa]
Lampsacus [Sampsames]
Lasthenes
Lebanon [Libanus]

Levi

Leviathan

Levites

Levites [levitical priests]

Libnah [Lobna]

Libya [Libyans]

Libya [Put]

Libyans

Libyans [Put]

Lord [Sovereign]

Lucius

Luhith [Luith]

Lycia

Lydda

Lydia [Lud]

Lydians [Lud]

Lydians [Ludim]

Lydians [Lydia]

Lysias

Lysimachus

Maachati [the Maacathite]

Maaseiah [Maasias]

Maccabees [Machabees]

Maccabeus

Macedonian

Macer [Macron]

Madmenah [Medemena]

Magog

Mahseiah [Maasias]

Maked [Mageth]

Malachi [Malachias]

Mallus [Mallos]

Manasseh [Manasses]

Manilius [Manius]

Mareshah [Maresa]

Marisa [Maresa]

Mattan [Mathan]

Mattathias [Mathathias]

Matthias [Mattathias]

Mauzzim [fortresses]

Mauzzim [of fortresses]

Mede

Mede [Media]

Medeba [Madaba]

Medeba [Medaba]

Medeba [Nadabath]

Medes

Medes [Media]

Megiddo [Mageddon]

Melchias [Malchiah]

Melzar

Memmius

Memphis

Menelaus

Mephaath

Merodach

Merodach-baladan [Mero-
    dach Baladan]

Merrha [Merran]

Mesaloth [Masaloth]

Meshach [Misach]

Meshech [Mosoch]

Micah [Micheas]

Micaiah [Micheas]

Michael

Michmash [Machmas]

Midian [Madian]

Migdol [Magdal]

Migron [Magron]

Milcom [Melchom]

Milcom [their king]

Minni [Menni]

Miriam [Mary]

Mishael [Misael]

Mizpah [Maapha]

Mizpah [Maspha]

Mizpah [Masphath]

Mnestheus [Menestheus]

Moab

Moabites

Modein [Modin]

Molech [Moloch]

Molech [Sakkuth]

Mordecai [Mardochias]

Moresheth [Morasthi]

Moreshethite [of Moresheth]

Morter [Mortar]

Mosel [from Uzal]

Moses

Myndos [Myndus]

Nabateans [Nabutheans]

Nanea

Naphtali [Naphthali]

Naphtali [Nephtali]

Nathan

Nazirite [Nazarite]

Nazirites [Nazarites]

Nebaioth [Nabaioth]

Nebo [Nabo]

Nebuchadnezzar [Nebuchadrez-zar]

Nebuchadnezzar [Nebu-chodonosor]

Nebushazban [Nabusez-ban]

Nebuzaradan [Nabuzardan]

Neco [Nechao]

Nehelamite [of Nehelam]

Nephi [naphtha]

Nephthar

Nergal [Neregel]

Neriah [Neri]

Neriah [Nerias]

Nethaniah [Nathanias]

Netophathi, that were of [the Netophathite]

Nicanor

Nile

Nimrim [Nemrim]

Nimrod [Nemrod]

Nineveh [Ninive]

Nisroch [Nesroch]

Noah [Noe]

Nob [Nobe]

Not my people [Lo-ammi]

Numenius

Obadiah [Abdias]
Odares [Odomera]
Oholah [Oolla]
Oholibah [Oolibah]
Omri [Amri]
Onias
Oreb
Orion
Orthosias [Orthosia]

Palestine [the Philistines]
Palestine, people of [Philistines]
Pamphylia
Paran
Pashhur [Phassur]
Pathros [Phatros]
Pathros [Phatures]
Patroclus
Pekah [Phacee]
Pelatiah [Pheltias]
Pelusium
Pentecost
Persepolis
Perses
Persia
Persian
Persians
Persians [Persia]
Pethuel [Phatuel]
Petra [Sela]
Pharaoh [Pharao]

Pharathon [Phara]
Phaselis
Phasiron [Phaseron]
Philarches
Philip
Philistia
Philistines
Philistines [Philistia]
Philometor
Phinehas [Phinees]
Phoenicia [Phenicia]
Phrygian
Posidonius
Ptolemais
Ptolemeans [Ptolemais]
Ptolemy [Ptolemee]
Pygmeans [men of Gamad]

Quintus

Raamah [Reema]
Rabbah [Rabba]
Rabbah [Rabbath]
Rabmag [Rebmag]
Rabsaris [Rabsares]
Rabshakeh [Rabsaces]
Rachel
Ramah [Rama]
Ramatha [Ramathin]
Raphon
Razis [Razias]

Rechab

Rechabites

Regem-melech [Rogom-melech]

Remaliah [Romelia]

Rephaim [Raphaim]

Reuben [Ruben]

Rezeph [Reseph]

Rezin [Rasin]

Rhodes

Rhodocus

Riblah [Reblatha]

Rimmon [Remmon]

Romans

Romans [of Kittim]

Rome

Sabaim [Sabeans]

Sabaoth, Lord of [LORD of hosts]

Sabeans

Salu [Salomi]

Samaria

Samgarnebo [Semegarnabu]

Samos [Samus]

Samuel

Sarah [Sara]

Sarsechim [Sarsachim]

Satan

Saul

Saura [Avaran]

Scenopegia

Scythians

Scythopolitans [people of Scy-thopolis]

Seba [Saba]

Second [Second Quarter]

Seir

Seleucia

Seleucus

Senir [Sanir]

Sennacherib

Sepharvaim

Seraiah [Saraias]

Seron

Sesac [Sheshach]

Shadrach [Sidrach]

Shallum [Salom]

Shallum [Sellum]

Shaphan [Saphan]

Sharezer [Sarasar]

Sharezer [Sereser]

Sharon [Saron]

Shealtiel [Salathiel]

Sheba [Saba]

Shebat [Sabath]

Shebat [Sabath]

Shebna [Sobna]

Shechem [Sichem]

Shelemiah [Selemias]

Shemaiah [Semei]

Shemaiah [Semeias]

Shephatiah [Saphatias]

Shephelah [Sephela]

Sheshach [Sesach]

Shiloah [Siloe]

Shiloh [Silo]

Shimei [Shimeites]

Shinar [Sennaar]

Shittim [Setim]

Sibmah [Sabama]

Sibraim [Sabarim]

Sicyon

Side

Sidon

Sihon [Seon]

Simeon

Simon

Sivan

Sodom

Solomon

sons of the Assyrians [Assyrians]

Sosipater

Sostratus

Spain

Spartans

Sud [Sodi]

Susa

Susanna

Syene

Syria

Syria [Aram or Edom]

Syria [Aram]

Syria [Coelesyria]

Syriac [Aramaic]

Syrian tongue [Aramaic]

Syrians

Syrians [Arameans]

Tabeel

Tabor [Thabor]

Tahpanhes [Taphnes]

Tahpanhes [Taphnis]

Tahpanhes [Zoan]

Tamar [Thamar]

Tanhumeth [Thanehumeth]

Tanis

Taphsar

Tarshish [Tharsis]

Tarsus [Tharsus]

Tartan [Thathan]

Tekoa [Thecua]

Telassar [Thalassar]

Tema [Thema]

Teman [Theman]

Tephon [Thopo]

Tharseas [Tarsus]

Thassi [Thasi]

Theodotius [Theodotus]

*Thou hast obtained mercy [Ru-
    hamah]*

Thracians

*Ticon, the house of [as far as
    Hazer-hatticon]*

Tigris

Timnath [Thamnata]

Timothy [Timotheus]

Tirhakah [Tharaca]

Titus

Tob [Tubin]

Tobias

Tobijah [Tobias]

Togarmah, house of [Beth-togarmah]

Topheth

Topheth [Topeth]

Toubianites [Toubiani]

Tripolis

Trypho [Tryphon]

Tubal [Thubal]

Tyrannus [Auranus]

Tyre

Tyrians

Ulai

Uphaz [Ophaz]

Uriah [Urias]

Uz [Hus]

Uzziah [Ozias]

Without mercy [Lo-ruhamah]

Xanthicus

You are my people [Ammi]

Zabadeans

Zabdiel

Zabulun [Zabulon]

Zacheus

Zadok [Sadoc]

Zarephath [Sarepta]

Zeboiim [Seboim]

Zechariah [Zacharias]

Zedad [Sedada]

Zedekiah [Sedecias]

Zephaniah [Sophonias]

Zerubbabel [Zorobabel]

Zimri [Zambri]

Zimri [Zamri]

Zion [Sion]

Zoar

Zoar [Segor]

Bibliography

Carleton, J. G. *The Part of Rheims in the Making of the English Bible*. Oxford: Clarendon, 1902.

Cartmell, J. "English Spiritual Writers: x. Richard Challoner." *Clergy Review* n.s. 44, no. 10 (October 1959): 577–587.

A Catholic. "A new Version of the Four Gospels, with Notes, Critical and Explanatory." *Dublin Review* 2, no. 2 (April 1837): 475–492.

Biblia Sacra: Vulgatae Editionis Sixti V Pont. Max. iussu recognita et Clementis VIII auctoritate edita. Vatican City: Marietti, 1959.

Challoner, R. "The Touchstone of the New Religion: or, Sixty Assertions of Protestants, try'd by their own Rule of Scripture alone, and condemned by clear and express Texts of their own Bible." London, n.p.: 1735.

——. ed. *The Holy Bible translated from the Latin Vulgat: Diligently compared With the Hebrew, Greek, and other Editions in divers Languages. And first published by The English College at Doway, Anno 1609. Newly revised, and corrected, according to the Clementine Edition of the Scriptures with Annotations for clearing up the principal Difficulties of Holy Writ.* 4 vols. Dublin(?): 1752.

——., ed. *The Holy Bible, translated from the Latin Vulgate, Diligently compared with the Hebrew, Greek, and other editions in divers languages. The Old Testament, First published by the English College at Douay, A.D. 1609 and The New Testament, First published by the English College at Rheims, A.D. 1582. With annotations, references, and an historical and chronological index. The whole revised and diligently compared with the Latin Vulgate Published with the approbation of His Eminence James Cardinal Gibbons Archbishop of Baltimore.* Baltimore: John Murphy, 1899.

——., ed. *The New Testament of Our LORD and SAVIOUR JESUS*

CHRIST. Translated out of the Latin Vulgat; diligently compared with the original Greek: and first published by the English *College at* Rhemes, *Anno 1582. Newly revised and corrected according to the* Clementin *Edition of the Scriptures. With Annotations, for Clearing up modern Controversies in Religion; and other Difficulties of Holy Writ.* 2 vols. Dublin(?): 1752.

Cotton, H. *Rhemes and Doway: An Attempt to shew what has been done by Roman Catholics for the Diffusion of the Holy Scriptures in English.* Oxford: University Press, 1855.

de Hamel, C. *The Book: A History of the Bible.* London: Phaidon, 2001.

Dodd, C. [H. Tootell]. *The Church History of England, From The Year 1500, to The Year 1688. Chiefly with regard to Catholicks.* 8 vols. Brussels [London], 1737–1742.

Duffy, E., ed. *Challoner and His Church: A Catholic Bishop in Georgian England.* London: Darton, Longman & Todd, 1981.

English College of Doway. *The Holie Bible Faithfully Translated into English, out of the Authentical Latin. Diligently conferred with the Hebrew, Greeke, and other Editions in diuers languages. With Arguments of the Bookes, and Chapters: Annotations. Tables: and other helpes, for better understanding of the text: for discoueirie of corruptions in some late translations: and for clearing Controversies in Religion.* 2 vols. Doway: Lavrence Kellam, at the signe of the holie Lambe, 1609–1610.

English College of Rhemes. *The Nevv Testament of Iesvs Christ, Translated Faithfully into English, out of the authentical Latin, according to the best corrected copies of the same, diligently conferred vvithe the Greeke and other editions in diuers languages: Vvith Argvments of bookes and chapters, Annotations, and other necessarie helpes, for the better vnderstanding of the text, and specially for the discouerie of the Corrvptions of diuers late translations, and for cleering the Controversies in religion, of these daies.* Rhemes: Iohn Fogny, 1582.

Frede, H. J. *Kirchenschriftsteller: Verzeichnis und Sigel.* Freiburg: Herder, 1995.

Gilley, S. "Challoner as Controvertionalist." In E. Duffy, ed., *Challoner and His Church: A Catholic Bishop in Georgian England.* London: Darton, Longman & Todd, 1981, pp. 90–111.

Greenslade, S. L., ed. *The Cambridge History of the Bible: The West, from the Reformation to the Present Day.* Rev. ed. Cambridge: Cambridge University Press, 1975.

Gryson, R. *Altlateinische Handschriften: Manuscrits Vieux Latins*. Freiburg: Herder, 1999.

The Holy Bible, Conteyning the Old Testament, and the New: Newly Translated out of the Originall tongues: & with the former Translations diligently compared and reuised: by his Maiesties speciall Comandement Appointed to be read in Churches. London: Robert Barker, Printer to the Kings most Excellent Maiestie, 1611; rpr. Thomas Nelson, 1990.

Kaske, R. E. *Medieval Chirstian Literary Imagery: A Guide to Interpretation*. Toronto: University of Toronto Press, ca. 1988.

Knox, T. F. Introduction. In *The First and Second Diaries of the English College, Douay, and an Appendix of Unpublished Documents, Edited by Fathers of the Congregation of the London Oratory, with an Historical Introduction*. Records of the English Catholics under the Penal Laws. Chiefly from the Archives of the See of Westinster 1. London: David Nutt, 1878.

Metzger, B. M., and R. E. Murphy. *The New Oxford Annotated Bible: New Revised Standard Version*. New York: Oxford University Press, 1991.

Milgrom, J., comm. *The JPS Torah Commentary: Numbers*. Philadelphia: The Jewish Publication Society.

Pope, H., and S. Bullough. *English Versions of the Bible*. St. Louis: Herder, 1952.

Quentin, H. *Biblia sacra: iuxta Latinam Vulgatam versionem*. Typis Polyglottis Vaticanis, 1926–[1995].

———. *Mémoire sur l'établissement du texte de la Vulgate*. Collectanea Biblica Latina 6, 1922.

Rahlfs, A., ed., and R. Hanhart, rev. *Septuaginta: Id est Vetus Testamentum graece iuxta LXX interpretes, Editio altera*. Stuttgart: Deutsche Bibelgesellschaft, 2006.

Sabatier, P. *Bibliorum Sacrorum Latinae versiones antiquae, seu Vetus Italica, et Ceterae quaecunque in Codicibus Mss. & antiquorum libris reperiri poterunt: Quae cum Vulgata Latina, & cum Textu Graeco comparantur. Accedunt Praefationes, Observationes, ac Notae, Indexque novus ad Vulgatam è regione editam, idemque locupletissimus*. 3 vols. Rheims: Apud Reginaldum Florentain, Regis Typographicum & Bibliopolam, sub signo Bibliorum aureorum, 1743–1749.

Weber, R., ed. *Biblia Sacra Vulgata*. 5th ed. Stuttgart: Deutsche Bibelgesellschaft, 2007.